'Fieldwork is a key component of social work education and so a book that introduces students, practitioners, and academics to fieldwork with a global lens is timely and extremely welcomed. Introducing the readers to current practices and concerns from Europe, North and South America, Australia, and Oceania, this handbook gathers key issues shared by the international community to provide effective and innovative fieldwork. As an international profession, it is crucial that social work students receive up-to-date, relevant, and innovative information that will inform their training and their future practice; make connections with the global community of social workers; and link its practice with current thinking and debates. As this book includes voices from many countries and perspectives, it invites readers to think both locally and globally about undertaking the linkage of practice with theory as a crucial element of fieldwork. Informed by theory and evidence-based practice, this timely and much need book identifies the challenges and its future directions. In pursuit of social justice practice, this book makes an important contribution to twenty-first-century fieldwork for the education of social workers across the globe. I thoroughly recommend its inclusion into the global and national social work curricula.'

Carolyn Noble, *Professor of Social Work, Australian College of Applied Psychology, Sydney, Australia*

'This handbook is an impressive and important contribution to promote sustainable futures of fieldwork education. It actualises the complexity of becoming a social worker across entangled local, national, and global contexts. The reading awakened memories and questions from my own field placement as a student and teacher for international fieldwork education. How had textbooks prepared me to work toward anti-oppression, capacity building, hope, and creativity? What did I know about the geopolitical history of my place(ment)? How could I practice critical reflexivity to un-learn privilege and change oppressive structures? This book demonstrates the richness and multiple forms of social work, where structural privilege and marginalisation, but also resistance and innovation, shapes spaces for fieldwork education. As a contribution to global social work education, I warmly recommend it to be read through the lens of glocality, a fusion of local and global, that promotes seeing the many contributions as interlinked across communities and regions in the world.'

Mona B. Livholts, *Professor of Social Work, University of Helsinki, Finland; Executive Board Member European Association of Schools of Social Work, EASSW*

The Routledge Handbook of Field Work Education in Social Work

This *Handbook* provides an authoritative account of international fieldwork education in social work. It presents an overview of advances in research in social work field education through in-depth analyses and global case studies.

Key features:

- Discusses critical issues in teaching social work and curriculum development; health care social work; stimulated learning; field education policies; needs, challenges, and solutions in fieldwork education; reflexivity training; creativity and partnership; resilience enhancement; integrated and holistic education for social workers; student experience; practice education; and ethical responsibility of social work field instructors.
- Covers social work field education across geographical regions (Asia and the Pacific; North and South America; Australia and Oceania; Europe) and major themes and trends from several countries (U.S.A.; Canada; Australia; China; Hong Kong; Sweden; Aotearoa New Zealand; England; Ukraine; Spain; Estonia; Italy; Ireland; Slovenia; Poland; Romania; Greece; Norway; Turkey; and the Czech Republic).
- Brings together international comparative perspectives on fieldwork education in social work from leading experts and social work educators.

This *Handbook* will be an essential resource for scholars and researchers of social work, development studies, social anthropology, sociology, and education. It will also be useful to educators and practitioners of social work in global institutions of higher studies as well as civil society organisations.

Rajendra Baikady is U.R.C. Special Post-Doctoral Fellow and Senior Research Associate at the Department of Social Work and Community Development, University of Johannesburg, South Africa.

Sajid S.M. is a senior social work educator and Professor of Social Work at Jamia Millia Islamia, New Delhi, India.

Varoshini Nadesan is Lecturer and Postgraduate Supervisor at the Department of Social Work and Community Development, Faculty of Humanities, University of Johannesburg, South Africa.

M. Rezaul Islam is Professor in Social Work at the Institute of Social Welfare and Research, University of Dhaka, Bangladesh.

The Routledge Handbook of Field Work Education in Social Work

Edited by Rajendra Baikady, Sajid S.M., Varoshini Nadesan, and M. Rezaul Islam

Routledge
Taylor & Francis Group
LONDON AND NEW YORK

Cover image © Getty Images

First published 2022
by Routledge
4 Park Square, Milton Park, Abingdon, Oxon OX14 4RN

and by Routledge
605 Third Avenue, New York, NY 10158

Routledge is an imprint of the Taylor & Francis Group, an informa business

British Library Cataloguing-in-Publication Data
A catalogue record for this book is available from the British Library

Library of Congress Cataloging-in-Publication Data
A catalog record has been requested for this book

ISBN: 978-1-032-12607-4 (hbk)
ISBN: 978-1-032-20552-6 (pbk)
ISBN: 978-1-032-16494-6 (ebk)

DOI: 10.4324/9781032164946

Typeset in Bembo
by Deanta Global Publishing Services, Chennai, India

Contents

Figures

Tables

Contributors

Kylie Agllias has held multiple roles in Australian field education across her career, including Field Education Coordinator at the University of Newcastle, University Liaison, and External Field Educator. Her core research and practice interests are social work pedagogy and family estrangement.

Beth Archer-Kuhn is Associate Professor with the Faculty of Social Work at the University of Calgary, Canada. As a Teaching Scholar through the Taylor Institute for Teaching and Learning, Archer-Kuhn has been exploring student-centred pedagogies, inquiry-based learning, immersive learning, critical reflection, and transformational learning within higher education. Recent publications include *Canadian Reflections on the COVID-19 Pandemic in Social Work Education: From Tsunami to Innovation*; *Inquiry-based Learning in Higher Education: A Pedagogy of Trust.*

Gurid Aga Askeland is Professor Emerita at the Faculty of Social Work and Family Therapy, V.I.D. Specialized University, Oslo, Norway.

Jessica Ayala is a Teaching Professor and Vice Dean in the Faculty of Social Work at the University of Calgary, Canada. Her areas of interest include online and blended learning, field education, and social work education. Ayala was Educational Leader in Residence for Online Learning at the Taylor Institute of Teaching and Learning during the pandemic and contributed to the Academic Crisis Management Team at the university.

Mary Baginsky is Senior Research Fellow in the NIHR Health & Social Care Workforce Research Unit, King's College London, UK. She is an experienced social research and evaluation professional with significant experience in academic, public, voluntary, independent, and private sectors and has published widely. She has worked in and with government departments and agencies in the UK and overseas, local authorities and partnerships, higher education institutions, charities, and service providers.

Rajendra Baikady holds a dual appointment as a URC Special Post-Doctoral Fellow and as a Senior Research Associate at the Department of Social Work and Community Development, University of Johannesburg, South Africa. In addition to this, he is also a principal investigator (Summer Research Fellowship) at the International Socioeconomics Laboratory, Harvard University, USA. He completed his first Post-Doctoral Fellowship at the Hebrew University of Jerusalem, Israel (2019–2020) and was awarded the Golda Meir Fellowship by the Lady Davis Trust at Hebrew University of Jerusalem, Israel. He is a Fellow of the Royal Society of Arts in the UK.

Paula Beesley is Senior Lecturer in social work and Academic Practice Lead at Leeds Beckett University, England, UK. She is a qualified social worker and practice educator, with a wealth of experience in child protection social work and practice education. Her teaching interests centre around skill development and placement learning. She is the lead author of *Developing Your Communication Skills in Social Work* (2018) and author of *Making the Most of Your Social Work Placement* (2020). She is undertaking a PhD on the effectiveness of supervision in social work placements.

Bindi Bennett is a Gamilaroi cis-gendered mother, researcher, and social work lecturer at the University of the Sunshine Coast. Her interests include equine therapy, trauma, Aboriginal social work, Aboriginal identity and wellbeing, as well as increasing cultural responsiveness in social work education. Bennett has more than 20 years' practice experience in the fields of Aboriginal social work, child and adolescent mental health, schools, and health.

Jennifer Boddy is Associate Professor and Deputy Head of School (Learning and Teaching) with the School of Human Services and Social Work, Griffith University, Australia, and she is a member of the Griffith Criminology Institute in Australia.

Marion Bogo was Professor at the Factor-Inwentash Faculty of Social Work, University of Toronto, Toronto, Ontario, Canada. She is the former Field Director, Dean, and first appointee to the first Endowed Chair in Social Work at the university. Her long-standing programme of research focuses on social work field education, the conceptualisation and assessment of professional competence, and, more recently, simulation-based education. She has published more than 135 journal articles and book chapters and seven books, and has disseminated her research in invited presentations internationally. She consults internationally to schools of social work on social work education approaches.

Cemre Bolgün is a full-time faculty member in the Department of Social Work at Manisa Celal Bayar University, Manisa, Turkey. His academic studies are usually on social policy, international migration, social exclusion, child poverty, and public attitude toward social work. Specifically, he conducts research on social cohesion and intergroup relations between the local community and displaced persons. His major responsibilities in the department are research, counselling, and supervision.

Elena Cabiati is Associate Professor at the Catholic University of Milan and Brescia, Italy. She teaches methodology of social work and intercultural social work in bachelor's, master's, and PhD programmes. She is a member of the Relational Social Work Centre (Department of Sociology) and her main research interests are in social work with ethnic minority people, social work education and child protection. She is a board member of the European Social Work Research Association, and she is a social worker.

Annamaria Campanini is a professor at the Department of Social Work, University of Milan-Bicocca, Italy and President of the International Association of Schools of Social Work (IASSW).

Giovanni Cellini is a Research Fellow at the Department of Cultures, Politics and Society of the University of Turin, Italy, where he teaches as a contract professor on the degree course in social work. A specialist social worker, his main research topics are social work in the welfare system and in the penal penitentiary sector, the helping professions and managerialism, the social work methodology, and social work education.

Sevaste Chatzifotiou is Associate Professor of Social Work at the Democritus University of Thrace (Komotini, Greece), Department of Social Work. She holds an MA in Social and Community Work Studies from the University of Bradford, UK. She also holds an MA in Social Research Methodology and a PhD in Domestic Violence against Women and Social Support in Greece from the University of Manchester, UK.

Honglin Chen is Professor of Social Work at the Department of Social Work, at Fudan University, China.

Dominic Chilvers has a background in psychiatric social work in the UK and New Zealand and has been an educator for ten years. He is the Principal Academic and BSW Programme Leader at Ara Institute of Canterbury, New Zealand and the Chair of the Council for Social Work Education New Zealand. Chilvers's doctoral research investigated the factors that influence how social work field educators work with students on placement, and he continues to research in the teaching and learning space.

Lo Kai Chung is a registered social worker in Hong Kong. He has been involved in frontline, supervisory, and social work teaching experiences in non-governmental organisations (NGOs) and universities for more than 15 years. As a practice consultant at the University of Hong Kong (HKU), he is responsible for supervising placement students and serves as setting coordinator of multicultural social work and community development services. His research interests lie in the area of multicultural social work, social work with fathers, social community development, and social work education.

Małgorzata Ciczkowska-Giedziun is an assistant professor in the Department of Social Pedagogy and Educational Research Methodology T the University of Warmia and Mazury in Olsztyn, Poland. Her scientific and research activities are connected with social work with the family, family pedagogy, and social pedagogy. She specialises in issues of multidimensional family support.

Helen Cleak is Adjunct Associate Professor in the Department of Community & Clinical Health, La Trobe University, Australia, and has an international research profile in field education with institutions such as Trinity College, Dublin, Ireland, and Queens College, Belfast, Northern Ireland. She has a strong practice and academic background in coordinating field education programmes and her co-authored book, *Making the Most of Field Placement* (5th ed.) has been adopted as the major fieldwork text in most Australian social work programmes.

F. Corradini is a research fellow at the Department of Sociology at the Catholic University of Milan, Italy, and has a PhD in Organisation Sciences. She collaborates with the Relational Social Work Research Centre. She is a lecturer in social work practice theory at the bachelor's degree level in social work and an academic tutor in unconventional practice placement at the master's degree level.

Carole Cox is Professor at the Graduate School of Social Service, Fordham University, USA. She is a Fellow of the Gerontological Society of America and a Fulbright scholar. She also serves as a representative of the International Association of Gerontology and Geriatrics (IAGG) to the United Nations. She is the author of eight books and more than 60 journal articles dealing with dementia, grandparenting issues, human trafficking, and social policy. Her book is entitled *Social Policy for an Aging Society*.

Hang T. Dao is lecturer in the Faculty of Sociology, Vietnam National University of Social Sciences and Humanities, Hanoi, Vietnam. She has been part of the Department of Cultural and Educational Issues, which mainly concerns social groups' cultural, educational, and religious issues and the influences of these fields on human life. She has been involved in some research related to students' issues, employment, religious and migration issues, and consumption behaviour.

Ágnes Dávid-Kacsó is Professor of Social Work at Babes-Bolyai University's Faculty of Sociology and Social Work, Cluj Napoca, Romania.

Marilena Dellavalle is an Associate Professor at the Department of Cultures, Politics and Society, University of Turin, Italy and has a PhD.

Elsa Døhlie is a Retired Associate Professor of Social Work at VID Specialized University, Oslo, Norway.

Zhao Fang is Professor of social work at the Department of Social Work at Fudan University, China.

Naomi B. Farber is Associate Professor at the University of South Carolina, College of Social Work, USA. Her scholarship has examined high-risk sexual activity, early childbearing. and family formation among low-income women. Currently. she is focusing on the history of the social work profession and education.

Niamh Flanagan is Assistant Professor/Lecturer in the Department of Applied Social Studies, Maynooth University, Ireland, where she teaches child and family policy, policy for practice, and research for practice. She has lectured in research methods and social policy in several third-level institutions and has specialised in teaching research for practice to social workers, youth workers, and community workers.

Fabio Folgheraiter is Full Professor in Social Work at the Catholic University of Milan and Brescia, Italy. He teaches theory and methods for social work in bachelor's, master's, and PhD programmes. He is the Director of Relational Social Work Research Centre at the Catholic University of Milan (Department of Sociology), and he is the founder of the relational social work method.

Christian D. Frost is Lecturer in Social Work with the School of Human Services and Social Work at Griffith University in Australia.

Kateřina Glumbíková is Assistant Professor at the Faculty of Social Studies, University of Ostrava, Czech Republic. Her research is focused on the issue of reflexivity in social work with vulnerable children and their families, and includes evaluation of social housing and homelessness of mothers and women without a shelter.

Juha Hämäläinen is Professor of Social Work at the Department of Social Sciences, University of Eastern Finland, Finland. He is also appointed as Visiting Professor at University of Ostrava, Czech Republic.

Kathryn Hay is Associate Professor, Massey University, New Zealand and teaches across field education, policy, and research methods courses. She is Associate Dean of Work-Integrated

Learning in the College of Health. Her research interests include work-integrated learning; social worker engagement in disaster management; and the readiness to practice of newly qualified social workers. She is on the editorial boards of social work and work-integrated learning journals in New Zealand and the Asia-Pacific.

Kiel Hennessey is an Aboriginal man, whose people descend from the Warrie-Gah peoples of the Wiradjuri Nation. Hennessey has more than 18 years' experience working in reciprocal relationships across government, non-government, and university sectors in the fields of social services, education, and health.

Jennifer Hewson is Associate Professor in the Faculty of Social Work, University of Calgary, Canada. Her research interests include age-friendly communities; social participation, isolation, and inclusion; and policies and practices related to programme and service delivery in the older adult sector. Her teaching has focused on gerontology, research and evaluation, community and international development, leadership in the social services, and field education.

Andrew Pau Hoang is a Post-Doctoral Fellow in the Academy for Leadership in Teacher Education and a member of the Social Contexts and Policies of Education Academic Unit at the University of Hong Kong. He researches school support services with an emphasis on how education, social welfare, and mental health systems condition the experiences of youth at risk and the multiple professionals dedicated to supporting them.

Huong T. Hoang is Associate Professor and Vice Dean of Faculty of Sociology, Vietnam National University of Social Sciences and Humanities, Hanoi, Vietnam. Her areas of interest and research are religion, social policy, and social research methods. She has taught courses on the sociology of religion, spirituality and social work, social problems and social policy, and social policy practice for undergraduates and graduate students. She has published a book, eight chapters, and several articles and papers in various journals and national and international conference proceedings.

Staffan Höjer is Professor of Social Work at University of Gothenburg in Sweden. He is also appointed as a research associate at Stellenbosch University, South Africa.

Rachael Howard is a Burra woman from Gundungurra Country who grew up on Wonnarua Country and now lives on Arrernte Country, Australia. She is working in remote communities outside Alice Springs delivering culturally safe and responsive mental health, drug, and alcohol support; case management; and community development.

M. Rezaul Islam is Professor in Social Work at the Institute of Social Welfare and Research, University of Dhaka, Bangladesh; International Academic Adviser at the Department of Social Administration & Justice, University of Malaya, Malaysia; Senior Research Associate, Department of Social Work, University of Johannesburg, South Africa; and Academic Fellow at the Faculty of Arts and Social Sciences, University of Sains, Malaysia. He was Visiting Professor at the University of Malaya, Malaysia from 2012 to 2016.

Graham Ixer has a long career in children's social work, academia, national policy, and regulation. He has had a research interest in practice learning and published an edited book, *Practice Learning: Perspectives on Globalisation, Citizenship and Cultural Change* (2006), in which he brought together a number of leading researchers and practitioners from across the world to address different perspectives on practice learning. He was head of social work education at the General Social Care Council responsible for regulating social work in England, including practice learning and field education.

Navrátilová Jitka is Professor of Social Work at Masaryk University's Faculty of Social Studies, Brno, Czech Republic.

Lise Johns is a full-time lecturer/researcher in the School of Human Services and Social Work at Griffith University in Australia. She is also a Program Advisor for the Bachelor of Social Work and a research consultant for Palliative Care Social Work Australia (PCSWA).

Lucy Porter Jordan is Associate Professor in the Department of Social Work and Social Administration and an associate dean of Faculty of Social Sciences, University of Hong Kong. She holds a PhD in social work from the University of Washington, Seattle, Washington, USA. Her practice is in social policy and development and capacity building in the NGO sector. Her major research areas are migration, families, youth comparative Asian studies, and social and health inequalities.

Angela Judge-Stasiak has been supporting distance social work students in the Faculty of Social Work at University of Calgary, Canada since 2015. Her professional experience includes student service, career development, placement coordination, and field supervision in higher education. Judge-Stasiak has been studying social work field education through graduate studies and is currently working on a Doctor of Education program focusing on computer-based simulations to enhance field education.

Alicia Kalmanovitch is a PhD student at Carleton University's School of Social Work Ottawa, Ontario, Canada. Her interests lie in policy, Holocaust scholarship, and social work education. A registered social work and field supervisor, her practice experience is in community development, homelessness, and policy analysis.

Steven Keed is a Wiradjuri man from Dubbo currently living on Ngunnawal Country, Australia. He works in mental health and teaches a course at Australian Catholic University on Working with Aboriginal and Torres Strait Islander peoples.

Carolyn Knight is Professor Emeritus at the School of Social Work, University of Maryland Baltimore County, USA. She is a social worker with more than 30 years of experience working individually and in groups with adult survivors of childhood trauma. She has written about and presented workshops on the trauma-informed conceptualisation and its application to clinical practice and supervision. She is co-author, with Professors Alex Gitterman and Carel Germain, of the 2021 social work practice text, *The Life Model of Social Work Practice* (4th ed.).

Kersti Kriisk is a lecturer in the School of Governance, Law and Society, Tallinn University, Estonia. She guides social work undergraduate and graduate students in their field placements and collaborates with practitioners in this context. Her research focuses on social policy priorities and expenditure on social protection in local governments.

C. Landi is a research fellow at the Department of Sociology at the Catholic University of Milan (Italy) and has a PhD in Sociology. She collaborates with the Relational Social Work Research Centre. She is a lecturer in social work procedures at the bachelor's degree level and an academic tutor in unconventional practice placement in social fieldwork at the master's degree level.

Éva László is a Professor of Social Work at Babes-Bolyai University's Faculty of Sociology and Social Work, Cluj Napoca, Romania.

Jie Lei is Associate Professor of Social Work at the School of Sociology and Anthropology, Sun Yat-sen University, China and has a PhD.

Lorraine Letkemann is Senior Instructor and Director – Office of Field Education in the Faculty of Social Work at the University of Calgary, Canada. She also serves as the Regional Coordinator for the Southern Alberta Region and teaches in both the BSW and MSW programmes. Most recently Letkemann and the provincial field education team navigated through the challenges of providing meaningful practicums to hundreds of students during the pandemic.

P. Limongelli collaborates with the Relational Social Work Research Centre. She is an academic tutor in unconventional practice placement in social fieldwork at the bachelor's degree level at Catholic University of Milan (Italy). She has a PhD in Applied Sociology and Social Research Methodology. She worked for many years in a family centre, where she developed long experience working with families, in particular women, belonging to ethnic minorities.

Mark Lynch is Director of Simulated Learning within the School of Human Services and Social Work at Griffith University in Australia.

Jane Maidment is a professor at the University of Canterbury, New Zealand and has a long history of research and practice within field education. She completed her PhD on this topic in 2000 and has continued to research in this and other social work education-related fields since. Edited book titles include *Practice Skills for Social Work and Welfare* (2016), *Social Policy for Social Work and Human Services in Aotearoa New Zealand* (2016), and *Supervision in Social Work: Contemporary Issues* (2015).

Irine Mano is a qualified social worker and a Social Work Practice Learning Tutor at Anglia Ruskin University in Cambridge, UK With an MSc in Practice Education, Mano is passionate about supporting social work students navigate their placements successfully and provides training for practice educators.

Jill Manthorpe is Professor of Social Work and Director of the NIHR Health & Social Care Workforce Research Unit, Associate Director NIHR School for Social Care Research, and NIHR Applied Research Collaborative (ARC) South London Social Care theme lead, The Policy Institute at King's College London, UK. She has undertaken several studies of social work education and taught on undergraduate and post-graduate social work training programmes for many years.

Jan Miner was Director of Field Instruction at Fordham University's Graduate School of Social Service in New York City, USA between 2000 and 2016. Trained and certified in psychoanalytic psychotherapy, she maintained a clinical practice in New York City for 25 years. She has taught research methods since 1997 at Fordham University (New York City). Currently, she teaches in Fordham University's online Master's in Social Work (MSW) programme and in the Bachelor's in Social Work (BSW) and MSW programmes at Nazareth College in Rochester, NY.

Mariah Moran is a doctoral candidate from the University of South Carolina, College of Social Work, USA. She is interested in social work education and re-examining fundamental questions about the profession through the writings of historic figures. Moran's research also includes the pragmatic, perceptual, and existential factors associated with geographic mobility in the rural American Southeast and how mobility is related to well-being, decision-making, and social relationships.

Brenda Morris is the MSW Practicum Coordinator at the School of Social Work at Carleton University, Ottawa, Ontario, Canada; co-founder of the Alliance of Ontario Social Work Field Education Directors; former Board Director of the North American Network of Field Educator and Directors; and a member of the Canadian Association for Social Work Education Field Education Committee.

Varoshini Nadesan holds postgraduate qualifications in both social work and child and youth care. She has 20 years' graduate experience as a social work practitioner at the Department of Social Development in KwaZulu/Natal, six years' experience at the South African Council for Social Service Professions (SACSSP) in Pretoria as National Manager for Professional Conduct, and nine years' experience as a lecturer and senior lecturer at the University of Johannesburg, South Africa.

Phillip Pallas is Lecturer in Social Work and Deputy Program Convenor of the Bachelor of Social Work (Honours) at the University of Newcastle, Australia. He is a University Liaison for the field education program and has held roles as an External Field Educator.

Eleni Papouli is Assistant Professor of Social Work at the University of West Attica (Athens, Greece), Department of Social Work. She holds an MA in International Child Welfare from the University of East Anglia, Norwich, UK, and a PhD in Social Work from the University of Sussex, UK.

Navrátil Pavel is Professor of Social Work at Masaryk University's Faculty of Social Studies, Brno, Czech Republic.

Jarosław Przeperski is Head of the Center for Family Research at the Nicolaus Copernicus University in Toruń, Poland; assistant professor in the Social Work Department; and an expert on family matters in the Polish Ministry of Justice and the Ministry of Family, Labour and Social Policy. He is the author of many expert opinions and publications in the field of public family and welfare policy.

Monika Punová is Assistant Professor at the Department of Social Policy and Social Work at Masaryk University, Brno, Czech Republic, where she has been a long-term guarantor of fieldwork education of social work students. She also collaborates with the Research Institute for Labour and Social Affairs as a researcher. She is the founder of several non-profit organisations providing social work to youth at risk and vulnerable families in the Czech Republic (Lata, Ratolest Brno, Klíč pro rodinu).

Pavlína Rabasová works at the Faculty of Social Studies, Department of Health and Social Studies, University of Ostrava, Czech Republic. She holds the position of Assistant Professor specialising in the following areas: health and illness, nursing, palliative care, informal care, pedagogy, and ethics in health care. She is also a guarantor of professional practical training.

M. L. Raineri is Associate Professor of Social Work at the Department of Sociology, Catholic University of Milan, Italy. She collaborates with the Relational Social Work Research Centre. She teaches Social Work Practice Theory at the bachelor's and master's degree levels in social work. Her research interests are about social work theory and practice, namely, the practical expression of relational social work at case, group, and community levels and about students' practice placements and students' supervisor training and support.

Liljana Rihter is an assistant professor, researcher, and the Dean of the Faculty of Social Work, University of Ljubljana, Slovenia, where she teaches subjects involving the methodology of research on all three levels of social work studies. Her research work encompasses various themes: methods and models of evaluation of social protection programmes, vulnerable groups, dementia, working poor, precarious work, analysis, needs-assessment, and poverty.

María del Valle Medina Rodríguez is Adjunct Professor at the Department of Social Work at the University of Granada, Spain. She has been a social worker and mediator at the Ímeris Association since 2000. Her main research interests are childhood, juvenile justice, and restorative justice.

Roser Manzanera Ruiz is Associate Professor at the Department of Sociology and teaches in the Degree in Social Work and Sociology at the University of Granada, Spain. Her main research interests are international social work and development, globalisation, gender, and social change.

Sajid S.M. has been a senior social work educator for 35 years and has been Professor of Social Work at Jamia Millia Islamia (JMI), New Delhi, India since 2001. He also served as Registrar, Pro-Vice-Chancellor, and Officiating Vice-Chancellor of Jamia Millia Islamia from 2010 to 2014. In addition, he also held the positions of Honorary Advisor, Centres of Higher Learning and Research, Jamia Millia Islamia, from 2008 to 2011 and Director, Academic Staff College, Jamia Millia Islamia from 2007 to 2008. He established the Nelson Mandela Centre of Peace and Conflict Resolution, JMI and was its Founding Director.

Leanne Schubert has held multiple roles in Australian field education across her career including Field Educator (internal and external), University Liaison at The University of Newcastle, and was briefly the National Professional Practice Lead at The Australian Catholic University Oversighting Field Education pedagogy.

Enrique Pastor Seller is Accredited University Professor in Social Work and Social Services by the National Agency for Quality Assessment and Accreditation (ANECA), Spain, Professor at the University of Murcia's Department of Social Work and Social Services, Spain, and has 15 years' professional experience as Director of Social Services Centres. He has six years of research experience and is the author of numerous articles, chapters, and books published by prestigious international journals and publishing houses; he is also a member of editorial committees of journals in ISI WoS, Scopus, etc. and is a visiting professor and researcher at prestigious international universities.

Tetyana Semigina is Professor at the Academy of Labour, Social Relations and Tourism at the National University of Kyiv-Mohyla Academy, Ukraine, and works on international projects. She has authored more than 400 publications on social work and social and health policy.

Karen M. Sewell is Assistant Professor with the School of Social Work at Carleton University, Ottawa, Ontario, Canada. She is an experienced clinical social worker with more than 20 years of practice experience, and a research profile demonstrating commitment to children's and youth mental health, social work education, transformative social work pedagogy, including simulation-based learning, and the social work profession.

Steven M. Shardlow is Emeritus Professor of Social Work, Keele University, UK and Researcher, University of Hertfordshire, UK.

Shweta Singh is Associate Professor in the School of Social Work at Loyola University Chicago, USA. Her MSW is from the Tata Institute of Social Sciences at Mumbai, India and her doctorate is from the University of North Carolina at Chapel Hill, USA. She has engaged in comparative research on linkages between education, work, and well-being for women and girls. Her work is informed by her theory 'identities of women'.

Marie Špiláčková is Associate Professor in the field of Social Work at the Faculty of Social Studies of the University of Ostrava, Czech Republic. She has focused her education and research on the theory and methodology of social work with emphasis on historical research in social work and urban planning. She supports professional discourse with the aim of strengthening awareness and thinking about the history of social work in various dimensions.

Fiona Stevens is Lecturer in Social Work and Field Education with the School of Human Services and Social Work at Griffith University in Australia.

Béla Szabó is Professor of Social Work at Babes-Bolyai University's Faculty of Sociology and Social Work, Cluj Napoca, Romania.

Prospera Tedam is Associate Professor of Social Work at the United Arab Emirates University where she has been since 2018. She was previously a Senior Lecturer in Social Work at the University of Northampton, UK (2006–2016) and Principal Lecturer at Anglia Ruskin University, Cambridge, UK (2016–2018). Tedam qualified as a social worker in 1996 and has practice experience in children and families' social work.

Iva Tichá is a social geographer and works at the Faculty of Social Studies, Department of Health and Social Studies, University of Ostrava, Czech Republic. She holds the position of Assistant Professor specialising in the following areas: demography, networking, public administration, and project education. She is also a professional practical training administrator.

Anne Tiko is a lecturer of psychosocial work in the School of Governance, Law and Society, Tallinn University, Estonia. Her research focuses on delinquent youth, families at-risk, children at psychosocial risk and their support.

Sarah Todd is Professor and the Director of the School of Social Work at Carleton University, Ottawa, Ontario, Canada. Her scholarship is focused on community practice and social work education. Her current research explores how practitioners navigate uncertainty in practice in the hopes that we might develop better tools to help train students to work effectively with uncertainty in practice. She is also a 3M Teaching Fellow.

Karmen Toros is Professor of Social Work in the School of Governance, Law and Society, Tallinn University, Estonia. She is actively involved in social work education and training of child protection workers. Her research focuses on child welfare and protection, strengths-perspective in child protection practice, and is particularly interested in assessment of child well-being. She has been conducting research on the assessment practices of child protection workers in Estonia with an aim to lay the foundation for creating a comprehensive assessment system and effective assessment practice.

Charalampos Tsairidis is Assistant Professor of Statistics at the Department of Social Work, Democritus University of Thrace, Komotini, Greece. His teaching and research interests mainly focus on mathematics (pure, applied, financial), statistics, operational research, and information demography.

Steven Wahle is a PhD student at University of South Carolina, USA, studying the history of social work as a profession with a particular interest in veteran resources in the US. Wahle has worked for Veterans Health Administration in direct practice and community building.

Elaine Wilson is a professionally qualified social worker having graduated from University College Dublin, Ireland, with a master's degree. She worked as a Senior Medical Social Worker and Acting Head of Department in St. Vincent's University Hospital, Dublin. Having worked as an oncology social worker for a number of years, and having developed a particular interest in this area, she took up a Research Fellowship position with The Cancer Clinical Research Trust.

Johnston H. C. Wong is Professor in Social Work and Social Administration. He started his career as a youth worker in Hong Kong. His early academic interests focused on youth and family work, branching out to psychological stress and unemployment. His research areas cover social indicators studies, healthy villages and cities, social laws in China, social work in disaster, health care, and for older people. He received the International Crisis Intervention Leadership Award from ICISF and the President Citation Award from ACPA.

Buğra Yıldırım is a full-time faculty member in the Department of Social Work at Manisa Celal Bayar University, Manisa, Turkey. His academic studies are usually on medical social work, social work education, paediatric asthma, caregiver burden, the biopsychosocial aspect of chronic illness, health policy, disease management, social work theory, social innovation, and social entrepreneurship in the future of social work.

Veronika Mia Zegzulková is a doctoral student of the social work study programme at the Faculty of Social Studies of the University of Ostrava, Czech Republic. She works at the Department of Social Work as an administrator of professional practical education. Professionally, she deals with social work in an international and global context at the level of pre-graduate education. As part of her pedagogical activities, she focuses mainly on preparing students for entry into the practice field and individual social work.

Tamara Rape Žiberna is a teaching assistant and researcher at the Faculty of Social Work, University of Ljubljana, Slovenia. She is the coordinator of fieldwork (in the third year of study) at the Centre for Practice and a teaching assistant of subjects involving the methodology of research. Her research work focuses on themes concerning fieldwork and teamwork in social work.

Foreword

The Routledge Handbook of Field Work Education in Social Work is a welcome addition to the literature on social work education and comparative research. It offers a wealth of contributions on field education across four continents. The book comes at a time of increased interest in international social work and in learning from others. It is also a time when educators in diverse contexts are struggling to provide quality field education for students, as field education across the globe is facing both old and new challenges.

As the editors point out early in their introduction, field education is an essential part of the preparation of social workers; indeed, it is now sometimes referred to by the US Council on Social Work Education and others as the 'signature pedagogy' of the field. From the earliest days, educators have recognised that practical experience must accompany academic learning to prepare social work practitioners. This differentiates a profession from a purely academic subject. A review of the history of social work education bears this out.

Between 1950 and 1972, the United Nations (UN) conducted five world surveys of social work education. In the very first of these, issues and variations in 'practical training' were discussed (UN, 1950). Supervision, the need to integrate theory and practice, and the balance between observation and learning by doing were highlighted in the overview and in country summaries. The International Association of Schools of Social Work continued the global survey of educational programmes, issuing the *World Guide to Social Work Education* in 1984. The criteria for inclusion as a social work programme were few in number and quite modest. It clearly stated, however, that 'The course of study should include theoretical study as well as substantial continuing field practicum with an arrangement for appropriate instruction in both class and field' (p. ix). This volume profiled social work programs in 61 countries across six continents, an expansion from the 46 countries listed in the 1950 UN publication.

In 2004, the International Association of Schools of Social Work and the International Federation of Social Workers issued the first ever *Global Standards for the Education and Training of the Social Work Profession*. The standards were revised in 2020 (IASSW/IFSW, 2020). Both versions include lengthy sections on field education under curricula and state that field education must 'be sufficient in duration and complexity of tasks and learning opportunities to ensure that students are prepared for professional practice' (IASSW/IFSW, 2020, p. 13). Other standards include providing qualified supervision, training for field instructors, a field manual with clear policies, and methods of evaluating students and field settings. New to the 2020 version is an aspirational standard that programmes should 'Create practice placement opportunities that correspond to at least 25% of the overall education activity within the courses (counted in either credits, days, or hours)' (p. 14). This is clearly an effort to reduce the variability in attention paid to the field component.

Organising and delivering quality field education continues to be a challenge for schools of social work. Many of the issues identified 70 years ago continue, including providing regular, professionally competent supervision and the need to help students integrate their classwork with field education. Over the past three decades, social work has expanded to numerous new locales, most notably to the countries of the former Soviet Union and China. The 2020 world census of social work education identified more than 3,500 programs in 159 countries (IASSW, 2021). In some places, social work is a completely new subject, and educators have had to initiate placements in areas without trained supervisors or even settings that defined themselves as social work settings (Healy & Thomas, 2021). In other countries, including such diverse places as Jamaica and Ethiopia, expansion in the number of schools of social work and increases in the number of students enrolled has outpaced the availability of suitable field placements (Kebede, 2019). Mentoring students into the profession is less likely to occur if experienced social work supervision is missing.

The Routledge Handbook of Field Work Education in Social Work includes overviews of field education and treatment of special subjects in 26 countries ranging from the United Kingdom to China, Slovenia, Turkey, Canada, and New Zealand. Several chapters provide student perspectives on their learning in the field. Special topics addressed include the experiences of indigenous students in field placement and considerations for ensuring that international placements are optimally designed and supported. Reflexivity as a component of learning and way of integrating learning is addressed by several authors. Finally, the impact of the COVID-19 pandemic is covered in three chapters at the end of the volume. Field education faced disruptions and unusual challenges, in terms of the needs and demands of service users, threats to the health of students and field instructors, and widespread closures of in-person services. Learning from these experiences will inform education in future emergencies. In their conclusion, the editors lament that the topic of technology is not adequately addressed in the present book. Presumably, the expansion of virtual service delivery during the pandemic will offer lessons for future consideration of technologies in field education.

In concluding the book, the editors remind readers that 'Competency of students and graduates from a school of social work largely depends on the quality of the field education agency, availability of faculty support, competent supervisors, and expertise in introducing an innovative fieldwork practicum'. In the United States, and perhaps other contexts, increased pressures for research and publication have diminished the involvement of full-time faculty in field liaison and engagement, widening the divide between classroom instruction and field learning and severing what was, in earlier times, a close collaboration between academia and the field. At the same time, neoliberal pressures push agencies to meet higher efficiency standards through increased caseloads and outputs. This leaves less time for field instruction and is resulting in fewer available placements for the growing social work student population. These trends may heighten the stresses on the dominant model of field education for social work and call out for creative solutions. Comparative study and increased sharing across borders can help in developing new models. This volume is an excellent start and a most welcome addition to the literature.

Lynne M. Healy, *MSW, PhD*
Board of Trustees Distinguished Professor Emerita
University of Connecticut School of Social Work, USA

References

Healy, L.M. & Thomas, R.L. (2021). *International Social Work: Professional Action in an Interdependent World* (3rd ed.) New York: Oxford University Press.

I.A.S.S.W. (1984). *World Guide to Social Work Education*. New York: Published by the Council on Social Work Education for the International Association of Schools of Social Work.

I.A.S.S.W./I.F.S.W. (2020). *Global Standards for the Education and Training of the Social Work Profession*. Accessed from: www.iassw-aiets.org

I.A.S.S.W. (2021). Global Directory of Schools of Social Work Census 2021. Forthcoming at www.iassw-aiets.org

Kebede, W. (2019). Social work education in Ethiopia: Past, present and future. *International Journal of Social Work*, 6:1. DOI: 10.5296/ijsw.v6i1.14175

United Nations (1950). *Training for Social Work: An International Survey*. New York: United Nations.

Acknowledgements

We are grateful to each of the volume's contributors, all of whom are eminently qualified to write about social work field education in their own countries, regions, and regimes. We acknowledge their enthusiasm, cooperation, and expertise in bringing out this remarkable handbook on fieldwork education in social work.

Rajendra Baikady gratefully acknowledges support from the Hebrew University of Jerusalem, Israel, in the form of a post-doctoral fellowship during 2019–2020 during which the idea for this handbook project was conceived and initiated. He is also thankful to his supervisor Professor John Gal for his continued support and encouragement.

Finally, we thank Antara Ray Chaudhary and Shashank Shekhar Sinha for proving an opportunity to put together this handbook and Rimina Mohapatra and her team at Routledge for their editorial support and cooperation in producing this handbook. Choosing Routledge as the best possible publisher for this handbook was justified at every stage of work with these colleagues.

Rajendra Baikady
Sajid S.M.
Varoshini Nadesan
M. Rezaul Islam

Introduction

Signature Pedagogy – A Practice Laboratory of Social Work Education

Rajendra Baikady, Varoshini Nadesan, Sajid S.M., and M. Rezaul Islam

Social work is a globally recognised human service profession committed to the principles of equality, social justice, and human rights. Social work, as an academic programme, is offered at various levels in several countries across the globe. Fieldwork within social work is a professional training component that equips graduates to apply theoretical aspects learnt in the classroom to real-life conditions. While there are continued inconsistencies with regard to professional standards, course curriculum, availability of qualified educators, supervisors, and practice learning agencies, social work, as a social change agent, has gained the confidence of the public in several countries, especially in the West. Since its inception, social work education has maintained its focus on 'practice learning', which is widely referred to as either fieldwork, field instruction, field placement, field education, field practicum, or internship, which is also an integral component of social work education both at undergraduate and postgraduate levels. Field education offered at all levels of social work teaching programmes is expected to make social work professionals more ethical and value-oriented change agents in contemporary society. Further practical teaching and training offered during graduate studies helps graduates to demonstrate social work competencies and develop their own professional use of self (Bogo, 2010; Finch et al., 2019).

Field education plays a crucial role in preparing social work graduates for their professional practice. Literature in the social work field extensively demonstrates that fieldwork practicum or fieldwork practice is as important as theoretical teaching. However, there are studies that have found a gap between the linkage of theory and practice within social work academia. Many universities accord equal emphasis and weight to the theoretical component and the field instruction components of social work education. Because students are expected to work with human beings and intervene in real-life situations, it is imperative that field education is implemented with the help of a better structured curriculum and tested situations, methods, and tools under the close supervision of both the faculty and field supervisors. Given the impact of globalisation, neoliberalism, the market-oriented development agenda, and constantly changing social realities, it is important to develop evidence-based, culturally competent, and learner-centred fieldwork curricula and practice modules in institutions of social work across the globe. In addition to this, it is imperative to mention that demand for indigenous social work models and field practice methods are in greater demand presently than ever before. Social work educators,

DOI: 10.4324/9781032164946-1

practitioners, and learners across the globe are raising their voices for context-specific curriculum, as many of the countries that teach programmes in social work have, until recently, been highly influenced by Western ideology (Gray & Coates, 2010; Gray, 2010; Baikady & Cheng, 2020; Baikady et al., 2020).

A systematic scanning of the literature produced on 'field education in social work' shows that the contributions addressing field education at local, national, international, and transnational levels is limited. Most of the available literature is rooted in a particular national or local context. Further, issues of changing social contexts, interdependency, and global connectedness demands for a global approach in training and educating social workers who can then engage in practicing social work at micro-, meso-, and macro-level across the globe. Technological advancement, availability of movable resources, and the possibility of cross-border teaching and international field practice placements further encourages a global and international approach in training social work graduates for a global society. The global definition of social work (IFSW/IASSW, 2014) further makes it clear that 'respect for diversity' is among the central principles of social work that encourages and demands diversity and interconnectedness in the social work curriculum. Scholars across the globe are debating on indigenisation and developing context-specific curriculum for training social work graduates. However, this also brings up valuable questions such as to what extent we need indigenisation, how international components can be accommodated within the context-specific social work curriculum and practice modules, and how learning from global social work helps in developing context-specific social work teaching and practice modules. While some of the authors in this volume (Chapter 12) discuss these issues extensively, we believe that further discussion and debates are needed in international social work practice and placement, particularly related to field education training.

'The Global Agenda for Social Work and Social Development 2020–2030' (IASSW/ICSW/IFSW, 2020) aims for global transformation while ensuring social justice, equality, and human development across the regions and regimes. Further, the first theme of the Global Agenda, namely '*Ubuntu: Strengthening Social Solidarity and Global Connectedness*', aims for promoting global social work education and practice across the globe. We believe that, parallel to this, social work academia across the globe, especially in developing countries with more privileges of development and advancement, should come forward in developing and strengthening social work education and practice in countries where there are little or no resources to support an emerging educational discipline. There is also a need for social work teaching programmes to collaborate with United Nations (UN) agencies and development initiatives to equip its graduates with the most advanced knowledge in social development. This extended and exclusive handbook on fieldwork education in social work brings together a handful of evidence-based contributions tested and verified by the experts in the field with an intention of contributing to global literature on fieldwork, education, and practice.

Fieldwork in Social Work Education: A Practice Laboratory

Fieldwork in social work practice is considered to be a testing ground for students and graduates. Through field practice, students and graduates apply their theoretical learning to real-life situations and test, enhance, and strengthen their skill, approach, and knowledge-base on practical aspects of social work. Fieldwork is a learning-by-doing opportunity for students and graduates in which they are supervised, guided, and mentored by experienced social work educators and field supervisors in the placement agency. During the fieldwork practicum, students and graduate learners are expected to undertake a number of activities within the learning space and to analyse these learnings with their respective supervisors and peers. These activities, conducted in communities and other learning spaces, serve as a vehicle in the socialisation process of students and prepares them for future professional practice. Field education is one of the key components in social work education and plays a significant role in the success of social work education and practice (Wang & Chui, 2016). Furthermore, during the field practicum process, theoretical knowledge is applied to real-life situations, thereby fostering understanding and interventions in social issues and problems that social workers confront in society. Hence, field education is principally considered to be a missing link between theory and professional practice (Parker, 2007). Acknowledging the importance and unconditional role fieldwork plays in preparing the next generation of social workers, field instruction was designated as the signature pedagogy of social work education by the Council on Social Work Education (CSWE, 2008).

Social work is an established practice-based profession (IFSW/IASSW, 2014). Theoretical learning that underpins classroom and practice learning collaboratively play a major role in preparing well-trained and value-oriented social work graduates who can then apply their skills and knowledge in practice within the boundary of professional ethics and conduct. Field education provides a rich learning experience to students, enabling them to practice what they were taught in the classroom. Moreover, students tend to find learning by doing more memorable than theoretical inputs provided in the classroom. Thus, field practicum, in general, plays a role of a practice laboratory and provides required infrastructural space for the social workers to test and validate their skills and capabilities while preparing them for future practice.

Contemporary Challenges and Concerns for Social Work Field Practicum

Evidence in literature shows that fieldwork practicum had been the central focus in social work education since the introduction of social work education in the 1900s (Doel & Shardlow, 2005; Bogo, 2010; Reamer, 2012). However, even after several decades of teaching, learning, and research, the fieldwork component of social work across the globe continues to experience shortcomings and challenges. Countries across the globe, irrespective of their history and the number of established schools, experience a shortage of well-trained supervisors at both schools and fieldwork placement agencies. The lack of qualified supervisors in many countries leads to limited learning opportunities for students and graduates during their social work programmes, thereby providing an obstacle for the engagement of professional practice. Additionally, the quality of field education students and graduates receive plays an important role in producing ethical, competent, and knowledgeable social work practitioners.

Finding agencies with the capacity to provide guidance for trainees during their field practicum is a greater challenge in many of the developing countries in the world. Students are generally sent for field practicum in the governmental and non-governmental organisations or agencies that are involved in social welfare and social development. By doing so, schools of social work and fieldwork supervisors expect students to learn and experience of the functioning of the agency, areas of interventions, welfare provisions, and the community intervention strategies that the agency follows. Unfortunately, in many countries, a large number of organisations are headed by unqualified social workers or persons who have vested interests in helping the profession but do not understand professional social work practice. This makes it difficult for social work students and graduates to get the required guidance and supervision during their field placement. Arguably, students continue to experience ethical dilemmas during their field practice and find limited space and avenue to clarify their doubt, particularly in the absence of the trained supervisor.

Despite increasing demand for trained social workers, many countries lack well-established teaching programmes and practice learning opportunities. Countries in which social work is a new academic discipline face enormous challenges in setting up practice teaching opportunities for its students. Thus, it is not an uncommon challenge that finding suitable placement agencies, trained supervisors, and availability of a uniform, structured fieldwork curricula for field practice hampers teaching and learning. One example is that of China, a country that is progressively advanced and identified as part of the Global South. Despite 30 years of social work development, social work academics in China still face challenges, such as a lack of qualified supervisors both within the schools of social work and in the fieldwork placement agencies. Another example is the continent of Africa, the countries of which face high levels of poverty, unemployment, crime, and exploitation based on gender, race, and economic status. Except for a few countries, such as South Africa and Nigeria, social work, as a service profession, is not yet well established in most countries on the continent.

Several chapters in this handbook discuss the various contemporary challenges faced by fieldwork practicum in different countries. Chapters in this volume, written by subject experts from different parts of the world, raise arguments on the status of field education while highlighting context-specific challenges and possible solutions for better implementation of fieldwork practicum. Many of these authors put forward insightful learning experiences that can influence practice-education-related polices not only in their countries but also in the international context.

Scholars in social work argue that social work field practice has received more attention than any other aspects of the social work curriculum (Bogo, 2015). However, despite growing scholarship and research on field education in the past several decades, the need for preparing social work practitioners capable of direct community interventions is rarely debated. This may be attributed to the focus in the literature regarding the training of social workers for clinical practice in social work (Bogo, 2015).

However, some schools of social work spent decades strengthening relationships with communities and agencies for developing students' placement protocols (Lewis et al., 2016; Xiong & Wang, 2007). The success of social work teaching programmes and learning during field practice can be ensured when schools of social work find themselves equipped with building cordial relationships with the field practice organisation and community. Agency placements play an important role in teaching students and graduates about agency functioning and responsibility, whereas community placements help students and graduates to develop interpersonal communication skills, understanding social issues and problems, and community dynamics and strength. Hence, it is important that students, during their postgraduate education, get exposure to both agency placements and community placements.

Developing and incorporating indigenous literature in social work field practicum is a challenging task in many countries. Currently, the importance of developing indigenous knowledge bases is critical, as Western knowledge and models are not producing expected results for problem-based interventions. Developing, validating, and disseminating context-specific literature and evidence-based theories is an ongoing debate; however, this has yet to be achieved in social work academia. Social work academia, in many countries, continues to face issues related to knowledge transfer despite advancement in science and technology.

The ability to build collaborative relationships among the schools within and outside the country is becoming more challenging and compounded by limited resources. The growing impact of globalisation and market-based economic planning across the globe have resulted in gross inequality and imbalance in resource distribution. Training and teaching about inequality and social justice for students, graduates, and social work professionals is more important now than ever before. In contributing to the transformation agenda for society and to bring about social change within local and global societies, social work students and graduates should receive comprehensive training, including exposure to external situations through field-based learning and placements.

Despite the advancement and development in social work across the globe, literature, debates, and innovations in terms of international field practicum and internship placements remain limited. The need for developing students' perspectives on global social work and imparting skill sets required for international field practice placement is a long discussed, yet not well-established, phenomenon in the global social work field. The incorporation of international content in social work education has been a point of discussion for several decades (Boyle et al., 1999; Caragata & Sanchez, 2002; Dominelli & Bernard, 2003; Mathiesen & Lager, 2007; Xu, 2006). However, there appear to be rare debates on developing a well-informed, evidence-based curriculum for international social work training and practice in the social work context. Several schools of social work have developed their own guidelines for field placements to monitor students' progress in their field learning; however, the absence of an internationally recognised and accepted curriculum that predominately focuses on fieldwork practicum is much needed in the promotion and advancement of international social work education and practice.

In 2015, the UN formulated 'Sustainable Development Goals' (SDGs) and set the reduction of inequality within and among countries as one of the major targets to be achieved by 2030. Since then, a lot of discussions centred around the incorporation and applicability of the SDGs in research, teaching, and practice. As a result, there has been considerable literature produced on different aspects of the SDGs and their achievements so far. However, despite the commitment of social work to the principles of social justice, equality, and human development, the emphasis on fieldwork orientation on global development goals is lacking. Arguably, there is little systematic literature on how global development goals can be incorporated into social work field education across the globe and contribute to the success of the UN 2030 agenda.

Need for an International Handbook on Fieldwork Education in Social Work

This is a handbook that brings together innovative fieldwork education and teaching programmes from 20 countries across the globe. However, the obvious question is 'Why create a large, extended handbook on '*fieldwork education*'. We feel that there is a clear need for a handbook on fieldwork education in social work with a global approach. Debates on challenges faced by countries in the Global North and Global South appear to be similar yet different. It is important to provide in-depth, up-to-date, and expert-validated literature on issues related to fieldwork education and its challenges across the globe. This handbook is written at a time when social work education, training, and professional practice across the globe is in a state of transition and is facing several challenges, including a of lack of professional recognition and accreditation. Contributions in this handbook provide cross-national perspectives on how social work field practicum is practiced and taught in different parts of the world, innovative practices, and the challenges faced by social work field education and how they are addressed in countries across the globe. This handbook is a comprehensive yet humble attempt to bring social work educators and fieldwork supervisors from international contexts together to discuss, deliberate, and learn from each other's experiences. This *Handbook on Fieldwork Education in Social Work* will fill the gap in literature by generating high-quality academic contributions dealing with field education at different levels of social work education from universities and colleges across the globe. Thus, this book is expected to be the first in social work academia to discuss field education from schools across the globe in a single volume.

While this handbook may offer innumerable advantages for social work academics, practitioners, researchers, and students, we elaborate on the following significant takeaways from our experience in compiling and editing this handbook:

Space for Global Innovations

Fieldwork in social work has been debated extensively, yet it lacks debates relating to the inclusion of indigenous knowledge applied to practice. There has been consistent effort to bring in international dimensions in both social work education and practice. Several efforts have been made through international field placement, collaborative research, teaching, and policy practice to replicate the innovative practices that are followed in some parts of the world. This handbook brings to the fore several such innovations in terms of fieldwork supervision, placement opportunities, introduction of new focus areas in the curriculum, ethical dilemmas experienced by students and their supervisors, and international collaboration and its impact on the development of social work field practice. Further, this volume itself is a product of our collaborative work with authors from across 20 countries in different parts of the world. There are also individual chapters that are the result of international and transnational collaboration between author groups.

Learning from Each Other

The *Handbook of Field Work Education in Social Work* comprises 36 well-researched contributions by subject-matter experts and fieldwork supervisors across 20 countries covering different regions of the world. Similar to economic and natural resources, social work education and practice opportunities are unevenly distributed among the developed and developing countries and among countries in the Global North and Global South. The availability of trained fieldwork educators, agencies for student placement, possibilities of open community placement, and economic and institutional resources are not equal, uniform, or stable in each country where social work is taught and practiced. There are several countries in which social work was introduced very recently, and there has been limited advancement in infrastructural and availability of resources. Additionally, some countries view social work as an academic discipline and as a service profession that is systematically controlled and mandated by the 'state' and 'state machineries'.

Building a Bridge: Internationalisation of Fieldwork Practicum

The demand for the internationalisation of the fieldwork practicum is on the rise. The demand for more international content in social work curriculum is also reflected in literature (IFSW, 2005; Cox & Pawar, 2006; Payne & Askeland, 2008; Dominelli, 2010). Universities across the globe are involved in collaborative research, teaching, and practice learning. Further, there is a dire need for social work education to develop social work teaching and learning programmes that prepares professionals to address global concerns, such as human rights, poverty, inequality, and social justice. Social work education in the twenty-first century needs to focus its attention toward training social work graduates to address global concerns. Alongside economic development, the social condition of countries appears to be deteriorating. The issues of human rights violations; injustice on the basis of race, gender, and economic status; and the widening gap between different income groups are a few factors that service professions should incorporate in their theoretical and practical education for future professionals. At a time when discussion on developing indigenous and culturally specific social work education in many countries is ripe, there is a need for incorporating the internationalisation of teaching and learning programmes, as this is marginally emphasised, especially in the developing world.

This handbook is a combination of both indigenous literature and international literature on social work field practicum. Staffen Hojer et al. (Chapter 3 in this volume) discuss their collaborative effort in developing social work field practicum in Chinese schools of social work. They present a collaborative approach which may assist countries where social work has fewer years of development and the profession constantly faces 'state' interference in its functioning. Admittedly, during the early stages of social work, many Western countries initiated the first schools of social work in the Global South, which have since grown into hundreds of teaching programmes.

Scope and Nature of the Handbook

The *Handbook of Field Work Education in Social Work* identifies and delineates social work field education from various national and international scopes. It comprises specially commissioned chapters combining cutting-edge, original research, and reviewed articles of high-quality, written and reviewed by subject experts and editors. Thus, this handbook provides an unparalleled overview of social work fieldwork education and its challenges in different societies. The findings and discussions presented by authors in this handbook predominantly set the agenda for future directions and for discussion on social work education, field education, and professional practice. The focus of the chapters are both theoretical, evidence-based, and empirical, bringing out policy analysis and outcome, to enable academicians and practitioners working on policy impact and advocacy work. This handbook is a collaborative outcome of experts across the globe and is, therefore, intended as a primary reference for scholars, educators, students and practitioners in different countries across the globe. The book has been divided into five parts:

Part I: Transforming Practice Teaching: Perspectives from Asia and the Pacific
Part II: Strengthening Field Education in Social Work: The North and South American Experience
Part III: Current Realities of Social Work Field Education in Australia and Oceania
Part IV: Social Work Field Education in Europe
Part V: Social Work Field Education under COVID-19

The aim in this handbook is to provide in-depth analyses of:

(i) Geographically based social work field education (Asia and the Pacific, North and South America, Australia and Oceania, Europe).
(ii) Key concepts that underpin debates concerning social work field education (theoretical approach, black African students, challenges for field education, integrated and holistic education).
(iii) Key concerns from different countries (Canada, Australia, China, Hong Kong, Sweden, Aotearoa/New Zealand, England, Ukraine, Spain, Estonia, Italy, Ireland, Slovenia, Poland, Romania, Greece, Norway, Turkey, Czech Republic).

(iv) Key international comparative perspectives on fieldwork education (China and Europe; social work and other social sciences).
(v) Principal perspectives of stakeholders (educators, practitioners, and learners; indigenous student experiences; novice social workers).
(vi) Key issues in teaching social work practicum and curriculum development (health care social work, trauma informed perspective, stimulated learnings, policies related to field education, analysis of needs challenges and solutions, reflexivity training, creativity and partnership in field education, resiliency enhancement, ethical responsibility, values and virtues, lived experiences of students).

The chapters in this handbook do not follow a rigidly prescribed framework, but in each chapter, the reader will find:

(i) Country specific information on field practice education.
(ii) An overview of social work education.
(iii) Historical background of field education.
(iv) Key features of the fieldwork practicum.
(v) What particular strategies are used for fieldwork practicum.
(vi) Challenges faced by field education.
(vii) Innovations, solutions to challenges. and a way forward.

One interesting factor is the differences in presentations and author submissions. Authors are rarely similar in their approach. Thus, there are some differences noted in each of these chapters. However, the structure is the same and readers will find a reasonably common approach: introduction, conceptual underpinnings, key issues, implications for social work field education, and conclusions and recommendations regarding future research.

Concluding Remarks

In our effort to develop the first ever handbook on fieldwork education in social work, we have worked diligently to include a variety of related aspects and a range of perspectives on fieldwork education in social work, setting out its challenges in different regimes and regions across the world. This handbook of fieldwork in social work education contains up-to-date contributions from leading writers in the field. This does not mean that we have covered everything in terms of conceptual understanding and geographical coverage. However, we hope that readers, students, educators, and researchers in social work will continue to explore the development of social work internationally and its applicability to the contemporary world. We see fieldwork practice and other related practice components in the social work discipline as a unifying factor that brings together an enriched understanding on a variety of theories and principles that deal with societal realties. We envisage the outcome to enable educators and researchers to develop a well-organised fieldwork practicum and structured supervision frameworks in social work as a means to achieve social justice and equality in constantly changing societies. We do believe that social work has emerged; rather, it continues to evolve as a strongly committed profession for ensuring equality, social justice, and human rights in each region and regimes it serves. Therefore, we envisage this handbook to serve as a guiding light for field practicum developers, students, and practitioners and provide well-thought-out solutions to the issues experienced while conducting practicum in practice settings. We are confident that our effort will go a long way in ensuring an equal and just society for all.

To conclude, we wish to inform readers of the second volume *The Routledge Handbook of Social Work Field Education in the Global South*, covering fieldwork education and its challenges in developing countries. The handbook on the Global South includes 28 well-researched contributions, covering 20 countries in the Global South. We believe that, together, these two volumes provide a true portrait of global social work with respect to social work practice, teaching, and learning. This handbook will inevitably support skill development, enhanced competencies, and fulfil requests for guidance and cross-cutting perspectives on social work field education amidst difficult times. Notwithstanding, the impact of the COVID-19 pandemic has made an indelible mark on social work education and impacted field instruction practice. We believe that some of the experiences and perspectives presented will serve as important tools to guide academics and supervisors as they navigate through similar and unique interruptions in learning.

References

Baikady, R., & Sheng-Li, C. (2020): Challenges for social work education in China: Findings from three metropolises, *Social Work Education*, DOI: 10.1080/02615479.2020.1795109

Baikady, R., Sheng-Li, C., & Channaveer, R. M. (2020): Eight decades of existence and search for an identity: Educators' perspectives on social work education in contemporary India, *Social Work Education*, DOI: 10.1080/02615479.2020.1773780

Bogo, M. (2010): *Achieving Competence in Social Work through Field Education*. Toronto: University of Toronto Press.

Bogo, M. (2015): Field education for clinical social work practice: Best practices and contemporary challenges, *Clin Soc Work J.*, 43: 317–324. DOI: 10.1007/s10615-015-0526-5

Cox, D., & Pawar, M. (2006): *International Social Work: Issues, Strategies and Programs*. Thousand Oaks, CA: Sage.

Doel, M., & Shardlow, S. M. (2005): *Modern Social Work Practice: Teaching and Learning in Practice Settings*. Burlington, VT: Ashgate.

Dominelli, L. (2010): *Social Work in a Globalizing World*. Cambridge: Polity Press.

Finch, J., Williams, O. F., Mondros, J. B., & Franks, C. L. (2019): *Learning to Teach, Teaching to Learn* (3rd ed.). Washington, DC: Council on Social Work Education.

Gray, M. (2010): Indigenization in a globalizing world: A response to Yunong and Xiong (2008), *International Social Work*, 53(1): 115–127.

Gray, M., & Coates, J. (2010): Indigenization and knowledge development: Extending the debate, *International Social Work*, 53(5): 613–627.

ICSW/IASSW/IFSW. (2020): 2020 to 2030 global agenda for social work and social development framework: 'Co-building inclusive social transformation. Retrieved from https://www.ifsw.org/2020-to-2030-global-agenda-for-social-work-and-social-development-framework-co-building-inclusive-social-transformation/

IFSW. (2005): Global standards for the education and training of the social work profession, adopted at the general assemblies of international associations of schools of social work and the international federation of social work, Adelaide, Australia. Available at: http://www.ifsw.org

IFSW/IASSW. (2014): Global definition of social work. Retrieved from http://ifsw.org/get-involved/global-definition-of-social-work/

Lewis, L.A., Kusmaul, N., Elze, D., & Butler, L. (2016): The role of field education in a university–community partnership aimed at curriculum transformation, *Journal of Social Work Education*, 52(2): 186–197. DOI: 10.1080/10437797.2016.1151274

Payne, M., & Askeland, G. (2008): *Globalization and International Social Work: Postmodern Change and Challenge*. Aldershot: Ashgate.

Reamer, F. (2012): Essential ethics education in social work field instruction: A blueprint for field educators, *Field Educator*, 2(2). http://fieldeducator.simmons.edu/article/essential-ethics-education-in-social-work-field-instruction/

Wang, Y., & Chui, E. (2016): An exploratory path model of social work students' satisfaction with field education experience in China, *Social Work Research*, 40(3): 135–145. DOI: 10.1093/swr/svw010

Xiong, Y., & Wang, S. B. (2007): Development of social work education in China in the context of new policy initiatives: Issues and challenges, *Social Work Education*, 26(6): 560–572. DOI: 10.1080/02615470701456210

Part I

Transforming Practice Teaching

Perspectives from Asia and the Pacific

1

Reclaiming a Macro Lens, Recasting Multilevel Practice

Social Work Field Education in Hong Kong

Andrew Pau Hoang, Lo Kai Chung, and Lucy Porter Jordan

How might we make sense of the phenomenon that the selection of field practicum in the community development (C.D.) field—and macro practice more broadly—is increasingly rare amongst Bachelor of Social Work (B.S.W.) and Master of Social Work (M.S.W.) students in Hong Kong? As social work educators, we have consistently observed our students' preferences for micro-level theories and practices to engage with individuals, families, and groups through case management, counselling, and therapeutic services. However, the macro-level praxis of community capacity building and planning, policy advocacy, and organisational and social change is equally important to Hong Kong's social development, the well-being of its most marginalised and disadvantaged residents, and social workers' professional identity. This is especially true given the region's high level of economic inequality, crisis of public housing, unequal opportunities for quality education, and continued social unrest over public governance.

Social workers have long been on the front lines of addressing these enduring public issues. In fact, Hong Kong social workers have historically been most visible in terms of their social and political participation (Chow, 2008). During the colonial period (1842–1997), social workers—particularly those in community work settings—played an active role, alongside the lower classes, opposing their domination by colonial bureaucrats and ruling interests (Wong, 1993; Chiu & Wong, 1998). Although their 'radical' political actions were suppressed in the 1970s, social workers earned greater legitimacy over the next two decades by taking active roles in opening the political system and standing for elections to represent silenced and deprived communities. Despite the staunchly conservative welfare ideology of the colonial government, social workers played a major role in increasing government social welfare expenditures leading up to the change of sovereignty in 1997. However, the welfare landscape of Hong Kong—and, therefore, the possibilities for domains of social work practice—has transformed significantly since the establishment of the social work profession and the region's reintegration with mainland China. Of particular concern is how field education opportunities—and, therefore, future social work practice—in C.D. have become increasingly stifled. This chapter examines some of the historical contributions of C.D. and the social and political conditions of its present formation as a setting for social work education and practice. Advocating for a revival of C.D. services is

DOI: 10.4324/9781032164946-3

beyond the scope of this chapter. Nonetheless, we argue that a macro lens in social work needs to be reclaimed and that the practice-guiding principle of 'person-in-environment' should be honoured through field education that cultivates a multi-level practice orientation among social work students.

We begin by providing a brief background of social work field education and C.D. in Hong Kong. Social work has gained an increasingly professionalised status, despite the widespread acknowledgment that welfare programmes—particularly in the C.D. field—continue to be slashed. We situate this problem in relation to the devaluation of macro social work, whose telos is social action and social change and the concomitant advancement of micro-focused, remedial social work approaches. These approaches emphasise helping individuals adapt to and improve social functioning within existing social environments. We connect the past to the present (and society to the field) by highlighting the trend of consistently low student enrolment in C.D. placements based on data collected from the field office of our university. This trend is largely consistent across the region and is connected to the depoliticisation of social work observed by scholars since at least the mid-1980s (Chiu & Wong, 1998). C.D. continues to be hollowed out by the diminishment of opportunities for students to receive field education and training in this area of social work practice. In our substantive discussion, we consider how the present social context of depoliticisation dovetails with the intensification of neo-liberalisation and managerialism in social work education and training. With an emphasis on implications for field education, this chapter concludes by engaging with recent calls to reclaim and reimagine macro social work education (Netting et al., 2016), including social workers' political roles as an aspect of professional practice (Lam & Blyth, 2014). Despite the precariousness of C.D. as a welfare institution, we argue that its broader macro praxis can and must be salvaged. To this end, we offer suggestions for what it means to 'reclaim and recast' social work field education and practice in the region.

Social Work in Hong Kong

The social work profession was established in Hong Kong following World War II, when relief organisations from Western countries set up offices in the region (Chow, 2008). Professional social work education in tertiary institutions began in 1950 at the University of Hong Kong, and many other educational institutions soon followed by establishing their own social work programmes. Leading up to the 1990s, however, this was not the only path for individuals to become social workers. Practitioners who occupied a 'social work post' at a social work agency for more than a decade before the early 1980s were also considered social work professionals (Social Workers Registration Board, 2016). The journey to social work professionalisation culminated in the establishment of the Social Worker Registration Ordinance (the Ordinance) on June 6, 1997. The Social Workers Registration Board (S.W.R.B.) was then established as a statutory body strictly governed by the Ordinance, ensuring professionalism by monitoring the quality of social workers and protecting the interests of service users and the general public (Chan, 2017). As of February 2020, there are 24,442 registered social workers serving the Hong Kong population of nearly 7.5 million (S.W.R.B., 2020).

The S.W.R.B. is responsible for setting criteria and standards of competency required for professional accreditation of the social work education and training institutions (Chow, Cheung, & Chan, 2018). In 2019, there were 14 such institutions which provided social work education programmes for qualification, ranging from Higher Diploma to Postgraduate/Master's-degree level (S.W.R.B., 2019). Such accreditation recognises fieldwork placement/practicum as the signature pedagogy of social work education and competency-based assessment (Chow et al.,

2018). Field education is regarded as a necessary component to be qualified for registration as a social worker and aims to reflect the multiple levels of assessment and intervention (from micro to macro) where future social workers can be expected to practice (Donaldson, Hill, Ferguson, Fogel, & Erickson, 2014).

Field Education in Hong Kong

Fieldwork placement is an essential methodology and process for social work educators to engage with students and provide them a platform to integrate classroom knowledge with experiential learning in different social work settings (Dash & Roy, 2020). Various terms synonymous with 'fieldwork' are often used, including field practicum, placement, practice learning, and field experience. They are all characterised by a specially designed learning experience in which students learn to become independent social work practitioners (Chan, 2017; Ford & Chui, 2000).

Social work students consider multiple factors before choosing fieldwork placements during their studies. Through our personal observations—including supervisory roles in field education—and statistical evidence from our field office, we have identified a trend in the declining number of students selecting C.D. or macro-focused interventions as their fieldwork placement. This finding is consistent with most countries that have relatively longer histories of social work education (Segal-Engelchin, Kaufman, Huss, & Amos, 2017; Donaldson et al., 2014; Rothman & Mizrahi, 2014), alluding to the marginalisation of macro social work in social work education and practice not only in Hong Kong but globally. Recognising the trend to overemphasise micro practice (also sometimes called 'clinical' or 'direct' practice), local scholars have argued for a pedagogical movement to return the 'social' element to social work (Chack, 1993) by enhancing critical reflection about the structure of society through fieldwork practice (Kam, 2014; Chan, 2017). We suggest that such shifts are facilitated by the ethos of C.D. education and practice.

Community Development as Social Work

The International Association for Community Development (I.A.C.D.) proactively connects fieldwork practitioners, academics, students, and volunteer community activists to promote the field of global C.D. In 2018, I.A.C.D. published the 'International Standards for Community Development' to promote professionalism in standards of practice. According to the standards document, C.D. is defined as:

> A practice-based profession and an academic discipline that promotes participative democracy, sustainable development, rights, economic opportunity, equality and social justice, through the organisation, education and empowerment of people within their communities, whether these be of locality, identity or interest, in urban and rural settings.
>
> *(I.A.C.D., 2018, p. 13)*

The concepts and practices of C.D. have been adapted to social work practice in Hong Kong since the 1960s (Kam et al., 1994). This began with addressing subsistence and survival needs through meal feeding services offered to residents to promote a sense of belonging and stability through groups, programmes, and community projects. The colonial government subsidised the pioneer Community Centre (C.C.) in the 1960s and Neighbourhood Level Community Development Project (N.L.C.D.P.) in the 1970s. These aimed to provide services for transient and deprived communities for whom welfare services and facilities were inadequate or non-existent. Since the 1980s, C.D. services have consisted mainly of C.C.s and N.L.C.D.P.s subsidised by the government, whose services target entire communities, mostly defined geographically (Fung, 2017; Fung & Hung, 2011). C.C.s employ social workers as part of integrated groups and community work teams, and N.L.C.D.P.s typically employ three social workers or community organisers (Kam et al. 1994). Although C.D. services are funded by the Home Affairs Bureau, they are managed by the Home Affairs Department (for C.C.s) and the Social Welfare Department (for N.L.C.D.P.s). They continue to enhance communication between Hong Kong residents and the government, with the primary objectives of serving the needs of disadvantaged groups, building community strength, promoting mutual aid, and encouraging community participation/cohesion (Home Affairs Bureau, 2005).

Community Development by What Means? To What Ends?

After Hong Kong became a Special Administrative Region of the People's Republic of China in 1997, the first policy statement of C.D. set out by the Legislative Council (L.C.) Panel on Home Affairs (1997)—and reviewed in 2005—defined C.D. as 'primarily concerned about encouraging people to participate in issues that affect their lives with a view to developing vibrant and sustainable communities. This is a process of enhancing civic awareness and social consciousness' (L.C. paper, 1997). Furthermore, non-government organisations (N.G.O.s) that provided C.D. services should:

> Mobilize community resources and encourage people to interact with one another through participation in a series of activities and networking groups. They aim at promoting self-help and mutual help in solving community problems and building up social support networks. *The services should ultimately strengthen community capacity and facilitate social integration, which contributes to a caring, just and harmonious society. The services should be provided in a flexible and non-partisan manner.*
>
> *(L.C. paper, 1997, emphasis added)*

Such definitions of C.D. and consequent directives can be seen as emphasising a social order theory orientation, in which macro services are aimed at remedial problem-solving as the main form of practice. Such an orientation exemplifies social development theories and evolutionary change models that largely accept the existing social order and seek social improvement rather than extensive social change (Midgley, 1995; Payne, 2014). Midgley and Conley (2010) defend social development theory as a form of activism and progressive social change. However, this paradigm of C.D. practice was soon contested by the Community Development Division of the Hong Kong Council of Social Service, which provided another iteration in July of that same year. Circulated amongst academics, N.G.O.s and community work practitioners, the term 'community development' was alternatively re-defined as:

> A process of raising social consciousness whereby people are encouraged through collective participation to *identify, express and act on their needs.* It is a community-oriented social work approach which comprises a series of *planned actions with the ultimate goals of achieving social* justice and *improving the quality of community life.*
>
> *(H.K.C.S.S., 1997, emphasis added)*

Substantiating—and arguably, departing from—the stance of the Home Affairs Bureau, the academics and community workers from N.G.O.s believed that consciousness-raising and planned social action with a community-oriented approach could better achieve the goals of promoting social justice. The term 'non-partisan manner' emphasised by the government was criticised as the deliberate depoliticisation of C.D. services. Scholars have identified these larger tensions reflected in contemporary social work education (Kerelian & Arat, 2017) and practice (Cheung, 2018). Should social workers emphasise social order or social change as process? Should they help build a caring, just, and harmonious society or work toward achieving social justice and improved quality of life as outcomes? Kerelian and Arat (2017) destabilise these binary oppositions and argue for a re-conceptualisation of social harmony inclusive of social justice. However, Cheung (2018) notes that social workers may, nevertheless, encounter the dual demands of building harmonious communities on the one hand and becoming responsible and contributing members of society on the other as contradictory.

In Hong Kong, Rothman's models of community organisation (1974)—including the ideal type of 'social action'—has had an influence on macro social work. Social action aims to redistribute power, resources, and decision making in communities and sometimes to change the policies of formal organisations (Leung, 1990). It is a core element of C.D. to achieve social justice and empower community members, utilising conflict to negotiate with power holders (Popple, 1995).

Contesting and disruptive tactics were popular among reform-minded social workers in the 1970s, organised by N.G.O.s funded by overseas churches. Such approaches fostered many policy changes since the 1980s and explains the pervasiveness of protest actions during colonial times (Fung, 2017). However, such social action approaches have often been deemed 'radical' and considered one of the crucial factors that have led to the downsizing of C.D. resources (Tung, 2011).

Social action has displeased Hong Kong policymakers and government officials in recent history (H.K.C.S.S., 2019). In 2008, an N.L.C.D.P. community worker received warnings from senior management of an N.G.O.—Young Women's' Christian Association (Y.W.C.A.)—to minimise criticism of the government for how it handled the flood damage of Tai O, a rural area. Later on, it was discovered that the head of the Home Affairs Bureau reflected to the Y.W.C.A. senior management that the team was 'inharmonious' to community stakeholders and the government, calling it the '*HeXie*' (壓抑異見聲音) incident (H.K.C.S.S., 2019). This occurrence signals how C.D. through social action deemed radical may not be welcomed by officials responsible for funding services.

Indeed, the resources from government subvention of Hong Kong's C.D. services over the past half-century have been inconsistent. This is partially explained by the government's attempts to eliminate N.L.C.D.P.s and transform C.C. programmes by merging them with 'community-based' family services. For example, the numbers of Integrated Family Service Centres (I.F.S.C.)—two-thirds of which are directly run by the Social Welfare department—and the social workers they employ have increased dramatically since 2004/2005. However, the focus of 'community-based' services in I.F.S.C.s is to support and strengthen individuals and families (Social Welfare Department, 2010, 2005), re-inscribing community work under a social order theory paradigm as remedial, direct practice. This can be analysed as one way in which governments 'manipulate the "community" as a policy tool' to compensate for welfare cuts (Fung & Hung, 2011, p. 459). Such efforts have not been without resistance, however, as large-scale mobilisations among service users, community workers, and academics in tertiary social work institutions have defended the distinctive operations of C.C.s (Fung, 2017). However, the lack of government resources—particularly for N.L.C.D.P.s—has been palpable since the handover. Community workers claim that C.D. services have been in a period of darkness since the 1990s (H.K.C.S.S., 2019). The decrease from approximately 54 to 17 project teams since 1995 is a significate indication.[1]

As transient communities were displaced or demolished, terminated N.L.C.D.P.s were not replaced by other projects delivering similar services (Fung & Hung, 2011). The Home Affairs Bureau deploys the resources of a single team from the Society for Community Organisation to operate the Care and Support Networking services that aid reintegration of ex-offenders, persons recovering from mental illness, and street sleepers in West Kowloon. The number of community centres operated by N.G.O.s under subvention by the Social Welfare Department remains frozen at 13, despite the population of Hong Kong increasing from 5 to 7.5 million between 1980 and 2020 (Census, 2020). In a period of precariousness surrounding C.D. services, how can field education cultivate in students the necessary macro practices, knowledge, and skills exemplified by, though not exclusive to, C.D.?

The Context of Macro Practice in Field Education

In the U.S.A. context, a focus on the clinical social work licence in many states has led to fewer role models and mentors to support new macro practitioners (Donaldson et al., 2014). Many social work graduates share that they have low levels of political skill and less preparation to work in larger systems and to adopt macro-level intervention strategies into their professional roles (Segal-Engelchin et al., 2017). Students are also worried about their future employment in C.D. settings:

> Macro students feel that their employment options will be constrained because they will not be qualified to work in the much larger clinical area if they are not able to get macro jobs or if they want to switch emphasis
>
> *(Segal-Engelchin et al., 2017, p. 53)*

As Hong Kong based social work educators, we also observe this sentiment among our students. Experience in fieldwork placement is a reliable indicator of students securing future employment in those areas. It is understandable that an attractive job future is an important consideration in choosing field placements. The decline of C.D. resources in Hong Kong means fewer placement opportunities, role models, and mentors for students seeking to cultivate a macro social work sensibility and skill set.

It is important to recognise how field placements in macro-practice benefit students. They facilitate involvement in local politics and advocacy organisations as part of training to prepare students for social change work (Segal-Engelchin et al., 2017). Different from interventions with individuals, families, and groups, community interventions often involve large groups of people and more complex resources and dynamics. Many community organising programmes are highly informal and unstructured, cultivating adaptability and collaborative responsiveness in contrast to the regulation and tight scheduling typical of more micro-focused work such as casework interviews (Kadushin & Harkness, 2014). As field placement is the first 'close to employment' environment for the majority of social work students, they are expected to strike a balance between learning and working with people in diverse organisational settings. Students, therefore, come across many difficulties in the field practicum experience (Lager & Robbins, 2004).

Many factors can affect students' performance in field placement (Fortune, McCarthy, & Abramson, 2001). The field experience is 'the product of the collaboration between academic institutions and agencies' (Ford & Chui, 2000, p. 25), and it is customary to hire fieldwork instructors or supervisors as the main liaison between institutions and students. Supervisors are also encouraged to further develop their skills and reinforce supportive roles in practice teaching

(Yeung, Tsor, & Kim, 1998). However, they can encounter difficulties when structuring opportunities for students' learning within agency settings. Ideally, field education situates practice within the larger social context and nurtures students' professional socialisation and developing skill sets. Cultivating critical reflection for reflexive practice, therefore, is essential to help students develop their social and cultural-analytical skills and ethical sensibilities. However, in some agency settings, the adoption of critical reflection is narrowly defined as the ability for new service ideas to help agencies meet funding requirements under managerialist pressures (Chan, 2017). Even the indigenously developed Social Work Practicum Assessment Tool (Chow, Cheung, & Chan, 2018), which has been cross-culturally adapted for usage in Hong Kong, does not include a critical examination of welfare policy loopholes as a criterion in evaluating practice competence, side-lining the relevance and importance of this kind of macro-focused critical reflection (Chan, 2017).

Community Development and Field Education at the University of Hong Kong

In the present context, consistently low numbers of Hong Kong social work students are choosing C.D. as their fieldwork placement. With support from the fieldwork placement team at our university, data was collected regarding the trend of students who have chosen C.D. as their fieldwork placement in the two required practicums (summer block and concurrent) required for qualification by the S.W.R.B. To reiterate, such trends are not only unique to our institution, but reflect regional and global trends in social work education (Donaldson et al., 2014)

Fieldwork placement arrangements from the department involve a matching exercise which begins 6 to 9 months before the first placement. Students are invited to submit two preferences among nine types of placement settings: C.D. services, services for the elderly, family services, medical setting social work services, multicultural social work services, rehabilitation services, school social work services, services for children and youth, and overseas/mainland fieldwork. Due to keen competition among students for the same placement, some settings (such as medical, family services, and overseas placement) require students to have outstanding academic results as part of the selection criteria. This requirement is not applicable to students choosing C.D. services. In light of other considerations, (location of service centres, students' previous front-line experience in the same setting, attachment/on-the-job placement, etc.) the fieldwork team announces the matching results and organises briefing sessions for students that are conducted by full-time supervisors in the fieldwork team who have front-line practical experiences in those settings. The following statistics (Tables and Figures 1.1 to 1.3) show the trend of B.S.W. (full-time), M.S.W. (full-time) and M.S.W. (part-time) students, respectively, who selected C.D. as their fieldwork placement between 2012–2020:

The numbers of students placed in C.D. settings over the past decade is consistently low, averaging about three students per year. The modest increases observed in 2014–2015 and 2015–2016 could have coincided with an increasing desire observed among our social work students to be involved in social action and social change initiatives raised by the Umbrella Movement between September and December of 2014. However, it is important to note that these statistics alone cannot ascertain the motivations of students selecting C.D. as their field placement.

Discussion

This chapter's point of departure was the problematisation of low numbers of social work students selecting C.D. as their field placement. Community work and C.D. services have played a pivotal role in Hong Kong's social welfare landscape, empowering the region's disadvantaged and silenced communities, advocating for social change and responsive governance. Social work

Table 1.1 Full-Time B.S.W. Students Choosing C.D. as Field Placement

Year	*Mode*	*B.S.W.*		
		# of placement students	*# of students placed in C.D.*	*% of total*
2012–2013	summer block	58	3	5%
	concurrent	70	2	3%
2013–2014	summer block	64	4	6%
	concurrent	64	2	3%
2014–2015	summer block	50	6	12%
	concurrent	32	3	9%
2015–2016	summer block	39	1	3%
	concurrent	45	2	4%
2016–2017	summer block	46	8	17%
	concurrent	45	3	7%
2017–2018	summer block	40	1	3%
	concurrent	43	3	7%
2018–2019	summer block	43	1	2%
	concurrent	40	1	3%
2019-–020	summer block	44	1	2%
	concurrent	44	6	14%

Source: All tables and figures in this chapter are by the authors.

Table 1.2 Full-Time M.S.W. Students Choosing C.D. as Field Placement

Year	*Mode*	*M.S.W. (F.T.)*		
		# of placement students	*# of students placed in C.D.*	*% of total*
2012–2013	summer block	45	3	7%
	concurrent	48	2	4%
2013–2014	summer block	49	3	6%
	concurrent	48	2	4%
2014–2015	summer block	62	4	6%
	concurrent	58	5	9%
2015–2016	summer block	65	9	14%
	concurrent	66	3	5%
2016–2017	summer block	43	3	7%
	concurrent	43	3	7%
2017–2018	summer block	51	1	2%
	concurrent	50	1	2%
2018–2019	summer block	64	0	0%
	concurrent	64	1	2%
2019–2020	summer block	64	1	2%
	concurrent	67	5	7%

has gained an increasingly professionalised status in the region, despite the widespread acknowledgment that welfare programmes continue to be slashed in the C.D. field. In the following discussion, we provide a structural analysis of this problem by highlighting the neo-liberal and managerialist ideologies that shape contemporary social work and the concomitant devaluation

Table 1.3 Part-Time M.S.W. Students Choosing C.D. as Field Placement

Year	*Mode*	*M.S.W. (P.T.)*		
		# of placement students	*# of students placed in C.D.*	*%*
2012–2013	summer block	20	2	10%
	concurrent	41	2	5%
2013–2014	summer block	13	0	0%
	concurrent	52	6	12%
2014–2015	summer block	14	1	7%
	concurrent	54	5	9%
2015–2016	summer block	11	0	0%
	concurrent	64	7	11%
2016–2017	summer block	19	0	0%
	concurrent	45	4	9%
2017–2018	summer block	19	0	0%
	concurrent	53	1	2%
2018–2019	summer block	18	0	0%
	concurrent	71	3	4%
2019–2020	summer block	10	0	0%
	concurrent	57	6	11%

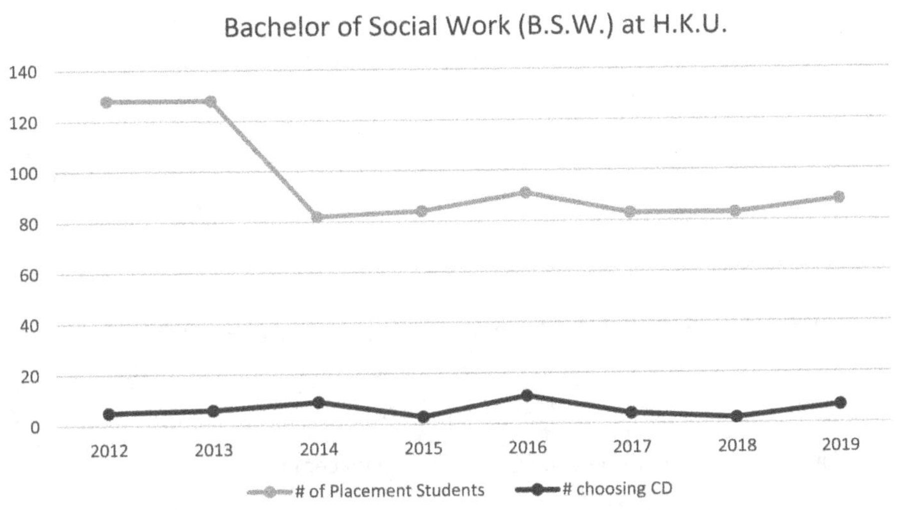

Figure 1.1 Full-time B.S.W. students choosing C.D. as field placement

of macro practices, whose telos is social action and social change. This leads us to suggestions for field education that are inspired by calls for a pedagogical movement: to *reclaim* the macro lens exemplified by C.D. for social work field education and to *recast* social work practice in the vertical register of multilevel practice.

Welfare Ideology and the Subvention System: Conditioning Field Education

Global transformations, including neo-liberalisation and managerialist reforms, adapted from Western countries—including the United Kingdom, U.S.A. and Canada since the 1990s—have

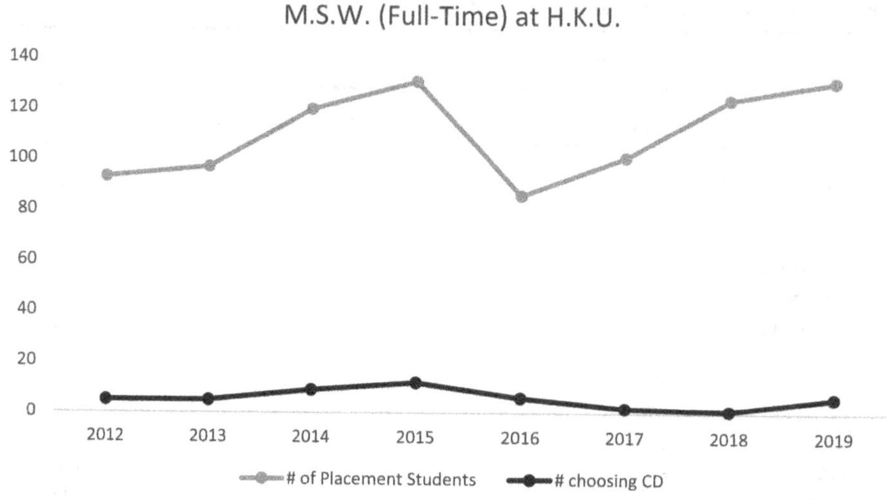

Figure 1.2 Full-time M.S.W. students choosing C.D. as field placement

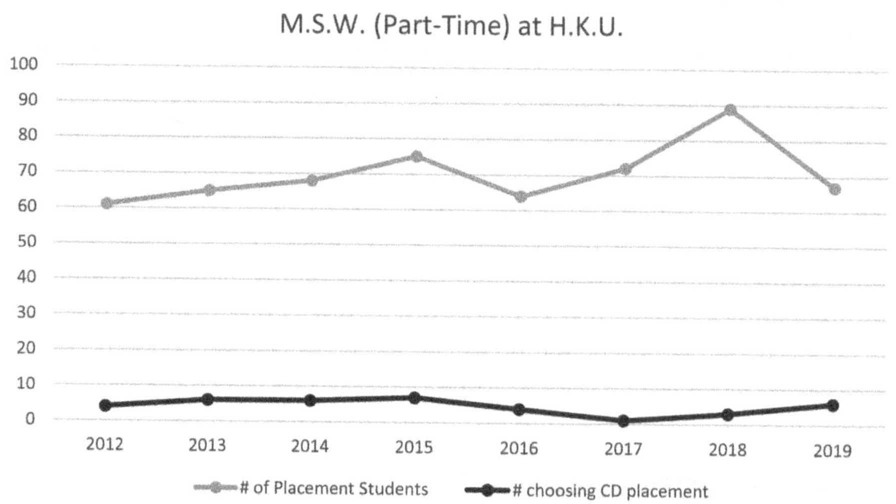

Figure 1.3 Part-time M.S.W. students choosing C.D. as field placement

inspired the new welfare ideology in Hong Kong. Although the community is a central element of the third sector to provide welfare support and economic development for disadvantaged groups, neo-liberalisation has weakened the capacity of C.D. to improve their welfare (Fung, 2017). In Hong Kong, one repercussion of such transformations has been the new funding/subvention system, which emerged in the early 2000s in the wake of the Asian economic crisis. This subvention system is comprised of a lump sum grant scheme and welfare bidding.

Previously, the allocation of public resources for social welfare followed a standard unit cost model. Social programme expenses were subvented (funded) according to the input and items utilised for the programmes (i.e., the actual salary requirements of all required posts). The new lump sum scheme involves a block grant for N.G.O.s (covering staffing, equipment, and general expenses), but with an important shift from 'input to output control through performance monitoring and business management practices' (Fung, 2017, p. 62). Under the welfare bidding system, funding supports for new service developments are allocated on a competitive basis, and the role of N.G.O.s has been reduced from partner to contractor in pursuit of value for money (Yan, Cheung, Tsui, & Chu, 2017). This has given rise to new institutional logics i.e., New Public Management (N.P.M.), based on instrumental rationalities and business management practices. Such logics are principally concerned with cost-efficiency, accountability, and competition. This can have adverse effects on professional practice, noted by Cheung (2018) who argues that social workers' professionalism has become disempowered, whilst their managers and administrators have become the ones who are most empowered.

Field education is conditioned by this managerialist climate in multiple ways, and the question of whether future C.D. workers are able to practice their profession within this new welfare system of 'actually existing neoliberalism' (Brenner & Theodore, 2002) is a significant concern. First, the change of funding mode means that social service agencies with funding cuts or which are unsuccessful in their bids for new social programmes and services will encounter major difficulties in providing fieldwork education and training. This means fewer placement opportunities for students. Second, the emphasis on managerial practices that emphasise students following procedures and routines can jeopardise their cultivation of a critically reflexive praxis regarding structural issues (i.e., welfare policy loopholes) and social change, reducing them to 'operators of standardized policies and procedures' (Yan et al. 2017, p. 979). Although social service agencies should be able to mobilise resources and networks for multilevel interventions, those subsidised by the government worry about encouraging 'troubled' workers (those workers deemed to cause 'trouble') by suggesting that social workers should not only work according to the tasks assigned by the agencies but to also practice according to their own professional discretion and values (Chan, 2017). This has led to a 'passive tendency of submitting to the preferences of funders and the government' (Fung, 2017, p. 68), leading some to conclude, rather boldly, that 'newer non-profit organisations with more progressive agendas stand little chance of obtaining state funding' (Lee, 2012, p. 550).

Social change has mainly been the purview of social workers in community settings rather than other fields of practice (Chiu & Wong, 1998). Among the nine placement settings offered in our department, C.D. services best encapsulate the potentiality of macro perspectives integrated with knowledge and skills. The comparatively wide range and number of remedial practice settings offered to social work students could inadvertently reinforce the idea of social work as micro work—what some have described as the 'supremacy' of personalist social work in Hong Kong (Chiu & Wong, 1998). Developing and implementing interventions at individual and interpersonal levels to solve problems by helping individuals improve self-regulation and personal functioning reflects the individualism of neo-liberalism, which diffracts social work into multiple forms of individualisation (Bourdieu, 1998). Social work students are steered toward individual, group, and family therapy in response to market–society demand. Furthermore, service users—who often do not access social services voluntarily—are increasingly seen as *consumers* of social services (Yan et al., 2017). Some see this as diluting social workers' sense of purpose and commitment to the professional ideals of social justice and social change (Yuen and Ho, 2007). Although such ideals remain important (in theory) to social work in the region, the means by which they are to be achieved through social work remains a point of contestation.

Reclaiming a Macro Lens, Recasting Multilevel Social Work

Existing macro-level services and intervention in Hong Kong—such as the C.C.s, N.L.C.D.P.s, and the single Care and Support Networking Team—have become constrained in many respects. Practices of social action and advocacy are often discouraged, which serves to depoliticise the civil society function of N.G.O.s and jeopardises the profession's basic values of social justice (Yan et al. 2017). Financial dependence upon existing lump sum grants through the subvention system cast a 'structurally determined limit' (Chack, 1993, p. 252) on social reform and make it unfavourable to advocate system change. This context delimits possibilities for social work's 'signature pedagogy' of field education and the uneven levels of practice settings in which students can (1) learn to think, practice and perform ethically with integrity, and (2) critically reflect upon what this means as an element of reflexive practice. Despite the potential pessimism implied by the crisis of C.D. services in the region and the sociopolitical issues this reflects, we write with increased hope and vigour that the macro praxis exemplified by C.D. services—community capacity building, social planning, policy analysis and advocacy, and organisational and social change—can be salvaged by 'reclaiming' a macro lens through social work field education, which needs to be reflected systemically in social work education more broadly. In what follows, we detail suggestions for how this might be achieved, such that the social work community can begin conversations about the rationales and means to promote multilevel social work. We hope that such suggestions stimulate efforts to address the 'estrangement' between state-sponsored welfare and emancipatory social work (Cheung, 2018).

Critical Reflection upon Sociocultural and Policy Contexts of Field Education

Social work programmes have been criticised for the disconnection between education and practice (Lager & Robbins, 2004). Students may find it difficult to build connections between their studies and field experiences during the course of their practicum. Students are also aware that classroom knowledge and social work values may sometimes be incongruent with the practice cultures of their agencies. This can lead to conflicts and struggles between social work ideals and practice. Therefore, intentional efforts to bridge this liminality by facilitating critical reflections upon the sociocultural and policy contexts of field education are needed (for example, through integrative seminars). We echo the assertion by Yan et al. (2017) that 'reflexivity does not come naturally. It needs to be nurtured' (p. 987). Whilst integrative seminars connecting classroom knowledge with practice exist in many social work programmes (Birkenmaier, Wilson, Berg-Weger, Banks, & Hartung, 2003), including case analysis within agency-based practice (Boisen & Syers, 2004), they should also strive to emphasise a structural reflexivity—the *historical and contemporary systems and processes that condition possibilities and impossibilities for praxis*. In other words, field instruction systems must also be analysed as social systems (Nadesan, 2019) that affect and are affected by societal transformations. In addition to integrating personal and professional identities and the bridging of macro and agency contexts to students' ongoing experiences, integrative seminars could also include:

1. Questioning the development of professional practice alongside ethical thought.
   a. What makes professional practice ethical practice?
   b. What/who determines what is professional and ethical in social work?
   c. How are professionalism and ethics shaped by the roles one inhabits (as a trainee versus as a registered social worker)?
2. Tracking important events and policies that change the context of social work education, training and practice.
   a. What shapes the field education objective to help students think, act and perform ethically with integrity, which exceeds the dispositions and skills of any individual social worker?

3. Locating discordances between education and practice as—not within individual competencies (e.g., students, supervisors) nor even endemic to specific fields of practice, but—reflective of the changing local and global landscape in which social work emerges and is variously compelled to adapt and/or resist.

Foregrounding Macro Social Work and its Relevance for Practice and Research

As the 'stepchild' of social work (Rothman & Mizrahi, 2014), macro social work courses are far fewer in number than their micro counterparts. General practice and foundation courses often make minimal usage of macro practice examples (Segal-Engelchin et al., 2017). We, therefore, suggest better integration of macro social work practice in the formal curriculum. For example:

1. Teaching strategies can be diversified by incorporating macro-focused field training and service-learning camps (Segal-Engelchin et al., 2017) and facilitating opportunities for conceptual linkages by teaching students how to work alongside impoverished communities.
2. Social work research methods courses can incorporate participatory approaches for community-based research projects (Dash & Roy, 2020; H.K.C.S.S., 2019; Fortunate, McCarthy, & Abramson, 2001). This suggestion is particularly important given the significant growth of emphasis placed on research at most Hong Kong social work tertiary institutions. Where social work faculties are encouraged to engage in more grant writing to secure research funding, and where 'field instruction is too often relegated to a second-class citizenship' (Lager & Robbins, 2004, p. 21), the two can work together to design and implement effective, evidence-based field instruction practices that meet the needs of service users, agencies, and social work trainees.
3. The concepts of social activation (stimulating the energies of people who have been excluded from existing social opportunities) and social capital (increasing the number and extent of people's social networks to increase the human resources available to everyone) remain foundational to macro social work theory. Students can put these concepts into action by being supported to
   a. Set up local concern groups, coalitions, or organisations that respond to social issues affecting their work. In a managerialist context in which professional autonomy is affected, the social work community must work together to guard against the diminishment of their energies with the multiple monitoring and performance evaluation technologies that exist at organisational and societal levels.
   b. Bring communities and service users together to form their own concern groups, which Barber (1995) calls 'politically progressive casework'.
   c. Rebuild strategic alliances between social workers and service users where such bonds have been dismantled, for example, due to redevelopment, urban renewal, or other 'tragedies of enclosure' (Mies, 2014).[2]
4. Given that social workers are expected to assimilate into the managerialist climate of Hong Kong's welfare institutions, it may also be important for students to learn how to write funding proposals, bid for resources, and work with funders and donors (Chan, 2006).

We offer these curricular suggestions in the spirit of calls for social workers to reclaim their political and professional roles to ensure equitable distributions of resources (Lam & Blythe, 2014), cultivating the development of macro practice skills, tasks, and attitudes for social work students where they may not be able to do so as part of a C.D. placement. Social workers need to be prepared to intervene at multiple levels, including the structural dimensions of state intervention and engaging with policy debates that condition present and future human injustices and suffering (Donaldson, Hill, Ferguson, Fogel, & Eriskon, 2014).

Conclusion

The imbalance between remedial and action/change-oriented practice remains a concern, as social issues require complex and long-term interventions at multiple levels of social work practice (Rothman & Mizrahi, 2014). Social work in Hong Kong continues to aspire toward principles of social justice, with a dual commitment to individuals and society. Focusing on the individual without addressing societal issues has been argued to be a 'crude form of practice' (Chack, 1993, p. 250). Field education must find ways to counteract the loss of community base associated with the region's economic strategies of maximising financial flexibility and preserving its conservative financial policies (Lee, 2012). As C.D. services have become crippled, the capacity of C.D. workers to improve the welfare of disadvantaged groups has become more difficult. That does not mean, however, that workers and students alike cannot find spaces to practice social action and inspire change.

Social work and social work education in Hong Kong must be reconceptualised to actualise the distinctive professional and disciplinary ideals of ecological, multilevel practice–inclusive of, but also beyond remedial approaches. This requires consolidation of existing ties with C.D. organisations, expansion of university-community collaborations in the C.D. field (academic and field education/internships) where possible, and curriculum modifications that revitalise macro-level social work into mainstream/generalist social work education programmes. 'Reclaiming a macro lens, recasting multilevel practice', takes the position that awareness of structural deprivation is necessary but insufficient for social work; such deprivations must also be the target of intervention. Cultivating a truly multilevel praxis orientation among social work students is needed to analyse social issues more holistically and to work toward improving welfare of the people of Hong Kong. This vision of welfare sees improved individual and interpersonal well-being as inextricably bound to the strengthening of community capacity for transformative social change.

Notes

1 The information of resources released for N.L.C.D.P.s terminated between 1997 and 2001 is not kept (Legislative Council, 2020).

2 Enclosure means 'piracy, violence, theft or appropriation of what belongs to the people' in the name of progress, modernisation, and growth (Mies, 2014, p. i108). This can include public streets, communities and even nature as 'the commons'. Ng (2017) argues that 're-commoning' the commons can be a strategy to re-root political processes back into the local community. Social workers can work collaboratively with services users to (re)build community capacity, for, as Mies (2014) argues, without a community to defend the dignity of a place, 'no resistance to enclosures will be possible' (p. i111).

References

Barber, J.G. (1995). Politically progressive casework. *Families in Society: The Journal of Contemporary Social Services*, *76*(1), 30–37.

Birkenmaier, J., Wilson, R.K., Berg-Weger, M., Banks, R., & Hartung, M. (2003). MSW integrative seminars: Toward integrating course and field work. *Journal of Teaching in Social Work*, *23*(1–2), 167–182.

Brenner, N., & Theodore, N. (2002). Cities and the geographies of 'actually existing neoliberalism'. *Antipode*, *34*(3), 349–379.

Boisen, L., & Syers, M. (2004). The integrative case analysis model for linking theory and practice. *Journal of Social Work Education, 40*(2), 205–217.

Bourdieu, P. (1998) *Utopia of endless exploitation: The essence of neoliberalism*. Paris: Le Monde Diplomatique.

Census and Statistics Department (Census). (2020). *Browse by Statistical Subject*. Retrieved from: https://www.censtatd.gov.hk/hkstat/sub/bbs_tc.jsp

Chack, K.-W. (1993). State-funded social work projects for social reform: Reflections from community organizing in Hong Kong. *International Social Work, 36*(3), 249–260.

Chan, R. (2006). Community economic development: Applications and limitations in Hong Kong. *International Social Work, 49*(4), 483–493.

Chan, Y.-M. (2017). Enhancing critical reflective practice in fieldwork education: An exploratory study of the role of social work agencies in the welfare context of Hong Kong. *World Academy of Science, Engineering and Technology [Humanities and Social Sciences], 11*(4), 811–821.

Cheung, J.C.-S. (2018). A social worker with two watches: Synchronizing the left and right ideologies. *International Social Work, 61*(2), 234–246.

Chiu, S.W.-S., & Wong, V.C.-W. (1998). From political to personal? Changing social work ideology and practice in Hong Kong. *International Social Work, 41*(3), 277–291.

Chow, N. (2008). Social work in Hong Kong –Western practice in a Chinese context. *China Journal of Social Work, 1*(1), 23–35.

Chow, E., Cheung, C., & Chan, G. (2018). Calibrating field practicum assessment in social work education with a competency-based evaluation tool in Hong Kong. *International Social Work, 61*(2), 260–273.

Dash, B., & Roy, S. (2020). *Fieldwork training in social work*. New York: Routledge.

Donaldson, L., Hill, K., Ferguson, S., Fogel, S., & Erickson, C. (2014). Contemporary social work licensure: Implications for macro social work practice and education. *Social Work, 59*(1), 52–61.

Ford, D., & Chui, W. (2000). Where East meets West: Fieldwork instruction in Hong Kong and England. *Asia Pacific Journal of Social Work and Development, 10*(2), 19–39.

Fortune, A., McCarthy, M., & Abramson, J. (2001). Student learning processes in field education: Relationship of learning activities to quality of field instruction, satisfaction, and performance among MSW students. *Journal of Social Work Education, 37*(1), 111–124.

Fung, K.-K. (2017). Neoliberalisation and community development practices in Hong Kong. *Community Development Journal, 52*(1), 55–75.

Fung, K.-K., & Hung, S.-L. (2011). Community work in Hong Kong: Changing agenda in the recent phase of economic globalisation. *Community Development Journal, 46*(4), 458–475.

Hong Kong Council of Social Service (HKCSS). (1997). *NGO paper on community development services*. Retrieved from: http://webcontent.hkcss.org.hk/fs/er/Reference/NGO%20paper%20on%20community%20development%20services.pdf

香港社會服務聯會 [HKCSS]. (2019) 社區發展資料匯編*2019*.香港: 超媒體出版.

International Association for Community Development (IACD). (2018). *The International Standards for Community Development*. Retrieved from: https://www.iacdglobal.org/international-standards-accreditation/standards/

Kadushin, A., & Harkness, D. (2014). *Supervision in social work* (5th ed.) New York: Columbia University Press.

Kam, P., Leung, C., Chan, L., Lam, H., Woo, M., Fung, K., & Wong, M. (1994). *Community Work: Theory and practice*. Hong Kong: The Chinese University of Hong Kong.

Kam, P. (2014). Back to the 'social' of social work: Reviving the social work profession's contribution to the promotion of social justice. *International Social Work, 57*(6), 723–740.

Kerelian, N., & Arat, G. (2017). Reshaping the social work education system toward cultural competency: The Hong Kong case. *International Social Work, 62*(1), 316–329.

Lager, P., & Robbins, V. (2004). Field education: Exploring the future, expanding the vision. *Journal of Social Work Education, 40*(1), 3–11.

Lam, C.-W., & Blyth, E. (2014). Re-engagement and negotiation in a changing political and economic context: Social work in Hong Kong. *British Journal of Social Work, 44*, 44–62.

Lee, E. (2012). The New Public Management reform of state-funded social service non-profit organisations and the changing politics of welfare in Hong Kong. *International Review of Administrative Services, 78*(3), 537–553.

Legislative Council Panel on Home Affairs (LC). (1997). *Policy Statement on Community Development*. LC Paper No. CB(2)1997/04-05(01). Retrieved from: https://www.legco.gov.hk/yr04-05/english/panels/ha/papers/hacb2-1997-1e.pdf

Legislative Council. (2020). *LCQ8: Community development services*. Retrieved from: https://www.info.gov.hk/gia/general/202001/08/P2020010800272.htm?fontSize=1

Leung, J.C.-B. (1990). Community development in Hong Kong: A study of 'top-down' and 'bottom-up' social policy planning and implementation. Doctoral thesis, University of Hong Kong, Hong Kong. Retrieved from http://hdl.handle.net/10722/34936

Midgley, J. (1995). *Social development: The developmental perspective in social welfare*. London: Sage.

Midgley, J., & Conley, A. (2010). *Social work and social development: Theories and skills for developmental social work*. New York: Oxford University Press.

Mies, M. (2014). No commons without a community. *Community Development Journal, 49*(S1), i106–i117.

Nadesan, V.S. (2019). A systems analysis of field instruction in social work education. Doctoral thesis, University of Johannesburg, Johannesburg, South Africa. Retrieved from http://hdl.handle.net/10210/400595

Netting, F.E., O'Connor, M.K., Cole, P.L., Hopkins, K., Jones, J.L., Kim, Y., Leisey, M., Mulroy, E.A., Rotabi, K.S., Lori Thomas, M., Weill, M.O., & Wike, T.L. (2016). Reclaiming and reimagining macro social work education: A collective biography. *Journal of Social Work Education, 52*(2), 157–169.

Ng, M.-K. (2017). Enclosure and recommoning in Wanchai, Hong Kong: The struggle of local community development in Asia's World City. *Local Economy: The Journal of the Local Economy Policy Unit, 32*(7), 640–655.

Payne, M. (2014). *Modern Social Work Theory*. (4th ed.). London: Palgrave Macmillan.

Popple, K. (1995). *Analysing community work: Its theory and practice*. Buckingham: Open University Press.

Rothman, J. (1974). Three models of community organisation practice. In F. Cox, J. Erlich, J. Rothman, & J. Tropman (Eds.), *Strategies of community organisation*. (pp. 25–45). Itasca, IL: Peacock Publishing.

Rothman, J., & Mizrahi, T. (2014). Balancing micro and macro practice: A challenge for social work. *Social Work, 59*(1), 91–93.

Segal-Engelchin, D., Kaufman, R., Huss, E., & Amos, O. (2017). Impacts of an intensive macro-oriented social work programme on first-year students' values, practice preferences and sense of practice competence. *British Journal of Social Work, 47*(8), 2346–2363.

Social Welfare Department. (2005). *Service description of integrated family service centres (IFSCs)*. Retrieved from: https://www.swd.gov.hk/en/index/site_pubsvc/page_family/sub_listofserv/id_ifs/

Social Welfare Department. (2010). *Building effective family services: Review on the implementation of the IFSC service mode*. Retrieved from: https://www.swd.gov.hk/en/index/site_pubsvc/page_family/sub_listofserv/id_ifscsm/

Social Workers Registration Board (SWRB) (2016). *Category of RSWs*. Retrieved from: https://www.swrb.org.hk/en/Content.asp?Uid=26

Social Workers Registration Board (SWRB) (2019). *Lists of Recognized Qualifications*. Retrieved from: https://www.swrb.org.hk/tc/hk.asp

Social Workers Registration Board (SWRB) (2020). *Statistics on registered social workers*. Retrieved from: https://www.swrb.org.hk/tc/statistic_rsw.asp

Tung, C.-F. (2011). *Strategy and controversy about community development service in Hong Kong: The case analysis of the Yau Tong Shan CDP*. Hong Kong: Author.

Wong, C.-K. (1993). *Social work and social change: A profile of the activist social workers in Hong Kong*. Hong Kong: Hong Kong Institute of Asia-Pacific Studies, The Chinese University of Hong Kong.

Yan, M.-C., Cheung, J.C.-S., Tsui, M.-S., & Chu, C.-K. (2017). Examining the neoliberal discourse of accountability: The case of Hong Kong's social service sector. *International Social Work, 60*(4), 976–989.

Yeung, V., Tsor, K.-L., & Kim, W.-C. (1998). Student satisfaction in social work placement in Hong Kong. *Asia Pacific Journal of Social Work, 8*(1), 80–88.

Yuen, A.W.-K., & Ho, D.K.-L. (2007). Social work education in Hong Kong at the crossroads: Challenges and opportunities amidst marketisation and managerialism. *Social Work Education, 26*(7), 546–559.

2

Developing Health Care Social Work Curriculum and Arranging Fieldwork Education in China

Johnston H. C. Wong

Meng, Ding, and Zhang (2012) proposed that medical social workers should be provided with well-planned pre-vocational and in-service training. They indicated that social workers in hospitals are unprepared to take up the challenge, as they listed many 'missing points' in existing social work education. Lack of knowledge regarding health problems and health care systems among social work graduates may be the most significant setback when they were employed in the health care field.

In a more recent paper, Jin, Chen, Pan, and Du (2017) discussed the problems of communication among the three parties involved in health care social work placement, namely the social work school, the hospital, and the social work agency. Tri-party settings are common because many social work projects in hospitals are funded by the government, as is the case, for example, in Shenzhen, instead of the hospitals. However, as social workers were not directly employed by hospital administrators, the latter have little interest in the work of the former. Hospitals in Shanghai presented a different situation, as the Shanghai City Health Authority simply requires hospitals to hire their own social workers. Hospital administrators in Shanghai would have high expectations for the contributions of social work in their system, as the hospital is footing the bills.

Liu and Fu (2018) pointed out that, to solve such expectation problems, it is important to adopt a competence-based fieldwork education that takes into account the challenges in health care settings. In their lengthy paper, they talked from a macro level of ethical values of empathy, to the micro level of case management and project management skills. Unfortunately, how these competencies can be acquired through field education is not discussed.

Upon closer scrutiny of these health care social work competencies, a dual supervisor approach in fieldwork education is unavoidable. Huang and Zheng (2019) studied the implementation of the dual supervisor system in health care and discovered that it is easier said than done. Again, the problem lies in the lack of communication between the medical supervisor appointed by the hospital and his or her counterpart, the social work supervisor appointed by social work colleges. Therefore, the aim of this chapter is first, to identify the necessary knowledge base and, second, the key competencies for health care social work in China and discuss how practice-related skills can be nurtured during fieldwork education.

DOI: 10.4324/9781032164946-4

To begin with, the international curriculum for health care social work will be examined in relation to the context of health problems and health care systems in China. Second, a systematic review of health care social work field education literature will be conducted to identify existing problems. Feedback on fieldwork education from a number of hospitals will be enlisted to demonstrate how communication and expectation problems can be overcome. Finally, a strategy for forming a provincial hospital–social work college cluster will be presented and discussed.

Health Care Social Work in China

Pioneers in Health Care Social Work

The first hospital social work services department in China, actually the earliest in the Asia Pacific region, was founded in 1921 at the Peking Union Medical College Hospital (here after referred as PUMC Hospital). Ida Pruitt, a girl who grew up in a village nearby the town of Peng-lai in Shantung, went to a school in Georgia, a teachers' college at Columbia, and finally received social work education in Philadelphia. She then joined the Massachusetts General Hospital in Boston and worked with Ida Cannon who published the first book on hospital social work (Cannon, 1952), and was named by Bartlett (1975) as the 'founder of medical social work' in the United States. Returning to China, Pruitt became head of the Hospital Social Service Department in the PUMC Hospital in 1917 and retained this role for 20 years (Peking Historical Archives Committee, PCCPC, Beijing Municipal Committee, 1987). However, development of hospital social work services was interrupted by war, political events, and economic constraints for decades.

Recognition for Health Care Social Work

Only after 2006, when the Chinese government reconfirmed its commitment to provide public hospital services and lay emphasis on humanistic care, was health care social work reactivated. The new era witnesses a rapid expansion of social work services in health care in more developed cities such as Shanghai and Beijing as well as in the Pearl River Delta and the Yangtze River Delta (Sung, 2012).

Since 2001, Shanghai has led in the establishment of social services departments in hospitals, while many nurses and doctors became social services practitioners (Liu, 2012). Shanghai City Government took a pioneering role in furthering social services and proudly presented the Shanghai model of social work progress (Xu, 2007). The most notable, of course, was the establishment in 2000 of the Social Service Department at the Shanghai East Hospital, which is affiliated with the Tongji University.

The occurrence of SARS in 2003 was significant to the whole of Chinese society. Community workers promoted public hygiene to combat SARS. Social workers in hospitals helped to comfort the sick and connect their families (Wang & Gu, 2004; Hua, 2004). The re-establishment of the social work department at the PUMC Hospital in 2007 marked a victorious come back (Liu, 2012). A Human Resources Department of the Ministry of Health Report published in 2007 stated that social work departments in hospitals have mushroomed in major cities of China such as Shanghai, Beijing, Guangzhou, and Shenzhen (Ministry of Health, 2007).

Furthermore, health care social work played an important role in responding to the devastating effects of the Sichuan earthquake that occurred on May 12, 2008, which shocked China. The number of deaths was more than 98,000, according to official figures. The number of injuries was twice or three times as many as the number of deaths. The China Association for Social

Work Education mobilised its members to serve in post-disaster work, in which rehabilitation and psychosocial recovery were the major emphases (Gao, 2009). With financial support from the Hong Kong Jockey Club, rehabilitation services organised by social workers were launched in several hospital rehabilitation centres and a network of rehabilitation community sites in the northwestern districts of Sichuan.

Contents of Health Care Social Work

Help in mediating doctor–patient conflicts is considered to be a major reason for creating social work services in hospitals (Wang, 2004). Worsening doctor–patient relationships and complaints about medical negligence were on the rise until the introduction of new laws recently. Many family members of deceased patients had disturbed the law and order in the hospitals and even harmed the medical staff to get compensation. Many hospital administrators generally expect social workers to mediate and improve the doctor–patient relationship.

A second area of work for health care social workers is to help those patients who lack the means to pay for major operations and treatment for serious diseases. Medical insurance still cannot cover all expenses, especially for rural residents and migrant workers from the rural areas. Social workers must find funding from local charity and business sectors. Other means of fund raising involve publicising patient situations and economic hardship on charitable platforms found on the internet. Patient informed consent is necessary because the release of personal data cannot be avoided in this situation.

In terms of service nature, the main focus of social work in hospitals shifted gradually from financial aid to psychosocial counselling and building of social support (Li, Tong, & Wu, 2012). More and more research papers explore the application of social psychological interventions to lessen the impact of sicknesses on patients' mental health and helping patients and their families to cooperate with physician-prescribed medication plans.

In terms of service targets, social work in health care penetrated into many sub-areas such as drug prevention and child health care. As services grew in variety and depth, some scholars consider 2012 as the 'beginning of a new era' for social work in health care in China (Liu, 2012).

Expansion of Health Care Social Work

In Guangdong, Shenzhen started to launch hospital social work in 2008. Eight medical social workers were contracted by the Civil Affairs Department of Shenzhen to serve six major hospitals (Wang, 2008). Jiangmen Rehabilitation Hospital, meanwhile, set an alternative example. They established a social work department in 2008 and then a subsidiary social work agency, the 'Li Min Social Work Agency', in 2009. Social care is catered for both in- and out-patients, and a community health approach is adopted (Guangdong Professional Association of Social Workers, 2014). Foshan and Guangzhou came into the picture relatively late, in 2012 and 2013, respectively. By 2014, altogether, there were 30 medical social workers from four agencies serving eight hospitals in Foshan (Tian, Zhang, & Zhao, 2014).

By 2013, more than 160 hospitals in China had begun to provide social work services (Zhao, 2014). The Shanghai Civil Affairs Department and the Shanghai Department of Health declared in 2015 that all major hospitals should establish social work teams (Zhu, 2012). In 2019, the China Ministry of Health endorsed the Shanghai Hospital Social Work Service Standards and made it a national policy.

Localisation of Health Care Social Work Curriculum

Knowledge Base for Health Care Social Work

Health care settings are highly professional environments. They adopt a model of interdisciplinary teamwork that was first developed in community mental health centres to provide the best care for patients (Cowles, 2003). Very detailed work procedures and protocols are normally required to meet good practice standards. Literature shows that the interdisciplinary approach is not without problems. Some notable issues include turf protection, different values and perceptions regarding problems and needs of patients, self-promotion, prestige and status discrepancies that prevent open communication, language barriers, lack of skills and knowledge areas, and differences in problem-solving processes (Cowles, 2003).

According to the National Association of Social Workers of the United States (NASW), the knowledge base for health care social work is composed of four major areas and 42 knowledge points. Table 2.1 shows all the areas and points of the knowledge base.

To summarise, we can tell that in the areas of 'roles and responsibilities' of health care social workers and 'research and evaluations', the knowledge base and skill competencies should be the same for healthcare social work services in China or other parts of the world. However, in the areas of 'health status' and 'health systems', China has its unique situations, and social work educators in China have to redefine these knowledge points, which are quite different from those of other countries. To fill the above knowledge gap, revised educational contents in the form of a localised health care social work curriculum is proposed in the next section.

Localising Health Care Social Work Curriculum

Despite tremendous progress, we still found that, in China:

> The health literacy level of residents is low, with the unhealthy lifestyles such as smoking, excessive drinking, lack of exercise, unbalanced diet etc., resulting in increasing health problems. In China, there are 270 million hypertensive patients; 13 million stroke patients and 11 million coronary heart disease patients; more than 97 million diabetic patients; nearly 100 million chronic obstructive pulmonary disease patients; about 3.8 million new cancer cases each year, with an annual increase of 3.9%. Chronic non-communicable diseases including cardiovascular and cerebrovascular diseases, cancer, chronic respiratory diseases, diabetes among others account for 88% of the total deaths and more than 70% of the total disease burden. The prevention and control of major infectious diseases such as hepatitis, tuberculosis and HIV/AIDS is still at severe situation. Mental health, occupational health and endemic diseases cannot be ignored. In addition, some health problems or related issues among those vulnerable populations need to be solved urgently, such as birth defects, myopia and obesity among primary and secondary school students, early childhood development, as well as chronic diseases in the elderly.
>
> (National Health Commission, 2019a)

To make sure the international curriculum is suitable for Chinese social workers, a number of factors must be taken into account.

1) Physical, mental, and behavioural health
   a) Disease profiles in China: Social workers need to study the major causes of death and disease in China. This information is easily available via World Health Organization

Table 2.1 Knowledge Areas and Knowledge Points Based on NASW Standards for Social Work Practice in Health Care Settings (NASW, 2014)

Knowledge Areas		*Knowledge Points*
Physical, mental, and behavioural health	a)	Interplay between the physiological elements of acute, chronic, and life-limiting illness and biopsychosocial–spiritual functioning;
	b)	Concepts and theories associated with life span development, neurobiology, and behavioural change;
	c)	Grief, loss, and bereavement;
	d)	Addiction, depression, anxiety, and other mental health conditions;
	e)	Sexual functioning;
	f)	Essentials of the *Diagnostic and Statistical Manual of Mental Disorders* (DSM-5);
	g)	Basic medical terminology;
	h)	Counselling and behavioural change intervention;
Health care systems	a)	The health care continuum;
	b)	The unique needs of marginalised, oppressed, and diverse populations;
	c)	The social determinants of health and health disparities;
	d)	Evidence-informed approaches to health care; integrated, primary, and behavioural health care; the chronic care model;
	e)	China health care reform policies, regulations, and delivery system changes;
	f)	Basics of health care financing, including rural and city medical insurance coverages;
	g)	Health care system trends, including ongoing health care infrastructure changes;
	h)	Accreditation and regulatory standards governing health care settings;
Roles and responsibilities	a)	Biopsychosocial–spiritual assessment;
	b)	Use of the strengths perspective
	c)	Case management, care coordination, patient navigation;
	d)	Discharge and transition planning;
	e)	Advance care planning;
	f)	Palliative care, including pain and symptom management;
	g)	Hospice and end of life care;
	h)	Identification of abuse (child/elder/dependent adult) trauma, neglect, and exploitation;
	i)	Crisis intervention;
	j)	Facilitation of benefits and resource acquisition to assist clients and families, including and understanding of related policies, eligibility requirements, and financial and legal issues;
	k)	Advocacy for clients and families within the health care institution and commitment to addressing quality-of-life concerns for clients and families;
	l)	Client, family, interprofessional, and community education;
	m)	Family systems issues, including the impact of health care concerns, illness, and disease on family relationships; lifecycles; and caregiving roles and support needs;
Research and evaluations	a)	Research and evaluation methodology;
	b)	Social work outcome/practice evaluation approaches;
	c)	Opportunities for social work participation in institutional quality improvement programmes and research projects;
	d)	Promotion of clinical trial enrolment with clients, and participation in community-based participatory research projects;
	e)	Ability to analyse research results and incorporate findings into practice, organisational quality improvement initiatives, and advancement of the social work field;

(WHO) country reports as well as information from the Chinese Center for Disease Control and Prevention (CCDC).

b) Health behaviours: Social workers should acquaint themselves with the health behaviour of the Chinese people, particularly related with smoking and diets. Diet and exercise patterns need more attention, as the smoking problem is relatively well documented. China has numerous regional diets, and they must have different effects on health. On the other hand, people's patterns of physical exercise are more homogeneous in terms of geographical region, except in remote areas

c) Chinese medicine: The faith and adoption of Chinese medicine in daily life is another important determinant in health. It is both a medical treatment method as well as a way of life. Chinese medicine's emphasis on holistic care and the recovery of the immune system is undergoing large-scale scientific validation. Previously, Chinese medicine was used as a supplementary tool in medical treatment in most major hospitals; however, Chinese medicine may, perhaps, be considered as a major treatment method in dealing with certain sicknesses, particularly non-communicable diseases (NCD). Therefore, Chinese medicine is playing a complimentary role rather than supplementary one.

2) Health care systems
   a) Equalitarian origin: After 1949, health care became the responsibility of the state. In the cities, hospitals' and clinics' services were operated by either local governments or state enterprises. Primary health care was emphasised by the Chinese leaders who were fully aware of the huge population size in rural and agricultural regions. Health care services are basically but comprehensively covered. The equalitarian nature of the system was often admired by Western observers
   b) Marketisation of hospitals: The situation changed from 1978 onward because of the Reform and Open Door Policy. As the whole society was turned toward marketisation, hospital care was required to follow market economy, and its social welfare orientation diminished. Most hospitals, though built by the government, must pay for all costs and reinvestment funds by charging patients for care (Liu, 2007). Hospital administrators who were preoccupied with balancing their books had little interest in offering additional services, such as social work, to care for the patients. Small rural hospitals were squeezed by giant medical centres in the cities.
   c) Health care financing and the medical insurance system: Putting the burden of escalating costs on patients forced low-income groups out of proper treatment. Recently, the Chinese government has pushed for medical insurance reform to improve coverage and comprehensiveness. Social workers are supposed to know insurance and social security rules and regulations very well.
   d) Legal knowledge: Health care services involve a lot of legal issues. The Chinese legislators have been very active in reviewing social laws in the last decade. For example, mental health laws, tort laws, laws related to compensation following traffic and industrial accidents, laws related to medical malpractice, anti-domestic violence laws, and laws on protection of children, women, and the elderly have taken effect in the past five years. Social workers in health care settings cannot afford to be ignorant of legal issues.
3) Roles and responsibilities:
   a) Mediation in doctor patient relationship: As mentioned above, the hospitals' budget requirements have created many hospital–patient conflicts. Social workers are needed to play the role of mediator. It is advisable to develop a mediation framework which is supported by administrative legislation.
   b) Prevention for communicable diseases: Social and community workers are actively involved in education regarding sexually communicable diseases, such as AIDS; common childhood illnesses; and the recent outbreak of COVID-19.

c) Prevention for addiction: Social workers have a role in helping to fight against drug addiction, smoking, and reliance on other substances.
d) Protection for the underprivileged: As social work services in the community are still under-developed and not provided for, the role of health care social workers is to see to the needs of the mentally ill, children with learning difficulties, and people with disabilities of all ages.
e) Protection for the elderly: China will soon confront an aging tsunami. Older people face physical as well as mental health degeneration. Health care social workers will have to help them adjust socially and psychologically in long-term care
f) General health education: Health literacy in China is low. In 2018, the health literacy rate was only 17.06% (NHC, 2019b). In major cities, such as Shenzhen, Beijing, and Shanghai, higher health literacy rates of around 35% were recorded. In view of this, social workers in health care settings are charged with the responsibility of providing health education to the public.

4) Research and evaluations: There was very little research on local medical social work in the last two decades. Therefore, health care social workers must incorporate scientific research into their practices and interventions as far as possible. Without evidence, it is difficult to prove to medical staff that social work is a scientific discipline.

To summarise, health care social work curriculum for China will be unique and distinct from that of other countries, as health behaviours are influenced by Chinese culture in general and Chinese medicine traditions in particular. Moreover, the socialist system also develops a unique health care insurance approach. The health services financing model in China, which is basically a public service but operated in a market environment, is different from that of the United Kingdom, the United States, and Germany. All in all, the need for localisation in social work education for health care is evident.

Bridging the Training Gap for Health Care Social Work

Using the keywords 'health care social work field practice', a literature review on recent Chinese studies regarding health care social work field education from CNKI.net showed that, as of May 13, 2020, there were 81 papers produced from 2003 to 2019. After reviewing the titles and abstracts of these papers, only 35 of them are directly related to fieldwork placement arrangements and teaching methods. Other papers described health care social work services for special patient populations, while fieldwork is mentioned only briefly.

In parallel with the lack of empirical studies, it is observed that social work field education for health care in China faces many difficulties and inadequacies, for example the absence of structured fieldwork curriculum and the shortage of social work teachers with practice experience. As discussed earlier, social work has its roots in Western societies, therefore, health care social work field training has to be modified, localised, and adapted to the situations of modern China.

Health financing in China creates a delivery system totally different from that of the National Health Service (N.H.S.) in the United Kingdom or the American private health care market, and it has many implications to our fieldwork environment. Chinese medicine, proven valuable in combating COVID-19, is a unique feature in our health care environment. How far would it affect social work field training in the wider health context has yet to be examined.

Targets and Levels of Training

In describing the development of medical social work in Malaysia, Crabtree pointed out that medical social work holds an important position as compared to other areas of social work services. Forming alliances with medicine also promotes the profile of the social work profession as a whole (Crabtree, 2010). It is an opportunity for social workers to develop this highly specialised and reputable area of social work. The Chinese government is fully aware of the need to improve and expand the provisions of social work in health care because China is an aging society.

In 2012, Shanghai declared that, by 2015, they aimed to provide one social worker for every 300–500 beds in comprehensive hospitals and one for every 100–300 beds in children's, mental health, and cancer and rehabilitation hospitals. In 2013, according to the Shanghai Department of Health and Family Planning (2012), the total number of hospital social workers in Shanghai was around 309, serving 103 hospitals at a ratio of 3 workers to 1 hospital. The Shanghai City Government reconfirmed its commitment on March 1, 2020 issuing its Notice of Medical Social Work Standards. It required all Category 2 and Category 3 (the highest rank) general hospitals to employ one qualified social worker for every 300–500 beds. For Category 1 hospitals and community health centres, there should be at least one social worker. For special hospitals, the ratio should be increased to one social worker for every 100 beds. In short, the recognition for health care social workers is increasing, particularly in the more developed coastal regions.

The need for social workers in community health is also a big concern, particularly after the outbreak of COVID-19. One possible manpower strategy is to retrain family planning workers to become community health workers. The Chinese government has relaxed its population control, abandoning the single child policy by allowing each married couple to have two children, if they wish to enjoy state privileges for children. Having more than two children is not regarded as inappropriate if the family can afford the extra expense. The new law became effective January 1, 2016. Consequently, family planning workers may have to expand their services by not focusing on birth control but, instead, on paternal and child health. The number of these workers on government payroll in 2015 was around 500,000, and some estimate that it will be over 1 million (China Health and Family Planning Committee, 2017). To help family planning staff to become community health social workers through retraining is a possible strategy, as they are better equipped with health knowledge.

Social work educators in China face the challenge of providing proper training that will enhance student competencies in health care practice. Training may involve formal education, continuing education, and retraining. Formal higher education for diplomas and bachelor's and master's degrees should be designed differently, as the curricula should aim at providing health settings specific skills. Retraining, on the other hand, may be different for students who are social work graduates or have a medical and nursing background. Field practicum is crucial in the process of educating health care social workers.

Designing Health Care Social Work Field Practicum

How can social work students be well equipped to practice in the world of health? We probably do not have sufficient qualified teachers (Liu, 2007). At present, few institutions of higher education in social work possess the dual pools of educators, namely experienced medical staff and social workers. Medical schools offering social work programmes have advantages, but their capacities are limited and unable to meet the manpower needs. Another option is to involve the medical and nursing staff in hospitals to act as field work co-supervisors. Establishing an alliance between hospitals and social work schools will enable more than 400 institutions of higher learning to offer programmes training health care social workers.

Field work instruction should be probably designed and focused on social workers' competencies. Volland, Berkman, Phillips, and Stein (2003) extensively reviewed available peer-reviewed literature at the time of their study and proposed that there should be three areas of core competencies. These include:

1) Self-directed practice competencies which involve
   a. Case management;
   b. Collaboration, team building, and conflict mediation;
   c. Programme planning, financial management skills, and ethical decision making;
   d. Grant writing, data management, and analytical skills; and
   e. Policy advocacy.
2) Population based competencies which cover
   a. Familiarity with treatment modalities;
   b. Familiarity with policies and regulations; and
   c. Familiarity with common terminologies.
3) Re-focusing on basic skills, that include:
   a. Assessment and documentation; and
   b. Analytic skills and collaborative research.

Volland et al. (2003) also pointed out that there were a number of trends, including the increase of chronic instead of acute and communicable disease, aging population, and the higher prevalence of social and environmental diseases. These trends are very similar to the current situation in China. For health care social workers in China, specific populations such as drug addicts and people lacking mental capacities are high priorities. As China tightened smoking controls only in the last two decades, the prevalence of sickness related to tobacco consumption is still on the rise. As society has become more affluent, another health issue will be high blood pressure and cardiovascular diseases. Based on the analysis in Volland et al., the major competencies proposed for health care social work in China are shown in Table 2.2.

This table shows that we can categorise health care social work competencies into seven areas. Each area is defined by competencies contents and timing of acquirement corresponding to different stages of professional roles. Four areas of competencies, including (i) general social work skills, (ii) basic health knowledge, (iii) contextual social work skills, and (iv) operation in health care settings, are to be acquired and enhanced during fieldwork placements.

Forming Provincial Hospitals and Social Work Schools Alliance

After identifying the above competencies, a cluster-based model that forms the 'Hospitals and Social Work Schools Alliance' is proposed to develop 'Centres of Excellence' in fieldwork education for health care social work. This is based on the concept of the Tripodal Model of Social Work Education by integrating teaching, practicing, and research (Wong, Ng, & Yang, 2013). The advantages of this model are that it pulls resources from the supply and demand sides together to solve the problem of shortages of experienced fieldwork supervisors. Because students may face communication and expectation problems between the medical profession on one hand and the social work profession on the other, it is necessary

Table 2.2 Major Competencies for Health Care Social Work in China

Competencies Areas	*Competencies Content*	*Competencies Developmental Timing*
General social work skills competencies	Case, group, and community work	Before field practicum
Basic health knowledge competencies	Familiarity with treatment modalities, common terminologies, and treatment effects on patients and their families	Before, during, and after field work
Contextual social work skills competencies	Psychosocial assessment and documentation, conflict mediation, and therapeutic case and group work skills, for example cognitive behavioural therapy (CBT) and crisis intervention skills	During field work
Operation in health care setting competencies	Interdisciplinary teamwork, admission and discharge planning, health promotion, and case management	During field work
Patient-population-based competencies	Common diseases among older people, women and children; people lacking mental capacities; people addicted to alcohol, drugs, and tobacco; and people with AIDS and other social diseases	Serving as entry-level health care social worker
Project management competencies	Programme planning, budgeting, financial management, grant writing, and data management	Serving as mid-level and experienced health care social worker
Services improvement competencies	Policy advocacy; collaborative research; big data analysis; social marketing; and public relations	Serving as senior social workers and researchers

to employ a well-organised dual-supervisor approach to help social work students, who may also come from medical and nursing backgrounds, to cross the borders of health and social work disciplines.

The Council of Social Work Education (CSWE) of the United States, in collaboration with the National Association of Social Workers (NASW) launched a scholarship programme in 2015, the Social Work Health Care Education and Leadership Scholars (HEALS), which aims to train social work leaders within health care practice. Ten social work programmes were selected as the hub for scholarships to support health care education for social work students and field instructors. In 2019, HEALS continued to be an effective boost for health care social work training.

The cluster idea employed by HEALS can be borrowed to form 'Hospital and Social Work Schools Alliances' in China. At present, the city of Shanghai is privileged, first, by a definite policy to develop health care social work and, second, with a high concentration of reputable universities. For example, Fudan University operates the Fudan Shanghai Cancer Center (Hospital) and Tongji University operates the Tongji Hospital. In all major cities, particularly the provincial centres, there are provincial hospitals and top universities.

Formation of Alliances can be led by the Healthcare Social Work Committee (CASWE-HSWC) of the China Association of Social Work Education. Clusters can be formed in more than 20 major cities and provincial capitals, including Beijing, Changchun, Changsha, Chengdu,

Chongqing, Fuzhou, Guangzhou, Harbin, Jinan, Lanzhou, Kunming, Nanjing, Nanning, Shanghai, Shenzhen, Taiyuan, Tianjin, Wuhan, Xiamen, Xian, and others.

In view of the need to provide a more structured field practicum in health care settings and prepare field instructors to supervise these students, a special Health Care Social Work Manual can be prepared under the leadership of the CASWE-HSWC With the committee's assistance, the provincial or metropolitan hospitals can collaborate with reputable social work schools in the area to form the provincial health care social work excellence practice centres. The centres will spearhead the development of health care social work by providing students with structured fieldwork opportunities and social work experiences.

A dual supervision system should be adopted by having one medical staff from the hospital and another social work faculty from the Alliance. In a study of health care social work field education in Japan, Xu (2018) suggested that the successfully acquiring competencies depends on having a highly structured practice project with clear guidelines, well described procedures, clear evaluation rubrics, and good coordination among the dual supervisors. As presented by Xu, social work schools in Japan have developed a basic fieldwork management structure for health care settings that clearly define the roles of the three parties, namely the student, the social work supervisor, and the medical supervisor. Clear definitions of roles and tasks for the student, the social work supervisor, and the medical supervisor before, during, and after placement can then be systematically listed and included in the Fieldwork Manual (please refer to Table 2.4). Proper field education project management, which is taken for granted at the more developed social work educational institutions, has yet to be designed and decided through consensus under the leadership of CASWE-HSWC.

Last but not least, health care social work should be culturally sensitive in many aspects. The subject of death for many people is a taboo. It creates psychological pressures for patients, their families, and medical staff when a person is seriously ill. Avoidance of talking about dying sometimes deters medical doctors from informing patients directly about the illness. Social workers are needed to share the important information to the patient's families. Doctor–patient relationships can become very tense when the patients and their families have financial difficulties. Mediation by social workers can help, but a proper legal and administrative mechanism should also be established. Placement students should not be required to handle medical disputes; however, they should be briefed about how to refer these cases to their administrative supervisors.

China Health Care Social Work into 2030

The WHO has advocated for the 'Health in All Policies' (WHO, 2014). The Chinese central government, echoing the international strategy for health promotion, has announced its Health China Action (NHC, 2019a). To China, health care becomes a new arena for social work practice.

New Fields of Intervention

Dziegielewski (2004) has pointed out that social work, which has more than 100 years of professional development in the United States, concentrated mainly on hospitals at the beginning and was later extended to families, communities, and vulnerable groups. Different from the US experience, health care social work in China has expanded since 2000 simultaneously and horizontally in hospitals, outpatient services, family planning activities, rehabilitative services, drug and substance abuse control, and community clinics. This is because health care social work in China has benefited from the new concept of holistic health in which both preventive and community medicine are stressed. This phenomenon can be referred as the 'latest development

Table 2.3 Fieldwork Management for Health Care Settings

	Roles	*Tasks Before Placement*	*Tasks During Placement*	*Tasks After Placement*
Student	Learners	Project planning	Implementation and recordings writing	Reflection and report writing
Social work supervisors and social work college	Educational and emotional support person	Project negotiation with medical supervisor	Weekly supervision	Evaluation and career development guidance
Medical supervisor and health institute	Educational and administrative support person	Identify needs and make project suggestions to student	Daily supervision	Evaluation and recommendation

Table 2.4 Updated Fields for Health Care Social Work

	Major health fields for social work interventions
1	Holistic health, global hygiene, and environmental protection
2	Positive mental and spiritual health
3	Behavioural health
4	Mental health
5	Preventive and primary health care
6	Hospital care and treatment
7	Disaster and emergency response, financial assistance
8	Population, public hygiene, family and community health
9	Distance medicine and Web-based counselling (Wong, 2020a)
10	Community crisis intervention and resilience building (Wong, 2020b)

effect', as social work policymakers in China can draw from the experiences of Hong Kong, the Asia Pacific region, or the West (Jie, 1997).

The structure and intervention levels of health care social work have been discussed by many scholars, and the idea of expanding services from hospital to community is not new (Liu, Yan, & Kung, 2010). However, the outbreak of COVID-19 further expanded our horizons to virtual services and distance medicine. It is also observed that social work agencies in the United Kingdom have launched self-administered cognitive behavioural therapeutic questionnaires to match with telephone counselling. During the Wuhan lockdown, social workers from all over China volunteered to provide psychological support via WeChat groups, and crisis interventions were provided online (Wong, 2020a). Community crisis intervention, in the form of community mental health social work, became a new technique to combat COVID-19 (Wong, 2020b). In Table 2.4 an updated list showing the sub-fields for health care social work in China is shown.

New Knowledge Set for Health Care Social Work

The NASW has proposed four Knowledge Areas, namely basic health knowledge, health systems knowledge, understanding of roles and responsibilities, and research knowledge and skills. As health care social work is expanding its scope from hospital to community and from public to private institutions, an upgraded 'knowledge set' is recommended for advanced students from graduate schools to advanced practitioners. In addition to the original four areas, it was deemed necessary to include legal knowledge and business management knowledge. On the other hand, basic social work theory and skills are assumed to be the background knowledge for social work undergraduates.

Knowledge Area 1: Social work knowledge

- Allows understanding of patients and family members.
- Enables social workers to provide counselling.

Knowledge Area 2: Medical and health knowledge

- Allows understanding of treatment and nursing procedure.
- Enables social workers to explain medical and health advice.

Knowledge Area 3: Welfare and health care policy knowledge

- Allows understanding of insurance coverage and community resources.
- Enables social workers to help patients find financial means

Knowledge Area 4: Legal knowledge

- Allows understanding of health care related legal problems.
- Enables social workers to protect patients' rights to their best interest.

Knowledge Area 5: Business and project management knowledge

- Allows understanding of the operation of health and welfare institutions.
- Enables social workers to deliver services more efficiently.

Knowledge Area 6: Global health and environmental issues

- Allows understanding of public health problems and disease management.
  Enables social workers to promote healthy lifestyles.

Knowledge Area 7: Research

- Allows for evidence-based practice and evaluation of effectiveness.

To win recognition from medical, nursing and allied health professions to the contributions of social workers in health care settings requires rigorous training for social work students. The challenge is for social work educators in China to design state of the art evidence based learning and field work education to prepare our students with the highest standards of professional knowledge and skills.

Conclusion

This chapter has described the development of field education for health care social work in China. Field practicum at present suffers from poor management and a lack of experienced supervisors. To solve the latter problem, collaboration among provincial/metropolitan hospitals and social work schools is proposed. The social work profession can adopt a standardised fieldwork management structure to enhance better fieldwork experiences and learning effectiveness. Field work education should be competence-based, therefore, seven competence areas and 32 competence items are identified which should be trained at different stages, from pre-vocational to senior management positions.

The outbreak of COVID-19 has given the development of healthcare social work a big push. Social work services will quickly be extended from hospitals to communities. Mental health care is also brought to the limelight by the central government. Provincial and municipal hospitals will be pushed to the forefront to launch community health education. Social workers will have a major role to play in this new wave of health care reform, provided our professional training can stand up to the challenge.

References

Bartlett, H. M. (1975). Ida M. Cannon: Pioneer in Medical Social Work, *Social Service Review, 49*(2), 1–20.

Cannon, I. M. (1952). *On the Social Frontier of Medicine*, Cambridge: Harvard University Press.

China Health and Family Planning Commission. (2017). Gazette of the National Health and Family Planning Commission of People's Republic of China, 2017, Issue No.02 (Serial No.163). Available at: http://www.nhc.gov.cn/ewebeditor/uploadfile/2017/07/20170711102129596.pdf

Cowles, F. L. A. (2003). *Social work in the Health Field* (2nd Ed.), New York: Haworth Press.

Crabtree, S. A. (2010). Medical Social Work in Malaysia, Issues in Practice, *International Social Work, 48*(6), 732–741.

Dziegielewski, S. F. (2004). *The Changing Face of Health Care Social Work: Professional Practice in Managed Behavioral Health Care*, New York: Springer.

Gao, J. S. (2009). Culture, Psychology and Clinical Technologies: Post Disaster Clinical Social Work an Exploration, *Society*, (3), 197–202.

Guangdong Professional Association of Social Workers. (2014). *Collected Reports on Development of Social Work Agencies for the Third Promotion Week for Lingnan Social Workers*, 20–24. Extracted from http://www.gdsgs.org/news/gd/1029.html.

Hua, J. X. (2004). Response Strategy for Public Critical Incidents: Social Work Interventions an Interdepartmental Approach, *Academic Forum*, (4), 162–166.

Huang, Y., & Zheng, L. Y. (2019). Practice of Joint Supervision in Medical Social Work in the Functional Perspectives, *Journal of Fujian Medical University (Social Science Edition), 20*(4), 25–29.

Jie, Y. (1997). Latest Development Effect the Road to Modernization for the Latest Developing Countries, *Jiejiang Social Sciences*, (3), 64–69.

Jin, Y. Y., Chen, Z., Pan, W. M., & Du, L. N. (2017). Tri-parties Social Work Field Practice Model in a Jiangsu Hospital, *Electronic Journal of Clinical Medical Literature, 4*(40), 7891–7893.

Li, B. S., Tong, Y. L., & Wu, W. (2012). Medical Social Work its Present and Thoughts for Its Future, *Journal of Fujian Medical University (Social Sciences Edition), 2012*(1), 1–5.

Liu, B. Z., & Fu, Q. B. (2018). On Core Ability of Medical Social Workers and its Cultivation Strategy, *Journal of Chongqing Technology and Business University (Social Sciences Edition), 35*(5), 60–68.

Liu, J. T. (1994). Developmental Social Welfare and Developmental Social Work Education, *Social Sciences Abroad, Beijing, 1994*(11), 13–16.

Liu, J. T. (2007). Fundamental Differences between the Nature of Public Welfare and Social Welfare in Healthcare Services, *Chinese Hospital Management, Harbin, 2007*(8), 4–8.

Liu, J. T. (2012). Medical Social Work since China Economic Reform its Past, Present and Future, *Social Work, 2012*(1), 4–10.

Liu, J. T., Yan, J., & Kung, L. Z. (2010). Strategic Position of Mental Health Social Work in the New Model of Holistic Medicine, *Fujian Forum (Humanities and Social Sciences), 2010*(3), 141–145.

Meng, F., Ding, Z. M., & Zhang, Y. Q. (2012). On the Missing Items in Pre-vocational and In-service Education for Medical Social Work, *Journal of Fujian Medical University (Social Science Edition), 13*(3), 31–34.

Ministry of Health (2007). *Medical Social Workers Survey and Policy Study*, Human Resources Department, Ministry of Health. Retrieved from: https://wenku.baidu.com/view/ab1830f3f61fb7360b4c65e0.html

N.A.S.W. (2014). *Standards for Social Work Practice in Health Care Settings*, https://www.socialworkers.org/practice/health

N.H.C. (2019a). *Briefing on Healthy China Action (Jul. 2019)*, National Health Commission of the PRC, http://www.nhc.gov.cn/xcs/s7847/201907/704b1ca3555e47c6a677e384a462bd7c.shtml

N.H.C. (2019b). *Monitoring Report on Health Literacy in China, 2018*, National Health Commission of the PRC, http://www.china.com.cn/zhibo/content_75139559.htm

Peking Historical Archives Committee (PCCPC) and Beijing Municipal Committee (1987). *Old Stories of Peking Union Medical College Hospital*. Beijing: Chinese Literature and History Press.

Shanghai Department of Health and Family Planning (2012). *Implementation Notice for Advancing the development of hospital social work talents teams*. Shanghai Department of Health, 2012-4-16. Retrieved from: http://www.nhc.gov.cn/tigs/s9661/201206/bfd7e9c94596437991832e3ec3b3438e.shtml

Sung, G. S. (2012). Rebuilding Medical Social Work and Reconstructing Harmonious Doctor-Patient Relations, *Tianjin Science and Technology, Tianjin, 2012*(1), 69–71.

Tian, H. Y., Zhang, C., & Zhao, L. D. (2014, March 27). Lacking People, Financial Resources and Support Where is Medical Social Work Heading? *Nandu*, FB14. Retrieved from http://epaper.oeeee.com/K/html/2014-03/27/content_2043429.htm

Volland, P.J., Berkman, B., Phillips, M., & Stein, G. (2003). Social work education for health care: Addressing practice competencies. *Social Work in Health Care, 37*(4), 1–17.

Wang, C. Z., & Gu, Z. M. (2004). Social Workers' Response and Effects in Public Health Critical Incidents, *Journal of Social Sciences of Shanxi Higher Education, 16*(5), 32–34.

Wang, W. P. (2004). Medical Reform Calls for the Development of Medical Social Work, *Medicine and Society, 17*(2), 1–4+11.

Wang, Y. (2008, October 29). First Batch of Social Workers Serving 6 Hospitals, *Shenzhen Evening News*, Retrieved from http://wb.sznews.com/html/2008-10/29/content_391776.htm

W.H.O. (2014). Health in All Policies: Helsinki Statement. Framework for Country Action. http://www.euro.who.int/__data/assets/pdf_file/0004/74704/E82997.pdf?ua=1

Wong, H. C. J., Ng, Y. F., & Yang N. (2013). The Tripodal Social Work Education Model --- Integrating Teaching, Research and Practice for Excellence, *Journal of Social Work*, 3. http://mall.cnki.net/magazine/magadetail/SHGO201303.htm

Wong H. C. J. (2020a). Different Stages of Disaster the Wuhan Experience during the COVID-19 Community Outbreak. *EC Psychology and Psychiatry, 9*(7): 47–52.

Wong, H. C. J. (2020b). Innovations in Community Crisis Intervention - Adopting the ACT and AtCER MODEL in the COVID-19 Outbreak, *International Association of Schools of Social Work COVID-19 Stories Featured*, April, 3. https://www.iassw-aiets.org/covid-19/4781-innovations-in-community-crisis-intervention-adopting-the-act-and-atcer-model-in-the-covid-19-outbreak/

Xu, L. (2007). Major Ways to Develop Social Work the Shanghai Exploration, *China Society Periodical, 2007*(18), 33–35.

Xu, R. (2018). Implications of Fieldwork Education in Japanese Healthcare Settings to China. *Social Welfare*, 2, 15–22.

Zhao, F. Q. (2014). Development of Social Work in 2013, Address to the Annual Conference of China Association of Social Workers, Beijing. Retrieved from http://news.swchina.org/trends/2014/0120/4564.shtml

Zhu, G.Y. (2012, July 16). Social Workers for all Hospitals by 2015, *Shanghai Morning Post*, A15. Retrieved from http://newspaper.jfdaily.com/xwcb/html/2012-07/16/content_843477.htm

3

Fieldwork Education in Social Work as One Way of Building Bridges between China and Europe

Staffan Höjer, Honglin Chen, Juha Hämäläinen, Jie Lei, Steven M Shardlow, and Zhao Fang

From 2010 to 2020, more than one million individuals have received social work training in China (Niu & Östbö Haugen, 2019), while, by the end of 2018, 1.2 million professional social workers were employed (Ministry of Civil Affairs, 2019). Nowhere in the world has such a rapid expansion of social work education occurred previously. This expansion has helped to create a rapidly emerging field of practice. Compared to other countries in which the professionalisation of social work was driven, initially, by the expansion of the different forms of practice, which then led to the creation and expansion of social work education, the professionalisation process in China occurred in a different sequence. First, the construction of an academic discipline, second the expansion of social work education, then the shaping of practice.

The development of social work in China may be characterised as 'late start and rapid development', which has provided an advantage to 'learn the experience and lessons from other countries and regions in that course, so as to avoid detours and make fewer mistakes' (Yan, 2019, p. 418). However, copying Western experience and, perhaps, most frequently U.S. experience, has not been without difficulty. Recently, there has been evidence of a groundswell of opinion calling for the need to develop an indigenous, localised social work in China (Yan & Tsang, 2008).

This combination of rapid development and imported Western approaches to social work has led to significant criticism about the appropriateness of different models of supervision that have been used in Chinese social work. There have been claims that the supervisory relationship in China differs from that found in Western countries, both on account of the different historical trajectory of Chinese and Western societies as well as the differing cultural contexts. In a study conducted in Shanghai of the supervisor–supervisee relationship, An and Szto (2019) identified key micro-level factors for an indigenous Chinese model of supervision. The findings from this study demonstrated that supervisory relationships are important to develop a supervisee's professional identity through identification and confirmation of professional values, development of social work knowledge, and understanding the ethical basis for social work practice. In many cases, An and Szto found that the experience of delivering *professional social work* was limited in

DOI: 10.4324/9781032164946-5

many agencies[1] , which made the field experience less than satisfactory for the student. They concluded that the current supervisory relationship was precarious and in need of development.

A major area for development in China is social work field education, in particular: supervision capacity in agencies, practitioner skills in field education, and systems and structures for cooperation between social work practice agencies and universities. A consequence of the rapid expansion of social work has been a lack of experienced social work practitioners with the skills and knowledge to undertake high quality supervision of students. Field education is a central element of social work education and, according to Holden et al. (2011), education is the signature pedagogy of social work and the key component that plays a significant part shaping a student's professional identity. The strong sense of professional identity is a core component that supports good practice, and its presence or absence may influence the turnover rate. In a Chinese study, one of the authors demonstrated that both a weak sense of professional identity and poor job satisfaction had a direct negative effect on social worker intentions to leave their post (Jiang et al., 2019).

There has been a long history of collaboration between Chinese and European university departments of social work. This chapter builds on the experiences from one such collaborative joint project entitled, 'Building Bridges between Europe and China to Strengthen the Social Work Profession' (BUIBRI), which focused on the development of fieldwork education in China. The intention that underpins this project is twofold: to develop fieldwork education in China and all participating countries through the construction of a programme to enhance fieldwork education by educating some 600 agency supervisors.

The aim of this chapter is to describe and analyse the aims, methods, and processes within the BUIBRI project, which has a central focus on developing fieldwork education. Through investigation of these processes, the chapter reviews the challenges that have arisen in a cross-cultural collaboration to develop best practice in field education by treating the project as a case study. The chapter has been organised as follows. After a brief introduction, subsequent sections provide: an overview of social work and social work education in China; a discussion of key issues that confront the development of agency-based supervision and field education in China; details about the partners, aims, and objectives of the BUIBRI project; how the training programme was developed; how this programme was realised in three regions in China; what was learned from both research using the construct of 'self-efficacy' among the supervisors and also from the evaluation of the programme; how transnational knowledge sharing is possible; and what we have learnt from the various challenges and successes.

The State of the Art of Social Work and Social Work Education in China

During the 1920s, several social work courses were started at a small number of universities in China. However, the real development of a social work discipline in China began in the 1980s. The development trajectory escalated following the sixth Plenary Session of the sixteenth Central Committee Meeting of the Communist Party of China (CPC) in 2006, at which an important regulation to build a large social work workforce was proposed. In subsequent years, as an element of national strategy and institutional infrastructure construction, the social work profession was developed rapidly with the assistance of 'top-down' government initiatives. Social work education in China has undergone a remarkable expansion over the past two decades. In 2000, there were only 28 universities with undergraduate social work programmes, graduating approximately 1,000 students per year. By 2010 there were undergraduate social work programmes at 258 universities with about 10,000 graduates in 2010. A Master of Social Work

(MSW) was introduced at 33 universities in 2010; by 2012, a master's programme could be found at 60 universities with an annual intake of 2,000 post-graduate students (Liu, 2012, pp. 156, 172, 195). By 2019, a total of 430 universities and colleges provided diploma or undergraduate social work programmes, while the number of universities providing MSW social work programmes had reached 150 (Ministry of Civil Affairs, 2019).

Over the past 30 years, the development of social work in China has taken its own unique path, which has three core components.

Government-led social work: during the early period of social work development in China, the government issued a series of documents and policies which strongly influenced the emergent forms, structures, and practices of social work. As a consequence, increasingly, social work has become a pragmatical tool of social management and has developed a social structure approach that is 'embedded' in the current administrative system and is, thereby, constrained by the government administration and is reliant on government administrative system and resources. Consequently, the professional independence of social work is, to a significant extent, circumscribed.

Education first: social work education delivered through universities has played an important role in the development of social work in China. A large number of university teachers have become professors in social work education, either by transfer from other disciplines (notably: sociology, psychology, and philosophy) or through further training in social work. In addition, many new colleges and universities that provide social work programmes have sprung up.

Clinical orientation: social work has been characteristically clinical in orientation. The dependence on the governmental sector for resources has further intensified the clinical nature of the social work professional mission and forms of social governance. In order to be recognised and supported by the government, the discipline of social work will need to expand its sphere of competence within the existing professional ecosystem – deepening the government's recognition of the discipline's professionalism and ability to provide irreplaceable and necessary clinical services. Clinical approaches and skills have been given prominence in the development of the idea of the 'social work professional', while the development of macro skills and the structural mission of the discipline have been downplayed.

Supervision in Field Practice Education in China

In compliance with the predominant international structure of social work education, field practice has become an integrated component in both undergraduate and MSW social work curricula in China. For example, the National MSW Education Committee (2012) requires that 'social work field practice', supervised by an agency-supervisor, should comprise one-sixth of all the learning credits in an MSW programme. Meanwhile, the minimum number of required hours of field practice for MSW students, for those with a social work education background and those without, were set as 600 and 800 hours. respectively. There are good reasons to believe that field education has become a central element of undergraduate programmes. For example, in a 2016 survey of final-year students across all universities and colleges in Guangdong Province,[2] one of the authors found that all of the sample ($n = 575$) had experienced social work field practice as an integral part of their study (Lei, 2020).

The arrangements for provision of supervisors in field practice varies across Chinese universities. There are three ways for students to be supervised during field practice by supervisors who are: members of the academic staff that provides the programme; employed as members of staff by the social work agency that provides the field practice; and dual supervisors who hold positions at both the university and the agency. The three Chinese partners in the BUIBRI project, Fudan, Nanjing Normal, and Sun Yat-sen University, all rely on dual supervisors for student placements. However, using supervisors employed by social work agencies may be the preferred approach. For example, in Guangdong Province, a recent study has shown that 52.9% of students were provided with an agency supervisor while 15.8% and 14.4% of students were supervised by university supervisors and dual supervisors, respectively (Lei, 2020).

Although the importance of field practice is well recognised in Chinese social work education, recent studies have identified some significant obstacles that impede effective delivery of field practice for students. In particular, the lack of a quality placement causes a number of concerns (Wu et al., 2016). First, contradictory to the field practice requirements, it is still possible for some students to go into the field without supervision. Some 16.3% of students in the survey by Wu did not have any supervisor during their placement. Second, there is a lack of qualified supervisors, both from universities and agencies. In these cases, students received unplanned, ad hoc supervision (Chen et al., 2018). These tended to be disorganised sessions because of the lack of preparation and often led to a poorer learning experience than those provided by qualified supervisors. According to a survey of 15 MSW programmes in China by Liu et al. (2013), three of the top four most significant challenges identified with respect to field education were: 'lack of well-trained supervisors', 'lack of qualified social work supervisors in the agency', and 'lack of motivation for faculty to supervise students' (Liu et al., 2013, p. 190). Third, the quality of supervision has become a pressing concern, which impacts significantly upon students' enthusiasm and performance during the placement. The quality of supervision has significant implications for students' development of professional identity (Cai et al., 2018). In the UK, field supervisors are required to be registered qualified social workers, have a minimum of 2 years of practice experience, and have a practice education qualification before they take full responsibility of teaching, supervising, and assessing students (British Association of Social Work, 2019). In China, field supervisors are not required to undertake any training before they undertake the practice education role, and some supervisors may not even have social work qualifications (Liu et al., 2013). The importance of the quality of supervision for the development of students' competencies through their engagement in field practice was demonstrated by a 2018 comprehensive survey of students (n = 848) drawn from almost all Chinese MSW programmes (Wang et al., 2018). Similarly, a qualitative study of MSW students at a Shanghai university revealed that most students, during field practice, had performed very passively by only accomplishing tasks to the minimum level of competence because they did not receive timely and sufficient supervision (Cai et al., 2018).

The BUIBRI project

The main goal of the BUIBRI project was to address the need to develop quality in the social work field education system in China. Many scholars have described challenges to organising and implementing field education in China at the policy, university, and organisation levels (Cai, Bo, & Hsiao, 2018; Chen, Wub, & Peng, 2018; Li, Han, & Huang, 2012; Ting & Zhang, 2012). Quality field education, especially the availability of qualified faculty and field supervisors and adequate field agencies for placement, has been identified as a crucial factor for social work students to develop professional identity and demonstrate the ability to integrate theories and research knowledge into practice (Liu, Sun, & Anderson, 2013; Ting & Zhang, 2012). Within this context, the BUIBRI project was planned to overcome these challenges by building systemic linkages between practice, research, and education. The BUIBRI project aimed at building a relevant relationship between social work education and working life by enhancing university–agency cooperation to provide support for students' practical placements.

The specific objectives of the BUIBRI project were as follows:

1) to develop the skills of social work teachers in field education;
2) to develop resources for social work learning and teaching;
3) to promote the recognition of social work as an academic discipline;
4) to develop social work as a research-oriented professional system based on academic education in cooperation with academics and stakeholders.

These objectives were achieved by developing teaching and study materials and constructing and delivering training programmes to a) a group of 30 trainers that consisted of faculty and agency supervisors who then developed further and delivered the training to b) 600 agency supervisors who then provided placements to c) 600 students in three locations in China: Shanghai, Nanjing, and Guangzhou. In addition, the project produced two handbooks in Chinese that contained guidance about principles and methods of field studies in social work education.

The BUIBRI project, as a collaborative initiative between European and Chinese institutions, operated by exchanging best practices in the field of social work education. The three involved Chinese universities were Fudan University, Sun Yat-sen University, and Nanjing Normal University. From Europe. three universities participated: University of Eastern Finland in Finland, University of Hertfordshire in the UK, and University of Gothenburg in Sweden. Associated partners of the BUIBRI project were the China Social Work Academy and the China Association for Social Work Education. BUIBRI project partner universities had a long-term prior collaboration with Chinese academic institutes and scholars in the field of social work through academic exchange programmes, jointly written scientific articles, and various research and educational projects. The main motivation for these Sino-European collaborative initiatives was an interest in European social work traditions by Chinese colleagues who were relatively unfamiliar with European approaches, as the initial reference point for the development of social work in China was often US experience (Li et al., 2012, p. 643). The endeavours and experience gained through years of Sino-European collaboration were brought together in BUIBRI to introduce elements of European social work into Chinese social work systematically. Although European social work is not a homogenous entity (Frost, 2008; Lorenz, 2008), it can be characterised as aspiring to develop social work as an integrated part of a statutory system of social welfare that protects people's social rights. The underlying assumption behind the BUIBRI project was that achievements of European social work, represented in this case by British, Finnish, and Swedish experience, could be creatively discussed, transformed, and used to assist in the construction of the field education system in China in a way that would address the needs of Chinese society through its cultural and political contexts. The approach adopted by the project was to investigate best practices by country and based upon the insights found to develop and implement training materials and programmes for the Chinese context.

Substantive Discussion

Training the Trainers (Developing the Training)

The development and delivery of cross-national social work education programmes are implicitly paradoxical by nature. Embedded within the idea of a cross-national social work education programme is the assumption of a universal social work rather than a context-specific indigenous social work which has been derived from local social, political, and economic conditions (for discussion of these issues see Gray, 2005). Yet, such cross-national social work education programmes are often purposed to contribute to the development of an indigenised social work practice. The processes of planning, delivery, and review in the BUIBRI project contained the paradoxical nature of the cross-national educational programme through collaborative dialogue across all four nations involved in the programme.

Planning the Programme

There were three major challenges in planning the programme: conceptual clarity and consistency; complexity of devising a programme that would teach skills needed to supervise students during a placement whilst simultaneously developing participants' ability to teach those skills to others; and negotiating the content of the programme across a multinational team with different approaches to and understandings about pedagogy, social work, and higher education.

The aims of the programme were stated in the form of learning outcomes, in line with recent pedagogical approaches (Biggs, & Tang 2011):

1. be able to actively reflect on the nature and form of practice education in the context of BUIBRI project;
2. understand the nature of learning and be able to develop and enable learning in practice;
3. understand and be able to manage the process of practice learning;
4. demonstrate the ability to facilitate learning and use effective teaching skills;
5. understand the principles of assessing students' competence and be able to apply these in practice learning;
6. be able to reflect on personal professional development.

Delivering the Programme

The initial element of the programme was delivered over three consecutive days in Nanjing for 30 participants, later called trainers, from three cities in China: Guangzhou, Nanjing, and Shanghai. Several follow-up days were held for the participants, some with an international team and some with Chinese members only. The content of the programme was organised around six themes:

- What Makes Good Practice Learning?
- Structuring the Student's Learning
- Theories of Learning
- Enabling Student Learning
- Assessing Students
- Continuous Professional Development for Supervisors

Most sessions were presented jointly by a Chinese and European project team member, symbolising the cross-national collaboration and a visible response to the programme paradox. English and Putonghua (often known as Mandarin Chinese) were the languages used. Although many, but by no means all, of the Chinese participants had a good understanding of English, sequential translation was necessary. As the context demanded, sometimes this was word-for-word, and sometimes it was a summary. As is always the case, learning through translation slowed the pace of the sessions. There were several occasions in which European members of the team used terminology that confused meaning. A notable example was the terms 'evidence-based', 'research-informed', 'research-led', 'research-based' social work. How many practitioners or academics whose first language was English would, with confidence, able to split these conceptual hairs? Compliance with the terms in the bilingual glossary was central to promoting understanding in both the teaching materials and during learning events.

During the delivery of the programme, a number of devices were purposively employed to reduce the impact of communication challenges and to promote learning in a second language. These approaches were designed to limit the amount of spoken English and increase the amount of time that participants spent working in a Chinese linguistic climate. Decks of slides that were either in Chinese or Chinese and English for each presentation that were prepared prior to the delivery session, and printed copies of the slides were available to participants. Small group discussions and exercises were held in Chinese; frequently, a Chinese member of the team facilitated the feedback with European members of the team, receiving summaries in translation, thus, reducing time taken for translation. A handbook was provided for the whole of the programme, which was available in two versions – one English and one Chinese (this handbook was modified according to the comments of participants about its usefulness; several iterations were produced). When presentations were made in English, presenters made efforts to simplify their use of language, speaking precisely with clear diction. Aside from these language issues, one-third of the participants spoke Cantonese as their first Chinese language, and these participants had varying levels of competence in Putonghua[3].

Throughout the delivery of the programme, both the Chinese and the European tutors were alert to the emotional experience of the participants. First, in that they were expected to both learn new skills and then teach those skills to others. At times, this expectation raised anxieties, not unreasonably for participants. Second, as pedagogical traditions are influenced by geography and discipline, the pedagogical approach taken would have, for many of the participants been a novel experience. The majority of the participants had been educated in a didactic tradition with a strong emphasis on listening to the teacher. While this approach formed a part of the programme, a number of sessions used an active and participatory approach to learning to encourage the participants to develop their approach to teaching as preparation for when *they* would be teaching other potential agency supervisors.

Educating the Supervisors (Training Programme in Action)

After the training for the 30 trainers in September 2018, ten trainers each returned to Guangzhou, Shanghai, and Nanjing to proceed with the subsequent phase of the BUIBRI project in which they would educate agency supervisors from each region. An education programme for 100 supervisors per year (600 in total over the duration of the project) was planned for delivery at each location (Guangzhou, Nanjing, and Shanghai), with one round in 2019 and the second round in 2020. Here, we present experiences from the first round of the programmes for 300 supervisors that were delivered in 2019. These training programmes were led by the trainers who had participated on the training for trainers programmes. Each project team organised the training in their own region accordingly. During the planning of these programmes, two participants from each university were present, as well as the trainers themselves to develop training jointly for use on these training programmes for supervisors.

At all locations, the education programmes for supervisors comprised an initial three-day residential workshop during which a very similar training programme was followed to that of the trainers', with follow-up days at various intervals. These programmes were structured using the six themes previously mentioned, and a new handbook was generated with its links to videos,

PowerPoint presentations, and exercises – all used as the training tools during the programmes. The focus of this training was on the development of skills for supervisors. Training materials were modified and developed to suit the regional context, and different forms of programme delivery emerged.

The Shanghai team commenced recruitment for the training in the spring of 2019 through the Shanghai Association of Social Work, the organisation in charge of social work registration in Shanghai. More than 200 applications were received; places on the programme were allocated to the first 100 candidates to apply who met the selection criteria, which addressed the need for diversity of practice focus among the social work profession and the applicants prior experience of supervision. The teaching team held several sessions to prepare training materials that were suitably adapted to the Shanghai context. For the delivery of the programmes, the 100 successful applicants were organised in to five groups of 20 according to geographical location. Each of these groups was led by two trainers who had participated previously in the training for trainers programme; each group was led by a different pair of trainers.

The arrangements in Nanjing were very similar to those in Shanghai. The Nanjing team recruited 100 candidates through major social work organisations based in Nanjing. The ten trainers prepared regionalised teaching material through a series of meetings prior to organising the training for all of 100 selected candidates.

In order to enhance the impact of the BUIBRI project, the Sun Yat-sen University team at Guangzhou decided to extend the partnership to include all of Guangdong Province. Their development strategy can be summarised as follows. First, the Sun Yat-sen University team invited six other universities and colleges to participate in the project. Three of these universities and colleges were located in less well developed parts of Guangdong Province (eastern, western and northern), both economically and in respect of social work provision. Students from these universities and colleges had been looking forward to finding a social work placement in the Pearl River Delta, the region with the strongest economic and social work development in Guangdong Province. Second, the Sun Yat-sen University team persuaded 13 social work agencies from the Pearl River Delta to provide positions for social work interns. Third, the ten trainers who had participated in the training for trainers programmes had all been selected from amongst the applicants from these universities, colleges, and social work agencies. Based on the training materials developed by the BUIBRI project, they delivered two rounds of training for 200 agency supervisors selected from the 13 social work organisations. Fourth, members of the Sun Yat-sen University team acted as facilitators and assisted the six universities and colleges to negotiate with the 13 social work agencies to secure placements for their students. Lastly, in order to fully mobilise the resources of 200 trained supervisors, all the social work agency partners agreed to assign these supervisors to students from other higher education institutions, even if they did not come from among the project partner universities in Guangdong.

In all three locations, the education programme was not only directed toward supervisors involved at the three participating universities, but it was also made available to supervisors at other universities in their region. From the beginning of the project, it was evident that the development of social work education would diverge and vary between the three locations. The contexts in each location were distinct, for example, the development of supervision for social work students was grounded in a longer and more established tradition in Shanghai and Guangzhou than in Nanjing. There were also localised differences in provision between Shanghai and Guangzhou. In order to build in a level of localisation specific to each region in the project, guidelines, organisational structures, pedagogic approaches, and examples used in learning were modified and adapted to ensure a good fit to the local context to create the best education possible for the local situation.

What was Learned and Impact of Programme

During the evolution of the teaching programmes, the content was discussed with the participants to understand which parts they found easiest to grasp and which they found to be the most useful for them in their future role as supervisors. After training, the participants from both Shanghai and Nanjing acknowledged the value of teaching methods, teaching approach, and course design and gave positive overall comments about the training programme. Some participants were very enthusiastic about novel ideas such as the sections about peer counselling or Gibbs Cycle of Reflection (Gibbs, 1988). Many participants expressed the view that they would like further training of a similar style. A very positive outcome was the development of a peer support group amongst the trainers; this is evidence of their commitment to the values and pedagogic principles embedded in both the training programmes and the BUIBRI project.

A variety of approaches have been used to measure the impact the programme for supervisors, which have included: participant satisfaction surveys during the programme using a three-data-point evaluation (prior to, immediately post, and several months after the delivery of the programme once the participants had supervised a student on placement) that was theoretically grounded in changes in self-efficacy (Holden et al., 2002); and a qualitative evaluation designed to triangulate different perspectives following the participants' application of the programme principles in their own teaching (this applies both training of trainers and educating the supervisors).

Participant Satisfaction Surveys

In Guangzhou, agency supervisors completed a short survey designed to ascertain their views about the quality of supervisor training. The participating agency supervisors were generally satisfied with 'training content' and 'training methods'. Five indicators with the top ratings were: 'to lecture clearly' (97.03%), 'supervision of practice learning' (96.04%), 'contents of good practice learning' (95.05%), 'guidance on the process of practice learning' (95.05%), and 'training materials' (93.07%). However, it must be noted that five indicators received the lowest ratings below 90%, including 'research-based practice' (66.34%), 'length of training' (83.17%), 'practice of critical reflection' (85.15%), 'to learn relevant theories' (87.13), and 'plan of teaching' (88.12%). There is clearly more to do to meet the training needs of agency supervisors.

Longitudinal Evaluation Using Self-efficacy

The investigation of 'self-efficacy', originally derived from Bandura's (1997) work, was used to measure changes in self-perception of individual ability to perform a given role – as social work trainer or educator – and to explore the 'fit' of this research approach in a Chinese cultural context. More than 300 participants in the BUIBRI programme have been surveyed to ascertain their views about their self-efficacy to perform certain tasks. During the first round of training, all 300 participants completed the questionnaire before (T1) and after their training (T2). These 300 supervisors would then train 300 students in 3 months using the same teaching materials that were used for their training. After completing the teaching task, they would be evaluated again by the same questionnaire (T3). Initial findings suggest that, as hypothesised, older more experienced supervisors had higher self-efficacy scores than younger and less experienced supervisors. There were also differences between the three locations. Supervisors from Guangzhou, with a longer tradition of having agency supervision and some supervision training, had higher scores before the training programme. Interestingly most of these differences disappeared after the training (T2). Everyone achieved higher scores, and, following the training, the differences between sites were not large enough to be statistically significant. A more detailed analysis also comparing supervisors with different backgrounds (gender, age, with and without a Bachelor of Social Work (BSW) etc.) is under way, but preliminary results point at good results for most groups. Overall, it appears that the training program has had a positive impact on self-efficacy for most participants and decreased the differences between different locations and in respect to background.

Qualitative Evaluation

We conducted three focus groups with the supervisors, one at each site, to evaluate the impact of the training programme on their experience of practice education. Six supervisors from each site attended these focus group interviews. Supervisors expressed the view that they found it difficult to absorb all of the training materials presented over a 3-day period and that it was challenging to apply what they learnt in the reality of day-to-day practice. However, most shared the view that the training had provided them with a more structural and systematic approach to support students. Supervisors remarked that the training instilled a significant shift in their work with students; they recognised that it is of fundamental importance to consider the students' perspective in their practice learning journey. They realised the importance of getting to know students as individuals, identifying their learning needs, and exploring their interests at the outset. Training about supervision helped them to appreciate that supervision not only serves an administrative function but also an emotional and educational function to support students' learning. Additionally, it was very clear that supervisors found Gibbs' Cycle of Reflection, which was introduced in the training, a useful tool (Gibbs, 1988). They commented that not only could they use the model to help students to reflect on their practice but also as an aid to reflect on their own practice as supervisors. Different templates used for induction, supervision, and assessment were introduced in the training. Most supervisors found that these templates provided useful insights about how to structure and plan induction, supervision, and assessment. However, they all found it difficult to implement these templates in their entirety because of the time needed to complete the paperwork and the need to develop an indigenous version.

In other ways, this project has generated additional positive outcomes. In all participating universities, conferences about social work and supervision in social work education have been held. From various locations, there are reports about results from the programme. For instance, the strategy employed by the Sun Yat-sen University to widen the project partnership within the Guangdong Province has generated positive outcomes. By February 2020, there were a total of 137 students who had finished their placements within the framework of the BUIBRI project. Seventeen of them had signed a long-term contract to work in the social work agencies in which they finished their placements. Moreover, the BUIBRI project has enjoyed good publicity, in part, because the Sun Yat-sen University held five more launching ceremonies about the project and its programmes for supervisors in Maoming, Meizhou, Zhuhai, and Shenzhen other than just in Guangzhou. Similar results can be reported from the other locations.

Discussion

The BUIBRI project has facilitated not only new knowledge and skills in social work but also new thinking about social work education in China. First, the project has introduced new perspectives, for example, about recent Nordic and other European social work developments and educational philosophy into the Chinese social work education community, which, to date, has been extensively influenced by American social work ideas, concepts, and structures.

Nordic social work educational frameworks place more significance on the social structures that underpin personal problems and difficulties than Chinese frameworks have to date, which have been more focused on clinical social work variants. Consequently, in addition to recognising the importance of clinical practice, Nordic approaches have promoted and emphasised the importance of improving systems and the establishment of social mechanisms to empower individuals. These approaches are grounded in a desire to provide a better environment that enables the individual to grow and develop. These philosophical ideas have begun to contribute to the development of social work education in China, through initiatives such as the BUIBRI project.

Second, the BUIBRI project has provided an opportunity for a dialogue between Chinese and European countries conducted through the conduit of social work. This dialogue has provided an opportunity for the academic and practice fields of Chinese social work to summarise and jointly collate the unique characteristics of the developing Chinese approach to social work and then juxtapose these ideas and concepts with those in use by European partners. From this creative engagement, both parties have been able learn from each other.

Third, China's social work practice has been developed subsequent to the emergence of an academic discipline of social work, which is an 'education first' pattern. Whilst this style of development has many advantages in China, it has become apparent that both a significant proportion of social work academics and the teaching materials used, for example textbooks, have not been responsive to emergent trends in social work practice. Some inherent deficiencies appear to be present from the beginnings of the social work education in the 1980s, which has become increasingly unable to respond to the needs of practice development. The implementation of the BUIBRI project has enabled a group of educators and practitioners to improve their professional knowledge and abilities. These trained educators and practitioners will sow seeds on the fertile land of Chinese social work that, hopefully, will flourish, influence, educate, and help more practitioners, supervisors, students, educators, and the people who use social work services.

Conclusion

The evidence has suggested, for a long time, that functional interaction between social work education and the practice field is a critical factor to promote the use of a research-based approach in practice (e.g., Orme & Powell, 2007; Piippo et al., 2013; Steens et al., 2018). This may concern social work education and practice in different societal contexts. The BUIBRI project has demonstrated that success in transnational knowledge sharing is associated with efforts to develop social work as a recognised academic discipline and a domain of research-informed professional expertise. In spite of the considerable influence of nation-specific characteristics about the policies and practices of social work, academisation is a common element of the striving to develop social work as a professional system which combines research, education, and practice (Dellgran & Höjer 2016). Perhaps the most important lesson to be derived from the BUIBRI project is that this common element provides a sensible platform for beneficial knowledge sharing between Chinese and European universities to enable fruitful mutual learning. The project created a basis for future collaboration in the field of social work education focused particularly on linking academic qualifications to professional accreditation in China.

Notes

1 In this chapter, when we talk about social work agencies, we mean both governmental and non-governmental organisers of social work interventions.

2 Guangdong is a province in south-eastern China, covering 179,800 square km with a population of approximately 106 million
3 The written version (simplified Chinese) of Cantonese and Putonghua are the same, but the spoken versions of these dialects of the Chinese language are significantly different.

References

An, Q., & Szto, P. (2019) Research on the relationship between supervisor and social work interns in China: A Shanghai case study. *International Social Work, 62*(2), 905–917.

Bandura, A. (1997). *Self-Efficacy: The Exercise of Control*. New York: Freeman.

Biggs, J., & Tang, C. (2011). *Teaching for Quality Learning at University* (4th ed.). Maidenhead, Berkshire: Open University Press.

British Association of Social Work. (2019). *Refreshed Practice Educator Professional Standards for Social Work*. British Association of Social Work.

Chen, Q., Wub, L., & Peng, T. (2018). Exploring gaps between MSW students' experiences and expectations of field supervision in a Chinese setting. *Social Work Education, 37*(2), 265–276. DOI: 10.1080/02615479.2017.1395406

Cai, Y., Bo, A., & Hsiao, S. C. (2018) Emerging social work field education trends in China. *Journal of Social Work Education, 54*(2), 324–336.

Dellgran, P. & Höjer, S. (2016) Academisation of social work. In Taylor, I., Bogo, M., Lefevre, M. & Teater, B. (eds.) *Routledge International Handbook of Social Work Education*. New York: Routledge. DOI: 10.4324/9781315712536

Frost, E. (2008). Is there a European social work identity? *European Journal of Social Work, 11*(4), 341–354. DOI: 10.1080/13691450802075691

Gibbs, G. (1988). *Learning by Doing: A Guide to Teaching and Learning Methods*. Oxford: Further Education Unit. Oxford Polytechnic.

Gray, M. (2005). Dilemmas of international social work: Paradoxical processes in indigenisation, universalism and imperialism. *International Journal of Social Welfare, 14*(3), 231–238.

Holden, G., Meenaghan, T., Anastas, J., & Metrey, G. (2002). Outcomes of social work education: The case for social work self-efficacy. *Journal of Social Work Education, 38*(1), 115–133.

Holden, G., Barker, K., Rosenberg, G., Kuppens, S., & Ferrell, L. W. (2011). The signature pedagogy of social work? An investigation of the evidence. *Research on Social Work Practice, 21*(3), 363–372. DOI: 10.1177/1049731510392061

Jiang, H., Wang, Y., Chui, E., & Xu, Y. (2019) Professional identity and turnover intentions of social workers in Beijing, China: The roles of job satisfaction and agency type. *International Social Work, 62*(1) 146–160.

Lei, J. (2020) *Report of social work under-graduate students in Guangdong Province* (unpublished).

Li, Y., Han, W.J., & Huang, C.C. (2012). Development of social work education in China: Background, current status, and prospects. *Journal of Social Work EDUCATION, 48*(4), 635–653. DOI: 10.5175/JSWE.201Z201100049

Liu, M.-r., Sun, F. & Anderson, S. G. (2013) Challenges in social work field education in China: Lessons from the Western experience, *Social Work Education, 32*(2), 179–196. DOI: 10.1080/02615479.2012.723682

Liu, Z. (2012) *Indigenisation: A Necessary Way of Building Social Work Institutions* (in Chinese), Beijing: China Society Press.

Lorenz, W. (2008). Towards a European model of social work. *Australian Social Work, 61*(1), 7–24. DOI: 10.1080/03124070701818708

Ministry of Civil Affairs. (2019). *Figures of social work development* (in Chinese), http://www.mca.gov.cn/article/gk/tjtb/201903/20190300015629.shtml

National MSW Education Committee. (2012) *Guidance of the MSW Curriculum* (in Chinese), http://www.cdgdc.edu.cn/xwyyjsjyxx/gjjl/szfa/shgzss/xgjs/275982.shtml

Niu, D., & Östbö Haugen, H. (2019) Social workers in China: Professional identity in the making. *British Journal of Social Work, 49*, 1932–1949.

Orme, J., & Powell, J. (2007) Building research capacity in social work: Process and issues. *The British Journal of Social Work, 38*(5), 988–1008. DOI: 10.1093/bjsw/bcm122

Piippo, S., Hämäläinen, J., Savolainen, A., Suonio, M., & Väisänen, R. 2013. Better integration of education and practice? Promoting research-based social work. *The Journal of Practice Teaching & Learning. Social Work, Health, Nursing, 12*(2), 67–86. DOI: 10.1921/jpts.v12i2.290

Steens, R., Van Regenmortel, T. & Hermans, K. (2018) Beyond the research–Practice gap: The development of an academic collaborative centre for child and family social work. *The British Journal of Social Work, 48*(6), 1611–1626.

Ting, W., & Zhang, H. (2012). Flourishing in the spring? Social work, social work education and field education in China. *China Journal of Social Work, 5*, 201–222.

Wang, Y-a., Qiao, D. P., & Chui, E. (2018) Student engagement matters: A self-determination perspective on Chinese MSW students' perceived competence after practice learning. *British Journal of Social Work, 48*(3), 787–807.

Wu, S., Huang, H., Sun, F., & An, Q. (2016). Is social work really being recognized? Problems with social work employment opportunities in Mainland China. *Social Work Education, 35*(2), 186–203. DOI: 10.1080/02615479.2015.1136614

Yan, C. (2019). Social work education in China: The development, difficulties and solutions. In *Paper at 2019 4th International Social Sciences and Education Conference (ISSEC2019)*, Xiamen, China.

Yan, M. C., & Tsang, K. T. A. (2008). Re-envisioning indigenization: When the bentuhuade and the bentude social work intersect in China. In M. Gray, J. Coate, & M. Yellowbird (Eds) *Indigenous Social Work Practice and Education around the World* (pp.191–202). London, UK: Ashgate.

4

Field Work Education in Social Work

Perspectives of Vietnamese Social Work Students

Huong T. Hoang and Hang T. Dao

Field education (F.E.) is one of the required standards for social work (S.W.) education and training, which is approved by the International Association of Schools of Social Work (I.A.S.S.W.) and the International Federation of Social Workers (I.F.S.W.) (Sewpaul & Jones, 2004). S.W. is a practice-based profession; thus, F.E. plays a leading role and is central to S.W. education (Council on Social Work Education, 2015). With this importance in all curricula of S.W. schools worldwide, fieldwork practice is a compulsory component.

S.W. education and training were introduced to Vietnam in the middle of the twentieth century by the French Red Cross in the South. Due to historical fluctuations, S.W. education was interrupted after Vietnam's reunification in 1975. The return of S.W. education to Vietnam was marked by the Ministry of Education and Training's (M.o.E.T.) approval of S.W. bachelor's degree training in 2004. In 2010, the Vietnamese government recognised S.W. as a profession. Since then, the number of training institutions offering S.W. programmes has increased dramatically from 4 to 33 institutions between 2004 and 2010 (Durst, Lanh, & Pitzel, 2010; Nguyen, Hugman, & Briscoe, 2010). The figure was 55 universities and colleges and 21 vocational schools in 2017 (Nguyen, 2017). From the initial construction of the national framework for the Bachelor of Social Work (B.S.W.), M.o.E.T. has defined F.E. as a compulsory module of the S.W. training programme.

Based on the philosophy of 'learning by doing', F.E. plays a role 'to connect the theoretical and conceptual contribution of the classroom with the practical world of the practice setting' (C.S.W.E 2008, Educational Policy 2.3 in Liu, Sun, & Anderson, 2013, p. 182). Through the F.E., students have opportunities to apply S.W. theories and methods in actual practice. F.E. practice experience helps students to play the role of the future social worker. With real clients and experienced social workers, students are able to develop their professional skills as well as their soft skills.

Owing to F.E.'s significance to S.W. education, there have been various studies conducted into F.E. According to Wertheimer and Sodhi, between 2005 and mid-2011, slightly fewer than 100 articles indexed in S.W. abstracts were about field placement. These articles covered numerous topics related to F.E.'s pedagogy and the challenges of implementing the field component

DOI: 10.4324/9781032164946-6

(Wertheimer & Sodhi, 2014, p. 49). Some studies on S.W. training topics included: philosophy, models, history, development (Durst et al., 2010), programmes, and curriculum (Durst et al., 2010; Schmidt & Rautenbach, 2016). In particular, several other studies focused on practical issues in S.W. practice training, such as practice formats/models (Curl & Cary, 2014; Olson-Morrison, Radohl, & Dickey, 2019), practice organisation and instruction (Dhemba, 2012; Eltaiba & Ndoye, 2018; Hodgson & Walford, 2006; Schmidt & Rautenbach, 2016), practice programme and curriculum (Liu et al., 2013; Olson-Morrison et al., 2019; Panda, 2012), planning in practice (Hodgson & Walford, 2006; Liu et al., 2013; Panda, 2012; Street, 2019; Sunirose, 2013; Tippa & Mane, 2018), the role of stakeholders in practice training (Dhemba, 2012; Guin, 2019; Panda, 2012; Street, 2019; Wertheimer & Sodhi, 2014), supervision (Panda, 2012; Street, 2019), practice assessments (Eltaiba & Ndoye, 2018; Street, 2019), learning process through F.E. (Papouli Eleni, 2014), and suggestions/prospects for effectiveness of practice (Liu et al., 2013; Tippa & Mane, 2018).

Regarding studies related to the assessment of S.W. education and training, especially S.W. practice training, research concentrated on learners' perspectives played a vital role. These studies focused on people who experienced the practice process, so their assessments indicated whether the programme training in general and practice training, in particular, match their needs, competencies, and expectations. The learners' evaluation studies were also an essential basis for reviewing and adjusting the objectives and training methods to bring benefits and satisfaction to learners and stakeholders. Many strongly debated topics are interested in the preparation process (Eltaiba & Ndoye, 2018; Kanno & Koeske, 2010) and practice experience (Petrila, Fireman, Fitzpatrick, Hodas, & Taussig, 2015); assessment of practice, including content and programme structure, learning materials, and stakeholders' support (Eltaiba & Ndoye, 2018; Guin, 2019; Tran, 2016); assessment of supervision (Eltaiba & Ndoye, 2018; Guin, 2019; Kanno & Koeske, 2010; Petrila et al., 2015); difficulties encountered in practice (Eltaiba & Ndoye, 2018; Guin, 2019; Tran, 2015); and the needs and expectations of students (Kanno & Koeske, 2010; Petrila et al., 2015).

Although being a new science in Vietnam, but with practical contributions to social development and support for disadvantaged and vulnerable communities, the state and researchers pay attention to S.W. education. There were many research projects, reports, and master's theses that have provided evidence concerning S.W. education in Vietnam, such as the history and the development of S.W. (Hugman, Durst, Le, Nguyen, & Nguyen, 2009; Hugman, Nguyen, & Nguyen, 2007; Nguyen et al., 2010), the current situation of S.W. education and training (Hodgson & Walford, 2006; Hugman et al., 2009, 2007; Nguyen & Bui, 2012; Nguyen et al., 2010; Tran, 2015), government S.W. projects (Hugman et al., 2007), and international collaboration in S.W. (Hines et al., 2015), S.W. programmes and curricula (Hugman et al., 2009; Nguyen et al., 2010), factors related to S.W. education (training capacity, material, facilities) (Nguyen et al., 2010), difficulties and challenges in S.W. education (Nguyen et al., 2010), supervision for students at field settings (Doan, 2018; Luong, 2018; Mai & Nguyen, 2012; Nguyen & Nguyen, 2018; To, 2018; Vo & Dang, 2018), suggestions for improving S.W. education (Hines et al., 2015; Tran, 2015), and student assessment of S.W. education and training (in terms of programme, material, lecturer, placements) (Tran, 2015). A newly published article by a group of S.W. lecturers designed qualitative research to explore the challenges for S.W. field education in Vietnam. According to this research, lacking qualified field supervisors, a loose collaboration between universities and field agencies, and inadequate student assessment methods are the main challenges for F.E. (Nguyen et al., 2020).

S.W. training has also been a key topic in many recent international conferences and seminars organised by the Department of Social Assistance (D.S.A.), Ministry of Labour, War Invalids and Social Affairs (M.o.L.I.S.A.), Vietnam Association for Vocational Education – Training and Social Work Profession (V.V.T.S.W.P.), Universities and Academies training S.W. In December 2018, the D.S.A. and the sociology faculty at the University of Social Sciences and Humanities collaborated to conduct an international scientific conference called 'SW practice training: International experience and Vietnam reality'. The workshop focused on analysing S.W. training in Vietnam from the perspective of educational managers, training institutions, and practice agencies. Scientific reports in this workshop showed that practice training still faced many problems such as disproportional practice time, students' lack of soft and professional skills, the students' behaviour, and the loose connection between stakeholders in practice. At this conference, scholars discussed the current situation and F.E. experience and suggested solutions and recommendations to increase F.E. effectiveness.

From the above, it is widely accepted that F.E. is an essential component of S.W. education. In the context of developing the S.W. profession, various aspects of S.W. training in Vietnam were discussed to improve S.W. training quality. However, the learner's perspective-based research has been rare and not comprehensive. The purpose of this study is to listen to S.W. students' voices about their experience and assessment of F.E. After briefly describing the critical features of F.E. in Vietnam, we will examine the students' choice of field settings and their difficulties in the field. We then explore the students' self-assessment in the pre-practice stage, the students' assessment about stakeholders' roles, including training institutions, faculty lecturers, and field supervisors, and their result from S.W. practice. Finally, we discuss S.W. students' recommendations to improve S.W. practice.

Methods

Document Analysis

The primary materials gathered in this study include the B.S.W. curricula that were officially published on the training institutions' websites. These curricula were chosen because their quality had already been verified. The results showed that 16 collected curricula reviewed the structure and the volume of fieldwork education in Vietnam. This study's second source is the documents related to education and training policies and S.W. development policies.

Qualitative Interview

To explore respondents' opinions of the organisation of S.W. practice and students' assessment of practice progress, we used qualitative interviews via telephone and other online tools. The respondents include four lecturers (two of them from Hanoi and the others from Dalat and Ho Chi Minh City (H.C.M.C.)) and three alumni.

Online Survey

S.W. students' perspectives on F.E. in S.W. were collected in March 2020, by using self-administered questionnaires. The study's information, consent form, and instructions to complete the web-based survey were provided at the beginning of the questionnaire. The participants needed to confirm their consensus on the study before completing the questionnaire.

The questionnaire includes closed-ended questions to learn about student experiences in S.W. practice, their assessment of the process of S.W. practice, and open-ended questions to learn respondents' perspectives on limitations as well as suggestions to improve the effectiveness of F.E. in Vietnam. Two groups of participants are S.W. alumni and S.W. seniors of 11 universities training in S.W. in the North, the Middle, and the South in Vietnam (Vietnam National University (V.N.U.) Hanoi-University of Social Sciences and Humanities (U.S.S.H.), V.N.U. H.C.M.C.-University of Social Sciences and Humanities, University of Labor and Social Affairs (campuses in Hanoi and H.C.M.C.), Trade Union University, University of Science and Education (University of Da Nang), Ton Duc Thang University, Vinh University, University of Sciences – Hue University, Dalat University, and Hanoi National University of Education).

Sample

The sample consisted of 289 females and 68 males, including 131 graduate students out of 357 respondents. Of the respondents, 23% of graduates were in jobs that were entirely in accordance with their majors, nearly 49% were in S.W.-related jobs, 11.5% were working in other fields, and 4.2% alumni graduated but have yet to find a job. For final-year students, more than half of them wanted to find a job suitable for their major after they graduate, one-third planned to find any jobs, about 14% planned to continue their studies, whilst the rest had no plan yet.

Overview of Field Work Education in Social Work in Vietnam

Based on analysing M.o.E.T.'s policies and examining the training institutions' F.E. curricula, this section presents the foundations for the content design of practical modules and the F.E.'s characteristics in Vietnam's S.W. institutions.

Legal Framework for Constructing the Social Work Practice Curriculum

In 2004, Vietnam M.o.E.T. approved the first national framework for the B.S.W. After transferring from the traditional higher education model, which was influenced by Russia's model, with the credit-based training system (M.o.E.T., 2007), the B.S.W. framework was adjusted in 2010 by Circular 10/2020/TT-BGDDT. This framework comprises regulations for the structure, volume, and minimum content knowledge for S.W. training at a bachelor's degree level. According to M.o.E.T.'s framework, students need to complete a minimum of 120 credits of coursework, including 14 credits of practicum and internship, to graduate for a B.S.W. With groups and community development practice, S.W. practice with individuals are compulsory modules for all S.W. students. S.W. training institutions must adhere to these regulations to construct or modify their programmes.

Currently, Circular 07/2015/TT-BGDDT stipulates the minimum amount of knowledge and the learners' competence outcomes for each training level of higher education and the process of elaborating, evaluating, and promulgating training programmes for undergraduate, master's, and doctoral degrees. Accordingly, each training programme needs to identify specific learning outcomes of knowledge, skills, and training institutions' autonomy and responsibility (M.o.E.T., 2015). Therefore, training institutions must be based on two Circulars to construct or modify their programme. Moreover, Vietnam still lacks a legal corridor for S.W. activities, creating barriers for vocational training as well as S.W. practical training (Nguyen, 2018). From Decision 32 of the Government, there have been some by-law documents governing the activities of S.W. Recently, the M.o.L.I.S.A. drafted and proposed the S.W. Bill to Congress and sought public comment. Thus, until the S.W. Bill is approved, a curriculum for S.W. field education will be built on the legal basis of M.o.E.T., as mentioned above.

The Objectives of Social Work Practice Training

According to the M.o.E.T.'s framework, the B.S.W. programmes must provide students with, for example, comprehensive and general skills, such as problem detection and assessment, intervention skills with individuals and groups, community management and development, policy development and advocacy, policy assessment, and research skills (M.o.E.T., 2010). These target skills are similar to those of the Australian Association of Social Workers (A.A.S.W.) practice fields identified in 'Practice Standards 2013'.

The M.o.E.T.'s framework curriculum for S.W. practice emphasises the range of direct S.W. intervention with individuals, groups, and communities 'Providing students with the opportunity to connect theory with practice through client intervention (individuals, groups, communities) under the guidance of the training institutions and field supervisors' (M.o.E.T., 2010). Compared to A.A.S.W.'s practice standards, which include working with individuals, families, groups, and communities as well as social policy practice, management, leadership and administration, education and training, and research and evaluation, Vietnam's M.o.E.T. requires a narrower scope of practice. Consequently, based on M.o.E.T.'s orientation, all collected B.S.W. curricula focus on three modules including S.W. practice with individuals, S.W. practice with groups, and community development practice.

Time Requirements for Field Work Programmes

Reviewing 16 of the B.S.W. programmes in Vietnam reveals that all S.W. curricula have at least 122 credits, which is higher than M.o.E.T.'s framework. One programme reaches 137 credits, and the median of total duration is 128 credits. For F.E., most of the universities used M.o.E.T.'s framework for three modules of practicum and one module of internship, equivalent to 13 to 14 credits. There are three programmes that added field visit modules, with 17 and 18 credits for F.E. According to M.o.E.T. (2007), one credit is equivalent to 45 to 90 practice hours in field settings; this means students need to complete at least 585 hours of fieldwork practice in the B.S.W. programme. Compared to M.o.E.T.'s framework, all universities allot from two to five credits of field placement in their S.W. programmes, but the proportion of F.E. in their programme accounts for 10%–11.5% of the total training duration, which is 11.7% lower than that in M.o.E.T.'s framework. About one-fifth of reviewed S.W. training programmes have a higher percentage of time for F.E. than M.o.E.T.'s framework.

Components of Field Work Curriculum

Reviewing 16 S.W. training institutions, although they are entirely proactive in designing their own curricula for F.E., most institutions copy M.o.E.T.'s framework for F.E. A field visit module is optional, depending on educational institutions. In general, the components of S.W. schools' fieldwork curriculum in Vietnam suggest the following:

Field visit: appears in some educational institutions' curricula. This module is often held in the first half of the course, providing opportunities for students to reach disadvantaged groups in social protection establishments in order to better understand the subjects, functions, and roles of S.W.

S.W. practice with individuals: this module requires students to apply the knowledge and intervention techniques with individuals in a specific client case in the field.

S.W. practice with groups: this module requires students to apply the knowledge and intervention techniques with groups in developing and implementing a group-level intervention plan to address social issues of disadvantaged individuals, groups, or communities.

Community development practice: this module provides opportunities for students to practice in a residential area, applying knowledge and methods of community development to solve prior community issues.

Internship: this module takes place at the end of the course, allowing students to take a social worker's role at a field agency.

Field Settings for Social Work Students

Training institutions have diverse field settings for S.W. practice, mainly including social protection facilities, S.W. service centres, governmental and non-governmental organisations (NGOs), or disadvantaged communities. Depending on the practical training programme's design, students or training institutions have the responsibility to contact fieldwork agencies. For example, community development practice at V.N.U.-Hanoi U.S.S.H. is organised by training institutions, whilst at Dalat University, students make contact themselves (Do, 2018). With the internship module, all students are given the right to choose their internship institutions independently. In this case, the training institution may offer students some criteria to select a practice site, such as the need for a supervisor (Nguyen, 2018).

Considering the student autonomy in connecting to practice areas, training institutions are currently applying the following three types of contact: (1) Students are fully active in contacting practice areas, while training facilities provide information and support formal procedures to communicate with practice establishments; (2) Students are partly active in communicating with the practice site in one of several specialised practice modules; (3) Students are only active in contacting the practice site for graduation internships. The third kind mentioned often occurs when training institutions have memoranda or cooperation agreements with practice institutions.

Field Work Education Formats

The training schedule for S.W. field placement at educational institutions is quite diverse. In general, if the training programme includes a field visit, it will be held at the end of the first year. Practicum modules are usually organised from the second school year onward, while the internship module occurs in the fourth year. Furthermore, in some cases, training facilities arrange the whole final year for fieldwork practice.

In terms of arrangement of field education, S.W. training institutions often use one of four forms: concurrent, block, a combination of concurrent and block, and in-service placements (Dhemba, 2012). A block fieldwork placement means that students spend from at least a month to a year, depending on the situation, at a fieldwork agency, without any interruption in learning. Meanwhile, concurrent fieldwork coincides with classroom activities (Dhemba, 2012). Although students have to divide their schedule between both learning and practice, they can integrate theoretical knowledge into practice and through fieldwork to understand classroom knowledge.

Currently, the M.o.E.T. does not have specific requirements for the educational format of the practice training. Therefore, in Vietnam, training institutions are actively organising practice activities to suit the conditions of human resources and training schedules. A combination of concurrent and block is the most prevalent model applied in most S.W. schools. Accordingly, some modules are held almost parallel to theoretical learning. In contrast, other modules (usually field visits, community development practice, and internship) are organised using the block placement form over the summer months. Meanwhile, at some other training institutions, all practical modules are arranged separately from theoretical training, usually at the end of the third year and the whole of the final year.

The Role of Stakeholders

In F.E. in Vietnam, training institutions provide students with a system of general knowledge, field-based knowledge, specialised knowledge, and research methods. Practical activities at field-work agencies, where students apply theoretical knowledge and skills, allow them to play a social worker's role. During the practice process, the training institutions connect with the practice agencies to create favourable conditions for students. The coordination between them is reflected in the unified plans, the agreements on methods and supervision, the agreements on evaluation, and solving any problems arising during the period of practice. Some training institutions have established relationships and signed agreements with practice agencies to provide more professional and specialised practice progress. However, this coordination is mainly based on a verbal agreement between the faculty lecturers and the practice agencies' staff who perform the supervisor's duties.

In terms of the supervisor's task standards, the A.A.S.W. (2014) issued 'Supervision Standards 2014', covering three aspects: education, support, and accountability. N.A.S.W. and A.S.W.B. offer three points: administrative, educational, and supportive (N.A.S.W. & A.S.W.B., 2013). However, there are not any official standards for the supervisor's task in Vietnam. Most of the field supervisors are not well-trained and professional (Doan, 2018; Ho, 2018; Luong, 2018; Nguyen, Vu, & Nguyen, 2018; To, 2018; Vo & Dang, 2018). As a result, the lecturers are in charge of providing theoretical knowledge and guiding and monitoring students in the field. The lecturers have tasks throughout the practicum and internship, such as commenting on the plan, meeting and talking with supervisors about students' activities, guiding students to solve problems, advising about any situations that may arise, checking progress, making suggestions, and editing students' reports. Meanwhile, field supervisors mainly perform administrative roles.

Results

Besides briefly reviewing fieldwork education in S.W. in Vietnam, to understand students' thoughts about social work programmes (S.W.P.), the findings are divided into four main parts: (1) students' fieldwork experience; (2) students' assessment in the process of S.W.P.; (3) students' assessment in the result of S.W.P.; and (4) the recommendations from S.W. students. This content is based on surveying students' perspectives through data from qualitative-quantitative combined methods.

Students' Field Work Practice Experiences

The results of this study begin by describing the students' F.W. practice experiences through their choice of field setting and the difficulties they face. Meanwhile, the field site gives students different experiences, and the difficulties they encounter indicate problems that may affect the practice results.

Type of Field Settings Experienced by Students

As mentioned in the field setting section, students have opportunities to experience different organisations or communities. The students share the type of field settings in which they practiced their skills as Figure 4.1 below.

Statistics indicated that students tended to experience an average of 2.2 practice institutions (mean = 2.2, std. dev. = 0.94), and the number of students participating in three different kinds

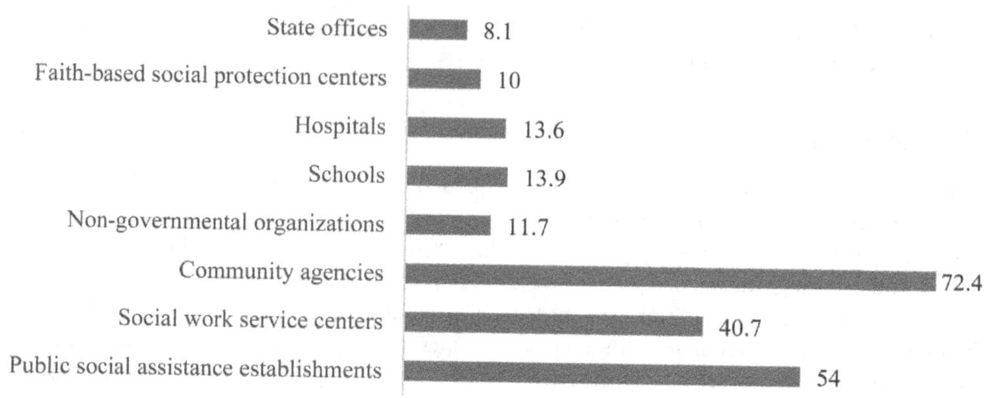

Figure 4.1 **Type of field settings experienced by students. Source: All figures and tables in this chapter are by the authors.**

of agencies accounted for the dominance (37.0%). Meanwhile, the highest number of different types of practice establishment was four, which means these students had varied opportunities to practice in distinct environments.

The majority of students practiced in the communities (72.4%), followed by public social assistance institutions (54.0%) and S.W. service centres (40.7%). Other types of practice sites, such as schools, hospitals, N.G.O.s, and faith-based social protection centres, each accounted for about 10% of the respondents. The state agencies, such as the People's Committee, the Division of Labor, War Invalids and Social Affairs, occupied the lowest rate, at 9.1%. Students said:

> There is still an emphasis on practicing at state-owned institutions and focusing on beneficiaries of government policies. Practicum has not allowed students to maximise their flexibility, creativity, and get acquainted with more new environments to accumulate more experience, knowledge, and have a broader view of S.W.
>
> If students do not contact field agencies for themselves, there are only state social protection centres or faith-based charity institutions that limit the working network as well as S.W. students' experiences in various fields.

Qualitative interviews indicated that training institutions encouraged students' proactive self-searching for field settings and flexibility in accepting the practice facilities' conditions. Approximately one-fourth of participants revealed that they were refused when connecting to field settings and needed the help of their lecturers, friends, or family's social network.

However, they thought that having students find their own field settings would 'cause many problems relating to facilities' activities in the practice process, and the main issues are settings do not meet requirements for S.W. practicum and supervisors have no professional knowledge on S.W.'.

There are no official standards for students in selecting field settings, so they could choose an inappropriate institution:

> During the internship, many students chose an agency where they have a close relationship to get the certificate, but they did not work there, or students chose a setting that is not good quality.

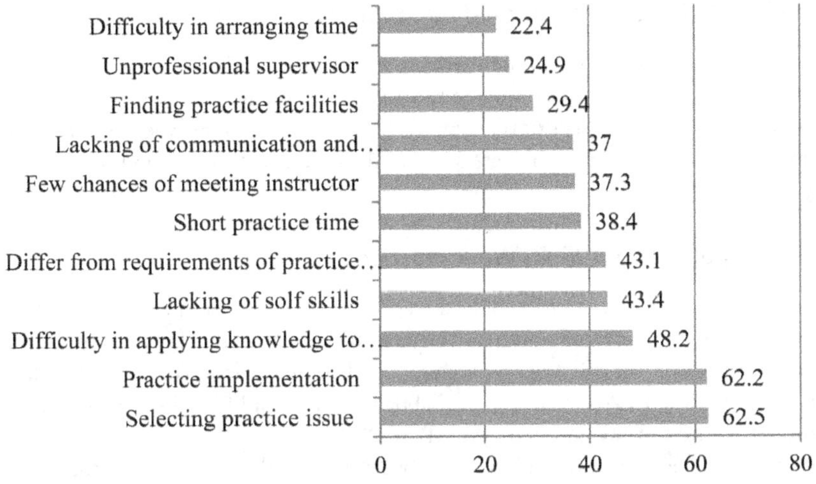

Figure 4.2 Difficulties encountered by students in the practice process.

The students' experience shows that their field facilities are quite limited and focus mostly on community agencies, public social assistance establishments, or S.W. service centres. Remarkably, this result indicated that the choice of fieldwork institution depends on not only students being active themselves but also on the support from their networks.

Difficulties Experienced by Students during Field Work

To verify the challenges students have undergone in practice, we included the lecturers' and social workers' ideas mentioned in previous research in the questionnaire, selecting practice issues and practice implementation, which were mentioned in qualitative interviews in our questionnaire. The results are shown as follows:

The survey revealed that the two of the most common difficulties many students encounter were selecting practice issues and practice implementation (62.5% and 62.2%, respectively). Some other challenges, including anxiety in applying the knowledge to practice, lacking soft skills, and the differing requirements of practice institutions and reports, constituted the majority of problems, with more than 40% of respondents in the survey. Some issues related to time arrangements and unprofessional supervision were not the students' main problems.

According to students, experience in unsuitable settings caused challenges for them in selecting their practice issues: 'The reality is that registering with an internship agency that does not relate to their profession, makes it difficult to choose appropriate subjects or research topics'.

Some students also felt that they lacked the specialised knowledge to work with their clients. They were able to meet various clients in the field, but they tended to select children or the elderly to complete their practice tasks. One student said that 'Our current skills let us approach simple types of clients'. Meanwhile, other students thought it would be better to practice in a specific field rather than by methods, as is what currently occurs.

As such, the consistency between quantitative and qualitative data shows that the main difficulties students face in the field are selecting practice issues and practice implementation.

The Process of Social Work Practice Assessed by Students

Students' assessment of various aspects in the fieldwork points out how these factors affect the process. These reviews include: (1) self-assessment of the pre-practice stage referred to how students understand S.W.P., (2) training institution's support, (3) faculty lecturer's role, and (4) field supervisor's role, implying the way in which these stakeholders are involved in the process and how fulfilling they are.

Self-Assessment of Preparation for Field Work Practice

According to the regulations ofVietnam's M.o.E.T., the syllabus outline should clearly state 'the number of credits, prerequisites (if any), theoretical and practical content and capacity, modules evaluation measure, study materials, and references, and conditions for experiment and fieldwork, practice modules' (M.o.E.T., 2014), and the syllabus outline should be disseminated and implemented according to the output standards (M.o.E.T., 2017).

Therefore, similar to the theoretical modules, at the beginning of the practical module, lecturers disseminated to students the subject's objectives, the learning outcomes, the content of the module, assessment methods, and specific requirements of final reports with the practical modules. In this study, to clarify students' understanding of the practice modules' contents, we used a scale of 1 to 10 for students to self-assess their comprehension level about the issues mentioned above. The following chart shows the results.

On a 10-point scale, most students assessed the level of understanding of the subject's objectives, learning outcomes of knowledge, skills, and evaluation measures of the modules at a fairly good level (median = 7). Other items assessed by students with a better understanding were the output standard of attitude, practice content, and the report's requirements (median = 8).

Students suggested that these were modules with practice content, so the requirements for practical skills and practice content were easily understood and visualised. Second, the final

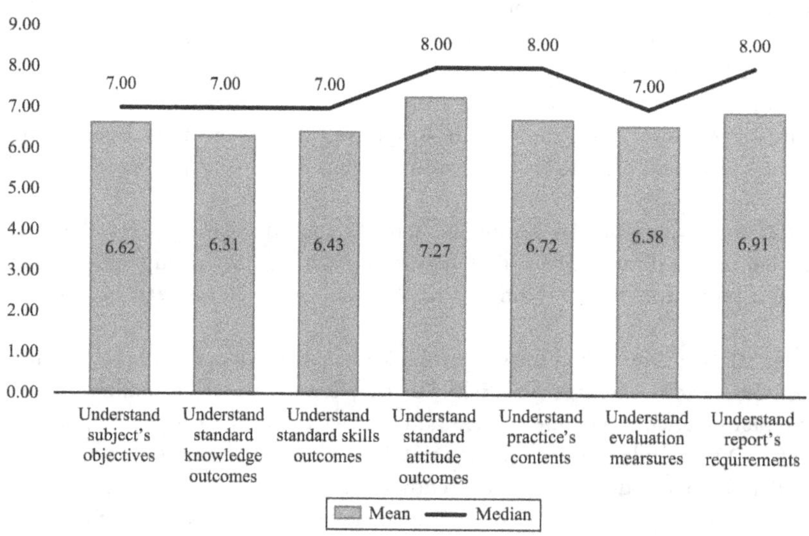

Figure 4.3 Students' assessment of preparation for fieldwork.

report was one of the most critical indicators (with the highest weight) for measuring practice achievement, so students were more interested in the report's requirements as the final result achieved in the practice and internship period.

Focusing more on how students prepared for fieldwork or professional internship, the results illustrated that the dominant choice of students was 'listening to instructors' (92.5%), which was followed by 'referring to the formers' report' (56%) and 'studying all materials provided by lecturers' (48.5%). Compared to that, the less active group of students tended to read parts of materials, while the more active group was likely to search for more references and documents to read (27.3% and 28.4%, respectively).

Thus, the result of preparation also pointed out that students more easily understood the final report's contents and requirements, as mentioned above.

The Training Institutions' Support Evaluated by Students

Training institutions play a crucial role in determining S.W. practice's content and method, cooperating with field agencies to create the best conditions for students to practice. Meanwhile, lecturers or instructors at training institutions provide theoretical knowledge of practice methods and guide other academic activities related to reports or outcome assessments.

From the students' perspective, the most common role of training institutions was to provide referrals to introduce students and connect to field agencies (82.5%) indirectly. Moreover, professional assistance (42.1%) and providing information about practice institutions (38.7%) also demonstrated the role of training institutions. While contacting practice agencies is not the main role of educational institutions, a small group of students needed this support (12.0%). Conducting interviews with lecturers showed that training institutions support students with information on field institutions if they cannot find any institution for practice.

Only 2.2% of the respondents think that the training institution supports practice funding. However, training institutions have direct and indirect financial support for students conducting fieldwork. Qualitative interviews with four lecturers also showed that, in some cases, the practical modules were held and connected by training institutions, offering financial support, including travel expenses, to the practice establishments, supervisors, and instructors/lecturers. Some

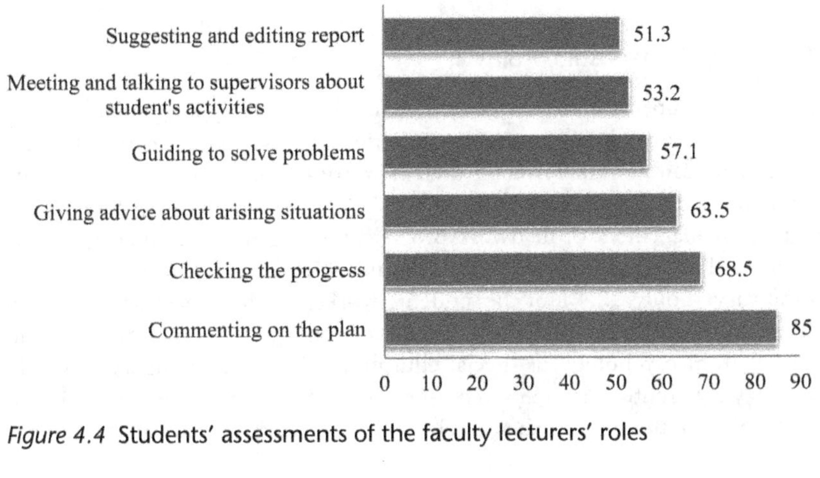

Figure 4.4 Students' assessments of the faculty lecturers' roles

institutions also assisted students with travel expenses depending on the practical modules, at VND15,000/day (65 cents/day) for internships or VND350,000–VND400,000/practical module ($15–17/module) (Nguyen et al., 2018).

In cases supporting students directly, training establishments also instructed students to use this money to build relationships with the agency or to support the field supervisors. Due to the training institutions' budget use, students were often less concerned about the administrative procedures relating to financial support.

Assessment of the Faculty Lecturers' Roles

Based on our understanding about lecturers' responsibilities in fieldwork collected from in-depth interviews, the six categories below represent the main role of a lecturer.

The lecturers' role is most evident in making suggestions to students' practice and checking progress during practice. Interviews with four lecturers demonstrated that students were required to meet face-to-face at least two or three times to report on progress during the practice. In addition, lecturers often used online communication channels such as Zalo (a Vietnamese social network platform) and Facebook to contact students regularly. When students practice at nearby locations, lecturers, as well as students, probably visit practice institutions to ask for official cooperation.

About 50% of the respondents assessed the lecturer as fulfilling their central role in guiding, giving advice, and supporting in the practicum process. Other tasks such as meeting, communicating with the field supervisors, commenting, and editing the reports did not seem to meet about half of the students' expectations in the survey. Through students' comments about organising better practical activities, several students experienced the feeling of being surprised at not having any particular direction when going to the practice agencies, and they wanted lecturers to be more involved in their practice process. For instance, through discussion with student groups (who had the same client sample), the practice plans should be clarified and oriented. Moreover, lecturers should actively check the progress of practice before coming to the field by promptly give feedback to inappropriate points in the client's intervention, be more meticulous and more rigorous in assessing the practice process as well as the report, and interact with supervisors to catch early problems in the field. Moreover, in some cases, students wish that lecturers/instructors came to the field for orientation and support.

The results indicate that the lecturer's role manifests itself in academic advice and remote monitoring from the student's perspective.

Assessments of the Field Supervisors' Roles

In the field, the professional supervisors or the person taking responsibility for students' professional activities play a significant role in the process and effectiveness of practice. Based on the A.A.S.W. and N.A.S.W. standards of supervisors, as well as practical requirements of the supervisor's role in Vietnam, the research has developed a framework for evaluating their functions in S.W. practice, including management of fieldwork progress, training process, support, contact, assessment, and feedback. The resulting findings are given in Table 4.1.

According to the survey, only 22.4% of the students worked with supervisors who were trained in S.W. About 65% worked under the guidance of some people from S.W. training programmes or others from psychology or special education. Hence, their supervisors' roles during the fieldwork were limited. Students reported that 'The on-site supervisor doesn't receive any professional S.W. training, so they rarely give comments on students' practicum

Table 4.1 Students' Assessments of Supervisor Roles

Supervisor Roles (n = 359)	*Valid %*
Providing information	81.1
Supervising	72.7
Commenting on the practice plan	69.6
Assessing practice progress	35.1
Selecting/assigning client	32.3
Guiding to interact with client	32.0
Noting and responding practice progress	23.1
Communicating to training institution about the practice	11.7
Informing training institution about arising issues	5.8

process. During my practicum and internship, I'm lucky to work with one supervisor who graduated B.S.W'.

The data showed that the primary roles of supervisors were providing information (about practice progress, organisational structure, clients, etc.) (81.1%), supervising students' practice activities (72.7%), and commenting on the plan (69.6%). According to respondents, the remaining roles were performed at low levels (less than 30%). A qualitative interview with alumni indicated that 'The limitation of lacking a qualified supervisor is that I don't know if I worked right or not, I didn't understand the client because I don't have enough time to collect their information'.

The data also presented the loose relationship between the training and the practice institutions because only 11.8% of supervisors communicated to the training establishments about the student's practicum, with approximately 6% of them communicating with the training institutions about problems that arose during the practice.

Thus, in the field, students mainly receive guidance from supervisors and less direct practical instruction.

The Result of Social Work Practice from the Students' Perspective

In addition to the aforementioned description of the practice process and the role of stakeholders, the research results also show two indicators to evaluate the F.E. results. First, students' assessment of the degree of theory to practice application shows the effectiveness of F.E. Second, the meaning of F.E. from students' viewpoints tends to demonstrate their interest in S.W.P., which has a significant influence on the result.

Students' Assessments of Applying Theory to Practice

The study explored the S.W. practice results by evaluating how they applied learned knowledge and skills to practice. Using a scale of 1–10, the content to be considered includes theoretical knowledge, S.W. skills with individuals, S.W. skills with groups, community development skills, and research skills. The median and mean values of students' assessments are presented in the following table.

Students tended to assess the application of theoretical knowledge and specific practical skills of S.W. at a fairly good level (median = 7), while that of research skills was average (median = 6).

Data from qualitative interviews showed the same situation when students thought that they did not have many opportunities to use theoretical knowledge or did not know how to apply this knowledge in practice. One of the essential things about fieldwork was that students interacted with real-life clients with complex circumstances and difficulties that they had never encountered before in their classes. From the qualitative data, the research found that, although the theoretical duration was considerable, it was challenging to cover all the disadvantaged groups in reality. Even in the classes of the most experienced lecturers, they had only provided the most typical model and unique experiences to illustrate the theoretical knowledge. For example, students still did not know how to work with children with rare or unusual forms of disabilities that had not been mentioned in class. Fundamentally, B.S.W.'s practice curriculum in Vietnam mainly classified different approaches. such as individuals and groups. but had not solved the more complex contents by client type such as S.W. with street children, orphans, disabled children, or abused children. Thus, the amount of time for theoretical knowledge was not enough for students to apply in reality.

It was also noteworthy that conducting scientific research requires students to combine theoretical, practical, and problem-solving skills, which seemed to be S.W. students' limitation in Vietnam. In addition, with the short duration of the practice period and the requirement to submit a report immediately after the end, achieving the most complete report was challenging for students.

Significance of Field work Practice for Students

Students' opinions about fieldwork were also indicators to measure the effectiveness of this activity. This study considered two types of S.W. students' views: perspectives relating to career and aspects relating to non-career. These indicators reveal factors that promote an individual, career, and social worker consciousness development. Specifics were shown in the table below.

Remarkably, students appreciated the opportunities they had in the practicum and the role of this in progressing career development and employment opportunities in the future. This was reflected in the fact that. through fieldwork, students could improve their S.W. professional skills (80.5%), raise their awareness about the role of social workers (73.5%), be inspired to pursue a career in the future (51.3%), and expand social networks in order to increase career opportunities (63.5%). These were also important goals that need to be achieved in field placements.

In addition, practice roles were performed in other areas. Notably, 88.3% of respondents thought that practice was to gain experience in life. Along with specialised skills and knowledge from this process, the interaction with clients and the S.W. service system (including supervisors, social workers, establishment's managers) gave opportunities to experience many actual situations in life, such as supporting disadvantaged people and improving communication skills.

Table 4.2 Median and Mean Values on Self-assessment of Applying Theory to Practice

Assessment of applying level (n = *359*)	*Median*	*Mean*	*Std. Deviation*
Theoretical knowledge	7	6.03	2.30
S.W. skills with individuals	7	6.40	2.31
S.W. skills with groups	7	6.43	2.29
Community development skills	7	6.41	2.38
Research skills	6	5.91	2.52

Table 4.3 Field Education's Significances from the Students' Perspectives

Field Education's Significances (n = *359)*	*Valid %*
Opportunity to gain experience in life	88.3
Opportunity to improve S.W. profession skills	80.5
Raising awareness about the role of social workers	73.5
Raising community awareness and social responsibility	71.0
Being inspired to pursue the S.W. profession in the future	51.3
Fieldwork is like extracurricular activities or a picnic	24.5
Expanding social networks and increasing career opportunities	63.5

Additionally, being exposed to disadvantaged circumstances also helps students raise community awareness and social responsibility (71%). This was one of the noble meanings of social workers' community support, and it was also a good way to show their citizenship.

About a quarter of students thought that the practice modules were like a picnic. On the one hand, this data showed that practicing activities also gave students many opportunities to interact with friends and other people and participate in mass activities. On the other hand, it was possible that students might not appreciate the importance and significance of fieldwork activities and, instead, considered them to be a sightseeing and recreational activity.

Recommendations from Social Work Students

From the above evaluations, the students suggest some solutions to improve the effectiveness of S.W.P. on the basis of the difficulties they experienced, their assessment of numerous dimensions, and the results they had from the process.

Analysing students' assessments of the limitations of practice training and the suggestions for improving practicum showed their ideas focused on the main issues as follows.

Increase the Duration of Field Placement

Of the respondents, 57.1% said that increasing the time for practice is essential, while 39.6% of them suggested maintaining the duration, and 3.3% recommended reducing it. The students' opinions from the open-ended question in the questionnaire indicated that they did not have enough time to apply their knowledge to solve the problems of the customer. A small number of people asked for the practice time to be reduced because of irrelevant experience at inappropriate practice agencies and lack of S.W. activities.

Diversified Choice of Practice Establishments and Practice Concept/Area/Fields

Students' current practice sites have mainly been state-owned institutions (social protection centres, S.W. centres). The training institutions' network with the practice agencies was limited, which led to the repetition in practice fields of their previous courses. As a consequence, there were some situations in which students did some illegal copying with earlier reports. In addition, clients became accustomed to students' presence, and their boring tasks and topics made the interaction between them less effective. Furthermore, the monotony of the practice sites resulted in students being less accessible to specific groups, such as autistic children, street children, people with addictions, and women who had been abused.

Pre-practice Support

Students proposed some support that might be effective with their pre-practice period, namely organising sharing sessions with their seniors and organising soft skills training, such as observation, questioning, communication, and rational behaviour. Strengthening the role of lecturers and supervisors to support students was also suggested. Because supervision in the field was not professional enough, students wished to meet lecturers more often to have answers to problems during the practice process. Students also need close monitoring to avoid being distracted.

Discussion

Before learning of student reviews about F.E., we reviewed the models of training S.W. practice in Vietnam. The results reveal that facilities closely followed the M.o.E.T.'s framework for F.E., though they have the right to adjust three-fifths of content and duration for the S.W. programme. Each institution has a particular objective and concern in teaching S.W.P., which maybe not equivalent to other institutions. For example, the University of Labor and Social Affairs spends one-quarter of the credits in the professional S.W. knowledge block for social welfare and social insurance, while 14 subjects in the Public Health University are related to health and health care (Hugman & Lan, 2019). However, they do little to adjust the duration time for F.E. compared to M.o.E.T. regulations. Comparing the total credits of F.E. in Vietnam to other S.W. training institutions globally, the time spent on F.E. is nearly equivalent to other countries. In Australia, the A.A.S.W. requires S.W. students to complete a minimum of 1,000 hours in at least two field education subjects. The School of S.W. at Columbia University requires students to complete 18 of 60 credits with 1,200 hours of practice. The School of S.W. at Loyola University Chicago requires 14 of 53 credits (equivalent to 840 hours), while 22 of 64 credits (about 1,680 hours) is required of students at the University of New England. In general, the amount of time allocated for training S.W. practice in Vietnam, which is from 13 to 18 credits, is similar to overseas training institutions, but the ratio of practice time compared to the total training time is nearly three times lower. As mentioned by faculty members in previous studies (Doan, 2018; Nguyen et al., 2018), students in this study also judged that F.E.'s duration time is inadequate for them to apply theoretical knowledge to practice. The time allotted in the field was sometimes wasted on irrelevant activities for S.W. practice. Training institutions in Vietnam have a strong emphasis on practice methods by following the 'Global Standards for SW Education and Training' (Hugman et al., 2009). However, after more than 15 years of S.W. training, institutions with different professional training orientations have applied a similar model for training in S.W. practice. Stakeholders all agree that the duration for S.W. practice is short, but facilities have not solved this problem. This fact reveals that training institutions are still confused about building their F.E. programmes in relation to the specialised areas in which they aim to train.

Examining students' evaluation of practical activities shows that a notable finding is that the current approach to constructing F.E. curricula in Vietnam has caused challenges and difficulties for students in the field. From the voices of students, two main difficulties encountered during the practice process are the selection of practice issues and the implementation of field placement. These two issues have hardly been mentioned in previous studies, nor have they been noticed in the scientific seminars on practical training in S.W. practice so far. While S.W. students at Qatar University highlighted that the main challenges they faced in field placement related to ethics and values (Eltaiba & Ndoye, 2018), Vietnamese S.W. students were confused about selecting practice issues and complementing intervention activities. In Vietnam, most S.W. schools held the practicum in the second and the third years after completion of general, fundamental, and some basic courses; professional courses are arranged at the end of the third year and the beginning of the final year.This arrangement of academic and practice modules applied in training institutions currently caused S.W. students to feel that they lacked professional knowledge for practice in the field settings.

In this study, one-fifth of the respondents reported that they met difficulties with concurrent fieldwork.This view is consistent with that of some previous research.The time constraints encountered when a practicum takes place at the same time as other courses are challenges for S.W. students in Vietnam (Nguyen et al., 2018; Nguyen & Nguyen, 2018; To, 2018) and Qatar (Eltaiba & Ndoye, 2018). However, only a minority group encountered this problem in our study.

Relating to the selection of field settings, notably, in the study conducted by Nguyen et al., (2020), students being active in choosing their field settings is considered as a strength. It gives them 'an opportunity to work independently and teaches them to be proactive in determining their professional interests'. While this study showed that only a handful of students had this ability, the majority encountered barriers. Although all educational institutions give students the right to contact practice settings, they had lax regulations on students' choices. As a result, students could select easy access agencies and that may not be suitable for S.W. practice. Due to the limitation of constructing a practice setting network, training institutions enhance the students' initiative by letting them search for their field setting. For some active students, this is a good opportunity for them to select the setting and the practice issue they are concerned about, while a small number of students felt this to be an obstacle.The current situation in Vietnam is quite different from S.W. training in other countries that have a developed S.W. education. Some S.W. schools in the U.S.A. have a F.E. manual that presents criteria for selecting field agencies (Columbia University School of Social Work, 2017; University of Houston Downtown, 2018). That is not to say that F.E. in Vietnam should have similar criteria. If applying these criteria for selecting field settings, it could be that there are not any agencies able to satisfy these requirements. In the near future, as the S.W. profession is developing in Vietnam, the number of qualified social workers is limited, and S.W. activities are still on the path toward professionalisation. The students' self-selection of location for practicum or internship is considered a training institutions' solution. Using flexible requirements for F.E. could open employment opportunities for S.W. students in the context of Vietnam.

Previous studies have indicated that the lack of supervisors with expertise in S.W., as well as the understanding of this position's role, was the major shortcoming in S.W. practical training in Vietnam today (Doan, 2018; Luong, 2018; Nguyen et al., 2018; Nguyen & Nguyen, 2018; To, 2018; Vo & Dang, 2018). Countries with a short history of training professional S.W., such as China, Qatar, or some institutions in Eastern and Southern Africa are face the same lack of qualified field supervisors (Dhemba, 2012; Eltaiba & Ndoye, 2018; Liu et al., 2013). According to the results of Hugman and Nguyen (2019, p. 14), there has been a lack of educational capacity in terms of human resources for S.W.P. In Vietnam, the compulsory requirement to teach a bachelor's degree is a master qualification; nevertheless, the number of lecturers educated in S.W. has been quite limited. Therefore, a large number have a master's degree or doctorate in sociology or psychology. With such limited human resources, it is impossible to assign lecturers to take on two roles simultaneously without negatively affecting the practice process.

To solve problems related to on-site supervisors, training institutions in Vietnam have implemented two solutions: (1) using faculty members who have S.W. training of some kind to provide the supervision; (2) training and supporting experienced workers in the social service agencies to do the supervision. More than ten years after Hugman et al. conducted their study in 2009, F.E. in Vietnam has experienced a slight improvement in finding solutions for on-site supervision. Our study observed that the two solutions mentioned above are still being used. Furthermore, we observed two institutions using other solutions. For instance, one training institution has a position of practice lecturer who can plan, organise, instruct, and support students during practicum and internship. Another institution signed contracts with professional S.W. agencies to provide F.E. services. These agencies are responsible for selecting or providing field settings, organising F.E., and providing qualified supervisors. Alternatively, faculty lecturers play double roles in teaching academic modules in the class and supervising in the field. These solutions are difficult to replicate because most facilities do not consider S.W. as a specific training field that needs to increase investment in human resources and finance. Nguyen et al., (2020, p.13) suggest long-term solutions such as establishing a field education office which coordinates the placements, arranges supervision, and develops a standard learning contract that can be individualised for student learning outcomes and assessment. In terms of a temporary solution, in the context of human resource limitations, non-S.W. agency practitioners who provide supervision should be identified to S.W. interns.

Field placement benefits students not only by providing effective learning opportunities but also by giving opportunities for experiencing life as well as expanding their social network. According to students, they self-assessed the application of the level of theoretical knowledge and skills as quite good but their research skills as medium. These findings are quite similar to results from the research conducted by Nguyen et al., (2020), which found that students developed their communication and team-working skills through S.W.P., but they needed more time to improve practical clinical skills and as still being limited in communication and computer skills.

Regarding the importance of S.W.P., the learning experience is accumulated from each of a student's placements. They helped recognise their passion for education and have better preparation for future employment (Nguyen et al., 2020). However, a number of students in this study still had not considered S.W. practice to be meaningful to their careers and employment orientation after graduation. These findings could help educators better understand their S.W. practice training for students.

These findings suggest that training institutions should pay more attention to learners' feedback about their F.E. in S.W. The present study raises the possibility that the gap between students' views and educators' views on students' challenges in the field settings may reduce the effectiveness of current solutions applied by institutions for improving training S.W. practice.

Conclusion

The research extends our knowledge of learners' experiences and assessments of F.E. in S.W. However, the results cannot be generalised to all S.W. students in Vietnam because of self-selection in sampling. In this study, although the online survey allowed access to students at major S.W. schools representing all three regions of Vietnam, the sample depended on voluntary respondents which could lead to systematic bias. Therefore, based on exploratory findings, this article recommends that training institutions should regularly ask learners about their need for practice training (at the beginning of the course) and their assessment of the process and effectiveness of practice (at the end of each course). The lecturers and instructors at the training institutions should also actively discuss with students their wishes and difficulties to regularly adjust and update the content of practical activities in accordance with students' actual experience. Universities can invite social workers, practice officers, and supervisors to participate in academic learning activities in the classroom to receive suggestions from practitioners and to make appropriate adjustments to the goals and methods of courses.

Acknowledgement

This research paper is solely funded by V.N.U. University of Social Sciences and Humanities, Hanoi.

References

A.A.S.W. (2014). *Supervision Standards – 2014.* Australian Association of Social Workers. Retrieved from https://www.aasw.asn.au/document/item/6027.

Columbia University School of Social Work (2017). *2018–2019 Field Education Manual.* Retrieved from http://www.socialwork.columbia.edu/field/.

Council on Social Work Education (C.S.W.E.) (2008) *Educational Policy and Accreditation Standards*, C.S.W.E., Alexandria, VA4.

Council on Social Work Education (C.S.W.E.). (2015). *Educational Policy and Accreditation Standards for Baccalaureate and Master's Social Work Programs*, Alexandria, USA, 1–16.

Curl, A., & Cary, S. (2014). A program evaluation of block and concurrent practicum formats. *Field Educator, 4*(2), 1–10.

Dhemba, J. (2012). Fieldwork in social work education and training: Issues and challenges in the case of Eastern and Southern Africa. *Social Work and Society: International Online Journal, 10*(1). Retrieved from https://www.socwork.net/sws/article/view/310/651.

Do, V. T. (2018). Nang cao nang luc thuc hanh, thuc tap cho sinh vien chuyen nganh Cong tac xa hoi thong qua viec xay dung mo hinh thuc tap chuyen nghiep tai cong dong [Enhance the capacity of practising for social work students through designing the model of community]. In *Hoi thao khoa hoc quoc te 'Dao tao Thuc hanh nghe Cong tac xa hoi: Kinh nghiem quoc te va thuc te Viet Nam' [Social Work Practice Training: International Experiences and Vietnam Reality]*, held by V.N.U.-Hanoi, U.S.S.H. and Department of Social Assistance, M.O.L.I.S.A. 21–22 December, Hanoi.

Doan, T. T. H. (2018). Thuc hanh Cong tac xa hoi trong dao tao dai hoc tai Hoc vien Phu nu Viet Nam [Social work practice in the bachelor of social work at Vietnam Women's Academy]. In *Hoi thao khoa hoc quoc te 'Dao tao Thuc hanh nghe Cong tac xa hoi: Kinh nghiem quoc te va thuc te Viet Nam' [Social Work Practice Training: International Experiences and Vietnam Reality]*, held by V.N.U.-Hanoi, U.S.S.H. and Department of Social Assistance, M.O.L.I.S.A. 21–22 December, Hanoi.

Durst, D., Lanh, T. H., & Pitzel, M. (2010). A comparative analysis of social work in Vietnam and Canada: Rebirth and renewal. *Journal of Comparative Social Work, 5*(2), 77–88. https://doi.org/10.31265/jcsw.v5i2.63.

Eltaiba, N., & Ndoye, A. (2018). The effectiveness of field education in social work education: A student perspective. *Advances in Social Work and Welfare Education, 20*(1), 170.

Guin, S. (2019). Fieldwork supervision through open and distance learning: An Indian perspective. *Asian Association of Open Universities Journal, 14*(2), 107–121. https://doi.org/10.1108/aaouj-08-2019-0031

Hines, A., Cohen, E., Nguyen, T. H., Drabble, L., Han, M., Sen, S., & Tran, D. T. (2015). Improving social work education in Vietnam through international cooperation: The 'social work education enhancement program'. *Social Work Education, 34*(6), 716–728. https://doi.org/10.1080/02615479.2015.1052391

Ho, S. T. (2018). Doi ngu kiem huan vien chuyen nghiep - yeu to quan trong dao tao thuc hanh cu nhan Cong tac xa hoi theo dinh huong thuc hanh [Professional supervisors: The crucial factor in training the Bachelor of Social Work]. In *Hoi thao khoa hoc quoc te 'Dao tao Thuc hanh nghe Cong tac xa hoi: Kinh nghiem quoc te va thuc te Viet Nam' [Social Work Practice Training: International Experiences and Vietnam Reality]*, held by V.N.U.-Hanoi, U.S.S.H. and Department of Social Assistance, M.O.L.I.S.A.. 21–22 December, Hanoi.

Hodgson, D., & Walford, H. (2006). Planning for learning and learning about planning in social work fieldwork. *The Journal of Practice Teaching and Learning*, 7(1), 50–66. https://doi.org/10.1921/17466105.7.1.50

Hugman, R., Durst, D., Le, H. L., Nguyen, T. T. L., & Nguyen, T. H. (2009). Developing social work in Vietnam: Issues in professional education. *Social Work Education: The International Journal, 28*(2), 177–189. https://doi.org/10.1080/02615470802243087

Hugman, R., Nguyen, L. T. T., & Nguyen, H. T. (2007). Developing social work in Vietnam. *International Social Work, 50*(2), 197–211. https://doi.org/10.1177/0020872807073985

Hugman, R., & Nguyen, T. T. L. (2019). Social work education in Vietnam. In I. Shaw & R. Ow (Eds.), *Asian Social Work: Professional Work in National Contexts* (1st Edition). London: Routledge.

Kanno, H., & Koeske, G. F. (2010). MSW students' satisfaction with their field placements: The role of preparedness and supervision quality. *Journal of Social Work Education, 46*(1), 23–38. https://doi.org/10.5175/JSWE.2010.200800066

Liu, M., Sun, F., & Anderson, S. G. (2013). Challenges in social work field education in China: Lessons from the Western experience. *Social Work Education, 32*(2), 179–196. https://doi.org/10.1080/02615479.2012.723682

Luong, T. L. H. (2018). Thuc hanh trong dao tao nghe Cong tac xa hoi tai Dai hoc Quang Binh. In *Hoi thao khoa hoc quoc te 'Dao tao Thuc hanh nghe Cong tac xa hoi: Kinh nghiem quoc te va thuc te Viet Nam' [Social work Practice Training: International Experiences and Vietnam Reality]*, held by V.N.U.-Hanoi, U.S.S.H. and Department of Social Assistance, M.O.L.I.S.A.. 21–22 December, Hanoi.

Mai, T. K. T., & Nguyen, V. G. (2012). Hoat dong kiem huan cua Nhan vien Cong tac xa hoi cho sinh vien tai cac co so – Nhung van de dat ra [Issues of the activities of the social workers' supervisions for students at the field settings]. In *International Conference 'Sharing of International Experience of Social Work and Social Protection'*. Hanoi: Viet Nam National University Publisher.

M.o.E.T (2007). *Decision 43/2007/BGDDT Ban hanh quy che dao tao dai hoc va cao dang he chinh quy theo he thong tin chi* [Promulgating the full-time training regulations at university and college according to the credit-based training system]. Viet Nam Ministry of Education and Training. Retrieved from http://vbpl.vn/bogiaoducdaotao/Pages/vbpq-toanvan.aspx?ItemID=71496&Keyword=.

M.o.E.T (2010). *Circular No.10/2010/TT-BGDDT ban hanh Chuong trinh khung Giao duc dai hoc nganh Cong tac xa hoi trinh do dai hoc, cao dang* [Promulgate the national framework of higher education for social work at the university and college levels]. Viet Nam Ministry of Education and Training. Retrieved from http://vbpl.vn/bogiaoducdaotao/Pages/vbpq-toanvan.aspx?ItemID=25098&Keyword=.

M.o.E.T (2014). *Decision 17/VBHN-BGDDT Quyet dinh ban hanh quy che dao tao dai hoc va cao dang he chinh quy theo he thong tin chi* [Decision on promulgation of regulation on formal undergraduate education applying academic credit system]. Viet Nam Ministry of Education and Training. Retrieved from https://moet.gov.vn/van-ban/vanban/Pages/chi-tiet-van-ban.aspx?ItemID=890

M.o.E.T (2015). *Circular 07/2015/BGDDT Ban hanh quy dinh ve khoi luong kien thuc toi thieu, yeu cau ve nang luc ma nguoi hoc dat duoc sau khi tot nghiep doi voi moi trinh do cua giao duc dai hoc va quy trinh xay dung, tham dinh, ban hanh chuong trinh dao tao trinh do dai hoc* [Promulgate regulations on the minimum amount of knowledge, the requirements on competencies that learners can achieve after graduation for each level of higher education and regulations on the development, appraisal and issuance of university training programs]. Viet Nam Ministry of Education and Training. Retrieved from http://vbpl.vn/bogiaoducdaotao/Pages/vbpq-toanvan.aspx?ItemID=66762.

M.o.E.T (2017). *Circular 12/2017/TT-BGDDT Ban hanh quy dinh ve kiem dinh chat luong co so giao duc dai hoc* [Promulgate regulations on accreditation of higher education institutions]. Retrieved from https://moet.gov.vn/van-ban/vanban/Pages/chi-tiet-van-ban.aspx?ItemID=1255.

N.A.S.W. & A.S.W.B.. (2013). Best practice standards in social work supervision. Retrieved October 8, 2019, from https://www.socialworkers.org/LinkClick.aspx?fileticket=GBrLbl4BuwI%3D&portalid=0.

Nguyen, H. T. (2018). Hoan thien co so phap ly ve dao tao thuc hanh nghe cong tac xa hoi o Viet Nam hien nay [Improving the legal framework for training of social work practice in Vietnam today]. In *Hoi thao khoa hoc quoc te 'Dao tao Thuc hanh nghe Cong tac xa hoi: Kinh nghiem quoc te va thuc te Viet Nam' [Social Work Practice Training: International Experiences and Vietnam Reality]*, held by V.N.U.-Hanoi, U.S.S.H. and Department of Social Assistance, M.O.L.I.S.A. 21–22 December, Hanoi.

Nguyen, H.T., Cohen, E., Văn Đỗ, T., Nguyễn, D. H.T., Ngô, T. M.T., Kiều, T.V., … Bùi, M.T. (2020). Social work field education in Vietnam: Challenges and recommendations for a better model. *International Social Work*, 1–16. https://doi.org/10.1177/0020872820930264.

Nguyen, T. K. H., & Bui, T. M. (2012). Tong quan dao tao Cong tac xa hoi o Viet Nam [Overview of Social Work Training in Vietnam]. In *International Conference 'Sharing of international Experience of Social Work and Social Protection* (pp. 3–10). Hanoi: Viet Nam National University Publisher.

Nguyen, T. T. L., Hugman, R., & Briscoe, C. (2010). The moving towards an 'Indigenous' social work education in Vietnam. *Social Work Education: The International Journal, 29*(8), 843–854. https://doi.org/10.1080/02615479.2010.517013.

Nguyen, T. T. L., & Nguyen, T. T. H. (2018). Dao tao thuc hanh cong tac xa hoi: Thuc trang, thach thuc va nhung goi mo tu kinh nghiem quoc te [Social work practice: Situation, challenges and international experience]. In *Hoi thao khoa hoc quoc te 'Dao tao Thuc hanh nghe Cong tac xa hoi: Kinh nghiem quoc te va thuc te Viet Nam' [Social Work Practice Training: International Experiences and Vietnam Reality]*, held by V.N.U.-Hanoi, U.S.S.H. and Department of Social Assistance, M.O.L.I.S.A. 21–22 December, Hanoi.

Nguyen, T. K. H., Vu, M. P., & Nguyen, T. Q. A. (2018). Dao tao thuc hanh Cong tac xa hoi tai cac truong dai hoc o Viet Nam hien nay co dao tao nganh Cong tac xa hoi [Training social work practice at the universities having Social Work Program]. In *Hoi thao khoa hoc quoc te 'Dao tao Thuc hanh nghe Cong tac xa hoi: Kinh nghiem quoc te va thuc te Viet Nam' [Social Work Practice Training: International Experiences and Vietnam Reality]*, held by V.N.U.-Hanoi, U.S.S.H. and Department of Social Assistance, M.O.L.I.S.A. 21–22 December, Hanoi.

Nguyen, V. H. (2017). Danh gia khai quat ket qua thuc hien de dan Phat trien Nghe Cong tac xa hoi giai doan 2010–2015 va dinh huong giai doan 2016–2020 [Assessment of the implementation's results of the social work profession developmental project in the period of 2010–2015]. In *Seminar 'Health Care: Sociological and Social Work Issues'* (pp. 27–39). Hanoi: Viet Nam National University Publisher.

Olson-Morrison, D., Radohl, T., & Dickey, G. (2019). Strengthening field education: An integrated model for signature pedagogy in social work. *A Journal of Scholarly Teaching, 14*, 55–73. Retrieved from http://www.insightjournal.net/wp-content/uploads/2019/07/4-Olson-et-al.pdf.

Panda, B. (2012). Strengthening fieldwork practicum in social work education. *Social Work Chronicle, 1*(2), 14–30. https://doi.org/10.26643/hrj.v1i5.6587.

Papouli Eleni. (2014). Field learning in social work education: Implications for educators and instructors. *Field Educator*, 4(2), 1–15. Retrieved from http://www2.simmons.edu/ssw/fe/i/Papouli_Field_Learning.pdf.

Petrila, A., Fireman, O., Fitzpatrick, L. S., Hodas, R. W., & Taussig, H. N. (2015). Student Satisfaction with an innovative internship. *Journal of Social Work Education, 51*(1), 121–135. https://doi.org/10.1038/jid.2014.371.

Schmidt, K., & Rautenbach, J. V. (2016). Field instruction: Is the heart of social work education still beating in the Eastern Cape? *Social Work (South Africa), 52*(4), 589–610. https://doi.org/10.15270/52-2-532.

Sewpaul, V., & Jones, D. (2004). Global standards for social work education and training. *Social Work Education, 23*(5), 493–513. https://doi.org/10.1080/0261547042000252244.

Street, L. A. (2019). FI perspectives on challenging behaviors in SW practicum. *Field Educator, 9*(May), 1–21.

Sunirose, I. P. (2013). Fieldwork in social work education: Challenges, issues and best practices. *Rajagiri Journal of* Social *Development, 5*(1), 79–94. Retrieved from http://ezproxy.puc.cl/docview/1547935865?accountid=16788%0Ahttp://todosibuc.uc.cl/openurl/56PUC_INST/56PUC_INST_SP?url_ver=Z39.88-2004&rft_val_fmt=info:ofi/fmt:kev:mtx:journal&genre=article&sid=ProQ:ProQ%3Asciencejournals&atitle=Fieldwork+in+Social+Work+E.

Tippa, N. G., & Mane, S. R. (2018). Problems & prospects of fieldwork training in social work education: A review. *Innovare Journal of Social Sciences, 6*(1), 1–2.

To, P. O. (2018). Kinh nghiem thuc tap tot nghiep doi voi sinh vien Cong tac xa hoi, truong Dai hoc Su pham Ha Noi [Experience of professional internship for social work students, Hanoi National University of Education]. In *Hoi thao khoa hoc quoc te 'Dao tao Thuc hanh nghe Cong tac xa hoi: Kinh nghiem quoc te va thuc te Viet Nam' [Social Work Practice Training: International Experiences and Vietnam Reality]*, held by V.N.U.-Hanoi, U.S.S.H. and Department of Social Assistance, M.O.L.I.S.A. 21–22 December, Hanoi.

Tran, V. K. (2015). Social work education in Vietnam: Trajectory, challenges and directions theoretical approach and research. *International Journal of Social Work and Human Services Practice, 3*(4), 147–153.

Tran, V. K. (2016). Challenges for social work education in Vietnam: Voice of social work students. *Social Work & Social Sciences Review, 18*(2), 7–24. https://doi.org/10.1921/swssr.v18i2.901.

University of Houston Downtown (2018). *Social Work Program Field Practicum Handbook Revised 2018018*. Retrieved from https://www.uhd.edu › social-work › Documents.

Vo, T. C. L., & Dang, T. M. L. (2018). Hoat dong thuc hanh Cong tac xa hoi trong chuong trinh dao tao cu nhan Cong tac xa hoi o Dai hoc Vinh [Social work practice in the Bachelor of Social Work at Vinh University]. In *Hoi thao khoa hoc quoc te 'Dao tao Thuc hanh nghe Cong tac xa hoi: Kinh nghiem quoc te va thuc te Viet Nam' [Social Work Practice Training: International Experiences and Vietnam Reality]*, held by V.N.U.-Hanoi, U.S.S.H. and Department of Social Assistance, M.O.L.I.S.A. 21–22 December, Hanoi.

Wertheimer, M. R., & Sodhi, M. (2014). Beyond field education: Leadership of field directors. *Journal of Social Work Education, 50*(1), 48–68. https://doi.org/10.1080/10437797.2014.856230.

Part II

Strengthening Field Education in Social Work

The North and South American Experience

5

Adopting a Trauma-informed Perspective in the Field Practicum

Current Realities and Future Challenges

Carolyn Knight

In 2001, Harris and Fallot introduced the term 'trauma-informed' (T.I.) to describe an approach to social, behavioural, physical, and mental health services that responded to the unique needs of clients with histories of trauma. T.I. *care* (the organisational context) and *practice* (services to clients) reflect five principles: trust, safety, choice, collaboration, and empowerment.

International health surveys reveal that more than two-thirds of respondents reported exposure to at least one trauma in their lifetime, and a majority experienced at least two (Atwoli et al., 2015, Kessler et al., 2017). Studies of clinical populations indicate that trauma survivors are disproportionately represented in behavioural and mental health, substance abuse, child welfare, K–12, forensics/correctional, and shelter settings (Şeker, Dinç, Işık, & Ögel, 2019; Zarse et al., 2019).

These findings suggest that social work students will encounter trauma survivors in their field placements. Some may be placed in trauma-focused settings such as rape crisis and refugee and resettlement programmes in which clients' recent experiences with trauma are addressed. Many more will be placed in settings in which the focus is on clients' current problems-in-living rather than the underlying trauma with which they may be associated. A T.I. orientation is needed in either setting, but it can be more challenging for clinicians to understand its application when their work with trauma survivors is concentrated on present-day problems such as substance abuse, domestic violence, and mental health issues.

T.I. practice requires knowledgeable supervision to support it. Therefore, supervision for clinicians and field instruction for social work students are essential elements of T.I. care (Knight, 2018). In this chapter, the author distinguishes the fundamentals of T.I. field instruction, integrating current research and theory and case material. This begins with a summary of the T.I. formulation, including its rationale. Field instructors cannot adopt a T.I. orientation if they do not understand its underlying assumptions and key principles. The author also identifies challenges associated with integrating a T.I. orientation into social work education.

Summary: Trauma-Informed Perspective

The T.I. formulation provides survivors with a corrective experience that stands in contrast to their experience with trauma (Hales, Kusmaul, & Nochajski, 2017).

DOI: 10.4324/9781032164946-8

Impact of Trauma Exposure on Survivors

Behavioural, Emotional, and Psychiatric Difficulties

Common long-term consequences of trauma exposure include behavioural problems such as substance abuse and self-harm/injury; emotional reactions such as depression, suicidal ideation, and stress; and psychiatric problems such as anxiety and dissociative disorders (Dye, 2018). Physical and health problems – especially chronic pain – also are common, reflecting the somatisation of emotional reactions. Neurobiological changes have been substantiated, which affect individuals' ability to manage stress and regulate emotions; this, in turn, exacerbates the emotional and psychiatric difficulties just noted (Sperry, 2016).

Changes in Cognitive Schema

Constructivist self-development (C.S.D.) theorists observed that, 'the individual [is an] active agent in creating...[their] reality' (McCann & Pearlman 1990, pp. 5–6). Survivors of trauma often develop a worldview characterised by a lack of safety and predictability and see themselves as powerless in the face of circumstances out of their control (Currier, Stefurak, Carroll, & Shatto, 2017; Samuelson, Valadez, & Jordan, 2017). Mistrust of self and others is common, especially among survivors of interpersonal violence. When trauma is interpersonal in nature and, particularly when it occurs in childhood, survivors' 'self-capacities' – including the ability to self-soothe, manage affect, and trust one's judgment – are compromised or remain undeveloped (Diehle, Schmitt, Daams, Boer, & Lindauer, 2014).

Resilience and Adversarial Growth

Whether an event is experienced as traumatic depends upon factors – particularly sociocultural – that are unique to those exposed to it (Perry, Modesti, Talamo, & Nicolais, 2019; Siddiqui & Qayyum, 2017). Yet, a recent meta-analysis indicates that most trauma research originates in Western Europe and the United States and, thus, reflects a Western worldview (Montagner Rigoli et al., 2019).

Social support has emerged as the most significant protective and risk factor (Pressley & Smith, 2017). This includes the presence or absence of resources, both at the time of and long after trauma exposure; validation and/or acknowledgement of the trauma; and reactions that convey acceptance and understanding or blame and accusation. Exposure to trauma also can result in what is referred to as adversarial or post-traumatic growth, which includes a reordering of priorities, a new or renewed sense of spirituality, enhanced feelings of empathy and concern for others, and enhanced feelings of self-efficacy (Bonanno, Romero, & Klein, 2015).

Trauma-Informed Practice and Care

Promoting Trust and Safety

These two principles reflect the impact that trauma has on survivors' core beliefs about self, others, and the world around them. T.I. *practice* enhances survivors' self-capacities and challenges core beliefs through (Knight, in press):

1. Providing a clear explanation of role, purpose, and nature of the help they can and cannot offer;
2. Establishing and maintaining clear and consistent boundaries;

3. Acknowledging limits of confidentiality;
4. Respecting clients' cultural and social identities;
5. Normalising, affirming, and validating clients' experiences, feelings, and reactions;
6. Helping clients develop self-capacities; and
7. Encouraging expression of feelings consistent with their role and purpose.

T.I. practitioners also recognise that the working relationship itself provides survivors with a corrective emotional and cognitive experience.

T.I. *care* addresses the needs of clients served by an organisation as well as the individuals that it employs. An organisation promotes trust and safety when it (Knight, in press):

1. Ensures physical safety and privacy for staff and clients;
2. Encourages respectful relationships between staff at all levels and between clients and staff;
3. Normalises and validates staff reactions to working trauma survivors; and
4. Provides clear and consistent expectations for staff performance.

Promoting Collaboration, Choice, and Empowerment

These three principles counteract the feelings of powerlessness and self-doubt that trauma survivors experience. T.I. practitioners promote them when they (Knight, in press):

1. Solicit clients' informed consent;
2. Treat clients as experts in their lives;
3. Work in partnership with clients to accomplish their goals;
4. Help clients appreciate the connection between current problems in living and past trauma; and
5. Assist clients in managing current problems in living and, when appropriate, coming to terms with past trauma.

These professional tasks and responsibilities are interdependent with and reinforce those associated with the promotion of trust and safety.

A T.I. organisation promotes these attributes when it:

1. Encourages staff and client input into its policies;
2. Provides staff with opportunities to enhance their professional growth and advance in their careers;
3. Reinforces the need and provides opportunities for self-care for staff;
4. Acknowledges and rewards staff achievements; and
5. Creates opportunities for staff to enhance their understanding of clients with trauma histories and ability to engage in T.I. practice.

Indirect Trauma

Two requisites of T.I. care – normalise and validate staff reactions and reinforce the need and provide opportunities for self-care – reflect the impact that working with survivors has on clinicians. Three distinct but interdependent manifestations of what the author refers to as indirect trauma (Knight, 2013) have been identified, two of which parallel those of survivors.

Secondary Traumatic Stress

Clinicians are likely to struggle with reactions analogous to post-traumatic stress, including hypervigilance, flashbacks, nightmares, and intrusive thoughts (Baciu & Vîrgă, 2018; Lee, Gottfried, & Bride, 2018). The most recent edition of the American Psychiatric Association's *Diagnostic and Statistical Manual* now includes this under the broad classification of 'Trauma and Stressor-Related Disorders' (2013).

Vicarious Trauma

Practitioners who work with trauma survivors are prone to develop a worldview characterised by cynicism, mistrust in others and their motivations, and to experience feelings of powerlessness (Blome & Safadi, 2016). While this term has been used to describe the full range of reactions that clinicians experience, it specifically refers to changes in core beliefs (Branson, 2019).

Compassion Fatigue

Compassion fatigue results when clinicians are unable to empathise with clients (Cohen & Collens, 2013; Figley, 1995). It can occur with any client population, but practitioners who work with trauma survivors are at particular risk because survivors are:

1. Difficult to engage in a working relationship due to attachment issues and their mistrust of others;
2. Likely to engage in self-defeating behaviours that can be frustrating to those with whom they work;
3. Present with an array of challenges that may overwhelm the practitioner; and
4. Display strong affect that may be upsetting to the practitioner.

Indirect Trauma, Burnout, and Countertransference

Indirect trauma is not the same as burnout or countertransference, but it can lead to both (Hriricova' & Lovavoa', 2018). Burnout results from the stressors associated with clinical practice, generally. Countertransference occurs when clinicians' personal reactions surface in their work, usually with specific clients. In contrast, indirect trauma – especially its first two manifestations – is the inevitable result of working with survivors. The 'vicarious trauma/countertransference cycle' (Pearlman & Saakvitne, 1995) results in avoidance of, blaming, and/or overidentification with the client.

Risk and Protective Factors and Vicarious Resilience

It is not a question *whether* clinicians will be indirectly traumatised by their work with trauma survivors, but *when* and *to what* extent. Research indicates that the following increase the risk of indirect trauma (Hensel, Ruiz, Finney, & Dewa, 2015; Molnar et al., 2017):

1. Less education, newness to the job, and most and least experience working with trauma survivors;
2. Unsupportive organisational/work climate;
3. Large caseloads and caseloads of predominately trauma survivors; and
4. Lack of attention to or penalties for exhibiting manifestations of indirect trauma in the workplace.

Findings regarding the risk of indirect trauma among clinicians with personal histories of trauma have been mixed.

Factors that mitigate the risk of indirect trauma include (Dane, 2000; Dombo & Blome, 2016; Sprang et al., 2017):

1. Perceived social support in one's personal life;
2. Satisfaction with life;
3. Organisational and supervisory climates that promote self-care and validate and normalise indirect trauma; and
4. Pre-and in-service training that helps clinicians anticipate, identify, and manage manifestations of indirect trauma.

Unfortunately, the protective factors associated with the employing organisation are typically unavailable (Berliner & Kolko, 2016; Wolf et al., 2014).

Analogous to post-traumatic/adversarial growth, working with survivors of trauma may benefit practitioners. Indicators of vicarious post-traumatic growth include (Frey, Beesley, Abbott, & Kendrick, 2017):

1. Appreciation for one's advantages in life;
2. Re-ordering of personal goals and priorities;
3. Heightened capacity for empathy;
4. Increased sense of competence; and
5. For clinicians with histories of trauma exposure, enhanced awareness of strengths and resilience.

Relevant Models of Clinical Supervision

T.I. field instruction is not a new approach to supervision. It reflects four models that already guide social workers engaged in this essential responsibility (Knight, 2019).

Discrimination Model

Bernard and Goodyear's (2014) discrimination model distinguishes three supervisory roles: teacher, consultant, and counsellor. The first two roles underscore the importance of field instructors helping students become more autonomous and independent practitioners, who transition from passive recipients of knowledge to active participants in their learning. These two responsibilities are consistent with the T.I. principles of choice, collaboration, and empowerment. The counsellor role suggests the need for field instructors to attend to trainees' affective reactions to their work and to the supervisor. They do not serve as students' therapists; rather, they assist students in managing manifestations of indirect trauma.

Relational/Reflective Models

Relational and reflective approaches recognise that the supervisory alliance is the means through which clinicians' practice competence is enhanced. Field instructors reflect on their contributions – both positive and negative – to the supervisory alliance. This includes being responsive to supervisees' cultural identities and sensitive to the role that power and privilege play in the supervisory relationship (Berger, Quiros, & Benavidez-Hatzis, 2018; Varghese, Quiros, & Berger,

2018). Field instructors also adapt their approach to their supervisees' unique interactional/attachment style (Bennett, Mohr, Deal, & Hwang, 2013; Wrape, Callahan, Rieck, & Watkins, 2017). The models' emphasis is consistent with the T.I. principles of trust and safety.

Interactional Model

Shulman's interactional model (2010) complements relational and reflective approaches with its emphasis on the importance and application of the parallel process, reflecting the principle, 'more is caught than taught'. The model presumes that the interpersonal dynamics that surface in the supervisory relationship mirror those that occur in supervisees' working relationships with clients and that supervisory skills parallel practice skills. Field instructors serve as subtle but powerful role models, providing them with a means of teaching social work students about T.I. practice and its five principles (O'Donoghue 2014).

Solution-Focused Model

The application of the principles of solution-focused practice to supervision has received less attention in the literature. This is surprising because solution-focused strategies provide supervisors with the means of identifying and building upon supervisees' strengths (McGhee & Stark, 2018). This is consistent with Bernard and Goodyear's conceptualisation of the consultant role as well as the T.I. principles of choice, collaboration, and empowerment.

Integrating Trauma-Informed Principles into Field Instruction

The author organises this discussion into three distinct sets of responsibilities. In practice, each reinforces and is interdependent with the other.

Foster Students' Understanding of Trauma and the T.I. Formulation

In their role as teachers, field instructors (F.I.) help their students to understand the impact of trauma on clients and appreciate how they can be helpful consistent with agency-defined roles. F.I.s must have a basic understanding of the following (Knight, 2019):

1. The meaning of trauma in clients' lives;
2. The short- and long-term effects of trauma exposure, including beliefs about self and others;
3. The association between present-day problems and past trauma;
4. The rationale for and characteristics of the T.I. conceptualisation;
5. Impact that trauma exposure has on clients' willingness and ability to engage in a working relationship; and
6. Skills and strategies of T.I. practice consistent with agency-defined roles.

In the following example, the F.I. assists her student, Hannah, in understanding what Hannah has framed as the client's 'resistance' and 'hostility'. The setting is a family services agency, and the client has sought assistance with her parenting, stating she has been 'lashing out' and worries that she will hurt one of her children. During the intake, the client revealed that she had been physically and sexually abused throughout her childhood by her mother and her mother's boyfriends and expressed a desire to 'do things differently' with her own children. In supervision, Hannah acknowledges her frustration with the client, who cancelled all subsequent appointments.

Hannah: Marta [the client] has missed three appointments now, giving me a different excuse each time. When I finally did see her and tried to talk to her about why she was seeking help, she wouldn't answer me, even though *she's* the one who sought us out.

F.I.: So, it sounds like you're feeling frustrated, maybe even angry with her for 'wasting your time' or not admitting she had a problem?

Hannah (hesitates): Well, not exactly angry, but....

F.I. (smiling): But you're not exactly happy with her, either, right?!

Hannah (smiling): Right.

F.I.: Let's take a couple of minutes to see things from Marta's perspective. You were repeatedly raped by mom's boyfriends; badly beaten up by mom; you *knew* your mom knew what her boyfriends were doing to you, but she didn't do anything. So, here you are as an adult with kids of your own. What's that like for you?

Hannah: I guess I'd feel scared that I would be like my mom. Ashamed that I was getting so angry at my kids.

F.I.: So, when you see your new social worker, how would that be?

Hannah: I guess I feel that she'd judge me.

F.I.: Right, and as a trauma survivor, Marta probably wonders whether she can trust you. She couldn't trust her mom, so she's not sure she can trust *anybody*. She wants to be different but worries she can't. And she's scared that you're going to betray her just like her mother did. Does this make sense?

Hannah: Yeah, it makes a lot of sense.

F.I.: So how about we talk about how you might approach her when you see her again. And how you might go about helping her accept your help?

The F.I. skilfully teaches *and models* a T.I. perspective as she helps Hannah understand her client's reluctance to engage with her. The F.I. reframes manifestations of transference, providing an explanation that reflects Marta's distortions in thinking about self and others: 'Can I trust this worker?' 'Can I trust *myself*? I'm afraid I can't'. The F.I. does more than just enhance Hannah's understanding of her client as a teacher. In the consultant role (Bernard & Goodyear, 2014), the F.I. asks the student to consider how she will approach Marta in their next session, promoting empowerment. The F.I. does not *tell* the student what to do; instead, she asks Hannah to think about what her next steps should be, given her newfound understanding of her client's actions.

Promoting Trust and Safety in Field Instruction

Clarify Expectations

A supervisory relationship that promotes trust and safety is one in which students understand what will be expected of them and what they can expect of their F.I. As they begin their work together, the F.I. conveys to students, 'This is how I suggest we work together. Do you understand? Does this make sense?' (Knight, in press). When framed this way, the F.I.'s explanation simultaneously promotes choice, collaboration, and empowerment. From the beginning, the F.I. reinforces for students that they are engaged in a partnership. Students are invited and expected to actively participate in their learning.

Encourage Open Discussion

The previous example suggests that the F.I. had successfully created a relationship in which her student can honestly reflect on her feelings (2014). The F.I. gently prompts Hannah to explore her reactions, suggesting that she might be angry at Marta for 'wasting her time'. This legitimises Hannah's frustration, which could result in compassion fatigue. This, in turn, assists Hannah in managing it.

F.I.s hold administrative responsibilities that have significant implications for their students' success in their education and future careers. They assign a grade. Research indicates that the very issues supervisees should discuss in supervision are the ones they avoid at least in part due to these administrative responsibilities (Best et al., 2014; Mehr, Ladany, & Caskie, 2015).

Students' worries that their missteps and personal reactions will reflect poorly on them mean that F.I.s will need to actively encourage and model honest discussion. When supervisors are transparent and willing to disclose their mistakes, negative reactions, experiences with self-doubt, this encourages their supervisees to do the same, lessening the intrusive influence of their administrative responsibilities (Petrila et al., 2015).

Clarify and Maintain Appropriate Boundaries

When T.I. F.I.s adopt the counsellor role, they help students acknowledge and manage feelings that surface in response to their work. Research suggests that supervisees' dissatisfaction increases when they perceive their supervisors are 'playing therapist' (Ellis, 2017; Ladany, Mori, & Mehr, 2013). Therefore, T.I. F.I.s must clarify the boundaries of their relationship and the rationale for exploring with students their reactions to their work.

A F.I. who works with undocumented immigrants provides the following explanation to his students at the start of their practicum:

> Most of our clients have experienced multiple traumas. They've seen loved ones murdered and raped. Family members disappear never to be seen again. And *then* they have to deal with our customs and immigration. While our job is to help them settle in, find housing, and employment, clients' trauma comes up *a lot*. So, I just want you to know that I'll be checking in with you to see how you're doing, how you're handling what you're hearing. Because the work we do *is* going to affect you. We have to take care of ourselves if we're going to be helpful to our clients. I'm not talking about being your therapist, I promise! I'm your supervisor and part of being your supervisor is helping you identify and manage the impact that your work has on you, so it doesn't get in the way of your work or interfere with your personal life.

The F.I. then provides the new intern with examples from his own practice that reflect vicarious trauma, secondary traumatic stress, and compassion fatigue. His transparency normalises indirect trauma, making it easier for his students to share their reactions when (not if) they surface.

Address Students' Affective Reactions

This task goes beyond asking about students' reactions to specific clients, as the F.I. did with Hannah. The F.I. makes an 'affective check-in' (Walker, 2004) a routine aspect of supervision as a way of assisting students in recognising manifestations of indirect trauma. The author's research indicates that students *will* experience indirect trauma in their practicum and further reveals that these reactions are rarely discussed in supervision, exacerbating their impact (2013; 2010).

When supervisors consistently address clinicians' experiences with indirect trauma, this lessens its impact and promotes vicarious post-traumatic growth (Cosden, Sanford, Koch, & Lepore, 2016; Naghavi & Salimi, 2018; Neswald-Potter & Simmons, 2016). It is important that F.I.s explain why students' affective responses will be important topics for discussion. To minimise the risk of re-traumatisation, F.I.s help students understand and manage their reactions rather than ask students to recount their clients' experiences with trauma. The focus is on helping students develop skills to engage in 'emotional containment' (Collins-Camargo & Antle, 2018).

This task enhances students' personal and professional insight as they come to appreciate how their work will impact them and the need for them to be proactive in engaging in self-care. In those instances in which students have their own history of trauma, the affective check-in takes on additional importance. The F.I. and student jointly explore whether students' reactions reflect indirect trauma or indicate that additional personal work on their trauma experience is needed. In the consultant role, the F.I. assists students in identifying next steps.

The author's institution requires students to regularly complete – and F.I.s to review– process recordings using the form that may be found here: https://socialwork.umbc.edu/field-education/field-forms/forms/.[1] Students are required to tune in to and note their personal reactions as these occur in their practice. This sends a message that such reactions are a normal and inevitable aspect of their practice and an important focus of supervision (see Appendix A for an abbreviated version).

The following two examples illustrate the affective check-in, as well as the importance of understanding its purpose. The setting in the first example is a rape crisis centre. The student hints at difficulties she is having as a result of her work with survivors, and her F.I. responds by exploring the reasons for this.

Serena: I can't believe how cynical I've become! It's like every guy I meet, I think they have an agenda. I'm waiting for them to come on to me or, worse, attack me. It's like I assume all guys are scumbags.

F.I.: I'm glad you could share this with me. I'm wondering if you've given any thought to why this might be the case? Where this cynicism stems from?

Serena (silent): I'm not sure (*pauses*). Maybe just what my clients have been through?

F.I.: Makes sense, but perhaps your clients' stories have triggered something personal for you?

Serena (puzzled): You mean like from my personal life?

The F.I.'s response reveals her lack of understanding of indirect trauma, framing Serena's developing cynicism as a manifestation of countertransference rather than as an indication of vicarious trauma. While the student felt comfortable enough to share her concerns, her F.I.'s response led her to question herself and undermined her confidence.

In contrast, in this next example – drawn from an inpatient psychiatric facility – the F.I. helpfully engages in an affective check-in:

F.I.: You might remember when you first started here, I told you that we would take time in our sessions to talk about your reactions to your work. You've been here about two and a half months, and I've asked about this before, and so far, you've seemed to be managing well. But, how about we take a look at this again? One thing I noticed with myself when I first started working here was that I had trouble leaving work at work. I'd think about my clients, worry about them, think about what they went through. It was hard for me to switch off the tape that was running though my head. Has that happened to you?

Harry: Well, I hadn't really thought about it, but yeah, I guess that sometimes it is hard to let go (*looks down and away*).

F.I.: I sense some embarrassment? Our reactions are part of our work. Can you tell me a bit more about what you're having trouble letting go of?

Harry: It's our new patient, Carlos. He seems so – I don't know – damaged. I hate to say that, cuz I try to find the strengths in clients, but he's been through so much. How does a person survive something so terrible?

F.I.: He sure has [the patient had been prostituted by his mother, who used the money to support her drug habit. He also was physically abused by her and regularly forced to appear in pornographic movies and photos with adults and children].

Silence

Harry: I have these images of him as a little kid and these men abusing him. It makes me sick to my stomach. And it makes me super angry!

F.I.: It *is* hard to conceive how awful people can be to one another, particularly children. Even after all these years, stories like Carlos's still make me really angry. How about we take some time to talk more about how your feeling and thinking about him and some of your other clients' experiences? I want you also to give some thought to how you can leave work at work. For me, one thing that has always helped is to remind myself that I don't have to take my clients' pain with me, that I *can* and *should* leave it at work.

Five aspects of this exchange are noteworthy. First, the F.I. previously clarified that addressing the student's affective reactions would be part of their work together; this paves the way for the discussion that he initiates in this supervisory session. Second, the F.I.'s willingness to be transparent and to reveal his own struggles facilitate his student's willingness to do the same.

Third, the F.I. focuses on Harry's reactions to his client's history of abuse, *not* on the specifics, lessening the risk that Harry will be re-traumatised. There may be times when F.I.s will need to explore with their students what triggered their reactions, but, in most cases, this is not necessary and can be counterproductive. Fourth, the F.I. normalises and validates Harry's experiences with secondary traumatic stress. Finally, the F.I. points out the importance of giving oneself permission to *not* think about clients. Consistent with the principles of solution-focused supervision, the F.I. will help Harry identify strategies that will help him manage his reactions, rather than telling him what those strategies are.

Attend to the Supervisory Relationship

Consistent with relational and reflective approaches to supervision, T.I. F.I.s are attuned and responsive to their students' unique learning needs and style. F.I.s appreciate the role that power and privilege play in their relationship and the interactions they have with their students. They also understand how their and their students' cultural identities and social position impact their relationship and their views of one another (Berger, Quiros, & Benavidez-Hatzis, 2018).

More than 25 years ago, Fontes described an approach to supervision called 'sharevision' in which supervisors promote a more egalitarian relationship with their supervisees and lessens the power differential between them and supervisees (1995). This is consistent with the discrimination model's emphasis on helping students move from passive to active learners. This approach lessens the power differential between F.I. and student, which, in turn, facilitates the open and honest discussion that T.I. field instruction requires, promoting the five T.I. principles.

T.I. F.I.s directly address barriers that may arise in their relationship with their students, sources of which include: the supervisors' authority and power, lack of agreement regarding or clarity about expectations for the participants in the field instruction relationship, inattention to students' affective reactions, and the instructors' lack of respect for or understanding of students' cultural identities and social positions. When needed, this may result in F.I. and student re-contracting the nature of and expectations regarding their relationship.

In the following example, the F.I. asks her student to consider what is getting in the way of their ability to work together. The setting is a community mental health programme that serves the LatinX community in a large U.S. city. Most of the clients are undocumented and fled Central America and Mexico to escape gang and drug violence and poverty. Most of the staff, including the F.I., are white. Her student, Marcella, is of Guatemalan descent; she was born in the United States, but her parents are undocumented. The exchange occurred about three months into Marcella's field placement. The student readily adapted to the setting, taking an active and enthusiastic role in her learning. More recently, however, the F.I. sensed, 'Something wasn't right':

F.I.: It's hard to believe but we're almost halfway through your internship! It seems like a good time to check in and see how things are going. You got off to a great start, and I really liked that you've been so involved in your learning and willing to take on new challenges. You've been working with some tough cases, like the Sanchez family, and Ms. Rosa. I've noticed in the last couple of sessions that you've been more quiet than usual. I'm wondering what that's all about? We talked a bit about how their stories have affected you, so I'm wondering if that is an issue?

Marcella: Yeah, I think it's starting to get to me a bit. Their stories are so sad, but I know I can't fix the world. I think I'm doing good.

F.I.: When we talked about Ms. Rosa last week, I suggested that maybe you were having a hard time managing your feelings about her terrible losses [the client fled El Salvador after her husband and teenage sons were murdered by gang members].

Silence

F.I.: You seem deep in thought. What are you thinking?

Marcella (looking away): I'm having a hard time with Ms. Rosa. And the Sanchezes, and Miguel, and Luisa [Marcella's other clients]!

F.I.: You seem upset...

Marcella (interrupting): Yeah, but you really can't understand.

F.I.: I can't understand?

Marcella: It's just different for you and Jean and Mark [the other social workers in the agency]. You all are ...[*looks away*]

F.I.: We're white?

Silence

F.I.: You're thinking that because we are white and more privileged, that it's hard for us to understand our clients or maybe how you are impacted by our clients?

Marcella (looking down, fidgeting): It's just different. I feel like I can really relate to my clients. So, when you tell me that I'm overidentifying with Ms. Rosa, it's a bit upsetting. Cuz you really can't understand things like I can.

F.I.: Ah...*now* I get it. You wonder how I – how we – can understand our clients and all they have experienced. That it feels like you might be in a better position to relate and empathise because of your own heritage. If I remember correctly, I think you told me your own parents had to flee Guatemala because of the violence?

Marcella: Yeah, it just feels like you are too far removed to really get what it's like.
FI: So, let's take some time to talk about what it means to 'relate' to our clients. And how about we also talk about what it's like for you for me – an older white woman – to supervise you – a young Guatemalan-American woman?

The F.I. and student proceeded to honestly discuss Marcella's personal experiences with racism and ethnocentrism. What emerged was her sense of guilt that she 'had it so good' while her clients' lives were so traumatic. The F.I. sensitively explores Marcella's reactions – first to her, and then to her clients, and then observes:

> When I first began as a social worker, I felt so much guilt that I had been so privileged and lucky in my life and that my clients hadn't. But that guilt made it hard for me to do my work. I don't feel guilty now, but I do feel humbled by my good fortune – and amazed at my clients' strength and resilience. I haven't had our clients' experiences – or yours or your parents' – and I wouldn't pretend to know what it's been like. But I think I've learned how to listen to my clients and treat them as experts in their lives. And you are the expert in *your* life and *your* learning. I'm glad we're having this conversation because I want you to be able to talk with me about whatever is on your mind, whether it's about your clients or me or you or our relationship.

The F.I.'s transparent expression of 'cultural humility' (Lipscomb & Ashley, 2017; Rosen, McCall, & Goodkind, 2017) is reassuring to Marcella, conveying her willingness to discuss the role that privilege and power play in their relationship. It also introduces to Marcella – in a non-threatening way – the possibility that Marcella's struggles with her clients may reflect what could be referred to as 'cultural guilt' about the advantages she had relative to her clients who – though they speak the same language and may even come from the same country – have very different experiences.

Promoting Choice, Collaboration, and Empowerment in Field Instruction

The skills F.I.'s employ to promote trust and safety also promote choice, collaboration, and empowerment by (Knight, in press):

1. Clarifying expectations for how they and their students will work together and solicit students' feedback;
2. Clarifying that students will take increasing responsibility for their learning, and they will help them to do this;
3. Sharing challenges they have faced, reducing the power differences between themselves and their students;
4. Helping students manage manifestations of indirect trauma; and
5. Soliciting feedback from their students about their work together, which may lead to the need for re-contracting (i.e., consider different ways of working that enhance students' comfort in the supervisory relationship and their learning).

Four additional skills explicitly promote choice, collaboration, and empowerment.

Encourage Independent Thinking and Action

When the F.I. engages in 'targeted questioning' (Collins-Camargo, 2006), students are encouraged to reflect on their work prior to receiving input from their supervisor. Consistent with a previous example, instead of saying, 'I think the reason why the client is missing her appointments with you is...' the F.I. asks, 'What do you think might be going on with the client that would lead her to miss her appointments?' The F.I. employs dialogue, not monologue, in the role of educator.

The F.I. refrains from prematurely providing students with an explanation or solution to a dilemma, encouraging students to do this for themselves. This may be threatening to students, given the F.I.'s evaluative responsibilities. However, if from the beginning, the F.I. has clarified this expectation and assisted students in becoming more independent *and* has been using the skills previously noted, this lessens the perceived risks associated with honest reflection.

In the process recording form previously noted, students identify the skills that they have used and provide their analysis of the session. Early in the field practicum, F.I.s often need to assist students with these two requirements. But, increasingly, students are required to complete these sections *before* discussing the session in supervision.

Build upon Students' Strengths

From the beginning, the supervisor identifies and builds upon students' strengths. In a previous illustration, the F.I. credits Marcella for her willingness to take the initiative and act autonomously. This does not mean that students' difficulties, missteps, and areas for growth are overlooked. In that same example, the F.I. helps her student recognise that her guilt interfered with her ability to be helpful. It is easier for Marcella to accept this constructive feedback because her F.I. also readily identifies her strengths.

It may be difficult for students to identify their strengths due to fears of appearing immodest or because they – like many of their clients – are preoccupied with their mistakes. A guiding principle of the solution-focused approach is to 'ask about exceptions' and 'find what works and do more of it' (Froerer & Connie, 2016). In field instruction, this means that the F.I. explores with students exceptions to the challenges they face so that they can build upon them.

Directly Assist Students with their Practice

While it may seem counterintuitive, when supervisors directly assist supervisees in their practice, this enhances supervisees' satisfaction with the relationship and promotes autonomous action and feelings of self-efficacy (Mor Barak, Travis, Pyun, & Xie, 2009; Rousmaniere & Ellis, 2013). This assistance ranges from participating in students' sessions with clients to using role plays and behavioural rehearsal to prepare students for their clinical interactions. The use of this skill – which has the potential to undermine students' developing competence – is complemented by those previously discussed that promote independence and autonomy.

Consider the following example drawn from an outpatient substance abuse programme[2]. The initial intake includes questions about clients' past experiences with trauma, particularly interpersonal victimisation. The student, Erin, has observed her F.I. and others conduct intake interviews and will be conducting her first intake on her own. In supervision, she and her F.I. prepare her for this very anxiety-producing experience.

F.I.: So, you're seeing Sylvia [the client] this afternoon. I'm wondering how you are feeling?

Erin: Nervous! But also excited. I'm glad I've gotten to observe. It makes me feel more like I won't mess up.

F.I.: Good to hear! I'm wondering what your thoughts are about asking Sylvia about any possible abuse history? I've been conducting these interviews for a lot of years, but I still find it hard to ask these questions. I hate to bring up a topic that might be painful for the client, and I hold my breath – hoping that when I ask, the client will say no!

Erin: I'm kind of feeling the same way. I know that if our clients have been abused, it's important we know about it as soon as possible to make it part of our treatment plan. But I'm scared that if she tells me something did happen, I won't know what to say. Like I did when I saw Carla [another client] and she told me about her father's murder. I just froze and sounded like an idiot.

F.I.: Carla's story really came out of the blue. You were understandably surprised and caught off guard. And as we discussed, it's okay to tell our clients this: that they caught us off guard, and we need a minute to collect our thoughts. But remember that when you saw Maurice [another client] and he told you about his rape in prison, you responded with a lot of support and empathy.

Erin: Yeah, I forgot about that.

F.I.: Well I didn't! So, how about it we talk about how you can apply what you did when you met with Maurice to your upcoming meeting with Sylvia. Suppose Sylvia does disclose she was abused in some way? Where do you go from there? Think about how you responded to Maurice. How might you do the same thing if Sylvia discloses some type of childhood trauma?

The F.I. reminds Erin of her success with a previous client when she was able to respond empathically to the client's disclosure of sexual abuse. The F.I. uses this exception to assist Erin in anticipating how she might respond should her client disclose a history of abuse. Consistent with the technique of targeted questioning, the F.I. refrains from telling Erin what to do. Rather, she asks Erin to think about how she might respond. As this supervisory session continued, the F.I. suggested she and Erin role play possible scenarios that might occur during the intake to further prepare Erin for the intake interview and reduce her anxiety.

Conclusion and Future Directions

The T.I. perspective epitomises the values, ethics, and principles of social work (Knight, 2015; Levenson, 2017). Yet, this perspective has not been widely integrated into social work education (Mersky, Topitzes, & Britz, 2019). When T.I. content is included in the social work curriculum, it is usually presented in a stand-alone advanced clinical course (Warfa et al., 2014).

Social work students *will* work with trauma survivors. Therefore, the generalist (i.e., baccalaureate) and foundation (i.e., first year master's) curricula must introduce them to the T.I. formulation. This is a challenging undertaking, as many social work educators, field coordinators, and F.I.s are themselves unfamiliar with or misunderstand what it means to be T.I. and mistakenly assume that a T.I. orientation is only needed in practice settings that are trauma-focused.

If social work students are going to respond in helpful ways to clients who are trauma survivors, they must have the guidance of F.I.s who understand and operate from a T.I. lens. Therefore, schools and programmes of social work must commit resources and efforts to providing F.I.s with continuing education opportunities to learn about this model and adopt it in their practice and supervision.

Notes

1 U.M.B.C. allows public use of this form.

2 An earlier version of this case illustration first appeared in Knight, C. (2019). T.I. practice and care: Implications for field instruction. *Clinical Social Work. 47*, 79–89.

Appendix 5.1A Process Recording Form

	Interview Content	*Practice Behaviours/ Skills Used*	*Student's Feelings/Reactions*	*Student's Analysis*	*Field Instructor's Comments*
W					
C					
W					
C					
W					
C					
W					
C					
W					
C					
W					
C					
W					
C					
W					
C					
W					
C					
W					
C					
W					
C					
W					
C					
W					
C					

References

American Psychiatric Association (APA). (2013). *Diagnostic and statistical manual of mental disorders* (5th ed.). Washington, DC: Author.

Atwoli, L., Stein, D. J., Koenen, K. C., & McLaughlin, K. A. (2015). Epidemiology of posttraumatic stress disorder: Prevalence, correlates and consequences. *Current Opinion in Psychiatry, 28*, 307.

Baciu, L., & Vîrgă, D. (2018). The prevalence of secondary traumatic stress among Romanian social workers: A replication study. *Social Work Review / Revista de Asistenta Sociala, 17*, 151–164.

Bennett, S., Mohr, J., Deal, K. H., & Hwang, J. (2013). Supervisor attachment, supervisory working alliance, and affect in social work field instruction. *Research on Social Work Practice, 23*, 199–209.

Berger, R., Quiros, L., & Benavidez-Hatzis, J. R. (2018). The intersection of identities in supervision for trauma-informed practice: Challenges and strategies. *The Clinical Supervisor, 37*, 122–141.

Berliner, L., & Kolko, D. J. (2016). Trauma informed care: A commentary and critique. *Child Maltreatment, 21*(2), 168–172.

Bernard, J. M., & Goodyear, R. K. (2014). *Fundamentals of clinical supervision* (3rd ed.). New York: Pearson.

Best, D., White, E., Cameron, J., Guthrie, A., Hunter, B., Hall, K., Leicester, S., & Lubman, D. I. (2014). A model for predicting clinician satisfaction with clinical supervision. *Alcoholism Treatment Quarterly, 32*(1), 67–78.

Blome, W. W., & Safadi, N. S. (2016). Shared vicarious trauma and the effects on Palestinian social workers. *Illness, Crisis, & Loss, 24*, 236–260.

Bonanno, G. A., Romero, S. A., & Klein, S. I. (2015). The temporal elements of psychological resilience: An integrative framework for the study of individuals, families, and communities. *Psychological Inquiry, 26*, 139–169.

Branson, D. C. (2019). Vicarious trauma, themes in research, and terminology: A review of literature. *Traumatology, 25*, 2–10.

Cohen, K., & Collens, P. (2013). The impact of trauma work on trauma workers: A meta-synthesis on vicarious trauma and vicarious posttraumatic growth. *Psychological Trauma: Theory, Research, Practice, and Policy, 5*, 570–580.

Collins- Camargo, C. (2006). Clinical supervision in public child welfare: Themes from a multi-site study. *Professional Development: Journal of Continuing Social Work Education, 9*, 102–112.

Collins-Camargo, C., & Antle, B. (2018). Child welfare supervision: Special issues related to trauma-trauma informed care in a unique environment. *The Clinical Supervisor*, 37, 64–82.

Cosden, M., Sanford, A., Koch, L. M., & Lepore, C. E. (2016). Vicarious trauma and vicarious posttraumatic growth among substance abuse treatment providers. *Substance Abuse, 37*, 619–624.

Currier, J. M., Stefurak, T., Carroll, T. D., & Shatto, E. H. (2017). Applying trauma-informed care to community-based mental health services for military veterans. *Best Practices in Mental Health: An International Journal, 13*, 47–64.

Dane, B. (2000). Child welfare workers: An innovative approach for interacting with secondary trauma. *Journal of Social Work Education, 36*, 27–38.

Diehle, J., Schmitt, K., Daams, J. G., Boer, F., & Lindauer, R. J. L. (2014). Effects of psychotherapy on trauma-related cognitions in posttraumatic stress disorder: A meta-analysis. *Journal of Traumatic Stress, 27*, 257–264.

Dombo, E. A., & Blome, W. (2016). Vicarious trauma in child welfare workers: A study of organizational responses. *Journal of Public Child Welfare, 10*, 505–523.

Dye, H. (2018). The impact and long-term effects of childhood trauma. *Journal of Human Behavior in the Social Environment, 28*, 381–392.

Ellis, M.V. (2017). Narratives of harmful clinical supervision. *The Clinical Supervisor, 36*, 20–87.

Figley, C. (1995). Compassion fatigue: Toward a new understanding of the costs of caring. In B. Stamm (Ed.), *Secondary trauma stress: Self-care issues for clinicians, researchers, and educators* (pp. 3–28). Lutherville, MD: Sidran Press.

Fontes, L. (1995). Sharevision: Collaborative supervision and self-care strategies for working with trauma. *Family Journal, 3*, 249–254.

Froerer, A. S., & Connie, E. E. (2016). Solution-building, the foundation of solution-focused brief therapy: A qualitative Delphi study. *Journal of Family Psychotherapy, 27*, 20–34.

Frey, L. L., Beesley, D., Abbott, D., & Kendrick, E. (2017). Vicarious resilience in sexual assault and domestic violence advocates, *Psychological Trauma: Theory, Research, Practice, and Policy, 9*, 44–51.

Hales, T., Kusmaul, N., & Nochajski, T. (2017). Exploring the dimensionality of trauma-informed care: Implications for theory and practice. *Human Service Organizations: Management, Leadership & Governance, 41*, 317–325.

Harris, M., & Fallot, R. (2001). *Using trauma theory to design service systems: New directions for mental health services*. San Francisco, CA: Jossey Bass.

Hensel, J. M., Ruiz, C., Finney, C., & Dewa, C. S. (2015). Meta-analysis of risk factors for secondary traumatic stress in therapeutic work with trauma victims. *Journal of Traumatic Stress, 28*, 83–91.

Hrircova, M., & Lovavoa, S. (2018). Stress, secondary trauma and burnout - Risk characteristics in helping professions. *Ad Alta: Journal of Interdisciplinary Research, 8*, 161–165.

Kessler, R. C., Aguilar-Gaxiola, S., Alonso, J., Benjet, C., Bromet, E. J., Cardoso, G., Degenhardt, L., … Koenen, K. C. (2017). Trauma and PTSD in the WHO World Mental Health Surveys. *European Journal of Psychotraumatology, 8*(Suppl 5), 1353383.

Knight, C. (2013). Indirect trauma: Implications for self-care, supervision, the organization, and the academic institution, *The Clinical Supervisor, 32*, 224–243.

Knight, C (2015). Trauma-informed social work practice: Practice considerations and challenges. *Clinical Social Work Journal, 43*, 25–37.

Knight, C. (2018). Trauma-informed supervision: Historical antecedents, current practice, and future directions. *The Clinical Supervisor, 37*, 7–37.

Knight, C. (2019). Trauma-informed practice and care: Implications for field instruction. *Clinical Social Work. 47*, 79–89.

Knight, C. (2022). Trauma-informed supervision. In K. O'Donoghue & L. Englebrecht, Eds. *The Routledge International Handbook of Social Work Supervision*, Chapter 36. Abingdon, UK: Routledge.

Ladany, N., Mori, Y., and Mehr, K. E. (2013). Effective and ineffective supervision. *The Counseling Psychologist, 41*, 28–47.

Lee, J. J., Gottfried, R., & Bride, B. E. (2018). Exposure to client trauma, secondary traumatic stress, and the health of clinical social workers: A mediation analysis. *Clinical Social Work Journal, 46*, 228–235.

Levenson, J. (2017). Trauma-informed social work practice. *Social Work, 62*, 105–113.

Lipscomb, A. E., & Ashley, W. (2017). Colorful disclosures: Identifying identity-based differences and enhancing critical consciousness in supervision. *Smith College Studies in Social Work, 87*, 220–237.

McCann, I., & Pearlman, L. (1990). *Psychological trauma and the adult survivor.* New York: Brunner/Mazel.

McGhee, M., & Stark, M. (2018). Promoting collegial teacher supervision: Applying solution-focused strategies in a clinical supervision cycle. *International Journal of Leadership in Education, 21*, 726–740.

Mehr, K. E., Ladany, N., & Caskie, G. I. L. (2015). Factors influencing trainee willingness to disclose in supervision. *Training and Education in Professional Psychology, 9*, 44–51.

Mersky, J. P., Topitzes, J., & Britz, L. (2019). Promoting evidence-based, trauma-informed social work practice. *Journal of Social Work Education, 55*, 645–657.

Molnar, B. E., Sprang, G., Killian, K. D., Gottfried, R., Emery, V., & Bride, B. E. (2017). Advancing science and practice for vicarious traumatization/secondary traumatic stress: A research agenda. *Traumatology, 23*, 129–142.

Montagner Rigoli, M., Rainho de Oliveira, F., Klock Bujak, M., Volkmann, N. M., & Haag Kristensen, C. (2019). Psychological trauma in clinical practice and research: An evolutionary concept analysis. *Journal of Loss and Trauma, 24*, 595–608.

Mor Barak, M. E., Travis, D., Pyun, H., & Xie, B. (2009). The impact of supervision on worker outcomes: A meta-analysis. *Social Service Review, 83*, 3–32.

Naghavi, A., & Salimi, S. (2018). An autoethnography of vicarious trauma and vicarious Growth in the context of rehabilitation counseling. *Iranian Journal of Psychiatry & Behavioral Sciences, 12*, 1–6.

Neswald-Potter, R., & Simmons, R. T. (2016). Regenerative supervision: A restorative approach for counsellors impacted by vicarious trauma. *Canadian Journal of Counselling and Psychotherapy, 50*(1), 75–90.

O'Donoghue, K. B. (2014). Towards an interactional map of the supervision session: An exploration of supervisees' and supervisors' experiences. *Practice: Social Work in Action, 26*, 53–70.

Pearlman, L., & Saakvitne, K. (1995). *Trauma and the therapist: Countertransference and vicarious traumatization in psychotherapy with incest survivors.* New York: Norton.

Perry, J. M., Modesti, C., Talamo, A., & Nicolais, G. (2019). Culturally sensitive PTSD screening in Non-Western youth: Reflections and indications for mental health practitioners. *Journal of Refugee Studies, 32*, 151–161.

Petrila, A., Fireman, O., Fitzpatrick, L. S., Hodas, R. W., & Taussig, H. N. (2015). Student satisfaction with an innovative internship. *Journal of Social Work Education, 51*, 121–135.

Pressley, J., & Smith, R. (2017). No ordinary life: Complex narratives of trauma and resilience in under-resourced communities. *Journal of Aggression, Maltreatment & Trauma, 2*, 137–154.

Rousmaniere, T. G., & Ellis, M. V. (2013). Developing the construct and measure of collaborative clinical supervision: The supervisees' perspective. *Training and Education in Professional Psychology, 7*, 300–308.

Rosen, D., McCall, J., & Goodkind, S. (2017). Teaching critical self-reflection through the lens of cultural humility: An assignment in a social work diversity course. *Social Work Education, 36*, 289–298.

Samuelson, K. W., Bartel, A., Valadez, R., & Jordan, J. T. (2017). PTSD symptoms and perception of cognitive problems: The roles of posttraumatic cognitions and trauma coping self-efficacy. *Psychological Trauma: Theory, Research, Practice, and Policy, 9*, 537–544.

Şeker, B. Ç., Dinç, M., Işık, S., & Ögel, K. (2019). Incidence and characteristics of psychological trauma in alcohol and Substance Abuse Disorder. *Addicta: The Turkish Journal on Addictions, 6*, 331–336.

Shulman, L. (2010). *Interactional supervision* (3rd ed.). Washington, DC: N.A.S.W. Press.

Siddiqui, S., & Qayyum, R. (2017). Developing culturally relevant intervention plan for psychological trauma: An application of community based participatory research approach for mental health. *Pakistan Armed Forces Medical Journal, 67*, 868–874.

Sperry, L. (2016). Trauma, neurobiology, and personality dynamics: A primer. *Journal of Individual Psychology, 72*, 161–167.

Sprang, G., Ross, L., Miller, B. C., Blackshear, K., & Ascienzo, S. (2017). Psychometric properties of the Secondary Traumatic Stress–Informed Organizational Assessment. *Traumatology, 23*, 65–171.

Varghese, R., Quiros, L., and Berger, R. (2018). Reflective practices for engaging in trauma-informed culturally competent supervision. *Smith College Studies in Social Work, 88*(2), 135–151.

Walker, M. (2004). Supervising practitioners working with survivors of childhood abuse: Countertransference, secondary traumatization, and terror. *Psychodynamic Practice, 10*, 173–193.

Warfa, N., Chalangary, J., St. Amour, A., Mollica, R., & Bhui, K. (2014). Cultural competence in psychological interventions for psychotrauma following natural disasters: An international perspective. *Clinical Neuropsychiatry*, *11*, 40–44.

Wolf, M. R., Green, S. A., Nochasjki, T. H., Mendel, W. W., & Kusmaul, N. (2014). 'We're all civil servants': The status of trauma-informed care in the community. *Journal of Social Service Research*, *40*, 111–120.

Wrape, E. R., Callahan, J. L., Rieck, T., & Watkins, C. E., Jr. (2017). Attachment theory within clinical supervision: Application of the conceptual to the empirical. *Psychoanalytic Psychotherapy*, *31*, 37–54.

Zarse, E. M., Neff, M. R., Yoder, R., Hulvershorn, L., Chambers, J. E., Chambers, R. A., & Schumacher, U. (2019). The adverse childhood experiences questionnaire: Two decades of research on childhood trauma as a primary cause of adult mental illness, addiction, and medical diseases. *Cogent Medicine*, *6*, 1–9.

6

Social Work Field Education in the United States

Carole Cox and Jan Miner

The purpose of this chapter is to describe the current status of social work fieldwork in the United States, including the demands and challenges faced. The Council of Social Work Education (C.S.W.E.) is the sole accrediting body for all 800 accredited schools of social work in the United States. The Council of Field Education within the C.S.W.E. provides leadership to all schools regarding the standards, knowledge, and training required by field educators. This central administration is important, as field education is considered the 'signature pedagogy of social work education' (Shulman, 2005), connecting the theoretical and conceptual contribution of the classroom with the practical world of the practice setting (C.S.W.E., 2008). It is referred to as the practicum of the profession, as it is where students apply what they have learned in the classroom while developing new training and skills. Competency in the field is demonstrated through observation by the field instructor who provides feedback.

Description of Field Education and its Challenges

According to the C.S.W.E.:

> The intent of field education is to connect the theoretical and conceptual contribution of the classroom with the practical world of the practice setting. It is a basic precept of social work education that the two interrelated components of curriculum – classroom and field – are of equal importance within the curriculum, and each contributes to the development of the requisite competencies of professional practice. Field education is systematically designed, supervised, coordinated, and evaluated based on criteria by which students demonstrate the achievement of programme competencies.

The designation of field as the signature pedagogy for social work education is consistent with the competencies for the professions (C.S.W.E., 2008, 2015a). Observative practice should occur in the students' field placements under the supervision of a competent field instructor who is able to give feedback. The 2015 Educational Policy and Accreditation Standards (E.P.A.S.) that apply the thresholds for professional competence that every social work school must meet reinforce this model by stating that the field placement provides the opportunity to demonstrate

DOI: 10.4324/9781032164946-9

competence through integration of the theoretical and conceptual materials that students learn in the classroom with the practical experiences encountered in the field. Accordingly, the field placement is the classroom in the community (Petracchi & Zastrow, 2010).

Social work competence is defined as 'the ability to integrate and apply social work knowledge, values, and skills to practice situations in a purposeful, intentional, and professional manner to promote human and community wellbeing' (C.S.W.E., 2015a, p. 6), and the expectation is that these generalist social work competencies will be demonstrated in the field placement and acknowledged and assessed in the field evaluation of the student's practice. The competencies address the areas of professionalism, ethics, skills, social and economic justice, research informed practice, diversity, ethical practice, human behaviour, assessment, intervention, and policy (C.S.W.E., 2015a).

Field Education Requirements

Accordingly, the C.S.W.E. (2008, 2015a) sets specific standards for field programmes, including the role of the field director, requirements for field instructors and field instructor training, criteria for the admission of students, and the required number of hours for Bachelor of Social Work (B.S.W.) and Master of Social Work (M.S.W.) students. B.S.W. students are required to have 400 hours per year and M.S.W. students are required to have 900 hours. Field instructors for graduate students must have a M.S.W. from an accredited programme in order to supervise a student, while undergraduate field instructors are required to have a B.S.W. or M.S.W. Individual programmes develop their own training and support for field instructors, criteria for field sites, and criteria that students must meet in order to begin fieldwork. However, these programmes must adhere to the specific guidelines set by the C.S.W.E. which include:

Selecting field placement settings;
Monitoring students on-site;
Maintaining communication between the university and the field placement site;
Evaluating student progress;
Evaluating the effectiveness of the field settings; and
Determining the criteria of qualified field instructors.

Areas of Concern

In 2015, the C.S.W.E. held a field summit attended by 50 field directors as a means of learning about current challenges and issues in the field. A survey of the four main areas of concern were identified as:

- Imbalance between supply and demand of adequate field sites;
- Diverse and complex student needs;
- Recruiting and maintaining high quality field sites and field instructors; and
- Economic trends and pressures.

The report noted concern about the educational opportunities for students in the field, highlighting that 'contextual factors such as changing student demographics, the state of the economy, agency environments and staff turnovers, students as consumers, students' competing obligations and economic status create complexities that are not easily addressed' (C.S.W.E., 2015b, p. 4). The findings also presented two dominant themes impacting field education: resources and leadership.

Related to economic trends and pressures was the need to develop better funding to support field education and increased resources, including personnel and technological supports. Institutional support for field education is a challenge and contributes to inadequate resources and staff. Moreover, the increasing diversity of student needs places additional pressure on field departments as personnel require time and training to properly address individual needs and demands. Comments provided by the survey participants included the need for a greater value placed on field and field education faculty and the inability of directors to improve their skills due to demands of the field office (p. 31).

The survey offered suggestions for strengthening the field department, including the greater availability of resources for field education, integrating the field with the curriculum, and identifying the director of field education as part of the management team with influence in decision-making (p. 33). The respondents believed that these suggestions would contribute to programmes and to the competency of students.

A subsequent survey, 'The State of Field Education Survey' (C.S.W.E., 2018) based on the findings of the 2015 survey, concluded with several recommendations for the commission:

- Examine programme structures and models of staffing that best support student learning and competency development and that best support the involvement of community partners. New models may emerge and be tested.
- Examine programme structures and models of staffing that facilitate the integration of field education within their respective programmes. Again, new models may emerge and be tested.
- Identify and promote mechanisms for leadership development for field faculty and staff members, including participation in C.S.W.E.'s annual programme meeting and participation in regional- and programme-level committees to share challenges, identify resources needed, explore new models, and develop knowledge about best practices.
- Address the need for field education to support the diversity and complexity of student needs by developing departmental policies and practices that recognise the need for and support adequate resources for the office of field education.
- Advocate for accreditation standards that mandate effective levels of resources for field education that consider the increased complexity of students' needs and the changed and changing practice environment, including staffing, time, and technology—in advance of E.P.A.S. 2022 and beyond.
- Further explore the relationship between larger programme size and the increased concern among directors of those programmes about lack of adequate time and staffing to achieve effective results.
- Conduct research and analyses of social work programmes and the integration of the field education component of the curriculum in those programmes.

As field education is a complex process in the United States, it is important to have some knowledge of the key actors in the programmes. The following section discusses these actors as well as the most common models of field education.

Key Actors

Field Directors

The role of field director is central to both the effectiveness of the department and the learning of students. The field director holds a position that designs, implements, and evaluates the field experiences of students to make sure that learning occurs while meeting with the expectations of the school, students, and agencies. Consequently, field directors should be key contributors to the curriculum and to the academic programme. They are also responsible for coordination of the teaching with the agencies and overseeing the students. Accordingly, they face the following competing demands (Buck et al., 2012):

- Keeping the programme in compliance with accreditation standards;
- Conceptualising how classroom learning is connected to the field;
- Designing curriculum for integrative field seminars;
- Providing supervision for liaison visits by field coordinators;
- Developing and implementing field instructor education;
- Creating policies and procedures by which field settings are selected and evaluated in relation to standards and programme outcomes;
- Developing and disseminating policy and procedures as set forth in the field manual, including field hours, admission criteria for student readiness to enter the field, placement, evaluation of students, and gatekeeping;
- Collaborating with programme faculty in creating an assessment plan for evaluation of student attainment of programme competencies and practice behaviours; and
- Ensuring the centrality of field education as the signature pedagogy of the curriculum.

A study of field directors (Wertheimer & Sodhi, 2014) found that the leadership of the position was impacted by whether the person was a faculty member or administrator/staff person, tenure or non-tenure-track faculty position, or position or part of the administrative team. Those who are tenure-track faculty and on the administrative team feel more valued and influential in the curriculum and in their ability to assume leadership roles in education. Those who serve primarily as administrators are liable to being marginalised and given lower status than those in faculty positions. This can lead to field education being treated as less important than classroom education.

The recent survey (C.S.W.E., 2015a) of field directors shows the majority (66.7%) hold M.S.W.s with very few (2.9%) having doctorates in social work. The median number of years in social work education was 15 years following that last degree, while the median number of years as a field director was 6 years. The majority of the respondents (64%) held contracted positions rather than being tenure-tracked, and almost half, 44.6%, reported no administrative/professional assistance for field education. Consequently, although the position is considered as pivotal to social work education, as it links the classroom to practice, the status of the directors is compromised and their roles as leaders in social work education impaired. By requiring that they have doctorates rather than just an M.S.W. and practice experience, they would have equal status with other faculty and, thus, more involvement in the curriculum and school leadership (Wertheimer & Sodhi, 2014).

Field Liaison

The C.S.W.E. standards (2008) require schools to ensure that the field education programme provides field instructor training and interactions with the field instructors and the sites. The field liaison represents the school and acts as an intermediary between the field agency, field instructor, and the courses. The role has been described as being an advisor, monitor, consultant teacher, mediator, and advocate (Faria et al., 1988). The liaison creates a link between the school and the field that clarifies the C.S.W.E. competencies with supervisors and, thus, shows how assignments can demonstrate necessary learning skills. The liaisons may also suggest teaching methods and provide other information to enrich the field experience for the student (Hendricks et al., 2013). They are also important advocates for the student in the field, as they help to assure the quality of the placement as an educational setting.

Liaisons are either full-time, adjunct, or part-time faculty who are based in agencies. In some programmes, they lead seminars which focus on integrating the experience in the field with the coursework. Liaison site visits to agencies are usually once a semester and involve the student, the field supervisor, and the liaison. During the visit, the assignments are discussed, which should include micro-, mezzo-, and some macro-level work. Liaisons are expected to be familiar with each level of practice so that they can offer support and act as a resource as needed.

A study of 408 undergraduate and graduate schools of social work in the United States and Puerto Rico (Ligon & Ward, 2005) found that liaisons were satisfied with their positions but were concerned about the quality of the field sites and field instructors as well as the number of students and agencies for which they were responsible. The findings of the survey also noted a need for more training for both liaisons and field instructors to ensure that the experience is effective and meets the learning needs of the student. A particular issue noted in the survey was that fewer than 75% of the liaisons used a learning plan, making it questionable as to how competency was actually being assessed.

Given concerns about the effectiveness of liaisons, one suggestion for strengthening the role is to ensure that a faculty member, rather than an outside person, act as the liaison This would help to maintain involvement in the student's field experience and further integrate it with the classroom. It would also help to build and strengthen relationships between the social work programme and the agency (Olson-Morrison et al., 2019).

Field Agency Supervision

The typical model that meets the C.S.W.E. accreditation standards is based on having a supervisor in the agency who is responsible for assigning work to the student and reviewing performance. This person is responsible for modelling social work behaviour and for evaluating the students. The key qualities associated with good supervision include skills in building a trusting relationship that includes critical clear feedback (Nickson et al., 2016) and maintaining a neutral perspective while helping students to integrate knowledge, skills, and professional values (Marc et al., 2014).

Agencies may also use task supervisors when the field supervisor is at another site as may occur when an agency has several offices. A task supervisor does not have to be a social worker, but they must have sufficient knowledge of the agency to interface with the student on a day-to-day basis. Typically, they give assignments, referrals and project work but do not evaluate the student or supervise, with the exceptions of administrative or policy procedures.

Findings from a study of both students and supervisors found that student preparation before the field placement, which includes understanding critical feedback and how to manage feelings of resistance, is important for a successful placement (Ketner et al., 2017). Student orientations and trainings and other supports can assist in strengthening supervisors and in helping them develop their own management skills. Supervisors should feel comfortable in sharing their own experiences with students, as this contributes to the quality of the relationship.

Off-site Supervisor

The off-site M.S.W. field instructor helps integrating theory and classroom work and socialises the student to the profession. This person often works with the task supervisor who is at the same site as the student. Often, the off-site supervisor is part of the university staff, in another department of the field agency, a volunteer, or paid separately by the social work programme. The duties of the off-site supervisor are the same as the field supervisor, evaluating the student and providing weekly supervision.

Several studies have discussed the advantages of using off-site supervision (Wiebe, 2010; Todd & Schwartz, 2009). A key advantage is that these placements permit students to engage in more grassroots community work where M.S.W.s are not necessarily employed. These often include more interdisciplinary programmes that focus on social and economic justice and marginalised communities as well as international organisations. The direct experience can be an important learning opportunity for students.

Among the disadvantages to off-site supervision are concerns that students will be less socialised into the social work profession and a lack of coordination among the social work programme, task supervision, off-site supervisor, and the students (Wiebe et al., 2009). Another disadvantage is that the use of task supervisors, who are not M.S.W.s, could undermine the profession, as it may result in students questioning the importance of the M.S.W. itself. Finally, it can be troublesome for students to travel to off-site supervisors, and as they are not an actual part of the agency, they may not be knowledgeable about all of its procedures.

Factors that appear to strengthen off-site supervision include planning and preparation around who meets with whom, who does the student evaluation, roles of each supervisor in case of a conflict, clear communication, have field liaisons visit jointly with both task and off-site supervisors, and offering students a group supervision seminar that can focus on socialisation into the profession (Maynard et al., 2015).

Student Supervision, Field Supervisor Training, Types of Placements, and Integrative Seminars

Student Supervision

Student supervision is a critical aspect of the field experience. It is through supervision that students learn how to apply their education to the real world. Supervision also enables field supervisors to see more closely the impact of what they are actually practicing while permitting them to develop their own management skills. The supervisory relationship lays the foundation for the overall experience, quality of learning, and skill development (Pehrson et al., 2009).

A major challenge for the field practicum is finding appropriate field placements for students with qualified field instructors. Large caseloads combined with less time to engage with students has led to an increase in the use of supervisors outside of the host agency and/or contracted social workers (Cooper-Bolinskey & Ketner, 2016). The traditional model has the student working in a social service agency under the supervision of a field instructor with a M.S.W. who is an employee of the agency. Although individual one-on-one supervision is often preferred, it is not always possible. Consequently, there has been an increase in group supervision with one supervisor for several students. Advantages to group supervision include the student being able to understand and acquire new skills and being able to watch and learn from peers (Zeira & Schiff, 2010).

Student supervision presents several challenges to supervisors. Large caseloads place greater demands on supervisors who often report that they have less time for supervision (Bogo, 2006).

Meeting the special needs of many students, as well as their other commitments, further challenges supervisors (Homonoff, 2008).

Data from a study of 13 field instructors (Street, 2019) found that the most challenging characteristics of students were resistance to feedback, direction, or supervision, including difficulty in listening to supervisors' suggestions or accepting them. Findings from the survey also noted that student inflexibility, acting as if they already knew what to do; having poor boundaries between personal and professional lives, leading to their disclosure of personal information; or focusing on their own needs through the client relationship were very problematic. In addition, the instructors were concerned that many students remained judgemental with biases and overlooked the importance of client self-determination, often appearing disengaged from the social work profession (Street, 2019). All of these challenging behaviours were seen as detracting from the value of the field experience and demanding of attention.

Field Supervisor Training

The C.S.W.E. requires that schools of social work provide orientation and training for field instructors and maintain a continuing dialog with instructors and their agencies (C.S.W.E., 2.2.10, 2015 Accreditation Standards), although it does not provide guidelines for how extensive this training should be. Some schools hold a basic orientation regarding programme structure and requirements that must be met by field instructors for supervision, completion of evaluations and signing of time sheets, and meeting with the student's faculty field liaison during the year. Field instructors may be invited to events that take place within the social work department during the academic year, and some schools hold events at years' end to thank the field instructors for their involvement in student education.

In specific geographic areas, schools develop more intensive training programmes for field instructors. Several schools of social work in a tri-state region in the northeast United States, in cooperation with one another, created a 12 session (24 hours) organised training course, 'Seminar in Field Instruction' (S.I.F.I.), which all field instructors are required to take. The S.I.F.I. is offered free of charge but is required of all new field instructors who accept students from any of the dozen schools involved.

The curriculum for the S.I.F.I. teaches field instructors how to create a learning climate, plan for viable assignments, use student process recordings in supervision as a teaching tool, develop an educational contract with the student, adapt to students' styles of learning, and conduct the evaluation process. Several sessions focus on teaching techniques designed to increase students' self-awareness. Much of the learning is experiential, with field instructors processing and learning from their own role as student within the course. The S.I.F.I. also serves an important role as a safe place for field instructors to brainstorm together to solve the many problems that surface when working with students. Field instructors receive a certificate of completion when they finish the course, and in the tri-state region where the course is required, S.I.F.I. certification is often a requirement in agency job listings.

Types of Field Placements

In meeting the field hour requirements established by the C.S.W.E., the two primary models are the concurrent field model in which the hours are taken concurrently with classes, and the block model in which the hours are completed in one semester, usually after the coursework. Research evaluations of these formats find little differences in their outcomes. Professional competence, assertiveness, depression, or self-esteem did not differ among students completing block or concurrent placements with each group achieving equal levels of competency (Theriot et al., 2006).

Concurrent placements usually are conducted over two semesters. Advantages to these placements are that, for many agencies, these placements are able to work with clients for long periods of time. This permits relationship and skill development with the field instructor able to measure progress. In addition, the placement offers the opportunity to immediately integrate the classroom learning with practice while also being able to bring the field experience into the classroom. This integration can enhance the learning for the individual student and the class.

Disadvantages of the concurrent placement is that they may be less flexible in that they are designed to be taken during normal working hours which can be a strain for part-time students or those with unconventional schedules. This disadvantage may also impact the field instructor who may be responsible for covering for the student during any absence, which may further impact the client who has to work with two different social workers.

Block placements offer students the advantage of total immersion in the field with the opportunity for consistent relationships with clients. They also provide for the development of close relationships with the field instructor and even the possibility of doing the placement in another area or even internationally. Obviously, the major disadvantage is the ability to integrate the field experience with the classroom learning. Another concern is that students in block placements have fewer interactions with faculty and, therefore, less opportunity for support and advisement (Curl & Cary, 2014).

A recent survey of M.S.W. students and field instructors on the advantages and disadvantages of concurrent and block placements found the primary advantage of concurrent placements, according to students, was the ability to be employed, flexibility, and to be able to balance responsibilities. Field supervisors felt there was an advantage in their being able to accommodate other commitments (Curl & Cary, 2014).

According to the survey, students viewed the primary advantage to block placements as the ability to finish their placement quickly and the opportunity to quickly develop skills and responsibilities. For field instructors, the advantages of the block placements were their ability to allow students to follow clients while also providing a continuity of care and helped to familiarise students with full-time employment in social work, including regular team meetings and professional relationships.

Integrative Seminars

Although not mandated, about three-quarters of schools of social work in the United States offer a version of an integrative or fieldwork seminar (Kilpatrick et al., 1994). Generally, the purpose of these classes, which are linked synchronously to the field practicum experience, is to provide a vehicle of linkage between classroom theory and real-life experience in agencies (Birkenmaier et al., 2003).

Depending on the school, a seminar may exist to augment course content in ways deemed important by the faculty. For example, in one northeast U.S. school, a seminar for students in placements that serve clients who use/abuse substances provides additional content that is approved by the state's Office of Addiction Services and Support. Students who complete this seminar and meet additional criteria within their graduate programme are deemed to have satisfied the educational requirements for certification as an alcoholism and substance abuse counsellor-trainee. At the same school, students in settings where social work and law intersect, specialised integrative seminars are offered that both social work and law students attend. Students in both professions share information and offer their unique perspectives in ways that expand each other's knowledge of the roles both professions play in clients' lives.

In many schools of social work, seminars function as an arena for peer supervision, peer support, reinforcement of social work values, and socialisation into the profession. Students in these seminars may present cases, either formally or informally, grapple with ethical dilemmas, discuss what is occurring in their field supervision, problem-solve with one another, and engage in activities that promote self-examination and self-awareness.

Seminar structures vary from having a minimal plan – with time for announcements followed by an 'open mic' approach, to ones that are topically organised and have tight agendas. Examples of topics at one school that requires a set agenda include mindfulness, learning and communication styles, cultural humility, navigating supervision, post-graduate certificate training, and preparing for the licensing exam.

One mid-Atlantic school offers a seminar during the final semester as a final step in a three-course sequence that leads to the completion of a research project that will integrate knowledge from policy, practice, theory, and research (Schneller & Brocato, 2011). In many schools, the seminar is a weekly or biweekly event. Some frontload the academic year, with seminars occurring more frequently in the beginning and tapering off as the year progresses. Other schools require seminars for foundation/generalist-level students but not for those in their advanced year/concentration. There are likely as many variations as there are schools that offer the experience.

Frequently, the instructor who leads the integrative seminar is also the field liaison for that group of students during that year in the programme. The instructor, also known as a field faculty advisor or fieldwork liaison, is also responsible for making site visits to the students in the field, typically once or twice during the placement, and is the person students are directed to consult should problems arise in the field placement. This dual responsibility enables the instructor to be more intimately involved with the student and the learning occurring in the field placement.

Conclusions

Field education in the United States is considered the signature pedagogy of the profession and is key in all social work programmes. An increasingly diverse group of students as well as agency limitations with regard to staffing and supervision present formidable challenges to the efficacy of field placements. Placements that are congruent with individual student needs and supervision that are knowledgeable and accessible are factors contributing to student learning. Unfortunately, supervisor–student ratios and untrained staff are becoming common and can seriously disrupt the learning experience. As agency budgets become increasingly restricted, these trends are likely to continue, and some schools may be in intense competition to attract and maintain agencies (Gushwa & Harriman, 2019).

Field directors and liaisons are critical to the quality of field departments. Increasing the status of field directors, making them commensurate with faculty, or giving them faculty status, as well as involving them in the curriculum, are ways that can reflect their value and assist in their continuation. Liaisons may feel supported if they are trained and involved in the students' learning. Knowing the exact expectations of the agency as well as the material that is being taught in the school are important means for strengthening their roles.

Supervision itself takes many forms. However, certain elements appear to be common to the definition of good supervision. Students should be prepared before they enter the placement field, and supervisors need to be knowledgeable and skilled. They must be able to give feedback to students and develop trusting relationships. Training programmes for supervisors can be very helpful in ensuring that they understand their roles as well as the curriculum and how it integrates with field. They may also act as supports to supervisors as they share common concerns and problems that they encounter with students.

Both concurrent and block placements have advantages and disadvantages, and it is not clear that one modality is superior with regard to learning. Students taking classes along with the concurrent placements have the opportunity to apply what they are learning; however, block placements offer the opportunity to be totally immersed in the agency and to finish the programme in a shorter period of time than concurrent placements. Given the comparability between the models, students should be encouraged to select the programme that best meets their specific needs and responsibilities.

Although not mandated, integrative seminars can play an important role in ensuring that the classroom learning is applied to the field setting and that the field experiences are linked to the classes. They can also act as places where students can share these experiences with their peers as well as with the instructor and, thus, problem-solve and develop self-awareness. Through discussing and sharing cases, listening to ethical dilemmas, and discussing their own experiences in the field, their learning experiences and development can be enhanced.

Finally, field education continues to be critical for social work education, as it enables theory to interact with practice. Just as nursing depends on being qualified to work with patients, social work demands the ability to work with clients. However, as education continues to change with greater use of technology and increasing online programmes, field placements may also change with the increasing use of online simulated cases. This shift will present a challenge to the profession, as it must ensure that this type of experience offers the same learning opportunities that are found in traditional placements.

Field education is also subject to massive environmental and social changes. The impact of the coronavirus throughout the United States has led to immense increases in need throughout society and a paucity of agencies and programmes to deal with it. Many agencies had to release student interns because of unsafe conditions, while in other instances, schools quickly took students out of the field causing disruption in agencies. Other disasters, such as the terrorist attacks of 9/11, hurricane Katrina, and super storm Sandy, caused agencies to focus on maintaining immediate services for clients, giving little attention to students and supervision. Field placements are particularly sensitive to social and environmental upheavals and agencies must engage in careful planning and preparation, along with the schools, to ensure that services, clients, and students are supported. This is critical for ongoing relationships and collaboration as well as for the well-being of students and staff.

Field education in the twenty-first century faces many challenges, yet such challenges may present new opportunities. Good experiences in the field are a link for students into the profession. Ensuring that fieldwork is commensurate with the needs and demands of students as well as with agencies in a rapidly changing world is not an easy task. It takes the commitment of social work educators and organisations to ensure that the field experience is a quality one for both students and agencies.

References

Birkenmaier, J., Wilson, R. J., Berg-Weger, M., Banks, R., & Hartung, M. (2003). MSW integrative seminars: Toward integrating course and fieldwork. *Journal of Teaching in Social Work, 23*(1/2), 167–182. https://doi-org.avoserv2.library.fordham.edu/10.1300/J067v23n01_11

Bogo, M. (2006). Field instruction in social work: A review of the research literature. *Clinical Supervisor, 24*, 163–193. DOI: 10.1300/J001v24n01_09

Buck, P. W., Bradley, J., Robb, L., & Kirzner, R. S. (2012). Complex and competing demands in field education: A qualitative study of field directors' experiences. *Field Educator, 2*(2). Retrieved from http://fieldeducator.simmons.edu/article/complex-and-competing-demands-in-field-education

Cooper-Bolinskey, D., & Ketner, M. (2016). Does type of supervision impact the quality of social work field education? *International Journal of Education and Social Science, 3*(7), 34–40. Retrieved from http://www.ijessnet.com/wp-content/uploads/2016/08/3.pdf

Council on Social Work Education. (2015a). *Educational policy and accreditation standards (EPAS)*. Alexandria, VA: CSWE. https://www.cswe.org/getattachment/Accreditation/Accreditation-Process/2015-EPAS/2015EPAS_Web_FINAL.pdf.aspx

Council on Social Work Education. (2015b). *Report of the CSWE summit on field education 2014*. Alexandria, VA: CSWE. Retrieved from http://www.cswe.org/File.aspx?id=79746; https://www.cswe.org/getattachment/05519d2d-7384-41fe-98b8-08a21682ed6e/State-of-Field-Education-Survey-Final-Report.aspx

Council on Social Work Education. (2018). *State of field education survey*. Final report. Alexandria, VA: CSWE. https://www.cswe.org/getattachment/05519d2d-7384-41fe-98b8-08a21682ed6e/State-of-Field-Education-Survey-Final-Report.aspx

Curl, A., & Cary, S. (2014). A program evaluation of block and concurrent practicum formats, Field Educator, 4.2. Retrieved from https://fieldeducator.simmons.edu

Faria, F., Brownstein, C., & Smith, H. (1988). A survey of field instructors perceptions of the liaison role. *Journal of Social Work Education, 24*, 135–144.

Gushwa, M., & Harriman, K. (2019). Paddling against the tide: Contemporary challenges in field education. *Clinical Social Work Journal, 47*, 17–22. DOI: 10.1007/s10615-018-0668-3

Hendricks, C. O., Finch, J. B., & Franks, C. L. (2013). *Learning to teach, teaching to learn: A guide for social work field education*. Council on Social Work Education.

Homonoff, E. (2008). The heart of social work: Best practitioners rise to challenges in field instruction. *Clinical Supervisor, 27*, 135–169. DOI: 10.1080/07325220802490828

Ketner, M., VanCleve, D., & Cooper-Bolinskey, D. (2017). The meaning and value of supervision in social work field education, Field Educator, 7.2. Retrieved from https://fieldeducator.simmons.edu

Kilpatrick, A. C., Turner, J. B., & Holland, T. P. (1994). Quality control in field education: Monitoring students' performance. *Journal of Teaching in Social Work, 9*(1/2), 107–120.

Ligon, J., & Ward, J. (2005). A national study of the field liaison role in social work education in the United States and Puerto Rico (2005). *Social Work Education, 24*, 235–243.

Marc, C., Makai-Dimeny, J., & Oşvat, C. (2014). The social work supervisor: Skills, roles, responsibilities. *Bulletin of the Transilvania University of Braşov*, 7(1), 221–230. Retrieved from http://webbut.unitbv.ro/BU2014/Series%20VII/BULETIN%20VII%20PDF/24_MARC,%20Makai,%20Osvat%201-2014.pdf

Maynard, S., Mertz, L., & Fortune, A. (2015). Off-site supervision in social work education: What makes it work? *Journal of Social Work Education, 51*, 519–534. DOI: 10.1080/10437797.2015.1043201

Nickson, A., Gair, S., & Miles, D. (2016). Supporting isolated workers in their work with families in rural and remote Australia: Exploring peer group supervision. *Children Australia, 41*(4), 265–274. DOI: 10.1017/cha.2016.41

Olson-Morriaon, S., Radohl, T., & Dickey, G. (2019). Strengthening field education: An integrated model for signature pedagogy in social work. *Insight: A Journal of Scholarly Teaching, 14*, 55–73.

Pehrson, K. L., Panos, P. T., Larsen, K. L., & Cox, S. E. (2009). Enhancement of social work field practicum student-supervisor relationship: Utilizing communication styles. *Journal of Practice Teaching & Learning, 9*(2), 72–92. DOI: 10.1921/146066910X518111

Petracchi, H., & Zastrow, C. (2010). Suggestions for utilizing the 2008 EPAS in CSWE-accredited baccalaureate and masters curriculums—Reflections from the field, part 2: The implicit curriculum. *Journal of Teaching in Social Work, 30*, 357–366. 10.1080/08841233.2010.515928

Schneller, D., & Brocato, J. (2011). Facilitating student learning, the assessment of learning, and curricular improvement through a graduate social work integrative seminar. *Journal of Teaching in Social Work, 31*(2), 178–194. https://doi-org.avoserv2.library.fordham.edu/10.1080/08841233.2011.560532

Shulman, L (2005) Signature pedagogies in the professions. *Daedalus, 134*, 52–59.

Street, L. (2019). Field instructor perspectives on challenging behaviors in the field practicum, Field Educator, 9. Retrieved from https://fieldeducator.simmons.edu

Theriot, M., Johnson, T., Mulvaney, M., & Kretzschmar, J. (2006). Does slow and steady win the race? The impact of block versus concurrent field on BSW students' professional development and emotional well-being. *Journal of Baccalaureate Social Work, 12*(1), 203–217.

Todd, S., & Schwartz, K. (2009). Thinking through quality in field education: Integrating alternative and traditional learning opportunities. *Social Work Education, 28*, 380–395. DOI: 10.1080/02615470902808326

Wiebe, M. (2010). Pushing the boundaries of the social work practicum: Rethinking sites and supervision toward radical practice. *Journal of Progressive Human Services, 21*, 66–82. DOI: 10.1080/10428231003782517

Wertheimer, M., & Sodhi, M. (2014). Beyond field education: Leadership of field directors. *Journal of Social Work Education, 50*, 48–68. DOI: 10.1080/10437797.2014.856230

Zeira, A., & Schiff, M. (2010). Testing group supervision in fieldwork training for social work students. *Research on Social Work Practice, 20*(4), 427–434. DOI: 10.1177/1049731509332882

7

It's Time to Deconstruct the Problematic Attitude of 'Fieldwork' of the 'Global North'!

Shweta Singh

Is it time to deconstruct the 'fieldwork' attitude of the 'Global North' as a problem attitude? In the Global North, it is difficult to find a bigger myth in the discipline of social work than that of 'fieldwork is the signature pedagogy of social work'.

The Myth: Unmaking Reflexivity

My perspective blends several standpoints – that of a social worker trained in India, a mixed-methods researcher and evaluator, a long-time instructor for a fieldwork agency-based evaluation course, and a poststructuralist-interdisciplinary theorist. My training as a social worker in Mumbai, India is central to meaning-making of social work fieldwork. I think fieldwork should serve as a life-changing and reorienting training for social workers. I have, over the years, been elated by the few students who love their fieldwork and aghast at the hollow engagement of several others. This is because the agencies did not have the intrinsic capacity to train or provide fieldwork experiences in Chicago, Illinois. Also, as a quantitative researcher, I am aware of the deficits of my untested model, but from a deconstructionist and intentional-constructivist epistemology, I highlight underlying power imbalances and the unfairness of the status quo in any system or process.

Therefore, I see exceptional merit in recognising the 'cultish' agreement that pervades a large section of U.S. social work academics, which is antithetical to both academic doctrines of interrogating universal truths and striving to empower of the marginalised. These trends tend to be cultivated and swiftly translated into globally-applicable models that become the unquestioned standard of practice. These eventually act as benchmarks for assessments. And then a small group of influential academics with global networks implement them in the Global South. This is a disservice to populations of our clients, consumers of our services, and practitioners and professionals who are actively engaged with reality. On a larger spectrum, it hinders training of social workers who can bring a multi-focality through a culturally humble, intellectually mature, structurally conscientious, knowledgeable interface from fieldwork to social work education.

Absence of Complexity

My own fieldwork during my Master of Social Work (M.S.W.), as a social worker, and subsequently, as an evaluator of social development programmes precipitated a reconfiguration of my

DOI: 10.4324/9781032164946-10

own dispositions toward society in general and the place of social workers in it. From expansive interactions, conversations, engagements, assignments, and detailed field-counselling in groups and individual sessions, I knew I was not an exception but the norm – a 5% chance of error norm. Hence, fieldwork with sex-workers in a red-light district, in the metropolitan district court, and in an urban slum were a study in human relations, social structures, policy building, and social advocacy tools. And then, later, of course, they were cemented as I continued as a professional practicing in villages of North India, the child labour industry, families, and shelter homes for women and children. Coming in close contact with some of the most vulnerable groups brought me a first-hand account of their resilience in the face of tough choices. My perception of these groups and their weakness in society changed to one of their marginalisation by society. In other words, society classified these individuals as being a poor fit for the system rather than highlighting the weakness of the system in not being flexible enough to accommodate the different life experiences and outcomes of these groups. Identifying the gaps between problems, its experiences by the individual, and the fit of the formulation of the problem as a theory were conundrums highlighted by the absence of a grassroots-oriented, non-judgemental, empowering, and dynamic theoretical framework.

Then, during the course of reviewing around 500 assignments, I found that even describing the programme or the service becomes an issue for a large section of students in the key assignment of my agency-based evaluation research course. Add in the complexity of ecology, the socio-psychological, economic components, and the fact that most agencies do not have programme details readily available, and the case get even more complex. At the most, students and I were able to collaboratively generate a broad demographic profile of clients receiving services in a programme. Even there, the buzzwords– 'needy', 'poor', 'limited-resource', 'marginal', and 'missing social support' were more likely than intersectional identities of clients. But the papers would go on to confess their commitment to apply the 'strengths-based' perspective and assertion that the clients all desired change.

As a newly emerged graduate of a reputed Ph.D. programme more than a decade ago, I cringed, but did not feel any significant sense of 'belonging' to a 'U.S.-based' intellectual community of academics. Instead, I experienced my identity as 'marginal' as an international, 'south Asian', 'brown' 'woman' for the first time in my life as a professional. Consequently, I was hesitant about articulating this as a concern to my peers. My perplexity grew at the stark contrast between my students and my own learning from fieldwork education, practice, and supervision. A few years later, still embedded in the ethos of Indian social activism, advocacy, and community-centric social work training, I did offer mild critiques and reflections to my colleagues at conferences – without much impact. I re-experienced the same poser of my Ph.D. programme –the application of a western model of binary interpersonal relationships to women's autonomy in the villages of North and South India. Much as I tried, I also could not find an expansive enough theory even within other disciplines; economics' rational best choices and psychology's behaviour and personality typologies drawn from Caucasian teenagers, were not convincing. Thus, I landed on the poststructuralism theories and built a framework around it to grasp identities of women in my defined contexts of South Asia.

Method and Context

Poststructuralism and Deconstruction

Discourse, language, power, knowledge, truth, and freedom are all examined; colonial designs are questioned in poststructuralism (St. Pierre, 2000). Rights, priorities, and outcomes are examined on a continuum in poststructuralist feminism and are applied here to understand fieldwork as a training tool and its ability to teach social work students about communities of meaning. Deconstruction, primarily, is tool of poststructuralist feminist inquiry.

According to Gannon and Davies (2007), poststructuralist feminism articulates the importance of language, drawing upon its genesis as a theory of literary criticism. It is able to expose 'subjugation' in language that becomes part of the overarching or meta-discourse – 'a system of being, thinking, and acting' (p. 82) on a topic. Through deconstructing, the objectivity of the teaching paraphernalia, the subjectivities underlying ideas, and the limitations of the discourse are highlighted. The principles underlying deconstruction are evaluating the power inequity, locating subjects in their contexts, comparing interpretations, and the inclusion of multi-focal ontologies.

Social work education, the generic umbrella of term 'critical thinking', becomes a ubiquitous learning outcome not only of fieldwork but everything else as well; while it is only a facilitation of a simplistic linear thinking and a meta-narrative that glosses over differences. Thus, allowing the delivery of similar curriculum and standardised practices to social work students. Deconstruction can bring this hidden absolutism to the front, point out the missing referential categories of groups, and lay bare the strategically placed metaphors and rhetoric that prevent deeper insights and submerge the issues and challenges in understanding the field from the outside.

Redefining Collective and Action in Social Work Fieldwork

This is imperative under deconstruction. The role that a relativistic interpretation paradigm can play outside of the literary criticism area is debated because of its emphasis on multiplicity. In social work, identification of stakeholders outside of programme inclusion criteria is rare. For a poststructuralist, the individual is not dispossessed by being in a community and neither does the collective own him or his rights and existence. From a critical pedagogy perspective, the liberation of the unemancipated other is anyways problematic, and the collective at both ends becomes questionable (Tavares, 1998). The identification of community as that of economic need is also, in large part, due to the denial of alternative forms of local economies that neoliberal solutions take away both in form and in discourse, thus, framing them as communities of need (Gibson et al., 2018).

Genesis of Social Work Professional Education

Social work's origins in most countries outside of the Western imperial powers often occurred while they were still colonised; hence, the implementations were simple – transplant the education to foreign lands to improve them, such as in India and Brazil in 1936, in Egypt in 1935, and so on. A couple of lines on the genesis of social work itself are warranted here. In most social work history books, British 'Poor Laws' from the1600s can be traced to the progressive era of the 'settlement movement' of Jane Addams, which, for postcolonialists and deconstructionists, can only be termed as a kind of 'consciousness building about poor folks' for economically self-sufficient groups. The delivery of social services and incorporation into policy within the U.S., from the 'depression era' to the 'war on poverty', built on the earlier poor-people-consciousness and offered a range of programmes that would 'improve' poor people's living conditions. These were all translated into colonised worlds' newly trained social work professionals' access to Mary Richmond's take on social casework and Jane Addams's views on community work. But beyond the dramatic genesis, in the U.S.A., social work/social services have been a dogmatic, largely political, policy fight over funding that is allocated or taken away from programmes for social welfare of the 'poor', the 'unemployed', groups that social workers are trained to further compartmentalised as 'family and child', 'health and mental health', 'substance and alcohol abuse', and so on (Singh et al., 2011). These meandering categorisations explain the survival of the rather ineffectual Systems Theory – often presented as the only theory in 'Western' social work education. The arguments for generalist practice have become stronger, as though the reason students are not able to relate to the field is because they take courses in a certain set framework that discourages community engagement. Meanwhile, the social work discipline marches on the very fringes of academic thought leadership, with competition from nascent disciplines, such as folklore studies, or radical ones, such as human geography. Embedded within this box, is social work fieldwork practice. A telling sign of the disconnect between fieldwork, scholarship, and teaching is the criticism of it from the social work practitioners.

How Did the International Fieldwork Sites, Particularly in the Global South Differ Then?

Fieldwork experiences of students and its manifestation in the Global South accentuates the argument for indigenising social work. While there are numerous reflexivity pieces about research-based fieldwork undertaken by academics, through the 1990s, in culturally unfamiliar spaces, they all overtly articulate reflexivity as well as its emergence (Smith, 2014) – this is the case in the parallel fields of anthropology, sociology, and psychology. It is a sort of salute to the heady mix of liberalisation, neoliberal criticism, and interpretive criticism happening in constructed and institutionalised intellectual academic spaces. The interesting thing is that these reflexivity undertakings appear in the same way and have similar angst toward or interrogation of their discipline. Research protocols demand 'language' and 'expression' be presented in the form of research writing. I propose that these expeditions remain 'viewing' experiences that are not really in a position to manifest change, even when they return with a funded intervention and recruit locals in their teams. They fail to acknowledge the colonial imprints, even when their roots or ethnic group affiliations can be traced to these same communities, their meanings do not overlap. The training and education circumscribe the relevance of local contexts, and their longer histories and complex structures get lost in the changes that the research will be bringing. Fieldwork research should be conducted by trained, locally-cognisant, and well-read individuals. Such research represents the challenges of 'engaging with communities' and undertaking 'stakeholder identification' within the constraints of agency-centred environments, and should reflect the struggles of social work students in the field.

Origins of Fieldwork as Beneficence Toward Agencies

Beyond the settlement house and Jane Addams, the genesis of fieldwork was 'applied philanthropy' and was a way of orienting students to poverty and adversity in the world. In 1897, the National Conference of Charities and Corrections highlighted the need for practical social work to understand the 'insane', the 'dependent', and the 'abandoned. The social sciences, populated largely by women students, were the only fields of study willing to go along with the emerging discipline. According to Lela B. Costin, in her book *Two Sisters for Social Justice: A Biography of Grace and Edith Abbott* (1983), Edith Abbott, while impressed with J.S. Mill and more committed to social good and work informed by professional training, she had less respect for the psychology casework approach wherein the goal was to impact people's personalities. Her focus on fieldwork was a well-constructed engagement that was closely tied to the school, with supervisors who were also full-time faculty members, leading to fieldwork supervision and engagement that was more than observation or inspection. Roughly around the same time, social work dropped its social sciences affiliation. It is interesting, from a deconstructive epistemology, that the person who wanted Abbott to have a leadership role was, according to Costin's historical research, Nisba Breckenridge, a key person in the Chicago Women's Trade Union League. One can imagine that her perspective was that of the population to be served, as women were not represented in the three groups listed above as clients. Social work fieldwork, then, was a field that focused on a community of regular and competent people trying to survive a misinformed and prejudicial system and circumstances. Critical insight and assessment were implicit in this understanding of fieldwork. According to authors such as Bishnu Mohan Dash (2017), in countries such as India, field education went through its own partially organic process. As social work, in general, passed through generalist and specialisations, so, too, did fieldwork, with construction of objectives and agendas in the 1960s and 70s. The realisation that regions and population diversity were a crucial dimension prevented any largescale standardisation and uniformity in the early years. A few surveys later, the portion of fieldwork education was set in terms of hours and credits, and then, under the leadership of the Delhi School of Social Work, concepts of block placements, structure, and process were streamlined. However, into the 2000s, the fieldwork component remained peripheral to social work education in India as in the U.S.A. With the increasing transmission of knowledge at the start of the twenty-first century, there is more influence of the U.S. social work has gained influence in India as well as other areas in the Global South.

Fieldwork Practice and Education

Though assessment is the new protocol and manuals the new intervention guideline, supervision remains an under-examined concept in social work fieldwork in U.S.A. The composition of fieldwork continues to be the (i) fieldwork supervision protocols, (ii) fieldwork supervisors, (iii) fieldwork agency/site, and (iv) fieldwork education – each of which is impacted by the classroom, curriculum, and instructor interface. Never mind the permutations that occur out of this – laid out as factors, their interrelationships are apparent; however, in most schools of social work, these remain under-articulated, and the paucity of field sites and supervisors means that there are not many measurables in place. Fieldwork education is also a largely neglected domain and is only now in a nascent stage of developing protocols and manuals that are more geared toward accountability and 'grading' than practice learning. In current manifestations of fieldwork, the supervisor has become such an important connection and yet remains an unpredictable variable. The advent of managerial social work has also not boded well for the connections between the field and the classroom, creating a superficial level of connection and coordination that is more about form-filling than any deep changes that used to be assessed with 3–5 hours of conversation every week between field staff and placed students.

Managerial Approach to Supervision in Fieldwork

In a study by Hanewinckel et al. (2018) comparing supervision in Brazil and England based on interviews with a sample of 17 supervisors and the authors' own reflections, the authors found that supervisors expressed confidence about supervising by meeting the required qualification protocol, though the supervisors with more extensive experience were able to offer more insights and fieldwork guidance. There have been other studies that have highlighted how the supervision practice is more geared toward assessment and management than a relational component that can serve as a meaningful field orientation or build mentoring relationships between students and supervisors. In under-circulated journals, such as *Supervision*, the issue of the under-researched topic of supervision has been presented, and various models attempt to outline the parameters of this relationship. They range from the interpersonal, psychodynamic (yet again) to the assessment of satisfaction with supervision as a service. The value of supervision has been discovered in field education practices of social work education, but agreement on its role and the essentials of its function are still being formed. Further, unlike in the Global North, supervision is not a licensed process, so standardisation, as seen operating in Western social work education, is not practical. But even more relevant is the fact that, in the context of the Global South, privilege and power cannot be presumed in the supervision relationship, especially in the context of emerging and surviving economies, as the student might be more privileged given that social work has become a popular profession for those in the middle class. And non-governmental organisations (N.G.O.s) can range across the continuum from grassroots organisations lacking resources to those flush with international funding.

A recent comprehensive dissertation described fieldwork and supervision modalities (Akileswari, 2018). Drawing from her research, realising the need for agency training, student involvement in agency work, and regular, documented conferences between the students and the supervisors has transformed supervision in India. In the last 40 years, it has been acknowledged that students' need for self-assessment of learning has expanded. The underlying principles, though, have not changed the relationship of equity and co-creation of learning space.

Role of Evidence-Based Practice and 'Trauma-Informed' Practice Education as Guidelines for Community and Client Engagement

Both of these ideas emerged in medicine and its subfields, and social work was among their early acolytes. A key presumption is that evidence is easily accessible and translatable, therefore, social workers are taught to find, decipher, and apply evidence. A parallel view sees little use for stand-alone research skills, while, in an older view, research was seen as a required evil in social work, with practice courses, especially, not investing much effort to incorporate such content. Evidence-based practice (E.B.P.) in social work rests on the premise of ample evidence for all kinds of scenarios and people, just like the field of medicine when conducting research under randomised controlled trial (R.C.T.) experimental designs. E.B.P. in social work counts on under-staffed agencies that find it difficult to supervise and have a designated individual act as a conduit for this researched practice (Drake et al., 2007). At the same time, even small social service agencies need a professionally trained social worker to carry out the technical case management for outreach jobs. The critiques of E.B.P. are plentiful in the Global North, but this is simply a power argument between the Global North and South over the colonisation of knowledge. In the Global South, the field was constructed to serve a larger number of people with less funding and fewer formally trained fieldworkers using practices based on evidence, whereas there is limited evidence on the practices that work in the Global North's most under-represented groups, such as immigrants, minorities, and the assorted intersectionalities of rural and inner-city neighbourhoods. The issue of representation is one of external validity and raises questions about the impact of such evidence in fieldwork practice with multiple unknowns and variables of all elements. Finally, there is a world of published evidence, as is the case in all other disciplines; however, all the top-ranked social work journals carry works regarding mostly Global North populations, and when populations differ, the lead researcher is most likely to be from the Global North, meaning that the ideas, theories, research questions, methods, and findings are all in alliance with those of the Global North.

This directly leads us to the emerging models that replace older ones or draw staunch allies amongst fieldwork educators and practitioners. The 'trauma-informed' model of practice is a good example. As a large number of social workers in Western society are therapists, their draw to diagnosis and counselling work requires their expertise to compete with psychologists and other counselling fields. The individualistic society and the exchange structure that has been fostered in social relationships demands simplistic relationship ideals of measured give and take, and the less expressive social ideals make the acknowledgement of feelings a task. This is the space in which trauma and its correlate post-traumatic stress disorder (P.T.S.D.) work; Western ideologies, with their linear interpretation, developed into meta-narratives, are limited in their ability to grasp the elaborate psychological experiences that are founded in multiple relationships and a traditional, collectivist consciousness. In numerous critiques, such as the those by Felix Lang (2018) and Orkideh Behrouzan (2018), trauma is outlined by the structural battering of poverty, oppression, and systemic racism, which is not a singular experience but a historical memory. The confrontation of oppressors and community are elements within trauma-informed practice so that participants can perceive their own agency. The survival of a large number of people with minimal resources and suboptimal living conditions might mean undertaking brain scans to identify trauma for millions of people. This is unfeasible and unlikely to happen. There is power in sharing sustained experiences of stress in that the retelling of the narrative results in repositioning and recognising agency and expanding it. For community work, especially for culturally diverse populations that do not identify with mainstream North American Caucasian eighteenth- and nineteenth-century culture, this interpretation can be super problematic. The articulation of practitioner's social justice commitment is not enough; local is always more relevant, and constructing mental and physical health in the local language is an exercise in power. The cultural location of vulnerabilities and interdependencies must precede merits of any confrontational strategies; this has been found in work done with immigrant populations, and cultural and moral interpretations continue to be subsets in ideological spaces. Given these aspects, being wary of and deconstructing each one of these new or emerging models to assess their utility and applicability in diverse groups within the Global North to identify potential deficits if applied in practice in the localised Global South should be seen as the first steps in social work academics in the Global South.

Western Social Work Academic Space

A key implication is that the Global South maintains an organic, fieldwork-centric education that strengthens connectivity between academics, non-profits, and social services. Plenty of social work articles espouse some of these ideas but mostly as an afterthought in policy, programme, research, and practice gaps. These, then, are mostly at the fringe and are not part of the influential writing that controls the parameters of social work education and funded programming. As part of the political, feminist, critical pedagogy restructuring fringe, I have reflected, over the last 20 years, on Western academic space and realised that these approaches to fieldwork practice and education are a direct outcome of the ridiculous sense of inferiority from the disciplines of psychology and public health that exist in a large section of academics within the social work discipline in the Global North.

Right now, social work is at the forefront of advocating for telemedicine, simulated fieldwork sites, and generalist practice, all of which have been derived from medicine, public health, and psychology. Training is also taking a new shape to help social workers fit in better with their interdisciplinary teams. As orienting people in other disciplines to the value of social work seems to have been ruled out by social work educators, the impetus is to train social workers to learn the content of other disciplines. In no way is my argument against the need for this work, but I definitely want to underscore the unfair practice social work educators are facilitating in making social workers carry the burden of fitting in while compromising the needs of the field, community, client, and agency by underselling social work's strengths and discipline. This peripheralises the real tools of social work, fieldwork supervision, groupwork methodologies, and community organising to yield space to paradigms from other disciplines. This is evident in that debates about micro and macro have still not left the station, Freud is still relevant in clinical social work, and community has become part of tacit learning. Macro, which could loosely translate into community work, should have been central and upfront, especially when discrimination, marginalisation, and invisibility of our core service receivers are problems in Western society. Even the curriculum barely reflects macro work, and the same is true for mezzo, and instead of seeing practitioners of groupwork as using truly innovative tools of social work, they remain on the fringes unless they have invested and motivated advocates. As the curriculum moves away from its organic roots, it has evolved into a site of contention, and the stakeholders who can make a difference are hardly ever the fieldwork agencies and freshly graduated students, as neither one of them is really aware of what they have lost. The emphasis on assessment of fieldwork has only resulted in reducing the hours mandated or left them unprescribed during the coursework. This is because the formalisation was not really based on learning parameters but on the awareness of limitations and constraints – student cost constraints, agency capacity constraints, and measurability of skill and competency.

Whatever the motivation for the contrived and natural transformation of the curriculum of Western social work and embedded fieldwork education, the take away is the futility of absorbing any of these changes as models or practice benchmarks for social work education in the Global South. The curriculum of social work in the West is paying the price for its cult-following tendencies and discipline-shaming roots by facing centuries-old unsolved social problems such as racism and not even being considered the first discipline to frame it. The search for both the underlying evidence and framing of trauma remain disconnected from the reality of practice and people. But the Global South has historical awareness of exploitation, colonisation, and self-actualisation. A culture of argument and debate and the absence of 'cult' cultures in academia can come up with better solutions. The socio-economic complexity and magnitude of our populations of need really demand nothing less than the most organic, local, disaggregated approach to social worker training, underscored by holistic supervision, and capacity building to continue working confidently and independently and in teams of government and non-government, local, national, or international and interdisciplinary taskforces (Gray et al., 2018). Social workers of the Global South would be able to convey the historical importance and social recognition to professional social workers and students who operate in grant-fostered, institution-mandated, multi-disciplinary teams in Global North.

Conclusion and Implications – A Quest for an Alternative Model

Eastern Wisdom and Meaning-Making of Fieldwork

Consider the field as a site for Buddha, who knew that, outside the walls of his palace and life of privilege, life included the reality of poverty and disease. He had gone out on a ride to see what the world was like and to understand it. He returned disenchanted, disheartened, and committed to knowing and doing more. After years of meditating and reflecting, he realised the purpose of life and his position in it. Then he roamed the world with what had been the sum of his reflections and formed them into teachings that could help people cope better with their circumstances. These were not a cognitive behavioural therapy (C.B.T.) approach but, rather, a lifelong narrative of discovery of one's place in the community.

In conclusion, I propose, that alternative models for fieldwork in the Global South are needed. Here, I propose one based on my ongoing work on the concept of *belonging* that is informed by the Identities of Women theoretical framework (Singh, 2007)

Why the Identities of Women Theoretical Framework is a Way to Conceptualise Fieldwork

The Identities of Women theory posits the importance of contexts, particularly for all kinds of marginalisation to be identified and addressed. Also, it believes in narratives and that the self-reflective articulation of agency and identity can lead to an actualised sense of self. It frames the dynamic nature of social relationships and perceives the institution on the axis of the individual rather than the other way around.

Under neoliberal certainties is the cyclical relationship of linear transitions with zero disruptions. Structured social work practices embrace the narrow conception of social problems, such as the division of society into those who work and those who cannot as a choice as culturally myopic but ideologically bound – it is an odd relationship between pedagogy and ecology of human life. As seen in Figure 7.1, the static nature of agency appears to dominate the fieldwork pedagogy and might work for training therapists who work with presumptive structures. In fact, the advent of social work education, which has grown in the last 5 years is an example of influence of this pedagogy. The Identities of Women theory approaches individual and group identity as a modifier of the experience of the surrounding systems, organisations' inability to accommodate that identity results in limiting community agency, social service agency, and student agency.

As seen in Figure 7.2, the dynamic nature of the space and interaction is complex and predictable only in parts. The key stakeholders are entities that impact ecology beyond what the social work education currently embraces. The nature of the discipline allows and encourages engagement with but not influence from disciplines such as psychology and medicine. A

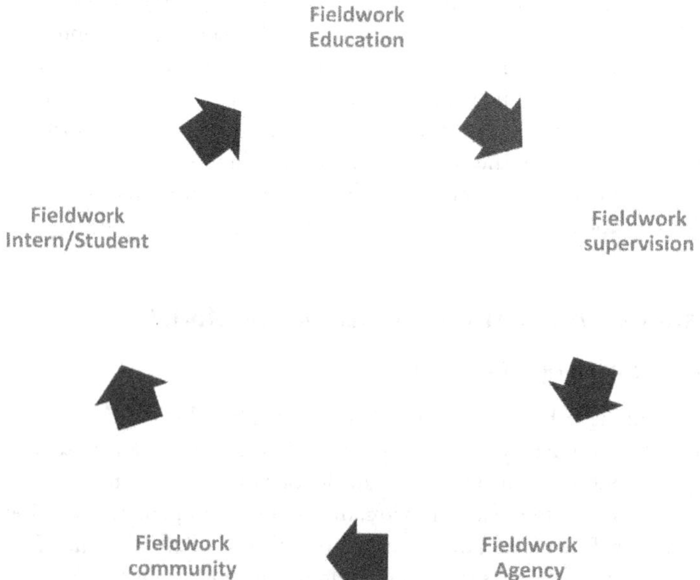

Figure 7.1 Cycle of fieldwork in Western social work pedagogy

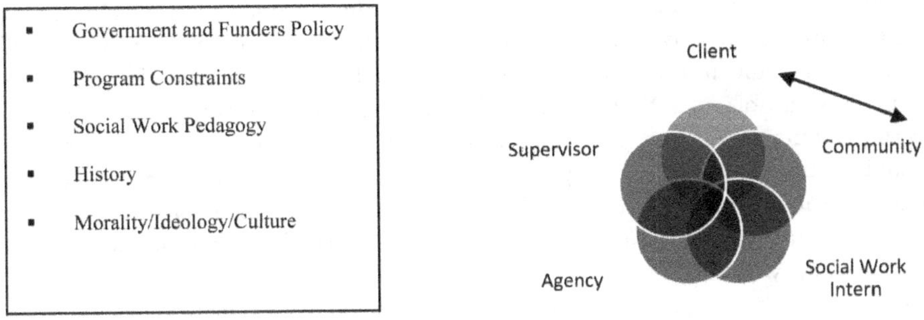

Figure 7.2 Assumptions and influences of social work are external

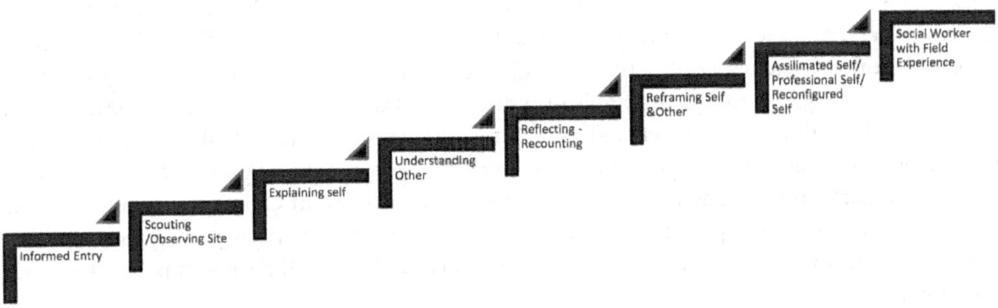

Figure 7.3 Continuum of belonging for social workers in fieldwork

sustained connectivity is necessary in facilitating a sense of belonging with every stakeholder. Meanwhile, the systems we think are out of the box and informing this relationship are just external influencers, and their role can only be to inform and guide this complex and largely unstudied interaction, as depicted by multiple intersecting circles.

Figure 7.3 is drawn from the women and work model of the Identities of Women theoretical framework. It depicts the steps that lead to an informed entry into social work with a comprehensive field experience. While needs from fieldwork education are not simple, students in this model are expected to be motivated, self-driven, engaged, aware of separation with the field, aware of the limitations of the field, and assess their own learning. The observation can be only an initial phase of engagement, where the orientation happens, and the student is able to scan the socio-economic and cultural landscape. In the third phase, the positioning of self is the first set of revelations in the growth and belonging trajectory. Then, the understanding of the other follows; this is the individual and overlapping circles from Figure 7.2. Then, the student reflects as the transition occurs, wherein the other and self both get reframed with an increasing grasp of the structures, dynamics, and context, as it frames these identities of the client, the agencies, and the community. Only when these have been assimilated, and advocacy-oriented engagement allows for optimal sense of self as a professional, does the experience become complete.

What is Belonging?

In the Identities of Women theoretical framework, the 'sense of belonging' is the experience of affiliation, acceptance of relevance, and easy identification with an institution, culture, social system by an individual or group. The sense of belonging contributes to an individual's comprehension of the abstract environment that includes the cultural ethos, social systems, institutions, and unmeasured dynamics, which is the pathway to natural transmission of ethics and ideas and results in the formation of strong ties. It can also lead to the self being experienced less as an isolated and individualised, and, instead, the self is perceived more in relation to the abstract other. Group pressure can be detrimental to the well-being of the individual and group. This construct applied to social workers' fieldwork practice, is the degree to which social work interns identify with the field as a system of relevance and importance in defining who they are in relation to it and what they aspire for themselves and for the community.

Belonging is the link between a monolithic conception of group identity and the rigid structures and institutions from which a group is excluded. Studies of the different experiences of black and white students at schools have found that developing a sense of belonging successfully addresses issues of behaviour, self-esteem, and detachment in children (Drolet et al., 2013). It has also been studied as a modifying variable that counters the negative effects of marginalised group identities (Sánchez et al., 2005). In my own early studies on girls' identity formation through multiple focus groups at schools in India, I found that adolescents identified the school as a key marker of their idea of self and the school. However, no one had asked them the question before, so it was not something they discovered until their participation in the focus group process. Similarly, in my study of narratives of immigrant women in Chicago, I found that their main grievance was feeling that they did not belong in the U.S.A. Each participant identified different institutions that aided this belief – such as relationships with peer-groups, teachers, and the physical space.

I propose that building an intentional engagement between the student and the community is important to both developmental and rehabilitative social work (Anand, 2017). The curriculum design and delivery need to be undertaken organically by the field supervisors, faculty supervisors, and community stakeholders and driven by a community-centric management. The role of departmental management and academic committees cannot represent the overlapping space of the community, agency, client, and social work intern except in a static, diagnostic way that is exemplified by trauma and narrow, evidence-based paradigms. If we look at this history of fieldwork in the West, we find a few decades in which storytelling, participant or non-participant observation, immersion, and critical evaluation were all encouraged and occurred systematically. Then the utilitarian ideas took over and the compulsion of other professional disciplines' science intervened.

Community as a Space for Belonging

The complex relationship between social identity and the dynamic nature of power within social situations and contexts has only been linear in developmental thinking, and only recently has this dynamism been addressed more actively (Nic a Bháird, 2013). The desire to make social intervention more meaningful for the community, sustain its impact, and build connectedness has led programme developers to intentionally incorporate more of the beneficiary culture into the interventions. In an interview and focus group study on staff and beneficiaries to study community engagement by an N.G.O. in Kolkata, Nic a Bháird (2013) reported the 'isolation, exclusion, and structural inequalities' that underlie the inequity in their power dynamics (p. 394). This study makes a useful contribution to our discussion regarding the reasons that the interventions of structured schooling fails because it ignores social dynamics and the resistance that will emerge from the stakeholders because no beneficiary community is homogenous and any intervention, even schooling, is perceived as an encroachment on established social order. On the other hand, a study by Shah (2016) on an N.G.O. programme for schooling girls in Gujarat shows that when the discourse becomes personalised and changes from an instrumental nature to a transformational one, schooling can be a tool for empowerment. The study's interviews highlight the staff's awareness that the girls in the schools will return to their own society, and they must be able to 'belong' to both so that the education does not become a problem for their survival within their own community (Shah, 2016, p. 17–18).

The intent to differentiate those who go into fieldwork, those who work at the agency, and those work in the community seems counterproductive. In a study of ten Ashram schools in the Wardha district of Maharashtra, a questionnaire identified key elements of the school (Dongre, Deshmukh & Garg, 2011). The study identifies the schools' limitations in terms of physical structures and values and their inability to accommodate cultures even when there is room to do so. The physical structure, while in proximity to the tribal settlement, does not seem to reflect the community; in fact, references to community seem to only have negative connotations of 'traditional', 'superstitious', and 'unaware'. The formation of a parent–teacher association also is not an organic artifact, as the local tribal communities have their own community governance and child-rearing norms, and these are not articulated at the culture at school.

Curriculum Design and Instruction

The culture differential is why, in the nine decades of social work in India, students wear what the field allows. The cultural assimilation is superficial, but nevertheless, it is the student's informed entry, showing an awareness of the explicit cultures of the community and the client within it. The person under a diagnostic microscope is not the client but the student and, by affiliation, the school that they come from. I remember my own struggles with wearing a sari in the field when doing fieldwork in a slum community near Mumbai, and yet, a year later, my sense of being in a community started with it.

The argument is beyond indigenous and local/global binaries; the big picture of the social work of the Global North is coming up deficient in fulfilling its obligations to the diverse people and their life trajectories in their own context. Then, the premise of superiority that pervades academics and its ivory-tower culture should have been shunned by social work, but, instead, it continues to embrace positions of power over community and then wastes resources with superficial outreach and engagement. The University of Chicago continues to draw flak for being in the middle of what has been a poverty island for nearly 200 years, and yet, its connections with the community are only decade old. The stranger culture of the Global North is contrary to the community and collectivism of the Global South, which is why people from rural and small-town cultures will share private details with their neighbours but will not be comfortable around strangers, no matter how qualified they are. This is the reason outreach for mental health services took so long, and still meets resistance in immigrant and minority cultures and communities in the West.

Further, the fieldwork, its curriculum, and its pedagogical design are constrained by micro practitioners of individual and family therapy. Tokenism pervades by allowing students, adjuncts and field agency representatives to participate in curriculum committees, but their input and insight remains unmeasured and their experiences undocumented. The conversation does expand as social work academia remains more urban and is limited because the communities it teaches or trains are not present in the academic curriculum designing. Here, again, the Global South has an inherent advantage, as the students in social work programs and the faculty and staff do belong to the communities they serve and train for.

Conclusion

The intentional ownership and articulation of fieldwork pedagogy must be undertaken by the Global South, as the field of social work remains unique and organic and has not been subjugated to any micro/macro tyranny of narratives. And this space must be incentivised for the local stakeholders – agency partners, teachers, and students – so that they can creatively make the 'sense of belonging' a reality for social work interns. Because, if we don't formalise and reclaim this pedagogical space, the U.S.-trained psychotherapist micro-social worker is waiting in the woods ready to save our 'Buddha' with some version of 'trauma-informed' couch therapy to cure Buddha and save his marriage. As in their worldview, Buddha's quest for truth and serving community might as well be a personality disorder that has yet to make an appearance in *DSM VIII* (McCollum, 2011).

References

Akileswari, S. (2018). A study on field work practicum and supervision in social work education. (Unpublished Doctoral dissertation) Department of Social Work, University of Madras, Tamil Nadu, India.

Anand, M. (2017). Role of rural camps in nurturing field practicum: Narrative from a faculty of social work, Delhi, India. *Social Work Education*, 36(5), 521–528. https://doi.org/10.1080/02615479.2017.1307334

Costin, L. B. (1983). *Two sisters for social justice: A biography of Grace and Edith Abbott*. University of Illinois Press.

Dash, B. M. (2017). Revisiting eight decades of social work education in India. *Asian Social Work and Policy Review*, 11(1), 66–75. https://doi.org/10.1111/aswp.12114

Dongre, A. R., Deshmukh, P. R., & Garg, B. S. (2011). Health-promoting school initiative in Ashram schools of Wardha district. *The National medical journal of India, 24*(3), 140–143.

Drake, B., Hovmand, P., Jonson-Reid, M., & Zayas, L.H. (2007). Adopting and teaching evidence-based practice in master's-level social work programs. *Journal of Social Work Education*, 43(3), 431–446. https://doi.org/10.5175/JSWE.2007.200600625

Drolet, M., Arcand, I., Ducharme, D., & Leblanc, R. (2013). The sense of school belonging and implementation of a prevention program: Toward healthier interpersonal relationships among early adolescents. *Child & Adolescent Social Work Journal: C & A*, 30, 535–551.

Gannon, S., & Davies, B. (2007). Postmodern, poststructural, and critical theories. https://doi.org/10.4135/9781483384740.n4.

Gibson, K., Astuti, R., Carnegie, M., Chalernphon, A., Dombroski, K., Haryani, A. R., Hill, A., Kehi, B., Law, L., Lyne, I., & McGregor, A. (2018). Community economies in Monsoon Asia: Keywords and key reflections. *Asia Pacific Viewpoint*, 59(1), 3–16. https://doi.org/10.1111/apv.12186

Gray, M., Agllias, K., Mupedziswa, R., & Mugumbate, J. (2018). The expansion of developmental social work in Southern and East Africa: Opportunities and challenges for social work field programmes. *International Social Work*, 61(6), 974–987. https://doi.org/10.1177/0020872817695399

Haanwinckel, B. Z., Fawcett, B., & Garcia, J. A. B. (2018). Contrasts and reflections: Social work fieldwork supervision in Brazil and England. *International Social Work*, 61(6), 943–953. https://doi.org/10.1177/0020872817695395

Lang, F. (2018). No such thing as society? A critique of hegemonic notions of trauma in the research on cultural production. *Middle East—Topics and Arguments*, 11, 154–158.

McCollum, E. E. (2011). Could EFT have saved the Buddha's marriage? A reflection on Beckerman and Sarracco. *Journal of Family Psychotherapy*, 22(1), 16–21. https://doi.org/10.1080/08975353.2011.551088

Nic a Bháird, C. (2013). The complexity of community engagement: Developing staff–community relationships in a Participatory Child Education and Women's Rights Intervention in Kolkata slums. *Journal of Community & Applied Social Psychology*, 23(5), 389–404.

Orkideh, B. (2018). Ruptures and their afterlife: A cultural critique of Trauma. *Middle East Topic and Argument (META)*, 11, 131–144.

Sánchez, B., Colón, Y., & Esparza, P. (2005). The role of sense of school belonging and gender in the academic adjustment of Latino adolescents. *Journal of Youth and Adolescence*, 34(6), 619–628.

Shah, P. (2016). Partnerships and appropriation: Translating discourses of access and empowerment in girls' education in India. *International Journal of Educational Development*, 49, 11–21.
Smith, A.-M. (2014). Old fieldwork, new ethnography. *Qualitative Inquiry*, 20(5), 699–708. https://doi.org/10.1177/1077800413513729
Singh, S. (2007). Deconstructing 'gender and development' for '*identities of women*'. *International Journal of Social Welfare*, 16(2), 100–109.
Singh, S., Gumz, E., & Crawley, B. (2011). Predicting India's future: Does it justify the exportation of US social work education? *Social Work Education*, 30, 861–873. https://doi.org/10.1080/02615479.2010.515303
St. Pierre, E. A. (2000) Poststructural feminism in education: An overview. *International Journal of Qualitative Studies in Education*, 13(5), 477–515. https://doi.org/10.1080/09518390050156422
Tavares, H. (1998). Poststructural feminisms and alter-pedagogical tales. *Review of Education, Pedagogy, and Cultural Studies*, 20(1), 77–98. https://doi.org/10.1080/1071441980200107

8
Social Work Field Education in Canada

Marion Bogo and Karen M. Sewell

Field education has always been recognised as a crucial component in social work education in Canada. The Policy and Standards for Accreditation of Schools of Social Work define and specify the factors involved in a quality field experience for students. This chapter will present this context of field education and, based on an analysis of empirical studies, identify the best practices to promote student learning. The chapter will also present the current realities facing Canadian social and health services that challenge the ability to provide this important educational element to prepare the next generation of social work practitioners. The chapter concludes with recommendations to make field education a priority for organisations and social work education programmes.

The Context of Field Education in Canada

The importance of field education was recognised in the earliest efforts to formalise social work education in North America (Farber & Reitmeier, 2019), including Canada. In fact, Canadian social work programmes patterned their curriculum after that of their neighbouring American schools, and until 1973, the US Council of Social Work Education accredited social work education programmes in Canada. At that time, the Canadian Association for Social Work Education – Association Canadienne Pour La Formation en Travail Social (CASWE-ACFTS), founded in 1967, took over the accreditation of Canadian schools of social work. Currently the CASWE-ACFTS sets educational policy and standards for evaluating more than 40 social work educational programmes offered at bachelor's and master's levels. The purpose of accreditation, as stated by this body, includes the promoting continuous improvement of programmes and advocacy for programmes so that they can provide quality education and 'maintaining rigour of social work education to ensure that graduates are able to provide high quality social work services' (CASWE-ACFTS, 2020, p. 3).

As this chapter is being written, the Canadian Education Policy and Accreditation Standards (EPAS) are under review with some upcoming changes to the earlier standards (CASWE-ACFTS, 2014). However, items related to field education largely remain the same. Typical of traditional approaches to accreditation, the document focuses on inputs such as content, structure, and resources. In contrast, the innovative Educational Policy and Accreditation Standards of the

DOI: 10.4324/9781032164946-11

US Council on Social Work Education (CSWE, 2015a) uses an outcomes-oriented competency-based approach. This framework focuses on what students are able to do in practice and delineates a number of competencies that are defined holistically in terms of knowledge, values, skills, and cognitive and affective processes.

The Canadian EPAS recognises the critical and distinctive nature of field education and that it takes place in a practicum setting. An emphasis is placed on the integration of classroom content, such as theory with actual practice through field learning. Specifically, the field is viewed as the place where students are able 'to further develop, refine, and enhance the values, knowledge, and skills reflective of the core learning objectives' (CASWE-ACFTS , 2020, p. 17). These content objectives include:

- Professional identity;
- Engagement with individuals, families, groups, and communities through professional practice;
- Development of a professional practice;
- Colonialism and social work;
- Indigenous peoples and communities;
- Francophone peoples and communities;
- Equity and social justice;
- Values and ethics in professional practice;
- Research;
- Policy analysis and development; and
- Organisational and societal systems change.

Canadian accreditation standards further describe inputs such as prescribing the hours for field education, requiring at least 700 field practicum hours for students in undergraduate Bachelor of Social Work (BSW) programmes. Advanced-standing Master of Social Work (MSW) students – those students with a BSW degree from an accredited university – can complete a minimum of 450 field practicum hours, a thesis, or a memoire. The later products must 'provide an opportunity for the integration and demonstration of advanced social work skills in practice, and/or policy analysis and/or research' (CASWE-ACFTS, 2020, p. 16). Students who do not have a BSW degree can enter a two-year MSW programme and must complete a minimum of 900 practicum hours.

The accreditation standards also require schools to provide information about the structure and resources for field education. The standards recognise that the delivery of field education involves both educational pedagogical knowledge and approaches as well as administrative capability in the school to locate and sustain field placements. In this respect, the accreditation process examines whether a school has enough financial resources to provide personnel for a field office and can advocate within the host university to support the field programme. Attention is paid to the position of the field education director, ensuring their involvement in the programme's governance, recognising the uniqueness of the responsibilities they carry, and considering the nature of their workload so that they are able to fully manage and continuously improve the field programme. One of the main roles is to seek and support field instructors. Field instructors are largely social workers employed in social and health services who voluntarily take on the role of field instructor for students in their placements. While employing organisations must agree, typically, there is no official policy to readjust these social workers' workload. Schools are expected to provide orientation and support as well as continuing education for all field instructors so that they master the pedagogical and assessment responsibilities of their role.

Best Practices for Field Education: Theoretical and Empirical Contributions

Students enter social work programmes based on a desire to serve others in a range of roles and highly motivated to learn practice. They look to their university programmes to prepare them for professional practice. Education scholar Lee Shulman stated that education for the professions is different from traditional education in the disciplines. In professional programmes students learn in order to help others – 'they [students] must come to understand in order to act, and they must act in order to serve' (Shulman, 2005, p. 53). Shulman continues, noting that professional schools have the responsibility to socialise their students to their profession's fundamental ways of thinking, performing, and acting with integrity. In academic courses, students learn a great deal of knowledge about theoretical concepts, policies and programmes, values, research methods, and key findings. There is, however, less opportunity to learn the complex practice behaviours, skills, and techniques associated with particular intervention models.

Social work, from its early inception, has used the field practicum as the place where students learn the important ways in which relationships are developed with clients, assessments are conducted, collaborative goal setting and planning takes place, and interventions are offered. In the field, students also learn how to function in an organisational context, a central feature of social work, which is largely an agency-based profession. In the field setting, students learn to work with peers, team members from a range of professions, supervisors, and managers. Students are also expected to learn to integrate the conceptual and substantive content acquired in their courses and apply this content to the contingencies presented by a range of client situations. Canada is a highly diverse society, and it is in the field where students have the opportunity to examine the degree to which concepts and practices are universal or limited to particular social identity groups and communities. A long-standing tradition in social work education recognises that services are largely delivered through the 'self' of the social worker. The term 'professional use of self' refers to the way in which the personal style and characteristics of each social worker is displayed in the professional role (Brandell, 2004). Academic courses are increasingly focused on helping students use self-reflection to identify conscious and unconscious beliefs, biases, and assumptions that might ultimately influence the judgements, decisions, and assessments they make. It is, nevertheless, in the field – in interaction with actual clients and colleagues – that uncensored reactions are experienced on both an affective and cognitive level. It is through reflection that students have the opportunity for meaningful development of self-awareness, understanding, and creating a professional practice approach that is client-centred. These activities are stimulated by meeting this fundamental and challenging dynamic when practicing in 'the real world'.

Educational theorists and researchers, as well as research from neuroscience, provide important insights about learning with implications for field education. While this vast body of knowledge is beyond presentation in this chapter, the following discussion integrates key points from this literature to support the selection of best practices for quality field education.

Socio-emotional Relationship between Students and Field Instructors

Through the years, social work educators have used a number of theories to understand the dynamics of teaching and learning in field education. Adult learning theory and, more recently, neuroscience concepts and research support a long-standing practice principle that the relationship between the student and field instructor is the crucial factor in producing a positive learning experience for students. Adult learning theory, developed by Knowles (Knowles et al.,

2005), was embraced by social work educators since first described in Knowles (1972). A number of key concepts fit well with social work's humanistic, student-centred values and are still relevant in contemporary classrooms, simulation-based learning, and field education. Knowles' (1972) theory presented propositions about how adult learning differs from the ways in which children learn and the implications for teaching. Relevant to field education, Knowles (1972) pointed out that, when adults are learning new material, they bring their own self-concept and self-esteem issues into the learning situation. These aspects of self are heightened as they engage in field learning, encounter complex situations, and strive to achieve competence to effectively intervene. Hence, students in the field are likely to experience the state of 'not knowing' as highly uncomfortable; while motivated to learn, they become acutely aware of all they do not know. A paradox of learning in all professional internships is that students are expected to provide an effective service while they are learning how to do so. Individual reactions to the perception of one's incompetence vary from over confidence, to actively engaging in learning, to avoidance and withdrawal. That self-concept issues are highly involved in learning has implications for the type of relationship needed in the field instructor–student dyad, which must attend to the emotional dynamics that are provoked.

Another important concept relates to personal knowledge derived from past experiences (Knowles et al., 2005). Students do not come to the practicum as a blank slate. Rather, they have developed beliefs and attitudes based on experiences and lessons learned in families and communities. Additionally, many students have been impacted by marginalisation and oppression due to self-identity characteristics. This knowledge is both useful in understanding practice situations but also can limit an expanded view because it includes information that can be articulated and named and also operates in an implicit fashion, and out of awareness. For new learning to occur, there must be a safe enough space and place for reflection, critical thinking, and developing self-awareness.

With the explosion in knowledge from neuroscience social work, educators have become interested in learning how understanding the ways in which our brains work can contribute to more effective teaching practices in the classroom and in the field (Miehls & Applegate, 2014). Of interest is that many of the new insights are congruent with the practices engaged in as a result of earlier theorising, scholarship and research, and practice wisdom about social work field education. Some time-honoured approaches in social work field education can now claim support from empirically based neuroscience contributions (Thomas et al., 2019). The emphasis from these studies on the inter-relationships between mind, body, and brain, and relationships are compatible with social work's systemic and holistic perspective.

Cozolino, a leading theorist on learning and the brain, with Sprokay, stated, 'The brain is a social organ innately designed to learn through shared experiences' (Cozolino & Sprokay, 2006, p. 11). Another leading scholar in education, psychology, and neuroscience, Immordino-Yang, with Gotleib (2017), articulated that co-regulation and the interactive shaping of the psychobiological self occurs through education environments. These notions suggest the importance of the social environment in which education takes place. This includes a type of social relationship wherein the educator provides attunement, keen perception, and understanding of the past and current experiences of students. With such understanding, field instructors can provide a type of supportive environment that facilitates learning. When learners feel supported, neural circuits are activated so that neural plasticity – the brain's ability to reorganise itself by forming new neural connections – can occur. This reorganisation enables an examination of cognitive and affective processes, including questioning and reconsidering affective responses, assumptions, and biases. Such an activity provides space and opportunity for new ideas and responses to become internalised.

A supportive socio-emotional environment is also the foundation for relaxed attention, which is needed for new learning (Cozolino & Sprokay, 2006). Energy for learning is compromised when individuals are diverted in learning situations with preoccupations about their vulnerability and the need to defend or protect the self. New learning situations that are challenging can stimulate stress and anxiety. Field practicum is such a case, as students will be working with complex situations in which the concepts and empirical studies they have learned about in school may be too abstract or general to provide useful guides for practice. Researchers have noted the presence of anxiety in social work students in relation to the practicum (Gelman, 2004; Gelman & Lloyd, 2008; Rompf et al., 1993; Sun, 1999). Anxiety was related to students perceiving their own lack of knowledge, skill, or experience working in specialised settings and with clients from unfamiliar communities. Some students reported feeling helpless and demoralised in the face of client problems that elicited emotional dysregulation in themselves. The fear of making mistakes and that clients would lack confidence in students' ability to be helpful were other themes. In a review of literature on sources of and responses to students' anxiety, Baird (2016) notes that the student–field instructor relationship can be a source of anxiety or a place where emotional regulation can take place. In a study of emotional responses in the field, Litvack, Bogo, and Mishna (2010) found that instructors who normalised student anxiety served as a mitigating factor in students' emotional responses to difficult situations encountered with clients, teams, and the organisation. This study also found that a negative relationship with field instructors contributed to a feeling of vulnerability in students.

Porges has developed polyvagal theory (2011), which proposes that our autonomic nervous system is constantly scanning internal (our bodies) and external environments looking for threats and places of safety. It is, then, understandable that we would look to others to assist in emotional regulation to feel less threatened, calmer, and, hence, more able to learn. The field instructor–student relationship has long been seen as the crucible within which learning occurs (Bennet et al., 2012; Bogo, 2010, 2015; Finch et al., 2019). In part, this principle of supportive interaction parallels what we are attempting to teach students in their work with clients. For students to have the experience of such a relationship provides them with a role model for their work with clients, helps them to learn experientially what such a relationship can feel like, and how it can motivate and encourage new learning and change. As Bennett et al., (2012) have pointed out, when students are practicing and learning in field settings, it is not unusual for them to become overwhelmed with the challenges presented by client situations and the difficulty in learning to practice competencies. These states can exacerbate feelings about self-concept and contribute to anxiety. Drawing on attachment theory, a safe, respectful, non-judgemental relationship with a field instructor provides a place to refuel, much like a 'holding environment'.

As social workers are increasingly working in situations of diversity and difference, it is important for them to engage in self-awareness, critical thinking, and recognition of how their cognitive and affective processes may be interfering with their aims of learning and conducting a practice free of discriminatory attitudes (Lee & Kealy, 2018). The importance of a particular socio-emotional environment is crucial for such a challenging task; our beliefs may be unexamined and largely operate in an unconscious manner and elicit great discomfort when brought into awareness. An environment is needed that works toward producing enough safety and a sense of trustworthiness to explore uncomfortable thoughts and feelings. Such an environment is aspirational and not easily achieved. However, if field instructors can demonstrate self-awareness, openness to questioning their own attitudes and behaviours, and discuss and reflect on such issues with students, they provide a role model as well as an experience of a process that can be emulated with clients.

These perspectives reflect the long-standing importance of the educational relationship that lies at the centre of learning, growth, and change identified by early theorists of social work professional education, such as Reynolds, Towle, and Perlman (Farber & Reitmeier, 2019). Additionally, a large body of research exists on factors that students perceive to support positive field education and that field educators view as important. Previous reviews found the following characteristics (Bogo, 2005, 2015). The importance of an available and collaborative relationship with strong support and high expectations that students are actively involved in their own learning. Learning is enhanced in organisations that provide a positive environment, welcome and value students, and offer multiple opportunities to learn from staff other than the primary field instructor. Students vary in their level of competence and confidence based on factors such as previous social work-related experience, developmental stage of the student, and learning styles. Accordingly, field instructors vary the degree of structure and autonomy provided.

Reflective Mutual Dialogues

Educational theorists contribute to our understanding of the importance of stepping back from a learning experience and extracting principles that may be generalisable to similar situations. While Kolb's (1984) original model of the learning cycle has been somewhat modified over the years, the fundamental idea still holds merit. The model attends to the ways in which concrete experiences are used to promote new learning. A cycle involves both active and passive and concrete and abstract processes. Concrete experiences do not automatically turn into integrated and internalised schemas. Rather, a process of reflection is needed to examine and critically analyse observations that can lead to forming abstract generalisations. Finally, these new insights are tested in future interactions in similar circumstances. This approach resonates with that provided by Schön (1983, 1987), one of the most influential theorists on professional practice. Schön (1987) argues that because professionals are frequently confronted with situations of great complexity in which typical practices are not useful, practitioners engage in a process of reflection, both during and after an interaction, to arrive at innovative responses. Such reflections enable heightened awareness of dynamics such as how the practitioner was thinking and feeling about the situation and influences their judgements, decisions, and actions. This activity has the potential to create new approaches to similar situations. Of interest is extensive research on more than 20 professions that found that practitioners use both reflection and principles originating from knowledge and research to address puzzling situations confronted in practice (Cheetham & Chivers, 2005).

Again, one can see that early and enduring approaches to field education and professional development through using reflection are consistent with these propositions from learning theory (Farber & Reitmeier, 2019). Much of field education is delivered through mutual dialogues between student and field instructor on a range of topics. While the focus of such discussions is primarily educational, instructors are responsible for service delivery and, hence, must also attend to administrative issues and ensure that clients are receiving the help they need. Hence, there is likely to be some discussion of agency policy and procedures, and this can include critically examining the impact of macro issues on micro practice.

The educational focus has many aims. Typically, the literature on field education proposes that the field is where students learn to integrate theory and practice. While classroom courses can present concepts with examples drawn from practice, it is in the field that 'real situations' can be used to identify and examine the concepts students are learning. This approach, however, supposes that field instructors are knowledgeable about the school's curriculum. Given the expanding and rapidly changing nature of knowledge and evidence-based practice, this may not be the case. Students can be encouraged to share information they are learning in their courses and discuss how these concepts are, or are not, transferable to their practice in the agency setting. Importantly, all social workers have an explicit and implicit knowledge base which they use to guide their practice. When the practitioner is working from an identified practice model, it is important to provide readings and resources so that reflective discussions can draw upon concepts and principles from that approach. Because many practitioners develop their unique professional practice model over time, it is helpful to articulate key notions in that model so that students can understand how their field instructor conceptualises practice. This provides a common terminology and set of principles and models the construction of such a model, which is an important goal for students.

Reflection is linked to developing holistic competence in social work (Bogo, 2018). Holistic competence consists of two dimensions:

> one dimension, meta-competence, refers to higher order, overarching qualities and abilities of a conceptual, interpersonal, and personal/professional nature. This includes students' cognitive, critical, and self-reflective capacities. The second dimension, procedural competence, refers to performance and the ability to use procedures in various stages of the helping process and includes the ability for example, in direct practice, to form a collaborative relationship, to carry out an assessment, and to implement interventions with clients and systems.
>
> *(Bogo et al., 2013, p. 261)*

An approach for bringing together the dimensions contributing to this view of holistic competence is available in the 'Integration of Theory and Practice Loop Model', developed by Bogo and Vayda (1998) and further elaborated in Bogo (2010, 2018). A loop portrays a process model that is ongoing and iterative, incorporating the activities of thinking, feeling, and acting. Similar to Kolb's model, and relevant to field learning, the process begins with accessing practice data which the student provides – preferably through direct observation or video recordings, although written records and verbal accounts are also used. Together, the field instructor and student examine the student's personal cognitive and affective reactions and reflections, which are used to link to the professional knowledge base – the concepts discussed above. Factors at the societal, organisational, interpersonal, and personal level are considered. These various themes are then brought together to capture new learning and plan for the next professional response. Finally, following the intervention, an evaluative conversation is held to determine the impact of the student's interaction with the client situation and to extract any principles that can be generalised for further practice.

Observation, Reflection, and Feedback

Bandura developed social learning theory, stating that new behaviours can be acquired by observation and imitation of others (Bandura, 1977, 1986). The cognitive processes include focusing attention on what is important, remembering that behaviour, modelling one's own behaviour on that which was observed, and being motivated to perform that behaviour. Cognitive educational theorists Schenck and Cruickshank (2015) and cognitive load theorist Sweller (1994) similarly point out that learning – and we would add especially in complex and potentially overwhelming field settings – presents a multitude of overwhelming stimuli. Students benefit from instructors who help students distinguish between what is important to observe and that which can be relegated to the side. Concepts, principles, and behaviours that are salient offer perspectives to frame the unit of attention. Importantly implicit cognitive processes engaged in by experienced practitioners need to be made explicit so that students can, in turn, develop the habits of thinking characteristic of their profession (Taylor & Care, 1999). Thus, opportunities to observe experienced social workers in action, followed by dialogues that link practice to underlying knowledge, begin to help students understand and integrate theory and action. This is similar to the stages of concrete experience, reflective observation, and abstract conceptualisation in Kolb's (1984) experiential learning cycle.

While observation of others is critical, providing numerous opportunities to practice is the essence of field education. As in learning any new activity, it is repetitious practice that enables one to move beyond a beginning or novice status. Ericsson's (2004) long-standing programme of research on expertise demonstated that it is focused and deliberate practice that leads to expertise. The notion of deliberate practice involves a number of points. Students need to have many practice events in order to engage in a cognitive process in which new learnings become understandable and personally meaningful, make sense, and become integrated into their professional self (Schenck & Cruickshank, 2015). This can occur through active engagement with relevant situations, through simulation (Katz et al., 2014), but, most importantly, through situations presented in field settings. Similar to the need for focus when observing others, for learning and improvement to occur, field instructors need to help students focus on what they need to learn. Repetitively doing tasks that one is proficient at does not engender new learning. Rather, it is receiving feedback on what needs improvement that will lead to a deliberate attempt to master new competencies. Hence, it is important for field instructors to observe students' practice and provide limited, specific feedback that students can use in their next interactions with the practice situation.

A study of students' reactions to feedback on their practice in simulation-based learning provides useful guidelines that pertain to feedback given in the field (Kourgiantakis et al., 2019). Following an innovative learning experience in which students took turns interviewing a simulated client and receiving feedback from their peers, a field instructor, the workshop instructor, and the simulated client, they provided written responses to a set of questions designed to elicit aspects of holistic competence (Kourgiantakis et al., 2019). Students reported that feedback enhanced their knowledge of key concepts being taught, improved their skills, and helped them to develop better professional judgement involving more critial thinking about assumptions made about the client situations and about a range of possible interventions. Students also noted that feedback increased self-awareness, highlighting issues that students may have overlooked and also validating their own perceptions. It appears that feedback serves an integrative function – bringing together the dimensions of the use of knowledge, skills, and cognitive and affective processes in the service of carrying out complex behaviors needed for practice. Such typical complex practices include relationship development and sustainment, arriving at a joint assessment and plan and some aspects of intervention.

Of importance to this discussion is students' perceptions of what aspects of feedback facilitated learning (Kourgiantakis et al., 2019). Specific and concrete feedback was the most helpful, especially when it included possible alternative responses. In contrast, seen as not useful, were abstract, vague, or general positive comments. It was the constructive feedback that students viewed as contributing to learning. Students spoke of the importance of timely, immediate feedback given in an empathic and warm manner. For field instructors, this means that direct observation followed by feedback will likely have the most impact. While review of video recordings has been recommended for field instruction, some use of direct observation, followed by feedback, provides the immediacy that will probably produce increased learning. We recognise, however, that given time constraints for instructor input in field education, this may not be possible in a consistent way.

As discussed earlier, the self of the student is highly engaged when learning to practice a new profession. Feedback that is not felt as positive can constitute a blow to self-esteem and self-confidence. While students may state that they welcome constructive feedback (as noted in the study above), their emotional response may be one that is deflating. The importance of the field instructor–student relationship is underscored. Reassurance from the field instructor regarding their commitment to help the student learn needed competencies is important at this juncture. Optimally, the relationship is experienced as a holding environment with support and encouragement for the student to stay involved and commited to learning.

Drawing again on insights from neuroscience, the goal is to support 'a moderate state of arousal' (Cozolino & Sprokay, 2006, p. 13); that which is not under-stimulated or so stressful as to distract. The goal is 'a state of high attention but without the debilitating anxiety' (p. 14). Recommended is a 'teacher's supportive caring, encouragement, and enthusiasm balanced with an appropriate level of challenge' (p. 14). Theoretically, this stance should undercut free-floating anxiety, which distracts from learning, as energy is directed to protecting oneself from emotional dysregulation connected to feelings of incompetence. An optimal level of anxiety can provide a spark for learning and, with directed focus, offers students a productive way to achieve learning goals.

In summary, ideal field education practices occur in positive and supportive environments provided by the organisation and team. The crucible for field education is the field instructor–student relationship; one that provides an attuned, understanding stance while also expecting students' high engagement in learning directed at reaching expectations. Aimed at developing holistic competence, observations of actual practice provide the data for feedback and for reflective discussions which link theory and practice and examine cognitive and affective processes. The later engenders self-awareness, which is so crucial for developing the personal/professional self. In contemporary diverse societies, understanding one's own assumptions and beliefs, the way they impact practice decisions and behaviors, and developing strategies for emotional self-regulation are all pivotal elements of social work practice.

Challenges in the Current Canadian Context

The previous section highlights empirical studies that have illuminated a number of best practices for field education. Likely, there have been more studies on this component of social work curriculum than any other. Moreover, these practices are consistent with concepts from selected learning theories, insights from neuroscience research, and practice wisdom regarding field education. It is disheartening, therefore, to hear of the many current obstacles that are preventing social work programmes and their field instructors from implementing these strategies. The following discussion highlighting barriers and challenges are based on studies conducted in Canada (Ayala et al., 2018a, 2018b; Tam et al., 2018) and issues echoed in studies from other countries.

In 2013, field coordinators signalled that a crisis in providing quality field education existed (Ayala et al., 2018a). The major issue identified was the scarcity of placements, attributed to neoliberal forces resulting in diminished resources in agencies. This, in turn, led to higher and more complex workloads for social workers with less time to provide education. When agencies are not committed to field education, the extra work involved in having a student falls on individual social workers who are already coping with more demands. Taking on a student appears too daunting.

Universities in Canada have also been subjected to budget cutbacks. Increases in the number of social work programmes and more enrolments in existing programmes have emerged as a solution (Regehr, 2013). With increased numbers of students requiring practicum, and with decreased agency resources to provide them, this conundrum appears to have become exacerbated with each passing year, producing saturation (Ayala et al., 2018b). The presence and expansion of online programmes across the country also means that field coordinators may often find themselves competing with universities in distant locations for practicum in their own communities. Lack of consultation between university administrators (who decide on expansion of student enrolment) and field coordinators (who are knowledgeable about the capacity of their community agencies to provide field practicum) is highly problematic. An additional stressor identified is the increased emphasis on experiential learning and field experiences in a number of disciplines as well as competition for practicum with related human service professional programmes.

The Canadian circumstance mirrors that of other countries. For example, in the US a field summit was convened in 2014 by the CSWE to respond to member schools' concerns about the gap between rhetoric and reality (CSWE, 2015b). Specifically, the EPAS in 2008 identified field education as the signature pedagogy of social work, the place where students are socialised to the fundamental ways of thinking, feeling, and behaving as a social worker (CSWE, 2008). To achieve this goal, field education is expected to be 'systematically designed, supervised, coordinated, and evaluated based on criteria by which students demonstrate the Social Work Competencies' (CSWE, 2008, p. 8) This statement was challenged because while research has demonstrated many of the crucial teaching approaches presented above, other studies found that actually implementing those practices in a systematic and pervasive manner was absent (Wayne et al., 2010). This sentiment is reflected in an aptly titled paper from New Zealand, 'Feeling lucky: The serendipitous nature of field education' (Hay et al., 2019). Students reported great variation and irregularity in the supervision they received in the placement and considered themselves lucky if they received instruction that met their expectations and those from the schools' programme. The U.S. field summit was also concerned with a lack of placements (CSWE, 2015b). In an analysis of articles published in the U.S.-based online journal *Field Educator*, Gushwa and Harriman (2019) highlight the challenges of a limited bank of quality field placements and adequate time for student supervision. They comment that 'challenges have increased markedly over a relatively brief period of time' (p. 17). Finally, researchers in Australia characterise locating quality field settings as a challenge, as they occur in a 'competitive and volatile health and human service sector' (Cleak & Zuchowski, 2019, p. 32). As in Canada, they note that the higher education system incentivised expansion of health-related programmes with expansion not only in numbers of students in existing programmes but also created more distance education programmes in which students also need field education experiences.

At a micro level, Tam, Brown, Paz, Birnbaum, and Kwok (2018) surveyed field instructors in two Canadian provinces regarding the barriers and challenges they faced in taking on students. Respondents valued students who were mature, dedicated, caring, and motivated. On the other hand, field instructors questioned university admissions criteria whereby students were admitted who presented challenges in learning as a result of personality style and attitude toward receiving feedback, past trauma, and lack of self-awareness. Similarly, when students' values conflicted with those of the profession and resulted in questionable decisions, judgements, and ethics, this posed a difficulty for field instructors. Students who lacked adequate attainment of knowledge and skills meant field instructors needed to teach foundational material. This concern was also identified at the US field summit (CSWE, 2015b) that recommended schools take on more of the responsibility for teaching and assessing students' competence, especially prior to entry into the field.

In the Canadian study, Tam et al., (2018) found important facilitators of quality field education included positive interactions and support from school faculty field liaisons and sufficient training for field instructors. Challenges related to a lack of support, unclear expectations for student learning and evaluation, and reluctance to fail a student. With increased university expectations that tenure-track faculty demonstrate productivity in research and publication, many Canadian social work programmes have hired adjunct instructors to act as field liaisons. This arrangement can support student learning and field instructors. However, as these personnel typically are not involved in curriculum planning and may not be highly conversant with the material students are learning, the goal of integrating theory and practice becomes more elusive.

Recommendations

Field education currently takes place in a complex context, producing multi-faceted issues that pose a challenge to quality field education. As we consider possible responses, it is useful to point out what can be done at various levels. At the micro level, McKee, Perlman, and Muskat (2015) propose changing the culture of the profession to plant the seed in current students, so they will be committed to socialise and educate future generations of social workers. They propose a number of strategies including field liaisons regularly discussing this commitment with students, a panel of recent graduates who are field instructors presents their experiences to students who are close to graduation, a full-day seminar on field education held close to the end of the programme, a course in the MSW programme on field education and staff supervision, and, where possible, final-year MSW students providing supervision to beginning BSW students. The later would be supervised by the MSW student's field instructor.

Schools can provide increased opportunities for students to learn practice through the use of simulation (Bogo et al., 2014). With more preparation with basic and foundational knowledge and skills, students would be better prepared to engage in field learning when they begin their practicum. Preparation can include in class and supplementary activities (Kougiantakis et al., 2019). When students are assessed in preparatory courses through competency evaluations conducted with the 'Objective Standardized Clinical Examination adapted for Social Work' (OSCE-SW; Bogo et al., 2014), results can be shared with field instructors. This occurred in one Canadian school, and field instructors responded to questions about the usefulness of this approach. They stated that this evaluation provided baseline information about student competence and was used to identify field learning goals which could be incorporated in the field learning contract (Bogo et al., 2017). Students' openness in discussing the evaluation led to early and active engagement with the field instructor.

Schools can also use the field seminar to more actively teach practice competence and help students to integrate theory and practice (Wayne et al., 2010). Field coordinators have noted a disconnect between the language used in schools and that used within agencies (Bogo & Sewell, 2019). In classroom courses, instructors can help students articulate their knowledge and skills in a way that is more easily understood by the field instructor.

Agencies can include offering field education in social workers' job descriptions and use this criterion in hiring interviews and performance appraisals. As an example, Perlman (2016) developed a social work education standard in a large metropolitan health sciences centre employing 72 social workers. The standard states, 'Staff are expected to offer an MSW practicum a minimum of once every two years if it is undertaken in a rotational model, or once every three years if it is the duration of a full placement' (p. 4). University-affiliated hospitals in Canada expect involvement in teaching in medicine and in many other allied health professions. It is imperative that social work professionals are included in academic health sciences commitment to education.

At the local and regional mezzo level, professional regulatory bodies can also promote field education when they accept providing education for students for a required continuing education credit. While seminars, workshops, and presentations to train social workers for their educational role are generally recognised, the actual teaching is not counted. It is an old adage that the best way to learn is to teach. The essence of this idea is that one has to incorporate and then retrieve information to be taught, thus reinforcing the teachers' understanding of the material (Koh et al., 2018). Teaching in the field contributes to further professional development for social work.

Additionally, at the mezzo level, the Canadian study (Ayala et al., 2018b) and the US Field Summit Report (CSWE, 2015b) recommend numerous initiatives in which local, regional, and national field coordinators advocate, coordinate, and initiate discussions and innovations related to field education. Suggestions also include strategic collaborations across the educational institution and with related disciplines and professions.

An important recommendation from both sources is that the field office and community partners work together to assess capacity when decisions about enrolment are made. Instructive in this regard is the experience in England, where the government provided funds for schools and the local authorities – the main employers of social workers – to form partnerships (Baginsky et al., 2019). The aim was to make sure that educational programmes met the needs of the actual employers. One aspect of the collaboration was working together on the number of students to be admitted in light of the local workforce plan and the number of field practicums that could be provided. Baginsky et al. (2019) report on the controversies and challenges in this initiative. Reviewing previous similar collaborations, they note that such partnerships often do not succeed because of the pilot nature of the projects and lack of continuing financial support. They concluded, however, that, at this point in time, most of the partnerships they studied were addressing the balance between recruitment and practicum availability.

In Canada, there are no documented examples of such recent initiatives. Bogo and Globerman (1999) studied inter-organisational relationships between schools and agencies in an earlier era of additional resources and when social work field instruction was viewed as a mark of one's expertise in practice and readiness to teach. Inter-organisational factors contributing to effective ongoing relationships included commitment to education, resources and supports, effective interpersonal relationships, and collaboration and reciprocity. Strong institutional leadership from the practice organisation and the social work programme resulted in 20 organisations, called Teaching Centres, providing practicum for 50% of the school's students at that time.

At a macro level, a strong recommendation that has been made through the years regards the necessity of involving the sector leadership in conceiving a systematic approach to produce the next generation of social workers. Social service and health organisations need competent practitioners and rely on university educational programmes to provide this workforce. And yet, organisations rarely enter into permanent partnerships to ensure this outcome. Rather, field coordinators (with limited power in the university) must develop and use their influence to persuade front-line social workers (with limited power in the agency settings) to agree to take a student. Clearly, this is a fragile approach to planning and preparing practitioners. Deans and directors of social work programmes need to engage with agency directors in social service and health organisations, as well as government agencies and funders, to address this issue. Regulatory bodies, professional associations, and national, regional, and local sector-specific organisations should also be involved in addressing this central component of stable ways of educating and preparing an effective social work workforce. Unfortunately, efforts in Canada in the past to bring together these organisations to collaborate on defining the profession and preparing for the future have not resulted in effective outcomes. A promising initiative occurred in June 2016. Three national social work organisations, the CASW, the CASWE-ACFTS , and the Canadian Council of Social Work Regulators (CCSWR-CCORTS), signed a historic 'Memorandum of Understanding' 'to foster communication, connection and collaboration among these three pillars of the profession' (CASWE-ACFTS, 2016). The aspiration was to address shared issues of concern with one voice, thus providing strong representation of the social work profession in Canada. To date, however, it does not appear that there has been any progress on the goals related to the crucial connection between field practicum, preparing the next generation of social workers, and the profession.

Canadian Responses to Field Education in the Face of a Pandemic

At the time of writing this chapter, the world is confronting the COVID-19 pandemic. In Canada, students are in the last quarter of their field practicum. The CASWE-ACFTS issued the following statement:

> all field education placements [must] be suspended and/or moved to Remote Learning Plans (RLP) effective March 20, 2020 until further notice. Field placements that do not involve community contact and that meet the criteria set out by university and local health authorities (e.g., research placements that can be carried out from home) may be exempted.

The statement also addresses the requirement of specific hours for field education:

1. Students who have completed 75% of the required placement hours to a satisfactory level will be evaluated as having met the field placement requirements;
2. For students who have completed between 60% and 74% of required placement hours to a satisfactory level, an RLP must be developed, implemented, and submitted for review and approval by the field education coordinator, manager, director, or any other such person as determined by the programme, in order to be evaluated as meeting the field placement requirements;
3. Students who have completed less than 60% of the required placement hours will be evaluated as not having completed the field placement requirements. Their placement hours will be recognised and brought forward to a future field placement once the suspension is lifted.

This unusual crisis situation has led field coordinators to seek creative ways for students to develop an RLP. LISTSERVs in North America have seen many suggestions passed between those responsible for field education. Because some Canadian field coordinators participate on LISTSERVs, sponsored by the US CSWE with American field counterparts, a plethora of online resources have been made available to Canadian schools and students. One can see that there are a wide range of accessible resources to augment and support learning for field practice.

Prior to this crisis, the national professional association, Canadian Association of Social Workers – Association Canadienne des Travailleuses et Travailleurs Sociaux (CASW-ACTS), has not been actively involved in field education. This association has a large bank of excellent webinars on a wide range of professional topics. Typically, these educational materials are available only to members of the provincial associations who, in turn, are members of the Canadian association (not all provinces are members). During the COVID-19 pandemic, the association made this rich resource bank of excellent webinars available to all schools of social work and their students. This collaboration during a crisis provides an example of the benefits of working together.

During the pandemic, the most difficult challenge is presented by the fact that field learning is based on being in a setting and interacting with clients, the field instructor, and staff. During this time, there has been a pervasive use of technology to connect with clients, and because the emphasis in field education has typically been on in-person interaction, the use of digital technology-assisted approaches is now considered an acceptable method for service and learning. Students must be aware of privacy, confidentiality, and security issues when communicating via telephone or information and communication technologies (ICT). If they have not learned this approach in courses, the field setting, or workshops, then schools and agencies need to develop and share this information before students embark on using this approach. Studies have shown that while there are many positives, including access and efficiency, there are also many challenges in using the wide range of ICTs, such as smartphones, social media, email (Mishna et al., 2014; Mishna et al., 2012). Some challenges include the lack of agency policy and guidelines or that they are too general and vague, relationship issues, and setting appropriate boundaries. These complex issues are not easily learned quickly in a crisis and without the benefit of knowledgeable instructor's guidance.

In addition to direct contact with clients, students are also involved in many activities in the field that can still take place remotely. These involve, where secure servers exist, writing case notes and assessments, participating in team and staff meetings, and interacting with field instructors. Organisational materials related to disruptions in service can be reviewed and critically examined with recommendations developed. Educational material for clients can be located or developed. Given the current crisis, it is likely that accreditation bodies and field educators will not only develop strategies for the short term but also engage in research and consultation to create long-term policies and procedures.

Another potential avenue for developing practice skills during this extraordinary time is simulation-based learning (SBL). SBL has increasingly been used in Canadian schools of social work to prepare for and augment students' development of competence in direct practice (Bogo et al., 2014). Stimulated by the research and development at the Factor-Inwentash Faculty of Social Work, University of Toronto former doctoral students have brought SBL to their appointments as faculty members in schools throughout the country (https://socialwork.utoronto.ca/simulation-learning/). While SBL with standardised clients may be considered as a way to replace part of, or supplement, field learning, it can never substitute for the authenticity of learning to practice with actual clients.

Conclusion

In common with social work education internationally, social work education in Canada has always prized learning to practice in real, authentic, community-based settings. The role of the field instructor is valued and seen as evidence of a practitioner's advanced knowledge and skill. Increasingly, over the past 30 years in Canada, similar to the US, Australia, and New Zealand, schools have faced a plethora of challenges to securing and maintaining stable field education sites and qualified, committed social workers as field instructors. Ironically, this situation has developed at the same time that theorising and empirical studies have illuminated the key processes in promoting effective learning for practice. Given the worldwide pandemic in 2020, as we write this chapter, Canadian schools are scrambling to figure out how to continue to offer this pivotal aspect of learning to practice. This highlights the importance of ongoing collaboration, advocacy, and work at the micro, mezzo, and macro levels to support field educators, coordinators, and agencies to ensure the preparation of competent social work practitioners. The future is uncertain at the very moment when we see the need for well-trained professionals to respond effectively to the health and mental health issues that threaten the well-being of populations.

References

Ayala, J., Drolet, J., Fulton, A., Hewson, J., Letkemann, L., Baynton, M., ... Schweizer, E. (2018a). Field education in crisis: Experiences of field education coordinators in Canada. *Social Work Education, 37*, 281–293.

Ayala, J., Drolet, J., Fulton, A., Hewson, J., Letkemann, L., Baynton, M., ... Schweizer, E. (2018b). Restructuring social work field education in 21st century Canada: From crisis management to sustainability. *Canadian Social Work Review, 35*, 45–65. DOI: 10.7202/1058479ar

Baginsky, M., Manthorpe, J., & Hickman, B. (2019). Social work teaching partnerships: A discussion paper. *Social Work Education, 38*, 968–982. DOI: 10.1080/02615479.2019.1616685

Baird, S. L. (2016). Conceptualizing anxiety among social work students: Implications for social work education. *Social Work Education, 35*, 719–732. DOI: 10.1080/02615479.2016.1184639

Bandura, A. (1977). *Social learning theory*. Englewood Cliffs, NJ: Prentice Hall.

Bandura, A. (1986). *Social foundations of thought and action: A social cognitive theory*. Englewood Cliffs, NJ: Prentice-Hall.

Bennet, S., Mohr, J., Deal, K. H., & Hwang, J. (2012). Supervisor attachment, supervisory working alliance, and affect in social work field instruction. *Research on Social Work Practice, 23*, 199–209. DOI: 10.1177/1049731512468492

Bogo, M. (2005). Field instruction in social work: A review of the research literature 1999–2005. *The Clinical Supervisor, 24*, 163–193.

Bogo, M. (2010). *Achieving competence in social work through field education*. Toronto, ON: University of Toronto Press.

Bogo, M. (2015). Field education for clinical social work practice: Best practices and contemporary challenges. *Clinical Social Work Journal, 43*, 317–324. DOI: 10.1007/s10615-015-0526-5

Bogo, M. (2018). *Social work practice: Integrating concepts, processes, & skills* (2nd ed.). New York, NY: Columbia University Press.

Bogo, M., & Globerman, J. (1999). Interorganizational relationships between schools of social work and field agencies: Testing a framework for analysis. *Journal of Social Work Education, 35*, 265–274.

Bogo, M., Katz, E., Regehr, C., Logie, C., Mylopoulos, M., & Tufford, L. (2013). Toward understanding meta-competence: An analysis of students' reflections on their simulated interviews. *Social Work Education, 32*, 259–273. DOI: 10.1080/02615479.2012.738662

Bogo, M., Lee, B., McKee, E., Ramjattan, R., & Baird, S., L. (2017). Bridging class and field: Field instructors' and liaisons' reactions to information about students' baseline performance derived from simulated interviews *Journal of Social Work Education, 53*, 580–594. DOI: 10.1080/10437797.2017.1283269

Bogo, M., Rawlings, M., Katz, E., & Logie, C. (2014). *Using simulation in assessment and teaching: OSCE adapted for social work*. Alexandria, VA: Council on Social Work Education.

Bogo, M., & Sewell, K. (2019). Beyond the 'crisis' in field education: Considering recent literature and forming recommendations. *CSWE 64th Annual Program Meeting*. Denver, CO.

Bogo, M., & Vayda, E. (1998). *The practice of field instruction in social work: Theory and process*. Toronto, ON: University of Toronto Press and Columbia University Press.

Brandell, J. R. (2004). *Psychodynamic social work*. New York, NY: Columbia University Press.

CASWE-ACFTS. (2014). *Standards for accreditation for Canadian social work education*. Ottawa, ON: Canadian Association for Social Work Education.

CASWE-ACFTS. (2016). Memorandum of agreement. Retrieved from https://caswe-acfts.ca/the-three-pillars-of-social-work-sign-historic-agreement/ March 31, 2018.

CASWE-ACFTS. (2020). *Proposed educational policies and standards for accreditation for Canadian social work education*. Ottawa, ON: Canadian Association for Social Work Education.

Cheetham, G., & Chivers, G. (2005). *Professions, competence and informal learning*. Cheltenham, UK: Edward Elgar.

Cleak, H., & Zuchowski, I. (2019). Empirical support and considerations for social work supervision of students in alternative placement models. *Clinical Social Work Journal, 47*, 32–42.

Cozolino, L., & Sprokay, S. (2006). Neuroscience and adult learning. *New Directions for Adult and Continuing Education, 110*, 11–18.

CSWE. (2015a). *Education policy and accreditation standards (EPAS).* Alexandria, VA: CSWE.

CSWE. (2015b). *Report of the CSWE summit on field education.* Alexandria, VA: CSWE.

CSWE. (2008). *Educational policy and accreditation standards.* Alexandria, VA: CSWE.

Ericsson, K. A. (2004). Deliberate practice and the acquisition and maintenance of expert performance in medicine and related domains. *Academic Medicine, 79*, 570–581.

Farber, N., & Reitmeier, M. C. (2019). (Re) Capturing the wisdom of our tradition: The importance of Reynols and Towle in contemporary social work education. *Clinical Social Work Journal, 47*, 5–16.

Finch, J. B., Wiliams, O. F., Mondros, J. B., & Franks, C. L. (2019). *Learning to teach, teaching to learn* (3rd ed.). Alexandria, VA: Council on Social Work Education.

Gelman, C. R. (2004). Anxiety experienced by foundation-year MSW students entering field placement: Implications for admissions, curriculum, and field education. *Journal of Social Work Education, 40*, 39–54.

Gelman, C. R., & Lloyd, C. M. (2008). Field notes-pre-placement anxiety among foundation-year MSW students: A follow-up study. *Journal of Social Work Education, 44*, 173–183.

Gushwa, M., & Harriman, K. (2019). Paddling against the tide: Contemporary challenges in field education. *Clinical Social Work Journal, 47*, 17–22. DOI: 10.1007/s10615-018-0668-3

Hay, K., Maidment, J., Ballantyne, N., Beddoe, L., & Walker, S. (2019). Feeling lucky: The serendipitous nature of field education. *Clinical Social Work Journal, 47*, 23–31.

Immordino-Yang, M. H., & Gotlieb, R. (2017). Embodied brains, social minds, cultural meaning: Integrating neuroscientific educational research on social-affective development. *American Educational Research Journal, 54*(1S), 344S–367S.

Katz, E., Tufford, L., Bogo, M., & Regehr, C. (2014). Illuminating students' pre-practicum conceptual and emotional states: Implications for field education. *Journal of Teaching in Social Work, 34*, 96–108. DOI: 10.1080/08841233.2013.868391

Knowles, M. S. (1972). Innovations in teaching styles and approaches based upon adult learning. *Journal of Social Work Education, 8*, 32–39.

Knowles, M. S., Halston, E. F., & Swanson, R. A. (2005). *The adult learner. The definitive classic in adult education and human resource development* (6th ed.). Boston, MA: Elsevier.

Koh, A. W. L., Lee, S. C., & Lim, S. W. H. (2018). The learning benefits of teaching: A retrieval practice hypothesis. *Applied Cognitive Psychology, 32*, 401–410. DOI: 10.1002/acp.3410

Kolb, D. A. (1984). *Experiential learning: Experience as the source of learning and development.* Englewood Cliffs, NJ: Prentice Hall.

Kourgiantakis, T., Bogo, M., & Sewell, K. (2019). Practice Fridays: Using simulation to develop holistic competence. *Journal of Social Work Education, 55*, 551–564. DOI: 10.1080/10437797.2018.1548989

Kourgiantakis, T., Sewell, K., & Bogo, M. (2019). The importance of feedback in preparing social work students for field education. *Clinical Social Work Journal, 47*, 124–133. DOI: 10.1007/s10615-018-0671-8

Lee, E., & Kealy, D. (2018). Developing a working model of cross-cultural supervision: A competence and alliance-based framework. *Clinical Social Work Journal, 46*, 310–320. DOI: 10.1007s10615-018-4

Litvack, A., Bogo, M., & Mishna, F. (2010). Understanding the emotional impact of field experiences on MSW students. *Journal of Social Work Education, 46*, 227–243.

McKee, E., Perlman, I., & Muskat, T. (2015). Students today, educators tomorrow: Shaping the social work curriculum to enhance field education. *Field Educator, 5*, 1–6.

Miehls, D., & Applegate, J. (2014). Introduction to neurobiology and clinical work. *Smith College Studies in Social Work, 84*, 145–156.

Mishna, F., Bogo, M., Root, J., & Fantus, S. (2014). Here to stay: Cyber communication as a complement in social work practice. *Families in Society, 95*, 179–186. DOI: 10.1606/1044-3894.2014.95.23

Mishna, F., Bogo, M., Root, J., Sawyer, J. L., & Khoury-Kassabri, M. (2012). 'It just crept in': The digital age and implications for social work practice. *Clinical Social Work Journal, 40*, 277–286. DOI: 10.1007/s10615-012-0383-4

Perlman, I. (2016). To educate students or not to educate students, that is no longer the question: An innovative approach to building professional commitment to social work field education. *Field Educator, 6*, 1–10.

Porges, S. W. (2011). *The polyvagal theory: Neurophysiological foundations of emotions, attachment, communication, and self-regulation.* New York: WW Norton & Company.

Regehr, C. (2013). Trends in higher education in Canada and implications for social work education. *Social Work Education, 32*, 700–714. DOI: 10.1080/02615479.2013.785798

Rompf, E. L., Royse, D., & Shooper, S. S. (1993). Anxiety preceding field work: What students worry about. *Journal of Teaching in Social Work*, 7, 81–95.

Schenck, J., & Cruickshank, J. (2015). Evolving Kolb: Experiential education in the age of neuroscience. *Journal of Experiential Education, 38*, 73–95.

Schön, D. (1983). *The reflective practitioner: How professionals think in action*. London, UK: Temple Smith.

Schön, D. (1987). *Educating the reflective practitioner*. San Francisco, CA: Jossey-Bass.

Sun, A. (1999). Issues BSW interns experience in their first semester's practicum. *The Clinical Supervisor, 18*, 105–123.

Sweller, J. (1994). Cognitive load theory, learning difficulty, and instructional design. *Learning and Instruction, 4*, 293–312.

Tam, D. M.Y., Brown, A., Paz, E., Birnbaum, R., & Kwok, S. M. (2018). Challenges faced by Canadian social work field instructors in baccalaureate field supervision. *Journal of Teaching in Social Work, 38*, 398–416.

Taylor, T. K., & Care, W. D. (1999). Nursing education as cognitive apprenticeship: A framework for clinical education. *Nurse Education, 24*, 31–36.

Thomas, M. S. C., Ansari, D., & Knowland, V. C. P. (2019). Annual research review: Educational neuroscience: Progress and prospects. *The Journal of Child Psychology and Psychiatry*, 60(4), 477–492. DOI: 10.1111/jcpp.12973

Wayne, J., Bogo, M., & Raskin, M. (2010). Field education as the signature pedagogy of social work education. *Journal of Social Work Education, 46*, 327–339.

9

Integrated and Holistic Education for Social Work

The Special Place of Field Education

Naomi B. Farber, Mariah Moran, and Steven Wahle

> The vestibule of learning is not to be entered carelessly or with muddy shoes. Beginners in social work do not need supervisors to make them aware of this. If they assume that they have only to learn some theories and memorize a few formulas for good practice, they are soon undeceived by the vital, dynamic quality of what they learn. It is life itself, often in the raw, which they encounter and to which they must make an adjustment before they can help others.
>
> (Reynolds 1942; 1985, p. 214)

The field practicum is the educational context in which students encounter most directly 'life itself'. Field education has been an integral part of preparing social workers for professional practice since educational programmes in the United States became formally aligned with institutions of higher learning in the early years of the twentieth century. The historically unquestioned importance of field learning was acknowledged by the Council on Social Work Education (C.S.W.E.) in elevating it to the status of the profession's 'signature pedagogy' (C.S.W.E., 2008). However, as accreditation standards, institutional environments within higher education, and the landscape of social work practice have all steadily changed throughout the history of the profession, the quality of field education often is compromised in ways that threaten students' development (Teigiser, 2009). Such compromises inevitably threaten the quality of services that social workers provide to clients.

This chapter examines selected continuing issues in American social work education that have significant impact on the fieldwork component. In responding to these fundamental issues over time, we have discarded valuable earlier principles whose loss diminishes social work education, hence the profession. Here, we identify seminal insights about the overall purposes and nature of social work education that offer direction for improving field education. Specifically, we posit that field education should be understood as one of three analytically distinct but functionally integrated aspects of a conceptually coherent process based on explicit attention to the complex and individual nature of students' development. This framework integrates Bertha Reynolds's (1942) concepts regarding the 'whole person' who learns with Charlotte Towle's (1954) analysis that places field education at the centre of more distal but inextricably unified

DOI: 10.4324/9781032164946-12

classroom and administrative levels, forming concentric circles of an organic model of social work education. Drawing on the insights of these influential educational scholars, the proposed framework: (1) identifies core developmental stages, (2) identifies levels constituting the institutional environment of professional social work education, and (3) provides examples of how the institutional levels should function to enhance professional development of students.

Background

Several years prior to Abraham Flexner's momentous assertion in 1915 that social work did not meet his criteria for being a profession, Mary Richmond, then executive secretary of the Charity Organization Society in Baltimore, decried the lack of formal training of 'charity workers' (Flexner, 1915). In 1897, she observed that,

> In these days of specialization, when we train cooks, our apothecaries, our engineers, our librarians, our nurses—when, in fact, there is a training school for almost every form of skilled service—we have yet to establish our first training school for charity workers, or, as I prefer to call it, 'Training School in Applied Philanthropy'.
>
> *(Meier, 1954, p. 7)*

Richmond argued that the transformation of applied philanthropy into a bona fide profession required students to be formally educated in schools where, 'emphasis is to be put on practical work rather than academic requirements' (Meier, 1954, p. 7), through close connections with both public and private charities, a view that was shared by other leaders.

Despite widespread commitment to an academic foundation for professional education, it was not clear what the model should be. Thus, for example, the founders of the New York School of Philanthropy faced '…the problem, in its incipience, as to whether the School should derive its function and the content of its curriculum from the universities or from the social agencies' (Meier, 1954, p. 32). The vision of academic and agency collaboration that resulted in the school's affiliation with Columbia University also guided the early development of other leading schools such as Simmons in partnership with Harvard University and the Chicago School of Civics and Philanthropy at the University of Chicago. While each school of social work developed a particular relationship with its institutional home, the overall path of social work education toward formally becoming part of higher education was established early on.

Once the question of whether social workers were better educated primarily in the agency setting or as part of institutions of higher learning was settled in favour of the latter, new professional schools were established quickly in a 'mushroom-like expansion' (Eubank, 1928, p. 265) across the United States and Canada. Yet, even with a common view about grounding social work in a scientific foundation taught in an academic setting, the programmatic expression of this principle took varied forms among the rapidly expanding number of social work programmes. In the context of such diversity, there remained unresolved basic questions among the 39 professional schools that existed in 1928:

> In a word, we may say that up to the present time there is no agreement among the schools as to: (1) the content of the class work curricula, (2) content of field work, (3) the amount of class work, (4) the amount of the field work, (5) the relative proportion of class and field work, (6) the nature and extent of field supervision.
>
> *(Eubank, 1928, p. 271)*

There continues—to this day—to be a lack of consensus about many aspects of the proper structure and content of professional social work education. Some differences among the leading schools reflected distinguishing aspects of their identities; for example, the emphasis on 'broad social science education' at the University of Chicago in contrast to the closer focus on casework developed by Porter Lee at the New York School (Farber and Reitmeier, 2019; Dore, 1999; Meier, 1954; Shoemaker, 1998). In addition, the rapidly expanding number of schools developed in varied local and regional contexts, ranging from dense urban locales with large immigrant populations to rural farm communities, each characterised by dissimilar features, such as cultural norms, service environments, and economic conditions. Such differences wrought concomitant variations in certain course foci and field placements.

Nevertheless, Sophonisba Breckenridge, at the University of Chicago, articulated an overall agreement regarding a 'combination of teaching in the field and teaching in the classroom' and the need to 'individualize the student as well as the client' within a 'generalized, as over against the specialized curriculum'. Within this framework, fieldwork provided students the opportunity to apply the theoretical and scientific knowledge gained in the classroom as well as 'to establish the kinds of relationships with persons needing treatment out of which constructive treatment may be expected to emerge' (Breckenridge, 1936, pp. 443, 447). The broader discourse reflected common themes and questions whose answers suggest a search for principled and deep coherence in educational purpose with programmatic individuality.

Among the shared core assumptions was that, as Gordon Hamilton asserted, 'The professional school certainly does not exist for mere imparting of knowledge or mere opportunities for research. It must exist—its main function must be—to produce people who know how to put together effectively knowledge and experience' (Hamilton 1942, p. 223). She observed that the 'startling differences' among schools in requirements for fieldwork, ranging from 221 to more than 900 hours, should be resolved with 'close consideration of the sequence of learning over 2 years, of the individual student's growth and the overall curriculum' (Hamilton 1942, p. 241). Hamilton further identified underlying principles to achieve the objective of educating autonomous professionals:

> I cannot overemphasize that *planning* [emphasis in original] educational sequences should not mean that a given student must *always* [emphasis in original] follow such sequences. Learning is not a mere accumulation of knowledge, and never knowledge in one precise order, but growth in understanding. For professional students, however, growth must be in a given direction. The several aspects of growth—greater assurance with techniques, greater ability to relate one's self with other persons and groups in a socialized development, identifying and forwarding the aims of social work in the larger world—must all be effectively integrated.
>
> *(Hamilton, 1942, p. 217)*

The American Association of Schools of Social Work (A.A.S.S.W.) began accrediting schools in 1932, but social work leaders remained concerned about the direction of professional education in relation to fundamental questions of purpose and method. At the 1944 meeting of the A.A.S.S.W., Hamilton expressed doubt that the current practices would produce social workers with 'mature skill' because, 'The pendulum everywhere in education has been swinging far over to technique, and I suspect that the emphasis on postwar education will be even more sharply technical and vocational…and we shall grow thinner and more superficial in essential competence' (Hamilton, 1944, p. 150). At the same conference, Frank Bruno added to Hamilton's sceptical assessment, specifying five 'special problems' facing social work education. These included:

(1) the graduate versus the undergraduate level and their relative place in the profession; (2) instructors, referring to their qualifications and status as full-time or part-time employees; (3) the sources of financial support of schools, with particular reference to the risks of relying heavily on tuition rather than endowments; (4) the organisation of fieldwork and its place in the curriculum; and, (5) the 'perennial conflict' over the relative emphasis on preparing practitioners for 'specific tasks' or for general 'professional competency' (Bruno, 1944; Farber and Reitmeier, 2019).

Notwithstanding, the dramatic burgeoning of schools of social work in their number, their importance as sources of professional knowledge supporting professional practice at all levels, and their entrenchment in contemporary institutions of higher learning, the apprehensions expressed by Hamilton, Bruno, and their colleagues are hauntingly familiar in their modern guises. We have surely answered Richmond's call to establish professional education but with scant attention to the prescience of our early academic colleagues regarding the complex ways that their concerns were and remain deeply intertwined. These challenges to social work education persist but without adequate foundational principles to guide us today in the context of dramatic changes within and outside of professional schools.

The educational principles of early influential educational scholars Bertha Reynolds and Charlotte Towle, together, provide important elements that facilitate a developmental process for students within institutional environments designed explicitly to graduate social workers firmly on their way to becoming competent and autonomous. These principles address essential questions: What is the purpose of social work education? What is the developmental path of successful social work students? What are the characteristics of educational environments that nurture positive development of students' potential in a desired direction? Answers to these basic questions of human nature and professional growth are necessary for schools of social work to make wise choices today not only about field education but also about their basic structure and, ultimately, their function.

Reynolds: The 'Whole' Learner Develops

Bertha Reynolds, a leading progressive practitioner and educator at Smith College, contributed to professional education in explicating how the necessary unity of both science and art in social work is achieved through processes of conscious instruction and learning. Reynolds's classic treatise, *Learning and Teaching in the Practice of Social Work* is based on the premise that, '…social work is a part of life. Learning is also part of life. It *is* [emphasis in the original] life, not only preparing to live. Just as living involves the whole person, so does learning' (Reynolds, 1942, p. 57). She observed that all learners are 'biological organisms that must survive and eat and find their mates', and they bring these and other universal human needs to the educational experience (Reynolds, 1942, p. 68). Because learners are 'whole' people, educational development requires students to examine, even challenge, aspects of their customary ways of thinking, feeling, and behaving as they gain new knowledge and skills necessary for practice. Good teachers are aware of how such changes might affect their students and then respond accordingly, striving for a balance between pushing toward growth that necessitates change and supporting learners at each stage of development.

Reynolds proposed five general developmental stages during which 'conscious intelligence' facilitates personal and professional growth in what Hamilton referred to above as 'a given direction'. Reynolds's developmental scheme provides a comprehensive perspective on how students in both field and classroom can move toward maturity as practitioners and so avoid becoming what Hamilton feared: social workers who are mere technicians.

Reynolds's first stage is a time of '*acute consciousness of self*' during which students are heavily invested in protecting themselves from the distress that can accompany feeling incompetent in the face of new demands. They may seem paralysed by a form of 'stage fright' and worry that they are incapable of responding appropriately to practice situations (Reynolds, 1942). This results from feeling overwhelmed by uncertainty and typically leads to learners relying on automatic reactions. In such circumstances, it is natural to revert to earlier and familiar patterns of behaviour. Thus, among instructors' roles in this stage is the responsibility to provide reassurance, security, and make students feel adequate to the tasks ahead – to remind students that they will encounter new situations all the time and that fear is a natural aspect of learning. Field instructors hold a special place in providing reassurance that, at this point, students are not expected to have expertise; and to help learners '…to find the solid ground of personal adequacy he already has on which to plant his feet while he struggles with the new experience' (Reynolds, 1942, p. 76).

In the second stage, a time of '*sink or swim adaptation*', students turn their awareness outward enough to perceive people's reactions to them and their performance as novices. In general, students in this stage do not yet have a deep understanding of what social work practice requires or the theoretical or practical reasons for various actions. Rather, they are highly motivated by expressions of (dis) approval of their behaviour in class and field. Consequently, if they receive encouragement from teachers to repeat successful efforts, they incorporate what is positively reinforced and continue to display those behaviours.

Learners' relationships with their teachers are especially vital for continued development. The trust established with their teachers in this stage will be vital in later stages to help learners critique themselves and adjust their approaches. It is especially important for students to experience them as both protective and stimulating as appropriate. Instructors—particularly in fieldwork—must be patient in increasing students' reality-based sense of security by calling forth the knowledge and skills that they already possess. If learners cannot also trust themselves, they cannot increase the ability turn their attention away from themselves and to view practice situations objectively.

Learners in this second stage are likely to seek direction in the form of asking teachers, 'What should I do?' for fear of making mistakes, saying the 'wrong' thing to a client. In both the classroom and field, teachers enhance learners' growth by asking them to identify how they proceeded in previous instances of uncertainty rather than reinforcing their desire to be supplied with the 'right answer'. Mature social work practice requires not simply accumulating relevant information but also, crucially, developing the capacity to apply it in unique client situations. Teachers should intentionally help learners assimilate knowledge with increasing confidence in their ability to use it commensurate with their developmental level, always balancing increasing expectations with reassurance of growing capacity.

According to Reynolds, most social workers attain, but often do not progress beyond, the third stage of '*understanding the situation without power to control one's own activity in it*' (Reynolds, 1942, p. 79). Movement into this stage brings a sudden 'concomitant of release of energy from pre-occupation with the self to freedom to study the situation as it is' (Reynolds, 1942, p. 79). This is an essential capacity for autonomous practice, but it must also be accompanied by greater integration of increased knowledge, significantly beyond 'spontaneous' responses characteristic of earlier stages. As they move through this phase, students also gain greater openness to assessing what more, or different, is required of them in order to become more proficient.

Despite, perhaps, feeling frustrated that students do not consistently perform with the expertise indicative of even a beginning professional, teachers should remember that this developmental pattern is usual and even expected. While providing honest feedback about what has not been effective practice, all teachers should help learners to continue to think independently. This means asking students to reflect more deeply about their responses, why they did not feel adequate to a given situation, and why they responded in certain ways. It is especially important to emphasise partial successes as evidence of growth instead of failure or inadequacy. Again, this requires teachers in the field and classroom to find a deliberate balance between communicating higher expectations and providing support.

Some social work learners continue to develop significantly and attain the next and fourth level of development: the stage of '"*relative mastery*", in which one can both understand and control one's own activity in the art which is learned' (Reynolds, 1942, p. 81). By this time, learners have taken in what was once new professional knowledge and skills to their way of thinking, feeling, and responding and can handle new situations and their demands more easily and with less anxiety. Perhaps most distinctive of this developmental stage is that,

> Conscious intelligence and unconscious responses are working together in an integrated wholeness of functioning. So much of the activity as is routine is taken care of with minimum expenditure of energy, leaving conscious attention to the study of new aspects of the activity as they arise in contact with the environment.
>
> *(Reynolds, 1942, p. 81)*

When this is achieved, learners have become genuinely professional and able to use themselves fully as instruments with professional purpose in novel situations.

Learners in the fourth stage are most likely completing their professional degree or are well into the early years of their social work career, perhaps serving as field instructors themselves. By this time, learners require little directive supervision in order to be competent social workers but need continuing stimulation. Today, this is commonly achieved through informal, perhaps, peer consultation and by staying abreast of or even participating in research.

While most learners do not reach stage five, the continuation of the profession depends upon those who are at the point of being focused on '*learning to teach what is mastered*' to students and junior colleagues. Reynolds likens the development from the fourth to fifth stage to earlier changes when the learner's increased expertise frees sufficient energy to permit shifting attention primarily outward to the needs of others, particularly toward meeting the needs of social work learners. She describes this freedom as the ability,

> to be able to see how each learner works best, what motivations favor learning and what ones need to be outgrown by a particular individual, what phases of the subject are obscure and what are clear already and can be used for building up security, at what point help is needed and when it is in the way
>
> *(Reynolds, 1942, p. 83)*

The well-developed teacher is student-centred rather than subject-centred and is capable of engendering development of the whole person as learner in class, in field, and/or in agency supervision. The fulfilment that comes from success in practice now also comes with the success of learners whom they teach and guide. Learners are fortunate when they encounter teachers whose perspective reflects the ideal that,

> If a teacher can be guided by *what is happening to the learner*, rather than what he himself wants to accomplish by means of the learner, he will be in a position really to teach what he has to give.
>
> *(Reynolds, 1942, p. 74)*

However, the reliable existence of such a felicitous combination of a learner's needs and an instructor's capacity requires an institutional context that holds education as a priority. It may not be, nor need be the sole priority, especially in the contemporary context of higher education, in which, for example, faculty have so many competing demands, but it must be the guiding value in making organisational decisions that impinge directly on students. Charlotte Towle's scholarship on professional education incorporates Reynolds's focus on the developmental trajectory of the whole person as learner and extends it to the educational environment itself as the crucible of the complex process of becoming a professional social worker.

Towle: The School as an Organic Whole

Charlotte Towle, long-time teacher of social work practice at the University of Chicago and internationally recognised scholar of the profession, articulated a vision of educational development in her definitive work, *The Learner in Education for the Professions: As Seen in Education for Social Work* (Towle, 1954). Consistent with Reynolds and other development-oriented educators, Towle emphasised the importance of the self—the whole person—in practice, thus, as a focus for professional growth. Accordingly, she asserted, professional educators must attend to the challenges of emotional as well as intellectual growth in a given direction:

> In professional education, we have the common obligation to impart certain essential knowledge and to conduct our educational processes so that they are a means to personality growth. Only thus may the student become free imaginatively to consider, understand, and relate to the needs, wants, and strivings of those whom he is to serve. Our educational systems must strengthen the student's integrative capacity, thus reinforcing his potentials for growth in that learning may proceed rather then become constricted or break down.
>
> *(Towle, 1954, p. ix)*

Such integrative capacity is partly innate and must be supported by sufficient motivation to learn, but for learners to develop fully toward professional competence, the educational environment must offer appropriate opportunity and nurture. Just as the professional relationship is the 'heart of helping' in practice (see Perlman, 1979, for a peerless explication of this concept), so is the educational relationship a key aspect of professional learning. Positive relationships throughout the educational experience help learners to cope with the discomfort of change and to meet the many and varied demands required in achieving integrative capacity while in school and as professionals (Farber & Penney, 2020; Urdang, 1999). Towle argues that they serve as the primary basis for relationships in practice. Thus, 'within a professional school the individual and collective teaching, helping, and administrative relationship with the student is the core of his preparation for professional relationship' in all facets of practice (Towle, 1952, p. 68). Educational relationships are not sufficient, but they are essential and should be explicitly cultivated within the school.

Towle distinguishes among three levels of educational relationships: with supervisors in the field placement, with instructors in the classroom, and, more broadly, with staff and others in the school administration (see Figure 9.1) all functioning in concentric circles revolving around the learner in concert as an 'organic whole' (Towle, 1954, p. 138).

Towle suggested that relational experiences at all environmental levels are potent in contributing to the student's overall development, be they positive or negative in their impact. So, maximising the effectiveness of education requires careful attention to how students' contact

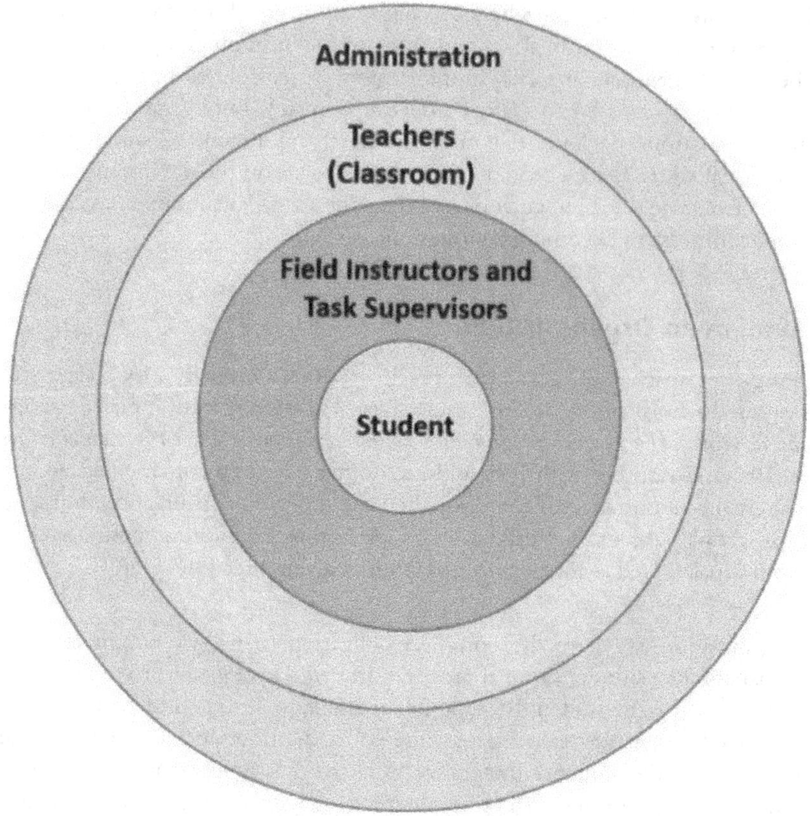

Figure 9.1 The organic educational environment (Farber and Reitmeier, 2019)

with all facets of the school influence specific aspects of their growth. Students must consistently experience a sense of 'oneness' among various contacts in the form of shared professional philosophies, values, aims, purposes in field, in the classroom, and in the school as an encompassing milieu. In order for learners to achieve the emotional and intellectual integration necessary for mature practice, the learning setting must itself function with clear, consciously devised integration within and among levels of the school. According to Towle, this 'implies also a universal attempt to understand the student as a learner in order to give help in the mastery of learning' (Towle, 1952, p. 69). She defines a high standard for educational practice that, in some respects, becomes ever more difficult to attain, yet it is as important as ever for setting a high standard for the profession.

Educational Development in the Contemporary Educational Environment

While there has been no explicit rejection of the developmental principles of Hamilton, Reynolds, Towle, and other seminal social work education scholars, educational priorities have shifted throughout the history of the profession. For example, after the C.S.W.E. succeeded the A.A.S.S.W. in 1952 as the accrediting body, evaluative frameworks alternated between meeting programme objectives and demonstrating competencies as outcomes, always with implications for programme priorities. Increasingly, other factors external to accreditation and professional standards have taken precedence in ways that profoundly affect our learners. For example, the impact of managed care and systems of reimbursement for social work services has been profound in ways that cannot be explored here (Urdang, 1999). However, their consequences in total are unmistakable within schools of social work. Of particular importance, here, are changes in expectations, priorities, and general academic culture of the institutions of which schools of social work are a part.

Although the importance of what students experience relationally within each environmental level has, by definition, remained potent since the time that Towle wrote, there seems to be less attention paid to these experiences and how they affect learning. As schools of social work became more deeply embedded in academic institutions, they also became more subject to trends within higher education that deeply affect how social work students are prepared for practice. Together, these changes pose serious risk to keeping students' development and, thus, the quality of education as a central value.

Administration

Towle placed the administration, representing the 'school as an institution', at the greatest distance from the student's immediate experience (Towle, 1954, p. 139). Today, however, administrative priorities have such extensive influence on the other environmental levels that their role in facilitating students' development requires greater deliberation.

One source of learning is students' participation in organisational governance, such as serving on school committees. Towle noted that this provides opportunity to form relationships with advisors, classroom faculty, and field supervisors who often serve in multiple instructional and administrative roles. Where students are in close contact with administrators carrying out these functions, they learn about agency practice, may develop mentors, and increase their confidence.

Of greater import is that administrators act as final authority, the school's representatives who 'set requirements, who are responsible for the whole beneficent or iniquitous system, and who finally pass judgment on him *in toto*' (Towle, 1954, p. 139). In this, and other consequential respects, the administrative level has taken on increasing prominence in a variety of significant ways. One notable change is that the size and role of academic administration have increased substantially over time, evident in the recent 47% increase in American university administrators in contrast to only 14% increase in faculty (Gambrill, 2014). The ascendency of 'bureaucracy and managerialism run amok' (Gambrill, 2014, p. 405) signals a shift in the investment of increasingly scarce resources toward administrative infrastructure and away from activities and personnel that more directly enhance learning, such as support for field supervisors and faculty. This dominance also heightens the overall impact of administrative priorities, reflected in policies and practices, on students and faculty.

Academic administration performs two crucial functions in carrying out the profession's responsibility for gatekeeping: setting standards for admission and requirements for graduation. While schools vary procedurally in how admission decisions are made and by whom, heavy reliance on tuition, especially in public universities, remains a prime motive in determining not only cohort size but selection criteria. Eubank identified this issue more than 90 years ago and likely would have been dismayed by modern forces that he could not foresee: How the sharp rise in the number of bachelor's and master's programmes accredited by C.S.W.E., declining pool of applicants who possess widely varying aptitude for social work, and severe economic pressures would result in many schools employing practically open admissions in order to remain viable (Stoesz et al., 2010).

Towle assumed that the rigorous assessment leading an applicant to be admitted to a school of social work, while not conclusive, was an acceptably reliable indication of a learner's 'educability', or the capacity and motivation to master the complex integrative demands of professional development. Towle defined 'educable adult' in the context of social work education as:

> ...individuals whose personality growth has not been seriously obstructed by the deprivations and unresolved conflict of the early years; those persons who have a well-developed ego-superego structure so that their emotional needs are unlike those of a child, in that there is greater capacity for self-dependence, while interdependence has replaced in considerable measure the dependency of early years. Their inner conflicts, in so far as they have been basically unresolved, are being adequately handled through constructive ego defenses.
>
> *(Towle, 1954, p. 85)*

It is not necessary to share the psychodynamic theoretical basis for this definition to appreciate the underlying standard of reasonable emotional maturity, among other qualifications, as a requirement for admission and certainly for graduation as a professional social worker. Such maturity allows a student to learn without undue stress, to interact with others in all environmental levels appropriately, and then to enter the profession with the capacity to put clients' needs first.

From the initial contact with applicants to the conferral of a degree, administrators and their staff communicate expectations and model behaviour that can further learners' development or serve other institutional interests. Current admissions processes rarely include interviews and other means of assessing an applicant's maturity or interpersonal qualities. Consequently, it is especially important that all interactions students have within the school are viewed as opportunities to deliberately reinforce certain behaviours and discourage others that are not consistent with professional conduct. For example, American social work educators often note students' 'sense of entitlement', expressed through demanding that their own preferences for convenience, responsiveness, high grades, and other desires be met unquestioningly and quickly by school personnel, including in relation to field placements. When administrative responses to students' conduct that may be reflecting cultural norms, or perhaps individual immaturity, are motivated primarily by concern for achieving admissions and retention goals or fear of legal action that could be financially or reputationally costly rather than by a commitment to professional growth, the student loses an opportunity to learn how to communicate effectively and professionally under stress. Likewise, if mental health difficulties, learning challenges, or other individual characteristics impede students' performance in the field or class, developmental-centred administrators' responses focus on assisting students reach the programme's educational goals rather than compromising standards in order to ensure graduation or avoid conflict. The responsibility to maintain standards supporting professional growth and ensuring that graduates are ready to practice ultimately lies within the administrative level of the institution; therein is a crucial source of push for development balanced by support for the student's individual needs.

Classroom

Closer to the student's immediate experience is the classroom, where instructors provide intellectual stimulation and essential knowledge for professional development. The singular importance of this environmental level lies in that,

> In the classroom several elements in learning move along together. The instructor is charged to impart knowledge, to inculcate certain habits of thinking, to foster appropriate

> feeling—all for the development of understanding for use. Although skills are developed largely in the field, much doing is taught in the classroom. In spite of the fact that it is difficult to separate knowing, thinking, and feeling the instructor must be able to differentiate them…in order to see their relatedness in the learning response
>
> *(Towle, 1954, p. 157)*

Through focused and productive educational relationships, instructors observe individuals' learning responses and can respond in ways that enhance development in all manner of their interactions.

At the most basic level, in the classroom, students learn what is to be applied in the field, and the professional literature is replete with creative andragogic strategies and techniques for integrating field experience with other coursework. However, in order for students to experience the full educational potential of this context, they need instructors who, as Reynolds observed, possess requisite developmental capacity themselves and who receive appropriate resources and support for their work as teachers. That is, the quality of students' opportunity to learn depends on the individual characteristics of their teachers but also heavily on the priorities of the administration that determines the composition and deployment of the faculty. These priorities have changed dramatically in recent decades.

One key development is that the entrenchment of schools of social work in modern institutions of higher learning has resulted in greatly increased contributions by faculty to the scholarly literature informing social work practice, which fulfils an urgent historic aspiration within the profession. At the same time, the greater value placed on research within the academy, in general, is reflected in changing priorities in many, if not most, schools of social work, where administrative decisions to hire and to retain faculty often favour greater effort in carrying out externally funded research (Hartman, 1990).

The impact of these changing academic practices is wide-ranging, but a few common and crucial implications for social work learners include: fewer instructors have extensive practice experience with which to guide and help integrate learning and to offer professional modelling and socialisation; instructors have less time to devote to their students' development as whole people; instructors may have low teaching loads with narrow focus, leading to less knowledge of the full curriculum and diminishing their capacity to facilitate deep integration and conscious learning across courses; and, more part-time or adjunct instructors who often are minimally integrated into the full range of administrative and faculty functions that affect students' development. With these shifts in the teaching environment come less opportunity, motivation, and capacity to address extra-procedural aspects of professional competence such as, for example, the role of emotional regulation, capacity for managing the normal anxiety that accompanies classroom and field learning, and for developing reliable use of self in all forms of practice (Sewell, 2020). The risks of failing to attend to these aspects of teaching the 'whole person' are unmistakable in the current status of field education with attending risks for the quality of professional practice.

Field

Towle placed field learning in closest proximity to the student in recognition that it is field supervisors who provide the 'core experience' as the 'major determinant of the student's development' (Towle, 1954, p. 138). It is often in the field where the fact that 'professional education constitutes a maturation push' is most dramatically evident (Towle, 1963). In the field placement, students directly apply what is learned in the classroom, learn new knowledge and skills for practice, engage in individualised supervisory relationships, and encounter and respond to, as Reynolds notes, 'life in the raw'.

Individualising the student's educational experience in the agency context presents a complex set of teaching responsibilities for the field supervisor in principle and even more so when social workers and agencies face the many challenging exigencies of contemporary practice. Each learner is at a particular stage of normal human development, for example late adolescent versus middle adulthood, with its typical features and needs. At the same time, the learner is at an educational stage of development that may be somewhat independent of the developmental themes associated with age. Each student brings to the learning situation a personal history that interacts closely with both aspects of development in determining strengths and areas for growth. This calls upon the supervisor not only to be highly sensitive to the learner's individual developmental needs but also to structure the field experience within an overall educational trajectory necessary to attain levels of proficiency defined by the school and C.S.W.E.

As Towle (1963) observed, the learner entering field at the foundation level,

> begins practice before he has knowledge, or before he has assimilated what knowledge he has. The need for help, therefore, is created by the discrepancy between demands and capacity to perform. It is created also by the discrepancy between demands and personality development implicit in performance capacity. Therefore, there arises the need for individualized help to safeguard the potential for emotional intellectual integration.
>
> *(p. 3)*

When students are in an advanced placement, they face higher expectations for performance in terms of expertise and independence, and their developmental needs should have changed accordingly.

Trends in administration and classroom environmental levels noted above have great bearing on field supervisory practice. For example, as administrative priorities have decreased willingness to perform certain gatekeeping functions, the responsibility for identifying significant performance problems often falls to field supervisors. There is some educational logic to this because, as Towle notes, 'It is as the student performs in the field, a situation in which he is related to the administrative, helping and teaching functions of supervision (underline in original) that in the last analysis, his educability is determined' (Towle, 1963, p. 4). However, it is unreasonable to burden primarily field supervisors with the task of pressing for a student to be asked to leave the programme or trying to help a student overcome serious deficiencies that may require different or more extensive support than knowledge and skills in to order to progress. It is neither educationally sound nor practically feasible in current practice contexts for field supervisors to extend their roles further into, for example, a more therapeutic realm, especially in the absence of support from the more distal levels of the school.

Another critical dimension of field teaching that is closely tied to the overall educational environment relates to students' capacity to form helping relationships, 'the sine qua non of all social work practice' (Urdang, 1999, p. 4). Insofar as the predominance of short-term and cognitively oriented practice approaches are reflected in social work curricula, classroom content and process focus less on students developing the deep awareness of the self and interpersonal dynamics necessary to form good professional relationships (Perlman, 1979; Urdang, 2010). When such developmental weaknesses are reinforced by administrative practice that is bureaucratically routine or fails to reinforce professional conduct, field supervisors are left to compensate educationally when students have shallow capacity for use of self or relational skills.

Skilled supervision addresses these and other expectable learning needs through such tools as process recordings, videotaping, live observations, and case consultation. Alone, however, field learning cannot make up for serious deficiencies elsewhere in students' educational experience or the unwillingness of administrators or faculty to impose rigorous expectations for students' performance. The capacity for supervisors to teach and the learning opportunities available in a field placement can fulfil their proper educational potential only when they function in close concert within a genuinely integrated holistic environment that places highest priority on the development of learners into competent and independent professionals. Achieving this standard also requires that field education receive the resources and commitment from schools commensurate with being our signature pedagogy and not be treated as an afterthought or residual function of the academic mission.

Recently, there has been increased interest among social work scholars in reintegrating a more holistic perspective on professional education and considering how to define and assess educational outcomes appropriately (Drisko, 2015). Current literature, though, is limited in size and conceptual coherence (Drisko, 2015). The more general movement for 'holistic education' seeks

> the broadest development of the whole person at the cognitive and affective levels (Singh, 1996). It aims for the fullest possible human development enabling a person to become the very best or finest that they can be and develop fully "those capacities that together make up a human being" (Forbes, 2003).
>
> *(Mahmoudi et al., 2012, p. 179)*

However, for the purposes of educating social workers who are ethically and legally accountable for exhibiting professional competence upon graduating, the notion of holism must be more precise and have demonstrable expression. Perhaps most helpful in the current literature is the work of Bogo and others who distinguish between 'meta competence' and 'procedural competence' (Bogo et al, 2013, 2014). This analysis suggests two 'inter-related dimensions' of holistic competence that importantly includes the capacity for self-reflection highly consistent with Reynolds's and Towle's understanding of students' development (Bogo et al., 2013, 2014). Reynolds's and Towle's work provide direction for carrying this work forward by lodging the responsibility of creating competent professional social workers through a holistic approach within consciously designed academic programmes. Institutions that commit to the charge of a holistic approach protect this valuable profession whose practice is far more complex than an accumulation of discrete skills, knowledge, and values. Holistic social work education and protection of the profession requires fully integrated systems of faculty, field, administration, and governing levels of organisation.

The 2022 E.P.A.S. standards of C.S.W.E. may increase emphasis on the multiple dimensions of competence that must be addressed in the explicit and implicit curricula in all levels of the educational environment. Yet, it is not clear that many schools are truly committed to or capable of achieving the changes necessary for an integrated and holistic environment that is closely focused on students' development beyond technical proficiency. Thus, there is reason to believe that the circumstances that gave rise to Hamilton's fears for our professional future have not been mitigated; indeed, some may be more worrisome.

Conclusion

As of this writing, questions abound over the future of the academy in general: Which schools will survive the cataclysm of the COVID-19 pandemic? What are implications of the attending financial distress for the hiring and retention of faculty and of what status? What is, what will be, and what should be the most common forms of instruction—in person and/or online? Schools of social work are currently grappling to find immediate answers to these and other troublesome questions that are likely to persist into the future. Depending upon how these critical issues are resolved by individual schools of social work and the institutions in which they are embedded, by higher education as a social institution and by the C.S.W.E. as an independent oversight body, the profession faces an even greater need to identify and act on core principles of professional education.

Schools of social work across North America struggle to regain their balance in terms of admitting and retaining students, delivering effectively sound curriculum, and carrying out the multiple missions guiding our professional schools. In such uncertain and challenging circumstances, we must be careful to reject answers that will lead to 'technical and vocational' rather than genuinely professional education. In order to avoid going in this undesirable direction, schools must make difficult decisions about students, faculty, and administration that will result in educating future generations of social workers who are mature, autonomous, and capable of continuous professional development. These decisions include taking full responsibility for gatekeeping by defining essential academic and personal qualities of students who are admitted to social work programmes; adjusting programmes so that only students who are truly qualified for professional practice with vulnerable people are admitted, and carefully assessing students' professional development and taking action to remove those few who are not meeting standards. In terms of teaching those students whose promise is acceptable, we must actively support the capacity of faculty to teach with attention to all of the multiple dimensions that constitute both meta-competence and procedural competence. It is equally important that administrative and faculty leaders vigorously advocate within educational institutions for hiring and retention standards that result in teachers who are not only good scholars but are also qualified to pass on to students necessary professional knowledge and skills. Meaningful expression of these principles includes setting and implementing fiscal and administrative priorities that directly facilitate these programme characteristics.

As social workers are wont to do, we ought to view the current challenges as opportunities—to rededicate ourselves to the fundamental principles that have animated our profession for more than a century and answer the questions facing us with constant reference to how we can educate social workers who will keep the historic faith of the profession. The path toward remaining true to our identity depends upon recognising and carrying forward the essential wisdom recognising that the whole person who learns requires a holistically integrated educational environment in order to become the bearer of the profession's most important knowledge, skills, and commitments.

References

Bogo, M., Katz, E., Regehr, C., Logie, C., Mylopoulos, M., & Tufford, L. (2013). Toward understanding meta-competence: An analysis of students' reflection on their simulated interviews. *Social Work Education*, 32(2), 259–273.

Bogo, M., Rawlings, M., Katz, E., & Logie, C. (2014). *Using simulation in assessment and teaching: OSCE adapted for social work (objective structured clinical examination)*. Alexandria, VA: CSWE.

Breckinridge, S. P. (1936). The new horizons for professional education for social work. *Social Service Review*, *10*(3), 437–449.

Bruno, F. J. (1944). Twenty-five years of schools of social work. *Social Service Review*, *18*(2), 152–164.

Council on Social Work Education. (2008). *Educational policy and accreditation standards*. Alexandria, VA: Author.

Dore, M. (1999). The retail method of social work: The role of the New York School in the development of clinical practice. *Social Service Review*, *73*, 168–190.

Drisko, J. W. (2015). Holistic competence and its assessment. *Smith College Studies in Social Work, 85*(2), 110–127.
Eubank, E. (1928). The schools of social work of the United States and Canada: Some recent findings. *Social Service Review, 2*(2), 263–273.
Farber, N., & Penney, P. (2020). Essential and neglected: Transforming classroom learning through relationship. *Journal of Teaching in Social Work, 40*(2), 95–113.
Farber, N., & Reitmeier, M. C. (2019). (Re) Capturing the wisdom of our tradition: The importance of Reynolds and Towle in contemporary social work education. *Clinical Social Work Journal, 47*(1), 5–16.
Flexner, A. (1915). Is social work a profession? In *Proceedings of the National Conference of Charities and Corrections at the forty-second annual session held in Baltimore*, Maryland, May 12–19, 1915. Chicago, IL: Hildmann.
Gambrill, E. (2014). Social work and avoidable ignorance. *Journal of Social Work Education, 50*, 391–413.
Hamilton, G. (1942). Some problems of the second-year curriculum of the professional schools. *Social Service Review, 16*(2), 212–223.
Hamilton, G. (1944). Planning for the future in schools of social work. *Social Service Review, 18*(2), 145–151.
Hartman, A. (1990). Education for direct practice. *Families in Society, 71*(1), 44–50.
Meier, E. G. (1954). *A history of the New York School of Social Work*. New York, NY: Columbia University Press.
Perlman, H. H. (1979). *Relationship: The heart of helping people*. Chicago, IL: The University of Chicago Press.
Reynolds, B. C. (1942; 1985). *Learning and teaching in the practice of social work*. New York, NY: Rinehart.
Sewell, K. M. (2020). Examining the place of emotions, affect, and regulation in social work education. *Journal of Social Work Education, 56*(1), 5–16.
Shoemaker, L. M. (1998). Early conflicts in social work education. *Social Service Review, 72*(2), 182–191.
Stoesz, D., Karger, H. J., & Carrilio, T. (2010). *A dream deferred*. New Brunswick, NJ: Transaction Publishers.
Teigiser, K. (2009). New approaches to generalist field education. *Journal of Social Work Education, 45*(1), 139–146.
Towle, C. (1952). The distinctive attributes of education for social work. *Social Work Journal, 33*(20) 63–94.
Towle, C. (1954). *The learner in education for the professions*. Chicago, IL: The University of Chicago Press.
Towle, C. (1963). *Lecture on supervision, papers*, Special Collections Research Center, University of Chicago Library.
Urdang, E. (1999). The influence of managed care on the M.S.W. social work student's development of the professional self. *Smith College Studies in Social Work, 70*(1): 3–25.
Urdang, E. (2010). Awareness of self—A critical tool. *Social Work Education, 29*(5), 529–538.

10

When the Going Gets Tough

Case Studies of Challenge and Innovation in Canadian Field Education

Brenda Morris, Sarah Todd, and Alicia Kalmanovitch

The Canadian context for field education is unique in that, unlike many other regions of the world, the accrediting, professional and regulatory bodies of social work function separately and autonomously. Canadian cultural, political, and legal environments further complicate the educational context given vast regional variations and differences. This environment is also shaped by global debates about the role of universities as primarily focused on creating democratic citizens that sit in tension with perceptions that universities' primary responsibility should be to prepare students for participation in the labour market (Collini 2012).

These tensions are also determined by the contemporary neoliberal state in which the commitment to public funds for higher education is often questioned and governments' commitments to resourcing universities has decreased (Lang 2005). Within this neoliberal context, field education in Canada is also faced with shrinking resources and a fully entrenched model of new managerialism at universities with management practices that prioritise continuous improvement, fiscal accountability, and measurable outcomes as primary measures of value and effectiveness (Barnoff et al. 2017; Moffatt et al. 2018; Todd et al. 2015). These same forces are also acting upon those organisations that partner with field educators to offer a comprehensive field programme (Baines 2017). As a result, social workers in the community struggle with workload intensification, further limiting the critical human resources needed to support social work students on placement. It is not only a question of constricting resources but also of increasing numbers of students seeking practicums that have resulted from a pattern of privatisation that has encouraged a never-ending expansion of university-based programme options for consumers. Given this, it is no surprise that the Canadian social work field education literature is largely challenge-focused, and recent research contributions have introduced the alarmist language of 'crisis' and 'complexity' (Ayala et al. 2018; Bogo 2015). However, the literature is also articulating promising practices and innovative strategies to address these complexities (Ayala et al. 2018; Bogo 2015; Crisp and Hosken 2016; McKee et al. 2015; Mishna et al. 2013; Pelech et al. 2009; Wiebe 2010). These strategies rely considerably on consultation, partnership development, and engagement with a broad range of stakeholders, settings, and methods of delivery at local, regional, national, and international levels in order to address current challenges. In schools and faculties of social work, today's field educators confront the challenge of delivering quality field

DOI: 10.4324/9781032164946-13

education and use existing literature to guide innovation, collaboration, and the identification of future avenues for research.

In this chapter, we identify key challenges and threats to the delivery of high-quality field education and use three case studies to highlight recent initiatives that are encouraging innovation, inclusion, and collaboration in the Canadian context. Canadian social work educators are creatively and collectively engaging the challenges of social work field education in novel ways that hold the promise of change, and we go on to argue that this requires complex and nuanced responses *across multiple levels (micro, mezzo, macro)*; responses that are both innovative and integrative in nature.

The first case study in this chapter explores the tensions that field educators encounter in their work and within which they see the greatest opportunity to create more transparency and inclusion. In the 'everyday' or micro aspects of their work, Canadian field educators in social work are increasingly attuned to the needs of those requiring placement accommodations for reasons of health or disability, and they struggle with the further complexities of responding when student mental health challenges threaten successful placement completion. In Canada, these responses must attend to a multitude of factors, including individual needs, system constraints, Canadian human rights and accessibility legislation, professional and regulatory accountabilities, accreditation standards, and institutional norms. Challenges emerge when the priorities of these individuals, systems, and laws collide with one another. Recent Canadian literature has mapped processes to attend to these factors and to increase transparency and inclusion (Todd et al. 2019). The first case applies these processes and demonstrates how they have been used to articulate essential requirements or core competences for social work education at one Canadian university.

At an institutional or mezzo level, these same educators are attending to the intensification of their own work and accompanying student expectations (Ayala et al. 2018) that have shifted in relation to the multiple effects of rising tuition fees, including the need to work part-time (and sometimes full-time) while going to school. As post-secondary education is increasingly commodified in the capitalist economy, and field educators are taxed by the 'complex and competing demands' of their roles (Buck et al. 2012), partnerships needed to produce a more predictable supply of placements are rare, and the availability of field placement settings risks falling short of student expectations. These expectations themselves are shaped by the context and students' anxieties about the labour market and the precarity of their generation's place within it. Drawing on these dynamics, the second case study focuses on how collaboratively engaging other stakeholders in enhancing field capacity, influencing national field education policy, and developing communities of practice (Agrifoglio 2015; Wenger 1998) is enhancing the ability of field directors to address this challenge.

Finally, we explore a challenge stemming from the macro conditions of social work field education in Canada. As universities realign their objectives to meet labour market needs (Blackmore et al. 2010; Brownlee 2015; Clark et al. 2009; Reimer 2004), increased demand for student work experiences creates tensions stemming from the differential terms and conditions of student work opportunities (co-op education, which is generally paid) versus professional learning opportunities (generally unpaid). The third case study explores the current discourse surrounding paid placements in social work and maps the development of policies and procedures to support such opportunities (where they exist) for Canadian social work students as well as the implications these interventions have for professional education.

In sum, the three case studies and discussion in this chapter provide three different snapshots of key tensions in the field and innovative approaches field directors use to address these challenges. In the conclusion of the chapter, we highlight how these cases are both specific to the

Canadian context and engage with themes impacting social work education around the globe. All local practices of field education grapple with social forces that are largely beyond an individual field educator's, student's, or school's control, but the integrative responses we highlight in these case studies are examples of strategies that can shape the future of field education at multiple levels, opening up spaces for transformation and possibility.

The Canadian Context

Canada is a highly decentralised federation of ten provinces and three territories. Member provinces and territories have significant control over their own regions, and key authority rests with the provinces and territories (i.e., regulation of education, health care, and labour regulations). Given the highly decentralised nature of the Canadian confederation, regulated professions are governed by a range of provincial, territorial, and/or federal policies and organisations with varying degrees of authority. While education is largely a provincial matter in Canada, social work education is regulated by a national body, the Canadian Association of Social Work Education (2014), which accredits schools of social work in Canada, thereby legitimating the degrees that students earn. This authority is, at times, challenged by provincial and territorial governments and regulatory bodies that all have a claim over the focus of social work education and the requirements and standards of the profession.

The social work profession has a national body, the Canadian Association of Social Workers, which while having little authority, works to support a national voice for the profession, collaborating with its provincial and territorial members and lobbying the federal government when needed. Meanwhile, in the provinces, there are both professional associations that represent the professional members' interests and regulatory bodies. The regulatory bodies hold professional members to account according to a variety of provincial laws and policies and generally articulate their primary role as that of public protection. There is quite a significant degree of variation within provincial standards – an inconsistency that has presented some challenges in terms of interprovincial mobility of social workers, particularly when social workers graduate from a school of social work in one province and intend to work in another.

For readers outside of the Canadian context, understanding the highly varied and uneven nature of the regulation and representation of the social work profession in Canada is important context for how field educators in the country must navigate and problem-solve the various issues that arise. The terrain is highly fragmented, resulting in regional differences that enrich and invigorate the profession but can also present barriers to effective collaboration and problem-solving across the country as a whole. Even the terminology used to describe field education can vary from region to region, further complicating field discourse and collaboration. For the purposes of this chapter, we will use the term *field educator* as an inclusive term for any person with direct involvement in the field placement experience. This includes agency-based field supervisors or instructors; field or faculty liaisons hired by the university to monitor student progress and support active field placements; field education coordinators, managers, or directors who hold responsibility for field education curriculum, placement processes, and field programme oversight in schools of social work; and academic scholars and faculty with expertise in social work field education. We also use the term *field director* as an umbrella term that includes only those in field education coordinator, manager, or director roles within schools of social work in Canada.

Methodology

This paper uses an intensive or case-based approach (Swanborn 2010) to explore the ways in which field directors in Canada respond creatively and collaboratively to the threats and challenges facing the delivery of field education in Canada. The three cases were developed from our experiences as field directors, professors, and students in social work education. Case-based methodologies allow qualitative researchers to understand complex phenomena and the relationship between those phenomena and their context (Baxter and Jack 2008; Meyer 2001). This ability to capture complexity and context made a case-study methodology the most appropriate approach for use in a project that aims to understand the multiple levels at which field directors intervene and reshape the shifting environment of field education in Canada.

Case study is a constructivist approach to research (Yin 2003) that recognises how phenomena are experienced differently based on one's social location, relational processes, and the specificities of the context. As a result, we have established clear boundaries around the cases that we have developed. While drawing on a range of literature from multiple perspectives, the cases are focused on framing the activities of field directors themselves. This means that the focus of the chapter is the relationship between field directors as subjects in their own realities; field education as the activities under study; and higher education, labour, and politics as the context.

Case studies are considered an ideal approach when trying to uncover how contextual conditions are relevant to a phenomenon (Yin 2003), and this is what we seek to explore in this chapter. Our use of case studies is solely for descriptive and explanatory purposes (Baxter and Jack 2008). This chapter explains and explores the field director role, particularly with respect to understanding how field directors work collaboratively and creatively to develop approaches to field education that are inclusive and responsive to a challenging environment. We offer no comparators or contrasting cases but, rather, use this approach to understand the often-obscured contributions of field directors in navigating and, thereby, shaping field education in Canada. The case studies were developed through a series of iterative conversations between the authors themselves and within further conversations with colleagues. They are built out of the authors' professional experiences as field directors, students, and administrators but were then enhanced through reflection and conversation – some components brought to the foreground, while others pushed to the background to help highlight relevant issues for the paper.

Micro-level: Student Mental Health Challenges on Placement

The prevalence of student mental health challenges in post-secondary education is well documented (Canadian Alliance of Student Associations 2018; Giamos et al. 2017) and a frequent source of concern for North American field educators (Allen and Trawver 2012). A 2019 American College Health Association-National College Health Assessment II survey of more than 55,000 students enrolled at 58 Canadian universities found that 33% had been diagnosed or treated by a professional in the past 12 months for one or more mental health conditions, most commonly for anxiety and depression (American College Health Association 2019), and the numbers in social work programmes reflect similar prevalence rates (Horton, Diaz, and Green 2009). This means that the need to support and respond to social work students who encounter mental health challenges during placement can be expected. Doing so is made more complex by regional variations in legislation relating to human rights, accessibility, the protection of personal health care information, and by national accreditation standards for social work education that require schools and faculties of social work to establish and enact professional suitability policies aimed at 'gatekeeping' the profession in the interests of protecting vulnerable service users and communities from harm (Canadian Association for Social Work Education 2014; Glenmaye and Bolin 2007). Field educators are frequently torn between their responsibilities to students, service users, accreditors, and institutions with few practical tools or policies available to guide the construction of 'good enough' responses that attend to multiple accountabilities. In 2019,

Todd, Asakura, Morris, Eagle, and Park from Carleton University's School of Social Work in Ottawa, Ontario, published *Responding to Student Mental Health Concerns in Social Work Education: Reflective Questions for Social Work Educators* within which the authors propose a series of reflective questions to help social work educators balance the rights and needs of students with the professional and institutional demands that students meet core competencies in their education. This work later prompted Carleton University's School of Social Work to draft essential requirements for their social work programmes (Carleton University 2018, 2019), whilst parallel development of similar tools was occurring across the province. Essential requirements articulate to students those core programme expectations that 'make the programme what it is' and, therefore, cannot be accommodated out of the student experience. Some examples of these are that students must be able to participate in a workplace on a regular basis with co-workers. Additionally, that they must be able to communicate respectfully and clearly in written or oral formats. These requirements also lay out programme expectations around a student's ability to demonstrate specific behaviours, such as meeting deadlines and appropriately managing confidential information. It is possible, even probable, that a wide range of students with a diagnosis of a mental illness can demonstrate these behaviours. It is also likely that people without a disability or diagnosis are unable to do so. As a result, the programme is able to refocus concerns, not on diagnosis, but, rather, on student ability to meet observable and measurable behavioural criteria (Todd et al. 2019). The following case study, encountered by field educators at the 'micro' level of direct practice with social work students on placement, will illustrate the utility of reflective questioning and clearly stated essential requirements when managing complex and high-risk scenarios during placement.

Case 1: Navigating Fluctuating Mental Well-being on Placement

The case of 'Martha' reflects a composite of student characteristics and contextual factors that, in our experience, are often encountered in social work field education. Martha is a 22-year-old white female student who is currently engaged in her fourth year Bachelor of Social Work (B.S.W.) practicum in a community-based organisation. All students, including Martha, are asked in the pre-placement phase whether they need any form of accommodation. Under Ontario human rights and accessibility legislation, students have a right to request accommodations (*Accessibility for Ontarians with Disabilities Act* 2005). Martha did not do so. During her placement, Martha quickly comes to the attention of the placement agency as a result of lateness and repeated absenteeism. When asked about the situation, Martha indicates that she suffers from anxiety and shares that this is what explains her absenteeism and lateness. She further explains that her attendance challenges are related to her recent change in anxiety medication. This is the point at which carefully considered responses are needed, and the reflective questions are extremely helpful in shaping interventions that attend explicitly to Martha's right to request accommodations and/or medical leave on placement and also take into account service delivery needs of the agency and the needs of clients. The situation also highlights the need for medical confirmation of health conditions around which accommodations are being requested (institutional and legislative norms). Martha is confident that, given that she has now adjusted to the new medication, her attendance will improve, and she appears to appreciate the negative impact that her lateness and short-notice absences have on clients and co-workers. She readily seeks and obtains a medical note substantiating the existence of a medical condition that has affected her attendance (the anxiety). Her physician also states that she is able to engage in placement with no further time off but that 'some flexibility' in hours might be needed. A meeting is organised with the faculty liaison (the university representative), Martha, and her field supervisor (the organisation's supervisor) to explore possible scheduling accommodations (later start time, shorter days, longer lunch, reduction in hours per week, etc.), but Martha indicates that it is her preference to continue with a regular work schedule, as she now feels better. Her field supervisor reviews procedures for timely reporting of any absences and communicates that given the impact on clients and staff, further short-notice absences or lateness cannot be accommodated. She again offers to strike a predictable accommodated schedule that would allow the agency to plan for Martha's attendance accordingly, but Martha states that such an accommodation is not necessary. Efforts are made to assess the possible impact of the work on Martha's health, and she states that this is not a significant factor. Arrangements are made to follow up with Martha and her supervisor again in two weeks. When this meeting time arrives, the field agency seeks termination of the placement because Martha has required further days of medical leave, has been late on several occasions, and has left placement early and suddenly during the two-week period.

The challenge in circumstances such as Martha's relates to determining what is considered a needed accommodation, versus what is seen as an essential requirement of the placement. Martha could argue that her placement was terminated because of a health condition that was responsible for her poor attendance record and suggest that her right to accommodations was breeched by the termination. However, Martha was unable to articulate or accept scheduling accommodations that would have allowed the agency to plan for and rely on her regular attendance, which can be viewed as an essential requirement, particularly given that the student was made explicitly aware that consistency was needed in order to mitigate impact on service users and co-workers and continue in the role.

Cases such as Martha's have led schools of social work across Canada to articulate the essential requirements for social work education, a concept referred to in other parts of the world as core competencies (Council on Social Work Education 2015; University College Cork 2020). In the context of human rights and accessibility legislation that stipulates that all individuals have the right to reasonable accommodations in the workplace (*Accessibility for Ontarians with Disabilities Act* 2005, *Human Rights Code* 1990), it is critical to be able to identify foundational 'musts' of the work that cannot be ignored if an individual is unable to perform them once all possible accommodations are offered. Figure 10.1 illustrates the relationship between accommodations and essential requirements as well as the implications of failing to meet essential requirements in social work education.

In the case of Martha, the placement was terminated as a result of essential requirements remaining unmet despite an explicit process to explore and maximise needed accommodations. With reference to Carleton University's articulation of essential requirements (2018, 2019), the requirement relating to attendance, participation, and timely completion states that 'students must attend classes and practicum settings consistently and reliably', and a further requirement relating to wellness and management of personal needs states that students must have 'the ability to recognise, identify and seek supportive resources, and when necessary to articulate their needs for accommodation' (Carleton University 2019). Unfortunately, Martha was unable to meet these requirements at the time of her placement, leading to its termination. She was, however, supported to complete the practicum component successfully at a later time when her health returned. This is another key aspect of how schools of social work are attempting to practice sensitively and supportively within the context of growing mental health concerns among university students. Canadian social work educators continue to work with students and colleagues to frame these challenges as having a temporal context. So, while in the past, there may have been a tendency to see Martha as the problem, field teams increasingly work to understand that it is Martha's mental health – at this time – that is presenting a challenge to her completion of

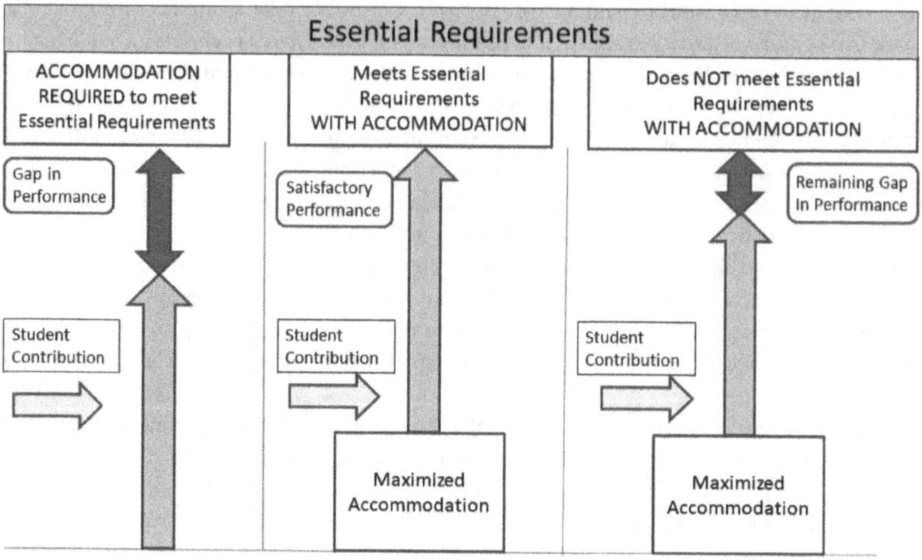

Figure 10.1 Accommodation to meet essential requirements. Source: Authors

the programme, and they work to foster hope and concrete opportunities for students to return when their mental health improves. By working collaboratively to make expectations more transparent and to increase opportunities for accommodation, such as taking breaks and returning, field education programmes are working to create systems that make the emerging post-secondary mental health crisis manageable within the context of field education. This approach seeks to protect students' rights and preserves the valuable community relationships upon which social work field education relies.

This micro-level case study provides insight into the innovative and integrative approaches field directors use to respond to the challenging and shifting realities of the individual students and the placement organisations that they are attempting to sustain. The case highlights how field directors use strategies of codification (reflecting upon and articulating expectations in ways that are transparent for students) and temporality in order to challenge the system, not to put students in boxes but, instead, to develop system responses that understand students as ever-evolving human beings. The goal is to construct innovative processes that aspire to accountability, responsiveness, flexibility, and transparency in order to ensure the values of social work are operationalised through the practices and policies of field education in action.

Mezzo-level: Addressing Practicum Insecurity through Partnership and Collaboration

This next section focuses on the work field directors do to intervene at the mezzo or organisational level of their work and how they similarly aim to create innovative and integrative responses to the challenges of contemporary field education. Within the mezzo level of practice, Canadian field educators are confronted with the dual realities of a rapidly changing field of practice (Baines 2017; Preston et al. 2014), resulting in an unstable supply of practicum opportunities for students (Bogo 2015; Tam et al. 2018). This is combined with increasingly high student expectations for specific sought-after practicum settings or arrangements. These expectations stem from factors such as anxiety about employment precarity, demographic and personal circumstances, financial strain, and/or an overall deep personal investment in educational success (Ayala et al. 2018; Buck et al. 2012; Lager and Robbins 2004; McConnell 2016). The Canadian literature reflects that social work and field education exist today in a neoliberal world filled with managerialism, economic rationalism, and decreased political efficacy of citizens, all of which influence the values and foci of social work practice on the ground as well as the conditions of work for social work practitioners themselves (Preston, George and Silver 2014). Continuous reduction of government and nongovernment funding for social services, sudden social programme terminations, and the combined stress of increased caseloads in a context of fewer resources have led to documented higher levels of stress and burnout among social workers (Jennissen and Lundy 2011; Regehr 2013; Tam et al. 2018) which, in turn, impacts social work field education by limiting the ability of agencies and organisations to commit to providing an adequate number of field placements, particularly those in which field instructors are themselves graduates of accredited schools of social work (Ayala et al. 2018; Canadian Association for Social Work Education 2014; Cleak and Smith 2012; Tam et al. 2018; Wiebe 2010) Add to this, the increased expansion of social work programmes across the country and the resultant competition for placements between schools and with programmes offering cooperative education (Ayala et al. 2018; McConnell 2016), and the tension between supply (unpredictable from one term to the next) and demand (increased student numbers and expectations) becomes extreme. This inevitable tension is one of the primary stressors reported by field directors across the country (Ayala et al. 2018; McConnell 2016; McKee et al. 2015) and, indeed, around the globe (Bellinger 2010; Buck et al. 2016; MacDermott and Campbell 2016; Noble and Irwin 2009; Zuchowski 2015).

Field directors are acutely aware of how the lack of institutional agreements between agencies and universities creates an unpredictable supply of placements that must be reviewed and renewed each term (Hunter and Poe 2014). These supply problems thwart student hopes and drain field resources that are expended each year in an effort to find and secure adequate numbers of placements to meet student and programme demand. Add to this an increasing need to arrange for accommodations on placement (McConnell 2016) and programme expansion across the country, leading to increased numbers of schools and, therefore, increased number of placements needed (Ayala et al. 2018; McConnell 2016). In sum, these conditions result in inadequate field capacity becoming a very significant, if not the top, threat to field education in Canada. In this chapter, we use the term 'practicum insecurity' to refer to the complex set of political, institutional, economic, and contextual factors that combine to threaten placement availability. We also acknowledge that the burden of the mounting tension between student expectations and institutional/programme demands, although understood as a systems issue, is borne primarily by individual field directors who ultimately hold responsibility for finding and securing placements for all social work students (Ayala et al. 2018). Field directors are, whether they like it not, the face that is managing practicum insecurity on behalf of all field stakeholders. It is an unenviable position.

According to a 2015 study of Canadian field education directors from eight out of ten Canadian provinces and all regions (n = 34), 74% reported challenges related to time and workload constraints and described their current workloads as unsustainable because of volume and complexity. These same respondents also described the significant impact this had on their morale (Ayala et al. 2018). The daily grind faced by field directors who have no direct influence on the factors that combine to create practicum insecurity, yet must manage it, has the potential to create burnout. At the same time, this stress can also be the catalyst for innovation and collectivisation, as described in the case study below.

Case 2: Building Capacity through Connection and Collaboration

Mainstream social work literature abounds with evidence of the need for active self-care strategies for practising social workers, particularly when workload intensification and emotional load create compassion fatigue and increased risk of burnout (Ray et al. 2013; Wilson 2016). However, authors writing from more critical perspectives draw attention to the relations of power and authority that underlie capitalism and neoliberalism. These authors argue that these structural issues, embedded in the systems of agencies, organisations, and communities within which social workers function, combine with workload stress to create untenable conditions of work that cannot be alleviated solely by individual self-care strategies, no matter how helpful they may seem at a micro level (Reynolds 2019). These authors point to the need for organisations to build cultures of collective care that 'prioritise caring for each other and to act more collectively to embed relational ways of acknowledging workers, managers and their work' (Wever and Zell 2018, p. 172).

In this context, an initiative undertaken by field directors in one Canadian province can be understood as both a response to the challenges of practicum insecurity and as a collective self-care strategy with potential to alleviate field director stress by developing a community of practice capable of influencing systemic issues. Although only one example of collective action on behalf of field directors in Canada, the Alliance of Ontario Social Work Field Education Directors (A.O.S.W.F.E.D. or The Alliance) is a recent illustration of how collective action at the systems level can help address individual and community-level stress in a positive manner.

Genesis and Mission Development

All Canadian field directors in accredited schools are members of the national Field Education Committee of the Canadian Association of Social Work Education (C.A.S.W.E.) and meet regularly to discuss and identify issues of concern in Canadian field education. In 2016, a signed intersectoral memorandum of understanding (M.O.U.) involving C.A.S.W.E., the Canadian Council of Social Work Regulators (C.C.S.W.R.), and the Canadian Association of Social Work (C.A.S.W.) reflected a national commitment to 'foster communication, connection and collaboration and to provide a framework to identify, prioritize, and address issues of shared concern' in social work nationally (C.A.S.W.E. 2016). This M.O.U. was met with resounding support from Canadian field directors, who wholeheartedly endorsed both the spirit and the intent to develop cohesive and coherent approaches to social work promotion, protection, and education. Provincial and regional variations in professional regulation, advocacy, and promotion, however, posed significant challenges to developing national action plans to address the specific concerns of practicum insecurity that collide with the needs and expectations of students, agencies, institutions, and the profession.

In 2017, field directors in Ontario (a single Canadian province), formed a group aimed at the promotion and development of quality field education for social work students. Originally known as the Coalition of Ontario Field Education Directors (C.O.F.E.D.), the group became the Alliance of Ontario Social Work Field Education Directors (A.O.S.W.F.E.D.) in 2018 and is comprised of more than 50 field directors from 15 accredited schools. The Alliance envisions quality field placements that are accessible to all students, providing rich social work learning and meaningful supervision across a range of settings, including practice, policy, leadership, administration, and research. These practicums allow students to meet specific curriculum objectives, including the development of social work skills, knowledge, values, and processes needed for competent professional practice.

Objectives and Initiatives

The Alliance has as its primary objective to understand, represent, and address the current context of field education through an annual process of identifying gaps and threats to field education. The Alliance works with stakeholder organisations/individuals to explore the potential for fruitful collaboration around member priorities. The annual process of revising and adapting to a rapidly changing environment in social work education is accomplished using consensus decision-making and, as such, represents a promising practice. It is notable that the 2019 Alliance priorities strongly align with issues raised in social work research, including field capacity/saturation (practicum insecurity), social work programme expansion, paid placements and equity concerns, accommodations, and gatekeeping responsibilities (Ayala et al. 2018; Buck et al. 2012; Bogo 2015; McConnell 2016; Sowbel 2012). The work of the Alliance can be understood as a direct response to these priorities and as a collective effort to address increasing pressures stemming from practicum insecurity and student/institutional demands. Other stated objectives propel the action agenda of the Alliance in that they seek to build relationships with identified stakeholders and actively address priorities and issues of mutual concern or benefit. Since its inception, the Alliance has worked collaboratively to pursue goals, such as the promotion of student field supervision within the professional community and the recognition of field supervision within regulatory frameworks. The Alliance also seeks to engage in national advocacy efforts to understand the impact of programme expansion on social work field education. During the COVID-19 crisis in Ontario, in April 2020, the Alliance partnered with the Ontario Association of Social Work on a remote practicum project that linked social work placement students to registered social workers who were able to supervise in a fully remote practice environment, thus allowing a number of students to complete placements as planned (Ontario Association of Social Workers 2020). These partnerships and collaborative measures have not only produced concrete results but have also improved the morale of Alliance members.

The final stated objective of the Alliance is that of mutual support and the development of a community of practice to achieve excellence in social work field education. The Alliance has been successful in creating opportunities for consultation, networking, collaboration, and knowledge transfer amongst its members, and these are practices that enhance the pursuit of stated objectives (enterprises) and enhance attendant social relations (Wenger 1998). Health Quality Ontario (2017), in its publication entitled *Improvement Through Collaboration: How to Build and Sustain a Community of Practice* suggest that communities of practice result in meaningful improvement in the quality of work accomplished by participants. Developing the Alliance in response to practicum precarity is an example of how field directors in Canada use innovative and integrative strategies to address challenges in field education. It represents a disruption to highly individualised and competitive institutional responses, instead, creating structures that push for integration and collaboration between systems and organisations that have been fragmented and, with ongoing fragmentation, have often come to understand themselves as in opposition. The type of response described in the second case study creates opportunities to build a new foundation of field education in Canada, to put the history of fragmentation in the past, and to build a collaborative, creative, and supportive future.

Macro-level: Developing Strategies in Response to Financial Need

In Canada, there has been a sustained critique of universities regarding their perceived inability to effectively connect students to the labour market upon graduation (Clark, Moran, Skolnik and Trick 2009). This critique has largely focused upon whether university programmes in

Canada are able to provide students with the skills necessary to fully participate in today's job market (Blackmore et al. 2010). Within this context, social work has fared quite well as a professional programme, with workplace training built centrally into its curriculum. However, this has not been without its tensions.

Students in schools of social work in Canada are required to complete 700 practicum hours as part of their Bachelor of Social Work (B.S.W.) programmes and a minimum of 900 hours as part of their two-year Master of Social Work (M.S.W.) programmes. These practicums provide students with the opportunity to develop their skills in workplaces under the supervision of a trained social worker. They also provide networking opportunities and key socialisation to the profession. In addition to the hours in on-site learning, students also participate in bi-weekly field seminars in which they are supported to integrate their classroom learning with their workplace learning. For each placement, students earn two full university credits. However, with the growing cost of university tuition (Statistics Canada 2020) and the increasing need for students to have part time jobs to support their personal living costs (Buck et al. 2012), this model has encountered some challenges. The organisation and number of hours required for a practicum make it almost impossible for students to maintain the paid employment that is often required for them to sustain themselves while in school. It should be noted that this economic pressure is faced by university students across this country and can be evidenced by the growing number of food banks at universities (Silverthorn 2016). Within this context, students often experience significant economic strain while in placement, and, along with this, they have begun to question the justice of the practicum system, which can exert on them a significant personal cost.

Case Study 3: Financial Needs and Strategies

Recently, students at a Canadian school of social work began to organise against the system of practicum-based learning (Bryan-Baynes 2018; Yao 2018). The students organised a petition and began to lobby the university to pay students for their time in practicum or to at least provide students with tuition relief while on a practicum. Part of the challenge of this activism was that, while it spoke clearly to the financial pressures the students were facing, it was based on significant misunderstanding of why practicums are organised the way that they are and how that is different from co-op based learning. From the perspective of schools of social work, the challenge here was not that the students did not have a clear and defensible position but, rather, that their position was one that aligned with the national student struggle for decreasing tuition costs overall rather than a specific inequity faced by social work students alone.

While schools of social work in Canada usually support students being paid for their practicums, the vast number of social services that offer student practicums do not have the resources to pay students for their practicum hours. In addition, many students have quite limited practice skills and require significant support to develop them, which means that students are already a significant cost for the organisation even before they are paid. For most organisations, the cost/benefit analysis of paid practicums, if they were required, would result in them not offering practicums at all. Organisations already report to us that the burden of having students can be significant for agencies already under significant pressure.

This situation has created an ongoing tension between students and field programmes in Canada and has required the development of creative solutions. The first strategy adopted by the School of Social Work at Carleton University has involved being more proactive in communicating with students about the differences between co-op education and practicum education. Students often have little understanding that the benefit of their practicums is that they receive university credit along with workplace skills and the opportunity to enter the field of practice and begin to build a professional network. That credit is, in effect, the recognition of their contribution and considered the 'greater right or benefit' under Ontario's Employment Standards Act (2000). While this has been obvious in the past, increasing tuition rates have left students with a sense that they have purchased their degree, which has obscured the fact that the tuition is paid to access the programme, but the programme itself still requires significant hours of work. What students had not understood was that they pay the same amount in tuition as students who complete cooperative education (co-op) or work placement. However, co-ops happen after degree completion, meaning students have already paid tuition for their degrees and are choosing to also pay co-op fees for an additional term. In effect, this makes co-op education more expensive than practicum-based learning. By sharing this information with students through our website and through information early on in their programme, we have been able to encourage social work students that their activism might be most effective if brought together within broader provincial and national campaigns to reduce overall tuition rates. Thus, we have worked to support students to understand that the problem is not specific to practicum education, but rather the challenges of practicum education are determined by the broader context of underfunding higher education and a privatisation of higher education in Canada.

While this reframing is centrally important, it is also vital that field education also recognises that these larger social forces reshaping higher education in Canada have significant material impacts on students and must also be attended to in how we design practicum programmes. In response to this, field directors at Carleton and beyond are working with national and provincial governments to secure greater numbers of paid practicums for students. For example, we regularly prompt organisations to consider providing an honorarium or stipend in any amount, when first determining whether or not a new practicum will be paid or unpaid. By creating a middle-ground that recognises students' financial strains and their contributions to the workplace, such an intervention has opened up the possibility to develop a field programme that acknowledges the financial needs of students in addition to the needs of community organisations. This mutual recognition goes a long way to building alliances throughout the profession.

In directly working with organisations and governments to expand paid opportunities for students, field directors are recognising that, as the cost of higher education has increased in Canada, the traditional ways in which practicum education has been organised have become untenable for many students. While schools of social work recognise that it is not possible, or even desirable, for all practicums to be paid, working to expand these opportunities is vital to making social work education accessible to a broad range of people, many who come from the communities that we most often serve. Without their active involvement in the profession, we run the risk of repeating past ethical transgressions in which the profession is unable to account for the experiences of those with whom we work. The commitment to designing social work education in a manner that is accessible is an ethical commitment made by field directors in the service of the profession itself.

Conclusion

In this chapter, we have used a case study approach to explore the creative ways in which field directors in Canada have navigated what is a fast-changing and challenging context of field education. We showcase the problem-solving and creativity that field directors use to foster connection and attempt to operationalise a vision of field education that is inclusive and collaborative. This is a significant disruption to the fragmented, protectionist approaches of the past and seeks to align field education with the principles of the profession. We have used case studies, built from our own experiences navigating field education in Canada, so that we might make visible efforts that often remain unseen despite their dramatic impact on students' experiences. We have highlighted three unique interventions focused on three different levels of field education – the micro experiences of individual students, the mezzo experiences of programmes themselves, and the macro experience of how practicum education in Canada is funded and organised. We undertook this approach in order to highlight both the specificity and the scope of work carried out by field directors and how those interventions in and of themselves actually re-create field education in a way that is disruptive of the neoliberal regimes that determine university-based education in Canada.

References

Accessibility for Ontarians with Disabilities Act. (2005). Retrieved from https://www.ontario.ca/laws/statute/05a11#BK0

Agrifoglio, R. (2015). *Knowledge preservation through community of practice theoretical issues and empirical evidence*. Cham, Switzerland: Springer International Publishing.

Allen, M., & Trawver, K. (2012). Student mental health and field education responsibilities and challenges of field educators. *Field Educator, 2*(1), 1–5. Retrieved from http://search.proquest.com/docview/1438556266/

American College Health Association. (2019). *American college health association-national college health assessment II: Canadian consortium executive summary spring 2019*. Silver Spring, MD. American College Health Association.

Ayala, J., Drolet, J., Fulton, A., Hewson, J., Letkemann, L., Baynton, M., & Schweizer, E. (2018). Field education in crisis: Experiences of field education coordinators in Canada. *Social Work Education, 37*(3), 281–293. https://doi.org/10.1080/02615479.2017.1397109

Baines, D. (2017). Anti-oppressive practice: Neoliberalism, inequality and change. In D. Baines. (Ed.) *Doing anti-oppressive practice: Social justice social work* (3rd ed.). Halifax, NS: Fernwood.

Barnoff, L., Moffatt, K., Todd, S., Panitch, M., & Parada, H. (2017). Academic leadership in the context of neoliberalism: The practice of social work directors. *Canadian Social Work Review, 34*(1), 5–21. https://doi-org.proxy.library.carleton.ca/10.7202/1040992ar

Baxter, P., & Jack, S. (2008). Qualitative case study methodology: Study design and implementation for novice researchers. *The Qualitative Report, 13*(4), 544–559.

Bellinger, A. (2010). Studying the landscape: Practice learning from social work reconsidered. *Social Work Education: The International Journal, 29*(6), 599–615. https://doi.org/10.1080/02615470903508743

Blackmore, J., Brennan, M., & Zipin, L. (2010). *RE-positioning university governance and academic work*. Netherlands: Sense Publishers.

Bogo, M. (2015). Field education for clinical social work practice: Best practices and contemporary challenges. *Clinical Social Work Journal, 43*(3), 317–324. https://doi.org/10.1007/s10615-015-0526-5

Brownlee, J. (2015). *Academia, Inc.: How corporatization is transforming Canadian universities*. Halifax, NS: Fernwood.

Bryan-Baynes, E. (2018, November 21). Quebec students take to the street to strike against unpaid internships. *Global News*. Retrieved from http://www.mcgilltribune.com/news/social-work-students-strike-against-unpaid-internships-112018/

Buck, P., Fletcher, P., & Bradley, J. (2016). Decision-making in social work field education: A 'good enough' framework. *Social Work Education: The International Journal, 35*(4), 402–413. https://doi.org/10.1080/02615479.2015.1109073

Buck, P., Robb, L., Bradley, J., & Kirzner, R. (2012). Complex and competing demands in field education: A qualitative study of field directors' experiences. *Field Educator, 2*(2), 1–17. Retrieved from http://search.proquest.com/docview/1761690504/

Canadian Alliance of Student Associations. (2018). Breaking down barriers: Mental health and Canadian post-secondary students [PDF file]. Retrieved from https://bp-net.ca/wp-content/uploads/2019/04/2018_Breaking-Down-Barriers-Mental-Health-and-Canadian-Post-Secondary-Students_CASA.pdf

Canadian Association for Social Work Education. (2014). Standards for accreditation [PDF file]. Retrieved from CASWE-ACFTS: http://caswe-acfts.ca/wp-content/uploads/2013/03/CASWE-ACFTS-Standards-11-2014.pdf

Canadian Association for Social Work Education. (2016). The three pillars of social work sign historic agreement. Retrieved from https://caswe-acfts.ca/the-three-pillars-of-social-work-sign-historic-agreement/

Carleton University. (2018). Essential requirements for MSW program - for students [PDF file]. Carleton University School of Social Work. https://carleton.ca/socialwork/wp-content/uploads/Essential-Requirements-for-the-MSW-Final-2018.pdf

Carleton University. (2019). Essential requirements for BSW program - for students [PDF file]. Carleton University School of Social Work. Retrieved from https://carleton.ca/socialwork/wp-content/uploads/Essential-Requirements-BSW-Program-April-4-2019.pdf

Clark, I., Moran, G., Skolnik, M., & Trick, D. (2009). *Academic transformation: The forces reshaping higher education in Ontario*. Kingston, ON: McGill Queens University Press.

Cleak, H., & Smith, D. (2012). Student satisfaction with models of field placement supervision. *Australian Social Work, 65*(2), 243–258. https://doi.org/10.1080/0312407X.2011.572981

Collini, S. (2012). *What are universities for?* London, UK: Penguin Books.

Council on Social Work Education (CSWE). (2015). Educational policy and accreditation standards [PDF file]. Retrieved from: https://www.cswe.org/getattachment/Accreditation/Accreditation-Process/2015-EPAS/2015EPAS_Web_FINAL.pdf.aspx

Crisp, R., & Hosken, N. (2016). A fundamental rethink of practice learning in social work education. *Social Work Education: The International Journal, 35*(5), 506–517. https://doi.org/10.1080/02615479.2016.1175422

Employment Standards Act. (2000). Retrieved from https://www.ontario.ca/laws/statute/00e41

Giamos, D., Lee, A., Suleiman, A., Stuart, H., Chen, S., Pullman, A., & Pidgeon, M. (2017). Understanding campus culture and student coping strategies for mental health issues in five Canadian colleges and universities. *Canadian Journal of Higher Education, 47*(3), 136–151. https://doi.org/10.7202/1043242

Glenmaye, L., & Bolin, B. (2007). Students with psychiatric disabilities: An exploratory study of program practices. *Journal of Social Work Education, 43*(1), 117–132. https://doi.org/10.5175/JSWE.2007.200404112

Health Quality Ontario. (2017). Improvement through collaboration: How to build and sustain a community of practice [PDF file]. Retrieved from http://www.entitesante2.ca/sante-en-francais/wp-content/uploads/2019/06/Health-Quality-Ontario-CoP-Toolkit.pdf

Horton, G. E., Diaz, N., & Green, D. (2009). Mental health characteristics of social work students: Implications for social work education. *Social Work in Mental Health*, 7(5), 458–475. https://doi.org/10.1080/15332980802467696

Human Rights Code. (1990). Retrieved from https://www.ontario.ca/laws/statute/90h19/v24

Hunter, C. A., & Poe, N. T. (2014). Developing and maintaining partnerships with practice settings. In C. A. Hunter, J. Moen, & M. Raskin (Eds.) *Social work field directors foundations for excellence*. Chicago, IL: Lyceum.

Jennissen, T., & Lundy, C. (2011). *One hundred years of social work: A history of the profession in English Canada, 1900–2000*. Waterloo, Ontario: Wilfrid Laurier University Press.

Lager, P. B., & Cooke Robbins, V. (2004). Field education: Exploring the future, expanding the vision. *Journal of Social Work Education, 40*(1), 3–12.

Lang, D. (2005). Financing higher education in Canada. In S. Michael and M. Kretovies (Eds.) *Financing higher education in a global market*. New York, NY: Algora Publishing.

MacDermott, D., & Campbell, A. (2016). An examination of student and provider perceptions of voluntary sector social work placements in Northern Ireland. *Social Work Education: The International Journal, 35*(1), 31–49. https://doi.org/10.1080/02615479.2015.1100289

McConnell, S. (2016). Final report on the provincial and regional meetings of CASWE-ACFTS field education coordinators and directors and recommendations for the design of a national online field instructors course [PDF file]. Retrieved from CASWE-ACFTS: https://caswe-acfts.ca/wp-content/uploads/2018/06/FieldProjectFinalReport2016.pdf

McKee, E., Muskat, T., & Perlman, I. (2015). Students today, educators tomorrow: Shaping the social work curriculum to enhance field education. *The Field Educator, 5*(2). Retrieved from https://fieldeducator.simmons.edu/article/students-today-educators-tomorrow-shaping-the-social-work-curriculum-to-enhance-field-education/

Meyer, C. (2001). A case in case study methodology. *Field Methods, 13*(4), 329–352. https://doi.org/10.1177/1525822X0101300402

Moffatt, K., et al. (2018). Worry about professional education: Emotions and affect in the context of neoliberal change in postsecondary education. *Emotion, Space and Society*, 26: 9–15.

Mishna, F., Levine, D., Bogo, M., & Van Wert, M. (2013). Cyber counselling: An innovative field education pilot project. *Social Work Education: The International Journal, 32*(4), 484–492. https://doi.org/10.1080/02615479.2012.685066

Noble, J., & Irwin, J. (2009). Social work supervision: An exploration of the current challenges in a rapidly changing social, economic and political environment. *Journal of Social Work, 9*(3), 345–358. https://doi.org/10.1177/1468017309334848

Ontario Association of Social Workers. (2020). *Ontario social work students in need of placements*. Retrieved from https://www.oasw.org/SocialWorkinOntario/BecomeaFieldPlacementSupervisor/

Pelech, W. J., Barlow, C., Badry, D. E., & Elliott, G. (2009). Challenging traditions: The field education experiences of students in workplace practica. *Social Work Education, 28*(7), 737–749. https://doi.org/10.1080/02615470802492031

Preston, S. G., George, P., & Silver, S. (2014). Field education in social work: The need for reimagining. *Critical Social Work, 15*(1), 57–72.

Ray, S., Wong, C., White, D., & Heaslip, K. (2013). Compassion satisfaction, compassion fatigue, work life conditions, and burnout among frontline mental health care professionals. *Traumatology, 19*(4), 255–267. https://doi.org/10.1177/1534765612471144

Regehr, C. (2013). Trends in higher education in Canada and implications for social work education. *Social Work Education: Social Work Education in North America: Research and Scholarship, 32*(6), 700–714. https://doi.org/10.1080/02615479.2013.785798

Reimer, M. (2004). *Inside corporate U: Women in the academy speak out*. Toronto: Sumach Press.

Reynolds, V. (2019). The zone of fabulousness: Resisting vicarious trauma with connection, collective care and justice-doing in ways that centre the people we work alongside. *Context, 164*, 36–39. Retrieved from https://vikkireynoldsdotca.files.wordpress.com/2019/09/2019-context-uk-zone-of-fabulousness-reynolds.pdf

Silverthorn, D. (2016). *Hungry for knowledge: Assessing the prevalence of student food insecurity on five Canadian campuses*. Toronto: Meal Exchange. Retrieved from https://static1.squarespace.com/static/5941c85ae4fcb533d8d82767/t/59ab0a93c027d8465d890e32/1504381735025/Hungry+for+Knowledge_11.04.2016a.pdf

Sowbel, L. R. (2012). Gatekeeping: Why shouldn't we be ambivalent. *Journal of Social Work Education, 48*(1), 27–44. https://doi.org/10.5175/JSWE.2012.201000027

Statistics Canada. (2020). Table 37-10-0003-01 *Canadian undergraduate tuition fees by field of study*. https://doi.org/10.25318/3710000301-eng

Swanborn, P. (2010). *Case study research: What, why and how?* Los Angeles, CA: SAGE.

Tam, D., Brown, A., Paz, E., Birnbaum, R., & Kwok, S. (2018). Challenges faced by Canadian social work field instructors in baccalaureate field supervision. *Journal of Teaching in Social Work, 38*(4), 398–416. https://doi.org/10.1080/08841233.2018.1502228

Todd, S., Asakura, K., Morris, B., Eagle, B., & Park, G. (2019). Responding to student mental health concerns in social work education: Reflective questions for social work educators. *Social Work Education, 38*(6), 779–796. https://doi.org/10.1080/02615479.2018.1563591

Todd, S., Barnoff, L., Moffatt, K., Panitch, M., Parada, H., Mucina, M., & Williams, D. (2015) Performativity culture in universities: Social work fabrications. *The British Journal of Social Work, 45*(2), 511–526. https://doi.org/10.1093/bjsw/bct139

University College Cork. (2020). Core competencies and health matters, school of applied social studies [PDF file]. Retrieved from: https://www.ucc.ie/en/media/support/academicsecretariat/ftp/corecompetenciesandhealthmattersAppliedSocialStudies.pdf

Wenger, E. (1998). *Communities of practice: Learning, meaning and identity*. Cambridge UK: Cambridge University Press.

Wever, C., & Zell, S. (2018). Re-working self-care: From individual to collective responsibility through a critical ethics of care. In B. Pease, A. Vreugdenhil, & S. Stanford, (Eds.). *Critical ethics of care in social work: Transforming the politics and practices of caring* (pp. 207–218). Abingdon: Routledge.

Wiebe, M. (2010). Pushing the boundaries of the social work practicum: Rethinking sites and supervision toward radical practice. *Journal of Progressive Human Services, 21*(1), 66–82. https://doi.org/10.1080/10428231003782517

Wilson, F. (2016). Identifying, preventing, and addressing job burnout and vicarious burnout for social work professionals. *Journal of Evidence-Informed Social Work: Trauma-Informed Care: Intervening Across Systems, 13*(5), 479–483. https://doi.org/10.1080/23761407.2016.1166856

Yao, J. (2018, November 20). Social work students strike against unpaid internships. *The McGill Tribune*. Retrieved from http://www.mcgilltribune.com/news/social-work-students-strike-against-unpaid-internships-112018/

Yin, R. K. (2003). *Case study research: Design and methods* (3rd ed.). Thousand Oaks, CA: SAGE.

Zuchowski, I. (2015). Being the university: Liaison persons' reflections on placements with off-site supervision. *Social Work Education: The International Journal, 34*(3), 301–314. https://doi.org/10.1080/02615479.2015.1005070

Part III

Current Realities of Social Work Field Education in Australia and Oceania

11

Social Work Field Education in Australia

Concepts, Challenges, and Twenty-First-Century Concerns

Helen Cleak

This chapter critically examines the historical development of field education in promoting and shaping the professional identity and competencies of social work graduates in Australia. In order to understand this development, attention is drawn to the national history of social work within a political and ideological context, including the development of the profession and a description of the health and welfare organisation where social workers are employed. Of course, social work practice is also shaped by higher education policies in which social work education operate, both globally and locally. This chapter then turns to a discussion of the profession's regulatory standards under which field education programmes function as well as offering a description of the current processes and content of field education programmes. The next section outlines the major challenges and debates that are currently shaping field education with particular reference to supervision models and their effectiveness in enhancing the student experience. This discussion underpins this with a consideration of the literature to debate the various factors that contribute to quality learning in field education and developing students' professional identity. Finally, this evidence base is used to draw implications for Australian social work field education in ensuring that quality and professional standards are maintained in a changing organisational, economic, and political context.

This chapter raises the triumphs and achievements of social work field education as well as the challenges and struggles and some predictions for the future. Underpinning this discussion is a strong focus on current research and contemporary literature to illustrate and provide evidence to highlight the content provided.

The Historical Development of the Profession

The social work profession in Australia has had a fairly short history and had its beginnings in the voluntary and charitable sector but became professionalised with the commencement of formal training for workers in 1940. There is little or no reference to the historical development of the social work profession (Mendes, 2005), although Garton (1990) notes that Australian social workers were trained on the British model, which emphasised the social causes of poverty,

DOI: 10.4324/9781032164946-15

rather than the American focus on psychology. Initially social work was composed of hospital almoners who were educated by training boards and were regarded as an elite group of specialist social workers (Miller, 2016). By 1940, the time was ready for the establishment of professional social work education in universities, which was lagging behind the developed world and the first degree-level qualifications were offered in the 1960s (Miller & Nichols, 2013).

Social work education has been somewhat of a success story in Australia with government policies favouring a welfare state approach to social problems with pensions and benefits available since Federation in 1901 and universal health care since the 1970s, and this has required the employment of qualified social workers to deliver a range of health and human services as well as to inform and advocate for needed changes at the policy level. However, it has been noted that, historically, social work, as a profession, has lacked power because of the absence of government registration and its concentration in large bureaucracies (Healy, 1998, cited in Mendes, 2005).

Social workers in Australia are primarily involved in casework and direct practice and are largely employed in the non-profit sector (government and non-government) and the greatest proportion of all social workers are employed in the health and community services fields (Healy & Lonne, 2010). Government projections show that employment for social workers grew strongly in the last 5 years and that growth is expected to continue for the next 5 years (Australian Bureau of Statistics, 2018). The undersupply of qualified social work practitioners within an ageing human services workforce has led to major government and non-government organisations (NGOs) employing staff with diploma-level qualifications, particularly in child protection, disability, and juvenile justice (Healy & Lonne, 2010).

These workforce projections have seen the demand for social work programmes within universities increasing. As a result, new social work programmes have proliferated in the last two decades, which has been further boosted by the Australian government's policy to deregulate enrolment quotas in higher education since 1986. In 1994, there were only 19 universities programmes (Fook & Cleak, 1996), but by 2017, the current number of accredited Bachelor and Master of Social Work courses in Australia had risen to 91 across 32 universities (Australian Association of Social Workers (AASW), 2017), most of which are centred in urban areas (Neden et al.,). Some of these courses are offered at a number of sites (some universities have both metropolitan and rural campuses), which means the actual number of programmes are even larger. Recent innovations in Australian social work education include the move towards online delivery, off campus, and distance education, partly as a recognition of the need to service Australia's rural and regional population. Distance education options are provided at 12 universities (Ross et al., 2019). The onset of the Covid-19 pandemic has accelerated the movement of most tertiary institutions to a blended learning model of delivery.

Development of Australian Social Work Curriculum

Australian social work has been influenced by programmes from the United Kingdom and North America from which much of the literature around conceptualisations of the social work profession, its knowledge, skills, and values has been derived. It has influenced the way that field education programmes have been constructed and implemented, and it is in the context of this understanding that this chapter will now review how Australian social work field education programmes have developed over time.

One of the distinguishing features of Australian social work is that it is based on a model of professionalism. The social work profession is not a regulated profession, but it is governed by the professional association, the AASW, which maintains strong control over professional standards and accreditation of social work programmes. Social work qualifying courses are accredited by the AASW every five years against clear guidelines for curriculum content and delivery, including detailed and comprehensive accreditation rules for the field education components of these programmes.

In his exploration of the profession in Australia, Mendes (2005) suggests that social work theory and literature in the 1960s emphasised psychoanalysis and casework at the expense of alternative theories and methods, such as sociology and community development. However, during the 1970s, there was a movement away from the earlier casework focus on addressing individual defects to the development of new skills, emphasising the promotion of social change, which was reflected in social work education. Systems and ecological approaches along with reflective methods in teaching social work students followed, as well as more content in relation to education about indigenous issues and an appreciation of safe cultural practice (Fook, 2003; ASWEAS, 2021). Accredited social work courses are generalist and generic in nature, and opportunities for specialisations are offered primarily in the form of elective undergraduate subjects or through postgraduate qualifications.

Field education placements are integrated into the course of formal study and have, historically, reflected the changing curriculum content discussed here.

Development of Field Education in Australia

Field education represents a significant component of all accredited social work programmes, with the AASW requiring students to undertake a minimum of 1,000 hours in field education over at least two placements and supervisors must have a minimum of two years practice post qualifying (AASW, 2021). Most programmes divide those hours into two full-time, 14-week placements and students follow the official working week in Australia, which is 35 hours per week. Thus, field education represents a significant proportion of the educational curriculum of the bachelor's degree (at least 25%) and master's degree (up to 50%) (Neden et al., 2018).

Universities have largely relied on the voluntary contribution of professionally qualified and experienced social workers to act as supervisors and have interpreted the nature of professional fieldwork in a 'clinical' manner in which the field educator assumes responsibility for the student's educational learning (Cleak et al., 2000). This simplistic model reflects the one-to-one relationship in which one student is assigned to one supervisor in one location and undertakes social work tasks that are offered at that agency and provides students with opportunities to apply and integrate what they have learned in the classroom. This apprenticeship model, in which the students followed and copied the expert social worker, were founded on key concepts from clinical practice which relied on the client–practitioner relationship to facilitate and support the change process (Bennet et al., 2012). University field education staff have continued to privilege the one-to-one supervisory relationship in which personal growth and development is achieved where role modelling, coaching, and experiential learning can occur (Bogo, 2015; Cleak & Zuchowski, 2019).

However, this one-to-one model has gradually been challenged by a range of global and local issues. First, the 1990s brought a changing educational and human services climate which increased pressures on practitioners to adhere to neoliberal, economic principles that demand lean, cost-effective services (Healy & Lonne, 2010; Bellinger, 2010), and this has resulted in a reduced commitment by the field to take social work students on placement. Through these influences, the field has seen a growth in work-based placements, a reliance on less experienced staff to supervise students, more requests for 'good' students, and less tolerance for student difficulties (Cleak & Smith, 2012; Neden et al., 2018).

The second concern facing field education programmes is the wide gap between the widely espoused importance of field education and the often ad hoc and scantily resourced arrangements which universities use to secure enough placements (Cleak & Zuchowski, 2020; Zuchowski et al., 2019). This has been evidenced since the 1990s, and the literature reporting on inadequate resourcing in field education programmes, its marginality in the curriculum, and the relatively low status of field education staff (Fook & Cleak, 1996).

As a result of these pressures, field education programmes have incorporated a range of other, often, innovative arrangements, despite the ongoing tendency to view these as atypical or somewhat 'second best' to the traditional model. One Australian study reported that these include inter-professional placements in which a number of disciplines are placed together, rotational-based placement models when students move through two or more practice areas, and collaboration between groups of universities and universities and agencies (Zuchowski et al., 2019; Cleak & Zuchowski, 2020). However, there are concerns about the agency's ability to have the time to supervise and create a pedagogically valuable learning environment that may not reflect practices that promote social work values (Neden et al., 2018; Cleak et al., 2020).

Lastly, there is an ongoing challenge being faced by many social work students who are required to spend 1,000 hours of unpaid time in placement. Social work students are usually older than other university students, and most are also in paid work (Baglow & Gair, 2019). The Australian government offers a means tested allowance to students classified as 'independent' prior to 22 years of age, so secondary school leavers are not able to access the youth allowance until in their third or final year of a social work degree. This youth allowance equates to 54% of other pension rates, so students often need to subsidise this by working (Neden et al., 2018).

The following section will now turn to the regulatory guidelines, policies, and processes that field education programmes are required to follow within social work programmes in Australia.

Regulatory Policies Governing Field Education in Australia

The AASW sets the standards and requirements for social work education in Australia, and all accredited courses are required to comply with a multiplicity of requirements and standards around course content, social work attributes, and practice standards. The Australian Social Work Education and Accreditation Standards (ASWEAS, 2021) also provide guidelines for supporting alternative placement models in field education but places limitations around the use of placements with external supervision, work-based placements, or the provision of credit for recognition of prior learning.

The ASWEAS (2021) outlines a range of attributes and required curriculum content areas, and social work programmes have the task of integrating these into the field education subjects.

The Current Requirements for the Structure of the Placement

- That students undertake a minimum of 1,000 placement hours in at least two field education subjects.
- Practice–theory integration seminars may be included within the required hours up to a maximum of 14 hours per 500-hour placement.
- No placement will be shorter than 280 hours.
- Placements must be structured in a way that is educationally viable so that educational goals can be achieved. Patterns of placement days may vary from 5 days per week to a minimum of 2 days per week. Placements that are 2 days per week must include at least two full-time (5-day) block periods.

There are guidelines for considering extenuating circumstances that would allow some flexibility regarding these requirements, such as students who have a disability that might lead to more impaired health or is simply untenable because of the nature of the disability. Work or family commitments or the financial cost are not considered as extenuating.

The Current Requirements for Placement and Supervision

- All placements must be able to provide appropriate social work tasks and meet the educational requirements of the field education programme.
- Each student is allocated a field educator who is a suitably qualified and experienced practitioner who has had at least 2 years of full-time employment post-graduation. In exceptional circumstances relating to distance, a field educator with less experience may be allocated for one placement only.
- There must be clear expectations for learning goals and performance outcomes that are documented in a learning plan.
- At least one placement will be in direct practice.
- The field educators must undertake training for the field education role.
- The field educators must be able to provide a minimum of 1.5 hours of formal supervision per student for each 35 hours of placement. At a minimum, half of this supervision must be provided on a one-to-one basis.
- The field educator will be able to observe the student's practice in placements where the focus is on direct practice.

Responsibilities of the Social Work Programme

- There must be a clearly identifiable field education unit with dedicated administrative support, and field education must be integrated into the social work curriculum. Field education coordinators must be social workers with a minimum of 5 years' post-qualifying practice experience.
- The social work programme assigns a field education liaison staff to each placement.

  Field education liaison staff must be either experienced social work educators or social workers with a minimum of 5 years' post-qualifying practice experience. They must maintain regular contact with the student with a minimum of three contacts, including at least one face-to-face contact. These may include group meetings and tutorials or video-conferencing in exceptional circumstances for one placement only.

Exemptions to These Arrangements

Existing policy offers a few alternatives to traditional placement arrangements.

Recognition of prior learning (RPL), is constructed in accreditation policy as the assessment of equivalence and transferability of learning acquired in one context in relation to another. The rationale is a balance between a social justice perspective that values the skills and expertise of experienced practitioners and reduces the requirement for such practitioners to repeat training and education. The argument against RPL is that policy and legislative contexts change frequently and that this is a professional learning experience involving reflection on past experiences and the creation of new learning (Neden et al., 2018).

The ASWEAS (2021) mandates possible RPL for part or the entire first placement in the Bachelor of Social Work and the Master of Social Work (Qualifying) degrees, but the more recent standards have modified the requirements for subsequent placements in which RPL has been granted ASWEAS (2021). The main features of RPL policy include:

- The field education programme must clearly articulate the rationale for how RPL will be used and assessed, and there must be an external, independent process to verify the accuracy of student's claims through the use of a panel.
- Only formal work experience, tasks, and duties in line with social work roles, tasks, and functions should be considered when granting RPL, not life experience.
- In order to be granted RPL students must provide evidence that they have met the standards and performance outcomes for the first placement. The work experience must include a minimum of 3 full-time equivalent years' practice in a relevant context in the previous 7 years and using social work practice skills, such as assessment and counselling, and methods, such as casework or community work.
- Assessment of a portfolio demonstrating how the student meets the professional practice standards – this could include job descriptions, referee reports from a qualified social worker, skills assessment, and critical reflection on placement or work experience.
- The granting of RPL has implications for second placement, including the condition that the second placement must be undertaken in an Australian setting, where there is on-site supervision, and the placement setting must be different to settings in the student's work history and any experience on which the RPL application was based.

Placements in the Student's Place of Employment

Field education placements can be undertaken in the student's workplace for one placement as long as it is in a different context and not involving the student's routine work responsibilities.

Common Processes in Field Education Programmes

Because of the ASWEAS requirements, the organisation and processes undertaken by field education programmes in Australia share a great deal of common practices. There has been no systematic review of how Australian social work programmes structure and organise their placements except for an early, nationwide Australian survey of 14 social work programmes from 16 schools in 1992 (Fook & Cleak, 1996). Their findings are largely relevant today and are described below.

Field education programmes have always relied on the voluntary contribution of agencies which provide the supervision and support of the student with no financial incentives. Most schools take responsibility for organising placements for students by a general mailout to prospective agencies followed by more specific personal follow-up via telephone or email. Only a small number of schools allow students to organise their own placements, and the final responsibility lies with the field education coordinator. In the past, schools used to offer students individual interviews to ascertain their interests and relevant experience before allocating placements, but the shortage of available placements has necessitated less choice and a reliance on the use of a detailed questionnaire of student details to allocate placements (Cleak & Wilson, 2018). In general, first-placement students are given less choice, are less likely to be individually interviewed by agency staff, and were more likely to be allocated a placement after some form of group discussion or educational session than final year students. Although the ASWEAS. require field education programmes to employ a permanent field education coordinator, there has been a trend for programmes to be part of a more general, administrative unit within schools which finds placements for a range of professions. For example, a health faculty member would usually establish an administrative placement team which would source placements for student nurses, allied health students, and social work students.

There has also been a history of competition between universities with very little collaboration between programmes around resource-sharing (Karger, 2012). However, in the State of Victoria, the six schools of social work tried to rectify this individualism in 1992, by leading a collaborative project that incorporated a joint database and shared administrative management of placement planning and implementation. This programme was based on the principle that all Schools should have equal access to quality field placements. This was followed in 2015 by the Victorian Schools of Social Work developing a standardised learning and assessment tool that was used by all social work students undertaking a placement (Cleak et al., 2015). This learning agreement is still being used by Victorian Schools today, but the collaborative database programme was disbanded once student enrolments and competitive practices overtook collective responses.

As outlined earlier, Australian social work programmes have followed a policy of not paying for student placements but have usually offered small incentives, such as library rights, in-house training, or research consultancies to agencies. However, a specific government initiative, beginning in 2011, introduced a policy of selective funding for some tertiary institutions to pay for clinical placements in health and allied health (including social work). The purpose of this plan was to build a health workforce for a projected shortfall for the next 30 years, but in order to meet the training needs, the government was required to support students' clinical placements within health, mental health, and aged care agencies (HWA, 2011). As a result, 'social work has been caught up in a system of payments being made for clinical student placements' using a competitive allocation process that has led to only some universities having access to the funding (Neden et al., 2018, p 350).

A recent national survey of field education programmes indicated that the struggle to find sufficient quality placements has changed the way that programmes are structured and their use of different supervisory relationships (Zuchowski et al., 2019; Cleak & Zuchowski, 2019; Cleak & Wilson, 2018). Neo-liberalism has changed the way health and human sevices are organised and delivered with agencies working within a more competitive and risk adverse environment with high workloads and resourcing issues, including reduced administrative support and limited budgets.

This section has highlighted the changing nature of placement practices in Australia, with earlier processes reflecting a philosophy of individual choice and a recognition of the importance of meeting the student learning needs by matching with an appropriate placement.

But since then, emerging issues have shifted these practices to reduced student choice and less access to quality placements. This will be discussed in more detail below.

Current Issues and Debates in Field Education

The following section will now turn to the current state of play of field education in Australia, using recent research and the literature to discuss the issues, challenges, and debates.

The present situation holds both constraints and opportunities for providing quality field education programmes across Australia. Although it has been argued that the profession might be disadvantaged because of the challenges outlined above, there is, simultaneously, an important opportunity to guide the development of the profession in ways which respond to and take advantage of the unique features of this situation. However, any creative and sustainable progress requires an evidence base to guide the practice, and this section will outline the current policies that have influenced the introduction of alternative field education models and processes. The discussion will be underpinned by the considerable research that has been undertaken in Australia to inform the present state of play plus the ongoing debate as the profession reviews the current guidelines.

Trends in Higher Education and Human Services in Australia

As outlined above, key policy changes within Australia's higher education sector triggered rapid growth in domestic and international student enrolments. International students now represent 28% of university enrolments in Australia, with the vast majority of these students coming from the Asia-Pacific region so that Australian academic institutions increasingly reflect a non-European population of students (Harrison & Ip, 2013). This trend is also evident in health profession courses, which have seen a particularly rapid increase in the number of international students over recent years in degrees such as social work (Ross et al., 2019).

One reason for the increase in international students enrolling in social work degrees can be attributed to an Australian policy that allows a person to live and work in Australia through a Skilled Independent Visa, as they are now classified as a high-demand field of employment by the Australian Government (Australian Government, 2017). There are no comprehensive figures that reflect the number of international students who are enrolled in social work courses, but a national study, which canvassed information from field education programmes, showed great variation between programmes in the number of international students being placed (Cleak & Zuchowski, 2020). Only one programme did not place any international students, there were five programmes that placed between 15 and 29 students, and one programme placed 106 international students during 2015. The challenge for social work programmes is that field educators consistently report that international students require more time and resources to supervise because they often face language, cultural, and educational barriers, and they also report that the education provider does not provide adequate training and support (Ross et al., 2019).

Apart from increased enrolments of international students, higher education reforms have also targeted enrolments of local students who have traditionally been under-represented in higher education. These students are from culturally, linguistically, and educationally diverse backgrounds; have low socio-economic status; are first in the family to attend university; are indigenous; or have disabilities (Hill et al., 2019; Cleak & Smith, 2012). The impact of this policy changed the composition of the student body who had varying English comprehension levels, and with more than a quarter of students now studying off-campus, students now present a range of different needs and expectations, which adds an extra layer of complexity in the processes of matching students to placements (ibid, 2019).

As described earlier, the accelerated growth in social work programmes was also fuelled by the recognition by the Australian government that it needed greater numbers of well-educated, highly competent health and human service professionals to meet changing community demands, new technology, an ageing population, and a forecasted shortfall in the health workforce (Health Workforce Australia, 2013; Cleak & Smith, 2012). As most health courses require clinical placements, the government allocated funds to build capacity within health and some human service agencies to provide placements for students (Buchanan et al., 2014). This funding offered incentives to pilot a range of different models of placement and supervision arrangements, including partnerships, student units with paid clinical supervisors, and group and external supervision (Hill et al., 2019). However, once this funding ended, most of these developments proved unsustainable in the longer term, although some state public health and mental health agencies introduced standardised fees for providing placements to be paid by universities (Department of Health, 2013).

Supervision Models

Difficulties in securing and retaining placements due to industry and educational contexts previously described has encouraged the introduction of alternative field placement structures and supervision arrangements. There has always been a range of other models that have been used to supplement the traditional one-on-one supervision approach to deliver teaching and support on placement, such as group supervision, co-supervision, and external supervision (Cleak et al., 2000). This section will pay particular attention to external supervision as there has been increasing evidence in Australia, as well as in the United Kingdom, that the use of external supervision by universities is increasing, and there is concern about the quality and viability of this model and whether it compromises optimal student learning (Curtis et al., 2012; Zuchowski et al., 2019; Cleak & Zuchowski, 2020). External supervision is used in field placements when there is no on-site social worker who meets AASW standards. Professional supervision is provided to the student for the duration of the placement by an external field educator appointed by the university (Cleak & Smith 2012).

An early Australian study by Fook and Cleak (1996) found that off-site supervision was commonly used but constituted a small number of placments. Seven schools used up to 10% external supervision, but for one school, approximately 60% of supervisors were off-site.

A study by Cleak and Smith (2012) explored social work students' satisfaction with the various models of supervision and found that, although external supervision was only provided to 10% of the cohort (*n* = 263), they were significantly less satisfied with their placement than students provided with one-on-one supervision with an onsite social worker.

A national survey in Australia was undertaken in 2015 to develop a snapshot of Australian field education programmes provided by accredited social work courses, including the current challenges and the supervision models being used (Cleak & Zuchowski, 2020; Zuchowski et al., 2019). Twenty-four field education programmes completed the survey which included at least one university from each state. The respondents reported that they sourced more than 5,000 social work and human service placements undertaken by students in Australia in 2015, of which the majority of placements occurred in the same period (July–November). This study confirmed that, although individual supervision was the most common model used, there was a wide use of external supervision with some of the larger programmes reporting that 50% of their students received external supervision. Group supervision was usually offered in conjunction with external supervision and other less used models were rotational-based models with different supervisors, student units with an internal supervisor, and student units with an external supervisor. The majority of the external supervisors and liaison people were contracted by the university to undertake this work and, worryingly, many had been employed for the first time in this role.

A follow-up study on student satisfaction with supervision and learning activities with their placements in Northern Ireland (*n* = 396) showed significant differences in satisfaction measures in relation to models of supervision with students being less satisfied when they received supervision from an external or long-arm supervisor and who had an unqualified on-site 'task' supervisor who may have a qualification but not in social work (Cleak et al., 2016).

An additional trend identified in the national survey showed that the usual process of programmes sourcing placements in their local catchment area had changed with most programmes now widening their geographical scope and placing students hundreds of kilometres away from the university campus and many programmes finding placements in another state or territory and, hence, increasing their competition with other programmes (Cleak & Zuchowski, 2020).

Little is known about the number of social work programmes that regularly send students overseas, but it appears that most programmes operate on a fluid, ad hoc arrangement (Cleak, Anand & Das, 2016). There are a range of difficult challenges in organising and supporting an international placement programme such as addressing student expectations, meeting accreditation requirements, and the resourcing costs for the students as well as for the universities. An additional challenge in organising international placements is identifying qualified supervisors for students and needing to use untrained staff to provide supervision who may be unfamiliar with the academic expectations and styles of learning and teaching (ibid, 2015). The limited evidence that exists in Australia showed that only that a small percentage of placements were overseas, with the 1996 survey reporting that only 1%–3% of placements were overseas, although one school reported approximately 17% of placements were taken overseas (Fook & Cleak, 1996).

Conclusion: What is Next for Research

The evidence offered by the literature and discussion show that the challenges and current debates in field education in Australia has been around for 30 years. The difference lies in the scale of the problem that has intensified the pressure on university programmes in securing and sustaining a pool of viable placements and the capacity of health and human services to provide adequate learning opportunities for students to meet their supervisory obligations. Successive decades have grappled with diminishing resources and increasing demand, and field education programmes have responded individually and collectively to continue to offer quality placements to social work students.

The COVID-19 pandemic currently gripping the world and closing intercountry borders, as well as an increasingly strained political climate between Australia and China, will invariably result in the downturn in international enrolments of social work students. This may go some way to ease the pressure on placements, although most Australian universities are having to cut costs by reducing staffing levels. The social work profession is maintaining its positive growth with high employment rates (Australian Bureau of Statistics, 2018) but is still facing considerable challenges both economical and ideological. And, unlike other countries, such as the UK, there has been little government intervention to fund and regulate field placements.

One positive initiative has been the establishment of a National Field Education Network (NFEN) in recent years, which has offered a forum for identifying and responding to social work field education issues and for recognising and sharing strengths, goals, capacities, and innovation (Rollins et al., 2017). This group meets regularly to share ideas, develop research plans, and fund submissions to promote an evidence base to improving practice.

The recent national survey found that field education programmes were open to considering innovative placement models while still meeting the requirements of the professional accreditation body (Zuchowski et al., 2019).

Clear areas for advocacy need to be identified at the local programmatic level, but other changes will necessitate structural change and additional resources at the government level.

One of these appear to be addressing the apparent misalignment between the learning aspirations contained within the current social work education standards and the current realities facing field education practice. However, this needs to be balanced by the research which reaffirms that student satisfaction with their placement experience and professional learning is strongly correlated to a positive supervisory relationship, opportunities to observe, be observed, and to reflect. This questions the use of alternative field education approaches. The future will require adequate investment in systematic research to ensure that the professional learning opportunities undertaken by social work students will not be compromised by short term expediencies. As the current president of the AASW stated,

> It is important that we negotiate this pressure sensibly to ensure that we maintain and further develop professional standards to maximise the quality of social work education. Any relaxing of standards needs to be done in the spirit of innovation and to address issues that we have identified as a profession, not for financial gain only for the universities.
>
> *(Craik, 2019, p. 129)*

References

Australian Association of Social Work [AASW]. (2021). *AWEAS field education standards*, available online at: https://www.aasw.asn.au/careers-study/educationstandards-accreditation (accessed May 17, 2021).

Australian Bureau of Statistics. (2018). Labour force, Australia, November 2018. Report 6202.0. ABS. Retrieved from http://www.abs.gov.au/ausstats/abs%40.nsf/mf/6202.0

Australian Government. (2017). Skilled independent visa (subclass 189). Retrieved from http://www.border.gov.au/Trav/Visa-1/189-

Baglow, L., & Gair, S. (2019). Mature-aged social work students: The challenges of poverty, study, and family responsibilities. *Australian Social Work, 72*(1), 46–57.

Bellinger, A. (2010). Talking about (re) generation: Practice learning as a site of renewal in social work. *British Journal of Social Work, 40*, 2450–66.

Bennet, S., Mohr, J., Deal, K. H., & Hwang, J. (2012). Supervisor attachment, supervisory working alliance, and affect in social work field instruction. *Research on Social Work Practice, 23*(2), 199–209.

Bogo, M. (2015). Field education for clinical social work practice: Best practices and contemporary challenges. *Clinical Social Work Journal, 43*(3), 317–324.

Buchanan, J., Jenkins, S., & Scott, L. (2014). *Student clinical education in Australia: A University of Sydney scoping study*. Sydney: The University of Sydney.

Cleak, H., Anand, J., & Das, C. (2016). Asking the critical questions- an evaluation of social work students' experiences in an international placement. *British Journal of Social Work*, 46, 2, 389–408.

Cleak, H., Hawkins, L., & Hess, L. (2000) Innovative field options. In L. Cooper, and L. Briggs (eds) *Fieldwork in the human services* (pp. 160–174). Adelaide: Allen and Unwin.

Cleak, H., Hawkins, L., Laughton, J., & Williams, J. (2015). Creating a standardised teaching and learning framework for social work field placements. *Australian Social Work, 68*(1), 49–64.

Cleak, H., Roulson, A., & Vreugdenhil, A. (2016). The inside story: A survey of social work students' supervision and learning opportunities on placement. *British Journal of Social Work, 46*(7), 2033–2050.

Cleak, H., & Smith, D. (2012). Student satisfaction with current models of field placement supervision. *Australian Social Work, 65*(2), 243–258.

Cleak, H., & Wilson, J. (2018). *Making the most of field placement* (4th ed.). Southbank: Cengage.

Cleak, H., & Zuchowski, I. (2019). Empirical support and considerations for social work supervision of students in alternative placement models. *Clinical Social Work Journal, 47*(1), 32–42.

Cleak, H., & Zuchowski, I. (2020). Mapping social work field education in the 21st century: A national survey of the Australian context. *British Journal of Social Work, 50*, 427–446.

Cleak, H., Zuchowski, I., & Cleaver, M. (2020). On a Wing and a Prayer! An Exploration of Students' Experiences of External Supervision. *British Journal of Social Work*, 1–19.

Craik, C. (2019). Social work education: Challenges and opportunities. *Australian Social Work, 72*(2), 129–132.

Curtis, L., Moriarty, J., & Netten, A. (2012). The costs of qualifying a social worker. *British Journal of Social Work, 42*(4), 706–724.

Department of Health. (2013). *Training and development grant: 2013–14 professional entry student placement subsidy*. Retrieved from http://www.health.vic.gov.au/fees.htm

Fook, J. (2003). Social work research in Australia. *Social Work Education, 22*(1), 45–57.

Fook, J., & Cleak, H. (1996). The state of field education in Australia: Results of a national survey. In J. Ife, S. Leitman, & P. Murphy (eds) *Advances in social work and welfare education* (pp. 29–42). Perth: University of Western Australia.

Garton, S. (1990). *Out of luck: Poor Australians and social welfare 1788–1988*. Sydney: Allen & Unwin.

Harrison, G., & Ip, R. (2013). Extending the terrain of inclusive education in the classroom to the field: International students on placement. *Social Work Education, 32*(2), 230–243.

Health Workforce Australia (HWA). (2011). *Mapping clinical placements: Capturing opportunities for growth–demand (university) study*. Canberra: Health Workforce Australia, Australian Government.

Health Workforce Australia (HWA). (2013). Health workforce Australia annual report 2012–2013. Adelaide.

Healy, J. (1998). *Welfare options*. St Leonards: Allen & Unwin.

Healy, K., & Lonne, B. (2010). *The social work and human services workforce: Report from a national study of education, training and workforce needs*. Strawberry Hills: Australian Learning and Teaching Council.

Hill, N., Cleak, H., Egan, R., Ervin, L., & Laughton, J. (2019). Factors that impact a social worker's capacity to supervise a student. *Australian Social Work, 72*(2), 152–165.

Karger, H. (2012): Lessons from American social work education: Caution ahead. *Australian Social Work, 65*(3), 311–325.

Mendes, P. (2005). The history of social work in Australia: A critical literature review. *Australian Social Work, 58*(2), 121–131.

Miller, J., & Nichols, D. (2013). Moving among friends: The establishment of professional social work education at the University of Melbourne, 1929–1941. *Social Work in Health Care, 52*(2–3), 110–124.

Miller, & University of Melbourne Social Work Alumni Association. (2016). *Leading social work: 75 years at the University of Melbourne.*

Neden, J., Townsend, R., & Zuchowski, I. (2018) Towards sustainability in Australian social work field education. *Australian Social Work, 71*(3), 345–357.

Rollins, W., Egan, R., Zuchowski, I., Duncan, M., Chee, P., Muncey, P., … Higgins, M. (2017). Leading through collaboration: The national field education network. *Advances in Social Work & Welfare Education, 19*(1), 48–61.

Ross, B., Ta, B., & Oliaro, L. (2019): Institutional responsibilities: providing placement for international students. *Social Work Education, 39*(5), 665–680.

Zuchowski, I., Cleak, H., Nickson, A., & Spencer, A. (2019). A national survey of Australian social work field education programs: Innovation with limited capacity. *Australian Social Work, 72*(1), 75–90.

12

'Getting Used to the First Nations Person in the Room'

A Discussion on Field Practice in Australia

Kiel Hennessey, Steven Keed, Rachael Howard, Bindi Bennett, Phillip Pallas, and Kylie Agllias

Whilst writing another chapter on Australia, the authors realised there is little to no literature led by Aboriginal people about their social work field placements. Given social work's desire for social justice, we thought it vital to begin to start these conversations and to address the large gaps that may not only be affecting Aboriginal and Torres Strait Islander peoples but may be relevant to First Nations peoples internationally. First Nations people rely on respectful and reciprocal relationships. For too long, First Nations people have had research done to them instead of with them. The non-Indigenous authors were very aware of the power imbalances and the history of social workers in this space. As part of their cultural responsiveness, the non-Indigenous (white) academics wanted to make sure that this chapter was led by First Nations peoples and experiences. The team was gathered based on existing relationships but also with a variety of ages and genders to have diverse voices. This process has been Aboriginal-led and in a recipricol and respectful process.

The term *First Nations* has been used predominantly, and sometimes interchangeably, with the term *Aboriginal* and *Torres Strait Islander*, and *Indigenous*, throughout this chapter. First Nations was chosen because there is no one good or accepted terminology. Terminology means different things to different people and is wrapped in the history and politics of the time. We felt First Nations would not only fit in Australia but may also be relevant for our international readers. In keeping with this standpoint, the chapter proceeds as follows: First, the authors introduce the history of Australia's First Nations peoples and their connection with Australian social work. This is proceeded by a review of a significantly limited body of literature which examines the experiences of First Nations students on field placement in Australia. In response to these gaps, the following section draws on the knowledge, insights, and lived experiences of the first four authors who proceed to discuss the field experiences of First Nations students, and educators, in Australia.

First Nations Peoples and Australian Social Work

The relationship between social work and First Nations peoples in Australia is complex. Australia has two distinct groups of First Nations peoples: Aboriginal and Torres Strait Islander peoples.

DOI: 10.4324/9781032164946-16

The term *Aboriginal* is used to describe the original inhabitants and descendants of mainland Australia and the island state of Tasmania. *Torres Strait Islander* describes original inhabitants and descendants of the Torres Strait Islands – a collection of islands off the northwest coast of the state of Queensland. *Indigenous* is a term used to refer to Aboriginal and Torres Strait Islander peoples as a collective within a national perspective and tends to be adopted in Commonwealth Government policy language. When applying for Indigenous-specific services or programmes, government agencies and community organisations usually accept three 'working criteria' as confirmation of Aboriginal or Torres Strait Islander status: being of Aboriginal or Torres Strait Islander descent, identifying as an Aboriginal or Torres Strait Islander person, being accepted as such by the community in which a person lives or formerly lived (A.I.A.T.S.I.S., 2020). However, it is important to recognise a movement internationally by Indigenous peoples to reclaim and reassert identity, language and terms of self-reference, becoming free of colonial descriptions or categorisations (see Kunoth-Monks, 2014; also, see Carlson, 2016 for a detailed examination of the politics of Aboriginal identity).

It is recognised that First Nations peoples within Australia have the world's oldest continuing culture or 'oldest civilisation' (Malaspinas et al., 2016). However, colonisation has caused significant disruption to First Nations peoples. 'Colonisation' is a contested term that deserves more space for discussion than is available in this chapter. Nevertheless, within the social work domain, Hidatsa Indigenous Professor of Social Work, Michael Yellow Bird, appears to use the word *colonialism* synonymously with colonisation, stating, 'Colonialism refers to the event of an alien people invading the territory inhabited by people of a different race and culture, to establish political, social, spiritual, intellectual and economic domination over that territory and people' (Gray, Coates, & Yellow Bird, 2008, p. 282).

Colonisation has had a significant negative impact on the lives of First Nations peoples in almost every corner of the globe (Gray et al., 2008). In Australia, the arrival of the British on 26 January 1788 initiated a series of events that have caused irrevocable disruption to the world's oldest continuing culture (Perkins & Langton, 2008) and continue to have an undeniable impact on First Nations peoples today (Briskman, 2014). Whilst there was some attempt at conciliatory relationships immediately following the European arrival (Langton, 2008), informed by then-Governor Captain Arthur Philip's orders to 'conciliate the affections of the natives', the ensuing frontier violence, the rapid spread of smallpox disease (Reynolds, 2001), and a campaign of massacres (Elder, 2003; Reynolds, 2000) devastated the Aboriginal population on the eastern seaboard and beyond (Perkins & Langton, 2008). There is a strong case that these key events in Australian history constitute genocide according to the United Nations definition (Tatz, 1999; Reynolds, 2001). Following the initial impact of British colonisation, the progression of policy that defines the relationship between the state and First Nations peoples are characterised by the terms *protection*, *segregation*, *assimilation*, *integration*, and *self-determination* (sometimes termed *self-management*).

The protection era (1880–1940) was informed by commonly accepted notions of biological determinism and social Darwinism (Davis, 2019). The rationale for this policy era is found in the common, historically, held belief that Aboriginal culture could not survive the rapid European expansion that was taking place (Davis, 2019). When it was realised that Aboriginal populations were not *dying out* there was a shift in policy toward assimilation (Davis, 2019). Aims of these strategies were to *manage* First Nations peoples and designed to *assimilate* them into the urban white population. The assimilation era (1951–1962) ensued with the aim of absorbing Aboriginal people into white society with the 'clear expectation of the cultural extinction of Indigenous peoples' (Dodson, 1996). This included the systematic removal of *half-caste* children from their families commonly known as the 'Stolen Generation' (H.R.E.O.C., 1997). This era has left a legacy of substantial fear for First Nations people in relation to government and welfare services (Calma, 2008; Green & Baldry, 2008). Briskman (2008) asserts, 'there is little doubt that the legacy of policies of oppression, the most enduring being protectionism and assimilation, has resulted in Indigenous People remaining on the lowest rung of the socio-economic ladder' (p. 84).

It was during the assimilation era that First Nations peoples advocated for civil and political rights, and policy shifted to an era referred to as land rights and self-determination. This early fight for self-determination can be seen in the establishment of the *Australian Aborigines League in 1932* and *The Aborigines Progressive Association in 1937* (A.I.A.T.S.I.S., 2020). Efforts toward self-determination become concerted after the 1967 Referendum in which powers were provided to the Commonwealth to legislate for Aboriginal people and to enter funding relationships with Aboriginal communities. *Closing the Gap* is the newest (and still current) initiative to address the health, social, and educational disparities between Indigenous and non-Indigenous Australians. Established by the Rudd/Gillard government to 'humanise the policy regime' initiated under former Prime Minister Howard's leadership (Thompson & Duthie, 2016, p. 50), the strategy seeks to promote better living conditions for First Nations people, particularly for those living in remote locations. Similarly, the policy is heavily criticised by Altman (2009) for failing to either 'value Indigenous difference… [or] to accommodate Indigenous aspirations' (p. 1). Simarlily, governments around the world implemented policies that sought to modernise and civilise a *primitive* or *backward* people (Walsh-Tapaiata, 2008).

Such policies had devastating impacts for those at the focus of their *protection* efforts. Social workers actively contributed to the trauma of colonisation by implementing government policies, thus, social work's track record with First Nations people is overwhelmingly negative (Ling, 2003; Nagpaul, 1972, 1993; Nimmagadda & Cowger, 1999; Tsang & Yan, 2001, Yip, 2004). It comes as no surprise, then, that social workers are often considered with suspicion by First Nations peoples. Simply, the atrocities of the past continue to inform First Nations peoples' view of social workers today.

Whilst historical accounts of British invasion and colonisation in Australia are readily available (see Reynolds, 2013; Broome, 2010), social work literature generally does not provide detailed historical accounts of contact history. Rather, social work literature is quick to link the arrival of the British and consequent government policies with the poor social and health status of First Nations Australians today (Bennett et al., 2012; Briskman, 2008, 2014). This deficit focus, while encompassing the realities of many First Nations peoples, belies stories of resistance and resilience and perpetuates dangerous stereotypes.

Social workers have a vested interest in improving the health and well-being of Aborignal peoples in Australia. Unfortunately, the above discussed historical legacies include poorer health and, on average, First Nations peoples can expect to live 10 years less than other Australians (Australian Institute of Health and Welfare, 2021). Along with poorer health and reduced life expectancy, First Nations Australians experience deficiencies in nutrition, higher rates of unemployment, and generally experience more housing inadequacies, such as overcrowding compared to other Australians (A.I.H.W. & Harrison, 2015). First Nations people are over-represented in the juvenile justice and adult prison systems. The latest government statistics, released in 2018, show that the national rate for Aboriginal and Torres Strait Islander children living in out-of-home-care was 10 times the rate for non-Indigenous children (A.I.H.W., 2018a, 2018b), and the average daily detention population of children and young people 10–17 years of age in Australia, Indigenous young people made up 59% despite Indigenous young people making up only 5% of the general population aged 10–17 (A.I.H.W., 2018c). In remote and very remote geographic locations, First Nations Australians were more likely to be living in overcrowded conditions and experience health conditions, such as high blood pressure and chronic kidney disease, at much higher rates than those in non-remote areas (A.I.H.W. & Harrison, 2015). Perhaps most alarmingly, First Nations men between 25 and 29 have the highest rate of suicide in the world (Commonwealth Youth Programme, 2016).

Of course, the Australian account of invasion, colonisation, and subsequent destructive impact is not an isolated one in world history. Colonisation and oppression are shared aspects of the lived experience of many First Nations people around the world. Whilst there are significant differences between First Nations peoples, many peoples have journeys that have 'been similar in that for a long time they lived in tune with their natural environment. This was then unfortunately followed by an abrupt change in direction, namely colonization' (Walsh-Tapaiata, 2008, pp. 107–108). International social work literature acknowledges the ongoing impact of colonisation on First Nations communities around the world (Walsh-Tapaiata, 2008).

Social workers have been complicit in the trauma, control, dislocation, acculturation, and colonisation of First Nations peoples (Gilbert, 2001, 2009; Green & Baldry, 2008). In Australia, social workers contributed to the trauma of First Nations people through the active involvement in what has become known as the Stolen Generations. The Stolen Generations is a term that refers to the forcible removal of Aboriginal children from families. This policy approach was in place between approximately 1910 until the 1970s (H.R.E.O.C., 1997). Based on the policy of assimilation, it is estimated that between one in three and one in ten First Nations children were forcibly removed from their families and communities (H.R.E.O.C., 1997). Children were removed and, in many cases, not permitted to speak language or retain cultural practices. The *Bringing Them Home Report* (H.R.E.O.C., 1997) highlights the intergenerational effects of removal, while Koolmatrie and Williams (2000) assert that forcibly removing Aboriginal and Torres Strait Islander children from families has 'left a powerful residue of unrecognised and unresolved grief that [has] pathological effects on Indigenous communities' (p. 163).

Given the complex and complicated historical relationship between the social work profession, colonisation, and First Nations peoples, there is a call within the literature for social workers to develop an understanding of this history as a precursor to effective practice. Gilbert (2001) argues that social workers cannot expect to develop effective working relationships with First Nations communities without having a thorough understanding of our shared history and First Nations peoples' experience of various government authorities. Within Aotearoa New Zealand context, Walsh-Tapaiata (2008) notes, 'for social workers who work with First Nations populations, it is critically important that they have a *correct* understanding of the history of that Indigenous population, recognizing the impact that history has had on them, much of which is still evident today' (p. 108). Further, adopting a structural perspective (Mullaly, 2007), she continues, 'personal troubles cannot be separated from public issues and social workers need to understand how they have historically contributed to the colonisation process, but also play key roles as agents for positive social change' (Walsh-Tapaiata, 2008, p. 108). Thus, the call goes beyond simply researching and becoming aware of historical facts toward interrogation of one's self and our propensity for racism. Gilbert (2001) stresses, 'Working with Aboriginal people requires soul-searching, forgiveness and preparedness to challenge our potential for racism' (p. 46)

Profession, Pedagogy, and Placement: A Review of Current Evidence

This section provides a review of current, available, and published evidence about (i) the socio-historic relationship between First Nations peoples and the social work profession, (ii) First Nations peoples' experiences with the teritary sector and social work education in particular, and (iii) First Nations social work students' experiences on field placement. It should be noted that this section is limited by the available evidence, so the core issues are supplemented and advanced through the First Nations authors' knowledge and experiences in section 12.4.

The Australian Association of Social Workers (A.A.S.W.)

The Australian social work profession has a complex relationship with First Nations peoples; Bennett's (2015) research found that the relationship between First Nations social workers and the professional body – the Australian Association of Social Workers (A.A.S.W.) – was largely undocumented and remained tenuous. However, the growing acknowledgement of social work involvement in the removal of First Nations children from their families – acts of overt and covert racism within the profession – and the disproportionate representation of First Nations clients in human service provision has underscored policy shifts in the A.A.S.W. in the last decade. Of most note, the *Code of Ethics* (A.A.S.W., 2010) and *Practice Standards* (A.A.S.W., 2013a) have been revised, and two *Reconciliation Action Plans* released (A.A.S.W., 2013b; 2017). The preamble of the *Code of Ethics* acknowledges and pays respect to First Nations peoples, commits 'to acknowledge and understand the historical and contemporary disadvantage experienced by Aboriginal and Torres Strait Islander peoples', and states that social workers must be responsible for 'culturally competent, safe and sensitive' practice (p. 5). Social work practice should respect diversity; value cultural knowledge, skills, history, and relationships unique to First Nations peoples; and recognise cultural elders, cultural duties, obligations, and responsibilities. Research must honour First Nations peoples' knowledge, obligations, and protocols (A.A.S.W., 2010). The *Practice Standards* (A.A.S.W., 2013a) document 23 standards across eight categories. Standard 3.1 is entitled: *Respect, strive to understand and promote the rights of Aboriginal and Torres Strait Islander peoples and their cultures.* It reiterates the aforementioned principles, as stated in the *Code of Ethics*.

The operationalisation of these principles in social work education is documented in the newly released *Australian Social Work Education and Accreditation Standards* (A.A.S.W., 2020). Within this document, the 'history and contribution of Aboriginal and Torres Strait Islander peoples' is one of five core content areas alongside content on 'power, oppression and exploitation' and 'culture, identity and discrimination' (A.A.S.W., 2020, p. 8). This document also features the guidelines for social work field education, although it does acknowledge that this is an area for further review and alignment. While this section clearly states that the higher education provider needs to offer a placement that is free from harassment and discrimination, it currently omits specific guidance in terms of diversity: There is no mention of pre-placement preparation, ongoing support for First Nations peoples students, or the role and place of cultural supervisors. In fact, reference to cultural support in the field, which was briefly mentioned previously (see A.A.S.W., 2012, p. 4), has been removed from the current 2020 reiteration.

The Tertiary Sector and Social Work Education

The authors were unable to obtain enrolment statistics for First Nations students in social work programmes in Australia at the time of writing. However, broader educational data may offer some insight. For example, the national census showed that 47% of Aboriginal and Torres Strait Islander people (20–24 years) had completed their final year of schooling (Year 12, Higher School Certificate) compared to 79% of the non-Indigenous population (Australian Bureau of Statistics (A.B.S.), 2016). While the Higher School Certificate is a direct pathway to university, research shows that less than half of First Nations students will take this route (Wilks & Wilson, 2015). Students who self-identified as Aboriginal and Torres Strait Islander comprised 1.9%

of all domestic onshore tertiary education enrolments in 2018, which equates to 19,981 students (Australian Government, 2019). While this rate has been steadily improving, it is still well below the population parity rate: Aboriginal and Torres Strait Islander peoples were 3.3% of the population in 2016 (A.B.S., 2018). An analysis of higher education data showed consistently lower enrolment, retention, and completion rates in the First Nations student population (Wilks &Wilson, 2015), which can be attributed to multi-faceted conditions, such as prior educational experiences and disadvantage, limited access to support (peer, family and institutional), financial hardship, ill health and well-being factors, competing family and community obligations, and racism and discrimination (Hearn, Benton, Funnell, & Marmolejo-Ramos, 2019; Taylor, Lalovic, & Thompson, 2019; Wilks & Wilson, 2015). This phenomenon was recognised in 2012 in *The Report of the Review of Higher Education Access and Outcomes for Aboriginal and Torres Strait Islander People*, which advocated for a collaboration between governments, the higher education sector, and professional bodies to improve educational access and a range of social and economic outcomes for First Nations peoples (Behrendt, Larkin, Griew, & Kelly, 2012).

A review of literature highlights the scarcity of information related to First Nations students in Australian social work programmes and even less in terms of their experiences while undertaking a social work placement. This may be somewhat indicative of the small numbers enrolled in tertiary education, but it is more likely reflective of the broader context. Consistent with international critiques, Australian commentators continue to foreground the ideological differences between Aboriginal and Torres Strait Islander and Western epistemologies and pedagogies, as well as the dominance of the latter (Bennett, Redfern, & Zubrzycki, 2018; Bessarab, 2015; Zubrzycki et al., 2014). Indeed, calls for a decolonised and co-constructed curriculum are well established (e.g., Bennett et al., 2018; Bessarab, 2015; Gair, Thomson, Miles, & Harris, 2003; Green & Bennett, 2018), and there is a growing literature on the translation of these principles to practice (e.g., Bennett et al., 2018; Duthie , King & Mays, 2013; Walter & Baltra-Ulloa, 2019). A comprehensive teaching and learning framework for integrating Aboriginal and Torres Strait Islander knowledges in social work was developed in 2015 (see Zubrzycki et al., 2014). This included a framework for the provision of culturally appropriate field education. Yet, many would argue that the current position of Australian social work programmes tends toward the embedding of First Nations *content* and a Eurocentric preparation for culturally responsive practice.

'In terms of recruiting Aboriginal and Torres Strait Islander social work students … most Australian social work programmes either do not have a specific student recruitment strategy or were unaware of the existence of such a strategy' (Zubrzycki et al., 2014, p. 60). An earlier sample of First Nations students reported a non-recognition of personal, community, and cultural worldviews and knowledges as well as their employment histories when entering social work programmes (Gair, Thomson, & Savage, 2005). They 'identified deficits in the curriculum including a lack of meaningful inclusion of Indigenous Australian cultural knowledges and the privileging of White theories' (p. 58). They suggested that significant and long-standing stressors and obligations, (including personal or family ill-health, long hours of paid work, and lack of access to educational equipment), impacted the prioritisation and, in some cases, the continuance of their social work education (Gair et al., 2005). Others noted that a lack classroom support impacted their academic experience and success (Gair et al., 2005).

These phenomenon can be further understood within the broader context: 'Universities generally believe their inclusion and embedding of Indigenous epistemologies in pedagogies and curricula will, of itself, circumscribe the parameters of its own transformative project, in overtly welcoming Indigenous worldviews and philosophies' (Larkin, 2019, p. 35). This belies the disparities between the employment of First Nations academics: There are small numbers of Aboriginal and Torres Strait Islander academics teaching directly into social work programmes in

Australia. Many non-Indigenous academics have reported that they lack confidence in embedding Aboriginal and Torres Strait Islander ways of knowing, doing, and being, as well as working with First Nations peoples to co-create such a curriculum (Bennett et al., 2018; Zubrzycki et al., 2014).

Bennett et al. (2018) also state that 'social work students and graduates often feel ill-prepared and anxious about their abilities to work collaboratively and respectfully with Aboriginal and Torres Strait Islander peoples' (p. 809). This is consistent with Gair's (2016) investigation of non-Indigenous social work students and the connections between activism, empathy, and racism. Self-reports suggested that lack of empathy and racism were not primary factors that prevented students from acting for social justice for First Nations Australians. Rather, they stated 'a lack of confidence, lack of knowing what to do, limited time, lack of information, and not wanting to offend' (Gair, 2016). What is important here, and given the focus of this chapter, is the way that these collective factors transform the daily experiences of First Nations students. First Nations students report experiences of racism within in the social work classroom, from lecturers and students (Gair et al., 2005; Zuchowski, Savage, Miles, & Gair, 2013). This includes explicit racist statements, complicity with totalising and deficit-focused depictions of First Nations peoples and communities, and ignoring racist comments and assumptions. Finally, and importantly, Fernando and Bennett (2019) highlight the potentially retraumatising effects of teaching Aboriginal content. They suggest that the (re)examination of historical intergenerational trauma and secondary trauma can have ongoing implications for Aboriginal and Torres Strait Islander students and requires educators who are skilled in enacting cultural safety and working with trauma.

Social Work Field Education

While First Nations student experiences may be referred to in Australian field education literature, this tends to be in the form of a brief acknowledgment in general research and/or commentary. The exception is one qualitative study, which explored the experiences of 11 Aboriginal and Torres Strait Islander students and graduates who had participated in at least one social work placement (reported in Gair, Miles, Savage, & Zuchowski, 2015; Zuchowski et al., 2013). Data was collected and analysed using a collaborative methodology including in-depth interviews and a focus group. Predominantly, the study by Zuchowski et al. (2013) found that First Nations students' 'social work/welfare placement experience was no different to everyday life, much of which is impacted by direct and indirect racism, discrimination and a lack of recognition and valuing of their cultural diversity' (p. 55).

Gair et al. (2015) reported that racism was intricately linked to historical and concurrent lived experiences including trauma, discrimination, and structural disadvantage. Students described being isolated and excluded on placement, through indifference, lack of cultural awareness, and ignorance; some were the only Aboriginal or Torres Strait Islander person located in the organisation. Students also described racism that was derived from inaccurate but dominant assumptions about Aboriginal and Torres Strait Islander peoples and communicated through positions of white privilege. This included comments about skin colour and educational status. Some reported their supervisor's resistance to relinquish the *expert position* and learn from, or utilise, the cultural expertise of the student (Gair et al., 2015). Conversely, in earlier research, some First Nations students reported that they were sometimes 'tapped' for cultural knowledge and tasked with educating their supervisors while on placement (Gair et al., 2005). Even when supervisors appeared to understand the historic experiences of First Nations peoples in Australia, this tended not to translate into an understanding of, or empathy for, the student's current lived experience (Gair et al., 2015). Explicit verbal abuse and derision were reported by some students (Gair et al., 2015).

In terms of student responses to racism, some tended to ignore the aforementioned acts and move forward to progress or 'get through' the placement (Gair et al., 2015). Interestingly, this is consistent with Aro's (2009) study of First Nations social work students on placement in child welfare services in Canada where:

> Two of five of the student participants noted that they feared that they would be isolated further, and branded as a troublemaker, if they spoke out about the oppressive practices they were witnessing. Rather than risk failing the practicum they chose to remain silent and 'get the practicum over with'.
>
> *(p. 87)*

In the Australian study, those who chose to challenge unacceptable comments and behaviours described feeling unsupported by staff and experiencing their supervisor's justification and inaction as debilitating (Gair et al., 2015).

The study by Zuchowski et al. (2013) also highlighted the strategies employed by First Nations students to successfully progress their placement. Students garnered support from a number of sources, including First Nations people within or external to the organisation, peers, and university staff. Students also described the development of their own 'unique practice framework which integrated social work knowledge and practice with cultural identity and understandings' (p. 59). In terms of improving the field education experience for future First Nations students, the participants recommended a specific and focused approach that included the screening of field educators for cultural suitability, the thorough preparation and support of First Nations students prior to placement, and the employment of cultural mentors or supervisors (which was effectively a formalisation of the supports that they had developed informally to support their own placement experience) (Gair et al., 2015).

Last, it is important to view this brief overview in terms of the Australian field education context explored in Chapter 15. Often overstretched and under resourced, field education programmes are increasingly unable to meet the number of placements they require. Field staff report conditions that often undermine placement matching and student support. Research shows that students are facing a number of challenges juggling placement, family commitments, and employment, and it is highly evident that vulnerable students and minority groups are disproportionately affected.

First Nations Students' Experiences in Social Work Field Education: A Way Forward

This section of the chapter responds to the gaps in research and literature identified in Section 12.3. It was developed through a dialogical process in which the authors met to discuss, compare, contrast, and critique their experiences of social work field education as a First Nations student and or educator. As such, it draws on the knowledge, insights, and lived experiences of the first four authors to advance current understandings of the core issues.

The Decision to Study Social Work

First Nations peoples are great supporters of concepts such as human rights and equity. Calma (2008) states that social workers by very definition are human rights workers. By becoming social workers, First Nations peoples are giving themselves the skills and knowledge to become advocates for one's own empowerment, self-determination, sovereignty, and collective human rights. More broadly, many First Nations peoples talk about reciprocity and giving back to families and communities. The pursuit of well-being for First Nations peoples is something that goes well with the core values and principles of social work (human dignity and worth). Many First Nations peoples are trying to make things better for the next generations to come. What better way to change a system than from the inside – to be part of a system to influence and create change.

Some universities seem to have been more successful at gathering numbers of First Nations students, and some have only small numbers enrolled. This could be because the area or format the university is in (e.g., rural versus urban, online versus face-to-face). However, it could have something to do with the reputation of the university, the cultural responsiveness of staff at orientation, the reputation of staff in the community, and the ongoing actions of the university and staff in relation to First Nations peoples (e.g., do they have a First Nations social worker employed as a lecturer).

Experiences of the Social Work Classroom

All the statistics, as noted in the previous section, highlight that keeping First Nations young people in school to Year 12 is a difficult task. First Nations students choosing to go into higher education are a minority and can sometimes be older with a large amount of lived experience. Although completion rates are steadily increasing, enrolment, retention, and completion rates from Aboriginal and Torres Strait Islander students are significantly lower than that of non-Indigenous students (Australian Government, 2020). This will mean universities will need to further respond to designing teachings that meet the needs of the next generation of First Nations peoples entering the university sector. Australian universities will need to be attractive to further cohorts, or the social work profession may suffer and will miss out.

Despite these challenges First Nations peoples can, do, and have completed both university and social work specifically. However, this decision can be difficult, and there are some reasons that we believe First Nations peoples are struggling to compete and these include:

Connection to land – Most universities are based in urban major cities. Often, students must relocate, leaving them feeling lonely, isolated, and unsupported. First Nations people's connection to land is fundamental to their well-being (Kingsley et al., 2013), and this is sacred and spiritual. To be parted from it, then, is like leaving the *Mother* for the first time and can be very distressing and overwhelming.

Financing university life – A high proportion of First Nations peoples come from low socio-economic backgrounds. Being able to pay for accommodation, texts, transport, and general living can be difficult, particularly in areas of high cost, such as Sydney and Melbourne. Sometimes, First Nations peoples can access a cadetship or scholarship, but these are competitive and might entail extra work hours at an organisation.

Indigenisation has been slowly implemented since the Behrendt et al. (2012) report highlighted the issue that Aboriginal knowledges needed to be incorporated into university degrees. Unfortunately, truth telling about the past has been limited in Australian education (Pascoe, 2014). This means that social work peers may have limited or skewed knowledge of Australian history, and, therefore, there may be dominance of the deficit narratives both in the content and in the conversations. Often, stereotypes are presented, meaning it seems as if social work is lagging behind in terms of cultural responsiveness. Aboriginal knowledges are generally such a tiny part of social work degrees. We have had feedback from students complaining that the only unit that makes sense to them is the one about working with Aboriginal people, where it focuses on topics such as knowing, doing, and being; intergenerational trauma; and traditional healing and counselling techniques, such as Dadirri (Ungummer, 2017) and yarning (Bessarab & Ng'andu, 2010).

Indigenising curriculum does not mean just asking in guest lecturers, though. Having an outsourced, drop-in *guest expert* can give the message that First Nations stories and experiences are not important enough for lecturers to learn and to then themselves to be part of that conversation. First Nations curriculum needs to take a horizontal and vertical approach. Academics need to ensure that there is an equal epistemology of Aboriginal ways of knowing, doing, being, and becoming (Martin & Mirabbopa, 2003). In this way, it is seen as equal and important rather than the risk of competing with mainstream content. If it is continued to be added as a week or a topic in a unit, it runs the risk of being forgotten or being tokenistic and not a priority.

The Placement Process

According to our experiences, it seems that social work has assumed that First Nations students only want to work with First Nations communities or only have something to contribute on First Nations issues. Educators themselves may be unaware of their own worldviews and biases and may not be provided with any cultural training. It was explained to us that, several times, the experience has been that students were placed in organisations and situations that triggered past personal or cultural trauma with no discussion of cultural protocols or cultural safety. All the First Nations authors had horror stories of being in a powerless situation in which they had to manage their own cultural trauma without support, being frightened that they would be pulled from placement, or placed on photocopying for the rest of their stay. Another experience is being treated like First Nations Google. Being asked for cultural advice and information from supervisors and the organisation. This has placed an extra burden on students to educate their supervisors. Students then have the extra burden of educating, supporting, and giving understanding about the historical, social, economic, political, and cultural components for First Nations peoples when this (as described by the A.A.S.W.) is up to social workers to be accountable and responsible for.

Another compounding factor to think about in placement is the fact that First Nations communities, organisations, or even representatives may not want a white or non-Indigenous student. They may fear the damage they may do if not culturally responsive enough or if people are unaware of the protocols or language. Often, non-Indigenous people who have never been to a First Nations community are shocked by the near third-world conditions, lack of services, and inflated prices of food and petrol. It can be overwhelming for the student and requires quite a commitment from supervisors. In this way, First Nations placements should be based on the principle that they are a privilege and not a right (Whitford, Taylor, & Thomas, 2013).

Racism

Being a minority in the room can expose First Nations students to racism and discrimination. Feelings of 'I don't belong here' and 'I can't do what they want me to do' and other confidence issues exacerbate racist experiences and some of the micro aggressions (Sue et al., 2007) students may face. Often, that student is the first person in the family to attend university, which, in and of itself, can be very daunting. At this stage, a strong First Nations student support centre can become like extended family.

Racism on placement from supervisors, clients, or even other students can create feelings of being unsafe personally, professionally, and culturally. It can be a big secret. Students struggle with the obvious power issues and then have to figure out whether they should tell (and who) or suffer in silence, just getting through so that they are successful in the placement and in their degree. To respond to this, many workplaces have written rules and policies and strategies to address racism. However, when racism is occurring, it is obvious that the workplace is not culturally safe, and then who can you trust? Students may be very anxious about discussing experiences of racism, as it involves significant personal and professional risks. In fact, they may have already had experiences in which speaking about racism has meant it was minimised, ridiculed, ignored, or even joked about. It is unknown if universities really know how to deal with racism and what to do if breaches of the A.A.S.W. code of conduct occur. The 'great Australian silence' is, then, replicated for students on placement.

Problematising of the First Nations students and their concerns can occur in field placements. Students can suddenly be described as 'trouble', 'passionate', or even 'unsatisfactory as a fit' if they are seen to be non-compliant or if they 'rock the boat'. In this way, it is a contemporary expression of a historical reality of continued oppression and racism in Australia.

Trauma and Intergenerational Trauma

The lived experience of trauma was explicit and inherent in the author discussions that evolved while writing this chapter. Examples included sending students (i) to placements without consideration of kin or familial relationships; (ii) to organisations with long trauma associations, such as child protection agencies; and (iii) to supervisors who appeared to be unaware of their own trauma-load, the lived experiences of First Nations students, or the potential for (re)traumatisation in this cohort. Most students do not describe such experiences in terms of trauma but more in terms of their daily lived experiences. This might say something about their expectations of people in authority (including their limited capacity or desire to keep First Nations students/people safe). It might also be explained in terms of the other issues described in this chapter. For example, students are often reluctant to say 'no' to a directive by a field educator in case it is interpreted as a lack of readiness for practice. Students are unlikely to reveal the traumatic experiences they may have endured for fear of further stigmatisation or judgement. Unspoken and, indeed, unrecognised trauma can go unnoticed and be misinterpreted by field educators as a lack of interest, incompetence, or worse. Again, students are more likely to endure traumatic experiences in order to pass placement and move onto practice than to set themselves up for potential exposure and confrontation.

Field Education as a White Process

'White privilege to a white person is like water to a fish. How are they supposed to recognize it if it's all they know?' (Alfarano, 2020, n/p). Social work and the curriculum and pedagogical practices have been built to continue the advantages of the majority (white Caucasian) and add to the benefits of access to social rewards that white people have received and continue to receive in Australia. Literature for addressing white privilege in field education is crucial to the field. The current lack of attention does not make it non-existent. Discussing the impacts that this has on the social work field education area will hopefully lead to race-based training of staff, managers, and supervisors

The whiteness of social work is often ignored, mainly by white people who continue to be awarded privilege and advantages within the social work profession. White fragility with behavioural responses of anger, victimhood, denial, and withdrawal (Diangelo, 2011) are rife in the institutions we work for and in social work itself. The continued status quo of whiteness is not currently being critically examined or transformed at a fast-enough pace, meaning continued racism and oppression to First Nations people, which trickles down to our students (Walter & Baltra-Ulloa, 2019). We must assume that whiteness permeates field practicum processes, thoughts, and practices because whiteness is a product of Western culture, and our universities are the embodiment of this (Walter & Baltra-Ulloa, 2019). This means that whiteness is the dominant position from which processes, decisions, and actions are made in field practice.

Recommendations: Implications for Social Work

Increased Cultural Capability of Field Educators/Supervisors

This involves the need for staff to have access to knowledge about working with First Nations peoples. It is the ability to undertake the reflective practices and pro-action needed to build cultural confidence and responsiveness. It is also requires the support of the university to make sure that all workers have good practice when it comes to the diversity of First Nations peoples and communities. Cultural supervision needs to be underpinned by a broader cultural capability strategy across all universities and the organisations in which we are sending students.

First Nations Peoples' Peer Networks across Year Groups

There needs to be formal or informal groups designed to bring together First Nations students from across the university sector. This provides opportunities to share and learn from each other and to provide personal and cultural support. Research suggests that giving First Nations peoples an opportunity to engage in cultural activities increases their mental, emotional, physical, and spiritual domains (Gallop & Bastien, 2016). Becoming role models and mentors to each other fundamentally supports Aboriginal ways of knowing, doing, and being (Martin & Miraboopa, 2003).

Cultural Mentorship Initiatives

Mentoring means having access to a First Nations person who is experienced as a cultural mentor/supervisor. Mentoring is about caring and sharing. It also means an investment of time and know-how. It is a real commitment from the supervisor to the supervisee to bring them up in terms of personal growth, skills, and knowledge. It is a meaningful relationship which should be respectful. We argue that field educators are inadequately prepared to deal with First Nations students. The quality of cultural supervision for both students and field educators should be assured from year to year. There should be cultural protocols in place for support and evaluation of the placement as a culturally safe and appropriate area. Field educators should also be screened and trained.

Conclusion

This chapter was created in response to a dearth of research and literature about the First Nations student experience of field education in Australia. It has critiqued and supplemented the existent literature through the knowledge, insights, and lived experiences of the first four authors. It reveals a field education experience that is potentially fraught with significant challenges, borne from Australia's colonialist history, and one which is poorly supported to create a culturally safe space for students. The authors have offered a way forward that includes practical strategies to improve the cultural capability of all field education staff and developing peer support networks and mentorship initiatives. While many of these suggestions have been tabled previously, with varying degrees of uptake, implementation will require an honest evaluation of the whiteness inherent in social work programmes and, indeed, the profession at large.

References

A.I.A.T.S.I.S. (2020). *We hereby make protest: The 1938 Day of Mourning*. Retrieved May 29, 2020, from https://aiatsis.gov.au/exhibitions/day-mourning-26th-january-1938

Alfarano, B. (2020). *Confronting the white elephant: White privilege in social services*. Retrieved May 29, 2020, from https://www.socialworktoday.com/archive/exc_0618.shtml

Altman, J. (2009). *Beyond closing the cap: Valuing diversity in Indigenous Australia*. C.A.E.P.R. Working Paper 54. Retrieved May 15, 2020, from https://caepr.cass.anu.edu.au/sites/default/files/docs/CAEPRWP54_0.pdf

Aro, C. L. (2009). *Indigenous social work student experiences in the child welfare specialization: Exploring the field education encounter*. Masters of Social Work, University of Victoria.

Australian Association of Social Workers. (2010). *Code of ethics*. Retrieved February 2, 2020, from https://www.aasw.asn.au/document/item/1201

Australian Association of Social Workers. (2012). *Australian social work education and accreditation standards (ASWEAS) 2012: Guideline 1.2: Guidance on field education programs*. Retrieved May 10, 2020, from https://www.aasw.asn.au/document/item/3553

Australian Association of Social Workers. (2013a). *Practice standards*. Retrieved February 2, 2020, from https://www.aasw.asn.au/document/item/4551

Australian Association of Social Workers. (2013b). *Reconcilliation action plan*. Retrieved May 10, 2020, from https://www.aasw.asn.au/document/item/5310

Australian Association of Social Workers. (2017). *Reconcilliation action plan: Innovate*. Retrieved May 10, 2020, from https://www.aasw.asn.au/document/item/9889

Australian Association of Social Workers. (2020). *Australian social work education and accreditation standards (ASWEAS) 2020 : Guideline 1.2: Guidance on field education programs*. Retrieved July 12, 2020, from https://www.aasw.asn.au/document/item/6073

Australian Bureau of Statistics. (2016). *2071.0 - Census of population and housing: Reflecting Australia - stories from the census, 2016*. Retrieved May 15, 2020, from https://www.abs.gov.au/ausstats/abs@.nsf/mf/2071.0

Australian Bureau of Statistics. (2018). *3238.0.55.001 - Estimates of Aboriginal and Torres Strait Islander Australians*, June 2016. Retrieved May 15, 2020, from https://www.abs.gov.au/ausstats/abs@.nsf/mf/3238.0.55.001

Australian Government. (2019). *Selected higher education statistics –2018 student data*. Retrieved May 15, 2020, from https://www.education.gov.au/selected-higher-education-statistics-2018-student-data

Australian Government. (2020). *Year 12 attainment*. Retrieved 29 May, 2020, from https://ctgreport.niaa.gov.au/year-12-attainment

Australian Institute of Health and Welfare. (2018a). *Child protection Australia 2016–2017 (Child welfare series No. 68)*. Canberra: A.I.H.W. Retrieved May 29, 2020, from https://www.aihw.gov.au/getmedia/66c7c364-592a-458c-9ab0-f90022e25368/aihw-cws-63.pdf.aspx?inline=true

Australian Institute of Health and Welfare. (2018b). *Child protection Australia 2016–17. Supplementary data tables*. Canberra: A.I.H.W. Retrieved May 29, 2020, from https://www.aihw.gov.au/reports/child-protection/child-protection-australia-2016-17/data

Australian Institute of Health and Welfare. (2018c). *Youth detention population in Australia 2018*. Bulletin no. 145. Cat. no. JUV 128. Canberra: A.I.H.W. Retrieved May 29, 2020, from https://www.aihw.gov.au/getmedia/55f8ff82-9091-420d-a75e-37799af96943/aihw-juv-128-youth-detention-population-in-Australia-2018-bulletin-145-dec-2018.pdf.aspx?inline=true

Behrendt, L., Larkin, S., Griew, R., & Kelly, P. (2012). *Review of higher education access and outcomes for Aboriginal and Torres Strait Islander People*. Final Report. Retrieved May 29, 2020 from https://docs.education.gov.au/system/files/doc/other/review_final_report_2012.pdf

Bennett, B. (2015). 'Stop deploying your white privilege on me!' Aboriginal and Torres Strait Islander engagement with the Australian Association of Social Workers. *Australian Social Work, 68*(1), 19–31. DOI:http://dx.doi.org.ezproxy.newcastle.edu.au/10.1080/0312407X.2013.840325

Bennett, S., Green, S., Gilbert, S., & Bessarab, D. (Eds.) (2012). *Our voices: Aboriginal and Torres Strait Islander social work*. Melbourne: Palgrave Macmillan.

Bennett, B., Redfern, H., & Zubrzycki, J. (2018). Cultural responsiveness in action: Co-constructing social work curriculum resources with aboriginal communities. *British Journal of Social Work, 48*(3), 808–825. DOI:http://dx.doi.org.ezproxy.newcastle.edu.au/10.1093/bjsw/bcx053

Bessarab, D. (2015). Changing how and what we do: The significance of embedding Aboriginal and Torres Strait Islander ways of knowing, being, and doing in social work education and practice. *Australian Social Work, 68*(1), 1–4. DOI:10.1080/0312407X.2015.973475

Bessarab, D., & Ng'andu, B. (2010). Yarning about yarning as a legitimate method in Indigenous research. *International Journal of Critical Indigenous Studies, 3*(1), 37–50.

Briskman, L. (2008). Decolonizing social work in Australia: Prospect or illusion. In M. M. Gray, J. Coates, & M.Y. Bird (Eds.), *Indigenous social work around the world: Towards culturally relevant education and practice* (pp. 83–93). Hampshire: Ashgate Publishing Ltd.

Briskman, L. (2014). *Social work with indigenous communities: A human rights approach*. Annandale, NSW: Federation Press.

Broome, R. (2010). *Aboriginal Australians. A history since 1788*. Crowsnest: Allen and Unwin.

Calma, T. (2008). *The role of social workers as human rights workers with Indigenous people and communities*. Australian Human Rights Commission. Retrieved May 15 2020, from https://humanrights.gov.au/about/news/speeches/role-social-workers-human-rights-workers-indigenous-people-and-communities

Carlson, B. (2016). *The politics of identity: Who counts as aboriginal today?* Canberra: Aboriginal Studies Press.

Commonwealth Youth Programme. (2016). *Australian youth development index 2016*. Retrieved May 29, 2020, from https://nacchocommunique.files.wordpress.com/2016/08/australian_youth-index-2016.pdf

Davis, M. (2019). *Family is culture: Independent review report of Aboriginal children and Young people in out of home care*. Retrieved May 29, 2020, from https://www.familyisculture.nsw.gov.au/__data/assets/pdf_file/0011/726329/Family-Is-Culture-Review-Report.pdf

Dodson, M. (1996). *Assimilation versus self-determination: No contest*. Retrievedaustrak from: https://humanrights.gov.au/about/news/speeches/assimilation-versus-self-determination-no-contest-dodson-1996

Diangelo, R. (2011). White fragility. *The International Journal of Critical Pedagogy, 3*(3), 54–70.

Duthie, D., King, J., & Mays, J. (2013). Raising awareness of Australian Aboriginal peoples reality: Embedding Aboriginal knowledge in social work education through the use of field experiences. *International Education Journal, 12*(1), 197–212.

Elder, B. (2003). *Blood on the wattle: Massacres and maltreatment of Aboriginal Australians since 1788*. Sydney: New Holland.

Fernando, T., & Bennett, B. (2019). Creating a culturally safe space when teaching Aboriginal content in social work: A scoping review. *Australian Social Work, 72*(1), 47–61.

Gair, S. (2016). Pondering the colour of empathy: Social work students' reasoning on activism, empathy and racism. *The British Journal of Social Work, 47*(1), 162–180. DOI:10.1093/bjsw/bcw007

Gair, S., Miles, D., Savage, D., & Zuchowski, I. (2015). Racism unmasked: The experiences of Aboriginal and Torres Strait Islander students in social work field placements. *Australian Social Work, 68*(1), 32–48. DOI:10.1080/0312407X.2014.928335

Gair, S., Thomson, J., Miles, D., & Harris, N. (2003). It's very 'white' isn't it! Challenging monoculturalism in social work and welfare education. *Advances in Social Welfare Education, 5*(1), 37–52.

Gair, S., Thomson, J., and Savage, D. (2005) What's stopping them? Exploring barriers hindering indigenous Australians from completing a social work degree at a regional Queensland University. *Advances in Social Work and Welfare Education*, 7(1), 54–62.

Gallop, C. J., & Bastien, N. (2016). Supporting success: Aboriginal students in higher education. *Canadian Journal of Higher Education, 46*(2), 206–224.

Gilbert, S. (2001). Social work with Indigenous Australians. In M. Alston & J. McKinnon (Eds), *Social work – Fields of practice* (pp. 46–57). South Melbourne: Oxford University Press.

Gilbert, S. (2009). Aboriginal issues in context. In M. Connelly & L. Harms (Eds.), *Social Work Context and Practice* (2nd ed.) (pp. 94–106). Melbourne: Oxford University Press.

Gray, M., Coates, J., & Bird, M. Y. (Eds.). (2008). *Indigenous social work around the world: Towards culturally relevant education and practice*. Hampshire: Ashgate Publishing Ltd.

Green, S., & Baldry, E. (2008). Building indigenous Australian social work. *Australian Social Work, 61*(4), 389–402.

Green, S., & Bennett. (2018). Wayanha: A decolonised social work. *Australian Social Work, 71*(3), 261–264. DOI:10.1080/0312407X.2018.1469654

Hearn, S., Benton, M., Funnell, S., & Marmolejo-Ramos, F. (2019). Investigation of the factors contributing to Indigenous students' retention and attrition rates at the University of Adelaide. *The Australian Journal of Indigenous Education*, 1–9. DOI:10.1017/jie.2019.5

HREOC. (1997). *Bringing them home: Report of the national inquiry into the separation of aboriginal and torres strait islander children from their families*. Retrieved May 29, 2020, from https://humanrights.gov.au/our-work/bringing-them-home-report-1997

Kingsley, J., Townsend, M., Henderson-Wilson, C., & Bolam, B. (2013). Developing an exploratory framework linking Australian Aboriginal peoples' connection to country and concepts of wellbeing. *International Journal of Environmental Research and Public Health*, *10*(2), 678–698.

Koolmatrie, J., & Williams, R. (2000). Unresolved grief and the removal of Indigenous Australian children. *Australian Psychologist*, *35*(2), 158–166.

Kunoth-Monks, R. (2014). *Rosalie Kunoth-Monks on Q and A in 2014* [video file]. Retrieved July 20 2020, from http://www.abc.net.au/news/2017-06-02/rosalie-kunoth-monks-on-q&a/8576100

Langton, M. (2008). Trapped in the Aboriginal reality show. *Griffith Review*, *19*, 143.

Larkin, S. (2019). Race and the Indigenous social work academic in the Australian academy. In B. Bennett & S. Green (Eds.), *Our voices: Aboriginal social work* (pp. 31–46). London: Macmillan Education UK/Red Globe Press.

Ling, H. K. (2003). Drawing lessons from locally designated helpers to develop culturally appropriate social work practice. *Asia Pacific Journal of Social Work*, *13*(2), 26–44.

Malaspinas, A.-S., Westaway, M. C., Muller, C., Sousa, V. C., Lao, O., Alves, I., … Willerslev, E. (2016). A genomic history of Aboriginal Australia. *Nature*, *538*(7624), 207–214. DOI:10.1038/nature18299

Martin, K., & Mirraboopa, B. (2003). Ways of knowing, being and doing: A theoretical framework and methods for indigenous and indigenist re-search. *Journal of Australian Studies*, *27*(76), 203–214.

Mullaly, R. P. (2007). *The new structural social work*. Don Mills: Oxford University Press.

Nagpaul, H. (1972). The diffusion of American social work education to India: Problems and issues. *International Social Work*, *15*(1), 3–17. DOI:10.1177/002087287201500103

Nagpaul, H. (1993). Analysis of social work teaching material in India: The need for indigenous foundations. *International Social Work*, *36*(3), 207–220. DOI:10.1177/002087289303600303

Nimmagadda, J., & Cowger, C. D. (1999). Cross-cultural practice: Social worker ingenuity in the indigenization of practice knowledge. *International Social Work*, *42*(3), 261–276.

Pascoe, B. (2014). *Dark emu black seeds: Agriculture or accident?* Broome: Magabala Books.

Perkins, R., & Langton, M. (2008). *The first Australians: An illustrated history*. Carlton: The Miegunyah Press.

Reynolds, H. (2000). *Why weren't we told? A personal search for the truth about our history*. Ringwood: Penguin.

Reynolds, H. (2001). *An indelible stain?: The question of genocide in Australia's history*. Ringwood: Penguin.

Reynolds, H. (2013). *Forgotten war* (p. 63). Sydney: NewSouth Publishing.

Sue, D. W., Capodilupo, C. M., Torino, G. C., Bucceri, J. M., Holder, A., Nadal, K. L., & Esquilin, M. (2007). Racial microaggressions in everyday life: Implications for clinical practice. *American Psychologist*, *62*(4), 271.

Taylor, E.V., Lalovic, A., & Thompson, S. C. (2019). Beyond enrolments: A systematic review exploring the factors affecting the retention of Aboriginal and Torres Strait Islander health students in the tertiary education system. *International Journal for Equity in Health*, *18*(1), 136. DOI:10.1186/s12939-019-1038-7

Tatz, C. (1999). Genocide in Australia. *Journal of Genocide Research*, *1*(3), 315–352.

Thompson, L. J., & Duthie, D. (2016). Towards culturally safe social policy processes for Aboriginal Australians. *International Journal of Interdisciplinary of Social and Community Studies*, *11*(4), 47–62.

Tsang, A., & Yan, M. C. (2001). Chinese corpus, Western application: The Chinese strategy of engagement with Western social work discourse. *International Social Work*, *44*, 433–454. DOI:10.1177/002087280104400404

Ungunmerr, M. R. (2017). To be listened to in her teaching: Dadirri: Inner deep listening and quiet still awareness. *EarthSong Journal: Perspectives in Ecology, Spirituality and Education*, *3*(4), 14.

Walsh-Tapaiata, W. (2008). The past, the present and the future: The New Zealand Indigenous experience of social work. In M. Gray, J. Coates, & M. Yellow-Bird (Eds.), *Indigenous social work around the world: Towards culturally relevant education and practice* (pp. 107–116). Surrey, England: Ashgate.

Walter, M., & Baltra-Ulloa, J. (2019). Australian social work is white. In B. Bennett & S. Green (Eds.), *Our voices: Aboriginal social work* (pp. 65–85). London: Macmillan Education UK/Red Globe Press.

Whitford, D., Taylor, J., & Thomas, K. (2013). Working in Indigenous health settings. In K. Stagnitti, A. Schoo, & D. Welch (Eds.), *Clinical and fieldwork placements in the health professions* (2nd ed.) (pp. 329–347). Melbourne: Oxford University Press.

Wilks, J., & Wilson, K. (2015). A profile of the Aboriginal and Torres Strait Islander higher education student population. *Australian Universities' Review, 57*(2), 17–30.

Yip, K. S. (2004). The empowerment model: A critical reflection of empowerment in Chinese culture. *Social Work, 49*(3), 479–487.

Zubrzycki, J., Green, S., Jones, V., Stratton, K., Young, S. D., & Bessarab, D. (2014). *Getting it right: Creating partnerships for change. Integrating Aboriginal and Torres Strait Islander knowledges in social work education and practice.* Sydney: Teaching and Learning Framework. Australian Government Office for Learning and Teaching. Retrieved May 18, 2020, from https://researchbank.acu.edu.au/cgi/viewcontent.cgi?article=1470&context=fea_pub

Zuchowski, I., Savage, D., Miles, D., & Gair, S. (2013). Decolonising field education: Challenging Australian social work praxis. *Advances in Social Work and Welfare Education, 15*(1), 47–62.

13

Aotearoa New Zealand Field Education Practice

Kathryn Hay, Dominic Chilvers, and Jane Maidment

Social work education in Aotearoa New Zealand has a significant history of more than 40 years, and field education has been an integral component of the curriculum since its genesis (Dale, Mooney, & O'Donoghue, 2017). Initially, only located in the university sector, since the late 1990s the number of social work programmes has burgeoned. There are currently 18 tertiary education institutions (T.E.I.s), including universities, polytechnics, wānanga[1], and private institutions, offering social work qualifications approved by the Social Workers Registration Board (S.W.R.B.). These institutions incorporate a range of pedagogical and andragogical approaches informed by Māori[2] and Western models, leading to significant differences in the curriculum and delivery of field education. This chapter discusses the context and nature of social work field education in Aotearoa New Zealand. Current challenges are explored following a brief introduction to the context of field education. Reflections on working with field educators (social workers who oversee placements in agencies) and placement agencies are presented prior to three examples of interesting placement learning opportunities. Considerations for learning and teaching are then examined. The final section of the chapter offers ideas for sustaining and enhancing quality field education practice that may have value beyond Aotearoa New Zealand.

It is noted that, while the authors have a collective experience of teaching and researching in the domain of field education for more than 50 years, this chapter offers only one perspective. The viewpoints in this chapter are, therefore, those of the authors and do not represent the opinions of other social work field education academics in Aotearoa New Zealand.

The Context

Aotearoa New Zealand is a country of approximately 4.8 million people. With two main landmasses, the North and the South Islands, the majority of the population reside in the North Island with approximately 1.4 million people in Auckland, the largest city. There are T.E.I.s in all the main cities, with Auckland housing five social work programmes. While most of the social work courses target local students and offer classes regularly on campus, five of the tertiary providers facilitate distance programmes, with students learning primarily online and occasionally attending on-campus classes. The effect of this dispersal of programmes is that students are living and undertaking their placements throughout the entire length of Aotearoa New Zealand.

DOI: 10.4324/9781032164946-17

A small number of students may have one placement overseas, most frequently in Australia or other English-speaking countries.

The regulatory body, the S.W.R.B., establishes the parameters of the social work curriculum, including field education requirements, processes, and assessment. Prior to admission, applicants to programmes must meet the threshold related to personal character as set by the S.W.R.B. 'fit and proper' policy (S.W.R.B., 2018a). The terms of this policy refer to the nature of any criminal convictions, physical and mental health status, or conditions that may impact upon an individual's performance of practice in the field. The purpose of this policy is to protect the interests of service users as well as ensuring students themselves have opportunities to address potential impediments to their career progression early in their social work journey. Vetting student circumstances under the auspices of this policy and carrying out a police check is required by T.E.I.s pre-placement to afford some safeguards to agencies accepting students.

Social work students must undertake at least two placements for a minimum of 120 days. The placements must be more than 50 days in length and be in two different fields of practice in differently structured settings (S.W.R.B., 2018b). There are no requirements for students to have one of their placements in a statutory setting, which allows for greater flexibility and student choice (MacDermott & Campbell, 2016). In fact, a range of learning opportunities are often available to students in health, community, Iwi (extended kinship group or tribe), Māori, non-government, education, justice, and child protection settings. The S.W.R.B. sets parameters for supervision of students, namely that a registered social worker must provide supervision.

Traditionally, social work education has occupied the lowest (Level A) government-funding band for tertiary education. Level A does not account for the time and labour-intensive activities associated with teaching social work, such as facilitating practice skills labs, field education co-ordination, liaison, and supervision. While there have been decades of lobbying the Tertiary Education Commission and previous iterations of this organisation for social work to be shifted to Level B funding, these efforts have been stonewalled.

The social work profession and the T.E.I.s have unique obligations to tangata whenua (the Indigenous Māori population), including a commitment to recognising rights and obligations under Te Tiriti o Waitangi[3]. Students are, for example, required to develop competence in practising social work with Māori, thus, demonstrating that they are culturally responsive and committed to enhancing well-being (S.W.R.B., 2020). Field education is one domain in which students have first-hand opportunities to evidence their knowledge and begin social work practice in this competency.

The Aotearoa New Zealand Association of Social Workers (A.N.Z.A.S.W.), the largest professional association for social workers in the country, represents and advocates for their members in policy and media settings and provides information and professional development. Historically, A.N.Z.A.S.W. was involved in assessing quality in social work education but now focuses on promoting best practice. In keeping with the commitment to biculturalism in the social work profession, there is a second professional body called the Tangata Whenua Social Work Association (T.W.S.W.A.). This association provides a forum for Māori social workers to liaise and support each other. These two organisations, at times, collaborate with the Council for Social Work Education Aotearoa New Zealand (C.S.W.E.A.N.Z.), which is the representative body for the T.E.I.s providing social work programmes.

Registration of social workers in Aotearoa New Zealand first became possible under the introduction of legislation in 2003. Recent changes to the original legislation resulted in the passing of the Social Workers Registration Legislation Act (2019). Provisions under this new act have made registration of social workers mandatory and require T.E.I.s to attest to the competency of graduates, rather than the S.W.R.B., strengthening the significance of the field educators' role in the practicum assessment process. Other changes as a result of the new act include protection of the title social worker; employers and registered social workers are now responsible for reporting to the S.W.R.B. concerns about fitness to practice if they are identified. Post-graduation, ongoing competency will not be assessed except in cases in which a complaint has been laid about a social worker. A proportion of continuing professional development logs are audited annually to monitor ongoing social worker education. Currently, a scope of practice reflecting key social work roles has been developed by the S.W.R.B. It is critical that the nature of field education placements in the future fit within this general scope of practice.

Contextual Challenges

A number of challenges are being faced by schools of social work that are likely to impact field education. The most far reaching of these is the national Reform of Vocational Education (R.o.V.E.), a significant restructure to bring together 16 institutes of technology and polytechnics (I.T.P.s) under the auspices of one entity from the beginning of April 2020. These changes will affect ten out of the 18 social work programme providers in Aotearoa New Zealand. The aim of this restructure is greater consistency in the delivery of vocational education with the view of also increasing the role of employers in shaping this provision. It is currently unclear what the implications of this restructure might mean for degree level programmes such as social work, but it may lead to a contraction in the number of sites of social work education delivery. The opportunity to develop a national social work curriculum and assessment structure for all programmes incorporated within this new entity could have implications for how field education is taught and evaluated. In the future, this unified collective will likely comprise a significant voice in the national social work education space.

With reference to the influence of employers on social work education, it is important to note there have been high profile critiques of both social work practice in the media and regarding social work graduate readiness to practice. One of these critiques came from a former Minister of Social Development (Bennett, 2014) whose Ministry was responsible for the statutory care and protection services for children and adolescents. A common refrain from this organisation is that new social work graduates are not sufficiently prepared to engage competently with complex cases and lack the specific knowledge of relevant legislation to navigate practice with reference to the statutory mandate. This critique, to some extent, reflects on the quality of field education learning and the assessment of performance while students are on placement. At this point, however, it is important to also note the rather lacklustre engagement of statutory organisations in the provision of field education in Aotearoa New Zealand, with just a third of all placements facilitated in 2018 being sourced within statutory organisations (S.W.R.B., 2018c), despite this sector being the major employer of qualified social workers.

Recent findings from the 'Enhancing Readiness to Practise' research (https://ako.ac.nz/knowledge-centre/enhancing-the-readiness-to-practise-of-newly-qualified-social-workers/), undertaken in Aotearoa New Zealand, identified that final year students and new graduates recognised the centrality of their practice placements as a pathway to employment. Participants in this research reported that the transition for them from student to practitioner was easier because they had been on placement in an employing agency (Hay et al., 2018). The tertiary sector has now widely recognised work integrated learning (W.I.L.) as a viable way to enhance graduate work-readiness and employability (Rowe & Zegwaard, 2017). Many of the diverse range of disciplines now using this approach have little real understanding of its complexities and the range of supports needed by students engaged in W.I.L. Academic staff within social work field education in Aotearoa New Zealand are well-positioned to contribute to the development of W.I.L. in other disciplines, although this expertise appears to be underutilised.

Working with Field Educators

Social work field education involves a dynamic partnership between the T.E.I. responsible for delivering the programme of study and the social service agency who hosts the student during the practicum (Maidment, 2000). Each organisation can have quite different objectives for a placement; on the one hand, a concern for teaching and learning, and on the other, a focus on recruitment or managing their client workload (Chilvers, 2017). Overlaid on this partnership is a complex interpersonal relationship between the student, the field educator who provides supervision and support for the student, and the field education coordinator who arranges the placement and oversees the assessment of the student. This system of relationships is critical to the success of any placement but involves tensions and complexities that can derail the process (Maidment, 2000). Field educators can feel marginalised within this system because they are not full members of the tertiary education team, yet their work with students is peripheral to the focus on client need within their social work team (Chilvers, 2017). This experience of liminality highlights the need for field educators to have opportunities to participate in professional learning communities that will support the development of an educator identity and the sharing of knowledge required for effective teaching practice.

The funding model for social work education in Aotearoa New Zealand does not allow for field educators to be paid for their work with students. Historically social workers have been expected to mentor students as part of their commitment to the profession and, although this continues, it is increasingly unsustainable (Bogo, 2015). Work with students is commonly in addition to a demanding social work caseload, and field educators in the host organisations report that they have to be careful not to allow students to take on work that they might be left to manage at the end of the practicum (Chilvers, 2017). Workload is a concern for many field educators, and the competing demands on their time can impair their ability to provide a high-quality learning experience (Hay, O'Donoghue, & Blagdon, 2006). Although work with students may be peripheral to the goals of social service agencies, the support of managers and colleagues is an important influence on the practice of field educators (Chilvers, 2017). Leadership is required to address workload challenges and to make field education a more central concern within social service agencies. Team approaches, in which one person coordinates and supervises the student but all members of the team engage with them, can be very effective and significantly improve the quality of learning for the student (Vassos, Harms, & Rose, 2018).

Field educators are primarily focused on their practice with clients and their understanding of adult learning and teaching may be underdeveloped (Douglas, 2011). They may also lack up-to-date theoretical knowledge (Al-Ma'seb, Alkhurinej, & Alduwaihi, 2015; Boisen & Syers, 2004). Perspectives on the role of field educators and the purpose of placement have changed over time with an increasing focus on educational principles in the contemporary period (Beddoe, 1999). In addition to the demands of adopting an identity as an instructor and assessor, social workers may struggle to translate well-known principles from their practice into the learning and teaching space. For example, Chilvers (2017) found that social work field educators in Aotearoa New Zealand were familiar with bicultural principles in their social work practice but failed to identify the influence of indigenous learning and teaching principles in their work with students. These findings highlight the importance of initial training and continued professional development for field educators and the potential role of a community of practice in addressing identified limitations.

Research undertaken in Aotearoa New Zealand suggests that the lack of training for field educators is one of the key barriers to achieving the objectives of placement (Hay et al., 2006). Field educators report that they value the training and preparation they receive, believe this increases their confidence, and welcome the additional knowledge for working with students (Chilvers, 2017). However, there is a lack of empirical research into the effectiveness of field educator training (Bogo, 2006) that would help to determine the appropriate duration, curriculum, or andragogy. Deal, Bennett, Mohr, and Hwang (2011) undertook one of the few randomised controlled trials of field educator training effectiveness, and their findings raise doubts about whether field educator training actually results in desirable teaching methods or improves the confidence of students in their instructors. In contrast, research into the ambitious 150-hour training for field educators in the U.K. suggests the model was effective (Rogers, 1996; Slater, 2007), but, ultimately, it proved too expensive and was discontinued as a mandatory accreditation requirement (Bellinger, 2010). Within Aotearoa New Zealand, the training of field educators has been modest with generally between four and 16 hours of study. A key focus of this professional development relates to the knowledge and skills required to facilitate effective supervision for students on placement. This training has usually been provided by individual T.E.I.s with little control over consistency or quality. However, there have been some excellent examples of collaboration, particularly in major centres, such as Auckland or Wellington, where multiple T.E.I.s need to recruit competent field educators.

Although training and professional development for field educators is critically important, raising the quality of field education is a complex process that involves a range of other factors (Chilvers, 2017). Professional standards for field educators are an additional mechanism for catalysing excellent practice. In 2016, a working party that included educators and other stakeholders developed a set of guidelines for field educators across Aotearoa New Zealand that were jointly published by the professional associations for practitioners and educators (A.N.Z.A.S.W., 2016). The objective was to 'identify competencies, guidelines and tasks to help measure progress and celebrate successes in excellent field education practices' (2016, p. 4). The document establishes a set of expectations in four key domains: administration, teaching and learning, assessment, and quality. Despite the voluntary nature of these standards, they are a powerful tool for promoting best practice and have been incorporated into several social work programmes across the country. The potential for its widespread use by field educators who are educating and supporting students during their placements is significant and may lead to increased consistency in field education practices. Similar guidelines for students, agency managers, and academic staff could prove equally useful in the next phase of quality improvement (Hay, 2019).

Working with Placement Agencies

The challenges of promoting high quality field educator practice are paralleled by similar difficulties related to working with social services agencies that host students. Agencies do not receive any payment for providing placements other than in-kind arrangements such as access to library facilities or discounted course enrolments. Field education contracting, therefore, often relies on the relationships that academic staff have with local social service providers. Although there are examples of collaboration between T.E.I.s, the common picture is one of competition for placements due to limited availability and a culture of patch protection between academic institutions (Hay, 2018).

Partnerships between T.E.I.s and social service agencies are generally managed on an individual contract basis. Some larger regional or national organisations may contract with T.E.I.s across several of their services or sites. However, these contracts are still arranged with individual T.E.I.s, rather than with a collective of interested institutions. In 2008, the Tertiary Education Commission (T.E.C.) facilitated a stakeholder project to discuss the future of social work education and proposed the establishment of regional field education agencies that would negotiate placements on behalf of a number of T.E.I.s (T.E.C., 2009). This proposal was never progressed, partly because of the perceived complexity in establishing and funding such organisations.

Each T.E.I. has one or more field education coordinators who are responsible for maintaining the relationships with social service agencies and securing sufficient placements annually. Enrolment numbers are not capped to the number of available placements, so coordinators must respond to the fluctuations in student numbers, geographical location, and preferences about fields of practice. Field education coordinators are faced with the challenge of securing placements for all students despite the preferences of managers who control the supply. Work undertaken by Hay and Brown (2015) indicated that host agency managers are more likely to offer placements to students who demonstrate flexibility, humility, confidence, and resilience. During the placement, there can also be challenges in responding to students' personal, interpersonal, and academic challenges. Academic staff normally visit students mid-way through a placement, and this provides the primary opportunity to maintain the relationship with the field educator, their line manager, and other key people in the agency.

A wide range of placement types are used across Aotearoa New Zealand. The 2018 S.W.R.B. report on field education indicated that only 29% of placements were in government agencies, including child protection, health, corrections, local government, schools, and the police (S.W.R.B., 2018c). The ratio between government and non-government placements varies across T.E.I.s, with some ranging from only 10% and others more than 50% within government settings. Although there is a history of group placements in Aotearoa New Zealand, the most common model is now an individual one. Student units were instituted in the 1990s and provided placements for groups of students who were supported by an experienced practitioner for supervision and training but undertook their practice across one or more services. Despite the success of this model, it has been almost completely discontinued; the cost of a dedicated field educator being a significant contributing factor (Hay & Teppett, 2011). Group supervision models may, however, continue to be a viable solution to the challenge of a lack of field educators that can support individual placements (Sussman, Bogo, & Globerman, 2007).

The constraints on available placement opportunities can be a catalyst for creative solutions, particularly within the non-government sector. This includes examples in which students complete placements in settings without social workers and external supervision is provided by an experienced registered social worker. In these kinds of settings, students can be involved in identifying the potential contribution from social work and the placements can provide rich learning for confident students. Natural disasters or other major community traumatic events have also been used as opportunities for creative placements that would not normally be available to students. For example, after the 2011 earthquakes in Christchurch and Lyttelton, students were involved in crisis response activities, such as brief household need assessments and food distribution. After the 2019 terrorist attack on El Noor mosque and the Linwood Islamic Centre, students were engaged in providing support for families to access immigration, visa, and income support information and organising transport for affected families. In 2020, students were involved in developing resources to assist families during the COVID-19 pandemic lockdown, providing telephone follow-up with clients and supporting families directly affected by the virus. The following vignettes highlight other examples of creative placements in Aotearoa New Zealand in recent years.

Examples of Placement Learning Opportunities

Hauora (Māori Health) Placement Vignette

The Oranga Tamariki Act (1989) places obligations on the Aotearoa New Zealand state child protection agency to establish partnerships with Māori organisations to improve outcomes for Māori children and their families (S.7.a.a). It is equally important for academic institutions to partner with Māori social services when organising field education. Bethlehem Tertiary Institute is one example of a tertiary provider that has drawn on the strength of relationships with local hapū, Iwi, and kaupapa Māori agencies to develop placement collaborations. This involved navigating complexities such as S.W.R.B. supervision standards, practitioner workloads, and student inexperience in Māori cultural contexts.

Nga Matāpuna Oranga is a primary health organisation (P.H.O.) funded by district health boards to ensure the provision of kaupapa Māori primary health and social services. Pirirākau Hauora and Whaioranga Trust are two agencies that have received support with workforce development from the PH.O. Pirirākau Hauora is a hapu based kaupapa Māori agency that provides health and well-being services, including a general practitioner, qualified nurse, massage therapist, family support, holiday programmes, kaumatua support, and mental health services. Whaioranga Trust is also a kaupapa Māori health and social services agency offering advocacy, traditional healing, home-based support for people with disabilities, and day programmes and workshops related to mental health and addiction.

With workforce development support from Nga Matāpuna Oranga, placements for students that would not otherwise have been possible, have been successful with both these kaupapa Māori service providers. This involved both agencies arranging mentors for the students and Nga Matāpuna Oranga facilitating access to Māori field educators currently involved in clinical and cultural supervision. The tripartite agreement also enabled the students to access kaupapa Māori workforce development workshops in and beyond the placement and to establish networks within Māori health and social services. Feedback from students and practitioners has affirmed the value of collaboration for all parties.

Library Placement Vignette

Public libraries have an important role in communities not only for the provision of books, internet access, information, and other literary materials but also as a central hub for people to connect and engage. In Aotearoa New Zealand, social workers are generally not employed by public libraries, even though this is customary in some other countries (Luo et al., 2012). Consequently, field education opportunities have not been available in the library setting. In 2018, Massey University was approached by Wellington Public Library and invited to establish a partnership for both research and placement. The focus for the placement was for the student to engage with users of the library and to provide support and advice to the library staff about how they could safely engage with vulnerable people. A component of the placement involved the student conducting small-scale research using focus groups with library staff as participants. Interviews with local service providers, library and city council staff, and library customers were also undertaken. Multiple customer needs were identified, ranging from technology help to needing a bathroom or shower or a place to shelter. The focus group findings revealed that staff encountered many challenges, including verbal and/or physical assault, predatory behaviour, children being left unsupervised, delusional customers, and balancing customer needs with library priorities. Many of the staff emphasised their limited knowledge of how to effectively address these challenges, particularly with time constraints and limited training opportunities.

The social work student compiled the research findings and presented possible future developments to enhance existing library structures, policies, and practices. She also engaged directly with library customers, utilising her social work values, knowledge, and skills, demonstrating to library staff the potential value of social worker engagement in the future. The value of this placement is ongoing with other libraries throughout the country showing interest in the placement and research findings.

General Practice Medical Centre Placement Vignette

While social work delivery has been a feature within the health sector in Aotearoa New Zealand since the late 1930s (Beddoe & Deeney, 2012), these services have predominately been located within hospital settings. In recent years, Pegasus Health, a P.H.O. located in Christchurch, has facilitated a swathe of social work student placements based in privately owned general practice medical centres. This initiative has taken place to further support the development of a multidisciplinary, integrated approach to the delivery of primary health care in the community. Within the context of an increasingly ageing population and widening disparity between those that can and cannot easily access resources, the inclusion of social work in general practice enables critical social issues for vulnerable populations to be readily addressed. This initiative has promoted the establishment of permanent social work positions in general practice, a trend likely to continue, broadening the scope for health social work in the community. The role of social work in primary health includes identifying and reducing barriers to equitable health care, promoting access for marginalised populations to primary health, facilitating referral, navigating and linking patients to other community supports, providing a resource to the general practice team on matters specifically related to family harm, and child protection concerns. Social work placements in primary health care have resulted in students carrying out a range of interventions, including resourcing practices to more readily be able to provide services to gender diverse populations and Māori patients in culturally appropriate ways; developing social work assessment methods and documentation procedures within general practice based upon Te whare tapa whā, an indigenous model for addressing well-being (Durie, 2009); creating a resource map of all community support systems in the general practice neighbourhood to be used by staff for referral purposes; defining the specific role of social work in general practice; and differentiating between these roles and tasks and those of other community workers.

Learning and Teaching in Field Education

Pre-placement

While all social work education curriculum content is germane to preparing students for immersion into practice, there are particular areas that assume immediate relevance prior to students going out on placement and for their ongoing professional development during the practicum. Many social work programme providers in Aotearoa New Zealand require students to have passed a course focused on understanding and demonstrating the appropriate use of practice skills prior to commencing their placement. These practice skills courses generally comprise material covering a constellation of content focused on four domains including: demonstration of particular communication micro skills (Maidment & Egan, 2016); understanding and applying critical reasoning to case material; demonstrating capacity to exercise particular traits associated with emotional intelligence; written and verbal articulation skills to report and document practice endeavours (Beddoe & Maidment, 2009). Specific to the Aotearoa New

Zealand context, Pākehā students (of European descent) are required to have knowledge of and role-play practise focused on appropriate ways to begin working with Māori.

Exploring the role of professional supervision in practice is a second curriculum area that is usually included in student pre-placement learning and teaching. Curriculum content generally covered on this topic includes theory associated with the supervision process, the roles and tasks of supervision, addressing theory–practice integration, exploring ethical and legal issues, boundary setting, and writing supervision and other records. In particular, students are encouraged to think about how they might most effectively make use of both formal and informal supervision opportunities for accessing professional guidance while on placement (Cleak & Wilson, 2018) and, at the same time, identifying their own key strengths and areas for development in the field.

Another area in pre-placement curricula includes practical considerations that, in some areas, overlap with examining features of emotional intelligence. This curriculum material includes topics associated with increasing professional literacy, such as development of a social work identity, preparing for a placement interview, workplace health and safety provision and expectations, engagement with teamwork, and navigating agency politics.

Theory-practice Integration

It is customary for social work education providers to include a series of assessment tasks during the placement that encourage students and their field educators to examine aspects of integration during formal supervision and for students to address through assignment completion. This vital area for learning and teaching has, across decades, been recognised as an enduring educational challenge for students and field educators alike (Al-Ma'seb et al., 2015; Clapton & Forbes, 2009; Pilalis, 1986). For students, the articulation of explicit links between theory and practice has been identified as a conceptually complex task (Carelse & Dykes, 2013). Students model their practice on field educators, often in the absence of in-depth theoretical consideration (Boisen & Koh, 2016) and within organisational settings in which theory taught in the classroom is deemed 'a hindrance' by practitioners in the field (Collingwood, Edmond, & Woodward, 2008, p. 73). These conditions are not ideal for privileging discussions about bridging the perceived gap between the classroom and field, theory and practice. Even so, many models for prompting integration and encouraging praxis have been promoted over the years. These include reference to specific models, such as the Practice Pyramid, focused on student identification of personal and professional knowledge bases and values used to inform practice (Gordon & Mackay, 2017); student completion of process recordings with dedicated space for specific reflection on theory used within practice or, alternatively, praxis in which current knowledge is analysed from the perspective of practice evidence (Canning & Mullin, 2008). Utilising process-driven supervision models, such as the integration of theory and practice loop, to ensure the inclusion of critical reflection on the theory-practice nexus is useful (Bogo & Vayda, 1998). Students may also engage with critical incident analysis (Lister & Crisp, 2007) in which they deconstruct a practice event with the view to identify components associated with using a critical lens to explore what happened and to reflect upon how different forms of knowledge and ethics can be teased out from the incident. Mapping and analysing the intersections between practice events as they occurred in the field with core social work curriculum areas can also be employed (Beddoe & Maidment, 2009).

Assessment

Any one, or a selection of, the above tasks, along with the student's practice performance in the field, are subject to academic assessment. Social work students are required to be assessed against the ten core competencies as set down by the S.W.R.B. before graduating (S.W.R.B., 2020). Surprisingly, direct observation of student work with service users is not a mandatory requirement in Aotearoa New Zealand. Some institutions have, however, included observation work as a specific component within their placement assessment schedules. This activity can greatly assist with the provision of constructive feedback for the student.

Because field education in Aotearoa New Zealand is founded upon a competency-based framework, placement assessment must include forms of evidence that capture the level of knowledge and proficiency in skill and understanding students have demonstrated in the field. Some programme providers encourage students to develop a portfolio that documents a growing body of context-relevant evidence related to how the competencies have been demonstrated. Different types of evidence can include but are not limited to audio or video recordings of client interviews; copies of PowerPoint slide presentations and feedback about presentations done for client or staff audiences; written materials, such as case studies, process recordings, literature reviews, policy documentation, or exercise material demonstrating integration; de-identified case notes or client assessment documentation; links to relevant resources developed by the student for agency use; and practice observation feedback templates. Most T.E.I.s have specific items of assessment for all students to complete while on placement with latitude for these assessment tasks to be used in a way that reflect the primary focus of the placement. This degree of flexibility also encourages students and their field educators to shape assessment items around specific learning goals set at the beginning of the placement, building upon current strengths but also addressing identified areas for student development.

Currently individual T.E.I.s have autonomy to decide how they would like students to be assessed in the field, although there has been recent discussion within C.S.W.E.A.N.Z. making some form of standardised field education assessment documentation across the country moot. While the S.W.R.B. core competencies remain the foundation for assessment of graduate competence, diverse forms of evidence can be used to demonstrate and document how these competencies have been met.

Enhancing Field Education in the Future

As evident in the discussion above, in Aotearoa New Zealand, social work field education is well-established. There are many examples of good practice in individual tertiary institutions and at a national level. Further developments, however, have been identified through practice experience and several research studies that can enhance both current and future field education practice.

The establishment of a national field education sub-committee (F.E.C.) of C.S.W.E.A.N.Z. in 2006 has been critical, as it offers an appropriate forum for ongoing discussion and development. The purpose of the sub-committee is to foster collaborative links across the T.E.I.s. Since its inception, the F.E.C. has focused on strengthening networks amongst the field education staff, sharing placement opportunities, actively engaging in the development of policy with the S.W.R.B., and writing professional suitability guidelines. F.E.C. members were significant contributors to the creation of the national Field Education Guidelines. Members who were on administrative/professional pay grades in their institutions have also been supported by the F.E.C. in their lobbying to become academic staff. The F.E.C. has a strong voice in C.S.W.E.A.N.Z. discussions, many of which pertain to field education matters, and it offers a collegial environment for support as well as the advancement of good field education practice.

This model of collaboration is important for advancing excellent practice in field education, as exemplified in the current focus on building on the existing examples of T.E.I. partnership to develop national field education training modules. These training packages, to be offered both in online and face-to-face formats, will be owned by C.S.W.E.A.N.Z. and, therefore, available for all T.E.I.s to use with their local field educators. Unfortunately, a lack of resources to enable the educators leading this initiative to dedicate sufficient time to the project is inhibiting progress (Hay, 2019). However, since many organisations host students from more than one T.E.I., the objective is to develop national training modules that will generate consistency in key messages as well as increase the number of field educators accessing training. C.S.W.E.A.N.Z. is also participating in a joint project with the National Field Education Network in Australia to review an online supervision training package for field educators that is provided by Charles Sturt University (http://www.csu.edu.au/handbook/subjects/HCS514.html). One objective of this project is to ensure the curriculum is appropriate to practitioners in the Aotearoa New Zealand context and that local and indigenous literature is incorporated. These initiatives illustrate the efforts in Aotearoa New Zealand to enhance the quality of field education by providing access to quality training for field educators across the country despite limited resources.

Beyond these professional development packages, the establishment of a learning community that can support field educators as they respond to the challenges they face in practice would be highly beneficial (Chilvers, 2017). As noted above, field educators are often isolated and may feel sidelined by both the social service agency and the academic institution (Chilvers, 2017). Professional learning communities, such as the Scottish Organisation for Practice Teaching (socpt.co.uk), offer spaces for the exploration of challenges, successes, and innovations. Although there are fiscal challenges, in Aotearoa New Zealand, there are several social work organisations that could potentially provide such a community for field educators. This structure could champion field education as well as facilitate learning opportunities and access to relevant tools and resources.

Establishing clear expectations for each of the key stakeholders in the tripartite field education relationship is essential and the Field Education Guidelines assist field educators and mentors. To increase clarity, consistency, and emphasis on high standards of field education practice for all the stakeholders, there is a future opportunity for the development of national guidelines for students and academic staff engaged in field education. Further, the development of quality measurement tools to assess placement experiences would add value to future field education practice. Quality benchmarks may be determined through a variety of processes including the implementation of evidence-based models in the social work programmes (Agnew et al., 2017; McRae & Johnston, 2016). Consideration of kaupapa Māori vis-a-vis mainstream education approaches, cross-sector consultation, and the incorporation of existing tools, such as national Field Education Guidelines, is also important for future field education teaching and learning developments (A.N.Z.A.S.W., 2016; Hay, 2018).

The S.W.R.B. stipulates that students must receive one hour of supervision per week with a registered social worker throughout their placement (S.W.R.B., 2018b). Unfortunately, recent research in Aotearoa New Zealand has identified that this requirement frequently goes unmet (Hay et al., 2018). Instead, students feel 'lucky' if they have a professional supervisor who meets with them regularly and provides a quality supervisory experience (Hay et al., 2018). Several recommendations from this research are pertinent including embedding the national Field Education Guidelines and engagement in national training modules as described above. Furthermore, additional resourcing by the T.E.C. could increase workload provision for both academic staff and field educators to strengthen relationships, enhance the student allocation process, and offer more flexible support during a placement. Offering students the opportunity to experience a supervisory relationship in the T.E.I. prior to a placement could also scaffold their learning about this essential component of field education.

As previously emphasised, students are to demonstrate their competence to practise social work with Māori. This requirement has implications for field educators, some of whom may not have confidence in their own capabilities in this competency or know how to best support students in their own development. Some agencies may profess to have minimal engagement with Māori clients, thus claiming limited opportunities for students to extend their practice experience. Here lies a challenge for T.E.I.s to teach students how to extend beyond agency boundaries to establish relationships with whānau (extended family group), hapū (kinship group, clan), and Iwi and connect with Iwi or Māori organisations. Chilvers (2017) established the importance of ongoing professional development in this area for many field educators as well as educators in kaupapa Māori pedagogy and bicultural practice. The participants in his research suggested using professional learning groups, as mentioned above, to initiate training. The social work professional associations are also well placed to facilitate appropriate training, however, workload provision is also required so that field educators can be released from usual daily practice. The recent development of a professional capabilities framework (P.C.F.), which indicated capabilities expected of newly qualified social workers in Aotearoa New Zealand (Ballantyne et al., 2019), could be usefully extended in the future to cover the expected capabilities of first and second placement students.

While placements offer students an important opportunity for professional socialisation and integration of their classroom learning into practice contexts, placements may not always be successful. An increasing concern of academics, as highlighted by Hay's (2020) recent research, is that of students witnessing poor professional practice by field educators or other agency staff. T.E.I.s are tasked with the often challenging and, certainly, competitive task of finding suitable placements, and an agency approval process is required by the S.W.R.B. How a 'good' agency is determined, however, is fraught and may be dependent on organisational, personal, and practical factors. While an agency may be supportive of student learning, there may be tensions between the student and the field educator that inhibits a positive experience. The converse may also be true. Quality assurance policies can assist with keeping students safe and allow them avenues for redress if something occurs. The current system is, however, individualised at the tertiary provider level. Exploration of a national system of agency approval, so that agencies are not repeatedly asked for documentation by multiple T.E.I.s, is necessary. Clear guidelines on risk management processes that can be adopted by all T.E.I.s would also provide a stronger framework for mitigating and managing challenges.

Conclusion

Having reflected upon the nature and context of field education in Aotearoa New Zealand, it is clear that field education occurs within a dynamic and highly contested environment. While field education coordinators need to be adaptive and flexible, their work is located within rigid organisational and funding structures. There exists a desire for collaboration and cooperation between field education coordinators working within the T.E.I.s that reflects the close relationships that exist within a small country. Despite these relationships, the current T.E.I. structure inhibits the potential for maximising collaborative work. Further, limited placement opportunities in social service agencies inevitably creates competition.

The voice of tangata whenua (Māori) is increasingly given space in T.E.I.s, however, significant work continues to be required to develop opportunities for students to deepen their exposure to indigenous forms of knowledge and practice. Different approaches for Māori and non-Māori students are necessary, which highlights the importance of the availability of diverse learning opportunities. The dominant voice of the statutory social work sector can also inhibit expansive approaches to field education generally, and student learning specifically. Student placements ideally enable them to embrace social work values, such as human rights and social justice, which can be more challenging in less flexible agency environments. Maintaining a broad vision for field education in Aotearoa New Zealand is, therefore, critical.

Despite these challenges, social work field education in Aotearoa New Zealand is characterised by a great deal of creativity, innovation, and knowledge building. Students have the opportunity to experience varied learning opportunities on placement, creating a sound foundation for their future career. Across the social work profession, there is an overt commitment to advancing quality field education within Aotearoa New Zealand as is evident in the continued offers of interesting placement opportunities for social work students.

Notes

1 Māori tertiary institution.
2 Māori are the indigenous population of Aotearoa New Zealand.
3 Te Tiriti o Waitangi is the founding document of Aotearoa New Zealand and was signed by the Crown and many Māori iwi (tribes) in 1840.

References

Agnew, D., Pill, S., & Orrell, J. (2017). Applying a conceptual model in sport sector work-integrated learning contexts. *Asia-Pacific Journal of Cooperative Education, 18*(3), 185–198.

Al-Ma'seb, H., Alkhurinej, A., & Alduwaihi, M. (2015). The gap between theory and practice in social work. *International Social Work, 58*(6), 819–830. https://doi.org/10.1177/0020872813503860

Aotearoa New Zealand Association of Social Workers (A.N.Z.A.S.W.). (2016). *Guidelines for field education.* Retrieved from https://anzasw.nz/wp-content/uploads/ ANZASW-Social-Work-Field-Education-Guidelines.pdf

Ballantyne, N., Beddoe, L., Hay, K., Maidment, J., Walker, S., & Merriman, C. (2019) Enhancing the readiness to practise of newly qualified social workers in Aotearoa New Zealand. *Report on Phase Three. The professional capabilities framework.* Retrieved from ako.ac.nz/assets/Knowledge-centre/NPF16-003-Enhancing-the-readiness-to-practice-of-newly-qualified-social-workers/dc910f0be9/Report-on-Phase-Three-The-Professional-Capabilities-Framework.pdf

Beddoe, L. (1999). From preaching to teaching? Changes in field education in Aotearoa New Zealand. *Social Work Review, 11*(2), 21–27.

Beddoe, L., & Maidment, J. (2009). *Mapping knowledge for social work practice: Critical intersections* (1st ed.). South Melbourne: Cengage Learning.

Bellinger, A. (2010). Studying the landscape: Practice learning for social work reconsidered. *Social Work Education, 29*(6), 599–615. https://doi.org/10.1080/02615470903508743

Bennett, P. (11 November, 2014). *Speech at the 'Protecting the Public–Enhancing the Profession' conference.* Wellington: Social Workers Registration Board.

Bogo, M. (2006). Field instruction in social work: A review of the research literature. *The Clinical Supervisor, 24*(1–2), 163–193. https://doi.org/10.1300/J001v24n01_09

Bogo, M. (2015). Field education for clinical social work practice: Best practice and contemporary challenges. *Clinical Social Work, 43*, 317–324. https://doi.org/10.1007/s10615-015-0526-5

Bogo, M., & Vayda, E. J. (1998). *The practice of field instruction in social work: Theory and process* (2nd ed.). Toronto: University of Toronto Press. https://doi.org/10.3138/j.ctt1287tjb

Boisen, L., & Koh, B. (2016) Integrating theory and practice methods in field instruction. In M. Hensley (Ed). *The field instructor's survival guide* (pp. 63–82). New York: Springer Publishing.

Boisen, L., & Syers, M. (2004). The integrative case analysis model for linking theory and practice. *Journal of Social Work Education, 40*(2), 205–217. https://doi.org/10.1080/10437797.2004.10778490

Canning, J. J., & Mullin, W. J. (2008). Student process recording in practice with children. *The Clinical Supervisor, 27*(1), 61–75. https://doi.org/10.1080/07325220802221496

Carelse, S., & Dykes, G. (2013, 2014). Integration of theory and practice in social work: Challenges and triumphs. *Social Work (South Africa), 49*(2), 165–182. https://doi.org/10.15270/49-2-62

Chilvers, D. (2017). *Social work field educator practice: Expanding the vision*. Unpublished Doctoral thesis, University of Canterbury, Christchurch. Retrieved from http://hdl.handle.net/10092/15038

Clapton, G., & Forbes, R. (2009). Barefoot tutors? Navigating the barriers between student, university and field in social work education. *Journal of Practice Teaching and Learning, 9*(1), 5–19. https://doi.org/10.1921/146066909X481420

Cleak, H. & Wilson, J. (2018). *Making the most of field education*. (4th ed.). South Melbourne: Cengage Learning.

Collingwood, P., Emond, R., & Woodward, R. (2008). The theory circle: A tool for learning and for practice. *Social Work Education, 27*(1), 70–83. https://doi.org/10.1080/02615470601141409

Dale, M., Mooney, H., & O'Donoghue, K. (2017). *Defining social work in Aotearoa: Forty years of pioneering research and teaching at Massey University*. Auckland: Massey University Press.

Deal, K. H., Bennett, S., Mohr, J., & Hwang, J. (2011). Effects of field instructor training on student competencies and the supervisory alliance. *Research on Social Work Practice, 21*(6), 712–726. https://doi.org/10.1177/1049731511410577

Douglas, J. (2011). Developing kia tene/off the cuff: A resource for field educators in social work in Aotearoa New Zealand. *Aotearoa New Zealand Social Work, 23*(4). 34–44.

Durie, M. (1994). *Whaiora-Māori health development*. Oxford University Press.

Gordon, J., & Mackay, G. (2017). The practice pyramid: A model for integrating social work values, theory and practice. *Journal of Practice Teaching and Learning, 14*(3), 64–80.

Hay, K. (2018). 'There is competition': Facing the reality of field education in Aotearoa New Zealand. *Aotearoa New Zealand Social Work, 30* (2), 16–27. https://anzswjournal.nz/anzsw/article/view/507

Hay, K. (2019). 'It's a whole orchestra': What are the instrumental elements in quality field education? *Social Work Education*. https://doi.org/10.1080/02615479.2019.1651261

Hay, K. (2020). What is quality work-integrated learning?: Social work tertiary educator perspectives. *International Journal of Work-Integrated Learning, 21*(1), 51–61.

Hay, K., & Brown, K. (2015) Social work practice placement in Aotearoa New Zealand: Agency managers perspectives. *Social Work Education, 34*(6), 700–715. https://doi.org/10.1080/02615479.2015.1062856

Hay, K., Maidment, J., Ballantyne, N., Beddoe, L., & Walker, S. (2018). Feeling lucky: The serendipitous nature of field education. *Clinical Social Work Journal, 47*(1), 23–31. https://doi.org/10.1007/s10615-018-0688-z

Hay, K., O'Donoghue, K., & Blagdon, J. (2006). Exploring the aims of social work field education in the registration environment. *Social Work Review, 18*(4), 20–28.

Lister, P. G., & Crisp, B. R. (2007). Critical incident analyses: A practice learning tool for students and practitioners. *Practice, 19*(1), 47–60. https://doi.org/10.1080/09503150701220507

Luo, L., Estreicher, D., Lee, P. A., Thomas, C., & Thomas, G. (2012). Social workers in the library: An innovative approach to address library patrons' social service needs. *Qualitative and Quantitative Methods in Libraries, 1*(1) 73–82. http://qqml-journal.net/index.php/qqml/article/view/45

MacDermott, D., & Campbell, A. (2016) An examination of student and provider perceptions of voluntary sector social work placements in Northern Ireland. *Social Work Education, 35*(1), 31–49. https://doi.org/10.1080/02615479.2015.1100289

Maidment, J. (2000). Methods used to teach social work students in the field: A research report from New Zealand. *Social Work Education, 19*(2), 145–154.

Maidment, J., & Egan, R. (2016). *Practice skills in social work and welfare: More than just common sense* (3rd ed.). Crows Nest: Allen & Unwin.

McRae, N., & Johnston, N. (2016). The development of a proposed global work-integrated learning framework. *Asia-Pacific Journal of Cooperative Education, 17*(4), 337–348.

Oranga Tamariki Act 1989, No. 24. Retrieved from http://www.legislation.govt.nz/act/public/1989/0024/latest/DLM147088.html

Pilalis, J. (1986). 'The integration of theory and practice': A re-examination of a paradoxical expectation. *The British Journal of Social Work, 16*(1), 79–96. https://doi.org/10.1093/oxfordjournals.bjsw.a055185

Rogers, G. (1996). Training field instructors British style. *Journal of Social Work Education, 32*(2), 265–276.

Rowe, A., & Zegwaard, K. (2017). Developing graduate employability skills and attributes: Curriculum enhancement through work-integrated learning. *Asia-Pacific Journal of Cooperative Education, 18*(2), 87–99. https://hdl.handle.net/10289/11267

Slater, P. (2007). The passing of the practice teaching award: History, legacy, prospects. *Social Work Education, 26*(8), 749–762. https://doi.org/10.1080/02615470601140443

Social Workers Registration Board (S.W.R.B.). (2018a). *Fit and proper person*. Policy statement. Retrieved from https://swrb.govt.nz/about-us/policies/

Social Workers Registration Board (S.W.R.B.). (2018b). *Programme recognition standards*. Retrieved from http:// swrb.govt.nz/about-us/policies/

Social Workers Registration Board (S.W.R.B.). (2018c). *Social work education providers*. Annual report. Unpublished report.

Social Workers Registration Board (S.W.R.B.). (2020). *Core competence standards*. Retrieved from https://swrb.govt.nz/social-workers/competence/core-competence-standards/

Social Workers Registration Legislation Act 2019. http://www.legislation.govt.nz/act/public/2019/0003/latest/DLM7396614.html

Sussman, T., Bogo, M., & Globerman, J. (2007). Field instructor perceptions in group supervision: Establishing trust through managing group dynamics. *The Clinical Supervisor*, *26*(1–2), 61–80. https://doi.org/10.1300/J001v26n01_06

Tertiary Education Commission. (2009). *Social work education in New Zealand*. Unpublished report.

Vassos, S., Harms, L., & Rose, D. (2018). Supervision and social work students: Relationships in a team-based rotation placement model. *Social Work Education*, *37*(3), 328–341. https://doi.org/10.1080/02615479.2017.1406466

14

Understanding Simulated Learning and its Relationship to Field Education

Jennifer Boddy, Lise Johns, Christian D. Frost, Mark Lynch, and Fiona Stevens

Simulated learning is gaining momentum at an increasingly rapid pace in many university health schools throughout the world (Aldridge, 2016), with social work education being no exception. Simulation may take many forms but broadly includes any technique aimed at replacing real experience with guided experience, often including an immersive component that replicates the real world in an interactive manner (Gaba, 2004). Such approaches to learning not only provide educators with the opportunity to observe students in practice but they can also enable students to better prepare for field education, ensuring they have the opportunity to practice competencies in a safe learning environment without the risk of harm to service users (Isaak et al., 2018). Thus, students can obtain skills in recognising and managing challenging workplace situations before placement. Additionally, simulations provide students with key learnings around interdisciplinary practice with experiential knowledge about how diverse disciplines contribute to client well-being. This is vital preparedness for placement and future practice.

While simulation has been utilised in social work education for several decades (e.g., through student role-plays see Doelcker & Bedics, 1987; and for simulated patients see, Berliner, 1982), it is still a dynamic field, in part, because of the continual emergence of new technologies associated with simulated learning. For instance, technological advances allow for online collaboration (Goldingay, Epstein, & Taylor, 2018), the development of virtual patient simulations (Dodds, Heslop, & Meredith, 2018), and digital realities (Trahan et al., 2019). However, the use of simulation across institutions varies and, despite advances in simulation, many students feel anxious about placement (Rosenthal Gelman & Baum, 2010), making simulation ever more relevant. Thus, new developments in simulated learning pave the way for further thinking about how to prepare students for field education and early graduate practice in ways that have previously not been possible.

This chapter will first describe the theory underpinning simulation and how simulated learning activities are implemented. Second, it will provide examples of simulations that have helped prepare students for social work field education and professional practice. Finally, the chapter will conclude with a framework for defining the various forms of simulation that contribute to practice learning. Throughout the chapter, the challenges in implementing simulated learning

 DOI: 10.4324/9781032164946-18

will be explored, along with key lessons for successful implementation and the range of benefits offered through different forms of simulation.

Pedagogy and Learning Theories Underpinning Simulation

Pedagogy is broadly defined as 'the art, science, or profession of teaching' (Pedagogy, 2020). However, the term is commonly used to describe the way educators deliver curriculum content, meaning the instructional techniques and strategies they adopt and the theories that underpin their planning (Persaud, 2021; Wall, Litjens, & Taguma, 2015; Erlam, Smythe, & Wright-St Clair, 2017). Effective pedagogical practices will not only depend on the educator's teaching style, experience, and the context in which they work but will also be developed from theories, research evidence, political drivers, practice background, reflection, and the field's expectations (Child Australia, 2017). Additionally, the *process* of learning and *how* students learn is also given prime consideration (Child Australia, 2017). The way the educator understands pedagogy will ultimately influence the learning environment being created (Erlam et al., 2017).

In contemporary tertiary teaching environments, social work educators are increasingly integrating simulated learning activities into their teaching practices. Simulation is considered to effectively facilitate learning outcomes in line with Bloom's taxonomy – a framework that can be used to categorise educational objectives (Bloom, 1956). Not only can it assist with creating assessment and evaluating their complexity, but Bloom's taxonomy also offers an order for cognitive behaviours. It starts with students first remembering and understanding key points to then applying their understanding in practice. Following the application to practice, students are able to analyse and evaluate the value of their work and then use this to create new things. It can be applied to multiple teaching situations.

However, confusion has arisen with some educators calling simulation a pedagogy, which Erlam et al. (2017) dispute. Simulation is not a pedagogy per se but, rather, a teaching/learning tool or modality that can be used to translate classroom knowledge into a safe, simulated learning context (Erlam et al., 2017; Nimmagadda & Murphy, 2014; Kaakinen & Arwood, 2009). As theory underpins the way educators teach, it should also be drawn upon to conceptualise simulation proposals. In fact, Kneebone (2005) cautions educators against sacrificing the theoretical component of simulation design by placing undue emphasis on the technological aspects. Kaakinen and Arwood (2009) purport that if student learning is the pivotal reason for a simulation, then applying a learning theory will further enhance the likelihood of students' attainment of skills, knowledge, and disposition. Whilst not exhaustive, constructivism, experiential learning, and social learning theories present as dominant conceptual theoretical frameworks within simulation focused literature, as they centralise learners and provide explicit descriptions of 'cognitive and social processes', which the student experiences (Kaakinen & Arwood, 2009, p. 12; Zigmont, Kappus, & Sudikoff, 2011; Roberson, 2019).

Constructivism is an overall explanatory theory on how learners acquire knowledge and learn, being considered one of the most influential teaching approaches to student learning (Roberson, 2019; Shapira-Lishchinsky, 2015). It purports that adult learners construct their own knowledge based on their unique prior experiences (Roberson, 2019). Students are considered as active participants in their personal learning journey, participating in an interactive process between themselves, their teacher, and their peers (Olusegun, 2015). The concept is founded on Vygotsky's (1978) sociocultural theory in which new knowledge is constructed via social interactions (Topicu & Myftiu, 2015; McPhail & Rata, 2016). The theory assumes a process of sorting and decision-making on how old information converges with the new (Qiong, 2010; Olusegun, 2015). Exposing students to a new experience creates a 'perturbation', a form of mental unrest that challenges the learner to make sense of the new information. Each learner will actively create, interpret, and reorganise their thinking in accordance to the new knowledge generated by the experience (Shapira-Lishchinsky, 2015, p. 2).

To apply constructivism to simulations, the educator stimulates student curiosity by reviving previous knowledge and evoking a reflective process in which students check new information against old. Ultimately, learners decide whether change should occur (Olugesun, 2015). The learner is forced to think through the newly presented information, leading to a deeper understanding of the topic (Shapira-Lishchinsky, 2015). By incorporating reflections within simulation activities, educators seek to engage students in the discovery process, aiming to encourage high-order cognitive skills such as analysis, synthesis, and evaluation (Slavich & Zimbardo, 2012).

Alongside reflections, immediate feedback is a crucial component of simulation-based learning (and steeped in constructivism), as students are expected to use it to construct new learning for subsequent simulations (Kaakinen & Arwood, 2009). Some research purports feedback as being the 'single most important feature of simulation-based medical education', as it reduces the 'decay' of acquired skills, allows opportunity for self-assessment, and offers prompt clarification for any misunderstandings (Issenberg et al., 2005, p. 21; Burns, 2015). Studies continually highlight that simulations based in constructivism assist students with ethical decision making, moral sensitivity, and moral judgement (Shapira-Lishchinsky, 2015) as well as having direct connections to patient safety (Lestander, Lehto, & Engstrom, 2016). Whilst constructivism contains several theories within its umbrella, experiential learning theory (E.L.T.) deserves illumination because of its focus on *experience* when constructing new knowledge (Mattar, 2018).

Constructivist, David Kolb's (1984) eminent E.L.T. offers both a theoretical foundation and a process for knowledge acquisition (Poore, Cullen, & Schaar, 2014). Kolb (1984, p. 41) defines learning as 'the process whereby knowledge is created through the transformation of experience' (as cited in Poore et al., 2014; Lisko & O'Dell, 2010). In other words, a person learns through action or by doing. According to Kolb, learning is continual with new knowledge being created by transforming experience into existing cognitive frameworks, subsequently changing a person's thinking and behaviour (Lisko & O'Dell, 2010). When Kolb refers to the creation of knowledge through the transformation of experience, he is referring to two forms of experience: concrete and abstract. Additionally, the two ways of transforming that experience into knowledge are through active experimentation and reflective observation (Tomkins & Ulin, 2016). This is depicted in Kolb's learning cycle, which now owns a powerful presence in many tertiary institutions and is considered the theory's most renowned manifestation (Tomkins & Ulin, 2016). The learning cycle is depicted as connecting these four aspects, involving the 'integrated functioning of the total person – thinking, feeling, perceiving and behaving' (Kolb & Kolb, 2005, p. 194).

The theory holds the premise that students have different learning styles. Because of this, not all students will enter the learning cycle at the same point. However, regardless of where the students enter the cycle, they will follow the cycle in a linear fashion (Roberson, 2019). The model is most conducive to underpin simulations as, through all four phases, the student's thoughts, feelings, perceptions, and actions are evoked. This is a key aim of simulations (Roberson, 2019; Stocker, Burmester, & Allen, 2014; Zigmont et al., 2011). The concrete experience is achieved by the setting, scenario, and 'clients'. The abstract conceptualisation is achieved by ongoing assessment of the client. The active experimentation occurs with the actual interaction between the student and the client. Finally, reflective observation occurs when feedback is considered and pondered upon (Roberson, 2019). As mentioned, reflection is not only a key component of constructivism, but it can also be used to provide evidence of whether a theoretical approach has been effective. One study involving 51 nursing students

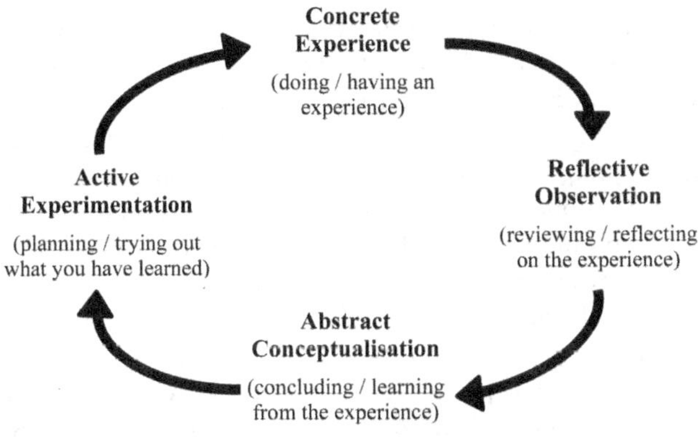

Figure 14.1 Kolb's learning cycle (McLeod, 2017).

revealed that, by writing a reflection after simulation, students identified a strong connection between reflection on their practice and patient safety. They also reported a new-found self-awareness of gaps in their knowledge. The researchers had utilised Kolb's E.L.T. theory to conceptualise the project, providing evidence of its effectiveness to underpin simulation-based activities (Lestander et al., 2016).

Bandura's (1977) social learning theory also warrants explicit consideration. Social learning theory focuses on how people learn from each other within a social context (Bethards, 2014). Although Bandura (1989) refined the theory by later including a cognitive component (thus, renaming it 'social-cognitive theory'), both theoretical versions emphasise observational learning (Peterson, 2004). Essentially, the learner observes a live or symbolic model and then repeats a process, strategy, or skill as demonstrated. Whilst the theory is regularly referred to in simulation literature in general, it is recently being applied specifically to the observer–learner role (Bethards, 2014).

Bandura (1977) proposed that observational learning involves four processes:

1) *Attention Processes* – the learner must have their attention on the modelled behaviour in order to learn. When applying to the observer–learner role, educators should emphasise concepts, not specific tasks, and link the concepts to scenario objectives.
2) *Retention Process* – the learner uses imaginal (envisioning performing the behaviour) and verbal systems (discussing the behaviour) in order to remember the activity. Simulation facilitators should, therefore, provide opportunities for observers to symbolically rehearse the modelled behaviours, ensuring debriefing opportunities.
3) *Reproduction* – the learner must have the ability (and be developmentally ready) to replicate the behaviour, which may require the input of others to provide feedback. In simulations, facilitators should provide opportunities for observers to participate in process-based roles, ensuring a facilitated discussion on how observed behaviour influenced decision-making.
4) *Motivation* – learners are more likely to adopt modelled behaviours if they are motivated by intrinsic or extrinsic factors. Intrinsic motivation comes from inside the individual, and extrinsic comes from external influences – e.g., the promise of a reward or a punishment (Bethards, 2014; Peterson, 2004). Simulation facilitators should, therefore, emphasise the importance of the observer role, ensuring observers are evaluated on their participation during the debriefing discussion (Bethards, 2014).

Bandura (2001) states there are many achievements people seek but cannot attain unless working in coordination with others. Scrutinising how others undertake a task is pivotal to the learning process. To further apply Bandura's social learning concepts to simulations, students are provided with opportunities to observe and learn whilst in collaboration and communication with peers (Burke & Mancuso, 2012). Adopting Bandura's principles to simulation-based learning involving an interprofessional team is an optimal design choice because it can provide an opportunity for students to observe peers (from other disciplines), attain insight into their own performance, and model behaviour and knowledge (Stocker et al., 2014).

Overall, constructivism, E.L.T., and social learning theories all have significant contributions for educators using a pedagogical approach to simulations (Erlam et al., 2017). Relevant learning theories should be carefully considered to conceptualise projects, with the aim of creating optimal, safe learning environments for social work students to attain learning objectives and test competencies as they embark on career pathways to help others.

Planning Simulation Activities

Building effective relationships and undertaking skilful assessments and purposeful interventions are key components that underpin the foundation of social work practice (Chenoweth & McAuliffe, 2014). Social work schools are increasingly incorporating immersive live simulations to help students develop these instrumental, vital skills. However, meaningful planning is required to ensure learning objectives and desired competencies are achieved.

Within more recent literature, there has been an acceleration of helpful recommendations on how to best design effective simulations. Helpful advice is provided on what to consider regarding constructing simulation materials (e.g., designing relevant vignettes, pre-post and post-simulation questionnaires, and reflection guidelines), adequately preparing students and actors, and providing immediate feedback (Lee, Kourgiantakis, & Bogo, 2020). Furthermore, Kourgiantakis et al. (2019b) provide best practices based on simulation-based learning literature. This includes (i) preparing and supporting facilitators, actors and students, (ii) articulating the theoretical framework assessment instruments, and competencies, (iii) designing case studies that are realistic and include diverse scenarios and clients, (iv) providing opportunities for students to engage, practice, give and receive feedback, and debrief, and (v) evaluating the simulation.

It is also important to add that, whilst the benefits of simulations are explicit, caution should be exercised. Lamé and Dixon-Woods (2018) alert educators that psychological harm could be evoked during simulation. Careful consideration must be given to case study design with some researchers recommending an avoidance of death-related scenarios for early learners as premature exposure could trigger distress (Lamé & Dixon-Woods, 2018; Winter, Patel, & Norman, 2017). This, again, highlights the importance of sound debriefing mechanisms, guided reflections activities, and post-simulation follow-up be employed (Kourgiantakis et al., 2019b; Lamé & Dixon-Woods, 2018). However, it should be noted the emphasis here remains on reactions that would be considered 'adverse' or 'potentially harmful', as some level of discomfort is commonly experienced by learners within simulations.

Finally, identifying students who may be potentially triggered by simulation content can result in educators and field education staff becoming more cognisant of students requiring additional support. This may need to be considered when specific field placements are being sought or result in alternative practicum options being offered. Educators and field education staff adopting good pedagogical approaches to simulations will embrace the learnings derived from the literature and effectively combine with their own teaching style and commitment to student learning. This, in effect, is a form of evaluative judgment which 'is relevant to self-management in professional practice with the juxtaposition of competence as opposed to confidence' and is often developed in simulation activities (Goldingay, 2020).

Simulation and Field Education

Numerous social work education programmes have identified field education as the discipline's signature pedagogy (Ledger, Hillman, Harreveld, & de Warren, 2017). The Council of Social Work Education (C.S.W.E.) (2015) states, 'the intent of field education is to integrate the theoretical and conceptual contribution of the classroom within the practical world of the practice setting' (C.S.W.E., 2015, p. 12). Subsequently, the benefits of simulation-based learning in relation to preparing for field placement has fast become an established concept within contemporary pedagogical literature (Dodds et al., 2018). However, the inclusion of simulated learning as a valid form of field placement is less common.

In the United States, a competency-based education framework has been adopted, meaning students' competencies in professional practice are identified and assessed prior to programme completion (C.S.W.E., 2015). Similarly, in the U.K., Frontline, which offers an intensive 2-year programme for people interested in becoming social workers, has a strong focus on simulated learning. Both contexts are underpinned by a competency-based framework, which tends to focus on acquisition and demonstration of skills rather than attributes or standards. Countries that have a focus on standards, such as Australia, New Zealand, and elements of the U.K. system, have tended to shy away from using simulation as a method or form of field education. However, this has created challenges.

In Australia, there has been a significant increase in students accessing higher education as a result of deregulation and marketisation in tertiary education (Cleak & Smith, 2012). Combined with increasing tertiary student enrolments, there is the ever-increasing expectation to provide flexibility within the teaching programme and field placement structures. Field educators tend to agree that it is important to offer diverse placement opportunities in order to be inclusive of the student cohort who may experience access and equity issues with regard to study (Spencer & McDonald, 1998). Further, there are many students who may have learning needs and other personal circumstances (Hemy et al., 2016), making flexibility important. Whilst the need to offer flexibility in tertiary education programmes is agreed, the increase in student enrolments has placed added pressure on field education to also meet these growing student numbers.

Some challenges outside of the universities' processes have included the restructuring of the Social and Community Services (S.A.C.S.) Award, legislating a wage increase of between 19% and 41% between 2012 and 2020 (A.C.O.S.S., 2020). This restructure did have an impact on some organisations' challenges in service delivery and staffing structures. One of the consequences of these financial pressures has been the ability to provide student field placements in human service organisations (Lucas & Vassos, 2019). Another significant challenge is that increasing workload demands have limited field educators potential to offer social work placements (Cleak & Zuchowski, 2018). As a result, these pressures on both the university to provide suitable field placement opportunities to increasing levels of student numbers and the constraints faced by the human services field to offer social work placements has challenged ongoing field education as a core component of social work education.

However, simulation cannot, as yet, be used as a form of placement in Australia, where field education practice is governed by the Australian Social Work Education and Accreditation Standards (A.S.W.E.A.S.) requirements of 1,000 placement hours. Yet, simulated learning and field education are grounded in a similar theoretical base, and both can be used for learning and assessment. Further, not only can simulations prepare students for 'real life' practice post-graduation, but they can also assist with preparing students for field placement, where many students support clients for the first time (Butler, Carello, & Maguin, 2017; Dodds et al., 2018; Fulton et al., 2019). It is within the practicum context that students are often first exposed to clients experiencing issues such as domestic violence, physical and sexual assault, child abuse and neglect, chronic illness, or life-limiting health conditions (Butler et al., 2017). For example, Kourgiantakis et al. (2019a) describe how simulation has been used and evaluated (n = 57) in a Canadian programme to not only provide students with an opportunity to enhance their skills and knowledge in mental health practice, but also to promote critical reflection and develop greater self-awareness and self-regulation. Students in this voluntary programme, titled Practice Friday, came together in small groups to take turns interviewing an actor playing the role of client. Feedback was provided by peers, a field instructor, and an academic based on observed competencies. Students were also required to reflect in writing and verbally on the interaction. Students reported a positive impact on their learning, with an increased knowledge, understanding, and proficiency in interviewing. They felt better able to critically reflect on practice, exercise professional judgement and decision making, integrate theory with practice, relate to client experiences, and demonstrate self-awareness.

Such opportunities can translate to better outcomes on placement. For example, Phillips et al. (2018) describe how 100 students enrolled in a virtual field practicum, that includes simulation with clients prior to going on placement, performed as well, if not slightly better in a range of competencies than those who did not undertake the simulation. Simulation, thus, bridges the 'theory–practice divide' and means educators do not simply teach students about practice but also provide opportunities for students to do practice. Simulations can, therefore, be a means to help prepare students for such encounters as well as provide an opportunity to *do* social work rather than only learn *about* social work practice in set coursework (Kourgiantakis et al., 2019b; Lee et al., 2020).

This is important because, as Bogo (2015) and Lee et al. (2020) point out, not all students have the same opportunities to learn while on placement. There is considerable variation in the tasks afforded students, with some having very limited opportunities to engage in clinical practice. Further, there is little consistency in how students are evaluated in placement, and some essential skills, such as those related to crisis intervention or working with complex mental health and behavioural issues, may never be practised on placement. Thus, simulation within the university setting, ensures that students can not only be taught about specific fields of practice, but also be required to demonstrate and engage in practice and for this to be evaluated in a consistent manner. Further, students who are granted more opportunities to practice skills tend to be rated more highly by field educators and describe a greater sense of competence in their own practice (Fortune, Lee, & Cavazos, 2007). This may be because simulation helps overcome the divide between university education and theory and challenges and prepares students to translate theory into practice on placement (Newton, Billet, Jolly, & Ockerby, 2009). Simulations provide a safe learning environment for students, as they are able to take incremental and considered risks within a student's comfort zone without the risk and fear of doing harm. Simulations can be adapted to suit the pace and tailored to the needs of the leaner (Doel & Shardlow, 1996; see also, Beddoe, Ackroyd, Chinnery, & Appleton, 2011).

Simulation can also complement field placements and has, in more recent years, been formally used as part of field education with positive results. Since 2015, simulations have been accepted by the C.S.W.E. as a means for students to accumulate field placement hours (as cited in Roberson, 2019). This shift emphasises the importance of understanding relevant learning theories and solid pedagogical practices when planning and designing simulations. One example, from Holland Bloorview Kids Rehabilitation Hospital in Canada, sought to provide social work students on placement with the opportunity to work on foundational interviewing skills and reported that students found the simulation less stressful than those previously undertaken in a classroom setting and that the process enhanced their confidence and practice skills (Sunarich & Rowan, 2017).

However, real-world placement experiences are still important. At times, students may perform well in simulations but struggle in 'real' situations (Beddoe et al., 2011). Simulation can be costly, and considerable work needs to be undertaken to ensure it is authentic, mimicking real-world practice. One example describes how field educators can be used as 'standardised patients' in order to ensure that meaningful feedback is provided to students regarding their performance (Rubin, 2019). This, however, requires that ample training is provided to social workers in order to use simulated scenarios and to support students to translate their knowledge into practice. It also requires the development of models for simulated practice, as described in the following section.

Model for Practice

The term simulation is used to describe a range of teaching and learning practices. In respect to social work education, the term simulation has been used to describe simulated clients, role-play, digital (virtual) realities, fictional clinical scenarios, live supervision, and case scenarios. Each are described below.

Perhaps the most prominent example of simulation, particularly within the field of health practice, is the use of *simulated clients* (also known as standardised clients, simulated patients, and standardised patients). In social work education, it often involves trained actors, professionals, or volunteer 'clients' from the community (Rubin & Francis, 2019). In all cases, the simulated client will be prepared by the educator to present a scenario in a standardised manner in order to provide consistency between learners.

Role play, which is also an extremely common experiential learning activity in social work training, includes student to student, student to teacher, or observing non-actors engage in role-play. It is different to simulated clients, as there is rarely preparation or strongly scripted scenarios. It can include the use of technology, such as video conferencing.

Digital (virtual) realities are a growing application of simulated learning. It has existed for several decades and can include the use of computer technologies to simulate and teach social work skills (see Abernathy & McBride, 1979; Meinert, 1972; Smith et al., 1980). It can include computer representations of real environments.

Fictional clinical scenarios are usually a capstone learning experience in social work in which students are required to prepare to take on fictional roles and act out a scenario, such as community action in response to poverty (Hitchcock et al., 2018) or disaster management (Pack, 2014)

Live supervision best exemplifies the thin line between the learning experiences of field education and simulation. Used primarily in field education, where there is direct observation of a student by a field educator, it is also used with students engaging in role-play with other students or actors (Andrews & Harris, 2017).

Case scenarios are used in most educational settings to help students apply learning to practice. A case scenario may be provided to students to work through independently, with questions used to guide student thinking. On the other hand, scenarios may be delivered live by a teacher-facilitator. In the case of live case scenarios, teacher-facilitators may adapt the scenario based on student responses.

The common components of the approaches to simulations, in our view, are authenticity, fidelity, adaptivity, and responsive feedback. These elements provide a component model of simulation design that can be used to inform the design of simulation both as a means to prepare students for placement and to supplement placement experiences. This model builds on previous studies that have been conducted to identify the common instructional design features of simulation-based education. Cook et al. (2013), for example, identified best practice in simulation-based education and that simulations should include the instructional design features of feedback, cognitive interactivity, repetitive practice, and a range of difficulty. While these features are necessary for effective learning, these alone do not differentiate simulation from other constructivist learning activities. Instead, the proposed component model of simulation design is not unlike Meinert's (1972) definition in which he identified four key points being present in simulations: '1) an object or physical model [fidelity]; 2) representing a system or system part [authenticity]; 3) possession of the capability of being manipulated [adaptivity]; and 4) the presence of the "essence of reality" in the manipulative process [adaptivity].' (p. 52).

Within our model, and as shown in Figure 14.2, the components of fidelity, authenticity, and adaptivity are used. *Authenticity* refers to whether the activity and its artifacts can be found in real practice. *Fidelity* describes the way in which the simulation resembles the real – that is, the degree to which the sensory components (visual, auditory, etc.) are accurate representations of the real-life scenario. The sensory features of a simulation replicate the real context and assist in suspending disbelief. The purpose of fidelity is to increase the likelihood of students suspending disbelief and treating the simulation and, by consequence, their choices as real and impactful (Hamstra et al., 2014). What is less clear is whether lower fidelity simulations decrease the likelihood of students suspending disbelief, and whether the suspension of disbelief improves learning outcomes. While often the area of most attraction, it is probable that fidelity is one of the least important aspects of effective simulation-based learning activities. It should be noted that the definition of fidelity is contested and that assessments of simulation based on degree of fidelity lack interrater reliability (see Hamstra et al., 2014). *Adaptivity* refers to whether the activity is responsive to the choices and actions of the learner. *Responsive feedback* refers to whether the feedback is immediate, relevant, and appropriate. It can be from self (reflections), peers, participants, and experts; without feedback the 'learning' is not complete (see E.L.T., metacognition). Feedback may include guided self-reflection; if responsive feedback is not incorporated in the activity, then metacognition is not guaranteed, and the activity should not be considered a learning activity. Responsive feedback is made explicit in the proposed model on the basis that the other three components may exist and no learning take place. For example, many non-serious games have high levels of fidelity, authenticity, and adaptivity; without responsive feedback, they cannot be understood as a learning activity.

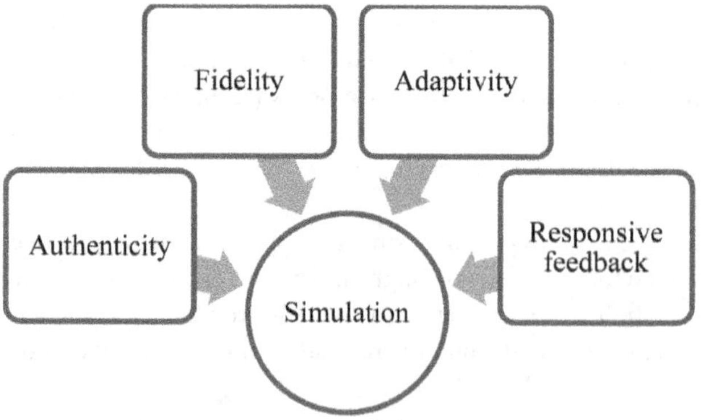

Figure 14.2 Components of simulation.

Table 14.1 Component of Simulation Activities

	Authenticity	*Fidelity*	*Adaptivity*	*Responsive feedback*
Simulated clients	Med – High	High	High	High
Role play	Low – Med	Low	Low – Med	Med – High
Digital realities	Med – High	Low – High	Low – High	Low – High
Fictional clinical scenarios	Low – High	Med – High	Med – High	Low – High
Live supervision	Med – High	Med – High	Med – High	High
Case scenario	Low – High	Low	Low – High	Low – High

As shown in Table 14.1, we argue that each simulation activity can be understood as having differing amounts of each component. For example, *simulated clients* are usually high in fidelity with the use of simulated learning environments. Usually highly authentic, engaging students in tasks that mimic practice. Authenticity may be increased with the use of artifacts such as systems for record keeping that are replicas of practice contexts. The fidelity of a simulated patient scenario can be increased with the use of simulated learning environments. While not essential, it increases the likelihood of the student being able to suspend reality and improves context-based learning and, subsequently, context-based recall. Highly adaptive, but less so than 'real' world clients, trained actors will be given constraints around where to guide the scenario. Adaptivity is high, as actors respond differently based on the actions taken by the students. Feedback is typically gained by expert observers, peer observers, and responses from the actor.

Role plays are usually low in fidelity but may include simulated learning environments. Adaptivity is highly dependent on the individual's understanding of the role they are playing. Feedback often includes self-reflection and group discussion. *Digital (virtual) realities* have varying degrees of fidelity based on the technology, that is. graphical representations, photographs, and virtual and augmented realities as well as authentic practices, such as observational assessments (e.g., risk in environments) and clinical tasks (e.g., writing case notes). Feedback can be embedded in the technology, indicating correct or incorrect behaviours, or via discussions with a teaching team. *Fictional clinical scenarios* are highly immersive, which increases fidelity; however, more preparation is required to make it authentic. As it is only loosely scripted, the adaptivity is the result of different behaviours by students in roles. Feedback occurs through debriefing and discussion. Fidelity will be increased in *live supervision* through the use of real practice environments or simulated learning environments. Authenticity and adaptivity are dependent on whether real clients or fellow students take on the role of the client. Feedback is provided during the activity. *Case scenarios* are very low on fidelity, asking students to suspend disbelief.

Conclusion

Simulation includes a range of different types of activities that have varying degrees of authenticity, fidelity, adaptivity, and responsive feedback. Each activity is grounded in an experiential and constructivist approach to learning and will be created using different variables such as real/virtual space, client, authentic artefacts, and teams that mimic practice. Moving forward, it will be important for accrediting bodies to more actively include the use of simulation not only as a means to prepare students for field education and practice but also as a means of field education. This is particularly important given current constraints and demands on field education globally. Simulation activities give learners the opportunity to practice and observe the impact of different interactions. It provides a powerful example of witnessing alternative realities. In the case of simulation-for-assessment, a student's competence can be assessed equitably against set criteria, removing the risk that some students have an easier or harder assessment than others. This helps address criticisms of placement, whereby learning and assessment can be inconsistent across students. It means educators can more easily control the experience which can also help reduce student stress levels. It can also assist educators to scaffold student learning experiences, and assessors can be more confident that specific practices were accessible in the scenario. Simulation can and should, thus, be used to support and supplement field education.

References

Abernathy, W. B., & McBride, E. (1979). Teaching referral skills through computer simulation. *Psychiatric Services, 30*(3), 164–166. https://doi.org/10.1176/ps.30.3.164

ACOSS (2020). *Challenges for Australia's community sector: ERO supplementation.* Retrieved from https://www.acoss.org.au/challenges-for-australias-community-sector-ero-supplementation-February 2020.

Aldridge, M. D. (2016). How can nurse educators perform patient simulation efficiently? *Teaching and Learning in Nursing, 11*(1), 8–14. https://doi.org/10.1016/j.teln.2015.09.001

Andrews, P., & Harris, S. (2017). Using live supervision to teach counselling skills to social work students. *Social Work Education, 36*(3), 299–311. https://doi.org/10.1080/02615479.2016.1270929

Bandura, A. (1977). *Social learning theory.* Upper Saddle. NJ: Prentice-Hall.

Bandura, A. (1989). Human agency in social cognitive theory. *American Psychologist, 44*(9), 1175–1184. DOI:10.1037/0003-066X.44.9.1175.

Bandura, A. (2001). Social cognitive theory: An agentic perspective. *Annual Review of Psychology, 52*, 1–26. Retrieved from https://go-gale-com.libraryproxy.griffith.edu.au/ps/i.do?p=ITOF&u=griffith&id=GALE|A73232700&v=2.1&it=r&sid=summon

Beddoe, L., Ackroyd, J., Chinnery, S. A., & Appleton, C. (2011). Live supervision of students in field placement: More than just watching. *Social Work Education, 30*(5), 512–528. https://doi.org/10.1080/02615479.2010.516358

Berliner, A. (1982). Enhancing social work education through the use of drama students as 'clients' in role play. *Arete*, 7, 61–67.

Bethards, M. L. (2014). Applying social learning theory to the observer role in simulation. *Clinical Simulation in Nursing, 10*(2), 65–69. https://doi.org/10.1016/j.ecns.2013.08.002

Bloom, B. S. (1956). *Taxonomy of educational objectives. Vol. 1: Cognitive domain.* New York: McKay, 20–24.

Bogo, M. (2015). Field education for clinical social work practice: Best practices and contemporary challenges. *Clinical Social Work Journal, 43*(3), 317–324. https://doi.org/10.1007/s10615-015-0526-5

Burke, H., & Mancuso, L., (2012). Social cognitive theory, metacognition, and simulation learning in nursing education. *Journal of Nursing Education, 51*(10), 543–548. https://doi.org/10.3928/01484834-20120820-02

Burns, C. (2015). Using debriefing and feedback in simulation to improve participant performance: An educators perspective. *International Journal of Medical Education, 6*, 118–120. https://doi.org/10.5116/ijme.55fb.3d3a

Butler, L., Carello, J., & Maguin, E. (2017). Trauma, stress, and self-care in clinical training: Predictors of burnout, decline in health status, secondary traumatic stress symptoms and compassion satisfaction. *Psychological Trauma: Theory, Research, Practice, and Policy, 9*(4), 416–424. https://doi.org/10.1037/tra0000187

Chenoweth, L., & McAuliffe, D. (2014). *The road to social work and human service practice.* (4th ed.). Melbourne: Cengage Learning.

Child Australia. (2017). *What is pedagogy? How does it influence our practice?* Retrieved from https://childaustralia.org.au/wp-content/uploads/2017/02/CA-Statement-Pedagogy.pdf

Cleak, H., & Smith, D. (2012). Student satisfaction with models of field placement supervision. *Australian Social Work, 65*(2), 243–258. https://doi.org/10.1080/0312407X.2011.572981

Cleak, H., & Zuchowski, I. (2018). Empirical support and considerations for social work supervision of students in alternative placement models. *Clinical Social Work Journal, 47*(1), 32–42. https://doi.org/10.1007/s10615-018-0692-3

Cook, D. A., Hamstra, S. J., Brydges, R., Zendejas, B., Szostek, J. H., Wang, A. T., Erwin, P. J., & Hatala, R. (2013). Comparative effectiveness of instructional design features in simulation-based education:

Systematic review and meta-analysis. *Medical Teacher*, 35(1). https://doi.org/10.3109/0142159X.2012.714886

Council on Social Work Education (C.S.W.E.). (2015). *2015 Educational policy and accreditation standards*. Retrieved from https://www.cswe.org/getattachment/Accreditation/Accreditation-Process/2015-EPAS/2015EPAS_Web_FINAL.pdf.aspx

Dodds, C., Heslop, P., & Meredith, C. (2018). Using simulation-based education to help social work students prepare for practice. *Social Work Education*, *37*(5), 597–602. https://doi.org/10.1080/02615479.2018.1433158

Doel, M., & Shardlow, S. (1996). Simulated and live practice teaching: The practice teacher's craft. *Social Work Education*, *15*(4), 16–33. https://doi.org/10.1080/02615479611220321

Doelcker, R. and Bedics, B. C. 1987. Differential use of role-play in social work education. *Arete*, *12*(3), 53–60.

Erlam, G., Smythe, L., & Wright-St Clair, V. (2017). Simulation is not pedagogy. *Open Journal of Nursing*, *7*, 779–787. https://doi.org/10.4236/ojn.2017.77059

Fortune, A., Lee, M., & Cavazos, A. (2007). Does practice make perfect? Practicing professional skills and outcomes in social work field education. *The Clinical Supervisor*, *26*(1–2), 239–263. https://doi.org/10.1300/J001v26n01_15

Fulton, A. E., Dimitropoulos, G., Ayala, J., McLaughlin, A. M., Baynton, M., Blaug, C., Collins, T., Elliott, G., Judge-Stasiak, A., Letkemann, L., & Ragan, E. (2019). Role-playing: A strategy for practicum preparation for foundation year MSW students. *Journal of Teaching in Social Work*, *39*(2), 163–180. https://doi.org/10.1080/08841233.2019.1576573

Gaba, D. M. (2004). The future vision of simulation in healthcare. *BMJ Quality and Safety*, *13*(1), 2–10. https://doi.org/10.1136/qshc.2004.009878

Goldingay, S. (2020) How do we prepare social workers to manage their own self in practice situations? The need for incremental exposure via technology. *Digital Social Work Cafe*.

Goldingay, S., Epstein, S., & Taylor, D. (2018). Simulating social work practice online with digital storytelling: Challenges and opportunities. *Social Work Education*, *37*(6), 790–803. https://doi.org/10.1080/02615479.2018.1481203

Hamstra, S. J., Brydges, R., Hatala, R., Zendejas, B., & Cook, D. A. (2014). Reconsidering fidelity in simulation-based training. *Academic Medicine*, *89*(3), 387–392. https://doi.org/10.1097/ACM.0000000000000130

Hemy, M., Boddy, J., Chee, P., & Sauvage, D. (2016). Social work students 'juggling' field placement. *Social Work Education*, *35*(2), 215–228. https://doi.org/10.1080/02615479.2015.1125878

Hitchcock, L. I., Peterson, D. T., Debiasi, L., Shipman, S., Varley, A., & White, M. L. (2018). Learning about poverty through simulation: A pilot evaluation. *Journal of Social Work Education*, *54*(3), 517–531. https://doi.org/10.1080/10437797.2018.1434427

Isaak, R., Stiegler, M., Hobbs, G., Martinelli, S. M., Zvara, D., Arora, H., & Chen, F. (2018). Comparing real-time versus delayed video assessments for evaluating ACGME sub-competency milestones in simulated patient care environments. *Cureus*, *10*(3). https://doi.org/10.7759/cureus.2267

Issenberg, B., McGaghie, W. C., Petrusa, E., Lee Gordon, D., & Scales, R. J. (2005). Features and uses of high-fidelity medical simulations that lead to effective learning: A BEME systematic review. *Medical Teacher*, *27*(1), 10–28. https://doi.org/10.1080/01421590500046924

Kaakinen, J., & Arwood, E. (2009). Systematic review of nursing simulation literature for use of learning theory. *International Journal of Nursing Education Scholarship*, *6*(1), 1–20. https://doi.org/10.2202/1548-923X.1688

Kneebone, R. (2005). Evaluating clinical simulations for learning procedural skills: A theory-based approach. *Academic Medicine*, *80*(6), 549–553.

Kolb, A., & Kolb, D. (2005). Learning styles and learning spaces: Enhancing experiential learning in higher education. *Academy of Management Learning & Education*, *4*(2). 193–212. https://doi.org/10.5465/AMLE.2005.17268566

Kolb, D. (1984). *Experiential learning: experience as the source of learning and development*. Englewood Cliffs. NJ: Prentice Hall.

Kourgiantakis, T., Bogo, M., & Sewell, K. M. (2019a). Practice Fridays: Using simulation to develop holistic competence. *Journal of Social Work Education*, *55*(3), 551–564. https://doi.org/10.1080/10437797.2018.1548989

Kourgiantakis, T., Sewell, K., Hu, R., Logan, J., & Bogo, M. (2019b). Simulation in social work education: A scoping review. *Research on Social Work practice*. 1–8. https://doi.org/10.1177/1049731519885015

Lamé, G., & Dixon-Woods, M. (2018). Using clinical simulation to study how to improve quality and safety in healthcare. *BMJ Simulation and Technology Enhanced Learning*, bmjstel-2018-000370. https://doi.org/10.1136/bmjstel-2018-000370

Ledger, S., Hillman, W., Harreveld, B., & de Warren, D. (2017). Field education as signature pedagogy – insights for Australian social work. *Advances in Social Work and Welfare Education, 19*(1), 62–70.

Lee, E., Kourgiantakis, T., & Bogo, M. (2020). Translating knowledge into practice: Using simulation to enhance mental health competence through social work education. *Social Work Education: The International Journal, 39*(3), 329–349. https://doi.org/10.1080/02615479.2019.1620723

Lestander, Ö., Lehto, N., & Engström, Å. (2016). Nursing students' perceptions of learning after high fidelity simulation: Effects of a three-step post-simulation reflection model. *Nurse Education Today, 40*, 219–224. https://doi.org/10.1016/j.nedt.2016.03.011

Lisko, S. A., & O'Dell, V. (2010). Integration of theory and practice: Experiential learning theory and nursing education. *Nursing Education Perspectives, 31*(2), 106–108.

Lucas, James J., & Vassos, S. (2019) Pedagogical intent and placement diversity in social work field education: One university's experiences. *Advances in Social Work and Welfare Education, 21*(1), 51–66.

Mattar, J. (2018). Constructivism and connectivism in education technology: Active, situated, authentic, experiential, and anchored learning. *Revista Iberoamericana de Educación a Distancia, 21*(2), 201–217. https://doi.org/10.5944/ried.21.2.20055

McLeod, S. (2017). *Kolb's learning styles and experiential learning cycle [Web log post]*. Retrieved from https://www.simplypsychology.org/learning-kolb.html

McPhail, G., & Rata, E. (2016). Comparing curriculum types: 'Powerful knowledge and 21st century learning. *New Zealand Journal of Educational Studies, 51*(1), 53–68. https://doi.org/10.1007/s40841-015-0025-9

Meinert, R. G. (1972). Simulation technology: A potential tool for social work education. *Journal of Education for Social Work, 8*(3), 50–59. https://doi.org/10.1080/00220612.1972.10671927

Newton, J. M., Billet, S., Jolly, B., & Ockerby, C. M. (2009). Lost in translation: Barriers to learning in health professional clinical education. *Learning in Health and Social Care, 8*(4). https://doi.org/10.1111/j.1473-6861.2009.00229.x

Nimmagadda, J., & Murphy, J. (2014). Using simulations to enhance interprofessional competencies for social work and nursing students. *Social Work Education: The International Journal, 33*(4), 539–548. https://doi.org/10.1080/02615479.2013.877128

Olusegun, B. S. (2015). Constructivism learning theory: A paradigm for teaching and learning. *IOSR Journal of Research and Method, 5*(6), 66–70. https://doi.org/10.9790/7388-05616670

Pack, M. (2014). Northern exposure: Integrating disaster management in a humanitarian and community studies program in the Northern Territory of Australia. *Advances in Social Work and Welfare Education, 16*(2), 73–85.

Pedagogy. (2020). *Merriam-Webster Learner's Dictionary*. Retrieved from http://www.learnersdictionary.com/definition/pedagogy

Persaud, C. (2021). *Pedagogy: What educators need to know* [Web log post]. Retrieved from https://tophat.com/blog/pedagogy/

Peterson, C. (2004). *Looking forward through the lifespan*. NSW, Australia: Pearson Education Australia.

Phillips, E. S., Wood, G. J., Yoo, J., Ward, K. J., Hsiao, S. C., Singh, M., & Morris, B. (2018). A virtual field practicum: Building core competencies prior to agency placement. *Journal of Social Work Education, 54*(4), 620–640. DOI:10.1080/10437797.2018.1486651.

Poore, J. A., Cullen, D. L., & Schaar, G. L. (2014). Simulation-based interprofessional education guided by Kolb's experiential learning theory. *Clinical Simulation in Nursing, 10*(5), 241–247. https://doi.org/10.1016/j.ecns.2014.01.004

Qiong, J. (2010). A brief study on the implication of constructivism teaching theory on classroom teaching reform in basic education. *International Education Studies, 3*(2), 197. https://doi.org/10.5539/ies.v3n2p197

Roberson, C. J. (2019). Understanding simulation in social work education: A conceptual framework. *Journal of Social Work Education*, 1–11. https://doi.org/10.1080/10437797.2019.1656587

Rosenthal Gelman, C., & Baum, N. (2010). Social work students' pre-placement anxiety: An international comparison. *Social Work Education, 29*(4), 427–440. https://doi.org/10.1080/02615470903009007

Rubin, M., & Francis, G. (2019). Engaging field educators as standardized patients in social work education. *Field Educator, 9*(1), 1–20. https://www.proquest.com/docview/2237490740/fulltextPDF/BF94152AD41349CEPQ/1?accountid=14543

Shapira-Lishchinsky, O. (2015). Simulation-based constructivist approach for education leaders. *Educational Management Administration & Leadership*, *43*(6), 972–988. https://doi.org/10.1177/1741143214543203

Slavich, G. M., & Zimbardo, P. G. (2012). Transformational teaching: Theoretical underpinnings, basic principles, and core methods. *Educational Psychological Review*, *24*(4), 569–608. https://doi.org/10.1007/s10648-012-9199-6

Smith, N. J., Parmar, G., & Paget, N. (1980). Computer-simulation and social work education: A suitable case, *British Journal of Social Work*, *10*(4), 491–499.

Spencer, A. & McDonald, C. (1998) Omissions and commissions: An analysis of professional field education literature, *Australian Social Work*, *51*(4), 9–18. https://doi.org/10.1080/03124079808411239

Stocker, M., Burmeister, M., & Allen, M. (2014). Optimisation of simulated team training through the application of learning theories: A debate for a conceptual framework. *BMC Medical Education*, *14*(1), 69. https://doi.org/10.1186/1472-6920-14-69

Sunarich, N., & Rowan, S. (2017). *Social work simulation education in the field*. Field Educator. https://fieldeducator.simmons.edu/article/social-work-simulation-education-in-the-field/

Tomkins, L., & Ulus, E. (2016). 'Oh, was that "experiential learning"?!' Spaces, synergies and surprises with Kolb's learning cycle. *Management Learning*, *47*(2), 158–178. https://doi.org/10.1177/1350507615587451

Topçiu, M., & Myftiu, J. (2015). Vyotsky theory on social interaction and its influence on the development of pre-school children. *European Journal of Social Science Education and Research*, *2*(3). 172–179. https://doi.org/10.26417/ejser.v4i1.p172-179

Trahan, M. H., Smith, K. S., Traylor, A. C., Washburn, M., Moore, N., & Mancillas, A. (2019). Three-dimensional virtual reality: Applications to the 12 grand challenges of social work. *Journal of Technology in Human Services*, *37*(1), 1–19. https://doi.org/10.1080/15228835.2019.1599765

Vygotsky, L. (1978). *Mind in Society: the Development of Higher Psychological Processes*. Cambridge Massachusetts: Harvard University Press.

Wall, S., Litjens, I., & Taguma, M. (2015). *Pedagogy in early childhood education and care (ECEC): An international comparative study of approaches and policies*. Research Brief. Retrieved from https://assets.publishing.service.gov.uk/government/uploads/system/uploads/attachment_data/file/445817/RB400_-_Early_years_pedagogy_and_policy_an_international_study.pdf

Winter, R. I., Patel, R., & Norman, R. I. (2017). A qualitative exploration of the help-seeking behaviors of students who experience psychological distress around assessment at medical school. *Academic Psychiatry*, *41*(4), 477–485. https://doi.org/10.1007/s40596-017-0701-9

Zigmont, J., Kappus, L., & Sudikoff, S. N. (2011). Theoretical foundations of learning through simulation. *Seminars in Perinatology*, *35*(2), 47–51. https://doi.org/10.1053/j.semperi.2011.01.002

15

Social Work Field Education in Australia

Issues and Trends

Kylie Agllias and Leanne Schubert

Australian Social Work: The Practicum in Context

Australia's modern welfare state was formalised in the 1940s to guarantee the wages of workers, a safety net of income support, and a range of universal services delivered by national, state, and local governments alongside approved providers. More recently, neoliberal economic reform has consistently eroded these provisions, through the privatisation of services and institutions, competitive tendering for community grants and funding, and stricter policing of particular populations under the ideological guise of *individual responsibility* and *mutual obligation*. While Australia is one of the world's wealthiest nations, relative poverty and income inequality remain high (Credit Suisse Research Institute, 2019; Davidson, Saunders, Bradbury, & Wong, 2018). Income inequality is higher than the Organisation for Economic Co-operation and Development O.E.C.D. average but more equal than in some other English-speaking countries, such as the United Kingdom and the United States of America (A.C.O.S.S. & U.N.S.W., 2020). A number of groups are overrepresented in the lowest 20% income bracket: the unemployed (77%), older people (39%), and sole parents (36%) (A.C.O.S.S. & U.N.S.W., 2020). However, income inequality is a symptom of a broader and more complex vulnerability for specific groups such as Aboriginal and Torres Strait Islander peoples, culturally and linguistically diverse populations, and/or those with a mental illness or disability (A.C.O.S.S. & U.N.S.W., 2020; Davidson et al., 2018).

Australian social work has been described as a generalist, secular, and professional model, derived from Western rationalist perspectives, featuring a distinct critical and social justice orientation (Agllias & Gray, 2020). Formal social work education developed alongside the welfare state in the 1940s and the professional accrediting body, the Australian Association of Social Workers (A.A.S.W.), was established in 1946 (Camilleri, 2005). While the A.A.S.W. has a current membership of c. 12,000 social workers, that number does not represent the entirety of social workers employed in Australia (A.A.S.W., 2019). Despite concerted efforts by the A.A.S.W., the profession has yet to achieve national registration and protection of title. Additionally, social workers are often employed under generic position titles, making it difficult to establish accurate numbers and employment patterns. Social workers are employed in diverse fields and levels of practice across the government, non-government, and private sectors, including health and

DOI: 10.4324/9781032164946-19

mental health, child protection and family work, income support, community development, policy, and research.

Reports suggest that growth in the number of social work positions has been strong for a number of years, and this growth is expected to reach beyond 2022 (Craik, 2019). Commonwealth and state governments have responded to current projected shortages in the health, community, and human service workforce through initiatives to increase university enrolments across a number of professions (Cleak, Hawkins, Laughton, & Williams, 2015). Indeed, the removal of quotas for university enrolment in 1986, alongside the introduction of a demand-driven funding model, had already provided universities with an incentive to expand (Cleak & Zuchowski, 2019). Combined, this has resulted in a rapid growth in Australian higher education student numbers and, particularly, in *health-related programmes*, including social work (Cleak et al., 2015; Cleak & Zuchowski, 2019).

The Australian Council for Heads of Schools of Social Work (A.C.H.S.S.W., 2020) represents the Australian universities that teach tertiary level social work studies, and they report 13,000 students currently engaged in social work education. Eligibility for membership of the A.A.S.W. is a 4-year Bachelor of Social Work qualification or a Master of Social Work (a three-plus-two qualifying degree), from an accredited tertiary institution. At the time of writing, the A.A.S.W. (2020a), listed 83 accredited programmes across 30 universities in Australia. Of these, five programmes were newly established (and provisionally accredited), and five were being phased out. Twenty-three were Masters of Social Work (Qualifying). Eighteen offered a distance education option (A.A.S.W., 2019).

It is within this socio-historic context that this chapter proceeds to examine the role and nature of field education in Australian social work and the accreditation standards that guide its implementation. The authors then discuss current trends and issues in field education, through a review of available evidence, as well as their own experiences in a range of field education roles. The chapter concludes with a future-oriented commentary on field education practice, process, and research.

The Role, Nature, and Types of Social Work Field Instruction

Current Standards in Field Education

First, it is important to understand the role of the A.A.S.W. in determining the nature, structure, and provision of social work field education. The A.A.S.W. sets the criteria for the accreditation of all social work courses via *the Australian Social Work Education and Accreditation Standards* (A.S.W.E.A.S.) (A.A.S.W., 2012b). These standards guide, and mandate, particular elements of social work education, including governance and organisational requirements, core curriculum content, and field education standards (Ledger, Hillman, & Harreveld, 2017).

While the A.S.W.E.A.S. guidelines direct the structure of placements, the field education curricula are also shaped by, and must be consistent with, the Australian Association of Social Workers *Code of Ethics* (2010) and *Practice Standards* (2013). The code of ethics is based on three core social work values: respect for persons, social justice, and professional integrity. There are 23 standards across eight categories: (i) values and ethics, (ii) professionalism, (iii) culturally responsive and inclusive practice, (iv), knowledge for practice, (v) applying knowledge to practice, (vi), communication and interpersonal skills, (vii) information recording and sharing, and (viii) professional development and supervision. Developmental performance outcomes are currently derived from these documents to assess novice through to graduating students.

The A.S.W.E.A.S. (2012b) state that field education courses must 'have the status of a full academic subject', and 'employ strategies to ensure that students integrate social work knowledge, skills and values' (p. 15), such as theory to practice classes or seminars. The standards also emphasise the cooperative principle of field education, including the student, field educator/practitioner, agency, and educational provider. The A.A.S.W. requires two field placements within the context of all A.A.S.W. accredited programmes. Students must successfully complete a minimum of 1,000 hours in these two placements. These hours are to be completed within the normal working hours/days of the organisation hosting the placement. The A.A.S.W. also clearly outlines the minimum requirements for student supervision on placement, namely 1.5 hours of supervision per 35 hours of placement time. Placements must offer more than observational opportunities. Of the two placements, one must be 'direct'. While the distinctions are somewhat artificial, a direct placement generally refers to a clinical or casework focus with individuals, families, or groups, while an indirect placement refers to policy, research, administrative, community, and project-type work. However, the reality is that placements are increasingly indirect or of a mixed nature in which there are elements of direct and indirect practice (A.A.S.W., 2012b).

The Role of Field Education

The practicum remains central in Australian social work education. It is considered the primary location for skill development; for processing and integrating theory, knowledge, and professional values; and applying these to practice (A.A.S.W., 2012a; Cleak et al., 2015; Vassos, 2019). Field education is a collaborative endeavour involving the social work profession, tertiary institution, the host agency or organisation, the field educator(s), and the student. The A.A.S.W. (2012a) requires that each social work programme has 'a clearly identifiable field education unit including administrative support' and staffing that reflects a 'commitment to the centrality of field education in the social work curriculum' (p. 5).

Practicum has been traditionally facilitated through an apprenticeship model which 'emphasizes and reinforces the idea that personal growth and development is achieved through the traditional one-to-one relationship, where role modelling, coaching, and experiential learning can occur' (Cleak & Zuchowski, 2019, p. 33). However, Cleak and Smith (2012) suggest that the resource intensive processes around the implementation and maintenance of placements has increasingly shifted Australian social work field education away from the *apprenticeship model*, in which the student observes the field educator and infers theory from practice, toward an *articulated model* 'which promotes a close relationship between classroom teaching and field experience' (Cleak et al., 2015, p. 50). This model focuses on the inclusion of directed tasks and self-reflection, which are guided by the aforementioned accreditation standards and code of ethics (Cleak et al., 2015).

Ledger et al. (2017) argue that field education, in the Australian context, cannot be considered the signature pedagogy of the profession in the same way that it has been in the U.S. They define *signature pedagogy* 'as the habitual and pervasive way in which a profession teaches and socialises students in preparation for practice' (Ledger et al., 2107, p. 63). They suggest that framing field education as signature pedagogy would depend upon its 'centrality, importance, as a critical juncture and where the key learning for social work students occurs' in addition to meeting Schulman's original criteria (see Shulman's 2005a, 2005b seminal works). To date, they note an absence of Australian research and literature to this end. They also observe that 'Australian social work education and practice is experiencing radical change' (Ledger et al., 2017, p. 65), suggesting that it is in the best interest of the profession to examine these changes and reposition field education at the forefront of research and innovation.

These sentiments coalesce with a number of shifts and debates in Australian social work education. Some have played out in the ongoing development of the latest *Australian Social Work Education and Accreditation Standards*, a document which has been delayed a number of times since 2017. For example, the Australian Council for Heads of Schools of Social Work's submission to the *ASWEAS 2016 Review* critiqued the current graduate attributes on the basis that they were reflective of an input-focused curriculum, inconsistent with the *Practice Standards*, and unamenable to evaluation during programme accreditation (A.C.H.S.S.W., 2016). In terms of field education, the A.C.H.S.S.W. (2016) endorsed the continuance of the 1,000-hour field placement but noted the unsustainability of 'the current placement learning model of agency-based, single supervisor one to one supervision and three liaison contacts' (p. 2) in the emerging higher education and human services context. The latest A.S.W.E.A.S. (A.A.S.W, 2020b) revision has recently been released and, while it offers some progress on the alignment of graduate attributes, the field education issues persist, and the document acknowledges this area requires further review.

Similar issues and debates are also evident in literature and research, and many are connected to sustainability within the university and the human services sector. For example, a national survey of Australian social work field education programmes highlights calls for further clarity in the A.S.W.E.A.S. in order to leverage adequate resourcing from tertiary institutions, while others advocate for further flexibility on the basis of sustainability concerns (Zuchowski, Cleak, Nickson, & Spencer, 2019). Some support the development of a common assessment framework for field education with suggestions that standardisation would ease the complexity of the existing A.S.W.E.A.S. arrangements and streamline the assessment process for field educators taking students from different universities (Cleak et al., 2015; Neden, Townsend, & Zuchowski, 2018). Others have critiqued standardisation on the basis of reduced flexibility and responsivity as well as warning against rationalist implications (Neden et al., 2018).

The A.C.H.S.S.W.'s (2016) submission also advocated for a 'more flexible and diverse interpretation of the range of learning opportunities and associated activities within Field Education' (p. 2), including 'simulations; agency visits and associated work; pre-placement readiness and preparation; integrative seminars; and broader appreciation of recognised prior learning (RPL) and recognition of work-based learning' (p. 2). Finally, they viewed 'signature pedagogy as offering a more powerful articulation across the curriculum, including both classwork and field education' (p. 2). They went on to suggest that:

> signature pedagogy has the potential to broadly define the core aspects of a teaching and learning methodology that is distinctive to social work education. This conceptualization could move beyond the binary of classroom and field, and focus more acutely on the integration rather than its individual components – a reflexive pedagogy that is used in both classroom and field.
>
> *(A.C.H.S.S.W., 2016, p. 2)*

The Nature and Types of Practicums

The growing need to move beyond the intensive 'one-to-one' placement model, in which one student is supervised intensively by one field educator, has provided the impetus to develop and evaluate different placement arrangements (Cleak & Smith, 2012; Cleak & Zuchowski, 2019). It has also resulted in the development of different models of supervision to accommodate these arrangements, including external supervision, group supervision, co-supervision, rotational supervision, student units, and interdisciplinary team supervision (Cleak & Zuchowski, 2019; Vassos & Connolly, 2014).

While there is little evidence regarding the merits of the different models of supervision, the rapid increases in student numbers have seen a growth of placements in non-traditional placement settings where students are not surrounded by social workers (such as non-government organisations and school settings). Among these new models of supervision, the most common type outside the one-to-one model is the external supervision model. This is where the student is placed in an agency where there is no social worker on site. The allocation of tasks to be completed and their day-to-day oversight, which is often described as task supervision, is provided by a non-social worker. This arrangement is then supplemented by the provision of social work specific supervision which is provided by a qualified social worker who is external to (i.e., not employed by) the agency. The social worker usually visits the agency regularly and focuses on linking theory and practice related to professional practice issues.

While there is little research to indicate the precise numbers of Australian students placed in different fields of practice and organisational contexts, placements are varied and the range of activities that students undertake diverse. The primary activities students engaged in on placement were identified by Smith, Cleak, and Vreugdenhil in their 2015 study of 263 students on placement. Regular activities undertaken included reflection on practice skills (73%), engagement in weekly social work supervision (72%), discussion of feelings (66%), receipt of constructive feedback regarding their progress (66%), reflection on their own social work practice (65%), and preparation and assistance to learn new skills (64%). Students observed practice less frequently with only 33% having the opportunity to do this regularly. The opportunities for students to have their practice directly observed regularly was also limited with only 36% engaged in this activity. Somewhat alarming was the finding that 24% of this student group had the opportunity either rarely or not at all to observe the practice of social workers in their agency or engage in activities related to 'conceptualising' or linking their practice to either the *Code of Ethics* (25%) or theory (22%) (Smith et al., 2015). These findings warrant further consideration given the value one would anticipate from a student observing an experienced supervisor who was modelling practice skills, making critical decisions, and applying theory to practice. Similarly, students are likely to benefit from supervisory support to unpack, critique, and develop their observations in a safe conceptual space.

Strengths, Challenges, and Debates in Australian Social Work Field Education

The following sections provide an evidence-informed thematic overview of the current strengths, challenges, and debates in Australian social work field education as follows: (i) 'Tertiary education sector: Sourcing, Resourcing, and Supporting Social Work Placements'; (ii) 'Social Work Students on Placement: A Juggling Act'; (iii) 'Field Education: Pedagogy and Readiness for Practice'; and (iv) 'Host Agencies and Educators: The Benefits and Challenges'.

Tertiary Education Sector: Sourcing, Resourcing, and Supporting Social Work Placements

University enrolments are higher than ever in Australia, with rates of domestic students increasing across the last decade (Norton, Cherastidtham, & Mackey, 2018). Shifts in tertiary education funding policies and deregulation have seen rates of international – or fee-paying – students boom. Both cohorts are paying more for their education, in an increasingly competitive environment, possibly amplifying their expectations about the quality of the educational experience (Norton et al., 2018). However, this market-style arrangement is being played out in an environment of long-term government funding cuts across the sector. When combined, these factors place a significant onus on under-resourced social work educators to balance university-driven retention targets and high student expectations, while maintaining educational and professional standards.

As stated, the practicum is widely recognised as critical to professional development, but some would argue that its status is more contested and less esteemed in the reality of the broader tertiary education context, in which field education programmes may be viewed as more expensive and resource intensive than those offered by other degrees (Neden et al., 2018; Noble, 2001; Zuchowski et al., 2019). Field education programmes can become more or less viable and manageable depending on the professional background and understanding of the heads or administrators of academic departments.

Despite the A.A.S.W.'s (2012a) requirement that all social work staff actively contribute to field education, the reality is that most field education programmes are managed primarily through a dedicated field education position (in addition to varying degrees of administrative support). Anecdotal evidence suggests that these positions are often at the lower end of the pay scale, are held by staff who are newer to academia, and may be perceived as less attractive or less prestigious than purely academic roles. This coalesces with the observations of the authors, who suggest that the unique nature of field education coordination can easily set up an artificial distinction between field staff and other members of a social work programme. The very demanding and practical nature of field coordination often belies the skill and expertise required to enact the role and can result in its designation to more recently appointed staff members, almost as a rite of passage. In addition, its close association with *social work practice* might designate it as a less relevant or pressing activity for senior academics whose promotional opportunities are more closely aligned with research and teaching outputs. This may also be reflected in Zuchowski et al.'s (2019) findings, in which field education staff stated they were eager to conduct related research but limited in their capacity to do so.

One of the most significant challenges to field education is the competition between social work programmes, which are tasked with sourcing field placements from an often overstretched and deregulated human service industry (Cleak & Zuchowski, 2019; Pack, 2018; Vassos, 2019). The previously documented sector issues have created significant competition for quality placements, and, particularly within the major metropolitan regions, such as Sydney, Melbourne, and Brisbane. 'In the urban context of Sydney, which is the largest city in Australia, the competition is so great for placements that the search for appropriate field agencies outstrips the supply of placements' (Pack, 2018, p. 3). Additionally, the national push to extend *Work Integrated Learning* into a range of tertiary programmes has increased enrolments in allied health degrees, and the blurring of professional distinctions in job positions, titles, and roles has created competition from a range of professions that are also seeking student placements. In some cases, welfare and allied health placements may be more attractive to organisations and field educators because of a simpler supervision and assessment regime and/or shorter duration. Regardless of the origin of such issues, in a survey of 24 schools of social work, 50% noted that *placement and supervisor shortages* challenged their field education programme (Zuchowski et al., 2019).

Research has shown that universities have responded to these challenges through a number of measures, such as sourcing placements outside of area, adjusting and aligning placement dates, and, in some cases, developing collaborative approaches. For example, the Victorian Combined Schools of Social Work (C.S.S.W.) is a small group of universities that have worked together since the 1990s to develop a standardised assessment tool, joint field database, and shared management system (Cleak et al., 2015). More recently, some Queensland universities have developed a collaborative approach to the allocation of placements in Brisbane, using a system of equitable distribution of placements between competing institutions (Zuchowski et al., 2019). Interdisciplinary placement models, including interdisciplinary student units, have also been used in some universities.

Acquiring placements can also be difficult in rural and remote locations in Australia, despite desires to attract more social workers in these regions (Jones-Mutton, Short, Bidgood, & Jones, 2015). Shortages of social workers and other key health workers, combined with overstretched services, may reduce the availability of placements. Additional considerations, such as ensuring suitable student accommodation, travelling long distances, external supervision arrangements, and crisis support need to be resolved by universities when securing placements in these contexts.

The number of social work students seeking and undertaking international placements is more limited but no less important. International placements offer significant learning opportunities and experiences, such as exposure to different cultures and welfare systems and especially conceptualising the connections between global and local issues. Particular challenges arise in relation to ensuring equivalence is maintained with respect of A.A.S.W. standards and ensuring that students are adequately supervised and supported. For example, Fox (2017) reports that one of the key issues for this group of students is managing isolation. She conceptualises five core components of isolation – geographical, cultural, emotional, pedagogical, and technological – suggesting that it is crucial for field education programmes to understand the breadth of student experiences in order to ensure that resources are available to support them from preparatory to post-practicum phases.

Changes within the tertiary education landscape have also resulted in marked changes to the Australian social work student cohort. Baglow and Gair (2019a) recently noted that 'progressive higher education policies, a social inclusion agenda and widening tertiary access all have increased the numbers of working-class, mature-aged, first generation and Indigenous university students' (p. 277), which results in tertiary educators faced with a far greater range of abilities and complexities across the social work student cohort. Increasingly, students are balancing employment and caring duties with study, which has implications for the types, nature, and structure of placements they require. For example, field education managers are often besieged by students wanting to be placed 'close to home', sometimes in areas where placement options are few.

Issues related to academic and professional literacy, health, mental health, disability, and disadvantage can impact student readiness for placement and require additional time and consideration when matching students, field educators, and placement settings. Sometimes these issues are more acute than readiness for practice and might pose a threat to the viability of the placement itself, such as the compliance challenges associated with a student who presents with a criminal history (Young, Tilbury, & Hemy, 2019). More than a decade ago, Hicks and Swain highlighted the 'increasingly complex issues of the duty of care (to student, agency and field teacher) and the duty to disclose (to student, to field teacher) which schools of social work must negotiate' (2007, p. 69). Research and anecdotal evidence suggest there are a number of students in recent cohorts requiring extra support or who are considered at risk, which can pose associated dilemmas (Zuchowski et al., 2019). Field education coordinators are often tasked with balancing a duty to warn about potential risks (to clients, students, field educators, and host agencies) with a duty to student privacy and confidentiality, e.g., when serious mental health issues are known. A discussion about the nature and development of such risks continues in the next section of the chapter ('Social Work Students on Placement: A Juggling Act').

Prior to the advent of COVID-19, international students were an ever-growing cohort in Australian social work programmes; with international border restrictions lifting, it is anticipated that this trend, in time, will be restored. Research suggests this group may also require additional placement preparation and support (Zuchowski et al., 2019). Ross, Ta, and Grieve (2019) recently investigated the experiences and perspectives of 83 field educators working for an Australian university regarding the supervision of international social work students via an online survey. More than 60% of educators reported that 'they supervised international students differently to domestic students' (p. 195), and those differences were often framed negatively in terms of extra time and support rather than viewed as an opportunity for mutual learning. Challenges often focused on language competence and knowledge of Australian welfare systems and cultural norms. Similar issues were reported in Zuchowski et al.'s (2019) study, in terms of domestic students from culturally and linguistically diverse (C.A.L.D.) backgrounds, in which limited local knowledge, language barriers, and lack of confidence were described.

The lack of understanding regarding diversity has the potential to emerge as a growing divide between academia and practice. While these factors are indicated in the research, they do not convey some of the nuanced complexities present in these situations. For example, in an observation of the placement allocation process at one university during 2019 (by Leanne), students who were assessed as eligible for placement by academics were being rejected for placement by field educators at a pre-placement interview as unsuitable. The reasons for this were varied and similar to the research findings and included the student's lack of working knowledge of the Australian welfare context, language competence, and concerns regarding a student's capacity to undertake an 'assessment', with one field educator citing the lack of available time to teach the student all that they would need to do in order to function adequately in that practice environment. Thus, in this instance, the concerns were less about diversity and more about the resources needed versus the resources available to ensure the student would meet the set professional standards.

Finally, the aforementioned considerations are often operationalised within a climate of diminishing resources and limited tertiary sector support. Zuchowski et al.'s (2019) survey revealed workload and resourcing issues across a number of field education programmes in Australia. This situation may be exacerbated by ever-shifting compliance requirements that field education staff must oversee, such as immunisation, national police checks, and working with children checks (a situation that is even more arduous for international students). While the implications of these complex and intersecting factors have not been fully investigated to date, there is no doubt that they potentially limit the development and innovative capacity of staff who are best situated to respond to emerging issues. Zuchowski et al.'s (2019) research found:

> that field education programs have been using incremental innovation in field education, including collaboration, partnerships, and new ways of responding to the changing student body. However, it is argued that radical structural change and additional resources will be needed for innovation to be more than merely incremental.
>
> *(p. 75)*

Social Work Students on Placement: A Juggling Act

While most students report positively about the placement experience, these sentiments often parallel concerns about balancing family, life, and work commitments during this period. The student placement *jugging act* is often intricately tied to experiences of financial stress and poverty (Agllias et al., 2016; Baglow & Gair, 2019a; Gair & Baglow, 2018b; Ryan, Barns, & McAuliffe, 2011). The National Study of Social Work Students (N.S.S.W.S.) (A.A.S.W., 2015) was conducted as a follow-up from an advocacy project initiated by the A.A.S.W. in 2014. In this study, social work students (n = 2,320) were asked if there was a time when they had insufficient funds to cover their needs. Many students reported times when they could not afford the basics as follows: educational resources (54%), clothing (39%), transport (36%), and, most alarmingly, food (33%) and medication (29%). The impacts of income insecurity included long hours of paid work, non-attendance of class in order to work, being over tired, reducing study load or deferring, lower grades and pressure to plagiarise, and difficulty with maintaining accommodation (A.A.S.W., 2014, 2015). Baglow and Gair's (2019b) examination of this data concluded that 'the results from the N.S.S.W.S. study for social work students are deeply worrying, with mature-aged students being more financially disadvantaged than younger students, and students receiving Austudy [a type of Government income support] being most disadvantaged' (p. 95). It is important to note that the most disadvantaged groups – such as lone parents, Aboriginal and Torres Strait Islander peoples, refugees, and people with a mental health condition or disability – are those most likely to be reliant on some form of government income support.

Social work placements across Australia are lengthy and costly. Hence, students' financial concerns generally peak when they go into the field for placement (A.A.S.W., 2015). The N.S.S.W.S. found that 69% of students surveyed reported an additional financial burden, 46% had to reduce hours of paid employment, 31% quit work to undertake placement, and 13% had to postpone placement. When students reduce the amount of paid work they undertake. they are not adequately compensated by government payments, which might result in an accumulation of debt or reliance on others for support (Baglow & Gair, 2019b; Gair & Baglow, 2018a; Johnstone et al., 2016). For some students, there are additional hidden costs in terms of the time and costs associated with travelling to and from placement. This is prevalent in metropolitan areas where students may need to travel from one side of a city to another.

It has been established that all university students are a high-risk group for stress and mental health concerns. Gair and Baglow's (2018b) examination of the N.S.S.W.S. highlighted the impact of social work placement on such vulnerabilities and its potential to increase stress and burnout while exacerbating existing mental health conditions. Johnstone et al.'s (2016) research also found that financial stress and inflexible placement arrangements increased social work student stress and compromised the learning experience. Importantly, this research revealed a reluctance of students to:

> disclose the level of hardship and the impact this was having on their placement experience. Students' explanations of this reluctance ranged from a fear of being seen as not coping with placement, acceptance that financial hardship is part of placement experience, and a belief that their level of hardship was not deserving of support.
>
> *(p. 489)*

This is an important finding and mirrors the authors' observations of students weighing the pros and cons of disclosing issues that potentially impact their placement and making decisions about who they should disclose to and how much they should disclose. Most frequently, these decisions concern mental health/health/disability status, caring duties, and financial concerns.

While the research is limited, the authors are highly cognisant of the ways that cultural and linguistic diversity are experienced by students on placement (and managed within the context of field placement). In one study, Aboriginal and Torres Strait Islander students reported significant experiences of covert and overt racism while on placement, which included experiences of isolation and lack of empathy through to abuse and derision (Gair, Miles, Savage, & Zuchowski, 2015). Importantly, the issues for Indigenous social work students in the Australian context are examined in detail by, Hennessey et al. in Chapter 12 of this volume. Another under-researched area is international students on social work field placement. International social work students experience a range of challenges on placement relating to language proficiency, teaching methods, understanding of welfare systems, and integration pressures (Irizarry & Marlowe, 2010; Ross et al., 2019).

Field Education: Pedagogy and Readiness for Practice

Placement is generally considered as supporting better theory to practice immersion. Recent Ph.D. research explored some of the processes related to this idea. Callen (2017) found that 'while Field Educators developed linkages between theories and practices with students, they did not focus primarily on this. Nor did they use the concept of integration' (p. ii). Further, Callen found Australian field educators did not use 'models, competency-based teaching or evidence-based practice' (p. ii). Callen's research suggests this process of theory to practice immersion may be more fluid with field educators developing their 'own epistemology for supervision' which involved a flowing process of didactic and facilitative discussion and reflection as theoretical concepts were 'co-produced' with students as needed according to the field educator's assessment of the student's ability and the context in which the issues were raised (Callen, 2017, p. ii). Thus, supervision is considered part of the role of helping students reach their learning goals in order to become competent practitioners. Field educators maintained a view of themselves as practitioners and not as educators and demonstrated little knowledge of university curricula and generally did not refer to the A.A.S.W. supervision requirements (Callen, 2017). Concerningly she concluded that:

> Overall, they appeared to take the context of their practice for granted and did not discuss the discourses at play in their work. These supervisors seemed to work largely in isolation, raising questions about the adequacy of preparation for social work in an Australian environment which is hostile to the values of the profession.
>
> *(Callen, 2017, p. iii)*

While Callen paints a starkly negative picture, her identified limitations are only part of picture. Within the human services landscape, an earlier study of 661 community sector workers showed social work education and placement was more successful in developing preparedness for practice compared to those entering the industry with no qualifications or other professional qualifications, such as psychology (Cortis & Meagher, 2012).

Waugh (2019) suggests that:

> For students, field education is pivotal in their degree as it is where they perceive 'real' social work happens, and where they 'see' the relevance of their university input (knowledge, skills, and values) in making sense of the complexities and uncertainties facing service users and human service organisations.
>
> *(p. 121)*

In fact, research shows that students remain positive about their placements and the generosity of supervisors (Pack, 2018). In classrooms across the country, they continue to report their growing sense of the social work landscape, their own identity as social workers, and their potential within the profession that results from their direct experiences. Smith et al.'s (2015) retrospective survey of social work students (n = 263) supports this: 'Almost 90% of students reported feeling competent about their practice and 90% reported having a sense of social work identity' (p. 525). Of note, the study revealed a pedagogical connection between the regularity of undertaking the learning task or activity with a supervisor or supervisory support and feelings of competence and social work identity. Drawing from the same data, Cleak and Smith (2012) explored the impact of different placement models on learning, finding a high level of student dissatisfaction with supervision that was provided by a social worker who was external to the agency. Additionally, 'students receiving external supervision were significantly less likely … to understand the unique role of social work and to feel some competence in practicing social work interventions' (p. 256). Jones-Mutton et al.'s (2015) research suggest that the off-site external supervisors' role can be challenging due to relational dynamics, limited understanding of the agency context, the ability to influence learning opportunities, and to swiftly clarify confusion about the social work role.

Finally, fieldwork education is not solely about the transmission of knowledge and skills from the field educator to the student. Research has shown a greater role for universities in terms of preparation for placement for both students and field educators (Pack, 2018; Ross et al., 2019). Pack's (2018) survey found some students and field educators would have liked further preparation for placement, and it is certainly the view of the authors that this would be beneficial to many. Literature in the field education space consistently stresses the need to support field educators to acquire adequate knowledge of the social work curriculum and training in the provision of student supervision (Hill et al., 2019; Pack, 2018). Ross et al. (2019) also argue that enhanced training for placement educators, which involves an 'inclusive approach towards cultural and linguistic diversity' (p. 188), would mitigate many of the challenges experienced by C.A.L.D. and international students.

Host Agencies and Educators: The Benefits and Challenges

The Australian policy context, as described earlier in this chapter, has exerted considerable pressure on human service organisations in terms of increased workload and accountability, often with reduced resourcing (Zuchowksi et al., 2019). Potential host agencies and field educators regularly verbalise these challenges when discussing their capacity to fully support a student on placement. It cannot be denied that there are inevitable demands that come with taking a student on placement. Field educators can find students time consuming with little, if any, clinical relief provided by their agencies (Hill et al., 2019; Pack, 2018). Closely aligned are notions of risk and safety. Pack (2018) highlighted the reality that 'safety of supervisees, and the safety of the social service organisation offering the fieldwork placement and their clients, are key issues underlying all fieldwork supervision' (p. 1). This concern for safety directly intersects with the emergent concerns regarding the intersection of student presentations and stresses as noted earlier. A study of field educators (n = 101) found that workload relief, more training, and better university preparation would encourage them to take on more student placements (Hill et al., 2019).

A continuing trend is the presence of significant benefit to the placement organisation in that placement opportunities serve as an environment for workforce development. However, there can also be a range of other benefits to the organisation in the form of new projects. For example, the completion of pieces of relevant research or the development of needed practice resources (Pack, 2018). One of the major benefits for both field educators and students continues to be the co-learning that occurs during a placement. Students invigorate the practice environments with their enthusiasm and bring fresh perspectives and ideas for consideration

(Pack, 2018). Similarly, interagency networks and professional relationships are often established and developed through external supervision arrangements (Jones-Mutton et al., 2015).

Conclusion: A Way Forward

In concluding this chapter, several suggestions signal a potential way forward on a number of social work education fronts. These diverse suggestions are drawn together from the various aspects of field education discussed thus far and include the increased use of online technologies to support field education, relationship building, strategies that promote sustainability, and finalisation of the review of A.A.S.W. requirements. Further, important and specific recommendations are made in Chapter 12, in relation to Aboriginal and Torres Strait Islander students.

We begin with the last point first, as it is critical for the future of Australian field education. Urgent resolution of the accreditation standards (A.S.W.E.A.S.) review is required to ensure a clear future direction for Australia social work field education. As noted by Waugh (2019), the A.A.S.W., the National Field Education Network, and the schools of social work must work collaboratively to achieve this if the consequences of the building 'perfect storm' (p. 123) – of more students, less placements, and inadequately resourced field education teams, overworked social work field educators – is to be avoided. Without this, there is an increased risk of a growing divide between the professional association, academia, and practice.

In any review process, contemporary developments need to be considered. In a current practice environment framed by the COVID-19 pandemic, social workers across Australia have adapted their practice to deliver services online using a range of technological advances. The skills acquired in this adaptation opened potential space for the development of new, online forms of supervision that might be applied to the practicum. Traditionally, online or telephone supervision have been used to support rural and remote placements. The potential for extending this mode of supervision to urban contexts is opening new placement alternatives. This warrants further investigation while acknowledging that not all organisations will have the requisite technology for this approach.

While the A.A.S.W. has some restrictions around the use of external supervision, this arrangement is becoming the new normal. Thus, it is imperative to understand the elements of external and off-site external supervision that work and those requiring development into the future. Zuchowski's (2015) recommendations are a positive start point: 'it needs to be carefully planned around the students' learning needs, focused on social work practice and supported by building and maintaining collaborative relationships and communication processes' (p. 13). Additionally, the authors recommend that external supervisors have a good understanding of the organisation in which the student is placed and have a working relationship with the task supervisor prior to the commencement of any student on an external placement to set the tone for this. Current timeframes and workload involved in setting up external supervision for placements tend to prevent this given it is common for social work supervisors to be appointed some weeks after the student has commenced the placement.

Further developments for international students are needed, and Diamandi, Hudson and Zuchowski's (2018) multi-pronged approach is an appropriate starting point. This considers assisting students improve their spoken and written English, be introduced to social work practice in the Australian context, and build skill and confidence to ensure greater success at the pre-placement interview. Additional strategies such as curriculum redesign, the use of hurdle requirements, integration seminars, training for field educators, or even the establishment of a campus-based community centre may extend this. By contrast, Goel, Leane and Muncey (2018) suggest the solution may rest in the development of innovative approaches to the creation of placements in less traditional areas of practice.

Given a changed practice landscape in which the provision of learning opportunities for students are less expected or desired by agencies (Cleak & Smith, 2012), the authors hold this may be best addressed by nurturing supportive and constructive relationships between universities and placement agencies. This is necessary to help combat the lack of practicums. Despite the time and resource intensive nature of this approach, in our experience, it is the most effective means of placement procurement being maintained.

In response to the growing concerns regarding risk and compliance noted above, the authors concur with Zuchowski et al. (2019) who identified the need for radical structural change and additional resources to develop innovative ways to manage and address these processes. To this end, further investigation of the potential for some of the associated administrative tasks to be reallocated to become part of the pre-admission requirements, coupled with advocacy for either a reduced fee structure for students or extended approval periods, to prevent recurrent costs incurred during a student's candidature when some approvals lapse prior to completion of their studies.

Whatever the path forward, sustainability of placements in the future is paramount (see Crisp, 2019; Neden et al., 2018). Crisp's (2019) advice is relevant not only for students but also for social workers in practice, social work educators, and the guiding professional organisations in determining the future of field education; thus: 'Rather than learning sets of facts, which may quickly become redundant in this ever-changing world, the need for social workers to be able to critically reflect on situations and respond appropriately is critical' (p. 3) in coming together to innovate and address the critical shortage of placements across Australia without creating a two-tier hierarchy in which some placements are paid by the organisation and others self-funded by the student (Crisp, 2019). Thus, care will be needed as the pressure to develop university paid placements (to the agency for the provision of supervision and support of the students rather than direct to the student) in line with other allied heath disciplines, such as occupational therapy, physiotherapy, and speech pathology, where this model already exists. Evidence mounts for this model for social work, if equity across the country is to be maintained.

No matter which of these forward-looking strategies are taken up, each requires a commitment to one critical factor for their execution: resourcing. Resourcing field education requires, at a minimum, the time and energy for people to come together and work collaboratively to create solutions. In wholehearted agreement with Waugh (2019), the authors view increasing resources as critical to the future development and expansion of the repertoire of innovative initiatives within Australian field education.

References

A.C.O.S.S. & U.N.S.W. (2020). *Inequality in Australia*. Retrieved June 23, 2020, from http://povertyandinequality.acoss.org.au/inequality/

Agllias, K., Howard, A., Cliff, K., Dodds, J., & Field, A. (2016). Students' experiences of university and an Australian social work program: Coming, going, staying. *Australian Social Work, 69*(4), 468–480. DOI: 10.1080/0312407X.2015.1090464

Agllias K., & Gray, M. (2020 forthcoming). *International social work and social welfare: Australia and Pacific Islands*, Encyclopedia of Social Work. Retrieved from, https://oxfordre.com/socialwork/view/10.1093/acrefore/9780199975839.001.0001/acrefore-9780199975839-e-565

Australian Association of Social Workers. (2010). *Code of ethics*. Retrieved February 2, 2020, from https://www.aasw.asn.au/document/item/1201

Australian Association of Social Workers. (2012a). *Australian social work education and accreditation standards (ASWEAS) 2012: Guideline 1.2: Guidance on field education programs*. Retrieved September 8th, 2019, from https://www.aasw.asn.au/document/item/3553

Australian Association of Social Workers. (2012b). *Australian social work education and accreditation standards (ASWEAS) 2012 V 1.4*. Retrieved February 2, 2020, from https://www.aasw.asn.au/document/item/3550

Australian Association of Social Workers. (2013). *Practice standards*. Retrieved February 2, 2020, from https://www.aasw.asn.au/document/item/4551

Australian Association of Social Workers. (2014). *Student income support survey: Full results and discussion 2014*. Retrieved April 2, 2020, from https://www.aasw.asn.au/document/item/6502

Australian Association of Social Workers. (2015). *National study of social work students: Briefing paper – Important emerging findings*. Retrieved April 2, 2020, from https://www.aasw.asn.au/document/item/8772

Australian Association of Social Workers. (2019). *Annual report 2018–2019*. Retrieved November 10, 2019 from https://www.aasw.asn.au/document/item/12468

Australian Association of Social Workers. (2020a). *AASW accredited courses*. Retrieved February 2, 2020, from https://www.aasw.asn.au/careers-study/accredited-courses

Australian Association of Social Workers. (2020b). *Australian social work education and accreditation standards (ASWEAS) March 2020*. Retrieved July 1, 2020, from https://www.aasw.asn.au/document/item/6073

Australian Council for Heads of Schools of Social Work. (2016). *Submission to ASWEAS review*. Retrieved March 2, 2020, from http://achssw.org.au/projects/asweas-review-submission/

Australian Council for Heads of Schools of Social Work. (2020). *Who we are*. Retrieved February 3, 2020, from http://achssw.org.au/

Baglow, L., & Gair, S. (2019a). Australian social work students: Balancing tertiary studies, paid work and poverty. *Journal of Social Work, 19*(2), 276–295. DOI: 10.1177/1468017318760776

Baglow, L., & Gair, S. (2019b). Mature-aged social work students: Challenges, study realities, and experiences of poverty. *Australian Social Work, 72*(1), 91–104. DOI: 10.1080/0312407X.2018.1534130

Callen, A. D. (2017). *Social work field education: Field educator as travel guide between two worlds: Integrating theory and practice in field education. (Doctor of Philosophy)*. Sydney: The University of Sydney. Retrieved from http://hdl.handle.net/2123/18485

Camilleri, P. J. (2005). Social work education in Australia: At the "crossroads". *Portularia, 5*, 171–184. Retrieved from: https://ro.uow.edu.au/sspapers/2086/?utm_source=ro.uow.edu.au%2Fsspapers%2F2086&utm_medium=PDF&utm_campaign=PDFCoverPages

Cleak, H., Hawkins, L., Laughton, J., & Williams, J. (2015). Creating a standardised teaching and learning framework for social work field placements. *Australian Social Work, 68*(1), 49–64. DOI: 10.1080/0312407X.2014.932401

Cleak, H., & Smith, D. (2012). Student satisfaction with models of field placement supervision. *Australian Social Work, 65*(2), 243–258. DOI: 10.1080/0312407X.2011.572981

Cleak, H., & Zuchowski, I. (2019). Empirical support and considerations for social work supervision of students in alternative placement models. *Clinical Social Work Journal, 47*(1), 32–42. DOI: 10.1007/s10615-018-0692-3

Cortis, N., & Meagher, G. (2012). Social work education as preparation for practice: Evidence from a survey of the New South Wales community sector. *Australian Social Work, 65*(3), 295–310. DOI: 10.1080/0312407X.2012.707666

Craik, C. (2019). Social work education: Challenges and opportunities. *Australian Social Work, 72*(2), 129–132. DOI: 10.1080/0312407X.2019.1566479

Credit Suisse Research Institute. (2019). *Global wealth report 2019*. Retrieved February 2, 2020, from https://www.credit-suisse.com/about-us/en/reports-research/global-wealth-report.html

Crisp, B. R. (2019). Educating for social work practice in the 2060s. *Australian Social Work, 72*(2), 251–256. DOI: 10.1080/0312407X.2019.1567801

Davidson, P., Saunders, P., Bradbury, B., & Wong, M. (2018). Poverty in Australia, 2018. ACOSS/UNSW Poverty and inequality partnership report No. 2. Retrieved from https://www.acoss.org.au/wp-content/uploads/2018/10/ACOSS_Poverty-in-Australia-Report_Web-Final.pdf

Diamandi, S., Hudson, C., & Zuchowski, I. (2018). Field education for International students in Australia: Preparing students and the sector. *Advances in Social Work & Welfare Education, 20*(1), 80–92. Retrieved from https://journal.anzswwer.org/index.php/advances/article/view/151/135

Fox, M. (2017). Student isolation: the experience of distance on an international field placement. *Social Work Education, 36*(5), 508–520. DOI: 10.1080/02615479.2016.1215418

Gair, S., & Baglow, L. (2018a). Australian social work students balancing study, work, and field placement: Seeing it like it is. *Australian Social Work, 71*(1), 46–57. DOI: 10.1080/0312407X.2017.1377741

Gair, S., & Baglow, L. (2018b). 'We barely survived': Social work students' mental health vulnerabilities and implications for educators, universities and the workforce. *Aotearoa New Zealand Social Work, 30*(1), 32–44.

Gair, S., Miles, D., Savage, D., & Zuchowski, I. (2015). Racism unmasked: The experiences of Aboriginal and Torres Strait Islander students in social work field placements. *Australian Social Work, 68*(1), 32–48. DOI: 10.1080/0312407X.2014.928335

Goel, K., Leane, V., & Muncey, P. (2018). Innovations in field placement for international social work students: Forging university partnership with community sector in elderly care. *Advances in Social Work and Welfare Education, 20*(1), 93–107. DOI:10.3316/informit.810843767812891.

Hicks, H., & Swain, P. (2007). Direct, facilitate, enable—The juxtaposition of the duty of care and the duty of disclosure in social work field education. *Social Work Education, 26*(1), 69–85. DOI: 10.1080/02615470601036583

Hill, N., Cleak, H., Egan, R., Ervin, L., & Laughton, J. (2019). Factors that impact a social worker's capacity to supervise a student. *Australian Social Work, 72*(2), 152–165. DOI: 10.1080/0312407X.2018.1539111

Irizarry, C., & Marlowe, J. (2010). Beyond mere presence – Making diversity work. *Social Work Education, 29*(1), 96–107. DOI: 10.1080/02615470902838760

Johnstone, E., Brough, M., Crane, P., Marston, G., & Correa-Velez, I. (2016). Field placement and the impact of financial stress on social work and human service students. *Australian Social Work, 69*(4), 481–494. DOI: 10.1080/0312407X.2016.1181769

Jones-Mutton, T., Short, M., Bidgood, T., & Jones, T. (2015). Field education: Off-site social work supervision in rural, regional and remote Australia. *Advances in Social Work and Welfare Education, 17*(1), 83–97.

Ledger, S., Hillman, W., & Harreveld, B. (2017). Field education as signature pedagogy-insights for Australian social work. *Advances in Social Work & Welfare Education, 19*(1), 62–70.

Neden, J., Townsend, R., & Zuchowski, I. (2018). Towards sustainability in Australian social work field education. *Australian Social Work, 71*(3), 345–357. DOI: 10.1080/0312407X.2018.1465576

Noble, C. (2001). Researching field practice in social work education: Integration of theory and practice through the use of narratives. *Journal of Social Work, 1*(3), 347–360. DOI: 10.1177/146801730100100307

Norton, A., Cherastidtham, I., & Mackey, W. (2018). Mapping Australian higher education 2018. Retrieved from https://grattan.edu.au/wp-content/uploads/2018/09/907-Mapping-Australian-higher-education-2018.pdf

Pack, M. (2018). Evaluating the field practicum experience in social work fieldwork programs using an online survey approach: Student and supervisor responses. *Social Work and Society, 16*(1), 1–20.

Ross, B., Ta, B., & Grieve, A. (2019). Placement educators' experiences and perspectives of supervising international social work students in Australia. *Australian Social Work, 72*(2), 188–205. DOI: 10.1080/0312407X.2018.1557230

Ryan, M., Barns, A., & McAuliffe, D. (2011). Part-time employment and effects on Australian social work students: A report on a national study. *Australian Social Work, 64*(3), 313–329. DOI: 10.1080/0312407X.2010.538420

Shulman, L. (2005a). Pedagogies of uncertainty. *Liberal Education, 91*(2), 18–25.

Shulman, L. (2005b). Signature pedagogies in the professions. *Daedalus*, Summer *134*(3), 52–59.

Smith, D., Cleak, H., & Vreugdenhil, A. (2015). 'What are they really doing?' An exploration of student learning activities in field placement. *Australian Social Work, 68*(4), 515–531. DOI: 10.1080/0312407X.2014.960433

Vassos, S. (2019). Challenges facing social work field education. *Australian Social Work*, 72(2), 245–247. DOI: 10.1080/0312407X.2018.1557232

Vassos, S., & Connolly, M. (2014). Team-based rotation in social work field education: An alternative way of preparing students for practice in statutory child welfare services. *Communities, Children and Families Australia, 8*, 49–66. DOI:10.3316/informit.502690115209585.

Waugh, F. (2019). Opportunities and challenges for increasing resources in field education. *Australian Social Work*, 72(1), 121–123. DOI: 10.1080/0312407X.2018.1534131

Young, P., Tilbury, C., & Hemy, M. (2019). Child-related criminal history screening and social work education in Australia. *Australian Social Work*, 72(2), 179–187. DOI: 10.1080/0312407X.2018.1555268

Zuchowski, I. (2015). Field education with external supervision: Supporting student learning. *Field Educator, 5*(2), 1–16.

Zuchowski, I., Cleak, H., Nickson, A., & Spencer, A. (2019). A national survey of Australian social work field education programs: Innovation with limited capacity. *Australian Social Work*, 72(1), 75–90. DOI: 10.1080/0312407X.2018.1511740

Part IV
Social Work Field Education in Europe

16

'She Subjected Me to Pressure from Everybody in the Team'

Aligning Black African Students' Experiences of Field Education with Social Workers' Motivations for Becoming Practice Educators in England

Prospera Tedam and Irine Mano

Social work placement is fundamental because it provides a projection of student's capability to interact safely in a person-centred, timely, efficient way and through equitable means to provide effective service to user groups (Hogston, 2006). Measuring the quality effectiveness of a student's professional skills set is, therefore, a critical element of the teaching, learning, and assessment strategies to ensure public safety in professions (Darling-Hammond and Liebermann, 2013). Heggen et al. (2014) highlight that placements socialise students into their professions, and placement experiences, plus knowledge gained, will often shape their practice beyond qualification. This puts placements as a major component facilitating experiential learning for professional and regulated courses in higher education. Maxfield and Parker (2012) posit that adequately supporting students in practice is an integral part of the effective preparation of students into capable professionals. Consequently, the authors suggest, therefore, that practice educators in social work, as facilitators of this experiential learning, have a very specific and challenging task to achieve: act as gatekeepers of the profession and conduct a holistic appraisal of the students' overall professional performance.

In England, social work students are required to complete a minimum of 200 days in practice as part of their bachelors or master's degree in social work (Social Work England, 2020). This practice period is referred to variably as 'practice learning', 'practicum', and 'field education'. In this chapter, we will use the term 'practice learning' or 'placements' while referring to the person who supervises and assesses the student as a 'practice educator'. This reflects current terminology in England. During this period of practice learning, the student is supported to understand the role of the social worker through developing professional relationships with service users, working to understand and assist them with difficulties they might be having and advocating on their behalf. This is overseen by a practice educator who is a qualified and experienced social

DOI: 10.4324/9781032164946-21

worker and whose role it is to support, coach, mentor, and assess the student at various points of their placement and make a decision on their readiness to practice at the point of qualifying.

A plethora of research exists about the role of the practice educator (Caspi and Reid, 2002; Stone, 2016; Field, Jasper, and Littler, 2016) and the importance of the practice educator–student relationship in the professional development of the student (Tedam, 2014; Bogo, 2015; Lefrevre, 2005; Glassman, 2016).

In this chapter, we contextualise the unique position of Black African students studying social work in England and introduce the findings from the Tedam (2015) study. We then outline the training required to become a practice educator in England and the role of practice educators once qualified. The focus is on the motivations of social workers to become practice educators and tensions that can exist between practice educators and social work students during practice learning when there is misalignment between motivations and student experiences. We argue that where there is a disproportionate failure rate of Black and minority ethnic (B.M.E.) students in practice learning specifically, and there is a need to critically examine what the underlying causes may be.

Students from ethnic minority backgrounds have been found to perform less well on social work courses than students from other backgrounds (Bernard et al., 2013). Significantly, whilst research found students of Black African backgrounds to be the second largest ethnic group enrolled into social work programmes in England, they were found to experience delayed progression and graduated with poorer degree classifications (G.S.C.C., 2007, 2009; Skills for Care, 2015). Research identified that sites of practice learning contributed significantly to the delayed progression and poorer outcomes for Black African social work students (Bartoli et al., 2008; Bernard et al., 2013; Tedam, 2014).

Context and Concepts

The Study: Black African Students' Experiences of Social Work Practice Learning in England – A Critical Race Inquiry

The doctoral study, undertaken by the lead author of this chapter (Tedam) in 2015, examined the social work practice learning experiences of Black African students in England. The study received approval in March 2014 by the University of Northampton Research Ethics Committee, and participants gave consent for use of the data beyond the thesis to include publications and conference presentations.

The study found that, worryingly, this group of students experienced over scrutiny and hypervisibility, racism, discrimination, and were often fast tracked to failure. Seven females and one male took part in this qualitative study informed by Critical Race Theory (C.R.T.). To be eligible to participate in this research they had to have completed at least one period in a practice learning setting in any part of England and in a duly accredited Higher Education Institution. In addition, participants had to self-define as Black African and stated their countries of origin as being Ghana, Nigeria, South Africa, Kenya, Uganda, and Zimbabwe. All participants had 'white' practice educators and only one participant had a positive practice placement. Tedam's (2015, unpublished) doctoral qualitative research concluded that a trusting and respectful learning environment is needed to ensure students from Black African ethnic backgrounds reach their full potential. The study also found that the experience of racism whilst on placement was, in some cases, relentless with varying levels of severity and impact on the student.

The idea of 'fast tracking to difficulty or failure' is one coined and used in Tedam (2012a, p. 4) to refer to the unwarranted speed with which some practice educators (P.E.s) instigate facilitative or fitness-to-practice procedures in relation to Black African students. This fast tracking is incongruent with a process in which students gain the practical skills and expertise required for the professions they are training to join. Measuring the quality effectiveness of a student's professional skills set is, therefore, a critical element of the teaching, learning, and assessment strategies to ensure public safety in professions such as social work and nursing (Darling-Hammond and Liebermann, 2013).

Becoming a Practice Educator in England

There are varying entry requirements in the English universities to train and qualify as a P.E.; however, the minimum requirements are that a social worker is at least 2 years qualified, has practice experience, and is committed to enabling the learning of another (B.A.S.W., 2019). To become a P.E. in England, social workers must work with a student on placement as part of their own training, undertake continuous assessments, and be subject to direct observations by a mentor. There are national Practice Educator Professional Standards (P.E.P.S.), approved by the British Association of Social Workers (B.A.S.W., 2019) which trainee P.E.s must meet, evidence, and pass in order to make them qualified to supervise social work students. These standards contain domains as well as values for P.E.s (for details see https://www.basw.co.uk/system/files/resources/peps-for-social-work.pdf)

For the purposes of this chapter, we focus on value (vii), which states that P.E.s must:

> Assess in a manner that does not stigmatise or disadvantage individuals and ensures equality of opportunity. Show applied knowledge and understanding of the significance of lived experience, poverty, racism, ill health, disability, gender, social class and sexual orientation in managing the assessment process and recognise and work to prevent and counter unjustifiable discrimination and disadvantage in all aspects of the assessment process.
>
> *(p. 4)*

Current P.E. training in England occurs at post-graduate (P.G.) level, and there are two stages of training which P.E.s can opt for.

> Stage 1 Practice educators at this stage will be able to supervise, teach and assess social work degree students up to, but not being solely responsible for, the final assessment prior to qualification. Stage 1 practice educators supervising final placement students will need to have their decision ratified and overseen by a PEPS 2 qualified PE mentor or assessor.
>
> Stage 2 Practice educators at this stage will be able to supervise, teach and assess social work degree students up to, and including the last placement. These practice educators will have the authority to recommend, based on appropriate evidence, that social work learners are fit to practise at the point of qualification.
>
> *(B.A.S.W., 2019, p. 13)*

While many social workers chose P.E. as a route to progression, research by Waterhouse, McLagan, and Murr (2011) found that most social workers who were unable to undertake P.E. duties felt that the pressure arising from high workloads, followed by lack of time, were the main barriers. It, therefore, goes without saying that if a social worker in this situation is compelled to take up the P.E. role without addressing these issues, students are likely to be disadvantaged.

The Role of the Practice Educator

P.E.s have multifaceted roles and functions which, according to Field et al. (2016), include a supportive role, educational role, and managerial role. In addition to these there are certain practice behaviours which P.E.s must demonstrate, which are not only crucial to their own professional development but also evidence of a commitment to enhancing the well-being and development of social work students. First, they must believe in their student's learning potential, and second, they must provide adequate learning opportunities for students to explore this potential (Wehbi, 2016). In the same vein, the quality of placements also plays a significant part in what the student can learn and how they learn. Suffice to say that there are other factors which contribute to the student's success on placement apart from a P.E.'s motivations to assess, and this includes, according to Flanagan and Wilson (2018), the volume of learning achieved by the student. Nonetheless, the P.E.–student relationship contributes significantly to a positive or negative experience on placement (Tedam, 2014), and the authors suggest, here, that P.E.s with the right motivations to support student learning will subsequently create an enabling environment for that learning to occur. Motivation is a complex concept that can often be difficult to define. Ryan and Deci (2008) propose that motivation exists in two forms: autonomous and controlled motivation. Autonomous motivation is self-determined and happens when an individual engages in an activity or behaviour purely because of enjoyment and pleasure in the activity itself, while controlled motivation, on the other hand, represents behaviour engagement which is determined by a desire to obtain outcomes that are not self-determined (Ryan and Deci, 2008).

> Controlled motivation is externally focused, associated with behaviours that are done to avoid negative consequences, obtain rewards, be viewed in a positive light by others, seek to avoid shame, etc. On the other hand, autonomous motivation is an internal experience of volition where a person identifies with the values of an activity and finds the activity consistent with their sense of self.
>
> *(Rodriguez-Keyes et al., 2013, p. 785)*

From the above definitions, autonomous motivation is more consistent with social work principles and values. It can be concluded from the literature that autonomously motivated P.E.s will be focused on best outcomes for the student, the service user, and the university as stakeholders within the practice learning relationship (Hodge and Lonsdale, 2011). In turn, it can be concluded that P.E.s working from the controlled motivation base may unwittingly jeopardise their assessments if working from a standpoint of supporting students with seeking reward as the main objective (Hodge and Lonsdale, 2011). The authors recognise that the negative experiences of Black African students on placement were linked to P.E.s lacking enough motivation to enable a learning environment congruent with cultural competency and learning difference for these students who are from a different background, as the case below indicates.

> It was my first supervision with my practice educator, she asked my country of origin and I said Kenya. She responded by saying 'Oh Kenya, that's where FGM is practiced'. I said yes. She paused and continued to ask 'are you a victim of FGM'?
>
> *(Tedam, 2015, p. 64)*

The inappropriateness of the final statement in this dialogue cannot be overemphasised and gives further credibility to the idea of the power of whiteness and the privilege which whiteness gives to its bearers. A white Irish female student, for example, would not have been asked this sort of question, nor would their country of origin have been linked to female genital mutilation, a global health and human rights concern. In addition to this, there is a gendered dimension in which a similar question would not have been asked of a male student under any circumstances. As this was Day 1 of a 100-day placement, the student was left feeling anxious (and rightly so) about the 99 remaining days. It is difficult to understand how any appropriately motivated P.E. could engage in discussions of this nature. Caspi and Reid (2002) argue that the emotional interaction between the student and the P.E. is an important component in practice learning because it provides the context for good quality work and learning. Consequently, a first supervisory session such as this should have been used to welcome the student, gain some understanding of her learning goals and needs and prior experience, and to share general information about the placement setting.

Williams and Rutter (2010) suggest that P.E.s are confronted with an enormous task to help students gain skills in knowledge acquisition, analysis, evaluation, and understanding of how to critically apply that knowledge to practice situations. A further critical strand of the P.E.'s role is to share practice wisdom, skill, and the ability to reflect on and critique one's own practice, thereby promoting professional currency and enhancing professional development and awareness of expertly navigating in a professional world to their student (Williams and Rutter 2010). This is a task which requires candidates with the skilful ability to employ their student's engagement and teach them in a manner in which they understand and can challenge to enable effective learning and teaching encounters (Howard, 2016; Pyles and Adam, 2016; Field et al., 2016).

Substantive Discussion

Motivation to Become Practice Educators

The following section discusses the three key themes that were identified from a review of the literature to understand the motivations behind social workers becoming P.E.s. The themes will be explored in the context of understanding motivational factors but also examining how these motivational factors contribute to a successful or poor learning experience for the student. Specifically, the experiences of Black African students will be examined in the context of each motivator. Peer reviewed articles based on research undertaken including 'What motivates social workers to become practice teachers' by Develin and Matthews (2008) and 'The impact of social work student failure upon practice educators' by Basnett and Sheffield (2010) were referred to when analysing the themes which became apparent on motivations for social workers becoming P.E.s. The themes arising from the literature review are:

- Giving back,
- Professional development and personal growth, and
- Gatekeeping for the profession

Giving Back

Social workers who have been asked their reasons for joining the social work profession have been reported as stating they want to help or give back (LeCroy, 2012). This is no different for social workers who decide to become P.E.s. The profession of social work is anchored on principles of empowerment and social justice (Thompson, 2009). The first reason for engaging in practice education was proposed as a sense of giving back to the profession through supporting other aspiring social workers to enter the profession (Globerman and Bogo, 2003). Values of self-worth, honesty, advocacy, empowerment, valuing humanity, and promotion of dignity and respect are central to the professional identity of social workers (Pullen-Sansfacon et al., 2012). Thompson (2009) has gone further to suggest that the competent social worker fully integrates professional values as a cross-over between their professional and personal life. Core values in social work include valuing the uniqueness of every person, the entitlement to justice, and the aspiration to freedom among many other things (Parker, 2007). It follows that the professional identity of social workers can only be transferred from P.E. to student through the adherence to social work values during placement (Pullen-Sansfacon et al., 2012; Tedam, 2014; Globerman and Bogo, 2003; Develin and Mathews, 2008; Waterhouse et al., 2011). As Parker (2007) puts forth, the health and care professions require individuals who live by the principles as set out by the professions in which they engage. Hence, by implication, P.E.s in these fields are expected to treat their students with the same level of respect as they would their colleagues and service users. This promotes learning and encourages students to challenge appropriately when they may disagree with their educator's point of view. Ultimately, it promotes the 'giving back' ethos for social work P.E.s as they are, thus, able to model professional practice congruent with social work values.

Participants in the Tedam (2015) study experienced the opposite of what is being described in the preceding paragraph. For example, one participant, Vicky*, who had a declared disability, felt that she had to be her own advocate when she turned up for a pre-placement interview to find that accessibility was problematic. Her prospective P.E. had not considered her needs and had booked a space which required the use of stairs. In the absence of an elevator, Vicky* had to tell her P.E. that she was unable to use stairs and spent time identifying another suitable location for the interview to take place.

From a contrasting perspective, the authors put forward that the above point also helps to safeguard the social work profession from poor or damaging practice. When students challenge their P.E., it can be viewed as a quality assurance mechanism. Finch and Taylor (2013) reported that students who successfully challenged their P.E.s challenged their way of thinking and injected new and contemporary ideas into them, thereby enabling the educator to reflect upon their own practice and find ways of improving it. Maclean and Lloyd (2013) propose that this process can work toward quality assurance of practice learning because it enables the P.E. to identify ways of improving current practice. It also affirms that the P.E. has an opportunity to improve their own practice if they are willing to learn something new from their student (Maclean and Lloyd, 2013; Parker, 2007). Finch et al. (2014) acknowledge that the notion of giving back was also linked to giving back proficient and safe practice to the service user. Overall, there is recognition that P.E.s have a mandate to safeguard service users or promote good practice of students by virtue of passing or failing students (Walker et al., 2008; Nicholas and Kerr, 2015). Through either passing or failing, there is an underlying obligation of a sense of contributing to the professions; in other words, giving back. Suffice to point out, here, that autonomous motivation is at play on the social worker's part to improve on their own professional development whilst, at the same time, gatekeeping the profession.

Develin and Mathews's (2008) findings also present that a significant motivational factor for P.E.s was to give something back. Probed further on what they thought they were giving back, the P.E.s identified that they 'essentially wanted to transmit, or pass on, the values that they saw as integral to the profession' (Develin and Mathews, 2008, p. 24). Waterhouse et al.'s study (2011) also echoed this viewpoint and identified that P.E.s who felt supported by their employers in their role as educators were also supportive and motivated to pass on the knowledge to their students. These P.E.s had been moulded and supported as students to evolve into competent practitioners and, therefore, wanted to give back in return (Waterhouse et al., 2011). Social work practice is centred on an ethos of enabling and empowering others (Tedam, 2014) and, true to this mission statement, practitioners interviewed by Waterhouse et al. (2011) wanted to role model empowerment to their students as a mechanism to help them understand the concept of empowerment for their own work with service users.

To empower another, one needs to feel empowered themselves (Thompson, 2009). Finch and Poletti (2014), in a study comparing social work practice education in Italy and England, reported that an existing perception of a lack of support for P.E.s from universities resulted in P.E.s inability to fail students. The nurturer/enabler dimension of the P.E. role took precedence in assessing students (Finch and Poletti, 2014; Develin and Mathews, 2008; Globerman and Bogo, 2003). Therefore, P.E.s made recommendations in the student's final report suggesting areas of improvement for the next placement in the hope that the following P.E. would fail the student as needed (Finch and Taylor, 2013). This is indicative of the P.E.s' lack of confidence in their own skills and knowledge to assess students, which, ultimately, hinges upon the perceived lack of support from universities when students have been deemed as a failed placement (Basnett and Sheffield, 2010; Finch and Poletti, 2014). Duffy (2003) posits that P.E.s feel their professional competence is undermined when a fail recommendation is proposed by the P.E. but not upheld by the university. Plenty and Gower (2013) highlight that the quality assurance processes with the universities' fitness-to-practice systems mandate investigations to ensure fair assessment of students. Hence, on the flipside to giving back, educators may identify themselves as at a loss to offer any valuable feedback when such an occurrence takes place, impacting further on their willingness to offer other practice education opportunities for future students. As a consequence, P.E.s may not feel empowered to fail students because of the quality assurance processes of student assessment as instigated by universities. Hence, it can be deduced that, in order to give back, P.E.s are motivated when they can work collaboratively with their student and the university (Bogo, 2015). Poor working relationships between local authority/independent P.E.s and the local universities can often result in lack of autonomous motivations for social workers to engage in practice education.

Whilst assessing, P.E.s also share their knowledge with their students to enable them to make links between theory and practice, and this requires a working professional relationship between P.E. and student. Tedam's (2014) research identified that cultural bias played a significant role in student failures in social work. Students in Tedam's study reported that they had negative experiences on placement on the basis of a lack of support, over scrutiny, unfair treatment, disrespect and patronising behaviour toward the student by the P.E., P.E.s finding it easy to fail African students, and a lack of confidence in student abilities and capabilities by their P.E.s (Tedam, 2014). Turned on its head, it presents that the P.E.s in this study were not interested in knowing the students as individuals as advocated by Bartoli et al. (2008) for a good assessment of student abilities. Consequently, the P.E.s lacked the capacity to enable, empower, or pass on knowledge effectively (Bartoli et al., 2008). Ultimately, the ethos of giving back becomes lost again, as it would imply that the educator is lacking in enough knowledge to give.

Interestingly, students failing a placement is a common practice, as it actually serves as a quality assurance mechanism, but it may not be viewed as such by the P.E. who personalises the learning experience of a student to their capability in teaching (Finch and Taylor, 2013). The value of transferring knowledge to a student is closely linked to educators developing and evidencing their own continual professional development, which is the second theme identified as a motivator for practice education in social work, which will be discussed further. There are some interesting discussions about giving back which need to be presented and analysed. Black African social work students found that their expectations of P.E.s, in terms of giving back, was not always positive nor worked in their favour. For example, in response to what Tolu* felt was a P.E. who was angry or hurt about something in her professional life, Tolu stated that she was keen to become a P.E. herself and that she would be the type of P.E. who protected her students and not leave them to be ill-treated by others in the team. She stated: 'when I eventually become a practice educator, I'm gonna protect my student because I felt my PE exposed me to members of the team and did not support me' (Tedam, 2015, p. 107).

Tolu* expressed frustration that social work educators taught concepts of anti-oppressive and anti-discriminatory practice within the classroom, yet there was a lack of adherence to similar principles in practice by P.E.s toward their students on placement. She expresses the need for P.E.s to 'protect' students, which is compatible with social work values and what social workers do daily with vulnerable service users.

Professional Development and Personal Growth

Professional development and maintaining professional growth are consistently highlighted as prime motivators for P.E.s accepting and supporting a student through a placement (Develin and Matthews, 2008; Waterhouse et al., 2011). The American Social Work Boards, Australian Association of Social Workers, and Social Work England all place practice education at the heart of a post-qualifying framework which is intended to accommodate the continuing professional development of all qualified social workers (Waterhouse et al., 2011; Chen, 2014). By implication, this motivates social workers to attain P.E. status, as this is often linked to progression to more senior positions once the P.E. status is achieved. In England, the Professional Capability Framework explicitly projects practice education as a pathway to professional development. This move emphasises the paramount importance of supporting students on placement as a professional development move. It has been highlighted that after 2 years of qualification, social workers are expected to start thinking of supporting other students on placement (Field et al., 2014). Linked to this point was the fact that experience in the field of practice also became illuminated as a key motivator for supporting students through the placement learning experience (Ersing and Loeffler, 2008). The common denominator, here, is professional development as experience is associated with skill and professional competency (Nicholas and Kerr, 2015). The process of teaching students is demanding and requires commitment on the part of the educator. Nevertheless, it is a process which stimulates critical thinking and reflective practice (Jones and Lomax, 2014). A review of the literature highlighted a common consensus that students bring with them a fresh look at practice and challenge the educator's own line of reflection and critical analysis, thereby promoting a sense of critiquing one's own practice to educators (Jones and Lomax, 2014; Field et al., 2014). Educators report that students keep them on their toes professionally and challenge firmly established ways of working and the professional practice which might be entrenched as best practice in organisations (Develin and Matthews, 2008; Doel and Shardlow, 2005; Maclean and Lloyd, 2013). Interestingly, research by Tedam (2015, unpublished) found that, in many instances, the previous experience of Black African students was not recognised. In one case, the student who had a previous degree in law was told she was arrogant and that her law degree was nothing to be proud of. Clearly, the P.E. in this instance missed an opportunity to discuss how the student's previous qualifications and learning might be used in the current placement. This also shows a misalignment between the P.E. motivation and the needs of the student.

The reflective cycle which the educator goes through in disseminating and dissecting knowledge in parts to the student, in turn, contributes to an enhanced sense of professionalism and currency (Globerman and Bogo, 2003; Nicholas and Kerr, 2015). This is related to the experiential taxonomy which suggests knowledge is attained through exposure to tasks in which we participate and engage with as individuals (Steinaker and Bell, 1979; Neary, 2002; Moon, 2015). Through exposure and participation in the assessment of their student's work, educators are, thus, expected to start internalising the learning process of their student (Develin and Matthews, 2008). Having internalised the learning, P.E.s can then disseminate knowledge, skills, and values to others. There is a heavy reliance, however, on the educator's skill, knowledge, and expertise without taking into consideration where the educator's level of skill should be pitched.

Again, Black African students bemoaned the types of work given to them whilst on placement, stating that the contours of such casework were often not at the right level and standard and resulted in them being unable to evidence that they had met the requirements for a pass. The only male participant, Tom*, concluded:

> They won't give you challenging cases cos they think you are not capable enough to work on them compared to whites. The cases they give you are not so difficult. They will give you less challenging cases which at the end of the day will not allow you to meet your learning outcomes and key roles.
>
> *(Tedam, 2015, p. 73)*

The P.E.s interviewed by Globerman and Bogo (2003) attached the notion of professional responsibility in relation to their organisation's commitment to professional education. The organisations where some participants were employed adopted an approach in which they positioned themselves as training centres for a variety of professionals (Globerman and Bogo, 2003). This approach, ultimately, encouraged ongoing learning, and having a student in the team promoted 'new ways of thinking, different perspectives, new literature and new ideas' (Globerman and Bogo, 2003, p. 70). When it is mandated by the agency's policy to offer student placement, P.E.s are more focused on ensuring the right outcomes for the students – a value attached to maintaining the good reputation and status of the organisation in which they work (Globerman and Bogo, 2003; Zuchowski, 2014; Finch et al., 2014). Thus, the motivation for practice education becomes to achieve best interests for the organisation and invariably for the student. Here again, there is the possibility that an organisation which does not adhere strictly to anti-oppressive practice could exacerbate negative experiences for Black African students. One female student commented, 'one factor which definitely affects placements for Black students is racism' (Tedam, 2015, p. 78).

She did not, at this point, specifically mention her P.E., however, her sentiments are echoed by another female student, placed in another part of England, who suggested that: 'my placement had no Black staff, even the cleaners were not Black, and I felt this impacted on the way they viewed me' (Tedam, 2015, p. 71). Such a sentiment is, by no means, isolated and is one that requires a social worker whose motivations for becoming a P.E. are congruent with the needs of Black African students.

Another female student who referred to her P.E. as scrutinising her work more than white students remarked in relation to her P.E., 'she subjected me to pressure from everyone in the team' (Tedam, 2015, p. 107). The use of the word 'subjected', in our opinion, suggests an oppressive environment which resulted in what can be interpreted as a kind of ganging up against this student. We recognise and acknowledge that social work students in some practice learning settings are being observed, mentored, and assessed by different members of the team, however, the student needs to be aware of this, and the process should be empowering and supportive. Tolu* was forced, here, to navigate multiple sources of pressure during her placement.

A dimension which presented itself from the Tedam study was that P.E.s seemed comfortable to fail students from a minority ethnic background. Masocha (2015) notes that minority ethnicities view their experiences of higher education different from their white peers, usually more negatively. This gap in consistent assessment could be attributed to the P.E.'s motivations for becoming a P.E. in the first place. Not adopting diverse teaching and assessment strategies that link into a student's worldview can result in the student's slow progression in learning or failure (Tedam, 2015). As already discussed in above paragraphs, the ethos of empowering is intrinsic to effective social work practice, hence, a lack of ability to displaying this value onto a student could bring into question the P.E.'s own practice (Higgins, 2014). Bogo (2015) concurs that this is sometimes a deterrent on social workers undertaking P.E. training, as it often means that their own practice falls under scrutiny from the student and the university. Black African students felt that their P.E.'s professional development was often at the expense of their own learning and development as student social workers. One female student stated that: 'my P.E. would be very nice to me in public and critical in private' (Tedam, 2014).

Inconsistencies of this nature created confusion for the student and exacerbated anxiety, therefore, creating further barriers to learning on the student's part. In addition, Black African students recommended that, from their experience, some P.E.s had much more to learn about anti-racist practice before they should be allowed to supervise students of minority backgrounds.

Gatekeeping for the Profession

Much of the literature about the P.E.s' role in England refers to them being gatekeepers of the profession. The term gatekeeping, according to Lafrance and Gray (2004), is difficult to examine in social work and refers to processes for identifying students who may be unsuitable for social work. They identify three main areas where unsuitability may be found. These are: (1) the personal family and life experiences that students bring to the profession, (2) the socialisation and educational processes they undertake, and (3) the outcomes or personal competencies anticipated when they graduate. In trying to make sense of these categories, we argue that the subjectivities inherent in these processes make it easy for personal bias and unfairness to creep into the P.E.–student relationship. Thus, the gatekeeping role is one of power, and it is the P.E.'s responsibility to demonstrate responsible use of power, especially when working with students from diverse backgrounds.

Caspi and Reid (2002) have suggested that there is a degree of interdependence in the student–P.E. relationship and that both have a responsibility to create and maintain a productive and conducive learning environment. For Black African students, this means not challenging P.E. attitudes and behaviours and taking ill treatment and discrimination on the chin. For the only student who had a positive placement experience, her personal strategy appeared to have worked. Maki* suggested that: 'if you are going into a placement agency and going to be meek, people will ride over you' (Tedam, 2015, p. 113). Although this strategy of assertiveness worked for Maki*, she was at risk of being labelled an 'angry Black woman', a stereotype which is used when Black women try to assert themselves and stand their ground (Reynolds-Dobbs, Thomas and Harrison, 2008). Gatekeeping of the profession is not easily achieved in an environment in which educators experience pressure from workload (Plenty and Gower, 2013), consequently, P.E.s must ensure that personal factors, such as stress and work overload, do not lead them to make unfair and unjust decisions about Black African students' progress in practice learning.

Conversely, the realities of balancing a student's learning style on placement and assessing that student's ability to demonstrate professional practice often presents a challenge in that assessment. Hence, it can be surmised that the educator role is pivotal to anchor successful, safe, and effective practice of social work students, but it is also clear that the role will only be beneficial if undertaken by candidates who hold the correct set of values, knowledge, skills, and principles of teaching and assessing students' developing professional capabilities. The authors propose that the complexity of undertaking this task requires candidates with the right motivations. Furthermore, it can be deduced that P.E.s with the right motivations will be able to provide a supportive learning environment which fosters a P.E.–student relationship in which the student feels able to challenge and open up to their P.E. (Field et al., 2016). A positive P.E.–student relationship is critical to facilitate successful learning and when this relationship is strained, practice learning also becomes strained. The authors suggest, therefore, that P.E.s in social work, as facilitators of the placement experiential learning, have the very specific and challenging task of conducting holistic appraisals of students' overall professional performance whilst acting as gatekeepers of the profession at the same time. Ultimately, passing or failing the student is a mandate which P.E.s must evidence fairly and without prejudice for particular groups of students to justify robust gatekeeping. The place of power in this gatekeeping role cannot be overemphasised, and this example illuminates how the misuse of power can impact students' learning and well-being on placement. Mavis* comments on her first experience with her P.E.:

> 'My first supervision was just awful. My PE asked, where are you from, why are you in this country? It felt like being in the Home Office interview. I felt that it was irrelevant what I was being asked.
>
> *(Tedam, 2015, p. 63)*

Mavis* likened her experience of her first supervision to the experience of being in the Home Office. The U.K. Home Office holds overall responsibility for working on and deciding on immigration cases in addition to counterterrorism, police, and drugs policy (Home Office Online). In relation to immigration, the process of being granted leave to remain in the U.K. is usually a long and protracted one (Bosworth et al., 2011). Immigration authorities need assurance and reassurance that they are granting the right people permission to live and/or work in the U.K. for a period or indefinitely. The process, therefore, requires applicants to be screened, interviewed, and checked in terms of their backgrounds and history. The Home Office interview is crucial in determining eligibility or otherwise for leave to remain (Bogner et al., 2010) and assesses applicants' credibility through disclosure of personal histories and information. The screening and interview process has been described by applicants as pressured, traumatic, painful, difficult, anxiety-provoking, and harsh (Bogner et al., 2010), resulting in applicants feeling powerless and distressed. It could be suggested that the P.E. had knowingly or unknowingly become part of what Warren and Mavroudi (2011) refer to as a surveillance culture, which ensures that immigrants remained restricted in many areas of social and economic mobility in the U.K.

Gibbs and Blakely (2000) ask somewhat direct questions about the purpose of gatekeeping in social work and express concern that gatekeeping may be a way to keep certain types of students away from the course or may mask educators' difficulties teaching diverse students. They argue that, although there are some social work educators who view their gatekeeping role as supportive and nurturing of the student, there are many who see it as an opportunity to 'close the gate' to students at different stages of a student's programme (p. 3).

Anti-racist Practice Education

It may seem obvious that anti-racist practice education should be both desirable and attainable in a profession that prides itself as working with people at the margins of society and promoting equality, fairness, and social justice for all. Unfortunately, this is not always the case and, consequently, we use this space to remind P.E.s about ensuring that anti-racist and anti-oppressive principles are apparent in their practice with all students and Black African students, specifically. One way of doing this is to draw upon a useful framework such as C.R.T. to understand, appreciate, and evaluate the experiences of Black African students who they are working with. As a framework, C.R.T. has been used to examine marginalisation and discrimination against Black people for whom education produces different outcomes in comparison to white peers (Savas, 2014). C.R.T. views racism as endemic and a daily occurrence for Black and minority ethnic groups. It also promotes and advances the voices of the otherwise voiceless and marginalised. C.R.T. recognises the intersectionality of identities and the importance of social class, religion, sexuality, gender, and the implications for outcomes for Black African students. The experiences of participants in the Tedam study mirrored the tenets of C.R.T., and, consequently, the use of C.R.T. as a strategy for developing anti-racist practice learning is important. In addition to C.R.T., Tedam (2020) proposes the use of the M.A.N.D.E.L.A. (Tedam, 2012a) and S.H.A.R.E. (Maclean et al., 2018) models to facilitate P.E.–student relationships and to promote anti-oppressive practice in placement settings. If P.E.s are to align their motivations with the experiences of Black African students, then the starting point must be the motivation to promote equality, fairness, and equity through assessment of and support to social work students undertaking practice learning. To be an anti-racist P.E. requires social workers to proactively work toward disrupting racism and racist practices. This also ensures protecting students from racist colleagues, service users, and institutional structures.

Implications for Practice

Practice/Field education is a central component of social work education and, in England and Wales, represents half of the qualifying programme. The centrality and value of practice learning means that students invest a significant amount of emotional and physical energy to ensure they undertake these placements with dedication, care, and professionalism. The authors believe that the majority of P.E.s in England are committed to social work values, which includes anti-racist practice, however, the practice learning experiences of the Black African students cannot be ignored. P.E.s are encouraged to adhere to the P.E. Values discussed earlier on in this chapter (B.A.S.W., 2019) and avoid complacency when it comes to keeping themselves up-to-date with research that can further enhance their P.E. practice with diverse students. Such a strategy might change the views of participants like Vicky*, who expressed toward the end of her interview: 'I wish I had chosen another career. One that does not involve practice educators' (Tedam, 2015, p. 87).

In considering the alignment of social workers motivations to become P.E.s and the experiences of particular students, we are reminded of alignment theory, used in businesses and organisations and which Sender (1997) suggests is the extent the extent to which strategy, structure, and culture create an environment that facilitates the achievement of organisational goals. Such a theory would be useful to address some of the issues discussed in this chapter.

It is important to devote some of this discussion to analysing the impact of the global pandemic COVID-19 and its impact on practice learning in the U.K. We have already highlighted the ways in which unconscious bias, discrimination, and oppressive practice can impact negatively on the practice learning experiences of Black African students in England. Situations such as what we are currently experiencing through COVID-19 have the potential to exacerbate unfair practice toward ethnic minority groups even further, particularly in relation to 'fast tracking to failure' (Tedam, 2012a, p. 24) and social distancing (Tedam, 2020).

It is interesting to note that there continues to be a shortage of Black African P.E.s, and the reasons for this have neither been fully understood or evaluated; however, it would be fair to surmise that if practice education is used as a route to progression in social work, then the barriers and glass ceilings for ethnic minorities in relation to promotions and advancement, generally, in the U.K. would apply in the case of social work.

Conclusion

In this chapter, we have acknowledged some of the motivations behind social workers becoming P.E.s and have examined the ways in which these motivations must align with the overall principles of fairness, equality, respect for diversity, and a genuine desire to support and mentor a social worker in training. Drawing upon a Master's (M.Sc.) thesis and doctoral research, the authors have made the case that the absence of core social work values and principles often leave social work students in precarious situations in which their experiences in field placements are fraught with misunderstandings and a feeling of unfairness in the assessment process. Writing specifically about Black African social work students in England, the chapter has outlined the need for anti-racist practice utilising CRT (Cole, 2009a) and Practice Educator Standards and Values (B.A.S.W., 2019) in spaces where practice learning occurs. The social work profession, like other allied health professions, is, at the time of writing, placed at the forefront of the fight against COVID-19, and it is natural that this will bring with it stress and anxiety on several levels. For this reason, it is important to remind social work P.E.s about the need to remain committed to the values and ethics of the profession. Additionally, Lawson (2011) cautions that motivation to achieve an outcome determines the relationship between intentions, behaviour, and outcomes; consequently, a key aim of this chapter has been to utilise the voices of Black African students to identify how their experiences of practice learning in England resulted the dissatisfaction, slower progression, and poorer outcomes. Finally, we propose that further urgent research is needed to understand P.E. perspectives of working with diverse students. This is important particularly in the wake of COVID-19 and the likelihood that already marginalised students are at risk of becoming even more disadvantaged because of the pandemic and the changes to social work field education in the U.K.

We also recognise the need for research that highlights the role of practice education in disrupting oppression and discrimination in all its forms. Such research would empower P.E.s and student social workers to actively promote anti-oppressive learning and practice environments for all.

References

Bartoli, A., Kennedy, S., & Tedam, P. (2008). Practice Learning: Who is Failing to Adjust? Black African Student Experience of Practice Learning in a Social Work Setting. *Journal of Practice Teaching and Learning*, 8(2), 75–90.

Basnett, F., & Sheffield, D. (2010). The Impact of Social Work Student Failure Upon Practice Educators. *British Journal of Social Work*, 40(1), 2119–2136.

Bernard, C., Fairtlough, A., Fletcher, J., & Ahmet, A. (2013). A Qualitative Study of Marginalised Social Work Students' Views of Social Work Education and Learning. *British Journal of Social Work*. 10.1093/bjsw/bct055

Bogner, D., Brewin, C., & Herlihy, J. (2010). Refugees' Experiences of Home Office Interviews: A Qualitative Study on the Disclosure of Sensitive Personal Information. *Journal of Ethnic and Migration Studies*, 36(3), 519–535.

Bogo, M. (2015). Field Education for Clinical Social Work Practices: Best Practices and Contemporary Challenges. *Clinical Social Work Journal*, 43(1), 317–324.

Bosworth, M., Hoyle, C., & Dempsey, M.M. (2011). Researching Trafficked Women: On Institutional Resistance and the Limits of Feminist Reflexivity. *Qualitative Inquiry*, 17(9), 769–779.

British Association of Social Work (BASW). (2019). Practice Educator Standards for Social Work. Online at https://www.basw.co.uk/system/files/resources/peps-for-social-work.pdf). Accessed 25.05.20.

Caspi, J., & Reid, W.J. (2002). *Educational Supervision in Social Work: A Task Centred Model for Field Instruction and Staff Development*. Columbia University Press.

Chen, G. (2014). *Mock California Supplementary Exam: CSE of Architect Registration Exam – CSE Overview, Exam Prep Tips, General Section and Project Scenario Sections; Questions, Solutions and Explanations*. California: ArchiteG Inc.

Cole, M. (2009a). Critical Race Theory Comes to the UK: A Marxist Response. *Ethnicities*, 9(2), 246–284.

Darling-Hammond, L., & Liebermann, A. (2013). *High Quality Teaching and Learning: Changing Policies and Practices*. Abingdon: Routledge Publishing.

Develin, D., & Matthews, M. (2008). What Motivates Social Workers to Become Practice Educators? *Journal of Practice Teaching and Learning*, 8(1), 18–30.

Doel, M., & Shardlow, S. (2005). *Modern Social Work Practice: Teaching and Learning in Practice Settings*. Aldershot: Ashgate Publishing.

Duffy, K. (2003). *Failing Students a Qualitative Study of Factors that Influence the Decisions Regarding Assessment of Students' Competence in Practice*, Report for Caledonian Nursing and Midwifery Research Centre School of Nursing. Glasgow Caledonian University.

Ersing R.L., & Loeffler D.N. (2008). Teaching Students to Become Effective in Policy Practice: Integrating Social Capital Into Social Work Education and Practice. *Journal of Policy and Practice*, 7(2), 226–238.

Field, P., Jasper, C., & Littler, L. (2014). *Practice Education in Social Work. Achieving Professional Standards*. St Albans: Critical Publishing.

Field, P., Jasper, C., & Littler, L. (2016). *Practice Education in Social Work: Achieving Professional Standards*. Northwich: Critical Publishing Ltd.

Finch, J., & Poletti, A. (2014) 'It's Been Hell': Italian and British Practice Educators' Narratives of Working with Struggling or Failing Social Work Students in Practice Learning Settings. *European Journal of Social Work*, 17(1), 135–150.

Finch, J., Schaub, J., & Dalrymple, R. (2014). Projective Identification and the Fear of Failing: Making Sense of Practice Educator's Experiences of Failing Social Work Students in Practice Learning Settings. *Journal of Social Work Practice*, 28(2), 139–154.

Finch, J., & Taylor, I. (2013). Failure to Fail: Practice Educators' Emotional Experiences of Assessing Failing Social Work Students. *Social Work Education: The International Journal*, 32(2), 244–258.

Flanagan, N., & Wilson, E. (2018). What Makes a Good Placement? Findings of a Social Work Student to Student Research Study. *Social Work Education: The International Journal*, 37(5), 565–580.

Gibbs, P., & Blakely, E. (2000). *Gatekeeping in BSW Programmes*. Columbia University Press.

Glassman, U. (2016). *Finding Your Way Through Field Work: A Social Work Student's Guide*. Sage.

Globerman, J., & Bogo, M. (2003). Changing Times: Understanding Social Workers' Motivation to be Field Instructors. *Journal of Social Work*, 48(1), 65–72.

General Social Care Council (GSCC). (2007). *Social Work Education in England: Delivering Quality, Recognising Success. Social Work Education Quality Assurance Report*. London: GSCC.

General Social Care Council (GSCC). (2009). *Raising Standards in Social Work Education in England 2007–8*. London: GSCC.

Heggen, K., Smeby, J.C., & Vagan, A. (2014). A Longitudinal Approach. In Smeby J.C. and Sutphen, M. (Eds) *From Vocational to Professional Education: Educating for Social Welfare*. London, Routledge.

Higgins, M. (2014). Can Practice Educators be the Bridge Between the Academy' and the Practicum? *Journal of Practice Teaching and Learning*, 12(3), 62–78.

Hodge, K., & Lonsdale, C. (2011). Prosocial and Antisocial Behaviour in Sport: The Role of Coaching Style, Autonomous vs. Controlled Motivation, and Moral Disengagement. *Journal of Sport & Exercise Psychology*, 33(1), 527–547.

Hogston, R. (2006). Quality Assurance and UK Nurse Education. *Nursing Standard*, 20(27), 41–47.

Home Office. (2015). About Us. Online at www.gov.uk/government/organisations/home-office/about. Accessed 25.04.2020.

Howard, G.R. (2016). *We Can't Teach What We Don't Know*. Columbia University, Teacher's College Press.

Jones, K., & Lomax, R. (2014). *Surviving Your Social Work Placement*. Basingstoke: Palgrave Macmillan.

Lafrance, J., & Gray, E. (2004). Gate-Keeping for Professional Social Work Practice. *Social Work Education: The International Journal*, 23(3), 325–340.

Lawson, R. J. (2011). Constructively Aligned Teaching Methods and Students' Approaches to Learning and Motivational Orientations. *Global Journal of Human Social Science*, 11(8), 59–68.

LeCroy, C.W. (2012). *The Call to Social Work. Life Stories*. London. Sage.

Lefevre, M. (2005). Facilitating Practice Learning Assessment: The Influence of Relationship. *Social Work Education*, 24(5), 565–583.

Maclean, S., & Lloyd, I. (2013). *Developing Quality Practice Learning in Social Work: A straightforward Guide for Practice Educators and Placement Supervisors*. Lichfield: Kirwin Maclean Associates Ltd.

Maclean, S., Finch, J., & Tedam, P. (2018). *SHARE: A New Model for Social Work*. Litchfield: Kirwin Maclean.

Masocha, S. (2015). Reframing Black Social Work Students' Experiences of Teaching and Learning. *Social Work Education: The International Journal*, 34(6), 636–649.

Maxfield, M., & Parker, M. (2012). Preparation for Practice Placement Experience. In Holland, K (Ed) *Placement Learning in Medical Nursing – A Guide for Students in Practice*. London, Elsevier.

Moon, J. (2015). *A Handbook of Reflective and Experiential Learning. Theory and Practice*. London: Routledge Falmer.

Neary, M. (2002). *Curriculum Studies in Post-compulsory and Adult Education: A Teacher's and Student Teacher's Study Guide*. Cheltenham: Nelson Thornes Ltd.

Nicholas, W.S., & Kerr, J. (2015). *Practice Educating Social Work Students: Supporting Qualifying Students on Their Placements*. London: McGraw Hill Education.

Parker, J. (2007). Developing Effective Practice Learning for Tomorrow's Social Workers. *Social Work Education*, 26(8), 763–779.

Plenty, J., & Gower, D. (2013). The Reform of Social Work Education and Training and Supporting Practice Educators. *Journal of Practice Teaching and Learning: Social Work, Health and Nursing*, 12(2), 48–66.

Pullen-Sansfacon, S., Spolader, G., & Engelbert, L. (2012). Migration of Professional Social Workers: Reflections on Challenges and Strategies for Education. *Social Work Education: The International Journal*, 31(8), 1032–1045.

Pyles, L., & Adams, G.J. (2016). Educating Transformative Social Workers: The Case for Holistic Pedagogies. In Pyles, L. and Adam, G.J. (Eds) *Holistic Engagement: Transformative Social Work Education in the 21st Century*. Oxford: Oxford University Press.

Reynolds-Dobbs, W., Thomas, K.M., & Harrison, M.S. (2008). From Mammy to Superwoman: Images That Hinder Black Women's Carer Development. *Journal of Career Development*, 35(2), 129–150.

Rodriguez-Keyes, E., Schneider, D.A., & King Keenan, E. (2013). Being Known in Undergraduate Social Work Education: The Role of Instructors in Fostering Student Engagement and Motivation. *Social Work Education*, 32(6), 785–799.

Ryan, R. M., & Deci, E.L. (2008). Self-determination Theory: A Macrotheory of Motivation, Human Development, and Health. *Canadian Psychology*, 49(3), 182–185.

Savas, G. (2014). Understanding Critical Race Theory as a Framework in Higher Educational Research. *British Journal of Sociology of Education*, 35(4), 506–522.

Sender, S. (1997). Systematic Agreement: A Theory of Organizational Alignment. *Human Resource Development Quarterly*, 8(1), 23–40.

Skills for Care. (2015). *Social Work Education in England. 2009–2014*. London: Department of Health, HMSO.

Social Work England. (2020). Guidance on Practice Placements. Online at https://www.socialworkengland.org.uk/media/2973/practice_placements_guidance_final.pdf. Accessed on 28.04.20.

Steinaker, N., & Bell, M. (1979). *The Experiential Taxonomy: A New Approach to Teaching and Learning*. New York: Academic Press.

Stone, C. (2016). The Role of Practice Educators in Initial and Post Qualifying Social Work Education. *Social Work Education: The International Journal*, 35(6), 706–718.

Tedam, P. (2012a). The MANDELA Model of Practice Learning. An Old Present in New Wrapping? *Journal of Practice Teaching and Learning*, 11(2), 19–35.

Tedam, P. (2015). Black African Students' Experiences of Social Work Practice Learning in England: A Critical Race Inquiry. Unpublished Doctoral Thesis. University of Northampton, Northampton. England.

Tedam, P. (2014). When Failing Doesn't Matter: A Narrative Inquiry into the Social Work Practice Learning Experiences of Black African Students in England. *International Journal of Higher Education*, 3(1), 136–145.

Tedam, P. (2020). Social Distancing and Field Placements. Advance Access https://journals.whitingbirch.net/index.php/JPTS/article/view/1372/1425. Accessed 28.04.20.

Thompson, N. (2009). *People Skills*. Basingstoke: Palgrave Macmillan.

Walker, J., Crawford, K., & Parker, J. (2008). *Practice Education in Social Work: A Handbook for Practice Teachers, Assessors and Educators*. Exeter: Learning Matters Ltd.

Warren, A., & Mavroudi, E. (2011). Managing Surveillance? The Impact of Biometric Residence Permits on UK Migrants. *Journal of Ethnic and Migration Studies*, 37(9), 1495–1511.

Waterhouse, T., McLagan, S., & Murr, A. (2011). From Practitioner to Practice Educator: What Supports and What Hinders the Development of Confidence om Teaching and Assessing Student Social Workers? *Practice: Social Work in Action*, 23(2), 95–110.

Wehbi, S. (2016). Challenging International Social Work Placements: Critical Questions, Critical Knowledge. In Gray, G., Coates, J., Yellow Bird, M. and Hetherington, T. (Eds) *Decolonising Social Work*. Abingdon: Routledge.

Williams, S., & Rutter, L. (2010). *The Practice Educator's Handbook*. Exeter: Learning Matters.

Zuchowski, I. (2014). Planting the Seeds for Someone Else's Discussion: Experiences of Task Supervisors Supporting Student Social Work Placements. *Journal of Practice Teaching and Learning*, 13(3), 5–23.

17

Teaching Field Social Work

Views from Ukrainian Academia

Tetyana Semigina

In this introductory section, I share some personal, first-hand accounts of my experience being a social work student and a teacher. From 1995 to 1997, I was a student at the National University of Kyiv-Mohyla Academy (NaUKMA) enrolled in the Master Programme in Social Work. This was the first postgraduate programme for social workers in Ukraine, and, at that time, no undergraduate bachelor's programmes were in existence in my country.

The Kyiv-Mohyla Academy was quite an unusual university within the rigid post-Soviet system of education. It was established in 1615 and was the first higher educational institution in Ukraine or even in the whole of Eastern Europe. The academy was shut down in 1817 by the authorities of the Russian Empire and was reopened in 1992 as a stronghold of Ukrainian national ideas shortly after Ukraine proclaimed its independence. The classes at the new (or rather renewed) university were bilingual, Ukrainian-English, taught by many guest lecturers from the 'Western' countries and based on the idea of liberal arts.

The innovative Master Programme in Social Work was introduced in 1994 with the support of the European Union Tempus-Tacis project. The project's co-partners were the London School of Economics (and later the Anglia Polytechnic University) and the University of Porto, Portugal. Many renowned professors of social work – Shulamit Ramon, Steven Shardlow, Jane Shears, Carol Munn-Giddings, Gill Bridge, Fernanda Rodrigues, David Brandon, and others – were invited as guest lecturers, while British social worker Jo Lukas became a resident lecturer and a project coordinator.

The teaching process was focused predominantly on the British generalist model of social work, so we, the students, had to delve into the aspects that had never existed before in the Ukrainian context. Some students believed it was their task to create new services and to train personnel. However, there was no Ukrainian literature on social work available at that time, and a few poorly translated British books were riddled with terminological problems for the aspiring learners.

It was expected that each student spent a third of her or his training in placement of field practice under individual supervision. This field education was a two-step process. First, we paid observational visits to a variety of statutory and non-governmental organisations, and then we had to make a choice as to which one to concentrate on. It was envisioned that such an approach would shape our interests and help us choose the placement for our master's thesis

DOI: 10.4324/9781032164946-22

research. We toured many institutions inherited from the Soviet times: boarding schools for children with disabilities, nursing homes, psychiatric clinics, narcological hospitals, institutions for street children, and other services that practiced social care without involving any social workers. The newly established social services for youth, disabled, and the elderly that we visited had little to do with the professional social work ideas we learned from our foreign lecturers at the University.

The Club Dzerela became my choice for placement (although my master's research ended up being in a different field). The Club was founded in 1994 by Raisa Kravchenko, an activist who became a field education coordinator at the school of social work where I studied and was later employed. In 1995, it was a self-help community of parents who had children with learning disabilities. Recollecting those times now, I am grateful for the chance to have tried myself in different roles working in Dzerela; these roles encompassed communication with parents and their children, assisting with the arrangement of various events (lectures, round tables, and meetings), sharing the information about the new club at the statutory institutions for people with mental health problems, and working to have the club officially registered as a non-governmental organisation.

One of the school's requirements was that the students keep a placement diary and a personal learning journal with the notes of the positive and negative experiences. These notes were to help us develop reflection skills and promote the analytical usage of the lessons from the experience. Another aspect of our field education was a student discussion forum organised by a supervisor. The forum allowed us to resolve the challenges of our placements and to look for alternate solutions to the problems we were dealing with.

All these experiences of the field education were so very unconventional and seemed exceptional to me. Prior to entering the school of social work, I got a bachelor's degree as a teacher of language arts and literature from the pedagogical higher educational institution. The field education there meant an 8-week placement: 4 weeks focused on teaching language during one quarter in a middle school and 4 weeks on teaching literature during another quarter in a high school. In reality, we were allowed to teach only two lessons in each term, and the visits to the school were mostly of an observational nature. At the same time, reporting on my field practice became a real nightmare, as I was obligated to gather copious amounts of different materials about the school and the pupils I was assigned to, my notes from the observed lessons, and a formal reference letter from the school master whom I had never met. Neither supervision nor feedback were ever provided to me. Therefore, I perceived the Kyiv-Mohyla Academy's approach as a pure innovation and have cherished my experience there ever since.

After graduation, I became a lecturer at the school of social work and tried to replicate the flexible, reflective style in my teaching. In the 2000s, I became a supervisor of the research placement for the master's programme students. We had weekly discussion meetings and tutorials, kept reflective diaries, and had a fairly good selection of the social services in which the students worked for one or two days per week. Yet, within a few years, the situation had gradually deteriorated: the scope of the field education got significantly reduced, the tutorials were abolished, the diaries turned into a formality (reduced to reporting on hours spent in a service), and the university had to sign a contract with a social service organisation to be able to allow its students to go to a lawful organisation. Eventually, red tape overtook the initial liberty and creativity of the field education, making it look more like a traditional, local post-Soviet custom than the modern social work style we strived for.

Why did this happen? What characterises the field training in social work today in Ukraine? What factors have influenced the transformation of approaches to the field education of the future social workers? And what should be done to meet the international standards? This chapter is aimed at finding answers to these research questions.

The holistic summative assessment approach (Linn, 2001; OECD, 2013) was employed for this study. It focuses on the institutional aspects of the field education arrangements. The research is based on the analysis of the documents (normative legal acts, the educational programmes of the universities and colleges) and the interviews with the professors who are engaged in the organisation of the field practice at their educational institutions (12 interviews based on a convenience sample were conducted with the professors from seven cities in Ukraine). We also analysed the teachers' reflections on their own professional experiences and the input from the representatives of the social institutions where the field practice is based, as well as the group discussions with the students of four higher education institutions in two Ukrainian cities – Kyiv and Lviv. Data were analysed for similarities and differences according to variables to identify convergent and divergent themes.

The paper starts by reviewing the chronology of the establishment of social work education in Ukraine. Then it presents analysis of the standards for social work education and content of different types of field education for the bachelor's programme in social work. The relations between the two sides of field education – social services and universities – are described, and the challenges and prospects for these relations are revealed. The discussion section is focused on such cross-cutting issues as a small scope of field education, a low level of social work professionalisation, and a low level of students' motivation.

The Development of Social Work Education

The Ukraine was a part of the Soviet Union. In 1991, the country proclaimed its independence and got rid of the article 'the' in its official name. The country inhered from Soviet times a network of social, medical, educational, and correctional residential statutory institutions authorised to provide support to those who were deemed worthy to get help and execute the social control over those whose behaviour was perceived as objectionable. No social worker education or professional social workers existed at that moment. Overall, the Ukrainian model of social institutions could be defined as 'paternalistic' (Semigina, 2019). All settings were based on the ideological perspective of social pathology (Ramon, 2000) and the medical model of disability (Bridge, 2005; Phillips, 2009).

With the societal and political changes in the country caused by the fall of communism, social services and educational institutions started the long process of alteration.

In Ukraine, social work, as an academic discipline, was officially established in the spring 1991 (it was regarded as a sub-component of sociology). At the same time, the social pedagogy profession and education was introduced. From 1991 to 2016, there were bachelor's and master's degrees in social work, as well as bachelor's, master's, and PhD degrees in social pedagogy. There was no strict borderline between the two disciplines. However, social pedagogues' education was rather propitiously tailored to the Ukrainian higher education scheme, as pedagogy was a traditional discipline taught at the university level (Semigina, Griga, & Volgina, 2005), while social work was regarded as something new and very applied.

The first departments and chairs of social work and social pedagogy were formed from 1991 to1996, predominantly at universities but also at some other educational establishments of higher learning (mostly pedagogical, cultural studies, technical). At the beginning, the education of social workers was a modified training of social pedagogues. The curriculum at the corresponding departments of teachers training colleges was simply 'reinforced' by adding several advanced courses in psychology and sociology.

The earliest bachelor's programmes in social work, which opened in Dnipropetrovsk, Chernigiv, Uzhgorod, Lviv, and other Ukrainian cities, rested on so called Western drivers – numerous European and Canadian projects. International academics were willing to contribute to the development of Ukrainian social work by sharing recent advancements in social work. At that point, all Ukrainian universities had been elaborating on their own programmes of social work education. The content of such programmes frequently related to the background of the chair and professors teaching in the social work department. In some universities, the focus on training was made on legal direction, some focused on sociological areas, and others had a psychological or management focus. So, self-organisation, diversity, and 'Western drivers' were key features of introducing social work as an academic discipline in Ukraine (Semigina & Boyko, 2014).

In the 2000s, the Ukrainian state instituted a more rigid approach within the educational policy. The government had adopted *The State Higher Education Regulations* (Ministry of Education and Science of Ukraine, 1999) as well as *The Order on Approval of Time Limits for Planning and Accounting of Educational Work* (Ministry of Education and Science of Ukraine, 2002). These documents limited the universities' autonomy.

In the mid-2000s, social work as a specialty was delivered in nearly 50 educational establishments of different types and forms of ownership (Semigina et al., 2005). The social work degree programmes found their place with faculties from different fields such as psychology, sociology, social management, and others. In 2006 and 2007, social work was reintroduced as a specialty for bachelor's (Cabinet of Ministries of Ukraine, 2006) and master bachelor's (Cabinet of Ministries of Ukraine, 2010) levels; however, with the 'new' academic domain: 'social welfare'. These decisions shoved social work back to its paternalistic origins, while social pedagogy was preserved as a branch of the pedagogical sciences and had all three levels of education (Ministry of Education and Science of Ukraine, 2011; Semigina, Kabachenko & Boyko, 2017).

In 2005, the first draft standard for social work education was created by the National Pedagogical University named after Mykhailo Dragomanov. It was heavily criticised by the leading universities and was not adopted. However, in 2009, the Sectoral Standard of Higher Education of Ukraine approved the 'social welfare' field of knowledge for the Bachelor in Social Work (Ministry of Education and Science of Ukraine, 2009). The standard required the university to teach the set of mandatory courses (e.g., history of Ukraine, philosophy, Ukrainian language, foreign language, history of Ukrainian culture, and political science) and ineluctably constrained the field education or internship, mainly to the micro level practice. The universities were obliged to align their programmes, and up until 2014, universities had no autonomy and proper rights (e.g., for student admission into the programme or to shape the programme curricula, including fieldwork).

With changes in political climate and Europeanisation starting in 2014, a new law, 'On Higher Education', was adopted (Verkhovna Rada of Ukraine, 2014). The law introduced principles of autonomy for institutes of higher education and stressed competence-based educational standards and new accreditation procedures. Universities were allowed to shape their own educational programmes and teach their own courses.

In 2015, a new list of academic specialties was approved (Cabinet of Ministries of Education and Science of Ukraine, 2015). At last, social work was recognised in Ukraine as an independent specialty with three levels of education (Bachelor, Master, Doctor of Philosophy), while social pedagogy was merged with social work. In 2017, the first PhD programmes in social work were licensed and enrolled their students.

In April 2019, educational standards for social work were first approved in Ukraine for the first (Ministry of Education and Science of Ukraine, 2019a) and second (Ministry of Education and Science of Ukraine, 2019b) levels of education, bachelor's and master's, respectively.

As of April 1, 2020, there are 88 higher education institutions with licensed bachelor's programmes in social work. There are 61 institutions of higher education with master's programmes, and 16 institutions – 15 universities and the Institute of Problems of Education of the National Academy of Pedagogical Sciences of Ukraine – that offer PhD programmes (Register of Educational Institutions, 2020).

Figure 17.1 presents a brief chronology of social work education's development in Ukraine with regard to the governmental educational policies. It is possible to define three stages of the development:

1) Initial introduction of social work and social pedagogy as academic specialties within sociology and pedagogy respectively, launching the first educational programmes with support from international organisations and in the context of relevant self-organisations;

Stage	Year	Event
Universities' autonomy	2019	New accreditation procedures of the educational programmes
	2019	The educational standards for Bachelor and Master programmes in Social Work
	2017	Official launch of PhD programmes in Social Work
	2015	New list of academic specialties (Social work was recognized as an independent specialty with 3 levels of educations; social work and social pedagogy were merged)
	2014	New Law on Higher Education (competence-based approach and more rights to universities in shaping programmes)
Rigid state regulation of universities	2009	The Sectoral Standard of Higher Education of Ukraine in the field of knowledge "Social Welfare" for preparation of Bachelors in Social
	2006-2007	New list of academic specialties (Social Work was viewed as a part of Social Welfare; Social Pedagogy as a branch of Pedagogy)
	2005	The draft standards for social work education emerged, but not approved
	2002	The Order on Approval of Time Limits for Planning and Accounting of Educational Work
	1999	The State Higher Education Regulations
Universities' self-organisation	1997	Social work was approved as an educational specialty
	1993-1996	Departments and chairs of social work and social pedagogy were formed (partially with the international support)
	1991	Social work was established as an academic discipline (within Sociology), as well as Social Pedagogy (within Pedagogy)

Figure 17.1 Chronology of social work education development in Ukraine with regard to the governmental educational policies. Note: The figure represents the author's views based on the analysis of legislation and regulations.

2) Introduction of the strict centralised regulations regarding educational programmes and recognition of social work as a social welfare specialty; and
3) Granting social work the status of an independent specialty and recognition to the universities' autonomy.

Standards and Requirements for Field Education

The standards for the bachelor's degree state that the goals for education are

> training professionals capable of solving complex specialized problems and applied problems in the social sphere or in the learning process, including the management of social processes and processes that take place in the individual development of the individual, which involves the application of certain theories and methods of social work and is characterized by the complexity and uncertainty of the conditions, and oriented towards further professional education.
>
> *(Ministry of Education and Science of Ukraine, 2019a)*

According to the current standards, the duration of bachelor's programmes in social work (based on a complete general secondary education) should be 240 credits of the European Credit Transfer and Accumulation System (ECTS). At the same time, a minimum of 50% of the volume of the educational programme is directed to the provision of general and special (professional) competences in the specialty defined by the standard of higher education.

In particular, professional competences include those that, in my opinion, require their assimilation through field education: (1) identification, social inspection, and assessment of the needs of vulnerable categories of citizens, including those who are in difficult life circumstances; (2) applying modern experimental methods of work with social objects in the field and laboratory conditions; (3) evaluating social problems, needs, features and resources of clients; (4) developing ways of overcoming social problems and finding effective solutions; (5) providing assistance and support to clients, taking into account their individual needs, age differences, gender, ethnic, and other characteristics; and (6) initiating social changes aimed at raising social welfare, etc.

The standards for social work education, approved by the Ministry of Education and Science of Ukraine (2019), contain no requirements for the scope of the field placements, its varieties, curriculum, and arrangements. These issues are assigned to higher education institutions by the abovementioned Law of Ukraine 'On Higher Education'.

The analysis of bachelor's programmes at 38 educational institutions shows that the volume of field education (all its varieties of visiting, learning placements, internship, undergraduate, etc.) ranges from 49.5 credits or 20.6% of the total volume of the educational programme (Borys Grinchenko University of Kyiv, 2020) to 4.5 credits or 1.88% (Odessa National Polytechnic University, 2020). The average amount of practice in the institutions studied is 8.45% of the total volume of the educational programme (240 ECTS credits). It should be added that the educational programmes at the two educational institutions that were included in the sample have an optional additional field education course: Kyiv University of Borys Grinchenko – selective internship for 6 credits; Izmail State Humanities University – selective social-pedagogical internship for 3 credits.

For example, at the Academy of Labour, Social Relations and Tourism (2020), the bachelor's programme envisions the following types of field education:

- Introductory/Visiting (one week of visits to different social services for two credits in the fourth semester);
- Learning (four weeks of full-time placement for 6 credits in the sixth semester);
- Internship (six weeks of full-time placement for 6 credits in the eighth semester).

The visiting field education is aimed at getting students acquainted with the organisational structure, content, and institutions that provide social services to different categories of clients. The placements should expand students' understanding of how different governmental and non-governmental organisations work with social work clients; support students' acquisition of competences in analysing the peculiarities of the activities of various social services; establish student's adherence to the norms of social work professional ethics; and enhance students' abilities to apply the basic concepts and categories of psychology, sociology, social work, pedagogy, social policy, and law.

The learning placement *objectives* are to deepen and consolidate students' theoretical knowledge of social work, obtained by studying relevant courses, to provide students with the conditions to acquire experience in working with a certain group of clients. Students are supposed to get acquainted with the content, normative documents, ethical norms, technologies, and forms and methods of work within a particular social agency and study how to assess a client's social situation, plan case management, and prepare a description of the client's individual case.

The internship is aimed at deepening and consolidating students' theoretical knowledge of social work, developing competencies necessary for the application of methods of individual and group social work in the context of social service, and gaining experience in practical social work with different categories of users in a particular field of social work. It is expected that students carry out professional intervention to solve a social problem of a client or a social group in accordance with the direction of the social agency (Academy of Labour, Social Relations and Tourism, 2020).

In interviews, social work educators and students provided similar expectations for different types of field education. However, the formal standards (adopted by the government or professional community) for various placements are missing.

So, the conducted research exposes the absence of any uniform requirements, approaches, or standards regarding the organisation of student practice in Ukraine.

Relations between Educational Establishments and Social Services

Practitioners interviewed during the study emphasised that the practice criteria required for future social workers to pass is not based on educational or professional standards but mainly on personal or institutional relationships.

Not all practitioners in the organisation understand the purpose of field education and are not interested in imparting knowledge and skills to students. Only a few higher education institutions try to liaise with field leaders (methodologists), conduct training for practice supervisors, hold conferences for practice practitioners, and visit communities where students practice.

According to the interviews, at present, tutorials are not widespread in Ukraine (students communicated weekly with instructors from their educational institution about their field placement), and sometimes students feel left behind and do not know who to share their problems with. There are no positions of a field education coordinator or director. The university professors play the role of a 'placement' tutor in addition to their theory teaching workload.

It is worth noting that both university professors and students talk about limited access to clients of social services during the field placement.

By 2015, there were many programmes in which students could get involved with working with clients; however, some of the programmes stopped funding and working with clients, and some did not admit students to service recipients any more. Adoption of the social work professional standards has worsened the situation, as social workers are afraid that students could not properly fill in all the numerous required forms.

Therefore, in Ukraine, students' social work field education, which should be oriented to the acquisition of skills to help clients and the formation of professional competences as stated by Ukrainian and international educational standards, does not always involve the work of students with clients. There are significant disparities in the organisation of practice in different higher education institutions and a lack of understanding of the models of organisation of practice and feedback from supervisors on the ground (the latter often involves the signing of a formal progress report).

Figure 17.2 presents a typical arrangement for social work field education. The relations between a social service (placement), a university, and a student seems to be rather formal with limited feedback.

Factors Affecting Field Education

The analysis of the interview results and reflection on my own experience gives reason to point out several factors that influence the organisation of the field education, its current difficulties, poor quality, and effectiveness. These factors can be conditionally combined into two large groups: endogenous and exogenous.

Endogenous or internal factors concerning higher education institutions can be attributed to insufficient motivation of teachers and supervisors, low motivation and readiness of students, lack of coordination of factional types of field education, and inadequate university policy on organisation of placements.

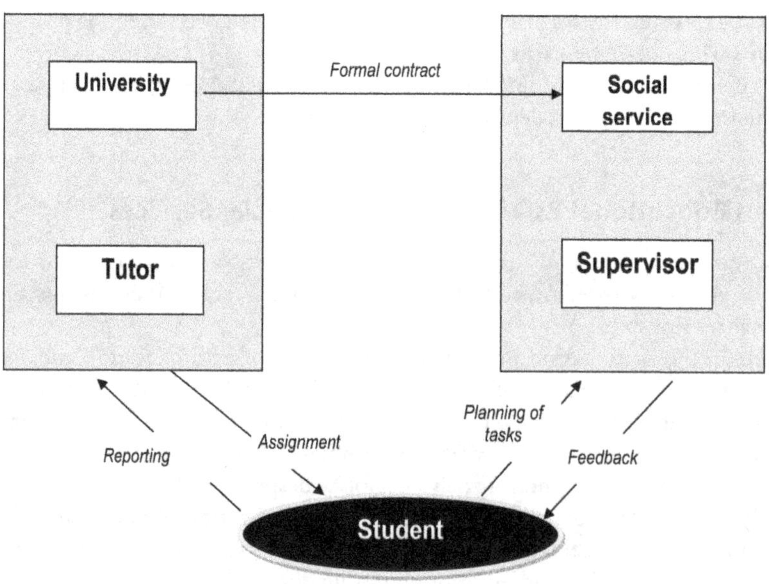

Figure 17.2 A model of social work field education arrangements.

In fact, not only users of social institutions (as required by *Global Standards for Social Work Education and Training* (IFSW, IASSW, 2000)), but also students have no influence on the organisation of field placements. Perhaps the new accreditation procedures for educational programmes, launched in Ukraine in the fall of 2019, will be capable of changing the situation to benefit diverse student and employer needs.

Among the exogenous, external factors that relate to the bases of practice and the current stage of social work development as a profession in Ukraine include professional requirements and standards oriented to quantitative indicators, undeveloped professional values, and limited range of social services, including innovative services, etc.

The factors that have an influence on students' field education arrangement could be grouped differently, paying attention to the problems of capacity of social institutions, resources, and timeframes for conducting the placement. In each case, the factors identified during the study testify to the complexity of organising field education for future social workers, the solution for which requires systematic actions from the educational establishment and beyond at the level of educational policy development and further professionalisation of the social sphere.

Summarising respondents' opinions shows four key ways that can enhance field education efficiency within Ukrainian universities (see Figure 17.3):

1) Introduction of dual education (a combination of apprenticeships in a social service and education at a school of social work; dual education is under discussion within the Ministry of Education and Science of Ukraine);
2) Working with integrated territorial communities (the voluntary association of communities in the course of decentralisation; a few universities are successfully working with such communities in social needs assessment and development of innovative social services);
3) A university clinic (where clients could apply to get help with solving their social problems); and
4) A modular training format (respondents suggest restructuring the educational process into cycles. For example, students may take courses on social work with HIV-positive people or/and on addiction and then to an agency that works with such clients for two weeks to practice skills).

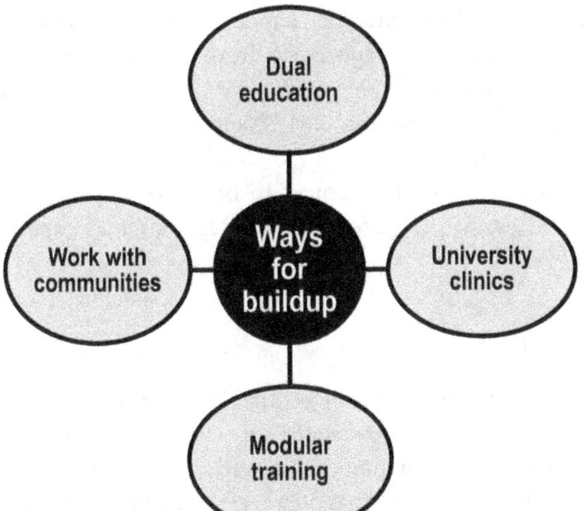

Figure 17.3 Ways to build efficiency in social work field education.

Each of these approaches has its own advantages and limitations. The most challenging now seems to be the introduction of dual education, as social services have no money to pay for the training of their employees. The other challenge lays within the universities, as governmental financial policy requires to have at least 12 students in the group in order to count the teachers' workload, so it is difficult to take elective courses for the needs of dual-education students.

Discussion on the Cross-Cutting Issues

A Small Scope of Field Education

Field education of various kinds – despite the declaration of its importance and fundamentality in Ukrainian literature (Polishchuk & Slozanska, 2014; Savelchuk, 2016; Veretenko, 2015) – actually has a rather modest share in the structure of preparation of social workers in Ukrainian institutions of higher education. This fact raises a question regarding the ability of educational programmes to provide a competency-oriented approach instituted by the new pro-European educational legislation.

However, the arrangement for social work field education is rather similar to the other academic specialties in Ukrainian universities. The issues of placements and internships are discussed by academics in different fields, such as tourism (Shchuka, 2010), health care (Babinets, Botsiuk, & Borovyk, 2019), music teachers (Horobets, 2012) and, accountants (Levchenko, 2016).

For many years, the Ukrainian educational policy was based on in-class teaching, and there were strict centralised requirements to calculate a professor's workload. As researchers pointed out, the Ukrainian state inherited a central control apparatus from Soviet times that focuses on meeting input and procedural requirements rather than monitoring performance and measuring outputs and outcomes (Darvas, 2002). The procedures of licensing and other state regulations were extremely top-down and bureaucratic (Buiashenko, 2017), thus, they discourage managerial efficiency and self-regulation of the universities.

In the nearly 6 years since new legislation was adopted, not many changes have occurred. The conducted research demonstrates that Ukrainian universities are still using the administrative, bureaucratic model of social work field placement described by Cleak and Zuchowski (2019), Slozanska (2017), Tverezovska and Viktorova (2017). The social work schools don't dare challenge the conventional traditions of diminishing field education. It happens, first and foremost, because of the predominantly authoritarian subordinate corporate culture within Ukrainian universities (Hladchenko, Anotonowisz, & de Boer, 2017; Nelipa, Batrymenko, Rudenko, & Liashenko, 2018), lack of focus on efficiency (Chernoknyzhna, 2018), and informal practices within the educational institutions (Polese et al., 2018).

All in all, Ukrainian social work educators must raise their voices in order to prepare their students according to the current international standards, professional perceptions, and experience of other countries.

A Low Level of Social Work Professionalisation

In mid-1990s international organisations initiated a variety of projects that brought new knowledge and social work models to Ukraine. This increase in new social services was observed in 2000s, and they were provided mainly by the non-governmental organisations, while all services (besides mandatory medical treatment of addicted people) that were established during the Soviet times are still operating in the country, keeping traditions of paternalistic approaches (Semigina & Boyko, 2014; Semigina, 2019).

It should be noted that, in Ukraine, the process of professionalisation of social work (as it is viewed by Weiss-Gal and Welbourne (2008)) has not been completed. There is no so-called professional monopoly, and social work, unlike most European countries, is a regulated profession that has a strong self-regulatory professional association responsible for assignment of professional qualifications and implementation of vocational and educational standards of practice. For example, in Australia, the professional association has developed a standard of practice for students in social institutions, which has made it possible to unify the expectations of the practice and ensure its consistency and harmonisation of the various components (Zuchowski, Cleak, Nickson, & Spencer, 2019).

In 2010s, the process of elaboration and introduction of around 30 quality standards for social services was initiated. It was assumed that this would broaden the spectrum of such services and improve their efficiency. However, professional standards ended up being used as managerial tools with traditional Soviet top-down bureaucracy. In recent years, the completion of the professionalisation process was substituted by the attempts to introduce a more performance-oriented style of management through adoption of social services standards. Yet, these standards were developed not by social workers, but for social workers, and as the means of control and paternalism. To some extent, researchers have observed similar tendencies in other countries (Ponnert & Svensson, 2016; Skillmark & Oscarsson, 2020). Contrary to other countries' experience of so-called pragmatic professionalisation (Liljegren, 2012), in Ukraine, the professional standards are instruments to coming back to indigenous knowledge that mainly refers to Soviet types of thinking, with the concepts of pathology, social control, and positivism as the core vision of professional activities.

The standards of social services and education of social workers should reflect the fact that modern social work is provided not only in outdated statutory services but also in modern settings and that the nature of this profession could be regarded as diverse and dynamic (Rosenberg, 2009).

Institutions of higher education in Ukraine should demonstrate leadership in development of social work and its institutionalisation. The key approach should be emphasis on long-term change and sustainability on strategies that target structural inequality and disadvantage (Mupedziswa & Kubanga, 2016). I fully agree with Dhemba (2012) that social work education, and especially field education, could play a pivotal role in knowledge transmission and in enhancing the profession's potential to play an influential role in social development. It is possible when educators are devoted to the developmental and empowering approach of social work and not a paternalistic one.

A Low Level of Students Motivation

Ukraine has inherited not only statutory quasi-social work services but also an education system designed to meet the needs of a centrally planned economy. In the post-Soviet times, the sector has not made the transition to programmes, curricula, and teaching practices that are appropriate to the needs of a new economy (Darvas, 2002).

Since the 1990s, Ukrainian tertiary education has expanded, with increased enrolments and more diversified programmes and degrees. For Ukrainian students and their families, a higher education diploma is important for avoiding unemployment and finding reasonably well-paying jobs. Thus, many universities function matter-of-factly as 'degree mills'. Social work is sometimes viewed as an 'easy' profession in which to get a diploma of higher education; and students know in advance that they will not work in social services (many graduates work as sales managers, public relations consultants, or have other jobs in business).

The conducted studies manifested that formal, (post-) Soviet requirements to field education are still in place, and social work teachers replicate the approach they used during their own studies. Today's students, who belong to the so-called Generation Z, wish to be involved in social causes and initiatives for social change (Vallone et al., 2016) and to learn through real-life experiences (Kubatova, 2016). These peculiarities of young students provide a strong ground for utilisation of community-based learning strategies allowing students to complete tangible, timely projects with community partner organisations (Gardner, Ronzio, & Snelling, 2018) and other collaborative developmental social work learning experiences (Gray, Agllias, Mupedziswa, & Mugumbate, 2017). Such approaches perfectly fit the current Ukrainian trend of creating united territorial communities where new services and projects could be introduced.

Speaking of modern young people, it is also worth mentioning the two other features of this generation: rationalism and sensitivity. Students are more interested in field education when it is structured around academic experience, with articulated learning objectives/competencies and procedures of evaluation (Barton, Bell, & Bowles, 2005; Sussman, Bailey, Richardson, & Granner, 2014). At the same time, students prefer different types of support and supervision during field education (Hemy et al., 2016). In some countries, studies are being conducted on how to prevent students from psychological trauma while undergoing internships and how to ensure proper supervision; culturally acceptable recommendations are being made on this basis (Tarshis & Baird, 2019; Weerman & Abma, 2019). Special attention is paid to the reflectional component of field education (Flanagan & Wilson, 2018; Sicora, 2019). Taking these ideas as inspirational turning points, Ukraine could transfer from the administrative model of field education to the collaborative model of the practical component of education.

Conclusions

Social work education in Ukraine was developed with international support and had all the chances to be in line with the international standards. However, in course of social work evolution, the 'Western' concepts of empowering were overshadowed by the traditional (indigenous) paternalistic way of thinking supported by the educational policy and overall political context of the country.

The research confirms that social work academics in Ukraine believe that the field education plays an important role in mastering professional competences envisioned by the Ukrainian legislation, the implementation of newly adopted educational standards for social work, and in professional socialisation of students. Yet, the analysis of bachelor's education programmes at 38 educational establishments in Ukraine revealed that the share of field education ranges from 49.5 credits to 4.5 credits, and the average amount of practice in the studied institutions is 8.45% of the total volume of the bachelor's training programme.

Studying the current state of field education at institutions of higher education in Ukraine confirmed the existence of a set of organisational challenges caused by the lack of good quality placements, formalised university policies, focus on meeting the needs of students and maintaining their motivation to master the skills of social workers, and resources.

Based on the research, possible solutions to develop field education in institutions of higher education (i.e., dual education, work with united territorial communities, develop university clinics, and modular training) can be drawn. Possible solutions to the professionalisation of social work will need strengthening of requirements for professional education and deepening innovative social services of a developmental nature that can attract students. The peculiarities of Generation Z reinforce collaborative community-based projects as an effective field education strategy for this cohort. This and other options must be explored more with respect to the students' perspective.

References

Academy of Labour, Social Relations and Tourism. (2020). Praktyky nashykh studentiv [Placement of our students]. Retrieved on 1 March, 2020 from: https://www.socosvita.kiev.ua/node/2084 [In Ukrainian].

Babinets, L. S., Botsiuk, N. Y., & Borovyk, I. O. (2019). Ambulatorna likars'ka praktyka yak klyuchova skladova pidhotovky simeynoho likarya [Outpatient practice as a key component of family physician training]. *Medychna osvita*, 2, 152–155, DOI: 10.11603/me.2414-5998.2019.2.10357 [In Ukrainian].

Barton, H., Bell, K., & Bowles, W. (2005), Help or hindrance? Outcomes of social work student placements. *Australian Social Work*, 58, 301–312, DOI: 10.1111/j.1447-0748.2005.00222.x.

Borys Grinchenko University of Kyiv. (2020). *Osvitn'o-profesiyna prohrama 231.00.01 Sotsial'na robota pershoho (bakalavrs'koho) rivnya vyshchoyi osvity [Educational and professional program 231.00.01 Social work of the first (bachelor's) level of higher education]*, Retrieved on 19 March, 2020 from: https://kubg.edu.ua/images/stories/Departaments/vstupnikam/il/2019/OPP_soc_robota.pdf [In Ukrainian].

Bridge, G. (2005). Disabled children and their families in Ukraine: Health and mental health issues for families caring for their disabled child at home. *Social Work in Health Care*, 39(1–2), 89–105, DOI: 10.1300/J010v39n01_07.

Buiashenko, V. (2017). Nederzhavni vyshchi navchal'ni zaklady i derzhavna polityka osvity v Ukrayini [Non-state higher education institutions and state education policy in Ukraine]. *Visnyk Akademiyi pratsi, sotsial'nykh vidnosyn i turyzmu*, 4, 22–35 [In Ukrainian].

Cabinet of Ministries of Ukraine. (2006). About the list of directions in which specialists are trained in higher educational institutions by educational and qualification level of bachelor. Order N° 1719.

Cabinet of Ministries of Ukraine. (2015). On approval of the list of branches of knowledge and specialties for which higher education applicants are trained. Order N° 266.

Cabinet of Ministries Ukraine. (2010). About the list of directions in which specialists are trained in higher educational institutions by educational and qualification level of specialist and master. Order N° 787.

Chernoknyzhna, K. (2018). *Efficiency estimation of the Ukrainian public higher education institutions: Inside and out.* Kyiv School of Economics.

Cleak, H., & Zuchowski, I. (2019). Empirical support and considerations for social work Supervision of students in alternative placement models. *Clin Soc Work J.*, 47, 32–42, DOI: 10.1007/s10615-018-0692-3.

Darvas, P. (2002). *Ukraine education reform policy note.* Retrieved on 22d March 2020 from: http://siteresources.worldbank.org/INTECAREGTOPEDUCATION/Resources/UkraineEducationPolicyNote.pdf

Dhemba, J. (2012). Fieldwork in social work education and training: Issues and challenges in the case of Eastern and Southern Africa. *Social Work & Society*, 10(1), 1–16. Retrieved on 3d March 2020 from: https://www.socwork.net/sws/article/view/310/651

Flanagan, N., & Wilson, E. (2018). What makes a good placement? Findings of a social work student-to-student research study. *Social Work Education*, 37(5), 565–580, DOI: 10.1080/02615479.2018.1450373.

Gardner, J. K., Ronzio, C., & Snelling, A. (2018). Transformational learning in undergraduate public health education: Course design for generation Z pedagogy in health promotion. *The Scholarship of Teaching and Learning*, 4(2), 95–100, DOI: 10.1177/2373379917721722.

Gray M., Agllias K., Mupedziswa, R., & Mugumbate J. (2017). The role of social work field education programmes in the transmission of developmental social work knowledge in Southern and East Africa, *Social Work Education*, 36(17), 623–635, DOI: 10.1080/02615479.2017.1310833.

Hemy, M., Boddy, J., Chee P., & Sauvage, D. (2016). Social work students 'juggling' field placement. *Social Work Education*, 35(2), 215–228, DOI: 10.1080/02615479.2015.1125878.

Hladchenko, M., Anotonowisz, D., & de Boer, H. (2017). Understanding the changes of the higher education governance in Poland and Ukraine. In R. Deem, H. Eggins (Eds.) *The University as a Critical Institution?* (pp. 55–74). Rotterdam: Sense Publishing, DOI: 10.1007/978-94-6351-116-2.

Horobets, T.V. (2012). *Metodychni zasady orhanizatsiyi praktyky z muzyky studentiv pedahohichnoho koledzhu [Methodical foundations of the organization of practice in music of students of the pedagogical college].* Kyiv: National Pedagogical University named after M. P. Drahomanov [In Ukrainian].

IFSW, IASSW. (2000). *Global standards for social work education and training.* Retrieved 20 November, 2019 from: https://www.iassw-aiets.org/global-standards-for-social-work-education-and-training/

Kubatova, J. (2016). Work-related attitudes of Czech generation Z: International comparison. *Central European Business Review*, 5, 61–70, DOI: 10.18267/j.cebr.167.

Levchenko, O. P. (2016). Student's manufacturing practice: Problems and ways to solve them. *Zbirnyk naukovo-metodychnykh prats' Tavriys'koho derzhavnoho ahrotekhnolohichnoho universytetu*, 19, 186–191 [In Ukrainian].

Liljegren, A. (2012). Pragmatic professionalism: Micro-level discourse in social work. *European Journal of Social Work*, 15, 295–312, DOI: 10.1080/13691457.2010.543888.

Linn, R. L. (2001). *The design and evaluation of educational assessment and accountability systems*. Los Angeles: University of California, National Center for Research on Evaluation, Standards, and Student Testing.

Ministry of Education and Science of Ukraine. (1999). The state higher education regulations. Order N° 1487.

Ministry of Education and Science of Ukraine. (2002). The order on approval of time limits for planning and accounting of educational work. Order N° 450.

Ministry of Education and Science of Ukraine. (2009). *Sectoral standard of higher education of Ukraine in the field of knowledge 'social welfare' for preparation of bachelors in social.*

Ministry of Education and Science of Ukraine. (2011). On approval of the list of scientific specialties. Order N° 1057.

Ministry of Education and Science of Ukraine. (2019a). *On approval of the standard for the specialty 231 'social work' for the first (bachelor) level of education.* Retrieved on 15 February, 2020 from: https://mon.gov.ua/storage/app/media/vishcha-osvita/zatverdzeni%20standarty/2019/04/25/231-sotsialna-robota-bakalavr.pdf

Ministry of Education and Science of Ukraine. (2019b). *On approval of the standard for the specialty 231 'social work' for the second (master) level of education.* Retrieved on 15 February, 2020 from: https://mon.gov.ua/storage/app/media/vishcha-osvita/zatverdzeni%20standarty/2019/05/06/231-sotsialna-robota-magistr.pdf

Mupedziswa, R., & Kubanga, K. (2016). Developing social work education in Africa: Challenges and prospects. In I. Taylor, M. Bogo, M. Lefevre, & B. Teater (Eds.) *Routledge international handbook of social work education* (pp. 119–130). London: Routledge.

Nelipa D., Batrymenko O., Rudenko S., & Liashenko I. (2018). Higher education management in Ukraine: Will generation change help us transform it faster? *Scientific Bulletin of National Mining University*, 3, 167–175.

Odessa National Polytechnic University. (2020). *Osvitn'o-profesiyna prohrama 'Sotsial'na robota', pershyy (bakalavrs'kyy) riven' vyshchoyi osvity [Educational and professional program 'social work', the first (bachelor's) level of higher education].* Retrieved on 19 March, 2020 from: https://drive.google.com/file/d/1_tn8ifwlssNMWnEPI5-5XbQMP2Lw-2aB/view [In Ukrainian].

OECD. (2013). The evaluation and assessment framework: Embracing a holistic approach. In *Synergies for better learning: An international perspective on evaluation and assessment.* Paris: OECD Publishing, DOI: 10.1787/9789264190658-6-en.

Phillips, S. D. (2009). 'There are no invalids in the USSR!': A missing soviet chapter in the new disability history. *Disability Studies Quarterly*, 29(3). Retrieved on 17 February, 2020 from: https://dsq-sds.org/article/view/936/1111.

Polese, A., Stepurko, T., Oksamytna, S., Kerikmae, T., Chochia, A., & Levenets, O. (2018). Informality and Ukrainian higher educational institutions: Happy together? *Policy Futures in Education, 16*(4), 482–500, DOI: 10.1177/1478210318758812.

Polishchuk, V., & Slozanska, H. (2014). Innovative approach to the organization of future social workers' practical training: Foreign experience. *Comparative Professional Pedagogy*, 4(2), 27–32, DOI: 10.2478/rpp-2014-0015.

Ponnert, L., & Svensson, K. (2016) Standardisation—The end of professional discretion? *European Journal of Social Work*, 19(3–4), 586–599, DOI: 10.1080/13691457.2015.1074551.

Ramon, Sh., (ed.) (2000). *Creating social work and social policy education in Kiev, Ukraine: An experiment in social innovation.* Cambridge: Anglia Polytechnic University.

Registry of Educational Institutions. (2020). *Unified state electronic database on education of Ukraine.* Retrieved on 1 April 2020 from: https://registry.edbo.gov.ua/search/

Rosenberg, J. (2009). *Working in social work: The real world guide to practice settings.* New York: Routledge.

Savelchuk, I. B. (2016). Pidhotovka sotsial'nykh pratsivnykiv za suchasnykh umov: Innovatsiyni tendentsiyi. *Bulletin of Zhytomyr Ivan Franko State University. Pedagogical Sciences, 1*, 120–125 [In Ukrainian].

Semigina, T. (2019). Health Care Social Work in Ukraine. In R. Winnett, R. Furman, D. Epps, & G. Lamphear (Eds.) *Health care social work: A global perspective* (pp. 218–234). Oxford University Press.

Semigina, T., & Boyko, O. (2014). Social work education in post-socialist and postmodern era: Case of Ukraine. In C. Noble, H. Strauss, and B. Littlechild (Eds.) *Global social work education – Crossing borders blurring boundaries* (pp. 257–269). Sydney: Sydney University Press.

Semigina, T., Gryga, I., & Volgina, O. (2005). Social work education in Ukraine. In F. Hamburger, S. Hirschler, G. Sander, & M. Wobcke (Eds.) *Ausbildungforsoziale Berufe in Europa. Band 3: Mit Beitragenuber Finnland, Russland, Belgien (Flandern), Frankreich, Luxemburg, Tschechien, Ukraine, Ungarn, Rumanien, Moldawien, Liechtenstein* (pp. 152–170). Frankfurt am Main: Institut fur Sozialarbeit und Sozialpadagogik.

Semigina, T., Kabachenko, N., & Boyko O. (2017). Piloting a social work doctoral programme: Ukraine's vignette. *European journal of Social Work*, 20(2), 265–276, DOI: 10.1080/13691457.2016.1202203.

Shchuka, H. P. (2010). Orhanizatsiya praktychnoyi pidhotovky maybutnikh fakhivtsiv turystychnoyi industriyi [Organization of practical training of future specialists in the tourism industry]. *Visnyk LNU imeni Tarasa Shevchenka*, 16, 117–125 [In Ukrainian].

Sicora, A. (2019). Reflective practice and learning from mistakes in social work student placement. *Social Work Education*, 38(1), 63–74, DOI: 10.1080/02615479.2018.1508567.

Skillmark, M., & Oscarsson, L. (2020) Applying standardisation tools in social work practice from the perspectives of social workers, managers, and politicians: A Swedish case study. *European Journal of Social Work*, 23(2), 265–276, DOI: 10.1080/13691457.2018.1540409.

Slozanska, H. (2017). Pidhotovka maybutnikh sotsial'nykh pratsivnykiv do zastosuvannya «casework» yak metodu sotsial'noyi roboty v terytorial'niy hromadi [Preparing future social workers for the use of 'casework' as a method of social work in the local community]. *Onovlennya zmistu, form ta metodiv navchannya i vykhovannya v zakladakh osvity*, 17(60), 111–114 [In Ukrainian].

Sussman, T., Bailey S., Richardson, K. B., & Granner, F. (2014). How field instructors judge BSW student readiness for entry-level practice. *Journal of Social Work Education*, 50(1), 84–100, DOI: 10.1080/10437797.2014.856233.

Tarshis, S., & Baird, S .L. (2019). Addressing the indirect trauma of social work students in intimate partner violence (IPV) field placements: A framework for supervision. *Clinical Social Work Journal*, 47, 90–102, DOI: 10.1007/s10615-018-0678-1.

Tverezovska, N. T., & Viktorova, L.V. (2017). *Orhanizatsiya i provedennya navchal'noyi sotsial'no-pedahohichnoyi praktyky studentiv [Organization and carrying out of educational social and pedagogical practice of students]*. Kyiv: Comprint [In Ukrainian].

Vallone, D., Smith, A., Kenney, T., Greenberg, M., Hair, E., Cantrell, J., Rath, J., & Koval, R. (2016). Agents of social change: A model for targeting and engaging generation Z across platforms. *Journal of Advertising Research*, 56, 414–425, DOI: 10.2501/JAR-2016-046.

Veretenko, T. G. (2015). Suchasni pidkhody do yakisnoyi pidhotovky maybutnikh pratsivnykiv sotsial'noyi sfery [Modern approaches to qualitative training of future employees of social sphere]. *Pedagogical Sciences: Theory, History, Innovative Technologies*, 52, 265–373 [In Ukrainian].

Verkhovna Rada of Ukraine. (2014). *On higher education: Law N 1556-VII*. Retrieved on 19 March, 2020 from: https://zakon.rada.gov.ua/laws/show/en/1556-18

Weerman, A., & Abma, T. (2019). Social work students learning to use their experiential knowledge of recovery. An existential and emancipatory perspective. *Social Work Education*, 38(4), 453–469, DOI: 10.1080/02615479.2018.1538335.

Weiss-Gal, I., & Welbourne, P. (2008). The professionalization of social work: A cross-national exploration. *International Journal of Social Welfare*, 17, 281–290, DOI: 10.1111/j.1468-2397.2008.00574.x.

Zuchowski, I., Cleak, H., Nickson, A., & Spencer, A. (2019) A national survey of Australian social work field education programs: Innovation with limited capacity, *Australian Social Work*, 72(1), 75–90, DOI: 10.1080/0312407X.2018.1511740.

18

Professional Placements in Social Work Training in Southern Spain

A Comparison with Other Social Sciences

Roser Manzanera-Ruiz and Maria del Valle Medina Rodriguez

Although work placements and internships are not new to the social work discipline in southern Spain, they have undergone profound transformations since their origins (Morales 2010). In 2011, when social work teaching in Spain was recognised as a university degree, training schemes saw many important changes that would influence the corporate identity of social work and strengthen it as a profession dedicated to social transformation as opposed to other university degrees. The objective of this chapter is to compare the contributions of practical training for students of social work and other social sciences, namely sociology. We aim to answer the following three questions: what skills do social work and sociology students acquire through practical and professional training? How does practical training contribute to critical professional practice in both disciplines and, more specifically, social work as a problem-solving profession? What are the strengths and weaknesses of placements in social work as well as their causes and consequences? We start from the idea that, although social work and sociology differ in essence, as the first is eminently practical and the second is more theoretical in nature, these differences became blurred when social work was officially recognised as a higher education study programme. Moreover, following the implementation of the Bologna Process in 2010 to facilitate the employability, mobility, and recognition of university degrees in Europe, work placements were embedded in programmes of study and became a core component in the curricula of both disciplines.

Although critical social work has been defined from a variety of approaches, all of them share a common assumption: the need for social workers to recognise and reflect on their social location in racial, class, gender, and heterosexual structures of domination as a cornerstone for a critical and anti-oppressive practice (Heron 2005). This perspective is what some authors, such as Mary Ellen Kondrat (1999), refer to as critical self-reflectivity. In this regard, students' position and their relationship with professors as well as academic and professional supervisors emerge as crucial aspects of their practical training in critical social work.

Our aim is to provide a reflection on our own teaching experience as professors of social work and sociology bachelor's degree programmes in southern Spain. To achieve the proposed objectives, a qualitative methodology has been used. Specifically, an analysis of secondary sources is carried out as well as semi-structured interviews with students who have recently completed

DOI: 10.4324/9781032164946-23

their practical training and the professionals, academic supervisors, and coordinators in charge of both the social work and sociology placements. As a result, the practical training schemes in these disciplines are similar in many European universities, with the only difference that training is optional in sociology degree programmes, while it is compulsory in social work. Therefore, the results of this study can be applied internationally at the European level.

This chapter is structured in four parts. In the first part, central concepts such as critical social work, practical training, and supervision are discussed, followed by a description of the methods used. In the second, as part of our results, we analyse and discuss the role of fieldwork education in social work and sociology undergraduate degree programmes in southern Spain, focusing specifically on the differences and similarities between both with regard to the competences. The third part reflects on placements in both disciplines, as well as their teachings, contributions, and limitations for critical professional practice and problem-solving social work. In the fourth part, the strengths and weaknesses of placements as well as their causes and consequences with a view to social work training and students' future professional practice are discussed. Finally, some conclusions are drawn.

Theoretical Background and Methods

Critical social work has been conceptualised in various ways and framed within a variety of discourses. These approaches range from an emphasis on the structural nature of personal problems or the analysis of the social control functions of social work, to a critique of the oppressive functions of social work and the corresponding commitment to personal emancipation and social transformation (Fook 2002, 2003). Other authors view professional social work as involving anti-oppressive practices or forms of participatory action research (Healy 2000, p. 3). One of the fundamental challenges of critical theoretical approaches in social work is their practical application. As Ferguson and Woodward (2009) noted, in practice, critical social work remains a minority approach in countries such as Britain, Canada, and Australia, as it largely contradicts the political values and priorities that define the neoliberal framework (Manzanera and Marin 2017).

Moreover, practical training involves entry into action and the critical formation of theoretical frameworks and, therefore, characterises a manner of doing – a concrete way of approaching the social reality in a coherent and intentional manner (Cruz 2011). Critical social work practice entails rejecting the interlocking power relations that permeate social workers' encounters with clients. To this, we must add the fact that many students are unfamiliar with contemporary radical social work and examples of radical social work practices and movements (Ferguson and Woodward 2009). For this reason, it is essential to determine whether theoretical and practical training of social workers promotes teachings aimed at recognising the different forms of structural oppression and acting on them (Manzanera and Marin 2017).

The current social work literature frequently mentions the importance of workers recognising their social location in racial, class, gender, and heterosexual structures of domination. As Heron (2007, p. 341) argues, reflecting on 'the privileges associated with social location is considered the cornerstone of such an anti oppressive practice, and Mary Ellen Kondrat's article on critical self reflectivity provides an important theoretical contribution to, and articulation of, what this would actually look like'. Some authors, such as Rossiter (2001), have highlighted the difficulties involved in practising critical social work when the profession forms part of the very system that victimises the people it is designed to help. However, based upon Foucault's recognition of the power–knowledge axis and his conceptualisation of the capillary form of power, Kondrat maintains that, in order to resist the reproduction of dominant power relations, it is necessary to analyse the subjectivity and position of the subject (Heron 2005, 2007, p. 342). In a similar manner, practical social work training in higher education reproduces these relations in three ways: the first through teacher–student relations, the second through placement supervisor–student relations, and the third through teacher–placement supervisor relations. With regard to practical training schemes, the last two types of relations are of most interest to us, here, as the first type is common to all higher education programmes of study.

Students' interaction with the academic or placement supervisors has been defined as a dynamic relationship between supervisor and social worker, whether professional or student, whereby the supervisors, by virtue of their knowledge, understanding of themselves and others, and their experience in social service techniques, provide real assistance to the supervisee, both professionally and personally (Tonon, Robles, and Meza 2004). Although this definition makes reference to the supervisors' own self-awareness, it does not mention their critical capacity or attitude in relation to the students or in their own practice. However, other contributions, such as Cruz (2011), do highlight this aspect of the supervisors' role. As regards the difficulty students encounter in aligning the institutional reality with the theoretical idealisation of their practical training, Cruz argues that supervisors must be reflective agents to allow them to discover the organisational traps. Supervisors, therefore, act as agents to link the theory to the institution's particular nature or approach, without ignoring the purpose of the method or methodologies applied. In this sense, the trap may be tensions that arise in relations with the academic institution; tensions that are not necessarily attributable to either party but which can create conflicts that affect the students' training processes. On the other hand, the supervisor or professional at the host institution is usually responsible for introducing the student to the reality of the working world and should apply the theoretical models, methodological tools, and protocols of action in which the student has been trained and which constitute the common theoretical underpinnings of our discipline. Indeed, this is the primary and most important responsibility of social workers at the collaborating institutions (Fernandez 2010, p. 238).

In this chapter, we employ a qualitative methodology that combines documentary research, semi-structured interviews with students, and systematic reflection, from a self-reflexivity approach, on the experiences of the professors, on-site supervisors, academic supervisors, and practising social workers involved in practical training. The use of a qualitative methodology based on small samples has enabled us to gain in-depth insight on the discourses, practices, and perceptions of the participants regarding placements in the higher education setting and the acquisition of competences for professional practice in the third sector. To this end, data were drawn from semi-structured interviews conducted with social work students, informal conversations with students and teachers, and observations in the classroom and workplaces. The sample comprised a total of 16 informants: two faculty-level placement coordinators, four fourth-year social work students, four fourth-year sociology students, three academic supervisors and three placement supervisors from the host institutions. The participants were selected for the study on the basis of convenience and the willingness to be interviewed. Snowball or chain sampling was also used to identify cases of interest referred by people who knew of informants of high interest. All of them were students at the faculty of social work and the faculty of sociology at a university in southern Spain. The interview script covered themes related to the professional skills acquired during the placements and fieldwork as well as the academic supervision and the practical application of critical social work knowledge. Prior to conducting the interviews, the participants were informed that all data would be kept strictly confidential and used solely for research purposes.

Practical and Professional Skills in Social Work and Sociology Degree Programmes in Southern Spain

Since the implementation of the European Higher Education Area (E.H.E.A.), the sociology and social work higher education programmes of study in Spain are organised according to a sequential, three-cycle system, which has put the two disciplines on an equal academic level. In both fields of study, after successfully completing 240 credits according to the European Credit Transfer and Accumulation System (E.C.T.S.) at the undergraduate level, it is possible to pursue a master's degree, which can vary in length from 1 to 2 years and is equivalent to 90–120 credits. The third cycle includes doctoral studies, which conclude with a dissertation. The study programmes were reorganised to adapt to the requirements imposed by the E.H.E.A. This meant that not only were the credits redistributed but that some core subjects were eliminated and others included. As a result, the bachelor's degree in sociology was reduced from 5 to 4 years in length, while the bachelor's in social work increased from 3 to 4 years with additional courses, subjects, and content. The reform was not limited simply to changing the curricular structures but aimed to place more emphasis on training through novel professional tools and theoretical approaches entailing methodological techniques and protocols of action typical of social work (Fernandez 2010).

The core curricular content of both degrees is similar in Spain, although universities have the autonomy to design their own academic offering and there are some differences in the type and content of the courses. As regards practical training schemes, each university establishes its own regulations. In the official sociology curriculum, placements are a compulsory subject with 6 E.C.T.S. credits and are organised at the faculty or school level. For this purpose, each faculty has its own placement office supported by the office of the vice-dean, which is responsible for setting up and overseeing the placements. Placement students are assigned an academic supervisor, but academic supervision does not involve the organisation of specific, structured seminars. Instead, practical training is viewed as forming part of the students' overall theoretical, practical, and methodological training with emphasis on the application of the knowledge acquired. However, unlike what Cruz (2011) suggests, the regulations do not make reference to the critical application of this knowledge. Rather, emphasis is placed on educational content that facilitates the students' labour market insertion and improves their future employability, including entrepreneurship. Nor is there any mention of the need for critical supervision of practical training that seeks the instrumental appropriation and transformation of reality. In the social work curriculum, practical training is allocated 30 E.C.T.S. credits, 24 of which correspond to placements at the host institutions and 6 to supervisory tasks. Supervision is understood as a process of reflection on the placement with professional support and involves tasks such as visits to the placement site and intermediate and final evaluations through periodic individual and group sessions in which the students critically reflect on their own professional practice and position. At a university in southern Spain, the teaching staff of the Department of Social Work and Social Services, all of whom are practising professionals, are dedicated exclusively to supervising placements, while professional supervision is carried out by the social workers at the host institutions.

In the bachelor's degree in sociology, practical training schemes are structured around 22 core competences (C.C.) and nine specific competences (S.C.). The C.C.s focus on aspects such as the analysis of problems in their field of study, the ability to communicate the results, and critical thinking for the analysis of socio-cultural factors associated with social problems. The S.C.s focus on learning and include the acquisition of technical, personal, and professional skills for the design of studies and the communication of the results or knowledge acquired.

For the bachelor's degree in social work, a total of nine C.C.s related to practical training have been defined. These C.C.s include analysing and reflecting on social problems from a critical approach for the development and implementation of intervention plans in response to problems and situations and the evaluation of the effectiveness of the implemented measures and plans.

The social work degree also establishes six S.C.s, which include the ability or capacity to evaluate social realities; interact with individuals, families, and groups in situations of vulnerability to promote their autonomy and individual responsibility; and support the development of networks.

Following the definition of critical practice as one in which professionals question their own interventions; take into account the social structure in which the case is located; work with participatory and engaging techniques; and contemplate the integrity, globality, and active role of users in their process of change, the competences that are most aligned with these notions correspond to the social work degree programme as shown in Table 18.1.

Both programmes of study establish the competences to be acquired by the students during the placements and emphasis the application of the knowledge acquired (see Table 18.1). The most important differences are related to the critical components the students are expected to acquire during their practical training and which are much more prominent in the social work degree. For example, the social work programme (see Table 18.1) places specific emphasis on competences related to critical, global, and analytical actions which seek to engage clients in their own change. In contrast, the sociology degree gives more importance to competences related to the acquisition of knowledge and the analysis of social problems but does not contemplate critical approaches to intervention.

The placement programmes in both degrees involve a wide range of people: academic supervisors, the professionals in charge of the students at the host institutions (on-site supervisors), coordinators or vice-deans, and the students themselves (see Table 18.2). Their duties also vary from one study programme to another. In the social work placements, the coordinators are responsible for overseeing the necessary resources, assigning students to groups for purposes of supervision, and planning teaching activities, such as theoretical–practical seminars and group supervision sessions, among others. The academic supervisors are experts in their field and hired by the university on a part-time basis as adjunct professors to oversee the groups assigned to them as well as coordinate and monitor the students during the placement in conjunction with the on-site supervisors. Finally, the on-site supervisors are responsible for overseeing the students' training process and must be social workers. The bachelor's degree in sociology is organised in a somewhat similar manner but differs in terms of the academic supervisors and professionals in charge of the students, as they are usually teachers with or without any professional experience outside academia. These differences strengthen the corporate identity of social work over other social sciences disciplines.

Practical Training in social Work and Sociology Study Programmes Aimed at Critical Professional Practice

As explained above, there are differences between the social work and sociology degree programmes not only in terms of the competences, number of hours, and placement credits but also in the way these training schemes are understood in the curricula. However, as the participants indicated in the interviews, the sociology and social work degree programmes share three common components with regard to practical training.

Table 18.1 Competences in Critical Social Work Practice

Critical professional practice	*C.C. and S.C. in sociology*	*C.C. and S.C. in social work*
Reflects on own interventions	C.C. Apply knowledge through the formulation of arguments and solve problems in the field of sociology C.C. Critical thinking S.C. Analysis and synthesis S.C. Cooperate in interdisciplinary and multicultural teams S.C. Decision-making skills and ability to adapt to new situations	C.C. Apply knowledge and competences through the formulation and defence of arguments and solve problems within their area of study C.C. Critically analyse one's own and others' circumstances C.C. Design, implement and evaluate social intervention projects S.C. Respond to crisis situations by evaluating their urgency, planning and developing actions, and reviewing their outcomes S.C. Evaluate possible needs and options to guide an intervention strategy
Takes into account the social structure where the case is located	C.C. Commitment to human rights and non-discrimination C.C. Commitment to gender equality S.C. Organisation and planning	C.C. Gather and interpret relevant data to inform judgements that include reflection on relevant social, scientific, or ethical issues C.C. Manage, present, and share social records and reports, keeping them complete, accurate, accessible, and up-to-date to ensure professional decision-making and evaluation
Works with participatory and engaging techniques	C.C. Work creatively C.C. Communicate information, ideas, and solutions to both specialist and non-specialist audiences C.C. Professional commitment C.C. Interpersonal skills S.C. Problem-solving	C.C. Communicate information, problems, and solutions to both specialist and non-specialist audiences C.C. Use mediation as an intervention strategy for alternative conflict resolution S.C. Interact with individuals, families, groups, organisations, and communities to bring about change and improve their living conditions using social work methods and models and regularly monitor changes in order to complete the intervention S.C. Design, produce, implement, and evaluate intervention plans with the client system and fellow professionals by negotiating the services to be provided and reviewing the effectiveness of the intervention plans with those involved in order to adapt the plans to changing needs and circumstances C.C. Prepare and take part in decision-making meetings to defend the interests of individuals, families, groups, organisations, and communities
Considers the integrity and globality as well as the active role of users in their process of change	C.C. Recognise diversity and multiculturalism S.C. Decision-making skills S.C. Conceptualise, design, and implement projects	C.C. Develop learning skills that are necessary to continue to undertake further study with a high degree of autonomy. S.C. Support the development of networks to address needs and work toward the planned outcomes by reviewing with individuals the support networks they can access and develop S.C. Promote the growth, development, and independence of individuals by identifying opportunities to form and create groups using group programming and dynamics to foster individual growth and improve interpersonal relationship skills

Source: The authors, based on the Spanish accreditation agency's (A.N.E.C.A.) verification report for the bachelor's degree in sociology and the bachelor's degree in social work, as well as course syllabi.

Table 18.2 Actors Involved in Practical Training

Degree	*Actors involved in practical training*	*Characteristics*
Sociology	Vice-dean in charge of placements	University teaching and research staff
	Academic supervisors	May or may not be sociologists and may or may not be practicing professionals
	Professionals in charge of students/ sociology placement supervisor	May or may not be sociologists and may or may not be practising professionals
	Students/Sociology placement intern	Must have successfully completed at least 120 core and compulsory course credits and 18 optional course credits.
Social Work	Placement coordinator	University teaching and research staff
	Academic supervisors	Always practising social workers
	Professionals in charge of students/ social work placement supervisor	Always practising social workers, except in 'non-conventional' placement sites
	Students/social work placement intern	Must have successfully completed 120 non-elective course credits.

Source: The authors

The first is related to the perceived differences in the value of practical training for critical intervention and the critical nature of the competences; that is, the participants recognised the importance of placements for their future professional practice that theoretical training does not provide:

> I learned a lot about [human] trafficking research ... I did the entire analysis of the survey and learned a lot about that topic and how to analyse a survey with open-ended questions. I also learned how to digitise surveys using a specific programme ... It helped me to apply theoretical knowledge that I could not have understood without the placements.
>
> *(Sociology Placement Intern 1)*

> It's one thing to see the theory on benefits at the faculty and a thousand other things, and quite another to see how all these teachings function in practice. This often leads you to critical reflection and to start thinking about how things could be better, about the injustices and inequalities that exist ... We can't forget that social work is also a struggle for social justice and equality.
>
> *(Social Work Placement Intern 1)*

Second, informants from both degree programmes recognise the important role the on-site supervisor plays not only in the development of basic practical skills but also in putting such skills into practice in a critical manner. From the interviews we were able to infer that, despite the fact that the placements reproduce certain power relationships, as Heron (2007) stated, it is also true that, depending on the nature of the relationship, it will have an influence on their critical training to a greater or lesser extent. This was expressed by the coordinator of the social work placements as well as a sociology and social work student:

> As for the placements, I believe that the institution and the professional the students do their placement with can contribute to this 'awakening' of the critical approach, taking into account the characteristics of the where they do them (what is its position regarding S.W.?),

and logically the background of the social worker who is supervising the student (does he or she see and act as an agent of change?). But, as I said at the beginning, students need to have previous training to be able to identify, discern, etc. whether or not what they are experiencing at the placement institution is critical social work. Likewise, through group and individual supervisions at the faculty, this reflective process can be carried out, that is, by accompanying students so they can assess whether or not their practical experience is framed within this critical positioning.

(Social Work Placement Coordinator)

I've seen how to apply sociology because I also had a sociologist as a mentor who guided me … and my internship supervisor took good care of me. … Other people have done placements more in social intervention, in social work, than in sociology … I think they [the internships] should be longer to be able to go more in depth … most people don't know how to apply what we've studied. We have a lot of theoretical training, but we don't know how to apply it. If they were longer, we could learn. … In sociology there are thousands of applications, you can be in a marketing department or work with social workers or analyse surveys.

(Sociology Placement Intern 2)

I think it depends a lot on the placement supervisors we've had, but in my opinion, I really think I did [acquire critical skills] thanks to my placement supervisor, seminar professor, and academic supervisor.

(Social Work Placement Intern 4)

Third, with respect to the training sites themselves and their organisational context, they either allow or hinder critical training. Thus, for example, if students do their training in the public administration, they will have less opportunity to engage in critical social work because the functions and tasks are very defined and restricted and tend to focus on managing and providing social resources. In contrast, if the placement is undertaken in a 'non-conventional' setting, the institutional context provides more opportunities for self-reflection and institutional criticism, as such sites do not depend on a rigid welfare services system and professional practice is not constrained by the imperatives of the institution and organisational traps (Cruz 2011).

The social work practicum, which is done over the entire academic year, is a subject in itself and allows the students to put into practice what they have learned over the years and also to apply professional techniques that they will continue to develop and improve on in their working life. I think this is a first step and an essential contribution that favours a critical vision of the profession, then there is the institution where the internship is done, which will put emphasis on different aspects, including the role of professionals and/or functions they sometimes have to assume and, of course, the critical vision of the person who supervises the placements.

(Social Work Academic Supervisor 1)

I think I was lucky in terms of the place where I did my placement because I have classmates who were put in charge of making photocopies … in my case I learned a lot about working in a team, organising my time, and having a responsibility. … It helped me to have a critical perspective because in the organisation where I did the placement, I was in contact with a sociologist, and I could see how he made a critical analysis of the information we got from some surveys. The degree does not include a gender focus, intersectionality, etc

> … lots of subjects are taught in an ethnocentric, unilateral way. … Then I saw that all these critical characteristics were included in the data analysis, plus I imagine the fact that it was a multidisciplinary team had an influence.
>
> *(Sociology Placement Intern 1)*

> I think this issue is closely linked to the place where you do your training. In some of them, like in my case, they really cultivate and encourage a critical spirit and, in fact, that is what their work principles are based on, which I consider tremendously positive in order to achieve the objectives of all intervention and social work.
>
> *(Social Work Placement Intern 2)*

As regards the sociology degree, the lack of critical skills is congruent with the very definition of the curricular placements, which, as explained, does not foster a critical perspective. Students are not expected to apply the skills learned in the rest of the programme in a critical way but to apply the knowledge acquired regardless of whether they do so in a critical manner or not. Contrary to what occurs in social work, sociology placements seek to fulfil a function that is more practical than transformative:

> As such they don't, [students] might have an opportunity, but they're not conceived for that purpose. It depends on what we mean by a critical perspective. There are some who criticise this connection with the labour market thing of working without getting paid. I don't think they foster that.
>
> *(Sociology Academic Supervisor 1)*

> We tried to adapt the programmes of study to the placements. … That was a lot of work because I had to contact the professional association, the Chamber of Commerce … and they informed me about the needs we could cover. That's one of the major problems in sociology or political science; that we ourselves are not able to say what we can do and what we cannot do. … Exactly, we tried to adapt the programmes of study.
>
> *(Vice-Dean of Sociology Placements)*

Work Placements in Social Work: Strengths and Weaknesses, Causes and Consequences

As discussed above, the bachelor's degree in social work is designed to provide students theoretical and practical training in order to acquire the skills needed to practise the profession from a critical perspective. Social work practice requires having knowledge on how to intervene, handle problems, and apply methods, models of intervention, and resources through the critical analysis of situations, people, and their potential and to question the social worker's position with regard to the institutions and public policies on which the profession depends.

The importance of work placements in higher education social work programmes is a revealing indicator of how social work in Spain has changed from an eminently practical discipline to one centred on theoretical developments and research. This focus provides future social workers the opportunity to apply the knowledge, skills, and competences acquired in their theoretical learning and position themselves critically before the situations, institutions, and professionals where they undertake their practical training. This knowledge is also complemented by other training activities and spaces such as academic supervision guided by professionals in the field and theoretical–practical seminars.

In the interviews conducted with those involved in the social work placements, five strengths were highlighted: the quality of the training; the length of the placements, which is considered to increase professionalisation; the diversity of social contexts and realities that the students are exposed to; the opportunity for students to put theory into practice under the supervision of professionals; and finally, mentoring.

As regards the first strength, the informants highlighted the fact that the internships were action-oriented and took place in a real context with direct contact and intervention with clients.

> I think we're very focused here on what direct intervention is. We want [the students] to experience that, the reality. And, above all, we try to make them aware of the most complex situations.
>
> *(Social Work Placement Supervisor 1)*

> I think the social work practicum is very important and, in fact, it's a fundamental part of the degree because, thanks to the courses we take before the practicum, we have some idea of what social work is. But, until you are in front of the people you're going to assist or try to help or whatever, you do not really know where you are, if what we studied is really useful, because one thing is the theory and another is to find yourself face-to-face with somebody and know how to react and be up to the job.
>
> *(Social Work Placement Intern 1)*

> The strengths of the practicum, well … I think mainly it's the direct contact with the professionals at the centres. The students have the opportunity, I think, mainly the opportunity to see or have a broader vision than what they learned in the theory [compared] to what they find in practice, which, on many occasions, especially in social work, is very different. It's one thing what the books say and quite another what you actually encounter.
>
> *(Social Work Academic Supervisor 1)*

The length and workload of the placements is yet another strength, as they provide the students the opportunity to experience and intervene in long-term interventions.

> The fact of the hours, right?, because it's 400 and something hours, isn't it?, and also in a [period of] time that's practically the whole year, which gives [the students] time to see many situations and mainly the follow-up of those situations.
>
> *(Social Work Academic Supervisor 1)*

The enormous variety of centres, fields, and types of institutions where students can do their placements is the third strength of this training scheme, as pointed out by those interviewed. This diversity gives students the opportunity to become familiar with and intervene in a wide range of groups with different realities and with different institutional resources.

> We do an amazing amount of things here. So, I think the fact that we see so much, so many areas, I think it's enriching, being able to work with different institutions, different entities, different sectors of the population, I think that would be like the most characteristic thing.
>
> *(Social Work Placement Coordinator)*

> I think so, because the knowledge I was able to acquire is very different from what we are used to in social work, and this can be a very good opportunity to focus my professional work in a different way.
>
> *(Social Work Placement Intern 3)*

The complementary and comprehensive training that the students receive in the seminars is the fourth strength of the placement scheme. The seminars address theoretical and practical issues related to the field in which the students do their training.

> What I do think is very good, in my opinion, are the seminars. Because, for me, I did the seminar for my centre, for community social services, I was lucky. And I think that I learned a lot, and it came in really handy.
>
> *(Social Work Placement Intern 1)*

> On the other hand, the seminar I did on health helped me a lot since we were able to learn more about specific topics related to health care.
>
> *(Social Work Placement Intern 4)*

Finally, both group and individual supervision by professionals who share their professional practice with that of the teachers was highlighted as an additional strength.

> The fact, too, that there are supervisors who work in [different] areas of intervention means you are also giving feedback to the students. I think that's also something that enriches and strengthens our practice.
>
> *(Coordinator Social Work Placements)*

> On the other hand, in the supervision sessions, I learned how to do the tasks for the practicum and about issues related to the assignments we had to turn in. I was also able to observe how a space can be created for reflection and the resolution of conflicts, doubts, or problems that come up as you progress through the placement centre.
>
> *(Social Work Placement Intern 3)*

Despite the above strengths, there are also weaknesses concerning the design and implementation of the placements; weaknesses that are likely to have a negative impact on the practical training the students receive in critical social work. Specifically, the informants mentioned four fundamental weaknesses during the interviews. First, there is a lack of placement sites and entities because there are more students than places available. Second, and related to the previous weakness, some placement sites and professionals do not foster the acquisition of critical skills. The third weakness has to do with the disjunction between theory and practice, as many of the theoretical courses on which the practical training is based are taught in the first years of the degree, while the placement takes place in the fourth year. Finally, the informants highlighted the disconnection and lack of coordination between the academic supervisors and the placement supervisors, which leads to different training outcomes.

As regards the first weakness, the lack of placement sites has two clear effects on the quality of the training. On the one hand, it affects students' motivation, as they are not able to choose the area or field of interest in which to be trained. On the other hand, some schools may not offer students placements aligned with the objectives of the subject.

> Well, the shortage of centres and sites, too. It's an important deficit that doesn't have anything to do with the centres themselves but well, of the, of the demand and the supply that doesn't, doesn't match up.
>
> *(Social Work Academic Supervisor 1)*

> Well, I think that one of the things that facilitates learning is the place where you do them [the work placements] because it's not the same to do them in a place where you don't really do social work as such, and you are doing other activities that are more focused on maybe adults, like bingo, games, or maybe helping children with their homework ... these are things that I think a social worker *can* do, but it's not our profession as such. So, I think an important thing is to know where, what place to go to because, depending on where you are, you'll learn much more about our profession or not.
>
> *(Social Work Placement Intern 1)*

The second weakness, which is closely related to the previous problem above, is that the available centres or entities sometimes do not offer enough activities so that the students can acquire the competences established in the placement syllabus.

> Another shortcoming is that there is no such thing as a ... I don't dare to generalise because that may not be the case, but perhaps there is a lack of awareness on the part of social work professionals who see social work students as a burden rather than as a someone who is learning. Seeing them as a burden means that, well, they think, I don't know if it's really like that, but the thought that, well, I don't get anything out of it, so I'm not going to make an effort. So, I think that this is also combined with what the professionals are like in their own company, whether it's public or private. But the situation in which you find yourself, at work, especially, also has a lot to do with your own sensitivity, apart from the information that here, the faculty, might provide.
>
> *(Social Work Academic Supervisor 1)*

The third weakness regarding the organisation and structure of the placements in the social work degree has to do with the time that elapses between the theoretical classes and the actual realisation of the placements. As mentioned, the placements take place in the last year of the degree, while subjects that are important for the students' practical training are taught in the first year.

> Because I also believe that it would be more beneficial for them to put what they see in theory into practice ... I mean, I teach, for example, introduction to the models in the first year, and then they intervene in the fourth year, I don't know ... maybe if they had some small practical experiences, like fewer hours in 2 or 3 years, it would be more enriching for the theory and practice. That's what I think, I don't know.
>
> *(Social Work Placement Coordinator)*

Finally, it is important to mention the lack of coordination between the academic supervisors regarding the content, objectives, and approaches of the students' placements.

> In the reports, [the students] are supposed to reflect on the institution, social work, the users ... During the group supervisions, [the students] are supposed to reflect on their position, but it doesn't depend on the students, the group supervisor guides [the students]

> to make such reflections, but it's not structured. ... There are nine supervisory groups, and each one functions the best it can or however it wants to. ... We have some common scripts that include a critical part relating to the institution, the users ... but it's not really self-reflection.
>
> *(Social Work Academic Supervisor 2)*

Therefore, despite fostering a critical spirit, there is little reflection on the position of the professionals, students, and supervisors or on their own relations, so we are still a far cry away from achieving what Kondrat referred to as self-reflectivity on the privileges associated with social location.

A Compendium of Lessons and Good Practices: A Comparison of Social Work and Sociology Training Programmes

As stated above, both academic disciplines incorporate practical training schemes in their degrees. However, their programmes of study differ greatly because of the very nature of the degrees. Although they may have originally been considered sister disciplines, social work and sociology have now grown apart. Social work is a discipline that involves resolving social problems from a critical approach, while sociology focuses on the analysis of these problems. These differences, which are almost epistemological – and which we won't discuss here for reasons of space – undoubtedly mark the nature and function of the practical training in both degrees. However, the following lessons can be drawn with regard to quality practical training that transcends these two fields of study.

The first has to do with the length of the practicums. As the respondents of both degrees pointed out, the practical training in social work is more extensive than in sociology. By doing internships for more than one semester, students are able to gain a better understanding of the inner workings of the placement sites, the corporate identity of the profession, the available resources, and social problems.

The second lesson is related to commitment. Professionals at the placement site who are committed to the practical training of students dedicate the necessary time and effort to teach the students and ensure that they learn. However, not all professionals are committed or dedicated. On the other hand, the academic supervisors must also be committed at both the individual and group level to successfully deal with issues that may arise in the students' practical training. However, these faculty members, especially in sociology, acknowledged that they had little time to dedicate to such tasks. And, of course, it is essential that the students themselves be committed to complying with the schedules and regulations of the placement sites and respecting users, as some respondents mentioned.

The third has to do with the coordination between the academic and placement supervisors. Both recognised the importance of keeping in contact and coordinating the activities during the students' training. Better coordination also means that the students can be assessed on a continual basis and enables identifying and acting on aspects that can improve the training processes. The fourth is related to periodic group supervisions during the internships. The social work students and supervisors recognised the importance of clarifying doubts and linking the theory to the practice. In sociology, this type of supervision is not organised or standardised, which is a major weakness of the training schemes in these degree programmes.

Having a coordinator with knowledge of the training programme to act as a liaison between the university and the placement sites is another good practice.

Mentoring has also been highlighted as a good practice to guide and provide ongoing support and feedback to individual students. Programmes of this kind need to be implemented more broadly in the sociology degree.

The seventh lesson is one of the most important aspects of practical training schemes: linking theory to practice. The transfer of knowledge from the academic to the professional world, as well as from the social reality to academia, serves to strengthen the synergies between both.

The eighth learning is the importance of offering a wide range of placements at sites that enable students to acquire the skills they need.

In relation to the previous learning, close collaboration between the university and the placement sites is essential to ensure that the training they provide is aligned with the objectives of the training schemes.

Finally, as the tenth lesson, it is important to mention that an integral component of placement processes is the development of a critical thinking stance, which must be fostered through the systematisation and analysis of the training received.

Conclusions

In Spain, the Bologna Process has broadened the scope of social work education. Moreover, the increasing importance of work placements in higher education has enhanced the dialogue between academia and society, thus, favouring the transfer of critical social work approaches to practical training. As regards the academic–formative structure of social work and sociology training schemes, the former are clearly of a much more critical nature. The competences to be achieved in both study programmes, as well as the design of the placements in terms of their structure and scheduling and the functions and duties of the various agents involved, demonstrate this. And although practical training in social work shares some similarities with other disciplines, such as sociology in terms of the academic and placement supervisors involved, these actors play an especially important role in social work, as they also serve to strengthen the corporate identity of the profession, unlike other social science disciplines. We have identified five strengths and four weaknesses of these practical training schemes. Among the strengths of the training provided, it is important to highlight its high quality; the timing, which allows for greater professionalisation; the diversity of social contexts and realities; the integration of theory and practice under the supervision of practising professionals; and the importance of mentoring. In contrast, we have also identified certain weaknesses. These include a shortage of placement sites to satisfy the demand; placement sites and professionals that do not foster the acquisition of critical skills; the disjunction between theory and practice, as the former is taught in the first years of the degree and placements are done in the fourth; and finally, the disconnection and lack of coordination between the academic and on-site supervisors, which make it difficult for the students to understand the importance of practical training.

References

Cruz, A. (2011). ¿Qué se enseña y se aprende en una práctica de entrenamiento profesional en trabajo social? [What is taught and learned in professional social work traineeships?]. *Prospectiva: Revista de Trabajo Social e Intervención Social*, 16, 161–196.

Ferguson, I., & Woodward, R. (2009). *Radical social work in practice: Making a difference*. Chicago: Chicago University Press.

Fernandez Riquelme, S. (2010). Prácticas y profesión en Trabajo Social: Relaciones académicas y proceso metodológico [Placements and profession in social work: Academic relations and the methodological process]. *Cuadernos de Trabajo Social*, 23, 229–246.

Fook, J. (2002). *Social work: Critical theory and practice*. London: Sage.

Fook, J. (2003). Critical social work: The current issues. *Qualitative Social Work Research and Practice*, 2(2), 123–131.

Healy, K. (2000). *Social work practices: Contemporary perspectives on change*. London: Sage.

Heron, B. (2005). Self-reflection in critical social work practice: Subjectivity and the possibilities of resistance. *Reflective Practice*, 6(3), 341–351.

Heron, B. (2007). *Desire for development: Whiteness, gender, and the helping imperative*. Waterloo: Wilfred Laurier Press.

Kondrat, M. E. (1999). Who is the 'self' in self-aware: Professional self-awareness from a critical theory perspective. *Social Service Review*, 73(4), 451–477.

Manzanera, R., & Marin, I. (2017). Professional competencies in social work education for the third sector in southern Spain. *Social Work Education*, 37(8), 92–107.

Morales, A. (2010). *Género, mujeres, trabajo social y sección femenina: historia de una profesión feminizada y con vocación feminista [Gender, women, social work and the women's section: History of a feminized profession with a feminist vocation]*. Granada: Universidad de Granada.

Rossiter, A. (2001). Innocence lost and suspicion found: Do we educate for or against social work? *Critical Social Work*, 2(1), 1–5.

Tonon, G., Robles, C., & Meza, M. (2004). *La supervisión en trabajo social. Una cuestión profesional y académica [Supervision in social work: A professional and academic issue]*. Buenos Aires: Espacio.

19

Estonian Undergraduate Social Work Students' Reflections on Field Placement

Challenges for Novice Social Workers

Karmen Toros, Kersti Kriisk, and Anne Tiko

Field placement is considered one of the most important components of social work education, as direct interaction with clients enables social work students to obtain understanding of the helping process and, therefore, facilitates development of professional skills in novice social workers (Lam, Wong, & Leung, 2007; Urdang, 2010; Steen et al., 2016). In describing field placement, Cleak and Zuchowski (2020) use the term 'transition to practice'. Similarly, Patil and Ennis (2018, p. 1371) acknowledge field placement within a social work undergraduate degree as a time of intense learning and linking of theory to 'real-world' practice. According to Wang and Chui (2016), field placement determines the success of social work education, discussing it in terms of the training of competent social workers. Therefore, it can be said that field placement is crucial for the development of the social work profession in general (McLaughlin et al., 2015).

Authors indicate that there has been a shift from the competence-based approaches to a reflective practice paradigm in social work education in the context of the growing complexity of social problems (Burr, Blyth, Sutcliffe, & King, 2016; Chow et al., 2011; Goh, 2012). Learning from the experiences during field placement in the form of self-reflection develops strengths and abilities and promotes widening students' horizons in constructing new solutions for ongoing and future cases that lead to improved practice effectiveness (Yip, 2006). Nevertheless, studies in recent years on social work field placement are rather limited, especially in the context of self-reflection. Mostly, these studies explored graduate students' experiences of field placement (Flanagan & Wilson, 2018; Fortune, Rogers, & Williamson, 2018; Gair & Baglow, 2018) or international field placement (Askeland, Døhlie, & Grosvold, 2016; Jönsson & Flen, 2020; Pawar, 2017) in general, with students from various countries, e.g., Ireland, the U.S.A., Australia, Sweden, and Norway. One study by Rehn and Kalman (2018) used narratives to explore undergraduate social work students' challenges during field placement, from which overarching themes of being emotionally overwhelmed and experiencing insecurity regarding interpretation of legislation, guidelines, and principles were identified. Matthew and Lough (2017) published a literature review based on 24 studies, including international placements, on

DOI: 10.4324/9781032164946-24

social work field placement, consisting of students globally. In conclusion, Matthew and Lough referred to the need to encourage students to use written and verbal reflections for identifying challenges they encounter related to the placement. Jönsson and Flen (2020) outlined a similar need to be strengthened while preparing social work students for their field placement based on their study – creating spaces for students' critical reflexivity to address emotional distress. 'Reflection' emerged as a theme in one more study and was identified as a strength of international social work field placement. According to Pawar (2017, p. 205), international field placement enabled a greater depth of reflection for students, highlighting the students' responsiveness to problems through the reflection model of learning.

In order to evaluate the students' needs for education in this context, it is necessary to understand future social workers' reflections and perspectives on whether social work education is supportive of practice in the field. This knowledge will help educators to better understand what changes or additional knowledge and skills are needed in the process of studies. Therefore, it contributes to the quality of social work education. The aim of this chapter is to explore undergraduate social work students' experiences and perspectives of their field placement in the framework of self-reflection. Specifically, what are their learning experiences during their field placement and challenges of the social work profession?

The Role of Self-reflection in Social Work Education and Field Placement: Key for Professional Growth and Competence

In social work, reflection is recognised as an essential element in practice, research, and education (Goh, 2012, p. 590). Burr et al. (2016, p. 1998) discuss that 'reflective practice has become a key part of both practice-based and class-based teaching in social work education'. Enhancing reflexivity promotes students' understanding of themselves and prepares them for their future careers as social workers (Chow et al., 2011). Self-reflection is acknowledged as a crucial attribute of competent professionals functioning in complex and changing societies (Kanthan & Senger, 2011). Mitendorf (2020) argues that social workers are faced with complex human situations and unexpected circumstances, which makes social work a demanding profession and, therefore, requires the capacity to reflect the complexity of the contexts of the profession.

Sööt and Viskus (2015) interpret self-reflection as a cognitive process, involving learning from the experience. Ross and Bruce (2007) construct self-reflection as more than just thinking but as linking to one's course of action. Yip (2006, p. 780) defines self-reflection as 'a process of self-analysis, self-evaluation, self-dialogue and self-observation'. Yip emphasises the importance of self-reflection to improve personal and professional awareness and professional growth, promoting construction of new meanings and solutions and learning from experiences. Yorke, Grant, and Csiernik (2016) discuss active self-reflection, which requires the capacity to continually self-monitor. Brammar and Lezova (2018) describe the process of self-reflection by using the word 'reflecting' and making meaning of self and wider experiences. Lam et al. (2007) perceive reflectiveness as thinking and exploring issues of concern, making sense of one's experiences, and interpreting these experiences, generating knowledge about self and the profession. The self of the worker is important in terms of of self-awareness (Trevithick, 2018). It can be considered as a tool, as understanding self leads to the understanding of contexts, values, ethics of social work, and service users embedded in the system. Rosen, McCall, and Truten (2017) indicate that the ability to engage in personal reflection fosters ongoing professional development and enables professional practice between social workers and various service users with different experiences than their own.

Fook (1999) advocates for reflectivity in the practice of professionals and expands the idea of self-reflection to critical reflection in social work – making meaning from the experience. Critical thinking about experiences and questioning these experiences encourage students to think more consciously about what they have learned (Pappas, 2010). Yan and Brown (2017, p. 1257) state that 'critical self-reflection is basis for the students to enhance their metacognitive skills, which in turn leads to improved learning'. The deeper the reflection, the stronger the individual's awareness of experiences and cognition (Yip, 2006). As social workers deal with various social problems in society, social work must look beyond its practice and values in order to understand the changing environments and contexts that shape the lives of people and communities (Mitendorf, 2020, p. 87).

Trevithick (2008, p. 1214) outlines that 'in everyday contexts, we seek and use knowledge in order to understand ourselves, others and the world around us'. In order to understand others, one needs to learn about herself/himself. Self-reflection is considered to enhance personal and professional development in practice (Chaddock, Thwaites, Bennett-Levy, & Freeston, 2014; Gale & Schröeder, 2014; Gün, 2010), increase professional growth and competence (Autry & Walker, 2011; Eng & Pai 2014), and, therefore, contributes to the quality of social work, in general, by constructing a new and deeper understanding of the experience (see Ip et al., 2012). Deeper reflection enables stronger self-awareness (Yip, 2006).

Students 'need educational support, guidance in becoming aware of how their own feelings, attitudes, and relationships with clients and how to deepen their capacity to develop a professional self' (Urdang, 2010, p. 532). Therefore, within the social work curriculum, field placement is a key component of social work education in which students can apply their knowledge and skills from theory into practice and make meaning of their experiences. In order to learn from these experiences, including exploring personal belief systems that influence their perceptions and interaction with clients, and evolve in this profession, social work training has the responsibility to ensure the environment and skills for students to engage in reflective practice.

Field placement is considered a fundamental component in social work education and a determinant of its quality; furthermore, students identify their experiences during field placement as central to their transition from studies to practice (Wang & Chui, 2016; Cleak & Zuchowski, 2020; Lam et al., 2007). Lam et al. (2007) elaborate that social work field placement is a 'rich context for reflective learning'. On one side, field placement enables students to link theory to practice (Patil & Ennis, 2018), and, on the other side, it is a 'safe place to practice' working with service users with the possibility of guidance and support from supervisors. In order to learn from the experiences during field placement and make meaning, we believe that reflection on those experiences facilitates the personal and professional growth of students – the future social workers.

Social Work Field Placement in the Estonian Context

The study reported in the current chapter was conducted among undergraduate social work students at Tallinn University, Estonia. Tallinn University (T.L.U.) is the only university in the Baltics in which social work studies take place on all three levels of higher education (bachelor's, master's, and doctoral studies), which means it has a leading position in the study and research field of social work in Estonia and the Baltic Republics. In the 1990s, Estonia was in a situation in which there was no efficient system of measures in social services, and the growth of social problems created the need for an entirely new social welfare system. The complexities of a society in transition presented real challenges for social work, but there were no professional social workers (Tamm, 2010). Therefore, Tallinn Pedagogical University (later renamed Tallinn University) started to educate social workers in 1991.

The aim of Bachelor of Social Work programme at T.L.U. is to create preconditions for the development of a social worker who has adopted the ethical principles of social work; has knowledge of social work theories, methods, social policy, and public health; and knowledge and skills for the performance and organisation of social welfare for various client groups in the public, private, and third sectors. The framework for developing social work curriculum is based on three important documents: (1) Standard of Higher Education of the Republic of Estonia; (2) Professional Standard for Social Workers; (3) Statute of Study Program of T.L.U. (Self-assessment Report, 2020). The compulsory subject-specific courses are related to different areas of practical social work at the individual, organisational, and society/community level, and the speciality electives pertain to different target groups of social work according to the student's specialisation interest in accordance with the Social Worker Level 6 Professional Standard. Field placement plays a key role in the study process. The relevancy of this experience is ensured through combined supervision by a specialist at the training location and a lecturer from T.L.U., together with a reflective training report (this plays an important role in self-analysis and conceptualisation of professional identity). Specific field placement courses include fieldwork in social work (6 credit points, 120 hours), observation internship (4 credits), and fieldwork in the community (4 credits); additionally, students can complete their field placement abroad (9 credits). The aim of the compulsory field placement is to create preparedness for applying professional values, skills, and knowledge in a working environment, specialising in one group of service users (e.g., social work with families, elderly, unemployed, etc.).

Method

A qualitative study on social work students' experiences and perspectives was conducted to explore their learning experiences during their field placement and the challenges of the social work profession. The framework of self-reflection was chosen, as it can lead to increased self-awareness and contribute to positive professional development during education as well as in practice environments. Siles-González and Solano-Ruiz (2016) stated that students' assessment of their own learning process contributes to the development of self-reflection and critical thinking.

Participants and Data Collection

This study includes reflections from 68 undergraduate social work students (94.1% female and 5.9% male) carrying out their compulsory field placements during 2016–2018 at T.L.U. Students were asked to reflect in writing and were encouraged to critically reflect on their fieldwork experiences and emphasise what they learned from this by keeping in mind two themes: knowledge and skills required for working with service users and theoretical knowledge learned from social work studies in the context of field placement. We wanted to capture the themes and issues that were most salient to them. Reflections of field placement were part of students' field placement portfolios. According to Finch (2008), portfolios can foster the integration of theory, action, and self-reflection, which are essential elements of professional education and enable educational outcomes as students navigate their social work studies.

The length of the written text varied from approximately two to four pages. Some of the students provided in-depth reflections, associating experiences with their perspectives on professional social work, how these experiences could impact them as a social worker, and identifying their strengths and challenges for becoming a competent social worker; other students gave more general descriptions of their field placement.

Regarding service users, almost one-third of students carried out their field placement with at-risk children and families (n = 25), followed by choosing the experience of working with various service users in local government (n = 19), unemployed persons (n = 9), adults with special needs (n = 5), children with special needs (n = 3), delinquent youth (n = 3), elderly (n = 3), and adults with substance abuse problems (n = 1).

During data collection, confidentiality and anonymity of information regarding reflections and study participants were considered – students' identities were kept confidential and anonymised by giving each student a number; no names of supervisors or links between students' field placement and students are provided in this chapter.

Data Analysis

Thematic analysis for data analysis was conducted by the first author using principles outlined by Braun and Clarke (2006). This particular method for identifying and analysing patterns in qualitative data was chosen because, according to Clarke and Braun, thematic analysis works well with people's experiences or understandings and construction of phenomena in particular contexts. Transcripts were manually coded using word processing software. Analysis of the data began with multiple readings of reflection notes to gain an overall understanding of texts, followed by discovering initial codes from the data (open-coding) and sorting the codes into potential meaning units for labels. Codes were then reviewed again, and the specifics of each theme further refined, combining codes into themes. Three main themes in the context of becoming a professional social worker emerged from the analysis (see Table 19.1), which is presented in the following section. The data was read again to extract quotes to illustrate the connections between the raw data and the conclusions drawn. As this study explores the understanding of a phenomenon in its context, precise numerical representation of responses is generally not provided (Rubin & Babbie, 2008). Nevertheless, themes and labels are presented in an order that approximates their relative frequency in the data.

Table 19.1 Students' Reflection on the Field Placement: Main Themes and Labels

Main theme	Labels
Lessons learned: Important insights	The right choice of the profession; reality of the profession; building self-confidence; creating connections between theory and practice; areas for professional development; improved self-reflection skills; complexity of social work profession: burnout, high volume of bureaucracy
Supportive components for effective field placement	Social-work-studies-related – theoretical knowledge from social work studies: professional ethics; networking; project writing and management; 'field placement-related research'; specific theories: ecological systems theory, communication theory, organisational behaviour theory, social cohesion, solution brief therapy Field-placement-related: supportive teamwork experience; supportive relations with the field placements' supervisor Social-work-practice-related: prior experience in social work field
Skills required working with service users	Communication skills: verbal communication, self-expression, negotiation, and active listening with (a) service users, (b) colleagues; analytical skills; problem-solving skills; strengths-based thinking; time management; assertiveness; self-reflection: group supervision; counselling; computer skills

Findings

Lessons Learned: Important Insights

Students' reflections reported on the usefulness of the field placement in the context of learning to become a professional social worker. Acknowledgment of the *right choice of profession* was a significant value found in field placement for several reasons: (i) general affirmation of the decision to study social work, as the following quote indicates: 'This experience [field placement] assured me that this is exactly the right profession for me, and I have made the right choice in choosing social work' (Student 10); (ii) specialisation – understanding the client group or the domain in the field as the best fit for a career or learning the opposite – that the specific field is not the best fit for a career in social work: 'The best part of it [field placement] is that now I am totally convinced that I want to work with children' (Student 2), and 'Field placement enabled me to think deeply, if this kind of the organisation is the right place for me or I would get stuck being in a comfort zone' (Student 5); and (iii) the changing decision from not being sure to being sure about choosing the profession:

> Prior to the field placement I was not sure whether I would like to work directly with service users … I wanted to learn, if my personal traits, values, and perspectives are in line with this profession. I thought that the work directly with service users would be mundane, but I was wrong; my perception changed totally.
>
> *(Student 47)*

The knowledge of choosing the right profession was linked with *self-confidence*. On one side, the belief that students had found the right path increased self-confidence, and on other side, experiencing field placement and successfully testing the choice of career assured students' positive coping as novice social workers. The following quote reflects this student's explanation of how field placement increased her self-confidence: 'I feel that the time I spent at the field placement boosted my self-confidence to communicate with service users and identify various options to provide assistance for them' (Student 35). Several students expressed their feelings of uncertainty prior to the field placement because of their lack of experience with service users. Nevertheless, the possibility of practicing their knowledge and skills acquired during their studies, in combination with support from the supervisor, improved their self-confidence. Student 2 wrote: 'As I had no previous involvement with social work's practical side, I felt insecure. I had doubts. How will I manage to perform my field placement? … At the end of the field placement, I felt so much more self-confident'. Students found it challenging to start working as novice social workers without the support of senior colleagues and expressed the need to have a supervisor in the beginning of their career.

Furthermore, field placement enabled students to *create connections between theory and practice*. Here, students had different views, whether they found that their theoretical base supported their practice or that practice facilitated their understanding of theory. Student 65 believed her social work training and theoretical knowledge was an essential part of the successful field placement; she 'tried to relate existing knowledge with new experiences from the field working with the service users'. Student 63's experience was the opposite in that her social work practice has given her a better understanding of theory. Some other students' experience made theory and practice appear as far apart from each other as two different worlds: 'I have studied social work in theory, but practice is totally different' (Student 59); 'During the field placement, I felt that, on a theoretical level, we discussed situations with clients differently in the classroom compared to the real life I experienced with working with service users' (Student 66). Even though these experiences varied, field placement was considered to either fill in the gaps or support existing knowledge; either way, the experience of field placement was the 'guide to the real life of social work', providing a glimpse of their future professional life.

The experience of field placement and working with supervisors and service users brought up *areas for professional development*, such as positive thinking ('I noticed that a positive attitude enhances children's trust', (Student 51)), self-efficacy ('without it, you cannot implement knowledge that you actually have already in practice … you must take risks and try', (Student 59)), coping with pressure, collaboration ('I realised the importance of the collaboration for achieving outcomes', (Student 31)), etc. In addition to learning about what needed to be 'improved', students pointed out the significance of the field placement in terms of self-development. Student 17 described it as follows: 'It was great to see my personal development, which may be seen as trivial for others, but huge for me, and I am so proud of myself'.

A separate discussion can be made regarding *improving self-reflection skills*, which was one of the crucial components of field placement, which not only provided social work practice experience with service users but also enhanced their self-reflection skills. In the process of data analysis, we noticed that not all of the students had engaged in 'self-reflection mode' but, rather, described situations they experienced. Nevertheless, several students emphasised the process of learning to self-reflect during their field placement and acknowledged the importance of self-reflection to become a competent and professional social worker, as the following student wrote: 'I learned to better analyse myself and the profession in the wider sense and what it means to be professional' (Student 11).

Although students shared positive aspects of the field placement, as indicated previously, they also expressed their thoughts on the *complexities of the social work profession*. Two themes were mentioned the most: burnout and the high volume of bureaucracy. Working with service users revealed their high workload, the hardships service users undergo, and understanding that, in reality, the idea of being able to 'fix the world' becomes 'it is not always possible to help everyone', etc. Contributing to the well-being of vulnerable people by becoming a social worker was now considered a possibility, but, at the same time, it was sort of a wake-up call about how complex and demanding this profession is. Students elaborated on their thoughts on the situations that can make them more vulnerable to burnout; the inability to help service users was frequently described, as the following student wrote:

> Social work involves working with a lot of unfortunate people, which made me realise that often they themselves do not want help for different reasons, and this makes the situation even worse and painful, as you cannot help them, although you want to, and this can cause burnout.
>
> *(Student 52)*

Burnout was noted quite a lot by the students, including reflection on how to avoid burnout or cope with it based on their experiences from the field placement. For example, this student indicated using humour to cope: 'I noticed the humour, the black type of humour among social workers, which I believe is a sort of protection for burnout' (Student 55). Burnout was considered one of the biggest challenges in their future profession – specifically, how to avoid burnout and/or cope with the demanding societal issues that increase the probability of experiencing burnout.

Bureaucracy was implied as a negative part of social work in terms of taking time away from direct work with service users. Nevertheless, for some students, bureaucracy and 'being an official' was the main focus of their reflection about field placement – becoming an official:

'I discovered that it was not difficult at all, the bureaucracy, logical and simple' (Student 45), 'I have made the right decision for myself becoming a social worker and I cannot wait to start working as an official' (Student 60). What we noticed, was that the terms students used in their reflections, indicated to two approaches: direct work with service users and working as an official.

Supportive Components for Effective Field Placement

Based on students' experiences, we divided their reflections into three groups related to: social work studies, field placement, and social work practice.

In the first group, social work studies, theoretical knowledge from social work studies was discussed, particularly, the importance of being prepared for the field placement by having knowledge in several domains. Most often students discussed *ethical principles* – good preparedness from the studies and how this enabled them to understand and analyse situations they encountered during the field placement, as Student 25's quote demonstrates: 'strong knowledge of ethics guided me during the entire time of the field placement'. Another student emphasised the code of ethics as the framework for the field placement: 'It is hard to link theory with practice in social work, especially without previous experience in the field, but if you link practice with social work ethics, this enables you to understand the concept of practice and leads to professionalism' (Student 67). Furthermore, students reflected on situations in their field placements, where they questioned workers' ethics regarding respecting service users' self-determination and valuing the relationship between the service user and the worker.

Networking, in the context of collaborating with other agencies and service users' extended family and community, was another theme emerging throughout students' reflections. Theoretical knowledge acquired during studies allowed students to understand its specifics, as this student outlined: 'Theoretical knowledge of networking helped to follow the process during a family group conference, and the feeling of knowing made me feel much more confident and able to relate to the meeting' (Student 2).

Social work curriculum incorporates courses on *project writing and management*, as this is one part of a social worker's daily duties – writing projects and applying money to develop services for service users. Therefore, it was not surprising to read about this theme from students' reflections. Students shared their experiences on reading projects but also being part of the writing process, which was greatly appreciated – on one hand, to implement knowledge in practice but, on the other, being trusted with this important task. Student 11 shared her ideas as such:

> Project writing was especially a highlight of my field placement experience. In the classroom, we had participated in all phases of writing the project as a group work and got the feedback, but I was not quite sure if this is the same with writing a 'real project'. As my field placement time was in the midst of project deadlines, I was able to be part of writing the project for ADHD [attention deficit hyperactivity disorder] children to the Ministry of Social Affairs and share my opinions of with other social workers. We got the financing, and it felt great to be part of the team, and, of course, the real experience of project writing will be useful in the future.

This quote reflects the importance of having knowledge, implementing theory in practice, and being able to be actively involved in real work during the field placement.

Although most of the students believed that the theoretical base studied at the university is setting the ground for field placement, some students expressed their point of view that social work training at the university does not prepare much for the future profession, but students themselves must experience and attend various in-service training to prepare themselves, as the following quote illustrates:

> University provides theory, which in general is rather complicated to apply in practice, therefore, I think that, in order to become a good social worker, you have to work hard yourself and learn through practice, especially through solving cases, taking additional courses.
>
> *(Student 38)*

Some of the students found it crucial to prepare for the field placement by reading literature and *research* in the given field. Students used terms 'evidence-based' and 'research-based' in this context, underscoring this to be the result of studies from several courses – to get familiar with the theme and current trends supporting the practice to be more efficient. One student summarised the idea as such: 'You don't have to invent yourself but use the knowledge from evidence-based practices' (Student 64).

Various *specific theories* – most commonly ecological systems theory, communication theory, organisational behaviour theory, social cohesion, and solution brief therapy – were mentioned to be crucial to know for field placement to be more efficient and able to understand how theories relate to practice. Student 68 shared her ideas on this topic regarding ecological systems theory:

> I recognised several theories while working with clients, or more precisely, how theories can help in the practice setting. I had discussions with social workers, how different theories work in practice, and I learned that, for the most part, practitioners use ecological systems theory to understand their clients, how different systems influence each other.

In order for the field placement to be efficient, students identified main factors that they considered important provided by the field placement and the supervisor. *Supportive teamwork* was considered highly important, as during their studies, students realised that social work cannot be done alone but must be conducted as a team. Being part of an effective and supportive team, increased students' self-confidence and motivation: 'That team of social workers made me feel part of the team and that my contribution was valued, which enhanced my self-confidence' (Student 29).

Most of the students were satisfied with their supervisors, characterising them as competent professionals, asking students' reflections during the field placement, as Student 19 explained: 'My supervisor always asked me what I think and what kind of observations I have from meeting with service users'. Student 37 had a similar experience, and she expressed the excitement of being asked what she would have done differently if she were in the supervisor's shoes: 'I felt as an equal, not just some trainee … Supervisor asked my opinion, vision, but also, what would I do or have had done differently' Some of the students expressed dissatisfaction with their supervisors, mainly for not being actively involved in working with clients.

The third component related to efficient field placement relates to *prior experience in the field of social work*. Students with previous experience (e.g., volunteer work, social worker in the family) found that having some background knowledge about services or specific group of service users made it easier to adapt to new situations and service users. Similarly, students who had had no previous experience shared their opinion that of having some previous experience would have helped them to 'learn the system' faster. Here, the need for a longer field placement was stressed by more than half of the students – the current length and hours are not enough, as it takes time to get to know the system. Students indicated that case management is a long process and the length of the field placement today does not enable them to experience the whole process and all the phases of it. Moreover, most of the students were not able to work independently with clients due to the short duration of the field placement. The following student used the word 'being an observer' to describe this situation: 'The length of the field placement is too short, and I found myself rather in the position of the observer' (Student 9).

Skills Required when Working with Service Users

In addition to lessons students learned from the field placement and supportive components for effective field placement, they discussed a lot about skills that are required to work with service users. Most outlined skills are presented in Table 19.1. In this section, we will not focus on all the skills but, rather, two skills they 'discovered' during the field placement.

Strengths-based thinking was seen of a great value in working not only with service users but also with colleagues and networking partners. Students considered strengths-based thinking as a skill that needs to be developed and advanced, starting, first, on a personal level – seeing strengths and resources within themselves – followed by recognising strengths and resources within others. Students noticed how strengths-based thinking empowers service users: 'Social workers at the centre [at the rehabilitation institution for adults with substance-use disorders] believe that every person has resources, inner strengths … This kind of approach encourages them to look forward and gives strength to cope with daily tasks' (Student 1); 'I realized that this [identifying strengths and building on strengths] was something social workers used a lot in their work with service users – the communication and the language they used – attention on strengths' (Student 58). Nevertheless, students questioned their ability to shift the paradigm from traditional problem-based thinking to strengths-based thinking, arguing that there is a need to have more focus on supporting students to develop strengths-based thinking during their social work studies.

Self-reflection was discussed in the first main theme of improving their self-reflection skills, but also in regard to systematic way of reflecting – *self-reflection skills in the context of group supervision*. Student 13 described her thoughts on the usefulness of peer group supervision:

> I found self-reflection skills to be so important … peer group supervision is a life saver in a way [In Estonia, supervision has not been available for all social workers, which led to the 'creation' of other ways for supervision, such as peer group supervision]. This is not only service users' case-related but fosters a systematic way of thinking about the practice and helping to find new ideas, solutions for complex situations.

Several students were able to take part of peer supervision groups, which was a highly valued experience.

Discussion

In this discussion, we focus on two main findings emerging as most challenging issues for the students based on their field placement experience reflections regarding their future profession as novice social workers: burnout and strengths-based thinking. Furthermore, we also focus on bureaucracy-based social work (social workers as 'officials'), which some students found to be the essence of social work. These challenges are discussed in the context of self-reflection.

Self-help Tool for Burnout: Peer Group Supervision

Martin, Myers, and Brickman (2020) argue that social work profession includes the risk of emotional, psychological, and physical well-being, making it crucial for social work students to be equipped to handle the complexities of this profession. Chow et al. (2011) have referred to reflexivity as a survival skill, which, in the context of this study, can be beneficial to prevent burning out, specifically providing students with supportive learning techniques and environment (see Ganzer & Zauderer, 2013). We find several important elements here: providing students with the skills to use self-reflection, being able to get supervision (for reflection on difficult cases and their personal struggles as social workers), and securing mentors for novice social workers at the beginning of their journey of social work profession. Encouraging students to reflect on their experiences can help them to make sense of troubling events (Robert, Piemonte, & Truten, 2018, p. 447). Urdang (2010) believes that being self-reflective can help prevent burnout; it is especially important in the case of supervision being downsized. Several authors state that supervision is fundamental to the social work profession, enabling reflection of practice in a safe environment (Nickson, Gair, & Miles, 2016; Wilkins, Forrester, & Grant, 2017).

Studies in Estonia bring out social workers' need for supervision. According to Toros and Lasala (2019), social workers working with children and families consider supervision to enhance self-reflection; furthermore, they consider supervision crucial for reducing stress and burnout (Toros, Tiko, Välba, & Kangur, 2016). Nevertheless, supervision is scarce for social workers in Estonia. This has led social workers in Estonia to find alternative ways to reflect on their daily practices and difficult cases among fellow workers in a supportive environment. They have discovered the effectiveness of peer group supervision. In the Estonian language, peer supervision is called '*kovisioon*', which directly translated means 'co-vision'. This solution helps social workers to find solutions and new perspectives together in a collaborative process. The format social workers in Estonia use is structured peer group supervision. Borders (1991) stated that the structured peer group format encourages skill development, instructive feedback, and self-monitoring. Acknowledging the feedback from social work students' field placement, we have incorporated a seminar for the third-year students regarding peer group supervision. The modified format for training students discussed in this paper is based on the structured group supervision model described by Newman, Nebbergall, and Salmon (2013) and peer supervision training by Aava (2013), consisting of five phases: information, clarification, analysis, feedback, and reflection. We believe peer group supervision supports the professional growth of all involved in the group process by stimulating critical thinking.

Strengths-based Approach: Empowerment of Service Users and Self-empowerment

The importance of strengths-based thinking has been outlined in various studies. For example, Gibson, Samuels, and Pryce (2018) found that strengths-based skills are essential to fostering stronger rapport with families and building relationships. Similarly, Toros (2014) found that the strength-based approach enhances collaboration with service users. Palmer-House (2008) concluded that strengths-based thinking promotes empowerment and relationships between the worker and service user but also enhances self-empowerment.

Social work students in our study reflected on the value of strengths-based thinking, although they found it difficult to master the skill of identifying and building on resources and capacities of service users. A study conducted in Estonia among child protection workers reported on workers' self-criticism and self-perceived weaknesses, rather than them seeing their own strengths and potential (Toros & LaSala, 2019). The study underscored the need to help social workers adopt and apply systematic and, possibly, less critical self-reflection, as such may lead to improved services to clients. Segev and Nadan (2016) argued that, in social work education, the external reality is brought into the classroom mainly through the experiences of students in their fieldwork. Therefore, a more systematic approach to developing conscious use of the strengths-based perspective throughout the field placement is required, focusing on students' own strengths and perspective of their strengths and resources and assignments, identifying strengths in the process of working with clients combined with self-refection to determine what works, what doesn't, and what would they do differently the next time.

Bureaucracy-based Social Work: Opposite to Core of Social Work

We noticed that some of the students discussed their experiences regarding their future profession in the context of bureaucracy-based approach, meaning they seemed to describe social workers as 'the official' rather than 'partner of the service user', emphasising paperwork, computers, and working in the office. Social work is a human interaction profession (Tamm, 2010) with the core of social work based on human relationships. As Parton and O'Byrne (2000) noted, social workers' expertise, traditionally, has been built on the ability to know how to establish relationships. Even though bureaucracy has been increased in daily social work practice, it raises the question of how to keep the people – service users – in the centre and promote relationship-based practice. Lesser focus on service users may affect relationships with service users. Munro (2011) argued that the quality of the relationship between the service user and professional directly impacts the effectiveness of the help provided. Furthermore, it compromises social work values (Rankine, 2019). The challenge we see here is not only the value conflict and the quality of support provided in this context but also the taking of the expert position and making decisions for the client, not with the client, as studies in Estonia indicate (Toros & LaSala, 2018; Välba, Toros, & Tiko, 2017). Therefore, it could be useful to strengthen critical self-reflection throughout the field placement on students' perspective of the core of social work, the role of the social worker, and approaches with service users in the frame of their experiences.

Concluding Thoughts

The transition from theory to practice – from the 'desk' to 'real' service users – might be frightening and raise lot of questions, challenges, and uncertainties. Even the best preparation might not seem like enough. Most likely, to some extent, every social work student has had these kind of thoughts. Nevertheless, equipping students with skills and tools to support their transition to 'real life' is one of the main tasks for social work educators. This chapter reported on the findings of social work students' experiences and perspectives during their field placement and the challenges of the social work profession in the framework of self-reflection. We consider self-reflection an empowering tool, which serves several purposes: critical reflection of experiences, including questioning these experiences; personal and professional values; values for social work practice; and helping to understand contexts and create new insights on the journey of becoming a competent and efficient professional. Rosenfeld (2014) asserts, if workers get into the habit of self-reflection, they will seek continuous learning throughout their professional careers. In order to develop the social work curriculum for better preparing students for their chosen profession, studying novice social workers' transition from studies to work with clients during their first year of their experience would enable deeper insight into the challenges and successes in the form of reflective journaling and interviews.

References

Aava, K. (2013). *Using Supervision Techniques in Teaching*. Tallinn: Tallinn University.

Askeland, G.A., Døhlie, E., & Grosvold, K. (2016). International Field Placement in Social Work: Relevant for Working in the Home Country. *International Social Work*, 61(5), 692–705.

Autry, L.L., & Walker, M.E. (2011). Artistic Representation: Promoting Student Creativity and Self-Reflection. *Journal of Creativity in Mental Health*, 6(1), 42–55.

Borders, D.L. (1991). A Systematic Approach to Peer Group Supervision. *Journal of Counseling and Development*, 69, 248–252.

Brammar, L., & Lezova, K. (2018). How Can Creative Practice Facilitate Reflection on Self-Learning? Implications for Narrative Career Counselling. *Australian Journal of Career Development*, 27(2), 108–115.

Braun, V., & Clarke, V. (2006). Using Thematic Analysis in Psychology. *Qualitative Research in Psychology*, 3(2), 77–101.

Burr, V., Blyth, E., Sutcliffe, J., & King, N. (2016). Encouraging Self-Reflection in Social Work Students: Using Personal Construct Methods. *British Journal of Social Work*, 46, 1997–2015.

Chaddock, A., Thwaites, R., Bennett-Levy, L., & Freeston, M.H. (2014). Understanding Individual Differences in Response to Self-Practice and Self-Reflection (SP/SR) During CBT Training. *The Cognitive Behaviour Therapist*, 7, 1–17.

Chow, A.Y.M., Lam, D.O.B., Leung, G.S.M., Wong, D.F.K., & Chan, B.F.P. (2011). Promoting Reflexivity Among Social Work Students: The Development and Evaluation of a Programme. *Social Work Education*, 20(2), 141–156.

Cleak, H., & Zuchowski, I. (2020). Mapping Social Work Field Education in the 21st Century: A National Survey of the Australian Context. *British Journal of Social Work*, 50(2), 427–446.

Eng, C-J., & Pai, H-C. (2014). Determinants of Nursing Competence of Nursing Students in Taiwan: The Role of Self-Reflection and Insight. *Nurse Education Today*, 35(3), 450–455.

Finch, J. (2008). 'Running with the Fox and Hunting with the Hounds': Social Work Tutors' Experiences of Managing Failing Social Work Students in Practice Learning Settings. *British Journal of Social Work*, 45, 2124–2141.

Flanagan, N., & Wilson, E. (2018). What Makes a Good Placement? Findings of a Social Work Student-to-Student Research Study. *Social Work Education*, 37(5), 565–580.

Fook, J. (1999). Reflexivity as a Method. *Annual Review of Health Social Sciences*, 9(1), 11–20.

Fortune, A.E., Rogers, C.A., & Williamson, E. (2018). Effects of an Integrative Field Seminar for MSW Students. *Journal of Social Work Education*, 54(1), 94–109.

Gair, S., & Baglow, L. (2018). Australian Social Work Students Balancing Study, Work, and Field Placement: Seeing it Like it Is. *Australian Social Work*, 71(1), 46–57.

Gale, C., & Schröeder, T. (2014). Experiences of Self-Practice/Self-Reflection in Cognitive Behavioural Therapy: A Metasynthesis of Qualitative Studies. *Psychology and Psychotherapy: Theory, Research and Practice*, 87(4), 373–392.

Ganzer, C.A., & Zauderer, C. (2013). Structured Learning and Self-Reflection: Strategies to Decrease Anxiety in the Psychiatric Mental Health Clinical Nursing Experience. *Nursing Education Perspectives*, 34(4), 244–247.

Gibson, K., Samuels, G., & Pryce, J. (2018). Authors of Accountability: Paperwork and Social Work in Contemporary Child Welfare Practice. *Children and Youth Services Review*, 85, 43–52.

Goh, E.C.L. (2012). Integrating Mindfulness and Reflection in the Teaching and Learning of Listening Skills for Undergraduate Social Work Students in Singapore. *Social Work Education*, 31(5), 587–604.

Gün, B. (2010). Quality Self-Reflection Through Reflection Training. *ELT Journal*, 65(2), 126–135.

Ip, W.Y., Lui, M.H., Chien, W.T., Lee, I.F., Lam, L.W., & Lee, D.T. (2012). Promoting Self-Reflection in Clinical Practice Among Chinese Nursing Undergraduates in Hong Kong. *Contemporary Nurse*, 41(2), 253–262.

Jönsson, J.H., & Flen, A.L. (2020). Global Social Work Ethics and International Field Training: The Experiences and Practice Dilemmas of Norwegian and Swedish Social Work Students. *International Social Work*, 1–4, DOI: 10.1177/0020872819889398.

Kanthan, R., & Senger, J-L.B. (2011). An Appraisal of Students' Awareness of "Self- Reflection" in a First-Year Pathology Course of Undergraduate Medical/Dental Education. *BMC Medical Education*, 11(67), 1–11.

Lam, C.M., Wong, H., & Leung, T.T.F. (2007). An Unfinished Reflexive Journey: Social Work Students' Reflection on Their Placement Experiences. *British Journal of Social Work*, 37, 91–105.

Martin, E.M., Myers, K., & Brickman, K. (2020). Self-Preservation in the Workplace: The Importance of Well-Being for Social Work Practitioners and Field Supervisors. *Social Work*, 65(1), 74–81.

Matthew, L.E., & Lough, B.J. (2017). Challenges Social Work Students Encounter in International Field Placements and Recommendations for Responsible Management. *Journal of Social Work Education*, 53(1), 18–36.

McLaughlin, H., Scholar, H., McCaughan, S., & Coleman, A. (2015). Are Non-Traditional Social Work Placements Second-Best Learning Opportunities for Social Work Qualifying Students? *British Journal of Social Work*, 45(2), 1469–1488.

Mitendorf, A. (2020). *Professional Social Work Narratives in a Young, Complex Neoliberal Society*. Tallinn: Tallinn University.

Munro, E. (2011). *The Munro Review of Child Protection. Interim Report: The Child's Journey*, from https://assets.publishing.service.gov.uk/government/uploads/system/uploads/attachment_data/file/624946/DFE-00010-2011.pdf.

Newman, D.S., Nebbergall, A.J., & Salmon, D. (2013). Structured Peer Group Supervision for Novice Consultants: Procedures, Pitfalls, and Potential. *Journal of Educational and Psychological Consultation*, 23, 200–216.

Nickson, A., Gair, S., & Miles, D. (2016). Supporting Isolated Workers in Their Work with Families in Rural and Remote Australia: Exploring Peer Group Supervision. *Children Australia*, 41(4), 265–274.

Palmer-House, K.E. (2008). The Perceived Impact of Strengths-Based Family Worker Training: Workers' Learning That Helped Empower Families. *Families in Society: The Journal of Contemporary Social Services*, 89(3), 428–437.

Pappas, M.L. (2010). Reflection as Self-Assessment. *School Library Monthly*, 27(3), 5–8.

Parton, N., & O'Byrne, P. (2000). *Constructive Social Work: Towards a New Practice*. New York: Palgrave Macmillan.

Patil, T., & Ennis, G.M. (2018). Critically Reflecting on the Australian Association of Social Workers Code of Ethics: Learning From a Social Work Field Placement. *British Journal of Social Work*, 48, 1370–1387.

Pawar, M. (2017). Reflective Learning and Teaching in Social Work Field Education in International Contexts. *British Journal of Social Work*, 47, 198–218.

Rankine, M. (2019). The 'Thinking Aloud' Process: A Way Forward in Social Work Supervision. *Reflective Practice*, 20(1), 97–110.

Rehn, M., & Kalman, H. (2018). Social Work Students' Reflections on Challenges During Field Education. *Journal of Social Work*, 18(4), 451–467.

Robert, J., Piemonte, N., & Truten, J. (2018). The Reflective Scribe: Encouraging Critical Self-Reflection and Professional Development in Pre-Health Education. *Journal of Medical Humanities*, 39, 447–454.

Rosen, D., McCall, J., & Goodkind, S. (2017). Teaching Critical Self-Reflection Through the Lens of Cultural Humility: An Assignment in a Social Work Diversity Course. *Social Work Education*, 36(3), 289–298.

Rosenfeld, R.B. (2014). The Examined Externship is Worth Doing: Critical Self-Reflection and Externship Pedagogy. *Clinical Law Review*, 21, 127–169.

Ross, J.A., & Bruce, C.D. (2007). Teacher Self-Assessment: A Mechanism for Facilitating Professional Growth. *Teaching and Teacher Education*, 23, 146–159.

Rubin, A., & Babbie, E.R. (2008). *Research Methods for Social Work*. Belmont: Thomson Brooks/Cole, Belmont.

Segev, E., & Nadan, Y. (2016). Facing Reality: Context-Oriented Reflection in Social Work Education. *British Journal of Social Work*, 46, 427–443.

Siles-González, J., & Solano-Ruiz, C. (2016). Self-Assessment, Reflection on Practice and Critical Thinking in Nursing Students. *Nurse Education Today*, 45, 132–137.

Steen, J.A., Mann, M., Restivo, N., Mazany, S., & Chapple, R. (2016). Human Rights: Its Meaning and Practice in Social Work Field Setting. *Social Work*, 62(1), 9–17.

Sööt, A., & Viskus, E. (2015). Reflection on Teaching: A Way to Learn From Practice. *Procedia - Social and Behavioral Sciences*, 191, 1941–1946.

Tamm, T. (2010). *Professional Identity and Self-Concept of Estonian Social Workers*. Tampere: University of Tampere.

Toros, K. (2014). Graduate Social Work Students' Approaches and Ways of Thinking in Child Protection Assessment: Case Vignette Reflections from Estonia. *Social Work Education*, 33(7), 890–895.

Toros, K., & LaSala, M.C. (2018). Estonian Child Protection Workers' Assessment Perspectives: The Need for Competence and Confidence. *International Social Work*, 61(1), 93–105.

Toros, K., & LaSala, M.C. (2019). Child Protection Workers' Understanding of the Meaning and Value of Self-Reflection in Estonia. *Reflective Practice: International and Multidisciplinary Perspectives*, 20(2), 266–278.

Toros, K., Tiko, A., Välba, E., & Kangur, P. (2016). *Abivajava lapse ja pere hindamine lastekaitsetöös: lastekaitsetöötajate refleksioone kliendi kaasamisest.* Uuringuraport. Tallinn: Tallinn University.

Trevithick, P. (2008). Revisiting the Knowledge Base of Social Work: A Framework for Practice. British Journal of Social Work, 38, 1212–1237.

Trevithick, P. (2018). The 'Self' and 'Use of Self' in Social Work: A Contribution to the Development of a Coherent Theoretical Framework. *British Journal of Social Work*, 48, 1836–1854.

Urdang, E. (2010). Awareness of Self—A Critical Tool. *Social Work Education*, 29, 523–538.

Välba, E., Toros, K., & Tiko, A. (2017). Family Engagement Within the Context of Assessment in Child Protection Practice: The Case of Estonia. *Child & Family Social Work*, 22(4), 1506–1514.

Yan, Z.Y., & Brown, G.T.L. (2017). A Cyclical Self-Assessment Process: Towards a Model of How Students Engage in Self-Assessment. *Assessment & Evaluation in Higher Education*, 42(8), 1247–1262.

Yip, K-S. (2006). Self-Reflection in Reflective Practice: A Note of Caution. *British Journal of Social Work*, 36, 777–788.

Yorke, J., Grant, S., & Csiernik, R. (2016). Horses and Baseball: Social Work's Cultivation of One's 'Third Eye'. *Social Work Education*, 35(7), 845–855.

Wang, Y., & Chui, E. (2016). An Exploratory Path Model of Social Work Students' Satisfaction with Field Education Experience in China. *Social Work*, 40(3), 135–145.

Wilkins, D., Forrester, D., & Grant, L. (2017). What Happens in Child and Family Social Work Supervision? *Child and Family Social Work*, 22, 942–951.

20

Fieldwork Education in Social Work in Italy

Annamaria Campanini, Marilena Dellavalle, and Giovanni Cellini

There is universal consensus in the literature that fieldwork education—as a learning experience mediated by theoretical knowledge—is a key curriculum component in social work programmes (Rehn & Kalman, 2016; Domakin, 2015; Gursansky & Le Sueur, 2012).

In Italy, as elsewhere, it is considered crucial to providing an education that can meet the social work profession's complex needs with a curriculum combining the scientific–cultural component with the methodological, deontological, and technical aspects in a virtuous circuit in which theory informs practice, which, in turn, informs theory (Tognetti Bordogna, 2015a; Raineri, 2015; Dellavalle, 2011). The underlying idea is that fieldwork instruction cannot be viewed as mere practice but as a way of learning from experience that becomes truly educational only if it sparks a process in which it is reflected on and internalised by the learner. This process can build skills in dealing with imperfectly defined real-life challenges subject to a panoply of cultural, social, relational, and organisational dynamics. It, thus, seeks to train professionals who not only know what to do in an immediate, practical sense but also know how to interpret, analyse, understand, and assess in order to provide clients with qualified support.

Fieldwork education has always been a part of the social work curriculum in Italy, ever since the country's very first schools for social workers were set up in the late 1920s. Over time, it has become an essential part of instruction, drawing on teaching methods and tools that assist students at the individual and group level to prepare for the profession, the daily life of the agencies and their organisation, and the cases they are called upon to handle. Theory and practice are, thus, seen as the twin pillars of a solid professional education.

Though it is true that work is still under way on ensuring the widespread use of active, interdisciplinary teaching methods that educate for competences as called for by the Bologna Process (Frost, Höjer, & Campanini, 2013), it cannot be denied that there has been an increasing awareness of the importance of field education at the university level, attracting interest whenever social work programmes are planned. The general opinion appears to be that field education should be organised in such a way as to provide students with the roadmaps and repertoires of knowledge that will enable them to come to grips with all of the changing, unusual, and often unpredictable circumstances that social work can throw their way (Fazzi, 2015).

This chapter will provide an overview of the state of the art of field education in Italy's current university system on the basis of a review of the literature, the findings of recent empirical

 DOI: 10.4324/9781032164946-25

research, and analysis of information provided on the websites of 37 social work degree programmes now offered at Italian universities. The differences between these programmes will also be discussed.

We will focus on a number of key aspects:

a. The recognition of field education as an instructional method and its visibility.
b. The teaching methods and tools used to build skills bridging theory and practice in different degree programmes.
c. The need to supervise the learning process during field education, thus, guaranteeing that the field experience adheres to shared educational goals at all times.
d. The relationship between the university and the world of the agencies where the social work profession operates. In this connection, the chapter will present several innovative initiatives involving new areas of action where social work's potential can come to fruition.

The Background for Field Education in Italy

Though social workers have been part of the Italian scene since the 1920s, the government first recognised social work as a profession in 1987, with legislation that also mandated university training for practitioners. Before that time, social workers were prepared for the profession in a system of predominantly private schools which, though lacking in official standing, were, nevertheless, able to develop and implement highly innovative teaching methods based on interdisciplinarity, student activation, and, above all, a blend of academic and experiential learning that was to become a feature of programme design worldwide (Fargion, 2009, p. 272). Field education was an essential part of these schools' approach well before it gained ground in universities.

The social work profession is regulated by a law dating to 1993; to practice in the profession, it is necessary to sit the national qualifying examination—open to degree holders only—and be listed in the Professional Register of Social Workers. Since 2001, university education has consisted of 3-year first cycle degree and two-year second cycle degree programmes covered by legislation that establishes the essential coordinates within which each university can independently develop its own curriculum. This has led to a certain diversification in programmes across the country.

Italian universities' involvement in social work education is to be valued chiefly for the positive effects it has had over time (Facchini & Tonon Giraldo, 2010, pp. 32–33): graduates find that their degree increases their employability, the social work disciplines have emerged from their former invisibility and gained academic recognition, and there are more opportunities for funding research which has boosted the scientific standing of theoretical work in the field and provided it with a larger audience. However, the field's scientific development continues to be held back by the fact that the Italian university system regards it as a subdiscipline of general sociology. Consequently, there are no departments of social work as there are in other European countries. This makes it difficult for specialists in the area to advance in their academic careers.

For many years, university social work programmes in Italy were marked by the distrust, if not, indeed, disdain, for the knowledge underlying the skills of application that Schön (1983) describes as 'an ambiguous, secondary kind of knowledge' (ivi, p. 28). Field education would seem to be the aspect that struggled most to assert its legitimacy, as witnessed by the fact that the number of hours that the private schools had devoted to it dropped sharply when social work training was transferred to the universities.

Currently, each degree programme requires students to complete a minimum of 18 credits, corresponding to 450 hours of field education, for the first-cycle degree, and 10 credits or 250 hours for the second-cycle degree. Each Italian university has set up its own organisation for this purpose. This has led to significant differences, some of which will be discussed later. In any case, the number of credits envisaged for field instruction does not seem to be entirely sufficient to meet learning outcomes, a problem which should be addressed as part of a thorough rethinking of the conditions, whereby the quality of university education can be improved. The issue has sparked considerable debate, especially after the National Association of Social Workers proposed that first-cycle degree programmes be extended from 3 to 5 years, but no consensus has yet been reached.

One area where Italian social work scholars are in agreement, and which informs many of the country's university programmes, is the idea that field education should be viewed in terms of instruction designed to activate the student and that puts the emphasis on personal experience, the setting where learning takes place, and forging links with theoretical knowledge.

The intent, here, is to instil an openness to reflection-in-action (Schön, 1983; Sicora, 2019), whereby field instruction becomes an educational tool precisely because it provides students with the skills needed to understand how theory can illuminate practice, and vice versa, and to grasp the complexity and interdependence of the problems encountered by practitioners.

For this reason, it is believed that passing a period of time at an agency, rich in stimuli as it may be, is not in itself sufficient as an opportunity to learn. What is needed is an approach that has been called 'dual mentoring' (Neve, 1995), which encourages students to adopt different levels of engagement and distancing as regards their daily work and personal experiences. In the field placement, such mentoring is provided by the in-agency supervisor who assists students in getting their bearings in the world of practice and provides them with support in this direct experience, as well as with the ethical, relational, and emotional content of social work practice. At the university, mentoring takes a variety of forms, including workshops conducted by social work faculty members and practitioners who help students interpret practice in the light of theory.

Challenging though it is, shuttling between theory and practice is essential in social work (Payne, 2014). It is an ability that must be developed at the outset of basic training and maintained throughout life to avoid drifting into professional stasis.

Integrating theoretical knowledge and the realities of practice is not something students can do on their own. It must be promoted and overseen by the university. The vital links between what emerges from first-hand experience and disciplinary knowledge—and which serve to interpret and guide action—cannot, in fact, be found *sic et simpliciter* by the student. To access these connections and visualise them, students must not only learn to find them—given that they are not immediately apparent—but also to drill down into what they mean through reflexivity and an openness to new information that can only be gained through organised mentoring and faculty involvement in reviewing the placement experience (Dellavalle, 2011).

The dual mentoring approach taken in a number of field education programmes (including those at the universities of Bologna, Genova, Torino, Milano-Bicocca, Roma Tre, Siena, and Venezia) apply a variety of methods:

- Supporting and monitoring each student's progress to ensure to the greatest possible extent that the work done during the placement is consistent with its intended learning outcomes, and prompt action can be taken if problems arise in the relationship with the supervisor or if the student is involved in activities that serve no educational purpose. This function is performed by the tutor, a social worker with extensive field experience who works together with the university faculty and liaises between them and the agencies.

- Guiding students in reviewing their placement experience in group workshops focusing on the methodological, ethical, relational, and emotional lessons learned during fieldwork (Mantovani, 2018) and helping students see the links between their experience and the interdisciplinary theoretical knowledge gained in the classroom.

The dual mentoring approach to field education calls for a close-knit relationship between agencies, the professional community, and the university. This relationship can be challenging, but it is here that the interdependence between theory and practice comes to life: this approach can trigger circular processes producing interchanges that are not only good for students but from which the agencies, practitioners and educational programmes can also draw mutual advantages (Fazzi & Rosignoli, 2016).

Nevertheless, it is not always easy for universities to find reliable field placements. Among the problems that are most frequently mentioned, and which we ourselves have encountered, is the fact that host organisations can be reluctant to accept students or allow social workers to reduce their workload when they take on supervisory duties (Gursansky & Le Sueur 2012) and, thus, be able to devote the necessary time and effort to trainees (Crisp & Hosken, 2016). A further problem is the hectic pace of social workers' jobs, which is partly due to the impact that managerialism has had on increasing the time spent in bureaucratic procedures (Bertotti, 2015).

Practitioners' willingness to take on supervision responsibilities is, thus, of key importance from a generative standpoint. Difficult organisational and operative conditions can reduce this willingness, while, in some cases, specific educational programmes may encourage it (Allegri, Attinà, & Dellavalle, 2020)

Field education can also be a space for experimentation in professional practice in a number of as-yet-unexplored areas in which social work practitioners are not yet found but could make a contribution. The challenge, here, is that of having the flexibility needed to abandon well-trodden paths and recognise that the multi-faceted welfare system offers a wealth of opportunities. Entering new spheres of action through field placements is part of the tradition of the social work schools that preceded today's university programmes: in the 1950s and '60s, trainees at these schools contributed to setting up new social work services dealing with hospitals, schools, and public housing (Dellavalle & Rocca, 2018; Cola, 2015).

Research on Social Work

Starting in the first decade of this century, scholarly research on the social work profession in Italy intensified, addressing such topics as the profession's role in the welfare system, educational programmes, and employment opportunities (Campanini, 2009; Facchini, 2010; Ruggeri, 2013; Tognetti Bordogna, 2015b).

A number of publications have dealt with field education in social work, presenting the findings of empirical studies that have addressed the topic from definitional, historical, and methodological perspectives, with particular attention to aspects such as students' perceptions, the role of supervision, and innovation.

Basic methodological aspects are addressed in Dellavalle (2011), which presents a practice learning model based on a review of the history and development of field education. Of particular interest are the description and analysis of the learning process in field education, which covers such essential topics as supervision, tutorship, and the mentor's role in reviewing the placement experience together with the trainee.

Regarding students' perceptions, interesting findings were reported from a qualitative pilot study that compared students at universities in three countries with three different welfare regimes: Italy, with its family-oriented system, Sweden (social democratic), and England (liberal) (Frost et al., 2013). Students in all three countries attached great importance to field placements and emphasised the need for more time in them. Indeed, the authors note that students see field placements as 'the most unequivocally appreciated element' of their education (ivi, p. 12).

Similar findings were reached in two Italian studies (Facchini, 2010; Tognetti Bordogna (2015b) which dealt inter alia with students' perceptions of social work education as a whole and of field education in particular: students' positive view of field instruction is reflected in their assessment of the entire degree programme.

The literature is unanimous in assigning considerable importance to supervision, as can be seen from a review (Novello & Soregotti, 2018) which predates the findings of a study conducted by Tognetti Bordogna & Decataldo (2018). The latter consisted of interviews with supervisors who worked with students at the University of Milano-Bicocca during academic years 2014–2015 and 2015–2016. One of the issues that was found to be particularly important was that of gatekeeping, which entails a heavy responsibility for supervisors and brings a wide range of abilities into play: field experience, empathy, ability to encourage critical reflection, and the capacity for innovation. Moreover, the supervisor has a vital role in 'showing' the organisation to students, enabling them to get to know it from the inside.

An 'ideal type' of the good supervisor—not a gatekeeper to the profession, but a motivated professional who encourages students to raise questions and welcomes exchanges of ideas and improvement—is described by Fazzi & Rosignoli (2012). Another topic of considerable interest for supervision is that of the 'dual learning process', so called because both supervisor and trainee learn from the experience. This was also addressed by Fazzi & Rosignoli (2016) in a later work, viz., a study carried out at the University of Trento, whose findings shed light on dual learning's importance in enabling supervisors to take the student's perspective, providing them with an opportunity for professional growth and increased job satisfaction.

Field education can be an area for introducing innovation, but it can also produce innovation.

An example of the first case is provided by Luppi (2019), who presents a project introduced by the social work degree programme at the University of Milano-Bicocca. The project involved social workers—faculty instructors, supervisors, and students—in observing and promoting placements in which the trainee is not under the supervision of a single social worker. Rather, coaching is based more on exchanges with peers, practitioners, students, and clients. In view of the changes now affecting the settings where practitioners work, the new approaches investigated in the project are more effective in introducing students to the challenges of the profession and enabling them to rediscover its community dimension.

In the second case, we refer to innovations that seek to broaden the social work profession's scope. In this connection, Dellavalle and Rocca (2018) present the findings of a study of an experimental project carried out by the Bachelor of Social Work programme at the University of Torino, which organised practice learning placements at third-sector agencies where social workers are not normally part of the staff. Such initiatives could create new opportunities for employment in today's welfare system, which is in the throes of a global crisis. The study's findings bear out the value of the experimental practice-learning project in two main areas. The first is in promoting the social work profession, as the student's work helped disseminate a favourable view of social work and correct misconceptions and, in a few cases, resulted in social workers being hired by the host agencies. Second, the experimental placements were able to stimulate students' ability to learn proactively.

Field Education in Italian Universities. Insights from a Qualitative Survey

Objectives and Method

This section will present the main results of a qualitative survey of the information provided on the websites of the Italian universities offering social work degree programmes.

It should be noted that ministerial orders and the National Agency for the Assessment of Universities and Research Institutes require universities to have degree programme websites, a requirement which has led to the digitalisation of information of the Italian universities' entire educational provision.

The survey's basic objective was to gauge the importance that Italian universities assign to social work field education programmes from the latter's public visibility on the internet, starting from the assumption that high visibility on websites means that these programmes are considered a valuable part of student instruction.

After reviewing the background, we proceeded to identify sources, read their content, and construct an analysis matrix in order extrapolate, analyse, and evaluate data about the general themes of interest to us here.

As regards the sources, the survey chiefly made use of *universitaly.it*, an online portal created by M.U.I.R., the Italian Ministry for Education, Universities and Research, to help students select a university programme. The portal provides details of the educational provision in all Italian universities and features hyperlinks to general information and the website for each degree programme. The survey collected information about field placements in the academic year 2019–2020 from the websites of all 37 social work degree programmes now offered in Italy. This economical research technique was selected for the ease of access it provides to the information needed for our study. In addition, we used the M.U.I.R. *Anagrafe nazionale degli studenti*, i.e., the national Student Records Office website, and *Almalaurea*, a site providing quantitative data about university graduates.

From a methodological standpoint, no sharp distinction can be made between documents that are suitable for quantitative analysis and those which can be dealt with using qualitative methods. Indeed, 'the same type of document can often be analyzed both with quantitative techniques and with qualitative techniques' (Corbetta, 2003, p. 454). Bearing this in mind, the documents retrieved online were chiefly analysed from a qualitative perspective. As the structure and content of the websites differed widely (some sites provided a wealth of details, while others offered very little information), it would have been quite difficult to divide the material into uniform units that could be measured and compared. Nevertheless, it was possible to extrapolate a certain amount of quantitatively useful data: the number of university credits and, thus, the number of placement hours envisaged in each degree programme; the number of years in which field instruction takes place; and the number of students who completed placements.

Qualitative analysis consisted of a close reading and critical scrutiny of the documentary material using the content analysis technique for general issues we considered relevant: ease of access to information about field education, the clarity of the general information about field education provided on the webpage (or pages), the completeness of the information and documents posted, the description of the field education programme's physical structure, the people engaged in it (e.g., the programme director, the academic tutors, and faculty members) and the activities involved (placements and classroom review).

Results and Discussion

The 37 social work degree programmes are offered across Italy in all but two of the country's 20 regions (Basilicata and Valle d'Aosta, two of the three least populous regions). In Rome and

Milan, Italy's largest cities, there are four and two programmes, respectively. Though programme names differ from university to university ('social work', 'social work sciences', 'sciences of social work', etc.), the programme that prepares students to become social work practitioners is identified by a single, specific degree class called social work.

The departments that run the degree programmes also differ among the various universities, though most are in the sociological/social policy disciplines.

Admission to these programmes is not governed by nationwide regulations, as is the case for other allied disciplines such as psychology and education sciences. Consequently, each university can decide independently whether to limit student numbers or introduce admissions exams.

In Italian universities, the open vs. selective admissions debate is still raging and, over the years, has brought major changes in the decisions made by a number of degree programmes. Twenty-four out of the 37 degree programmes have open admissions (64.86%), while 13 (35.13%) use an admissions exam to select a limited number of applicants, which ranges from a maximum of 150 (Roma Tre) to a minimum of 40 (Bolzano). Eight out of the 13 universities that limit student numbers are located in northern Italy.

The number of students accepted (whether through open enrolment or by examination) is particularly important, as it also affects field education. For open-enrolment degree programmes, the number of students is normally greater than for programmes that require an admissions exam. For example, at the University of Torino, which recently re-introduced open enrolment, students now number 340, compared to the limit of 120 when an exam was required. Large numbers of students call for a large number of placement slots and social workers to supervise trainees in the field. The risk is, thus, that it may not be possible to guarantee a good placement for all students, either because there are not enough agencies to host all the trainees, or because the agencies may not be sufficiently staffed to provide the required number of supervisors.

A Closer Look at Field Education

In order to highlight the similarities and differences between programmes, our survey focused on several specific topics extrapolated from the material on the websites: how field instruction is organised, the people involved with the students, admission procedures, how students are assigned to placements, tutorship and monitoring, final assessment, and the relationship between the university and the world of the agencies.

Under current legislation, students attending 3-year degree programmes must complete a total of 180 credits, each equivalent to 25 hours. At one university, however, each field education credit equals 35 hours. While the legislation requires that at least 18 out of the total number of credits be earned in field education, the national average is 19 credits or 475 hours, most of which are spent at the agency hosting the trainee. This figure is slightly below that indicated by Tognetti Bordogna (2015a), who found the national average to be 19.8 in the academic year 2012–2013.

The differences between universities are summarised below in Table 20.1.

This difference is by no means insignificant and brings us back to the debate about the advisability of increasing the number of credits required for field instruction, which could be accomplished by extending the current 3-year degree programme to 5 years, as urged by the National Association of Social Workers.

Unfortunately, the websites provide no information that would enable us to determine the ratio of hours spent at the agencies to hours spent reviewing fieldwork at each university.

In all the degree programmes, field education takes place in at least 2 years, the second and third in the programme. In most cases, the first year of field education is chiefly observational,

Table 20.1 Field Education Credits

Field education credits	*Total hours*	*Number of universities*
18	450–500	26
20–22	500–550	8
24	600	3
18	630	1

and involves fewer hours than the second, participatory year when the students work with increasing levels of independence. A few programmes (only six out of 37) feature a certain amount of introductory field instruction in the programme's first year. Most of the programmes (22 out of 37) provide some idea of how instruction is organised on their websites, though, as usual, the amount and quality of the information varies from site to site. Names and email addresses of the people to be contacted for technical and professional questions are provided, as well as those dealing with administrative matters.

It is not always clear from the websites whether field education is coordinated by a social work practitioner. Some sites state that the coordinator is an expert social worker, in accordance with the nature of practice learning and as called for in the literature. Not all sites give clear information or contact details for the tutor, despite the latter figure's importance (see Section 20.2).

To be admitted to a placement, all degree programmes require an entrance examination in social work and one or more exams in legal or sociological disciplines. Admissions follow a set procedure in which the student is required to submit an application within a specified timeframe. In some cases, a detailed description of the procedure is provided on the website. One degree programme even allows students to apply online using a dedicated platform accessed via the site. Other programmes give only general information about the admissions procedure, with an email address or telephone number to be contacted for the purpose.

The next step, after being admitted, is that of pairing students with the agency where their practice learning placement will be held under the supervision of an agency social worker. The websites indicate placement locations, the most common being social services run by local administrations, health care services (substance abuse and mental health services, hospital,; family planning and women's health centres, etc.), ministries (Justice, Interior), and private social organisations. Some degree programmes offer experimental practice learning arrangements in which the student is placed in an organisation where there are no social workers. Such cases involve what is known as delegated supervision, meaning that the supervisor is a social worker external to the host agency who is designated by the university (Dellavalle & Rocca, 2018).

Current regulations require that agencies hosting placements enter into a formal agreement with the degree programme. In most cases, the university selects the host agency on the basis of a number of variables, including student progress, the student's personal characteristics, and the agency's stated requirements. Over the years, the degree programmes have sought to forge alliances with outside agencies in their local areas in order share their experiences with training and strike a balance between their needs and those of the agencies. Nevertheless, our analysis of websites found situations in which the criteria used by the degree programme to pair trainees and host agencies were not clear, and others—which, according to the information available online, would seem to be in the minority—in which students themselves select a host agency which has an agreement with the university from a list, or even propose that new agencies enter into agreements and accept placements.

Shortly after entering the host agency, the student, supervisor, and tutor draw up a plan for the student's work in the placement and check the progress that has been made so far. This stage is crucial to setting up a feedback loop so that any difficulties encountered by the student at the beginning of the placement can be quickly identified and remedied. Twenty-six out of the 37 websites mention this planning stage.

As regards the goals pursued in the placement, the website pages dealing with field education programmes emphasise the connections between theoretical/methodological instruction and field practice. These connections are evident from the descriptions of mentoring and/or classroom review activities, for which a few websites—the minority—also provide calendars.

The last stage of the placement consists of the final assessment, in which the student's agency supervisor, the university tutor, and the social work faculty members all have a voice. All degree programmes require a written final report. The more complete websites provide guidelines regarding the report's content. The overall grade assigned to the student's field education performance is determined on the basis of the assessments of the written report and the agency placement. Assessment criteria are not indicated on the websites except for a very few cases. Lastly, it should be noted that a minority of the websites provide statistics about the number of students who completed placements.

The number of students who complete field education can be inferred from the number of graduates, given that field education is a mandatory requirement for the degree in social work. The ministerial website *anagrafe.miur.it* provides data on the number of graduates, the percentage of graduates in social work out of the nationwide total, and the breakdown by university and gender. Though these data would merit a secondary quantitative analysis, which is beyond our scope here, it should be noted that Italy's social work graduates in 2017–2018—and, thus, students who completed field education—numbered 2,584 (1,399 females and 185 males), corresponding to 3.97% of all recipients of 3-year degrees. The breakdown by university essentially reflects the distribution of the country's population, as most of the graduates were in the larger and more highly populated areas. The breakdown by gender, showing a marked predominance of women, confirms a trend that has long characterised social work worldwide (Bini et al., 2019).

Transparency and Completeness of Information on Field Education

Turning now to the qualitative analysis, we found that almost all of the degree programme websites enable anyone who habitually uses a computer to access information about field education.

Only four out of the 37 websites fail to provide this information or do so only in the broadest terms. In another five cases, the information is very limited, or the sites give only the contact details of the people in charge of the programme. It may be that these shortcomings arise because information about field education can be accessed only by students and faculty in a restricted area of the website (although this is not indicated in the public areas). This, however, would be at odds with the need to provide information to prospective students who are choosing a university or to undergraduates who wish to change degree programmes—a need which is met by the *universitaly.it* site (our source), which also contains a large amount of open access information and links to degree programmes.

Most of the degree programmes (27 out of 37) have a field education webpage accessed via links on the programme or university website. The level of accessibility, however, varies from site to site. Certain types of information are readily viewed in most cases, e.g., information about general programme content, scheduling, and contacts. Other types are not prominently displayed and can be found only after prolonged searching through the websites' pages.

In general, the survey found that the online information about field education provided by the 37 social work degree programmes varies widely. This reflects the differences, in some cases very pronounced, in how field instruction is organised and delivered.

One of the first differences is in the quantity of information available. A minority of the programmes have a single webpage summarising all of the information provided about field education without links to other content. On other sites, the homepage features one or more links to specific topics, some of which are administrative in nature (application forms and procedures, etc.), while others deal with the content and stages of instruction, planning, requirements for the final report, and so forth. As regards the latter information, e.g., the guidelines for planning and the final report, the situation is, once again, highly diversified, with sites that offer an abundance of material and others with very little. The quality of the information is also very uneven: though couched in readily understandable language on all sites, the information is partial in some cases and highly detailed in others, with references to the regulatory framework, procedures, and technical and professional aspects. In general, we can say that the Web editors use a concise written form which meets students' access needs.

A Close Look at Two Cases

In the highly variegated picture, we have sketched so far, the social work degree programmes at the universities of Torino and Milano-Bicocca are of particular interest. In both cases, the authors of this chapter gained direct experience as field education coordinators, tutors, and instructors. Both programmes have devoted considerable attention to their websites, though their form and content differ. While online content is a representation of 'reality' rather than reality itself, it is, nevertheless, clear that this attention shown to communicating with students via the internet—now an essential and indispensable channel—indicates a significant investment in field learning and its key role in the learning process.

The University of Torino social work degree programme has a webpage specifically for field education, with thematic hyperlinks to general information and to sections about the various stages involved. There are also links to areas on tutors, supervisors, agency contacts, a bulletin board, and the field education office's regularly updated Facebook page. In addition to general information, names and contact data for the programme directors and coordinators, and information is provided about admissions (enrolment and deadlines) and programme regulations. There is also a guide to writing the final report. For all stages of field education, specific pages provide details about procedures and links to forms. In the 'News' section, students can view timetables for activities held at the university: case review workshops, mentoring groups, workshops with faculty members, and classroom meetings with supervisors and students. Examination timetables are also posted, as well as final assessments and grades. The webpage has shown itself to be a useful tool for communication about how field instruction starts, is conducted, and concludes. It cannot replace the programme's training, teaching, and mentoring activities, which necessarily take place face to face through workshops, individual meetings with the tutor, and group work.

The website for the University of Milano-Bicocca social work degree programme has a link to the field education webpage, which offers concise general information. From this page, links provide access to a large variety of useful information and content, including the degree programme regulations which include sections on field education and how it is organised. Particular attention is devoted to the classroom lessons dealing with field education. Teaching materials are available on an e-learning platform that can be accessed only by students, though a list of the materials can be viewed. Reports on the organisation and activities of the field education office for the academic years 2013–2014 through 2017–2018 are open access. These documents show that the office has a clearly defined organisational structure, as we saw to be the case for its counterpart in Torino. As a major goal is to ensure that there is a sufficient number of host agencies for placements, there are ongoing efforts to recruit new agencies who are willing to enter into agreements with the degree programme and extend the scope of existing agreements. Lastly, a highly detailed document accessed from the homepage provides information on supervisors' final assessment. As for the University of Torino degree programme, it can be seen that close attention is given to the role of the supervisor and the educational alliance between agencies and the university.

Conclusions

We will now pass to an overall evaluation of our findings on the basis of the several key aspects, viz., the recognition of field education as an instructional method and its visibility, the teaching methods and tools used to build skills bridging theory and practice in different degree programmes, and the need to monitor and supervise the learning process, thus, guaranteeing that the field experience adheres to shared educational goals at all times.

First, the fact that field education is prominently presented on the degree programme websites enables us to conclude that its role as an instructional method is recognised.

We can also say that the variety found in the websites can be seen as an advantage, as excessive uniformity can denote rigid adherence to preconceptions, over-standardisation, and lack of independence. Nevertheless, it must also be recognised that the individual universities' independence in how they communicate on the Web is a problem, especially in cases where the lack of minimum requirements results in severely inadequate information or no information at all. Unfortunately, a few such cases exist among the 37 surveyed websites. Situations of this kind can create uncertainties about the educational programme or make it impossible to gain a clear understanding of it; as a result, there is a risk that the student will not be supported. In addition, too much diversification may translate into disparities between students in different degree programmes: the 'privileged' who have better tools and a broader range of content at their disposal, and the 'penalised' who have access only to limited information and poorer materials. In this connection, more thought should be devoted to the issue of transparency in general because greater transparency in communication between the university and students also means being better informed and having more opportunities to access knowledge.

Among their other purposes, as we have seen, the field education offices' websites serve as a vehicle for carrying out administrative tasks. This is another area where computer-mediated communication has demonstrated its usefulness to everyone involved in practice learning, from the programme coordinators and staff, to students, tutors, supervisors, and instructors.

As regards the content of the webpages dealing with educational methods, dual mentoring is a frequent theme in the presentations of field education programmes and the descriptions of the stages of the learning process. The roles of the university, the supervisor, and the student trainee are explained or otherwise clear from the posted documentation, and the picture, thus, conveyed of these roles is consistent with the findings of the literature (Dellavalle, 2011).

Not all of the websites provide information about tutors, though significant differences are, nevertheless, apparent: 13 websites have no specific information on the tutors, while the remaining 24 indicate the tutors' functions either directly on the webpages or through links to regulations and student guides.

All the websites provide information, though not always in detail, about the provision for classroom review of the placement experience, emphasising how practice and theory influence each other. Less attention, as we have seen, is paid to providing full information on assessment criteria and methods.

As for how students and agencies are paired for placements, there are significant disparities in the weight assigned to the degree programme's opinion in selecting the host. At times, someone at the agency may have more voice in choosing the students to be hosted, while the cases in which the students themselves choose the agency raise questions about the support provided to trainees by the university. In other words, there may be a risk that the university does not devote sufficient attention to assessing the agency's suitability as a host, which can have negative consequences for the student's placement experience.

The theme of the relationship between the university and the world of the agencies where the social work profession operates is neglected: the websites mainly indicate the agencies that are willing to host placements. In some cases, the websites indicate that placements are hosted in the public, private, and third sectors. Only the University of Torino website provided information on the objectives and methods of the experimental practice-learning programme in the posted 'Regulations' on the site.

Despite the many differences that were found, we can say, on the whole, that the degree programmes devote considerable attention to internet communication tools. Though this has undeniably positive aspects, it raises questions about the risks of excessive reliance on Web communication, which can depersonalise the interchanges between educators and students and, thus, eliminate the relational dimension, essential though it is. The actors involved in the placement experience must not withdraw from the direct interpersonal relationship, unmediated by technical aids. More in general, distance learning tools can be useful in exceptional or well circumscribed situations, but they cannot replace the relationship with the tutor, individual and group activities, and workshops in maintaining the links between theory and practice.

We will now turn to what is one of the greatest challenges facing Italian social work education, that of meeting the new international requirements.

At the European level, the Committee of Ministers issued a Recommendation to Member States in 2001 which confirmed the value of practice learning in providing professional training during education programmes. The preamble to the Recommendation recognises 'that the nature of professional social work demands the highest level of responsibility in decision-making and mature judgement on the part of social workers and that consistently high standards of competence, therefore, require appropriate education and professional training' (Rec. 2001/1). Later in the document, it is emphasised that there is a need to: 'provide a renewed European framework of principles for the effective education, training, practice and working conditions of social workers' (ivi).

Internationally, the Global Standards for Social Work Education and Training adopted at the I.A.S.S.W. and I.F.S.W. General Assemblies in Adelaide in 2004 state that field education must be an integral part of the programme, and consequently, adequate and appropriate resources should be made available for this purpose. The standards also state that field education should be sufficient in duration and complexity of tasks and learning opportunities to ensure that students are prepared for professional practice. They, thus, stress the need for planned coordination and links between the school and the agency/field placement setting.

The standards also offer a series of considerations about the need to provide supervisors and tutors with an adequate range of expertise and have appropriate qualifications as determined by the development status of the social work profession in the country concerned, as well as the need to provide for the continuing professional development of such staff.

The standards also go so far as to recommend that supervisors have opportunities to participate in planning the programme, particularly as regards field education.

Moreover, supervisors should be provided with a field instruction manual that details its procedures, assessment standards or criteria, and expectations. It is also recommended that there be a partnership between the educational institution, the agency, and service users in decision-making regarding field education and the evaluation of student's fieldwork performance. These are all very specific recommendations that provide clear guidelines for planning and organising the placement experience, which is universally considered a fundamental aspect of social work education.

These global standards are currently being reviewed and updated, and the drafts now being circulated call for field education to account for at least 25% of all instruction activities and for service users to be involved in making decisions about training students and assessing their abilities.

For the Italian social work system, then, the challenge is how to implement these standards and make the county's education programmes more effective and uniform.

We will conclude this chapter with a few remarks on avenues for future research.

The findings illustrated in the preceding pages point to the need for further thought about the relationship that agencies and the professional community have with the university. The Web is a (potentially) valuable communication tool not only for students but also for supervisors and staff at the host agency. The question that could be addressed by an empirical study is whether the professional community outside the academic world considers web-based communication to be effective and useful. In general, it can be said that the internet is a potential means of bringing together these two worlds—that of the university and that of the agencies and their practitioners. The information that degree programmes put on the Web can enable social work practitioners who act as field education supervisors or are interested in doing so to gain a better understanding of the content and organisation of the programme followed by their current or potential mentees. This is an aspect of no small importance for practitioners who received their training many years ago or in different settings.

Future research could also profitably address how the placement experience has changed in the light of the problems arising from the COVID-19 pandemic. Universities have had to develop new methods for regular teaching, and some of them have experimented with offering field instruction remotely, by agreement with agencies and practitioners. Studies that are now being planned in this connection could provide a basis for evaluating online methods and their potential for enriching field education under normal circumstances as well as in emergencies like COVID-19.

References

Allegri, E., Attinà, A. Dellavalle, M. (2020). La circolarità del rapporto tra teoria e pratica nel Servizio sociale. *Prospettive Sociali e Sanitarie*, 2, 18–20. https://prospettivesocialiesanitarie.it/cerca.php?aut=A.%20Attin%C3%A0&cerca=A.%20Attin%C3%A0

Bertotti, T. (2015). Resources reduction and welfare changes: Tensions between social workers and organisations. The Italian case in child protection services. *European Journal of Social Work*, https://doi.org/10.1080/13691457.2015.1030363

Bini, E., Vezzosi, E. Togni, C., Malatesta, D., Dellavalle, M., Ramos-Feijóo, C., & Waaldijk, B. (2019). Gender and social work. New historical studies and interpretations. *Contemporanea, Rivista di storia dell'800 e del '900*, XXII(2), 269–304, DOI: 10.1409/93532

Campanini, A. (2009). *Scenari di welfare e formazione al servizio sociale in un'Europa che cambia.* Milano: UNICOPLI.

Cola, P. (2015). Tirocinio sperimentale e supervisione delegata. In M. Tognetti Bordogna (Ed.), *Tirocinio come pratica situata* (pp. 176–184). Milan: FrancoAngeli.

Corbetta, P. (2003). *La ricerca sociale: metodologia e tecniche.* Bologna: Il Mulino.

Crisp, B. R. & Hosken, N. (2016). A fundamental rethink of practice learning in social work education. *Social Work Education, 35*(5), 506–517. DOI: 10.1080/02615479.2016.1175422

Dellavalle, M. (2011). *Il tirocinio nella formazione al servizio sociale: Un modello di apprendimento dall'esperienza.* Rome: Carocci.

Dellavalle, M., & Rocca, V. (2018). Experimenting with professional innovation through practice learning. *European Journal of Social Work*, 303–314. DOI: 10.1080/13691457.2018.1513396

Domakin, A. (2015). *The importance of practice learning in social work: Do we practice what we preach? Social Work Education*, 34(4), 399–413. DOI: 10.1080/02615479.2015.1026251

Facchini, C. (2010). *Tra impegno e professione: Gli assistenti sociali come soggetti del welfare*. Bologna: Il Mulino.

Facchini, C., & Tonon Giraldo, S. (2010). La formazione degli assistenti sociali: motivazioni, percorsi, valutazioni, in Facchini C. (ed.). *Tra impegno e professione. Gli assistenti sociali come soggetti del welfare*. Bologna: Il Mulino.

Fargion, S. (2009). *Formazione sul campo. Percorsi di crescita nella professione nel dialogo tra saperi esperienziali e saperi teorici*, in Campanini, A. (Ed.) *Scenari di welfare e formazione al servizio sociale in un 'Europa che cambia*. (pp. 271-294). Milan: Unicopli.

Fazzi, L. (2015). Are we educating creative professionals? The results of some experiments on the education of social work students in Italy. *Social Work Education*, 89–99. https://doi.org/10.1080/02615479.2015.1120716

Fazzi, L., & Rosignoli, A. (2012). *Guida per i supervisori di tirocinio per il servizio sociale*. Milan: FrancoAngeli.

Fazzi, L., & Rosignoli, A. (2016). Reversing the perspective: When the supervisors learn from their trainees. *The British Journal of Social Work*, *46*(1), 204–221. https://doi.org/10.1093/bjsw/bcu112

Frost, E., Höjer, S., & Campanini, A. (2013). Readiness for practice: Social work students' perspectives in England, Italy, and Sweden. *European Journal of Social Work*, *16*(3), 327–343.

Luppi, M. (Ed.) (2019). *Working papers Secondo Welfare—Innovare il tirocinio. La formazione di base degli assistenti sociali di fronte a nuovi bisogni e nuove politiche*. Torino: Centro Einaudi. https://www.centroeinaudi.it/percorsi-di-secondo-welfare/working-papers/9550-innovare-il-tirocinio-la-formazione-di-base-degli-assistenti-sociali-di-fronte-a-nuovi-bisogni-e-nuove-politiche.html. Accessed 24 July 2020.

Gursansky, D., & Le Sueur, E. (2012). Conceptualizing field education in the twenty-first century: Contradictions, challenges and opportunities. *Social Work Education*, *31*(7), 914–931. DOI: 10.1080/02615479.2011.595784

Novello, N., & Soregotti, C. (2018). *I supervisori di tirocinio nella letteratura internazionale*, in M. Tognetti Bordogna & A. Decataldo (Eds.), *Guido io. Ricerca sulla supervisione nei Corsi di Laurea in Servizio Sociale. Il caso di Milano-Bicocca* (pp. 13–33). Milan: FrancoAngeli.

Mantovani, F. (2018). *Laboratorio di guida al tirocinio in servizio sociale: Formazione, conoscenza di sé e competenze professionali*. Milan: FrancoAngeli.

Neve, E. (1995), L'attuazione del tirocinio: il doppio accompagnamento dello studente, in Bisleri C., et al., *La supervisione. Orientamenti ed esperienze di guida dei tirocini professionali*. Milan: FrancoAngeli, 125–141.

Payne, M. (2014). *Modern social work theory* (4 edn.). New York: Palgrave MacMillan.

Raineri, M. L. (2015). *Tirocini e stage di servizio sociale*. Trento: Erikson.

Rehn, M., & Kalman, H. (2016, June). Social work students' reflections on challenges during field education. *Journal of Social Work*, 12, 1–17. https://doi.org/10.1177/1468017316654362

Ruggeri, F. (Ed.) (2013) *Stato sociale, assistenza, cittadinanza. Sulla centralità del servizio sociale*. Milan: FrancoAngeli.

Schön, D. A. (1983). *The reflective practitioner. How professionals think in action*. New York: Basic Books.

Sicora, A. (2019). Reflective practice and learning from mistakes in social work student placement. *Social Work Education*, 38, 63–74. https://doi.org/10.1080/02615479.2018.1508567

Tognetti Bordogna, M. (2015a). *Il tirocinio come pratica situata: Le esperienze dei Corsi di Laurea in Servizio Sociale*. Milan: FrancoAngeli.

Tognetti Bordogna, M. (2015b). *Voglio fare l'assistente sociale: Formazione e occupazione dei laureati in servizio sociale in tempi di crisi e discontinuità*. Milan: FrancoAngeli.

Tognetti Bordogna, M., & Decataldo, A. (2018). *Guido io: Ricerca sulla supervisione nei corsi di laurea in servizio sociale: il caso di Milano-Bicocca*. Milan: FrancoAngeli.

Websites

Almalaurea. Un ponte fra Università e mondo del lavoro e delle professioni. https://www.almalaurea.it/

Anagrafe nazionale degli studenti. https://anagrafe.miur.it/index.php

I.A.S.S.W. (International Association Schools of Social Work). https://www.iassw-aiets.org/it/

I.F.S.W. (International Federation of Social Work). https://www.ifsw.org/

Universitaly. L'Università italiana a portata di click. https://www.universitaly.it/

21

A Critical Review of Practice Education in England

Graham Ixer, Mary Baginsky, and Jill Manthorpe

Most programmes of professional education and training across the globe have an element of practice learning. Whether the profession is medicine, nursing, law, teaching, or social work, practice learning is seen as a core element. Depending on the profession and country, these periods of practice learning that take place outside of the university or educational provider are known by various terms such as practice education, field education, or the practicum. It is the time when students (sometimes referred to as trainees) are expected to understand how knowledge informs their practice, and vice versa, and how theory links with practice. It is also a time when, ideally, they are supported by an experienced practitioner, their practice teacher, and colleagues.

Social work education in England has had a long tradition of structured and organised teaching and assessment of students whilst learning their craft in a practice environment. However, despite many positive aspects, there have also been many problems caused by constant change impacting on its development. In this chapter, we discuss two main changes: the first, the regulation of practice education and the second, the expansion of employment led routes, moving away from traditional programmes in universities and other higher education providers. It is unclear whether these changes bring about the outcomes expected, and research is currently ongoing.

Regulation

While English social university-based training started in the city of Birmingham in 1908, the regulation of social work education was not introduced until 1962. This was followed by the establishment of the Central Council for Education and Training in Social Work (C.C.E.T.S.W.) in 1970, the first statutory U.K. regulator for social work education (see Ixer, 2016). Since then, several government regulators have been given responsibility for the legal functions of social work education. C.C.E.T.S.W. lasted from 1970–2001 and was replaced by four devolved bodies. For England, this was the General Social Care Council (G.S.C.C.); for Wales, the Care Council for Wales; for Northern Ireland, The Northern Ireland Care Council; and for Scotland, The Scottish Social Services Council. These bodies jointly produced one U.K. set of codes for all social care workers and began to establish registration for all social workers, but devolution

DOI: 10.4324/9781032164946-26

has a significant impact in this context and others. In England, unlike the other countries, two government departments (Department for Education and Department of Health and Social Care) have been involved in regulation. This has sometimes led to less than coherent messages to the field. In part, as a result of the austerity measures that followed the financial crisis of 2008, but also reflecting a crisis of confidence in social work discussed later in this chapter, the Coalition Government closed the G.S.C.C. in 2012 and passed its functions to the Health and Care Professions Council (H.C.P.C.). Unlike England, the other U.K. bodies continued as national regulators and continue to have wider social care workforce responsibilities. It was not until 2019 that a new sector-specific body was established and H.C.P.C. functions transferred to Social Work England (S.W.E.). Because of the complexities of regulation in England, the main regulatory changes are summarised in a chronology as an appendix.

There are various routes to social work qualification in England, including post-graduate or undergraduate and employer-led, including apprenticeships. Despite many organisational and policy changes in England affecting social work education, one tenet of placement or practice experience is common, whatever the route to social work qualification. This is the importance attached to offering students varied and, where possible, contrasting placement experiences. Traditionally, for those on an undergraduate or post-graduate route, a first placement has often been in a voluntary sector or not-for-profit organisation, followed by a placement in a statutory social work organisation. The latter is usually in a local authority or the National Health Service (N.H.S.), although there has been some flexibility around accepting placements in organisations fulfilling or supporting statutory functions, such as fostering agencies. However, over the years, statutory placements have significantly reduced because local authorities are not required to offer placements and have often argued that they lack the resources to take students. S.W.E. has now directed that all students must have at least one statutory placement and defines this as providing 'the legal functions students need to experience across adult and children's services' that can be accessed. What is different now is that its guidance defines what legal functions mean (S.W.E., 2019a).

Steps to formalising Practice Education in England

Prior to 1970, the social work qualification consisted of a Letter of Recognition issued by the Home Office (Central Government), which acknowledged person-specific training. Under C.C.E.T.S.W., two new qualifications emerged: the Certificate of Qualification in Social Work (C.Q.S.W.) followed by the Certificate in Social Services (C.S.S.). The latter was mainly intended for residential childcare for which individuals trained whilst they worked, while the C.Q.S.W. was a 2-year university-based course with practice placements.

C.C.E.T.S.W. acknowledged both the importance of learning in practice and the centrality of the practice educator role in supporting students' learning, as well as in assessing them against minimum competence standards. Much later, C.C.E.T.S.W. announced its mandate for a 3-year degree unifying all other qualifications into one (1985). This was known as 'Paper 30 – the Diploma in Social Work', which was implemented 4 years later (C.C.E.T.S.W., 1989). C.C.E.T.S.W. also began to be more prescriptive about requirements and inputs in the length of placements. Courses were required to provide a minimum of 200 placement days normally spread over two placement periods. These were compulsory and could not be substituted by, for example, accredited prior learning. Because social work is delivered in many settings, placements could include schools, hospitals, prisons, voluntary and community projects, and statutory services. Students were also required, for the first time, to reflect on their practice.

The Diploma in Social Work was designed to help address the placement supply problem. Educational providers were required to work in partnership with employers to ensure an agreed workforce analysis that included resources available for placements. It was intended that such partnerships would plan and agree to placement numbers in advance based on how many social work graduates were needed in that area. The success of these partnerships relied upon the effectiveness of relationships between employers and education providers. However, strategic planning was limited, and most local authorities had neither the resources nor skills to collate accurate data to ensure effective strategic workforce planning.

Meanwhile, a Practice Teaching Award was introduced as part of a post-qualifying national programme; for the first time, recognition was given to the role and function of the practice educator who was responsible for training and assessment.

Practice Education Policy Shifts Since 2000

In 2003, the government attempted to raise the quality and profile of social work education by making it an all-graduate profession, while retaining the same placement requirements as the Diploma in Social Work. The deficits around workforce planning remained, so it was difficult to identify how many social workers were needed without reliable workforce data, which was largely absent. In essence, education providers (universities in the main) recruited into their programmes, some of them expanding their intake considerably, without linking this number to local workforce need and, in particular, placement capacity. Possibly as a result of this, several employers complained that students were not getting the right placement experience and, therefore, were being inadequately prepared (Baginsky et al., 2010). In part, this was because there was over-recruitment of students and an under supply of good quality placements.

Social work education often becomes the scapegoat for other failures in the social work system. This was evident in the proceedings of the government's Children Select Committee on Social Work (2009) where there was significant criticism of the standards of entry into social work education but also a concern at the failure of employers and higher education to work in partnership. Then, as presently (2020), there was high turnover amongst social workers, leading to high vacancy levels. Newly qualified social workers were expected to bridge the gap, assuming responsibility for some cases that should have been held by experienced practitioners. This distorted the narrative of social work at that time, and some of it remains today.

The government established a Social Work Task Force (S.W.T.F.) in late 2008. This met for the first time in February 2009. It came in the wake of the death of 'Baby Peter Connolly' and the subsequent Serious Case Review (S.C.R.) and trial (see Jones, 2014). Peter Connolly had been murdered by his mother and two others, and the case was a tipping point in the way the public and politicians viewed the profession of social work. The S.C.R. found that his death could have been prevented and that the practice of all agencies involved with the family had been inadequate.

Although the impetus for the S.W.T.F. arose in children's services, its remit covered social workers in any setting, as did its recommendations (S.W.T.F., 2009). The Social Work Reform Board (S.W.R.B.) was subsequently charged with implementing the task force's recommendations (S.W.R.B., 2012). Based on a S.W.T.F. recommendation, an optional 30 days of practical skills training, known as 'Skills Days', were introduced. These skills days were part of the original 200 days of placements. They were intended to address concerns from employers that university courses were too academic and, as a result, many social workers were graduating without the necessary skill set for the specific group with whom they were to work (Baginsky et al., 2010). What they did not do was address the situations into which newly qualified social workers were placed and had to manage, which were leading to many of the accusations of the inadequacy of their preparation. Later, the Practice Teacher Award was replaced by Practice Educator Professional Standards (P.E.P.S.), which set out the minimum requirements for practice educators in a two-stage process (British Association of Social Workers, 2019), but as they were neither enforced nor required by the regulator, they remained helpful good practice guidance.

Teaching Partnerships, Employer-led Routes and Their Implications for Practice Education

The pressure under which English social work departments operate, including high caseloads and high staff turnover, impacts on the numbers of placements available in the right places and when needed, as well as the relevant learning opportunities. In turn, these affect the quality of outcomes that can be expected and achieved. As the S.W.T.F. pointed out, responsibility is shared by employers as well as education providers. The supply of placements tied to demand for social workers and the principle of linking workforce need to social work education resurfaced in the Government's Teaching Partnership initiative (Department for Education (D.f.E.), 2019). A teaching partnership brings local employers and education providers together to prepare, plan, monitor, and evaluate the delivery of a social work programme with the aim of improving the quality of teaching, committing to provide placements, and raising the quality of social work applicants. It is reported to have 'stimulated a new level of collaboration' between employers and education providers which led to better relationships at all levels (D.f.E., 2019, p. 5). They provide a mechanism to get details of placements across several authorities and are reporting increases in volume and type of placement because there is agreement on the number of placements and their type. However, these are early days, and there is considerable variation between these partnerships as far as effectiveness is concerned (Baginsky et al., 2018). It remains to be seen how they will fare when they are no longer funded by central government.

More prominent in current social work education in England, and a move that has been of great interest internationally, has been the development of employer-led routes of social work qualifying. This is not new in the English context, as employers, mainly local authorities, have had a long tradition of sponsoring (paying for) selected employees to obtain a professional qualification while guaranteeing their placements. During the 1980s, such secondments accounted for almost half of all social workers who qualified (C.C.E.T.S.W., 1992). However, it was an expensive route, with employers paying university fees on top of salaries. Later financial pressures contributed to the decline of such programmes, although the Open University remains a substantial provider of social work education through its distance learning programme.

The government and local authorities have reversed this decline by introducing and funding new employer-led hybrid routes. 'Step Up to Social Work', 'Frontline', and 'Think Ahead' are post-graduate routes for selected applicants. An undergraduate apprenticeship route has also been introduced. The rise in employer-based routes indicates employers' greater interest in alternative approaches to university-based social work education. For employers, the attraction of employer-based routes is that 'practice' experience is their central component with far less time spent on classroom-based learning.

Step Up, Think Ahead, and Frontline are employer-led routes into social work. Step Up and Frontline for working with children and young people, although the qualification is generic so that graduates can choose to work in other sectors. Think Ahead is for mental health social work. Step Up is based on a partnership between a group of local authorities and an education partner or partners. These routes are designed to attract 'high performing' graduates that might otherwise not have viewed social work as a preferred career and are highly competitive. The government provides a bursary to cover living costs and pays all university fees and expenses.

These are fast-track routes to qualification. Step Up meets the same standards as other routes, which means that, upon successful completion, Step Up trainees are eligible to register as social workers 14 months after embarking on the training instead of the traditional 2 years for postgraduates and 3 years for undergraduates. By contrast Frontline and Think Ahead are run by independent organisations funded by central government. Trainees attend a residential course before working in a training team or 'hub' managed and supervised by an experienced practitioner.

The apprenticeship route is different in being a 3-year undergraduate programme. It meets the same social work standards as all other qualifying programmes, but apprentices stay in their social care employment settings and receive a salary while they train as social workers. In essence, they learn whilst they work. They undertake contrasting practice experiences to supplement their learning. In their last year, they work in a front-line social work team and follow a nationally agreed assessment process.

All four employer-led programmes illustrate how, in England, the traditional model of practice education is changing for both the learner, trainee or student, the practice teacher or mentor role, and, of course, for the employer of both parties.

The Role of the Practice Educator

At local level, traditional social work programmes ensure the quality of practice educators through their own procedures. Each programme must be approved by the regulator, S.W.E., as are the metrics used to measure outputs of learning. S.W.E. explains how programmes become approved but not individual compliance to a particular standard. Programmes self-report compliance to the standard and, unless there is a complaint or reason for the regulator to carry out an inspection, approved programmes have substantial autonomy, despite the calls over the last few decades for greater government oversight. The Professional Standards (P.E.P.s) discussed above are only voluntary (B.A.S.W., 2019). They do not address the standard of practice education but do outline the status, role, and task of the practice educator. So, for example, S.W.E. requires practice educators taking students on final placement to be currently registered social workers (S.W.E., 2019b), acknowledging that some practice experiences may be in settings where there are few registered social workers.

Moving to the individual level, practice educators often have considerable influence over their students' careers (Hackett & Marsland, 1997). Caffrey and Fruin (2019) argue that the role, accountability, and transparency of the practice educator's decision may be largely unchallenged. This could create issues of equality and fairness, especially if the practice educator, for whatever reason, views the student unfavourably and there is limited recourse for the student to challenge. This is because the issue of power is not necessarily shared and lies with the practice educator. This may be inevitable because, unlike the marking of an assignment, which can be scrutinised, usually by two members of teaching staff, the quality of the learning relationship between the practice educator and student is not subject to the same examination and measurement. Externality comes from the scrutiny of each practice educator's report by teaching staff and sometimes by an external examiner and a layperson representing service users or clients. Of course, such reports are the outcome of a comprehensive process based on a learning relationship in which details of discussions are neither recorded verbatim or possibly even acknowledged by the practice educator. They are likely to comment on the presence or absence of social work values of integrity, honesty, and respect, although such details are less commonly mentioned if there is no cause for concern in relation to the student. There are balances to maintain between overburdening the practice educator with a tight prescription of what to assess and enabling them to exercise their own professional judgement whilst hoping that this is done fairly.

It is less easy to address the more systemic challenges, such as the overall findings that certain groups do less well in social work education than others, despite social work being an inclusive profession. Hussain et al. (2007) used the regulator's data for 1995–1998 to show that those from an ethnic minority or who were disabled did less well than others not so defined, which was supported by social-work-specific research from Fairtlough et al. (2014). Reasons for this were complex, and these studies do not always take into account the demographics of practice teachers or teams. However, if such groups do less well than other groups, it opens the possibility of them being treated less favourably in the practice teacher relationship where the power dynamic continues to remain mainly with the practice teacher. Of course, without research on such outcomes, we cannot be sure.

Practice Education within Social Work Debates

Practice education in the English context reflects tensions about the place and form of professional education in social work. Employers who have complained about the disconnect between practice settings and universities, and opted for employer-led training, have sometimes reduced their placement offer to universities. Debates have continued about the purpose of practice education, how it can be quality assured in a fair way, and how new models of employer-led programmes are influencing traditional academic routes. The role of web-based learning and support in practice education remains to be considered in depth and, in the context of the global COVID-19 pandemic, may become a very familiar feature of social work practice education. Social work programmes are beginning to rethink the way they deliver education and question the rationale for such traditional modes of pedagogy.

Learning from England's Experiments: Back to the Employer!

A new world of practice education in England is emerging as a hybrid model integrating previous arrangements within new systems. It broadens ambitions that learning in placement should be about 'learning gain' for both the student or trainee and for the practice educator or team. There may be room to develop such an approach with an emphasis on what students or trainees have gained rather than focus on any deficits. Changing the focus of the conversation to what all parties have gained fits more with the Appreciative Inquiry model (Cooperrider & Whitney 2005). Such an approach switches the emphasis from deficit to asset and takes a more positive and appreciative approach.

Developing a hybrid model of practice education may help to build a consensus about practice education and sustain its effectiveness. It may help to address some of the long-standing inconsistencies in assessment, the criticisms of unfairness and bias, and the imbalance of power between the parties involved. There may be room to engage with others internationally and to explore whether the narrative of practice educator is one of authority and control over the learner or of emancipation and transformation, reflecting a commonality in learning relationships. As employer-led social work programmes are showing, the dyadic relationship between the practice educator and student is changing to something that is much more engaging and dynamic as students work in teams or groups. Working in different types of settings, such as group placements or in the 'hub' model of 'Frontline' and 'Think Ahead', might foster more open relationships and emphasis on learning for all. Making the role and process of practice education more transparent might help transfer some of the assessment responsibility from the educator to the student/trainee, allowing greater freedom on the latter's part to explore, imagine, practice, and challenge traditional ideas of praxis. The concept of praxis is a key idea in practice education, but, over the years, it has been challenged by a focus on outputs and outcomes for service users or clients. The process of praxis from a Hegelian perspective is about taking action to change the world. The world, to the student or trainee, is their placement or learning opportunity, and the action is that directed by the employer, regulator, practice educator, and education provider. There may be room to offer students greater freedom to take their own action supported, but not directed by, the practice educator in the context of their employment responsibilities. We would suggest that the student is a greater expert on their own learning than others. This learner-led process switches from pedagogy to what Knowles (2011) describes as andragogy, to an 'adult control' paradigm of education and is more likely to lead to 'deep level learning' (Entwistle 1988; Ramsden 1992).

The English experience is revealing how it is important for employers to work more closely with education providers and vice versa. This should help foster a joint understanding learning approach that seeks to develop social workers as confident and independent learners, but also foster co-design and collective ownership of this approach. It would encourage employers and education providers to view the education, and not just the training, of the next generation of social workers as a joint enterprise and dispel any tendency to view it as the education provider's sole responsibility. It would also make it more likely that both would own and accept responsibility for the assessment outputs and, ultimately, the programme's outcomes. Because current English standards on practice education are presented as 'outputs', they hold relevance to this new model. However, paying attention to inputs (process) also fosters greater consistency and scrutiny. This is critical to practice education because it develops the individual learner's ability to gain the skills that will support their own life-long learning and continuing professional development. It is the opposite of surface learning, which enables an individual to learn for a specific short-term goal, such as passing an exam, writing an essay, or meeting a practice educator's directed task.

Critical Analysis

To analyse the overall environment of practice education in England raises some critical questions that are rarely asserted and, when they are, rarely responded to, listened to, or acted upon. From the material we have presented in this short chapter, it is clear that social work programmes benefit from a partnership and collegiate approach to training and educating students. Generally, partnerships share resources, ideas, ownership, and risk. However, when there have been major tragedies in social work, mainly in children's departments, the government has intervened in social work education, citing universities, not employers, as providing poor standards of training that create social workers who are not equipped to manage the complexity of social work practice. The assumption, here, is that, if the input from universities were better, social workers would then be better equipped to support families and protect children, a theme raised in a government commissioned report on social work education (Narey, 2014). Such tragedies are a complex phenomenon. The government moved social work to being an all-degree profession, raised entry qualifications to narrow the profile of entrants, and brought in new routes to training at post-graduate level, all part of a proclamation of raising standards and, hopefully, reducing tragedies such as the death of the child Peter Connolly in 2007 (Department of Education, 2008). However, there is little evidence that correlates, for example, individual student academic profile at entry level with later practice outcomes, as suggested by Croisdale-Appleby (2014, p. 9). This leads to the question of whether continued government changes to social work education, often occurring after major tragedies, have not been able to produce the intended outcomes. It may be argued that regular change has created instability within the sector, much of which neither understands nor owns such changes (see Appendix 1 of change timeline).

Flux and change in English social work education have impacted on its sustainability, sector confidence, and consistency in outcomes. What is needed is evidence-based policy change that drives the right type of change at the right time. As described above, the government's 'Teaching Partnership' initiative produced positive outcomes in social work education (D.f.E., 2019). However, such partnerships rely on government funding and, as this runs out, sustainability is uncertain. Initiatives that are reliant on short-term government funding often face this problem. Should social work partners find other ways to achieve self-reliance when the incentive is not just financial but also benefits all through practice experience, ideas, values, and outcomes for end users? Should the regulator require employers to work within social work education partnerships? Because of a lack of research in this area, we are unclear of the difference and the impact different routes may have to improve social work practice. In reviewing the past 50 years of social work regulated education (see Ixer, 2013), there is a case for consolidating what we know and researching uncertainties.

There is much to celebrate in what has been achieved in England in helping to provide social work students with a rigorous education that helps to integrate the theory aspect of their experience into practice. The role of practice educator in supporting, educating, and assessing students in practice should not be seen in isolation to academic scrutiny, potentially allowing for fairness and equality to be addressed in all quarters. The practice educator has a similar role in all routes to qualification and continues to have a powerful influence over student learning outputs (e.g., making the recommendation of pass or fail). Such recommendations are completed in isolation from common U.K. academic protocols of quality assurance, such as double marking, moderation, external examination of the process, and so on. Developments among many programmes, such as a Practice Assessment Panel, are helping to break down this isolation and provide quality assurance of the evidence supporting the recommendation, although they do not review the process that leads to recommendations. This implies that programmes are only interested in outputs rather than how they are achieved. There have been suggestions that a register of minimum standards for all practice educators in England would bring quality consistency to the sector, but this would need substantial consultation and clear evidence of being worth the effort.

Conclusions

England has a complex and structured process of training and assessing students in practice that has been established over many years. As acknowledged, the problems with the current system of social work education, with regular changes in routes and standards, buffer against the good work that many practice educators, employers, academics, and students encounter. Moreover, new regulation brings about a new opportunity. S.W.E.'s regulatory philosophy seems driven by core values of enhancement rather than minimum standards and an openness to include social work stakeholders by engaging with them in every aspect of the regulatory process (S.W.E., 2019c). Nicky Morgan, M.P., then Secretary of State for Education in England, stated: 'I also want us to be confident that every new social worker joining the workforce has received high quality initial training' (Morgan, 2016). While practice education has always been held as important to the overall success of social work education, there is continued debate about what makes good practice education, but there is limited research to inform such a debate. A mix of input and output standards to bring consistency and greater quality to the system of practice education remains an ambition. A more systematic approach to researching this area should be an aim of the sector. The social work community needs to be able to evidence its approach, giving greater public confidence in a system that needs rigor, reliability, effectiveness, and sustainability.

Finally, at the time of writing, the world is experiencing a major pandemic, and universities in England, social work employers, and teams are quickly learning new ways of working. In one British university, the University of Winchester, the social work department created a virtual placement as an alternative to suspending placements during the early COVID-19 pandemic. The alternative of suspending or delaying the opportunity of students becoming social workers was seen as unfair. This provided new opportunities that seem limitless in relation to learning gain (see Appendix 2). Now may be an optimal time to rethink what is important to practice education; the agency that needs to employ good social workers; the body that provides the education, the practice educator or similar, who trains and assesses the student on placement; and most importantly, the student who should be at the heart of whatever process is in place for developing and preparing excellent social work practitioners Given the way COVID-19 has transformed the way social work and social work education are being delivered, the sector may rethink the purpose of social work education. COVID-19 might be the catalyst for a once-in-a-life-time change, helping the sector to examine, in particular for practice education, different or even better ways of training students in placement, such as the alternative placement idea. This challenge has been publicly raised by the new social work regulator (Conway, 2020). The pandemic may provide an opportunity to explore innovative ways to augment student learning in the practice environment.

Appendix 1

Chronology of Key Events

To give a clearer timeline of key events in social work education, the following is a chronology; however, these events must be seen in relation to other policy changes that impact social work education.

- 1962 – Formal regulation of social work training in the U.K. starts (Council for Training in Social Work).
- 1970 – Regulation for social work education under statue renamed Central Council for Social Work Education and Training (C.C.E.T.S.W.).
- 1972 – C.C.E.T.S.W. initiative to expand social work training across the U.K.
- 1973 – First ever values in social work developed (C.C.E.T.S.W.).
- 1974 – C.C.E.T.S.W. publishes 'Paper 4' integrating law in social work education.
- 1975 – Development of first 'student unit' to support students in placement.
- 1975 – 'Paper 9.1' development of the Certificate in Social Services (C.S.S.).
- 1975 – Tangible political support for social work education – first Secretary of State visit to a social work programme.
- 1976 – 'Paper 13' (C.C.E.T.S.W.) published 'Values in Social Work'.
- 1977 – 'Paper 17.1' (C.C.E.T.S.W.) begins the 'Post Qualifying' framework.
- 1979 – Press release calls for more black and ethnic minority people in social work.
- 1979 – New study published recognising role of independent assessors in placement assessment.

- 1980 – C.C.E.T.S.W. sets up its own quality assurance department with external assessors integrating practice with theory.
- 1980 – Birth of the C.S.S. and C.Q.S.W. qualifications.
- 1980 – New assessment of practice placements published.
- 1985 – First announcement of need for 3-year degree for qualification.
- 1987 – C.C.E.T.S.W. sets up specialist group to develop greater opportunities in social work for black people (Black Perspectives Committee).
- 1989 – Birth of 'Paper 30' integrating all qualifications into a unified Diploma in Social Work.
- 1991 – Publication of 'One Small Step Towards Racial Justice' to support new unified social work qualification outlined in 'Paper 30'.
- 1991 – Residential childcare initiative leading to specific childcare pathway in qualification and later a new post-qualifying award.
- 1992 – First coordinated response to finding good, quality placements acknowledging the problem.
- 1992 – New initiative to develop more good, quality practice teachers in placements, e.g., social work and joint nursing initiative.
- 1992 – Birth of National Occupational Standards for social work.
- 1992 – First discussion on replacing C.C.E.T.S.W. with new registration body.
- 1993 – Warner Inquiry led to special post-qualifying level childcare award in 1998.
- 1995 – New initiative to have only accredited practice educators to raise standards.
- 1997 – C.C.E.T.S.W. to be replaced by the General Social Care Council (G.S.C.C.).
- 1998 – Devolution across U.K. creates seven new bodies: three sector skills bodies in Wales, Northern Ireland, and Scotland, two in England covering adults and children, and one holding the U.K. Sector Skills license.
- 2000 – Birth of Sector Skills Council – sector-specific standards-setting bodies across the U.K.
- 2001 – First Code of Practice for the entire social care workforce.
- 2007 – Practice Learning Task Force set up to develop better supply of quality placements.
- 2008 – Social Work Task Force set up.
- 2012 – College for Social Work set up; closed 2016.
- 2012 – G.S.C.C. abolished, and functions transfer to the Health and Care Professions Council (H.C.P.C.).
- 2019 – Social work functions transfer from H.C.P.C. to Social Work England (S.W.E.).
- 2019 – S.W.E. publishes new standards on practice placements and new definition on what constitutes a statutory placement.

Appendix 2

At the start of 2020, the U.K. began to be affected by the global COVID-19 pandemic. By March 2020 all social work programmes in England were faced with the task of either suspending programmes or delivering in a different way. An example of creative practice was to continue with the placement but, instead, of risking students' health by going out into the placement environment, students were given a virtual placement. The following is an example of how one social work programme not only managed this but also learnt something new about other ways students learn.

The South Coast partnership is made up of six local authorities and a university.[1] They are part of the government funded Step Up to Social Work initiative. The students have three placements – 20-days as an introduction to children's social work, 50 days in an adults' settings, and finally, 100-days in children's statutory social work. The three placements are part of one module in which they have to meet learning outcomes through building a portfolio of evidence. Students had already completed a 20-day placement and were about to start their 50-day placement before the crisis and lockdown was implemented. Consequently, they were unable to start their planned placement in adult social services. However, unlike other programmes that suspended their placements, this partnership decided that the placement should continue as a virtual learning experience. The following is a snapshot of how this worked.

To suspend a programme brings huge consequences. During the early months of the Coronavirus crisis, no one knew when national restrictions would be over, putting students at risk of not being able to complete the course on time and not qualifying or entering the social work profession when they expected. Using a mix of approaches, the students entered a programme of 50-days of online learning, structured individual and group supervision, and tutorial group seminars. During this 50-day placement, students sought to identify a range of alternative evidence to direct placement experience as a contribution toward the final portfolio. They used recognition of prior learning processes whether in education or employment to present evidence that could be matched against the learning outcomes. They researched particular themes from their own learning pathways and identified particular issues about which they could write in two formative pieces of assessment. In essence, they could not only use prior learning and evidence from any source but also generate new evidence to contribute toward their final portfolio when their 100-day placement was complete.

This experience taught the programme a number of things that otherwise might be lost:

- Students come onto a programme with a vast amount of prior knowledge, social capital, and emotional intelligence that is not always recognised.
- Students learn at different paces.
- Step Up to Social Work students have vast experience and are independent learners who can be given more responsibility to manage their own learning and require less structured coaching and teaching. This, in turn, made the idea of a virtual placement possible.
- Because this group of students are more mature/experienced, they are able to use their peer group as a resource to aid and accelerate learning.
- A placement is not about the physical contact and experience of being in placement over a number of days but more about learning wherever it takes place.

It raises the possibility that, for students, learning may not need the standard number of days in placement. There is no evidence that shows whether students who have 200 days of placement are more ready to practice than those that experienced 100 days.

However, it is acknowledged that all students gain value-added experiences from placements that would be lost in virtual placements. Students enjoy these placements, but placements are sourced for learning and not enjoyment. The partnership has shown how learning can be refocused to explore alternative and more creative approaches to student learning, which must increase opportunities for students to excel in expressing their natural talents that might otherwise be lost.

It is recognised that these are early days, and the experience of a virtual placement has not been fully evaluated. However, there are many positive features that could support students to learn in alternative ways and support the principle forwarded in this chapter – a focus on learning gained rather than the number of days in a placement.

Note

1 Hampshire children's services, Wokingham children's services, Portsmouth children's services, Isle of Wight children's services, Southampton children's services, West Sussex children's services and University of Winchester.

References

Baginsky, M., Manthorpe, J. & Hickman, B. (2019) Social work teaching partnerships: a discussion paper. *Social Work Education, 38*(8), 968–982.

Baginsky, M., Manthorpe, J. & Moriarty, J. (2018) The framework for the assessment of children in need and their families and signs of safety: Competing or complementary frameworks? *The British Journal of Social Work*, 51(7), 2571–2589,

Baginsky, M., Moriarty, J., Manthorpe, J., Stevens, M., MacInnes, T., and Nagendran, T. (2010). *Social Workers' Workload Survey. Messages from the Frontline. Findings from the 2009 Survey and Interviews with Senior Managers*. London: Department for Children, Schools and Families; Department of Health.

B.A.S.W. (2019). *Practice Educator Standards for Social Work* (Originally published by the College of Social Work now held by the British Association of Social Work). Accessed 2/4/20 https://www.basw.co.uk/social-work-training/professional-capabilities-framework-pcf

Caffrey, B., and Fruin, H. (2019). An exploration of issues affecting the assessment of social work students on practice placement in England. *Journal of Practice Teaching and Learning*, 16(1–2), 68–82.

C.C.E.T.S.W. (1992). New initiative starts to slow results. *News*, 5. London: C.C.E.T.S.W.

Conway, C. (2020). *How Social Work England is Responding to COVID-19 – A Conversation with Colum Conway (CEO)*. Podcast at https://anchor.fm/what-works-for-childrens-social-care/episodes/How-Social-Work-England-is-responding-to-COVID-19---a-conversation-with-Colum-Conway--Social-Work-England-ef4pqf

Cooperrider, D., and Whitney, D. (2005). *Appreciative Inquiry: A Positive Revolution in Change*. San Francisco: Berrett-Koehler.

Department for Education. (2019). *Social Work Teaching Partnerships: An Evaluation. Interim Research Report - Early Findings*. London: Department for Education.

Crosidale-Appleby. (2014). *Professor Croisdale-Appleby's Review of Social Work Education Re-Visioning Social Work Education: A Department of Health Update*. London: Department of Health, December 2014.

Department of Education. (2008). *Haringey Local Safeguarding Children Board: Serious Case Review Child A*. London: Department of Education, 26th October 2010.

Entwistle, N. (1988). *Styles of Learning and Teaching*. London: David Fulton.

Fairtlough, A., Bernard, J., Fletcher, J., and Ahmet, A. (2014). Black social work students' experiences of practice learning: Understanding differential progression rates. *Journal of Social Work*, 14(6), 605–624.

Hackett, S., and Marsland, P. (1997). Perceptions of power: An exploration of the dynamics in the student-tutor-practice teacher relationship within child protection placements. *Social Work Education*, 16(2), 44–62.

Hussain, J., Millman, C., Scott, J., Hannon, P., and Matlay, H. (2007). Ethnic minority graduate entrepreneurs in the UK: Characteristics, motivations and access to finance. *Industry and Higher Education*, 21(6), 455–463.

Ixer, G. (2016). The concept of reflection: Is it skill based or values? *Social Work Education*, 35(7), 809–824

Ixer, G. W. (2013). Fifty years of professional regulation in social work education, in J. Parker & M. Doel (eds) *Professional Social Work*. London: Sage.

Jones, R. (2014). *The Story of Baby P: Setting the Record Straight*. Bristol: Policy Press.

Knowles, M. S. (2011). *The Adult Learner: The Definitive Classic in Adult Education and Human Resource Development*. Oxford: Butterworth-Heinemann

Morgan, N. (2016). *Delivering a Revolution in Children's Social Care Speech Delivered at Speech at Kensington Town Hall*, 14 January https://www.gov.uk/government/speeches/nicky-morgan-delivering-a-revolution-in-childrens-social-care

Narey, M. (2014). *Making the Education of Social Workers Consistently Effective: Report of Sir Martin Narey's Independent Review of the Education of Children's Social Workers*. Department of education (then DCSF), January 2014. Reference: DFE-00082-2014 D.

Ramsden, P. (1992). *Learning to Teach in Higher Education*. London: Routledge.

Social Work Education. (2019a). *Guidance on Practice Placements*. London: Social Work England.
Social Work Education. (2019b). *Qualifying Education and Training Standards 2019 Guidance*. London: Social Work England.
Social Work Education. (2019c). *Our Role and Legislation*. London: Social Work England.
Social Work Reform Board. (2012). *Building a Safe and Confident Future: One Year On*. London: Department for Children, Schools and Families.
Social Work Task Force. (2009). *Building a Safe, Confident Future. The Final Report of the Social Work Task Force*. London: Department for Children, Schools and Families.

22

Hearing the Student Voice

An Evaluation of Students' Experiences and Learning in Fieldwork Education in University College Dublin, Ireland

Elaine Wilson and Niamh Flanagan

This chapter describes and discusses the findings from research carried out with Masters in Social Work students in University College Dublin (Flanagan & Wilson, 2018; Wilson & Flanagan, 2019). The purpose of the research was to focus on students' experiences of fieldwork education and what aided or assisted their learning. Underpinning the research was a commitment to 'hearing the student voice', and so the research design was participatory and concerned with engaging the 'experts by experience' in the research process. Although there is increasing interest in the concept of participatory research, exploration of what works in social work fieldwork education, like many areas, has yet to explore this concept and, therefore, much of what we know about the mechanisms of fieldwork education are drawn from those who are not first-hand users of the service: practice teachers, tutors, and academics. This innovative research engaged the less dominant voice of the student, eliciting their opinions about what makes a good fieldwork experience and what tools aided their learning. Students designed and administered their own questionnaire, giving them hands on experience of undertaking a research project.

This chapter begins with an account of systems of social work fieldwork education in the Republic of Ireland, identifying administrative and educational processes, that link the university with placement providers. The chapter then moves on to focus on a participatory study of students' experiences carried out in University College Dublin. The professional Master in Social Work (MSW) is a two-year full-time programme with an intake of approximately 50 students annually.

The research findings illuminate the complex nature of the relationships between student and practice teachers and the paradox of student recognition. The chapter concludes with an appeal to social work educators to find more spaces for student voices.

Social Work Education in Ireland

Social work education has a long history in Ireland. In 1912, Alexandra College in Dublin was the first institution to establish social work training entitled 'Civic and Social Work'. In

DOI: 10.4324/9781032164946-27

1934, Trinity College Dublin established a diploma in social studies, followed immediately by University College Dublin's course in 1936. The contemporary form of social work education in Ireland began in 1973, when social work courses were approved by the U.K. Central Council for Education and Training in Social Work (CCETSW). This remained the case until 1997, when the National Social Work Qualifications Board (NSWQB) was established in Ireland. Since 2005, CORU has been Ireland's statutory regulator responsible for regulating 16 health and social care professional organisations. A central aspect of CORU's role is to ensure high standards of professional conduct, education, training and competence and thereby protect the public. In 2013, social work was the first profession to undergo statutory regulation with CORU, and social workers are required to maintain continuing professional development as part of their registration.

Currently, there are six third-level institutions offering social work education in the Republic of Ireland. These are University College Dublin (UCD), Trinity College Dublin (TCD), University College Cork (UCC), National University of Ireland Galway (NUIG), Institute of Technology, Sligo (IT Sligo), and Maynooth University. Four of the six institutions (UCD, NUIG, Maynooth, and IT Sligo) offer courses at post-graduate level, with the remaining two offering both post-graduate and undergraduate programmes. Approximately 230 students qualify as social workers across the Republic of Ireland annually. Similar to the UK, Australasia, and North America, fieldwork education is a required and integral component of the social work education curriculum.

Fieldwork Education in Ireland

In Ireland, a typical fieldwork education teaching team comprises the student and practice teacher, with a practice tutor acting as liaison between the university, student, and practice teacher (Wilson & Flanagan, 2019). The term 'placement' is more commonly used in Ireland to refer to the work experience a social work student undertakes in an agency. The number of hours a student must complete on placement is 1,000 hours over a minimum of two placements, which is determined by the regulator, CORU. The majority of the universities in the Republic of Ireland operate a 2-year full-time Master in Social Work programme, with a 14-week block placement in each year. Placements are generally organised by the university placement team, who liaise with statutory, voluntary, and community social work organisations who provide placement sites. Ideally, a student will have at least one statutory fieldwork experience, such as with Tusla (Child and Family Agency), the Probation Service, or mental health services.

As is common worldwide, the responsibility for facilitating the placement learning process is largely devolved to agency personnel, described as 'practice teachers' in Ireland and the UK. It is crucial that students can sample different pedagogical techniques to enhance their learning, and the practice teacher is central to ensuring that this happens. The relationship between practice teacher and student has been described as central to important teaching and learning processes (Kourgiantakis, Sewell, & Bogo, 2019), and it is through these processes that students develop holistic competency. Research indicates that students who have the opportunity to practice skills are more likely to have better work performance and be more satisfied with their placement experience (Kanno & Koeske, 2010; McPherson & Barnett, 2006). This research is supported by Lee and Fortune (2013, p. 647) who discuss the importance of social work 'doing' activities in the field placement but caution that real learning requires more than doing, or imitation of, practice teachers. Students need to be able to locate their professional selves within both the theoretical and practical space to become fully competent professionals. Lee and

Fortune (2013, p. 655) summarise it well, noting that students should be active both physically and psychologically during their placements.

Standard practice in the Republic of Ireland is that each student has an assigned practice tutor whose role is to provide support and guidance whilst also ensuring that the requirements of the university are met during the placement experience. Tutors can be either academic staff or external social work practitioners and, where possible, remain as tutors to the same students over the course of their academic career. Tutors work and support students before, during, and after placement. Assessment of the fieldwork is devolved to the practice teacher who gathers evidence using a variety of means such as observation, reflective practice, direct work with service users, and report writing. In addition, both practice teacher and student write a detailed, evidence-based report demonstrating the student's learning. Group supervision is uncommon in Ireland, so the exclusive nature of the practice teacher, tutor, and student relationship means that students from the same qualifying class can have different placement learning experiences. Unlike other jurisdictions, such as the UK, long-arm or off-site supervision is rarely used in the Republic of Ireland.

Research literature has identified that fieldwork experience or placement can produce significant anxiety in some students, particularly those going on their first placement (Gelman, 2004; Kanno & Koeske, 2010). Students may go on placement with low levels of confidence in their ability to manage what they encounter on placement or confusion about their role and social work identity. Gelman (2004) noted that one of the main factors for student dissatisfaction on placement could be related to poor preparation for the fieldwork experience. Interestingly, Kanno and Koeske (2010, p. 31) found only modest support for the expectation that good preparation would lead to greater student satisfaction with their fieldwork experience. They did, however, find that both direct and indirect supervision have a central role in supporting students on placement, with the students who received more supervision indicating greater levels of satisfaction. These findings were of particular interest in relation to our research, as the issues were raised and discussed by student participants.

Methodology

This participative research project evolved from a staff-initiated, student-to-student dialogue project which formed part of the MSW programme in UCD (Flanagan & Wilson, 2018; Wilson & Flanagan, 2019). The project combines experiential-learning and participative-research approaches, with students adopting the role of both research-learners and research-partners with staff. An experiential-learner approach has long been advocated by research educators (Joubert et al., 2017; MacIntyre & Paul, 2013; Rubin, Robinson, & Valutis, 2010), promoting experience and competencies in concrete tasks, with staff providing support and facilitation. Participative research adds a further dimension to experiential learning by introducing collaborative knowledge production as an output. Participatory research, in addition to prioritising knowledge creation, focuses on the roles that co-researchers play (Wilson & Flanagan, 2019). Thus, participatory research is done in active collaboration with students, rather than viewing them as the research subjects..

The dialogue project, described below, aimed to facilitate a conversation between first-year and second-year MSW students about experiences on placement. First-year students and staff worked as co-researchers on a survey of second-year students. Ethical approval for this predominantly quantitative study was awarded by the University Human Research Ethics Committee.

Instrument Design, Data Collection, and Analysis

Staff researchers conducted a preliminary literature review as a foundation for more extensive review of selected literature by student researchers. The research team employed blogs and in-class discussion forums to explore practice learning supports. The collaborative review of literature informed design of the e-survey instrument by the student–staff team. The identified supports were allocated to student teams who, with staff, designed both closed and open questions about each learning support, allowing the collection of both quantitative and qualitative data. Dependent variables were added to capture perceptions about the placement, such as satisfaction, learning, preparedness, and preparation. One student team undertook development of recruitment documentation, while another coordinated questions and trialled the e-survey instrument.

Study Design and Sample

Invitations to participate in the survey were issued to MSW students who had completed one of their practice placements. The cross-sectional survey was administered in two phases. In Phase 1 (2014), a first-year student–staff research team surveyed a convenience sample of second-year students. In Phase 2 (2015), staff researchers surveyed both student groups. The completed sample of 100 responses represented a 90% response rate from first-year students and a 60% response rate from second-year students. Two factors may have contributed to the disparity in the response rate. The first being that, at the time Phase 2 was being administered, second-year students were under pressure to complete their dissertations, while at the same, time first-year students were immersed in their research learning, of which this was a key learning experience.

Data Analysis

The Phase 1 survey, administered to second-year students, achieved a 77% ($n = 37$) response rate. Descriptive frequency tables were returned to first-year student groups for thematic analysis. This analysis was written up and presented by first-year student groups on an enclosed online social-writing platform and were subsequently redrafted into a poster and presented by students at the Irish Association of Social Workers' conference (First year MSocSc (Social Work) Students, Flanagan & Wilson, 2015).

Phase 2 of the study combined data from Phase 1 with data from a staff-run phase of the study administered the following year with minor amendments to the questionnaire and recruitment documentation. Both first-year and second-year students participated following their 2015 placement. This phase yielded a 66% response rate ($n = 63$) giving an overall response rate of 70% ($n = 100$) across the two phases. The authors undertook the analyses of the combined data set using IBM SPSS Statistics (a widely used statistical analysis package).

Limitations

Several research design decisions were carefully weighed in view of their limiting influence on the study. The study would have benefited from a longitudinal design and/or a link to academic or fieldwork assessment. However, these design elements would have required unanonymised data and associated ethical considerations which were deemed beyond the scope of this study in addition to the potential impact on response rates. The single-school convenience sample also limits the representativeness of the sample. However, as this model of research education was being applied for the first time, a multi-site study was earmarked for future developments.

Findings

On return from fieldwork placement, students were asked to report, both quantitatively and qualitatively, on their placement experiences: how they prepared; how prepared they were; who and what facilitated their learning; and how successful they perceived the placement to be. Crucial to our understanding of 'what works on placement' was to collate and correlate the perceptions of students, deemed to be experts by experience.

How Successful were Placements?

The success of placements, as perceived by students, was measured using two dependent variables, satisfaction with the placement and the amount of learning by the student on placement. These conceptual variables were intentionally undefined to allow students to provide a holistic measure of their satisfaction and learning. Students were generally satisfied with placement with 90% ($n = 90$) reporting that they were either satisfied or very satisfied (Table 22.1a). In addition, many students felt that they learnt a lot on placement, with a further one-in-three learning more than they had expected (Table 22.1b). Not surprisingly, students' perceptions of these two elements of successful placements, satisfaction, and perceived learning, were strongly correlated ($rs = 0.62$, $P \leq 0.001$), indicating that a personal sense of learning a lot played a significant, although not exclusive role in determining satisfaction with placements.

How Prepared were Students for Placement?

> I had been initially anxious (and excited) about starting placement and feel part of this related to feeling unprepared and unprofessional.

Table 22.1 Students' Perceptions of the Success of Placements

(1a) Students' satisfaction with practice placement

	n	%
1. Very satisfied	50	50%
2. Satisfied	40	40%
3. Neither satisfied nor dissatisfied	2	2%
4. Dissatisfied	6	6%
5. Very dissatisfied	2	2%
Total	100	100%
(*Md*=1.5)		

(1b) Students' perceived learning on placement

	n	%
1. Much more than expected	36	36%
2. I learnt a lot	47	47%
3. Some learning	16	16%
4. No learning	0	
Total	99	99%†
(*Md*=1.5)		No answer=1

† deviation from 100% due to rounding error

For many early-stage students, preparing for placements is a persistent anxiety. In addition to academic groundwork, most students ($n=90$, 90%) undertook additional personal preparation for placement. In all cases, this involved reading or researching, mainly to find out about the agency and its practices ($n=44$, 44%); reading policies, procedures, and legislation ($n=29$, 29%); reviewing theories and methods ($n=22$, 22%); undertaking recommended reading ($n=16$, 16%); reviewing lecture notes ($n=16$, 16%); and/or asking others about their experiences of placement ($n=14$, 14%). Interestingly, much of the preparation for placement did not have a significant effect on the students' levels of pre-placement confidence, on their overall satisfaction, or on their learning on placement. The type of reading that impacted students' pre-placement confidence was reading about the agency in which they were to be placed ($u=819.5$, $P \leq 0.01$).

After completing placements, students were asked to retrospectively rate their pre-placement confidence – how prepared they felt before going on placement – and to rate how prepared they were once on placement. Before placement, only 3% ($n=3$) of students felt they were fully prepared, and just under half of the students felt somewhat, prepared (Table 22.2a). The fact that over a quarter of students felt unprepared before going on placement is a concern. The kind of factors which contributed to this sense of unpreparedness for placement were procedural issues,

Table 22.2 Preparedness for Placement

(2a) Students' pre-placement confidence

	n	%
1. Fully prepared	3	3%
2. Somewhat prepared	45	45%
3. Neither prepared nor unprepared	24	24%
4. Somewhat unprepared	23	23%
5. Totally unprepared	5	5%
Total	100	100%
(*Md*=3)		

(2b) Retrospective assessment of students' actual level of preparedness for placement

	n	%
1. Fully prepared	5	5%
2. Somewhat prepared	49	50%
3. Neither prepared nor unprepared	26	27%
4. Somewhat unprepared	16	16%
5. Totally unprepared	2	2%
Total	98	100%
(*Md*=2)		No answer = 2

(2c) Comparison of pre-placement and actual preparedness

	n	%
1. More prepared than anticipated	25	26%
2. As prepared as anticipated	61	62%
3. Less prepared than anticipated	12	12%
Total	98	100%
(*Md*=2)		No answer = 2

such as needing more assessment skills, familiarity with procedures, and protocols or knowledge about the placement setting, agency, and its clientele. However, one student observed:

> I don't think it is possible to prepare everyone as the placements are all so different. It's important to relax and accept that you will learn as you go.
>
> We spend hours and hours in college preparing for the profession but, in reality, the majority of the learning is practical and while you are on placement.

Students were also asked to retrospectively rate their perception of how prepared they actually were for their placement (Table 22.2b). Responses suggest that, overall, the student body underestimated its preparedness for placement ($Z = -1.961$, $P \leq 0.05$) with the median rating of preparedness shifting upward to 'somewhat prepared' once students were on placement and the proportions reporting feeling unprepared for placement falling by 10% (Table 22.2b). Indeed, comparison of pre-placement confidence and actual preparedness revealed that as many as one-in-four students were more prepared than they anticipated (Table 22.2c). A group that is of concern are the 18% ($n = 18$) who, even in retrospect, felt that they were not prepared when they were on placement.

> My practice teacher told me to work on my confidence. He said that I had the skills and learning, I just needed to try and be more confident when working directly with my client.

Unfortunately, only half of this group ($n = 9$, 9%) indicated why they felt unprepared. Reasons cited focused on setting specific practices such as assessment, policies, and planning. One student voiced these concerns, calling for a greater focus on building pre-placement confidence.

> I felt unprepared and incompetent even though that was patently not the case – I got very positive feedback from placement.

Who Helped Students Learn on Placement?

As outlined above, a student on placement is typically supported by a practice teacher and a practice tutor who liaises between the university, student, and practice teacher. However, the research team hypothesised that the support system which students rely on when on placement is wider, comprising peers and agency staff, among others. Not unexpectedly, on-site supports, such as practice teachers and agency staff, represented the mainstay of support for students' learning, providing help that facilitated learning on a daily ($n = 60$, 64%) or weekly basis (teacher $n = 28$, 30%; agency $n = 19$, 20%). Supports from practice tutors were less frequent, usually monthly, or less, and from the academic staff, typically less than monthly.

Practice Teachers

Nearly two-thirds of students rated their practice teacher as 'very helpful' in facilitating their learning, and a further quarter rated their teacher as 'helpful' (Table 22.3a). Practice teachers clearly played a pivotal role, as ratings of their level of helpfulness were positively correlated with both placement satisfaction ($rs = 0.52$, $P \leq 0.001$) and levels of learning on placement ($rs = 0.43$, $P \leq 0.001$).

> [she gave] support and the feeling of being appreciated. I think her ability to empower me to do something and be independent in practice [was most useful]. A level of responsibility was given to me, and I feel I learnt a lot from that.

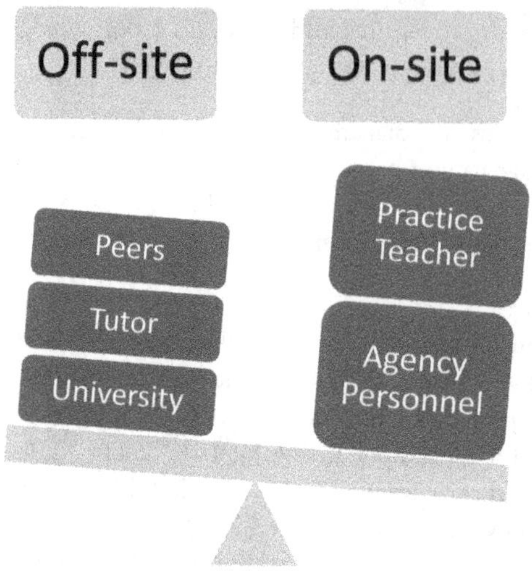

Figure 22.1 On-site and off-site support provided to students on placement.

Table 22.3 Helpfulness of On-site Personnel: Teachers & Agency

(3a) Helpfulness of practice teachers in facilitating learning on placement

	n	%
1. Very helpful	62	64%
2. Helpful	22	23%
3. Neither helpful nor unhelpful	4	4%
4. Unhelpful	4	4%
5. Very unhelpful	5	5%
Total	97	100%
(*Md*=1)		No answer = 3

(3b) Helpfulness of agencies in facilitating learning on placement

	n	%
1. Very helpful	52	54%
2. Helpful	30	31%
3. Neither helpful nor unhelpful	9	9%
4. Unhelpful	3	3%
5. Very unhelpful	2	2%
Total	96	99%†
(*Md*=1)		No answer = 4
		† deviation from 100% due to rounding error

The *frequency* with which practice teachers provided support also had a positive impact on satisfaction ($rs = 0.43$, $P \leq 0.001$) and learning ($rs = 0.48$, $P \leq 0.001$): the more frequently a practice teacher provided support, the more the students considered that they gained from the placement. The frequency and availability of formal and informal supervision, induction, and feedback, all of which are practice-teacher-driven, impacted ratings of satisfaction with practice teachers (P ≤

0.05). Moreover, findings suggest that practice teachers provided more frequent support to students who were less confident (rs = -0.36, $P \leq 0.001$) and felt less prepared (rs = -0.25, $P \leq 0.05$).

> Giving me a different way of interpreting what was happening, especially around my emotional processing of certain cases; ways of reframing cases; providing a supportive learning environment in which to learn and one in which I felt it was ok to make mistakes … it gave me confidence in myself that I could do the job.

Most practice teachers were also considered very/helpful (n=69, 78%) in guiding students' navigation of the link between theory and practice. In fact, guidance on theory use contributed most strongly to ratings of practice teachers (rs = 0.63, $P \leq 0.001$), satisfaction with placement (rs = 0.63, $P \leq 0.001$), and levels of learning on placement (rs = 0.50, $P \leq 0.001$). Assistance with the management of caseloads also had a significant impact on practice teacher ratings (rs = -0.53, $P \leq 0.001$).

A small number of students (n=9, 9%) reported that their practice teacher was very/unhelpful, and the correlations indicated that poor practice teachers can undermine a placement experience. Concerns about this, and the power attributed to such teachers, were articulated.

> It seems ridiculous that one person who is not employed by the college, can fail a student, when they have passed every single other aspect of their course.

Agencies

Agencies were rated as very/helpful in facilitating learning on placement by 85% of students (Table 22.3b), and positive ratings of agency support were correlated with satisfaction (rs = 0.56, $P \leq 0.001$) and learning on placement (rs = 0.38, $P \leq 0.001$). A student noted how valuable placement colleagues support was:

> Office support with colleagues in [the] agency [was useful] for different perspective on things. [The] team leader was great with helping me via research thesis information plus gave good feedback in relation to my progress.

Indeed, when information on 'additional supports' was sought, the most commonly cited was from team members (n=29, 29%). This support included guidance, support, advice, and provision of different perspectives, through both formal and informal talks.

> The team I was on was brilliant, from the team leader to the receptionist … the majority of the learning is practical ... that's why hav[ing] a good team is essential to your learning.

The importance of student integration into the team was also raised by a handful of students who noted that policies of giving students different access and rights to existing staff were unwelcome and created difficulties. The opposite, on the other hand, was a challenge for others. Joining a team was highlighted as a challenge because of its operational dynamics.

> The transitional challenges being experienced by one of my teams meant that this was a difficult environment to work in – I talked it over a lot with my practice teacher.

A range of additional supports were noted by students, including practice teacher and colleagues in the provision of assistance in managing caseloads and the assistance provided by administrative

Table 22.4 Helpfulness of Off-site Supports: Practice Tutors and University

(4a) Helpfulness of practice tutors in facilitating learning on placement

	n	%
1. Very helpful	28	29%
2. Helpful	35	36%
3. Neither helpful nor unhelpful	22	23%
4. Unhelpful	7	7%
5. Very unhelpful	5	5%
Total	97	100%
(*Md*=2)		No answer = 3

(4b) Helpfulness of the university in facilitating learning on placement

	n	%
1. Very helpful	9	9%
2. Helpful	34	35%
3. Neither helpful nor unhelpful	42	43%
4. Unhelpful	10	10%
5. Very unhelpful	2	2%
Total	97	99%†
(*Md*=3)		No answer = 3
		† deviation from 100% due to rounding error

staff. These supports were rated as 'useful' on average and, despite only typically being used monthly, both caseload and administrative support had an impact on satisfaction (rs = 0.464, $P \leq 0.001$; rs = 0.448, $P \leq 0.001$) and learning (rs = 0.389, $P \leq 0.001$; rs = 0.440, $P \leq 0.001$).

Practice Tutors

Support from practice tutors was significantly less frequent than support from on-site personnel ($P \leq 0.001$), and the ratings were commensurately lower (Table 22.4a). Practice tutors engage with students early in their academic career. They help students to identify their learning needs and factors that might affect their ability to learn on placement. Standard interaction with practice tutors occurs prior to, during, and at the end of placement in the form of a meeting and a phone call in the first three weeks to check in with both the student and practice teacher. Where difficulties emerge, tutors increase the amount of contact they have with students and practice teachers. Findings suggest that the helpfulness of practice tutors neither added to, nor subtract from overall satisfaction or learning on placement. Where helpfulness and frequency of support from tutors appeared to make a difference, albeit a moderate one, was on preparedness for placement (rs = 0.22, $P \leq 0.05$; rs = 0.33, $P \leq 0.001$). This may reflect the work that practice tutors carry out with students to ascertain learning needs and potential difficulties that could impact on placement learning. As well as this, the practice tutor helps the students to identify possible supports and tools that will help them overcome those difficulties.

> I went in [to the placement setting] on a particular day with my practice tutor to meet my practice teacher. This gave me a sense of what my practice teacher looks like, the type of person she is, and what the agency looks like.

As indicated, practice tutors' involvement in placements beyond the pre, during, and final placement meetings is based on need rather than routine. Only 21 (21%) students reported issues that triggered engagement of the practice tutors. These included discussion of a challenging case, inadequate supervision, poor student–teacher relationships, caseload management, and work familiarisation. However, a few respondents expressed hesitation to involve the practice tutors for fear it would undermine the student–teacher relationship or 'rock the boat'.

> Even thoughwe were informed that [practice tutor] supports were there, I ... had the feeling we should only go to them as a last resort.

Unfortunately, this study finds that requiring the support of the tutor was negatively associated with placement satisfaction ($u=546.5$, $P \leq 0.05$) and learning ($u=481.5$, $P \leq 0.01$). In situations in which practice tutors were heavily involved, there were significant issues, such as potential failure or fitness to practice proceedings, with students and practice teachers, who tend to be very stressed and concerned. The need for escalation to university support arose in a handful of cases. This sometimes resulted from a lack of clarity about, or confidence in, the practice tutor's role:

> Contact with your tutor isn't as helpful as contact with the college would be.

The University

In the placement ecology, the university plays a more distal role, with students typically receiving supports from the university less than monthly – significantly less frequent contact than with teachers, agencies, or tutors ($P \leq 0.001$). The responsibility for placements is devolved to the practice teachers, with practice tutors acting as the liaison between the university and student/practice teacher. University involvement in placements tends to be limited to significant issues that cannot be managed by the practice teacher, student, and practice tutor. However, some students pointed out that they did not call on the support of the university for fear of the impact on their placement.

> I did not feel like I could turn to ... the college about any of the difficulties that I was facing, as I was aware that they would talk to my practice teacher about it, and I felt that would make things worse with her. I think that had I had the opportunity to tell my tutor or the college in confidence, just to avail of advice, this would have made my experience wholly easier.

Support from the university was rated as very/helpful by 44% ($n=43$), 'neither helpful nor unhelpful' by 43% ($n=42$), and very/unhelpful by 12% ($n=12$). As with practice tutors, the level or frequency of university support did not have a significant impact on overall satisfaction or learning on placement. However, the helpfulness of the university did impact on pre-placement confidence ($rs = 0.26$, $P \leq 0.05$) and preparedness ($rs = 0.41$, $P \leq 0.001$).

Students were asked to rate the value of a range of other university supports, such as advice on how to deal with workplace stress, conflict, safety, access to placement reports of former students, and the mid-placement recall day. On average, each of these were rated as 'neither useful nor not useful'. Although these did not achieve high value ratings, neither did the value expressed correlate with dissatisfaction with placement nor learning on placement. Students perceived the principal value of the mid-placement university call-back day to be the opportunity for them to catch up, talk to, and get support from their peers ($n=30$, 45%). Students also valued the opportunity to listen to, discuss, compare, and learn from each other's placements, experiences, and cases. The day also provided an opportunity to ask questions, get reassurance from lecturers, reflect on placement, and freedom to air/discuss issues from placement.

> [it was] useful to reflect on what you had learned so far, as when you are on placement you are too busy to really think too much about what you are doing — great to catch up with peers and hear their experiences of placement — Useful for linking theory to practice.

Echoing the need for the university as a sounding board, nearly a fifth of the students stressed the need for regular check-ins and clear lines of communication between the university and students while on placement, particularly when things were not going well, either with the placement or personally.

> [would benefit from] more [college] involvement during placement, it's a long time until call-back day, and if you're struggling or having any [placement or personal] issues, it could almost be too late. Maybe an opportunity to link in more often [would be useful].

A number of suggestions were made about how to improve university support, particularly given the diverse nature of placement settings. These included the provision of setting specific preparation, more opportunities to talk with students who had experience of the placement setting, and the opportunity to review placement reports. Suggestions for greater skills preparation with regard to a wide range of areas (> 23) were cited. Most common among these were assessments, workplace stress, conflict and safety, child protection issues, and writing skills.

Perceived Lack of Support

Given the high correlation between the helpfulness of teachers, agencies, and tutors ($P \leq 0.001$) and between tutors and the university ($P \leq 0.001$), it is worth looking more closely at the student group who perceived little helpfulness from the four stakeholder groups. Four students (4%) rated teachers, tutors, agencies, and university staff as below helpful. A further seven (7%) reported help from only one of the four stakeholder groups, and two (2%) more reported help from off-site personnel only. Although small numbers make inferences unreliable, this group were not significantly different from their peers with regard to confidence or preparedness but were significantly less satisfied with their placement ($u = 299$, $P \leq 0.01$) and rated their learning significantly lower ($u = 285$, $P \leq 0.01$). While academic staff might not have been able to predict this scenario for individual students, it again underscores the importance of ongoing communication and support from the University.

> I had an absolutely dreadful experience on placement ... The college have a duty of care to their students and more support should be provided to students.

Peer Support

In addition to the supports from the formal practice infrastructure, students drew on support from other groups, most notably their classroom peers.

> It was scary going out on placement and the only other people who know and can appreciate what you're going through are your peers!!! Use and abuse the support!!!

Support provided by peers was highly rated, with 82% of students indicating that peers were very/helpful in facilitating learning on placement (Table 22.5a). However, help from peers was

Table 22.5 Peer Support in Facilitating Learning on Placement

(5a) Helpfulness of peers in facilitating learning on placement

	n	%
1. Very helpful	37	39%
2. Helpful	42	44%
3. Neither helpful nor unhelpful	13	14%
4. Unhelpful	3	3%
5. Very unhelpful	1	1%
Total	96	101%†
(*Md*=2)		No answer = 4
		† deviation from 100% due to rounding error

(5b) Frequency of peer support on placement

	n	%
1. Daily	33	35%
2. ≥ Weekly	36	38%
3. ≥ Monthly	15	16%
4. < Monthly	5	5%
5. Never	6	6%
Total	95	100%
(*Md*=2)		No answer = 5

not positively correlated with satisfaction, learning, or preparedness, but supported learning through other means.

> Meeting up with peers at meetings, didn't happen often, more so during visits, but was very helpful from an emotional support standpoint.

Despite diverse geographical locations, peer support was surprisingly frequent. Over two-thirds of students (*n*=69) received peer support weekly or more, and half of these received daily support (Table 22.5b). Most students employed a number of media for peer support, with the most commonly cited being social media (*n*=52, 52%).

> [I got peer] support via social media (Whatsapp groups, Facebook groups, individual social media contact), meeting up with members of the class outside placement for coffee to talk about placement and see how everyone is getting on, texts, calls. Support from non-UCD students within placement was also great.

Students also received peer support by meeting face-to-face (*n*=47, 47%), phone calls (*n*=27, 27%), texts/messaging (*n*=19, 19%), and meeting peers via work (*n*=7, 7%) while others pointed to the value of having a peer on the same placement (*n*=17, 17%). Although a small group (*n*=11, 11%) received less frequent peer support, such as less than monthly, these students had similar levels of alternative support to other respondents. Expanding on existing peer supports, students suggested linking first-year students with second-year students who had completed similar placements; structured group meetings/peer supervision; and establishment of setting-specific and geographic-specific forums.

Other Sources of Support for Learning

Open questions revealed that students' learning was further supported in other ways, most notably through interpersonal communications, for example, support from family and friends (n = 10, 10%) and valuable learning from service users (n = 6, 6%). Learning was also facilitated by site visits and contact with other agencies (n = 7, 7%) and documentary sources (n = 10, 10%), such as case files, libraries, internet, placement reports, policies, blogs, and learning journals.

Students also offered wide-ranging thoughts on what else might be supportive of learning when on placement. These included a buddy system, helpline, or colleague to talk to; interaction with other services; further training in suicide prevention, attachment theory, care and safety; specific information on writing reports/plans, understanding ethical frameworks; financial support; greater university support on crisis management; and suggestions on how to ameliorate the difficulties and stress associated with a 14-week placement, such as multiple shorter placements, or a longer interim break.

What Learning Tools Facilitated Placement Learning?

In addition to the placement infrastructure of teacher, tutor, agency, and university, a micro-level approach shifts the focus onto the learning tools that students used and valued on placement. Respondents rated 25 learning-support tools in terms of their usefulness and the frequency with which they were used during placement (Table 22.6). A comparison of these two variables

Table 22.6 Student Rating of Frequency of Use and Usefulness of Learning-Support Tools

		Average frequency of use Weekly or more	Monthly	Less than Monthly
Average rating of usefulness	Very Useful	• Observing others at work • Informal supervision • Co-working • Responsibility/ Independent work • Critiquing your own work		
	Useful	• Self-reflection • Formal supervision • Teacher feedback • Discussing case notes • Suggestions on improving knowledge and work • Brainstorming solutions	• Feedback on observations • Induction • Training • Assistance with managing caseload • Writing placement reports • Undertaking required readings • Receipt of administrative support • Writing case studies • Undertaking oral case presentations	
	Neither useful nor not useful		• Feedback on process recordings • Learning journal • Writing process recordings • Safety instruction	• Role play

allowed the research team to identify clusters of supports which ranged from mainstay tools, which are used frequently and highly valued, to tools which are infrequently used and not valued. The five mainstay tools included a mix of dyadic and independent learning tools: observing others at work, informal supervision, co-working, increased responsibility/independent work, and critiquing one's own work.

Social Work Cases

Three of the mainstay tools involved direct work with clients at different levels of responsibility: observation, coworking, and independent work. For students, work with clients clearly represents the crux of social work practice. There was near unanimous agreement ($n = 87$, 99%) among students that observing social workers at work was very useful ($n = 74$) or useful ($n = 13$). It was among the more frequently used tools, and many were given the opportunity to observe others at work on a daily ($n = 43$, 48%) or weekly basis ($n = 28$, 31%).

> Observing or shadowing other probation officers during my first few days [was useful]. It was useful to observe various counselling styles and the various teams in The Pprobation Service.
>
> You learn so much from watching your practice teacher. The fact she was interested in her job and cared for it. Her demeanour with clients, the importance of building that relationship even though you were there for assessment purposes.

Similarly, co-working was equally valued, deemed very/useful by 93% ($n = 82$). The opportunity to co-work was afforded to many on a daily ($n = 30$, 33%) or weekly ($n = 40$, 44%) basis. One student advised:

> Make sure you put yourself forward to co-work with people and get involved with the agency you are with. The time goes by so quick. Don't be afraid to ask questions in the agency; remember it is about you learning new things, and it is your first placement. Enjoy it; soon you will be back in college again.

Those who were fortunate enough to have this opportunity for direct work spoke of its value.

> I do feel that the biggest learning opportunity for me was being charg[ed] with facilitating a group and co-working this with another student. Huge learning curve and a lot of fun!!!

A third ($n = 30$, 33%) of students had the opportunity to take on increased responsibility or independent direct work on a daily basis and on a weekly basis for a half of the students ($n = 48$, 52%).

> I would have liked more independent work, my practice teacher insisted on being involved in all of my cases on some level, and I feel I would have learned more had I been left alone in some instances. Although I did appreciate his assistance and guidance.

All but one student had the opportunity to either observe, co-work, or work independently on a weekly basis. The one student who did not was, subsequently, dissatisfied with the placement experience. Although observation was rated highly by students, more frequent opportunities to observe social workers at work did not have a significant impact on overall placement satisfaction or levels of learning on placement. In contrast, the more co-working and independent work a student did, the higher their placement satisfaction (*rs* = 0.24, $P \leq 0.05$; *rs* = 0.21, $P \leq 0.05$) and perceived learning (*rs* = 0.25, $P \leq 0.05$; *rs* = 0.32, $P \leq 0.01$).

A further aspect of direct casework, which students found helpful, was discussion of case material. Such discussions ranged from informal 'brainstorming' solutions to use of process recordings. Review and/or discussion of case notes, although highly valued and frequently used, was not correlated with satisfaction or level of learning on placement. In contrast, 'brainstorming' solutions, although not quite as frequent or highly rated, was correlated with satisfaction (*rs* = 0.34, $P \leq 0.01$) and learning (*rs* = 0.31, $P \leq 0.01$).

> we would go through how the case was going and some of the discussions I was having with clients, and he would highlight examples of theories that I had been, unknowingly, applying.

Formal oral presentations of casework by students occurred less frequently; typically, more than once a month and were considered slightly less useful than the other two reviews of cases. It only had a moderate impact on satisfaction (*rs* = 0.28, $P \leq 0.01$) when occurring more frequently.

Supervision and Feedback

Practice teachers were contracted to provide a minimum of 1.5 hours of formal supervision weekly, with most providing significant amounts of additional informal supervision.

> [My practice teacher] offered me very good supervision ... a lot of opportunity to self-reflect and brainstorm about problems. Lots of opportunity to discuss anything I was worried about.

Informal supervision was the most frequently used with 90% (n=85) receiving at least weekly supervision, and many receiving informal supervision daily (n=57, 60%). Students clearly appreciated this support, rating it as very useful (n=72, 77%) or useful (n=17, 18%). Indeed, the frequency of informal supervision proved to have a significant impact on overall satisfaction with placement (*rs* = 0.43, $P \leq 0.01$) and perceived levels of learning (*rs* = 0.45, $P \leq 0.05$).

> I felt really supported on placement. I felt confident in my own abilities as a result of daily feedback from my practice teacher, and she was always available to me and encouraged me to take my own initiative and trust in my skills.

Given the ratings afforded to informal supervision, it is somewhat surprising that formal supervision was less valued (Z = -3.052, $P \leq 0.01$). Formal supervision was considered very useful by 62% (n=58) and useful by 30% (n=28), and the frequency of formal supervision impacted both satisfaction (*rs* = 0.27, $P \leq 0.01$) and perceived levels of learning (*rs* = 0.26, $P \leq 0.01$). The lower impact of formal supervision is partly attributed to its less frequent occurrence (Z = -4.683, $P \leq 0.001$) with comparable weekly supervision (n=80, 88%) but notably less daily supervision (n=4, 4%). Four students received less supervision than contracted, and this was reflected in poor practice teacher ratings, follow-up with tutors, and calls for more support across the board.

A variety of practice teacher feedback tools were evaluated in this study: general practice teacher feedback, suggestions on how to improve knowledge and work, feedback on observations on student work, and feedback on process recordings. Notably, each of the four types of

Table 22.7 Impact of Feedback on Placement Success

(7a) Frequency of feedback and impact on perceptions of placement success

	Median frequency†	*Correlation with satisfaction (rs)*	*Correlation with learning (rs)*
General practice teacher feedback	2 (*n*=96)	0.41**	0.47**
Feedback on observations	3 (*n*=96)	0.36**	0.53**
Suggestions for improvement	2 (*n*=95)	0.47**	0.48**
Feedback on process recordings	3 (*n*=95)	0.42**	0.41**

(7b) Usefulness of feedback and impact on perceptions of placement success

	Median useful‡	*Correlation with satisfaction (rs)*	*Correlation with learning (rs)*
General practice teacher feedback	1 (*n*=95)	0.72**	0.54**
Feedback on observations	3 (*n*=95)	0.48**	0.37**
Suggestions for improvement	2 (*n*=95)	0.56**	0.44**
Feedback on process recordings	2 (*n*=92)	0.45**	0.35**

† Daily=1, ≥ Weekly=2, ≥ Monthly=3, < Monthly=4, Never=5
‡ Very useful=1, Useful=2, Neither=3, < Useful=4, Not useful at all=5
** $P \leq 0.01$

feedback had a strong and statistically significant impact on both placement satisfaction and learning (Table 22.7), reinforcing the value students place on feedback and the fact that the more feedback students receive the more they perceive their placement as successful.

Most students received general feedback from their practice teachers daily (*n*=35, 35%) or weekly (*n*=48, 50%), and this feedback was considered the most useful type of feedback. Suggestions about how to improve knowledge and practice was also valued and was typically received weekly (Table 22.7).

> He was able to give me honest feedback about areas that I needed to improve on. He had a great skills base and was able to tell me about techniques that work.

Feedback on observations of students' work, while rated as very/useful by many, was not as highly rated or as frequently received as the more broad-based type of feedback discussed above. Feedback on written process recordings, sometimes considered an old-fashioned practitioner task, was rated as less useful than the other three types of feedback. However, it was still considered very/useful by many students, despite being provided less frequently than other types of feedback (Table 22.7).

Students identified many valuable features of practice teachers' feedback. Most common among these was advice on ways of working or how to take the next step in a case.

> It was most useful to hear his thoughts on what I should do and informing me of what services and resources are available. There were many things I didn't know were out there that he or other colleagues informed me about.

The constructive nature of the feedback and the value of positive reinforcement, encouragement, and confidence-building were echoed in open responses by several respondents.

> She focused on the positives and highlighted what I did that worked and encouraged me to always try and improve on what was effective with clients ... she always followed up to see if I agreed/disagreed with the feedback. We would tease out any aspects of my practice that might have needed to be improved on and why it needed to be improved on, why I was practicing in a certain way, and how I can overcome it, so I was always very clear on how to develop and improve my skills.

Other useful aspects of practice teachers' feedback included: challenging assumptions and understandings, linking theory and practice advice, help with written work and the practice teacher's knowledge and skills, assisting with planning and prioritising, recommending readings and resources, 'thinking on one's feet', and use of language. However, some were critical of negative feedback.

> [There was] nothing useful about my practice teacher's feedback. Constant focus on mistakes, which were not tolerated. No constructive feedback was provided; just received criticism. It appeared that I was expected to operate at the level of an experienced practitioner within that organisation.

High intercorrelations between the various types of feedback indicates that students who were afforded one type of feedback were more likely to be afforded other types too. The corollary being that some students received infrequent feedback across the board. Three (3%) received feedback less than monthly and a further seven (7%), less than weekly.

> The only positive feedback that I received from my practice teacher was during the mid-placement and final placement and in the placement report. Sometimes, when I received positive feedback from other professionals, my practice teacher would agree. Apart from that, I only received feedback when I asked her how she thought I did or when she gave me negative feedback.

Induction, Training, and Safety Instruction

All students received induction or training, which was considered very/useful by over 70% ($n=66$). Safety instruction was made available to three-quarters of students ($n=74$, 74%) but was considered notably less useful than induction or training ($P \leq 0.001$). Induction, training, and safety instructions did not contribute to perceived learning, and, at best, a useful induction programme made only a moderate contribution to satisfaction (rs = 0.339, $P \leq 0.001$). Qualitative comments from respondents go some way to explaining this, as safety training was largely considered the responsibility of the university.

Reflective Practice: Self-reflection and Critique

Responses to open questions about skills learnt on placement elicited commentary on reflective approaches ($n=10$).

> [My practice teacher] taught me to implement a 'what I did well' and 'what I could do better' approach to reflection, which ensured that the good work I was doing was always acknowledged too, instead of constantly critiquing myself, which can get a bit overwhelming.

Table 22.8 Frequency and Usefulness of Reflective and Critical Practices

(8a) Frequency of reflective and critical practices

	Reflective practice	*Reflective journal*	*Critiquing own work*
1. Daily	40 (44%)	17 (19%)	43 (47%)
2. ≥ Weekly	42 (46%)	33 (36%)	36 (40%)
3. ≥ Monthly	7 (8%)	14 (15%)	10 (11%)
4. < Monthly	2 (2%)	8 (9%)	2 (2%)
5. Never	1 (1%)	20 (22%)	0
Total	92 (101%)†	92 (101%)†	91 (100%)
No Answer	8	8	9

(8b) Usefulness of reflective and critical practices

	Reflective practice	*Reflective journal*	*Critiquing own work*
1. Very useful	51 (58%)	18 (21%)	55 (63%)
2. Useful	33 (38%)	27 (31%)	29 (33%)
3. Neither useful nor not useful	2 (2%)	22 (25%)	3 (3%)
4. Less than useful	0 (0%)	7 (8%)	1 (1%)
4. Not useful at all	2 (2%)	13 (15%)	0 (0%)
Total	88 (100%)	87 (100%)	88 (100%)
No Answer	12	13	12

† deviation from 100% due to rounding error

Despite the emphasis on reflective practice that is central to the social work programme, fewer than half of the students took time to engage in reflective practice or critique their own work on a daily basis, although most did so at least weekly (Table 22.8a). Notwithstanding this, both learning tools were rated as very/useful by almost all students (Table 22.8b). Keeping a reflective journal was used much less frequently and was considered less useful than the other reflective tools, although over half felt that it was useful.

> Even though it was not something that I had anticipated would be useful, the use of a reflective journal was really beneficial to me. I did not have the best time on placement with regards to my practice teacher, so it helped me to write down what I was learning despite the struggles that I had, which helped me to remain positive throughout placement.

However, despite their perceived value, none of these reflective tools were correlated with placement satisfaction or learning.

Student-driven Tools Needing Improvement

Some tools intended to support student placement learning were considered 'neither useful nor not useful' (Table 22.6). These included the writing of placement reports, case studies, required readings, learning journals, and process recordings. Notwithstanding the low rating of the usefulness of writing fieldwork placement reports, this tool was moderately correlated with both satisfaction ($rs = 0.22, P \leq 0.05$) and learning on placement ($rs = 0.23, P \leq 0.05$). Although the perceived learning value of documentary work was low, subsequent open questions on skills acquired, skills required, and training needed identified writing skills as an area of need ($n = 28$). The need for skills in practice writing were identified to include care planning sheets, sample case notes, court reports, and assessment frameworks. Suggestions were also made for specific training on writing.

> More emphasis [is needed] on how to write case notes, as this is one of the major areas in a social worker's job. Once a week, a practicing social worker should come to the [university] class, present a case: discuss the interview with their client, show how to present notes, and then show how to plan an intervention/construct a care plan (each week a different area of social work should be presented).

A final tool is the role play. Whilst, it is used in the academic learning environment, role play was the least frequently used learning tool on placement. The tool was used, on average, less than monthly and considered the least useful of all tools. However, it was associated, albeit inadequately, with greater learning ($rs = 0.261$, $P \leq 0.05$).

Skills Development

Other skills developed on placement which students cited in open questions included: communicating and listening skills; case management; relationship and rapport building; observation skills; counselling; information gathering; preparation; self-care/protection; resilience; when to disengage. The growth in other skills and values (being non-judgmental; authoritative; confident; innovative; empathetic; supportive; constructive; respectful; honest; open; truthful; dedicated; and non-presumptive) were also mentioned. Several practice teachers were clearly inspirational, imparting a dedication to their work which does not lend itself to a list of imparted skills.

> My practice teacher would go to the absolute end of the earth for a client; she stopped at nothing. I will always remember that of her; she would spend the time with clients and get them anything they needed that she had the power to get for them.

What Factors Influenced the Perceived Success of Placement?

Throughout the study the 'success' of placements was measured using two dependent variables: student's overall satisfaction with the placement and the student's perception of their learning. Correlation of these variables with learning supports allowed the authors to establish what role supports played in a positive placement evaluation. Student-driven tools such as self-reflection, critiquing one's own work, writing placement reports, case studies, required readings, oral case presentations, learning journals, and process recordings were at best inadequate in correlation with learning and satisfaction. Formal inputs such as induction, training, and safety instructions did not contribute to perceived learning.

The frequency of support from others such as assistance with managing caseload, administration support, and brainstorming solutions, were all positively correlated with learning and satisfaction. Although other dyadic tools, such as role-playing and discussing case notes, did not make a significant contribution to overall satisfaction, greater frequency of role-playing, although less valued, was weakly associated with greater learning. Somewhat contrary to the high value placed on working with cases through observing, co-working, and increased responsibility/independent work, it was not strongly correlated with perceived learning or overall satisfaction. Instead, greater frequency of co-working and increased responsibility/independent work were correlated with greater learning. Repeating the influence of dyadic support, all 'supervision and feedback' tools were significantly correlated with both greater learning and higher satisfaction. The frequency of formal supervision – a 'core tradition' (Beddoe, 2010, p. 1292) of social work – had the weakest correlation with learning and satisfaction, while the frequency of informal supervision was among the stronger correlations.

Discussion

Fieldwork education is well recognised within the research literature as being a central component of social work education (Bogo, 2015; Goodyear, 2014; Flanagan & Wilson, 2018). For many students, placements are the first opportunity to interact with social work clients and observe social work in practice. It is the first time that students can try out skills acquired in the academic setting. The role of practice teachers is a powerful one, both in terms of providing the necessary learning opportunities and assessment of students' readiness to enter the profession. Practice teachers have an ethical responsibility to ensure that students have sufficient experience on placement to gain the skills they require for social work practice.

This research, albeit small-scale, enabled the student voice to be the foreground, amplifying their opinions and experiences of what makes a good placement and the tools that assist in their learning. The response from students was very positive in terms of overall satisfaction with placements. As educators, it would be easy to become complacent considering such a positive response. However, the research highlighted several areas needing improvement.

One area identified by students was a lack of support from the university during placement. This was also associated with students not feeling sufficiently prepared for placement. Analysis of student responses indicated that, although students were receiving preparation for practice throughout the academic semester prior to placement, this was not recognised and/or working for students and, therefore, necessitated a different approach. An intensive '*preparation for practice*' module was introduced and delivered immediately prior to placement. The module specifically addressed issues raised by students in the research, such as a lack of clarity about stakeholder roles during placements. Time was dedicated to clearly identify the roles of all parties in the placement: practice teachers, practice tutors, and the university – with detail about support provision from each. Emphasis was put on describing the role and giving examples of where tutors might become involved beyond the standardised meetings. The practice learning handbook also explicitly detailed the roles and expectations of the responsible placement stakeholders.

The authors were cognisant of the fact that placements which necessitate heavy involvement of practice tutors and the university tend to be the those with which there are significant difficulties, such as the potential for failure or fitness to practice proceedings. These stressful and difficult situations are likely to trigger negative commentary on the role of those involved, and in the absence of clarity about roles, students may assume that the university can override decisions made by the practice teacher and become dissatisfied if this does not happen. Finch (2015) examined the role of practice tutors in managing students who are failing placements and concluded that the role of the tutor is multifaceted, complex, and poses distinct challenges. This complexity supported findings from the current research that the role of practice tutors needed to be more explicit. The lack of clarity regarding the role of practice tutors was not wholly unexpected, as there is a dearth of research literature on the role of practice tutors in social work practice education in general. The spotlight on the need for role clarity emerging from the current study prompted invitations to practice tutors and practice teachers to attend workshops together in which the overlap and distinction between practice teacher and practice tutor roles were discussed and elucidated.

Reflecting on the tools that students valued on placement, observation and observing social work practitioners were rated very highly. Supervision and feedback were also rated as core to learning on placement by students, with informal supervision being rated as more valuable than formal supervision. The value of informal supervision echoes LeFevre's (2005) finding of the importance of the practice teacher's availability to the student, as well as providing a collaborative and encouraging learning environment. Our research findings indicate that students placed a much greater emphasis on the role of external contributors to their learning such as their practice teachers or other team members (Flanagan & Wilson, 2018). This does not sit well with the idea that practice learning is rooted in theories of adult learning in which students are actively engaged and self-directed in their learning.

The finding is also unusual given that students in this study reported that practice teachers encouraged the use of self-reflection, and the students themselves recognised it as being an important skill (Flanagan & Wilson, 2018). The extent to which supervision and feedback overshadow the importance of autonomous learning in students' eyes is concerning. This finding underlines the need for social work educators to instil in students the confidence and trust in the value of their own role in learning, imbuing them with a sense of responsibility for their own learning. Adult learning requires students to be active participants in their learning and, whilst students will continue to have external learning tools at their disposal, they need to be proactive in both identifying and taking responsibility for learning. As noted in the introduction, the relationship between student and practice teacher is very complex, as is the relationship between student, practice teacher, practice tutor, and university.

Conclusion

Research, to date, has focused on hearing the voice of social work educators both in practice and in the university setting, and more research is required that invites the student voice to be heard. Valuing autonomous learning is a vital preparation for professional lives (Wilson & Flanagan, 2019), and more research is required on how best to equip students to do this. Encouraging students to navigate their own learning, particularly within in the practice learning setting, may engender the confidence to voice opinions about what is important for their learning as student social workers and in their future careers, in turn, improving the experiences for service users.

References

Beddoe, L. (2010). Surveillance or reflection: Professional supervision in 'the risk society'. *British Journal of Social Work*, 40(4), 1279–1296.

Bogo, M. (2015). Field education for clinical social work practice: Best practices and contemporary challenges. *Clinical Social Work Journal*, 43(3), 317–324.

Finch, J. (2015). Running with the fox and hunting with the hounds: Social work tutors' experiences of managing failing social work students in practice learning settings. *British Journal of Social Work*, 45(7), 2124–2141.

First-Year MSocSc (Social Work) Students, Flanagan, N., & Wilson, E. (2015). What facilitates learning on placement? *Unpublished poster presentation at: Irish Association of Social Workers Annual Conference*, Dublin, Ireland.

Flanagan, N., & Wilson, E. (2018). What makes a good placement? Findings of a social work student-to-student research study. *Social Work Education*, 37(5), 565–580.

Gelman, G. (2004). Anxiety experienced by foundation-year MSW students entering field placement: Implications for admissions, curriculum, and field education. *Journal of Social Work Education*, 40(1), 39–54.

Goodyear, R.K. (2014). Supervision as pedagogy: Attending to its essential instructional and learning processes. *The Clinical Supervisor*, 33(1), 82–99.

Joubert, L., Hebel, L., McNeill, A., Firth, S., McFadden, E., & Hocking, A. (2017). Teaching research in social work through academic practitioner partnerships: Knowledge, competency and confidence. *Advances in Social Work and Welfare Education*, 19(1), 37–48.

Kanno, H., & Koeske, G. (2010). MSW students' satisfaction with their field placements: The role of preparedness and supervision quality. *Journal of Social Work Education*, 46(1), 23–38.

Kourgiantakis, T., Sewell, K., & Bogo, M. (2019). The importance of feedback in preparing social work students for field education. *Clinical Social Work Journal*, 47(1), 124–133.

Lee, M., & Fortune, A.E. (2013). Do we need more 'doing' activities or 'thinking' activities in the field practicum? *Journal of Social Work Education*, 49(4), 646–660.

Lefevre, M. (2005). Facilitating practice learning and assessment: The influence of relationship. *Social Work Education*, 24(5), 565–583.

McIntyre, G., & Paul, S. (2013). Teaching research in social work: Capacity and challenge. *British Journal of Social Work*, 43(1), 685–702.

McPherson, L., & Barnett, M. (2006). Beginning practice in child protection: A blended learning approach. *Social Work Education*, 25(2), 192–198.

Rubin, D., Robinson, B., & Valutis, S. (2010). Social work education and student research projects: A survey of program directors. *Journal of Social Work Education*, 46(1), 39–55.

Wilson, E., & Flanagan, N. (2019). What tools facilitate learning on placement? Findings of a social work student-to-student research study. *Social Work Education*. https://doi.org/10.1080/02615479.2019.1702636.

23

Fieldwork in social work education in Slovenia

Needs, challenges and possible solutions

Liljana Rihter and Tamara Rape Žiberna

Historical Perspectives

The science and practice of social work has developed in three basic dimensions: knowledge creation (research), knowledge transmission (education), and knowledge application (practice, fieldwork) (Lyons, 2000). Fieldwork education is a valuable part of social work education because it develops the competencies and knowledge which are expected in the labour market and are required to respond to the needs of people, communities, and societies (Bălăuţă & Vlaicu, 2017; Rape Žiberna & Žiberna, 2017; Bogo, 2015; Cleak, Hawkins, Loughton, & Williams, 2015; McLaughlin, Scholar, McCaughan, & Coleman, 2015; Robertson, 2013; Bogo & Power, 1992) and realises the basic principles of social work, defined by the International Association of Schools of Social Work (I.A.S.S.W., n.d.) as a practice-based profession. The importance of fieldwork in social work education was emphasised at the outset as a special characteristic distinct from other professions (Kendall, 1959). It was regarded as important for students to be in contact with people (users of social work) already in the first year of their studies. In the United States of America, the first courses were practically oriented, while the importance of theory and practice later became the fundamental guideline. Social work students had contact with fieldwork under the supervision of an educator from the beginning of their education, allowing them to integrate theory and practice (Kendall, 1959). How to provide fieldwork education was a burning issue – what kind of skills, the extent of acquisition, what amount of time (and money) is required, and the appropriate methods for teaching it. Questions about a right balance between theoretical and practical knowledge were also raised, with the possibility and value of an internship after completing one's degree being placed at the forefront; yet, even today none of these issues have been clearly settled. The amount and importance of fieldwork education in social work has led some authors to argue that such experiences are the most valuable and have a more lasting effect than other forms of education (Sherer & Peleg-Oren, 2005, p. 316). Although it is generally agreed that fieldwork education is important, playing a key role in social work by facilitating a synthesis of what is learned at university (Parker, 2006), several studies also find that this aspect of university teaching is relatively overlooked (Domakin, 2014; Wilson & Kelly, 2010). We may agree with early authors (Kendall, 1959) researching this field that constant evaluation and reflection of social work

DOI: 10.4324/9781032164946-28

education are called for. Papouli (2014) points out that educators and field instructors rarely reflect on the process of students' learning in both classrooms and field settings because they are more focused on their own tasks and operations. Yet, the learning process is a considerable factor in achieving adequate competencies and professional identity. While professional (social work) education is usually categorised as formal learning and cognitive learning, Marsick and Watkins (2001) argue that informal learning occurs, especially in fieldwork placements. Informal learning is not neutral; it is experiential in nature and, therefore, connected to tacit knowledge; it also takes place in a social context as a constructivist activity in which person and environment interact (Papouli 2014). Approaches to fieldwork learning in social work education vary around the world, although Cleak and Zuchowski (2019) state that fieldwork is vital for social work students' transition to practice. This, then, makes it necessary to ensure the quality of fieldwork education, which is a real challenge (Bălăuţă & Vlaicu, 2017, p. 54; Bogo, 2015, p. 318; Robertson, 2013; Sherer & Peleg-Oren, 2005, p. 316; Cavazos, 1996) also because more organisations (faculty and fieldwork base) are being included (Barretti, 2007, 2009; Knight, 2001; Webb, 1988).

In Slovenia, fieldwork education has been a notable part of social work education ever since it was established in 1955 with a 2-year school (Zaviršek, 2005). Rapoša Tajnšek (2005) points out that, at the beginning, students were individuals already working in the social protection field or in departments of local or state authorities responsible for social well-being. Accordingly, they were engaged in fieldwork activities in their own organisations (in which they were employed), while, at the school, they had regular meetings and lessons about the methods and techniques of practical work. Historical records (Rapoša Tajnšek, 2005) show that, ten years after the study of social work began, students had one month of fieldwork between the first and second study years and three months in the last year. After 1973, fieldwork was carried out in the fifth semester when the main activities were seminar work about the organisation and functions of the fieldwork base, describing cases in terms of legal regulation and the method of work with the individual, using methods of group and community work, writing a journal of fieldwork activities, and preparing a diploma thesis (Rapoša Tajnšek, 2005, pp. 142–143). Flaker (2005) notes that the reforms which followed in the education sphere were not always supportive of fieldwork. In 1978, the 'absolvent year' (the period after completing all of one's exams in which to attend to all outstanding scholarly issues and before graduating) had been reduced to a single semester, and fieldwork, therefore, had to be included in regular semesters in the first and second years, although it was then performed differently, entailing voluntary work projects in which two teachers managed a project group of 15 students working in various fields (mainly with children and youth). With the transformation to four-year studies and the academisation of social work studies, fieldwork was reduced to a total of two and a half months. Still, on the other side, fieldwork manuals were produced to provide guidelines, and students were supervised by mentors in the faculty (teachers and assistants) and mentors in the fieldwork placements (social workers in the field). A further improvement in fieldwork education came after 2007 with the establishment of the Centre for Practice (hereinafter: the C.P.) and the Bologna reform of higher education in Slovenia (Mesec, 2015). At the C.P., various stakeholders (teachers, students, mentors from the field) participate in the planning, implementing, and evaluation (reflecting on) of fieldwork activities. This means that all of them participate in knowledge transfer, reflection, questioning, and the co-creating of new theories and practice (Mesec, 2015).

Compared to workplace learning theories (Hager, 2005), fieldwork learning in Slovenia has developed from the initial phase when fieldwork education was based on approaches that view workplace learning as a product (individual approaches) to the current phase in which fieldwork education is regarded more as a participatory process (socio-cultural approaches) or that learning is a process of construction and/or reconstruction. The above analysis of past curricula also shows that fieldwork has become more important over the decades.

Individual approaches in learning theory stress the following important characteristics of students with possible impacts on the achievement of competencies (Bogo, 2010; Papouli, 2014): a need to know (actively engaged students learn more), self-concept related to autonomy and self-directedness (students who accept responsibility for their actions are capable of making ethical choices), experiences (students with previous experience may learn faster), readiness to learn, orientation to learning (task-centred and/or problem-centred), and motivation to learn (internal motivation).

On the contrary, socio-cultural approaches emphasise the importance of the social context – the social, relational, and situational aspects. 'Students learn from, through, and with their interactions with others – their supervisors or field instructors, other students, work groups, other professionals, and more advanced or experienced others' (Papouli, 2014, p. 9). Students learn by observing practice and from instructions, underscoring the importance of values, behaviours, and attitudes in the working environment and also how their participation is perceived and carried out (Papouli, 2014).

Despite socio-cultural approaches being favoured in Slovenia, the system of fieldwork education must be constantly analysed and assessed to ensure it is able to respond to all challenges.

Current Programme for Fieldwork in Social Work Education in Slovenia

Fieldwork learning is a development process (Papouli, 2014). In Slovenia, Šugman Bohinc (2016) strongly recommends an epistemologically reflexive, ethically sensitive, and (self)critical attitude as well as narrative skills of collaboration in all social work education activities. In this way, students can develop their own professional behaviour so as to be able to answer the complex challenges of their partners in cooperation projects. This was elaborated on while planning a new programme for social work education according to the Bologna reform principles after 2007.

The core competencies students should acquire in the undergraduate programme of social work are: to identify, critically analyse, integrate, research, evaluate, plan, and utilise the resources of different (user and professional) systems; to co-create necessary solutions or desired outcomes in partnerships, as an ethical and professional response; networking; and to develop innovative approaches in support of resolving social distress in people's psychosocial problems in a special, social-work way that is different from other professions in the social protection field (Fakulteta za socialno delo, n.d. a).

In the current curriculum, fieldwork plays an important role. In the first and second years, students must complete 190 hours in each course – Practice I and Practice II. Of this, students perform around 100 hours of supervised work in different organisations and institutions. The courses are worth 10 E.C.T.S. (European credit transfer and accumulation system), e.g., credits out of 60 E.C.T.S. credits required for each year. The main goals of Practice I are: the student should become acquainted with social work, value context, and the life-world of the user as well as the network of social services; understand the contradictions arising from differences between user/professional perspectives; be involved in research and development projects in the field, learn, and practise basic social work skills (co-create projects of help and support in dialogue with users and knowledge of establishing the first contact and the working relationship; knowledge of leading a conversation, of documenting and writing, of research and reflection, and the use of ethics and personal responsibility; enabling access to important resources);

the competence of recognising and controlling one's own feelings and of searching for help by oneself. The core intention of Practice I is, therefore, to provide information and knowledge of mapping the life-world of the user in their local environment; of observing, listening, collecting, and forwarding information; safeguarding personal information; establishing the first contact and presenting themselves; becoming acquainted with special approaches regarding users' context; following the user perspective; knowing the characteristics of different types of conversations, writing notes and documents, and reporting; becoming sensitive to social inequalities on various levels; recognising and articulating values and positions concerning the phenomena of social exclusion, prejudice, and stereotypes; and becoming acquainted with the methods and techniques of intervision. While the aims of Practice I mainly refer to the situation of users, the aims of Practice II are broader. Students are required to know the characteristics of community and organisational project work; to learn how to research needs, to plan, organise, and manage projects under the supervision of mentors; and to develop a value stance on social inequalities and exclusion. They should cooperate in supporting individuals and communities and ensure users have an impact on it and support processes of integration and co-creation of changes in communities. They must reflect on concrete measures and practices derived from social policy and the implementation of legislation and its impact on individuals/groups (and understand the institutional context of some measures and improve it). Students should also be assertive while performing the planned tasks. They need to be sufficiently competent to know and use social work terminology, co-create unique projects of help and support, co-create innovations, recognise and manage their own feelings, and search for help if they need to. For the purpose of achieving these aims, the content of Practice II includes planning and implementing of a project or minor innovation, teamwork and groupwork, the methodology of assessing needs, and fieldwork in a public or institutional setting; strategies of planning services; strategies of fundraising and developing partnerships and coalitions; communication in the context of community and organisations; advocacy; mediation; negotiation; empowerment and ensuring users have an influence on the processes of social protection services; knowledge of legislation and using it to resolve the tangible issues of people and, similarly, as in Practice I, to develop a sensitivity to social inequalities and exclusions (especially for people with handicaps); to identify obstacles in the community; and methods and techniques of intervision (Fakulteta za socialno delo, n.d. b.).

In the third year, students must devote more hours (250) to the Practice III course. They complete 240 hours (over six weeks) of supervised fieldwork. The course is worth 15 E.C.T.S. credits out of 60 E.C.T.S. credits needed for the year. The main aims of Practice III are (Fakulteta za socialno delo, n.d. b.): to test social work skills and procedures with a focus on public power of attorney; to deepen the skills of establishing a working relationship, to co-create original projects for giving support and assistance, with an emphasis on family social work; to encounter a position of professional power and responsibility; and to learn about and test specific social work methods and skills in the chosen field of work (modules). Similarly, like in Practice II, students are required to deepen their knowledge of social work terminology, of dialogue with users in original support and assistance projects, of their understanding of the ways in which institutions function, and of using professional methods and techniques in special fields of work and managing their own feelings and search for help by themselves if needed. The content of Practice III includes learning about the fieldwork placement and its work and related legislation; planning the content of practice; knowledge of public power of attorney authority; training in basic skills (e.g., skills of co-creating a stimulating context to develop a successful dialogic practice of social work) and their application in social work; practising the method of intervision and other specific techniques according to the corresponding module.

Practice IV consists of 160 hours (10 E.C.T.S. credits), and its chief goals are to complete tasks and projects which students have started during their studies, deepen any knowledge and competencies previously assessed to be not fully sufficient or in need of improvement, develop job-search skills and career planning, seek employment opportunities, plan employment-related innovation, with a focus on considering a user perspective on needs assessment, plan service and service delivery, and evaluate the experiences and achievements during the fieldwork. Once again, similar competencies as in Practice II and Practice III should be achieved and deepened and certain additional knowledge, such as recognising the importance of social work while working with other professions (sociology, psychology, pedagogy, law, etc.), professionally reflecting on one's own fieldwork in a special field and on one's own personal involvement, and practising the ethics of participation. The content of Practice IV, thus, encompasses the epistemological perspective, user perspective, gender perspective, and issues of violence and other specific issues in social work practice; innovative approaches to researching needs and the planning of services, evaluation, the ethics of participation, the methods and techniques of intervision; and career planning (Fakulteta za socialno delo, n.d. b).

On the postgraduate level, individual project work and fieldwork account for 130 hours or 10 E.C.T.S. credits. The course's main goal is to give students the opportunity to test their practical competencies in fieldwork in a chosen field of social work. The student can also test the theoretical knowledge they have acquired in a concrete practical situation, and they are then expected to reflect on it. More specifically, students should acquire the following competencies: to link the theoretical doctrinal principles of social work with practical professional work; to directly apply basic concepts and participatory approaches in practice; to understand the way the institutions function and their relationship with the social environment with a view to improving institutional practices; to understand the protective and risk factors in different social work areas; to be able to consistently use social work terminology and language; to critically reflect professional language (discursive or epistemological analysis and its effects on social work practice); to critically reflect on the advocacy of social work professional autonomy in dialogue with various actors and institutions in the public sphere; to be able to explore and reflect on one's personal involvement in subsequent processes of social work; and to be able to reflect critically on one's own professional practices in the fieldwork. The content of individual project work and fieldwork may vary according to different modules in the postgraduate social work programme, yet some general guidelines reveal that fieldwork is the focus and that reflection on experiences plays a main role. The course is to prepare students to enter specific fieldwork in which students, under the supervision of a mentor, will prepare a plan for the fieldwork and innovation and implement it with constant monitoring (writing a journal, a report on the implemented innovation/project). Students must, therefore, test the usefulness of the knowledge they acquired from all courses in the programme. The course is related to the preparation of a master's thesis. Students may undertake empirical research or a project for the final thesis (Fakulteta za socialno delo, n.d. c).

The organisation of the fieldwork is coordinated by the C.P. In Slovenia, a coordinator from the faculty, a mentor from the faculty (a teaching assistant), a coordinator at the fieldwork base, a mentor at the fieldwork base (in smaller teaching bases, these are the same person), and a student are involved in implementing (and facilitating) the practice. At the Faculty of Social Work (more specifically at the C.P.), it has been observed that quality mentors are vital for a practice that is high in quality (Mesec, 2015).

Fieldwork represents about 20% of the undergraduate study programme and 17% of postgraduate programmes. This is in contrast with other countries, for instance Australia, where fieldwork represents 25% of the undergraduate study programme and about 50% of postgraduate programmes, while accreditation standards define the minimum fieldwork hours for social work education (Cleak & Zuchowski, 2019). In Slovenia, there is only one faculty of social work and there are no special accreditation standards for social work fieldwork (except for the general guideline in the Bologna reform of higher education also promoting fieldwork education). After completing studies (graduating), a social worker in Slovenia should apply for an internship (nine months) that ends with a professional exam and only then is a social worker licensed to work in the social protection field. In this way, internship provides an extra opportunity for supervised fieldwork.

We may conclude that, over the decades, fieldwork has gained in importance in social work education in Slovenia. During the Bologna process of harmonising the European higher education system, fieldwork was further improved with occasional monitoring and self-evaluations being provided. The primary purpose of the fieldwork is to connect social work courses (theory) with practical experiences under the supervision of a competent social worker (mentor at the fieldwork base) and a teaching assistant to enable reflection on and the development of practical skills according to the established social work principles and values. While students also learn about practice in a class setting, the majority of learning takes place in the field (Papouli, 2014). Field placement acts as a link between theory and professional work (Parker, 2007). Fieldwork enables students to learn without the pressures professional social workers encounter at work. Nevertheless, it is a challenge because students must integrate the (theoretical) knowledge and practice and acquire practical skills. Fieldwork can also contribute to personal development (Papouli, 2014).

Assessment of Fieldwork Education in Social Work in Slovenia

Main Challenges and Research Questions

Fieldwork education is a complex process for which organisation and implementation typically involves more stakeholders than in other parts of the teaching process, making ensuring the quality of the practical training quite a challenging task. Bălăuţă and Vlaicu (2017, p. 54) find that the quality of fieldwork depends on the fieldwork bases available and the effectiveness of their teaching. Bogo (2015, p. 318) adds that the nature of social work means that the true challenge is in determining to how to organise effective fieldwork. Robertson (2013) notes that maintaining the quality of fieldwork is an extremely sensitive, demanding, and time-consuming task. Thus, the result of such efforts does not necessarily need to be noticeable (in terms of the progress observed in the students' knowledge and ability), as also stated by Cavazos (1996). Sherer and Peleg-Oren (2005, p. 316) refer to the main stakeholders as the 'learning triangle' and consider that the mentors in the fieldwork base, the mentors from the faculty, and the students all play their role in preparing the social worker as an expert.

In the education of a future social worker, the influence of organisational culture and climate in fieldwork bases cannot be neglected. Bellinger (2010, p. 600) finds that organisations (fieldwork bases) rarely meet the criteria of learning organisations (see, for example, Škerlavaj et al., 2007). In the literature (Barretti, 2007, 2009; Knight, 2001; Webb, 1988), one also finds that both social work teachers from the faculty and mentors in the fieldwork bases act as role models for students in their socialisation into social work, and, thus, their role is critical. The quality of the latter's work in this area is also shown in student satisfaction (Knight, 2001; Fortune, McCarty & Abramson, 2001). Knight (2001) adds that a student's perception of their mentor's skills is very important. The expectations of students are also high because they see the fieldwork as the most important element of their studies (Sherer & Peleg-Oren, 2005). The qualifications of future social workers largely depend on the quality of support and mentoring students receive from the way their fieldwork is organised. As noted by Cavazos (1996), social work teachers also believe that the student–mentor relationship in the classroom is a key element of students' personal growth and learning, and more attention should, accordingly, be paid to this aspect.

The aim of this article is to briefly examine (using data from Slovenia) the satisfaction with different elements of fieldwork in social work of three major partners involved in the organisation of fieldwork. The results focus on an analysis of needs, challenges, and suggestions among all three partners (students, mentors from the faculty, and mentors in fieldwork organisations) that may lead to the improved quality of fieldwork education.

Methodology of Research

Population, Sample

The population comprises members of three sub-populations – students of social work, mentors located at fieldwork bases, and mentors from the faculty in the 2014–2015 study year.

Data were gathered from June to September 2015 from 186 students, representing 30.5% of all undergraduate social work students in Slovenia. All 610 students were invited (by e-mail) to participate in an online survey (using the 1Ka tool (1KA, 2020)).

The sub-population of mentors located at fieldwork bases comprises professionals (mostly social workers) who act as mentors (in fieldwork bases found across Slovenia) to students of the Faculty of Social Work at the University of Ljubljana in an undergraduate Bologna programme in the 2014–2015 academic year. According to the C.P., 242 mentors (i.e., those who had provided mentoring to at least one Faculty of Social Work student) were active during that academic year. All those meeting the above defining conditions were invited by e-mail in June 2015 to participate in an online survey conducted by the C.P. to evaluate student fieldwork, of whom 114 mentors (47.1% of those invited) participated in the survey.

In the 2014–2015 academic year, the Faculty of Social Work at the University of Ljubljana had 14 mentors (teaching assistants), 11 of whom participated in the mentioned online survey.

Data Collection and Analysis

The data were collected as part of the C.P.'s evaluation of fieldwork education in the 2014–2015 academic year. Two online surveys were conducted (using the 1Ka tool for Web surveys) – one for students and the other for mentors (from different organisations) and mentors from the faculty, such that the evaluation, similar to Higgins (2017), covered aspects of the three fieldwork stakeholders. The extensive questionnaires contained more than 70 questions (of various types), and the data were collected between 9 June and 30 September 2015. In this analysis, only selected questions (regarding satisfaction, challenges, and suggestions) from the questionnaire for mentors in the organisation are considered.

The analysis is based on secondary data, and the instrument itself was not adapted to the needs of the analysis. Two questions with numerical answers were analysed (using S.P.S.S. 24) and descriptive statistics were calculated. From the questionnaires for the mentors from the faculty and mentors at the fieldwork base, 17 open-ended questions were analysed about needs, challenges, and suggestions, and from the questionnaire for students, 16 open-ended questions were analysed.

Main Results

Satisfaction with Fieldwork

As shown in Table 23.1, all stakeholders agree that fieldwork in social work in Slovenia is good. Mentors from the faculty, on average, gave the highest score (around 8.4 on a 10-point scale) for their satisfaction with the fieldwork, while students in higher years of study, on average, gave the lowest score (around 7.9 on 10-point scale). Each participant made two assessments of the fieldwork – first at the beginning of the questionnaire (their first score) and then again at the end of the questionnaire, after the respondent's own analysis of the fieldwork (encouraged by a series of assessments of different elements of fieldwork).

Mentors from the Faculty

NEEDS OF MENTORS FROM THE FACULTY

The mentors from the faculty expressed their need for unification with respect to their expectations of students and the mentors' own understanding of the *instructions for fieldwork tasks*. Some mentors suggested that good practice examples of students' work and the instructions could support unification.

Regarding the *fieldwork tasks*, mentors from the faculty mentioned the complexity and quantity of tasks. Some think that students have too many fieldwork tasks, which is the biggest reason

Table 23.1 Satisfaction with Fieldwork

		Assessment of the fieldwork at the start of the questionnaire (on a 10-point scale, where 1 is very bad and 10 is very good)	*Assessment of the fieldwork at the end of the questionnaire (on a 10-point scale, where 1 is very bad and 10 is very good)*
Mentors from the faculty	*N*	11	9
	Minimum	4	8
	Maximum	10	10
	Mean	8.36	8.44
	Std. Deviation	1.69	0.726
Mentors at the fieldwork base	*N*	109	84
	Minimum	1	2
	Maximum	10	10
	Mean	8.35	8.25
	Std. Deviation	1.691	1.735
First- and second-year students	*N*	84	59
	Minimum	1	3
	Maximum	10	10
	Mean	8.15	8.25
	Std. Deviation	1.477	1.281
Third- and fourth-year students	*N*	101	76
	Minimum	3	3
	Maximum	10	10
	Mean	7.92	7.86
	Std. Deviation	1.747	1.547

they are done only superficially. Some tasks are more demanding than others, depending on the circumstances. They also suggest that students need greater training for some tasks.

The mentors' opinions on the *unification* among them concerning fieldwork are divided. Some believe that greater unification toward students, at least about the conditions and the instructions, could be beneficial and see the lack of some teachers' participation at the faculty's C.P. as a crucial barrier to any more unified approach to the students. Other teachers are convinced that greater unification (among the 14 people who constituted the C.P.) is impossible without introducing more stringent rules and reducing teachers' autonomy. There are also some teachers who agree with certain aspects of both presented sites.

CHALLENGES AND SUGGESTIONS

The mentors mentioned four groups of challenges. The first relate to *mentoring*. They identify a lack of competencies for mentoring students, supporting mentors in the field, and poor conditions for their mentoring to be of quality (too many students and organisations (mentors in the field) per mentor at the faculty). The second group of challenges refers to the *functioning of the C.P.* In this regard, teachers had different opinions on both – how it is working now and on how it should work. Some were more prone to continuity while others thought a lot of room remains for improvement. Others suggested more democratic governance, greater dialogue with students and mentors in the field, and sanctions for members of the C.P. who do not regularly attend C.P. meetings. Some mentors from the faculty suggested that greater unification of demands and grading criteria for students' assessment is very important. Other suggestions were that the C.P. should take on certain new assignments, such as the assessment of organisations and mentors in the field, a greater developmental role for the C.P. in implementing new knowledge in social work practice, etc. The third group of challenges refers to *students*. Mentors at the faculty reported having noticed students lacking in competencies, motivation and self-initiative. They also reported that students are not adequately equipped to conduct particular tasks. The final group of challenges refers to *fieldwork tasks*. Some mentors argue that students have too many tasks (so they are done only superficially), that they must write too many papers, and there is still a lot of room to improve the instructions.

Mentors at the fieldwork bases

NEEDS OF MENTORS AT THE FIELDWORK BASES

The mentors at the fieldwork bases mentioned three areas of *needs regarding mentoring the students of social work programmes*. They all refer to the relationship between the faculty and the mentors of the fieldwork. The first area is the proper and prompt education and empowerment of mentors, the second is better knowledge and understanding of the specifics of social work in different areas (e.g., in schools and health care) from mentors from the faculty, and the third is expectations of greater support for their work in specific areas from the mentors at the faculty.

Needs regarding the fieldwork tasks of students can be divided into three groups. Mentors detected that some students do not understand all of the instructions, and certain tasks (which demand more courage and competencies) seem too complex for particular students. Feasibility is sometimes jeopardised because of the obsolescence of the mentors' knowledge and because the nature of the work in some organisations demands the customising of the fieldwork tasks.

CHALLENGES AND SUGGESTIONS

The mentors at the fieldwork bases mentioned challenges and suggestions that may be divided into six groups relating to: students (these were the most often mentioned), the implementation of fieldwork, the students' fieldwork tasks, mentoring at the fieldwork base, cooperation with the faculty, and other.

Among the *challenges relating to students,* the mentors noticed that some students are not sufficiently equipped with knowledge (especially about legislation and about the instructions), and some are not motivated enough (e.g., they want fewer working hours, they do other things while doing fieldwork, show no curiosity, and have no questions) for fieldwork learning, have no expectations, and are very passive. On the other hand, some students can be very critical of the way work is done in their organisations (e.g., the Centre for Social Work (C.S.W.)). Students' lack of agility, self-initiative, and flexibility (also with respect to working hours) was also described as potentially able to obstruct work in the organisation. Individual students were described as immature (in their reactions to users) or not precise enough. Some also had problems with making eye contact and other communication skills with users. Students' responsibility, reliability, and confident use of knowledge are also missed sometimes. Mentors would like to see the students practise self-reflection and susceptibility and to have a stronger interest in user lifestyles. Some also noticed differences between full- and part-time students.

The mentors offered some *suggestions relating to students*. They think that students' fear of having a conversation with users would be reduced if, during their studies, they would engage in more user interaction. During different tasks and encounters, students would also gain more courage and self-confidence. Students should pay greater attention to developing their professional curiosity and ask more questions about the fieldwork. They should also be more proactive, have some expectations of the fieldwork, and be more independent in planning activities, generating ideas, etc. In some areas, mentors stressed the importance of positive energy and optimism for successful work with users. Because students are not well informed about the scope of the C.S.W.'s work, the faculty could do more to provide students with the information they require. Mentors also detected some students misunderstood the instructions for fieldwork (especially for tasks) and were unable to resolve open dilemmas by themselves. They noticed that students need more support, especially in teamwork and knowledge of different fields (education, health care, etc.).

Challenges, which some mentors relate to the *implementation of fieldwork*, were an inadequate implementation schedule for students' fieldwork (1 week and Mondays in the first and second years of study) and the fact that organisations (mentors) do not receive students every year. Some also mentioned having noticed that students who combined work in more than one organisation did not advance in their self-initiative and confidence in their work as they would have had they only worked in a single organisation. Mentors' *suggestions* about the *implementation of fieldwork* can be divided into those who expressed a wish to have a student every year (and keeping those who were exceptional), and those who suggest more precise and detailed information about the fieldwork curriculum for mentors and about work in different areas of work for students. Others' suggestions were that the compulsory initial training of students (which some organisations provide) should not be counted in the hours of students' fieldwork.

Mentors pointed to the over-complexity of the tasks (in the third and fourth years of study) and the need to adjust the tasks (which the student and supervisor must complete) to the circumstances as the main *challenge relating to tasks*. As a *solution*, they suggest a stronger emphasis on quality than quantity (fewer tasks that could be done better), clearer instructions for the students, and more fieldwork tasks related to legislation.

The mentors also mentioned some *challenges relating to mentoring*. Some think the time of the seminar for mentors (usually held in the second half of March) is inappropriate because they regard it as very important. Also identified as a challenge were certain instructions and especially the dilemma of how to attract more social workers (their co-workers) to mentor students, as this is a very demanding and responsible task for which social workers are not fully appreciated (by their employee), nor financially rewarded. Mentors *suggest* that more seminars (on different topics and in different parts of the year) should be available to them. They also think that a meeting at the start of each study year could help in determining what it is that organisations and mentors can offer and suggest a rethinking of the financial rewards for mentors.

They also expressed the importance of good cooperation with the faculty. The mentors are satisfied with their cooperation with the coordinator of the C.P., with the *challenge* continuing to be *cooperation with some mentors at the faculty*. Mentors also expressed feelings that mentors at the faculty are not well informed about what is happening in social work practice in different areas and would also like to obtain more professional support from mentors at the faculty. Their *suggestion* to them is for more intense cooperation (in the form of at least one meeting and a couple of phone calls) in every study year.

Besides fieldwork being very important to students and mentors, some *other challenges* were also mentioned by the mentors at the fieldwork base, such as the need for systemic changes (in the social protection field) and that every social worker should be familiar with the C.S.W.'s work. *Other suggestions*, such as longer periods of fieldwork are better, were also mentioned.

Students

STUDENTS' NEEDS AND SUGGESTIONS

Students expressed different needs (as shown in Figure 23.1) regarding *materials for fieldwork*. First- and second-year students mostly expressed needs regarding better notification and instructions, while their third- and fourth-year colleagues also expressed needs regarding the accessibility of materials, training to perform the tasks, and the instructions for tasks.

Students also expressed some needs related to *tasks* (Figure 23.2). First- and second- year students expressed needs regarding instructions and support, whereas third- and fourth-year students emphasised needs related to feasibility and support. Students in all years identified needs related to the number and complexity of tasks.

CHALLENGES AND SUGGESTIONS

The students agreed about the following challenges identified with regard to mentors from the faculty and at the fieldwork base:

- Not all mentors at the fieldwork bases are appropriate (well equipped with knowledge), motivated, and have enough time to mentor students when performing their work. They

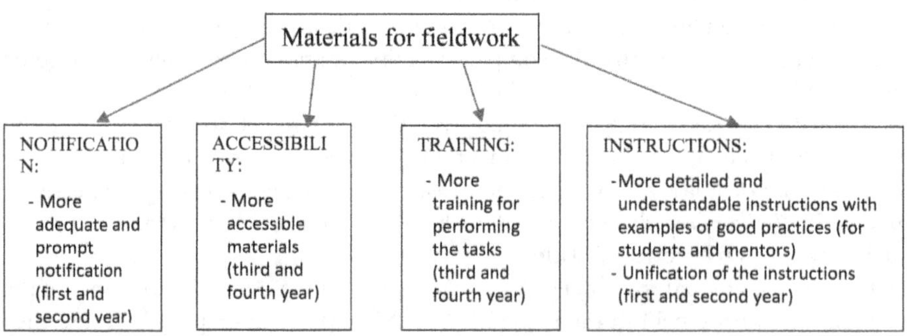

Figure 23.1 Students' needs and suggestions regarding materials for fieldwork.

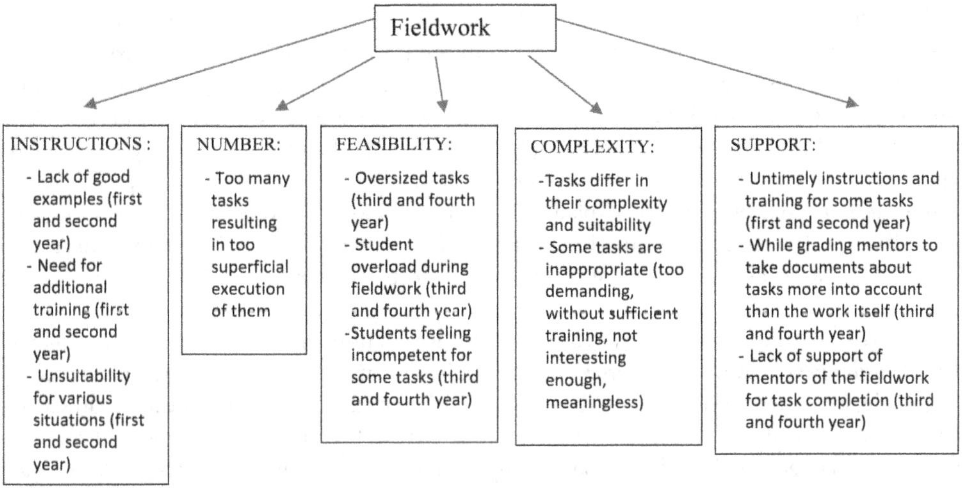

Figure 23.2 Students' needs and suggestions regarding fieldwork tasks.

are sometimes also not sufficiently informed about their role and have too many students at the same time as mentoring the fieldwork.

- Mentors from the faculty have too many students (the groups are too big); there are too many meetings with students; and their expectations, guidance, and grading differ. Some are also not very motivated to mentor or are unfamiliar with social work in different organisations.
- There is a lack of communication and cooperation between the mentors at the faculty and the mentors at the fieldwork base.

In relation to this, students *suggested* more motivated and accessible mentors (both faculty- and fieldwork-based) who are more interested in the students' progress. Students suggest that both be assessed by students and that the C.P. consider those grades while deciding on appropriate future mentors. Students think that fewer meetings with the faculty are needed (some could also be held on the internet) in smaller groups or individually and that mentors from the faculty should prepare for them and offer students clearer explanations of the required tasks, give students feedback on their assignments, help them with their dilemmas, and provide a lot of positive encouragement. Students suggest that mentors from the faculty should achieve greater unification among themselves of at least the basic demands and in their grading. At the end of the fieldwork, everyone involved should take the time and evaluate the fieldwork together. Students believe that, on one hand, the mentors at the fieldwork bases should be more motivated to mentor and be better prepared to share their knowledge and experiences and, on the other, allow students to try, as independently as possible, certain social work tasks. Some students also suggested compulsory education for mentors at fieldwork bases.

Students also see their lack of information and experiences regarding C.S.W. and the scarce opportunities to perform fieldwork there as challenging. As these public organisations are very important for social work in Slovenia, they suggest that every student should have at least part of their fieldwork at C.S.W. and that the faculty should give basic information about the administration and other specifics of C.S.W. to all students.

About the *content and organisation of fieldwork*, students feel they have too many tasks and not all of them are flexible enough or have a recognisable learning purpose for students. As a solution to this challenge, they suggest fewer, more flexible, and optional tasks and not as many papers about them. They also think that all mentors from the faculty should give them prompt, accurate instructions, illustrate them with examples, and have consistent expectations. Consequently, more of a student's fieldwork time and energy could be dedicated to working with users. More tasks could also be related to a selected module of a student. In the first and second years, students suggest that mentors from the faculty should process material for practice in classes, clarify the meaning and purpose of each task, explain the instructions for the required tasks in more detail, and explain the 'learning folder' (the final result of the fieldwork in which all papers related to the fieldwork are to be kept). They also think that case-based learning is the most appropriate approach and would also prefer to be given more tangible advice from mentors from the faculty.

Students in the third and fourth years of study also mentioned some *challenges in relation to fieldwork institutions*. In some cases, organisations applied for more students than they had (active) users, while some descriptions in the brochure, that led students to apply to the organisations for fieldwork, turned out to be false. Students suggest that, because they are not paid for their fieldwork, organisations should take care of students' lunch and transport costs while they are doing fieldwork; the faculty should harmonise the students' fieldwork tasks with organisations; and (especially for particular modules) more vacancies for fieldwork should also be arranged outside of the capital city of Ljubljana.

In the first two years, students also mention challenges relating to their motivation for fieldwork and insecurity related to their work in fieldwork placements (their ability to do some tasks and user satisfaction with their work). Third- and fourth-year students referred to several *challenges and suggestions related to fieldwork tasks*. They mention having too many tasks and, among those, some do not seem appropriate to them because students do not recognise the learning value in them or could not be done at the fieldwork institution. Certain tasks are too difficult, leading some students to resort to cheating (making up the data, etc.). Students also agree on the excessive number and complexity of the tasks. Students suggest fewer tasks and that, while grading students' fieldwork, the mentors from the faculty should give greater emphasis to the (social) work conducted as part of the fieldwork than to the papers (about work and completed tasks) gathered in the learning folder.

Students reported different levels of their own fieldwork progress, as shown in Figure 23.3. Some (mostly part-time) students reported making no progress or noted that things learned from the faculty are very different and not useful in social work praxis. Most students reported fieldwork-related progress in various areas – about knowledge (about organisation/institution, legislation) and also some personality traits (adaptability, organisation/self-organisation, independence, and initiative). In most cases, students mention gaining skills and competencies for social work, such as communication skills, loss of anxiety while working, improved writing skills, respect and understanding of users, and the use of social work skills and methods. Certain students mentioned great progress, while others identified different reasons mentioned below for accomplishing less in the fieldwork than expected:

- Mentors from the faculty did not always provide feedback (first and second years) and the mentors' expectations could be higher in last two years of studies (third and fourth years);
- Some mentors at the fieldwork bases did not have enough time for the students because of their own workload; some students (first and second years) had no contact with them and received no feedback; some students (third and fourth years) reported that mentors held personal reservations toward students related to their appearance or did not trust students (in the first and second years). Some mentors' expectations could be higher, as they should expect more from students (in the third and fourth years);

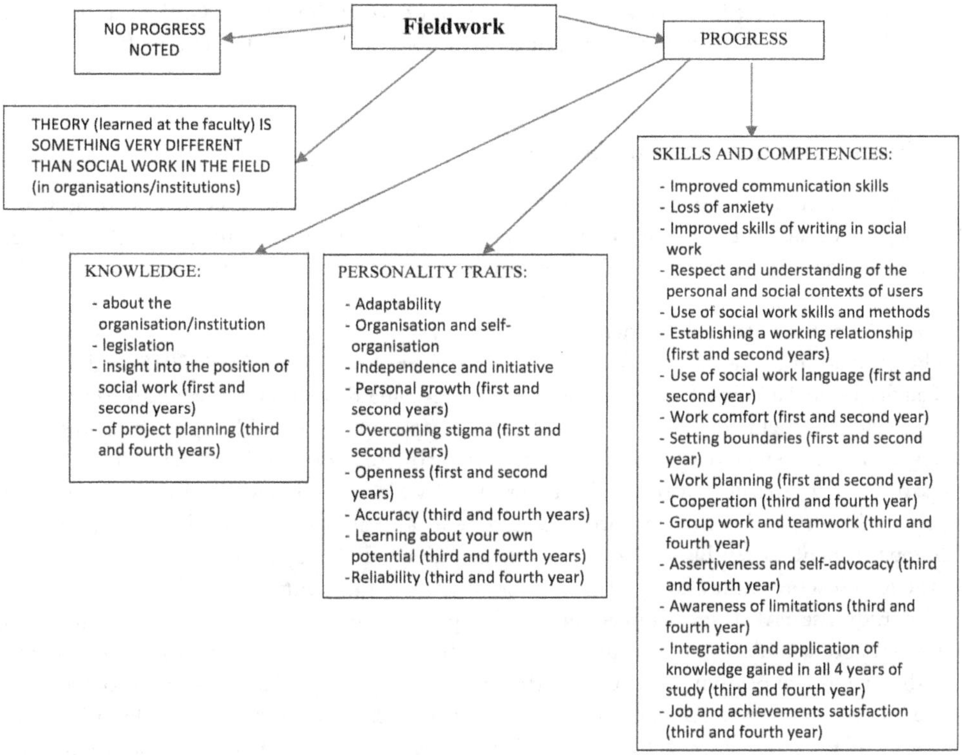

Figure 23.3 Students' fieldwork progress.

- In relation to properties of the organisation/institution (and areas of social work practice) in which fieldwork is conducted – there were no possibilities to take over or independently perform certain tasks (first and second years) or achieve greater progress;
- Students did not put enough effort and energy into the fieldwork to ensure greater progress, and some of their personality traits prevented any greater progress (in the third and fourth years); and
- Some elements of the implementation and organisation of fieldwork, such as too short a duration and unequal opportunities of students (mentioned in the third and fourth years) were also noted.

Students' *suggestions* for making better progress in the fieldwork in the first and second years were mandatory and prompt feedback to students from mentors (from the faculty) on papers, more lessons (knowledge) related to group work, supervisors should have greater trust in students and more contact with them, and they should encourage and enable students to do some work independently. In the third and fourth years of study, students emphasised the help of mentors at the fieldwork base as being crucial for their acquisition of competencies and that mentors from the faculty could do more to introduce and explain relevant legislation to them.

Students' *suggestions regarding other topics* also mentioned better preparation for fieldwork and improving the work of the C.P. As *challenges*, students also referred to different challenges in relation to both their status (full- and part-time students) and their module.

Students agreed that fieldwork is a very important part of their social work education and stressed the importance of fieldwork making up a substantial part of the curriculum in every year of study.

Conclusion and Remaining Challenges

Through the decades, fieldwork has gained in importance in social work education in Slovenia. This may be observed mostly in hours of study (credit points) related to fieldwork, although they remain lower than in some other countries (e.g., Australia). Like in some other studies mentioned before, our data also show that students appreciate and value the opportunities for fieldwork from the start of their social work studies.

The evaluation of the fieldwork at the undergraduate level in the 2014–2015 study year at the Faculty of Social Work, University of Ljubljana revealed that all stakeholders are, on average, satisfied with the fieldwork (scores around 8 on a 10-point scale). Although the scores of all participants in the research averaged out at around a score of 8, on average, the students were the least satisfied with the fieldwork. As also mentioned by Sherer and Peleg-Oren (2005), students perceive fieldwork as the most important component of their studies. This might also be a cause of disappointment if their high expectations are not met, which may, to some extent, explain the fact the lowest scores came from the third- and fourth-year students.

The study also reveals several needs and challenges. The main needs of the mentors from the faculty are about unifying the instructions for the fieldwork tasks among them. Some mentors from the faculty are of opinion that the quantity and complexity of the tasks are too extensive. Challenges relate to mentoring, the functioning of the C.P. (and the mentors' role in it), characteristics of the students, and the fieldwork tasks. Mentors at the fieldwork bases expressed needs with regard to mentoring students of social work programmes relating to the support of the faculty (proper and prompt education and empowerment of mentors, better knowledge and understanding of the specifics of social work in different areas, and expectation of greater support for their work). The second group of the challenges are similar as for the mentors from the faculty regarding fieldwork tasks for the students. The challenges they pointed out relate to students, the implementation of fieldwork, the fieldwork tasks of the students, mentoring at the fieldwork base, cooperation with the faculty, and others. Students expressed different needs regarding materials for the fieldwork and tasks. Challenges mainly related to the mentors from the faculty and the mentors at the fieldwork base.

The challenges to be deliberated on can, thus, be grouped in three categories: organisational issues (hours, planning, informing); content issues (type of exercises, themes); and additional support for mentors at the fieldwork bases (acquiring additional knowledge, support in conflict situations). It is also noted that every stakeholder mentioned challenges regarding other stakeholders, indicating their intense cooperation is particularly important.

Other authors similarly claim that the biggest challenges needing to be solved to meet expectations of higher quality in the fieldwork education in social work are the payment of mentors in the field (because their contribution of acting in this role is voluntary), continuous education, and the number of students per supervision group. According to some studies conducted abroad (United Kingdom, Australia), these issues are a consequence of neoliberal approaches to higher education which focus on efficiency and outcomes (Cleak & Zuchowski, 2019). In Slovenia, we also do not yet have a proper system for evaluating and financing the mentoring work of social workers at fieldwork bases, and the mentors are not materially rewarded for such training, nor are the students paid for the work they do during their placements, with the outcome being that it is difficult to impose certain additional requirements and then simply expect better quality to emerge. Papouli (2014) suggests that social work schools provide training programmes for fieldwork mentors and that the content of the programme should include an explanation of the two dominant learning theories (individual and socio-cultural). We can add that a third theory – learning as a process of construction and/or reconstruction (Hager, 2005) – should be included because only reflexive practice can ensure adequate results for all.

Moreover, the quality of fieldwork education can be a genuine challenge because, as mentioned by Papouli (2014), both mentors (from the faculty and at the fieldwork base) rarely reflect on the process of students' learning in both classrooms and field settings because they are more focused on their own tasks and operations. Yet, the process of learning is an important factor in acquiring adequate competencies and professional identity. Researchers in Australia have, for instance, found that fieldwork education in social work displays some worrying trends: an increasing student-to-staff ratio, insufficient social-worker-supervised placements, increased placements with external supervision, and the employment of casual staff to undertake core tasks such as supervision. There are growing demands on fieldwork placements (increasing number of students, ensuring the high quality of supervision) (Cleak & Zuchowski, 2019).

Students learn by observing practice and from the instructions – both mentors from the faculty and mentors at the fieldwork bases act as role models to students in their socialisation into social work and, hence, their role is considerable. As Papouli (2014) emphasised, values, behaviours, and attitudes in the working environment are very important, as is how participation is perceived and implemented. Here, some students in our data reported worrying practices (incompetent work of mentors) and personal traits (personal reservations about a student because of their appearance) of those who act as role models for students.

Our study also shows (as already noted by Papouli (2014)) the value of fieldwork for personal development because this was the second-biggest category (after skills and competencies) of progress in student fieldwork as self-reported by students.

One limitation of our study is that students who were on field placements abroad were excluded from the research and, therefore, information on international placements (which Pawar (2017) believes may hold some special characteristics and for which student needs could vary), that are also available to students, is missing. Moreover, only data concerning undergraduate study were analysed.

Continuing the evaluation of fieldwork education in social work has been a task of the C.P. at the Faculty of Social Work, University of Ljubljana ever since the Bologna reform. Evaluation is not seen as a control tool (with top-down predefined criteria) but more, as Higgins (2015) suggests, a critical pedagogical approach with the aim to enable the possibility of transforming the current practice. During the Bologna process of harmonising the European higher education system, fieldwork was further improved, with occasional monitoring and self-evaluations being provided. Based on the results of the presented study from 2015, the C.P. has already put into action certain suggested changes – mainly relating to the fieldwork instructions, tasks, and the length of the fieldwork in the final year of undergraduate study.

Only continuous monitoring and evaluation can provide information for improving fieldwork such that students acquire sufficient knowledge and competencies to carry out social work with self-confidence. In the Slovenian context, with changes in support of a neoliberal ideology of efficiency, managerialism, and bureaucracy, social workers of this calibre are urgently needed.

References

1Ka. (2020). One click survey. Retrieved April 2020, from https://www.1ka.si/d/en.

Bălăuţă, D. S. & Vlaicu, L. (2017). Perceptions of actors involved in social work field placement at the west university of Timişoara. *Revista de Asistenţă socială*, XVI(2), 53–60.

Barretti, M. A. (2007). Teachers and field instructors as student role models: A neglected dimension in social work education. *Journal of Teaching in Social Work*, 27(3/4), 215–239.

Barretti, M. A. (2009). Ranking desirable field instructor characteristics: Viewing student preferences in context with field and class experience. *The Clinical Supervisor*, 28(1), 47–71.

Bellinger, A. (2010). Studying the landscape: Practice learning for social work reconsidered. *Social Work Education*, 29(6), 599–615.

Bogo, M. (2010). *Achieving Competence in Social Work through Field Education*. Toronto: University of Toronto Press.

Bogo, M. (2015). Field education for clinical social work practice: Best practices and contemporary challenges. *Clinical Social Work Journal*, 43(3), 317–324.

Bogo, M. & Power, R. (1992). New field instructors' perceptions of institutional supports for their roles. *Journal of Social Work Education*, 28(2), 178–189.

Cavazos, A. (1996). Measuring BSW student learning in field instruction. *Journal of Social Work Education*, 32(3), 389–398.

Cleak, H., Hawkins, L., Loughton, J. & Williams, J. (2015). Creating a standardized teaching and learning framework for social work field placements. *Australian Social Work*, 68(1), 49–64.

Cleak, H. & Zuchowski, I. (2019). Mapping social work field education in the 21st century: A National survey of the Australian context. *British Journal of Social Work*, 1–20. DOI: 10.1093/bjsw/bcz151.

Domakin, A. (2014). Are we making the most of learning From practice placement? *Social Work Education*, 33(6), 718–730.

Fakulteta za socialno delo. (n.d. a). *Univerzitetni študijski program prve stopnje socialno delo*. Retrieved April 2020, from https://www.fsd.uni-lj.si/izobrazevanje/dodiplomski-studij/studijski_program/program_1%20_stopnje/.

Fakulteta za socialno delo. (n.d. b). *Učni Načrti*. Retrieved April 2020, from https://www.fsd.uni-lj.si/izobrazevanje/dodiplomski-studij/ucni_nacrti/program_1%20_stopnje/.

Fakulteta za socialno delo. (n.d. c). *Individualno projektno delo in Praktikum*. Retrieved April 2020, from https://www.fsd.uni-lj.si/izobrazevanje/podiplomski-studij/magistrski/studijski-programi/socialno_delo/ucni-nacrti/20190207091555179/.

Flaker, V. (2005). Od praktičnega poklica k dejavni znanosti. Memoarska analiza poti in prehodov izobraževanja za socialno delo (1975–2005). In: D. Zaviršek (ed.), *Z diplomo mi je bilo lažje delat!: znanstveni zbornik ob 50-letnici izobraževanja za socialno delo v Sloveniji* (pp. 65–119). Ljubljana: Fakulteta za socialno delo.

Fortune, A. E., McCarthy, M. & Abramson, J. S. (2001). Student learning processes in field education: Relationship of learning activities to quality of field instruction, satisfaction, and performance among MSW students. *Journal of Social Work Education*, 37(1), 111–126.

Hager, P. (2005). Current theories of workplace learning: A critical assessment. In: N. Bascia, A. Cumming, A. Datnow, K. Leithwood, & D. Livingstone (eds.), *International Handbook of Educational Policy* (pp. 829–846). Dordrecht: Springer.

Higgins, M. (2015). Evaluations of social work education: A critical review. *Social Work Education*, 34(7), 771–784.

Higgins, M. (2017). Conflicting and competing roles and expectations: The conundrum of failing social work students on placements. *European Research Institute for Social Work*, 17(1), 38–46.

IASSW. (n.d.). Global definiton of social work. Retrieved October 2019, from https://www.iassw-aiets.org/global-definition-of-social-work-review-of-the-global-definition/.

Kendall, K. A. (1959). Selected issues in field instruction in education for social work. *Social Service Review*, 33(1), 1–9.

Knight, C. (2001). The skills of teaching social work practice in the generalist/foundation curriculum: BSW and MSW student views. *Journal of Social Work Education*, 37(3), 507–521.

Lyons, K. (2000). The place of research in social work education. *British Journal of Social Work*, 30(4), 433–447.

McLaughlin, H., Scholar, H., McCaughan, S. & Coleman, A. (2015). Are non-traditional social work placements second-best learning opportunities for social work qualifying students? *British Journal of Social Work*, 45(5), 1469–1488.

Marsick, V. J. & Watkins, K. (2001). Informal and incidental learning. *New Directions for Adult and Continuing Education*, 89(89), 25–34. DOI: 10.1002/ace.5.

Mesec, M. (2015). Praktični študij na Fakulteti za socialno delo. *Socialno Delo*, 54(3–4), 239–249.

Papouli, E. (2014). Field learning in social work education: Implications for educators and instructors. *Field Educator*, 4(2). https://fieldeducator.simmons.edu/issue/volume-4-2-fall-2014/. Accessed 4 March 2020.

Parker, J. (2006). Developing perceptions of competence during practice learning. *British Journal of Social Work*, 36(6), 1017–1036.

Parker, J. (2007). Developing effective practice learning for tomorrow's social workers. *Social Work Education*, 26(8), 763–779. DOI: 10.1080/02615470601140476.

Pawar, M. (2017). Reflective learning and teaching in social work field education in international contexts. *British Journal of Social Work*, 47, 198–218.

Rape Žiberna, T. & Žiberna, A. (2017). Kaj je pomembno za dobro študijsko prakso v socialnem delu: Pogled mentoric iz učnih baz. *Socialno Delo*, 56(3), 180–197.

Rapoša Tajnšek, P. (2005). Fragmenti razvoja študijskega programa v prvih desetletjih izobraževanja za socialno delo. In: D. Zaviršek (ed.), *Z diplomo mi je bilo lažje delat!: znanstveni zbornik ob 50-letnici izobraževanja za socialno delo v Sloveniji* (pp. 135–145). Ljubljana: Fakulteta za socialno delo.

Robertson, S. J. (2013). Addresessing professional suitability in social work education: Results of a study of field education coordinators' experience. *Journal of Practice Teaching and Learning*, 11(3), 98–117.

Sherer, M. & Peleg-Oren, N. (2005). Differences of teachers', field instructors' and students' views on job analysis of social work students. *Journal of Social Work Education*, 41(2), 315–328.

Škerlavaj, M., Indihar Štemberger, M., Škrinjar, R. & Dimovski, V. (2007). Organizational learning culture - The missing link between business process change and organizational performance. *International Journal of Production Economics*, 106(2), 346–367.

Šugman Bohinc, L. (2016). Socialno delo v uresničevanju idealov pravične družbe. *Socialno Delo*, 55(5–6), 221–239.

Webb, N. B. (1988). The role of the field instructor in the socialization of students. *Social Casework*, 69(1), 35–40.

Wilson, G. & Kelly, B. (2010). Evaluating the effectiveness of social work education: Preparing students for practice learning. *British Journal of Social Work*, 40(8), 2431–2449.

Zaviršek, D. (2005). *"Z diplomo mi je bilo lažje delat!": Znanstveni Zbornik ob 50-Letnici Izobraževanja Za Socialno Delo v Sloveniji*. Ljubljana: Fakulteta Za Socialno Delo.

24

Prior to Embarking on First Fieldwork Education Exposure

Preparing Social Work Students through Five Experiential Learning Activities

Elena Cabiati and Fabio Folgheraiter

In this chapter, we focus on the preliminary year for social work students, which occurs prior to their first fieldwork education exposure. In the last 10 years, through the collaboration of social work students and practice teachers, social work educators at the Catholic University of Milan and Brescia developed five learning activities. These activities are carried out during the first year of the bachelor's degree to prepare students for the first practice placement experience that occurs in the second semester of the second year (from January to June). These experiential learning activities have the common aim of encouraging social work students to test their personal and relational skills and increase their awareness and confidence. The focus is not on the acquisition of social workers' specialist knowledge (commonly offered by specific courses). Through these experiential activities, students gained basic insights into the key principles of social work practice that are useful for increasing their ability to cope with imminent future field education challenges.

To Assist Students' Transition Toward Fieldwork: A Short Literature Review

Fieldwork education opportunities are incorporated in the academic curriculum as a method of preparing future social workers for social work fieldwork. There is extensive literature emphasising the importance of field education in the professional learning of students (Hay, 2019; Bellinger, 2016; Frost et al., 2013), and it is argued that the practice placement experience for all students is expected and demanding (Laidlaw et al., 2020; McSweeney & Williams, 2018; Flanagan & Wilson, 2018; Sarid et al., 2009).

Less discussed is how educators and practice teachers can support students in successfully coping with worries and difficulties linked to the first fieldwork education experience (McSweeney, 2018; Hughes, 2011). The transition from university to fieldwork practice is complex, especially if it is the first opportunity for the students to challenge themselves outside the university. Practice placement experience is expected by the students with enthusiasm and with some anxiety that has the potential to affect learning (Laidlaw et al., 2020; Gelman & Lloyd, 2008).

 DOI: 10.4324/9781032164946-29

'Practice shock' or 'practice anxiety' (Geirdal et al., 2019; Al-Ma'seb et al., 2015; Gelman & Lloyd, 2008) are terms often used to describe the impact on students of entering the practice, starting from their first practice placement up to the initial work period as social workers.

When students enter a placement, they are in a destabilising and disorienting space that, hopefully, gives them the opportunity to creatively alter their mindset (Doel, 2016, p. ix).

Previous studies focused on problems encountered by students on practice placement (Maidment, 2003; Barton et al., 2005; Kanno & Koeske, 2010). A number of the problems students faced suggested the need for additional opportunities before the placements to engage with material on safety in the field and ways to deal with workplace stress and conflict.

It is evident that the roles of educators and practice teachers are fundamental in building an adequate learning context. Preparing social work students for practice placement experience is challenging and demanding for educators and practice teachers, even after several years of experience.

Supervision plays a key role in the field education of social workers. As shown by previous studies, practice teachers value teaching and giving feedback to students that shapes their professional practice in the field setting (Ketner et al., 2017). Practice teachers and field instructors are fully committed to the field education goals, providing guidance, mentoring, using reflective feedback, and facilitating social work skills development in students (Kadushin & Harkness, 2014; Bogo, 2015).

Furthermore, most field instructors wish to introduce students to a good example of professional practice (Ketner et al., 2017); in other words, they feel responsible for being a good role model for students. While considering the differences between countries and contexts, for the majority of students, the first practice placement experience occurs during the second year of the bachelor' degree. Despite calls for better preparation of students for practice placement, few dedicated pre-placement resources have been developed (Grace & O'Neil, 2014).

Methods of preparing students before the first practice placement experience remains an issue being researched in the international arena. What are the most important skills that students need to gain for the first field education experience? More importantly, how can educators support students to gain these competencies? It is important to help students in their transition to fieldwork, both from a methodological and technical side rather than an experiential learning side.

For educators, the students' first practice placement is important: they live the experience through the students' eyes, assisting their growth as future professionals. Projecting the gaze toward the students' future as social workers, educators feel great responsibility for their success.

About the Context

This chapter presents experiences at the Catholic University in the cities of Milan and Brescia.

Milan and Brescia are two cities in the Lombardy region of northern Italy. In Italy, the Catholic University has five campuses: Milan, Piacenza, Cremona, Brescia, and Rome.

Social work education programmes are offered in Milan and Brescia.

In Italy, social work degrees have been offered exclusively within universities since 1987. The Italian government decided to adopt the structure of education following the Bologna Process in 2000.

The undergraduate programme in social work at the Catholic University's Milan campus recruits up to 100 first-year students per year, and the Brescia campus recruits up to 50 students. The social work education programme offered in Milan and Brescia is the same, and the majority of educators work in both campuses (in most cases they are employed at the Milan campus, but they move to Brescia for teaching and research activities).

The undergraduate social work programme consists of three years and offers students a broad foundation for generalist social work practice. Students enrolled in the three-year undergraduate programme are educated to intervene and provide services to individuals, groups, families, and communities.

According to the guidelines of the Italian Ministry of Education, University and Research, undergraduate social work programmes offer field education activities to social work students:

- In the second year, with *a practice placement experience* of 250 hours in social services organisations (i.e., hospitals and health care institutions, municipalities, mental health services, or child protection institutions). Through this traditional practice placement experience, students have direct contact with an expert social worker. The social worker assumes the role of practice teacher and he/she supervises the students' activity in the field. Through this experience, students make an organisational journey, discovering how social welfare institutions work.
- In the third year, with an *unconventional placement* of 150 hours. Unconventional practice placements are a type of field education in which students are given high levels of autonomy in planning and developing original projects that do not reproduce work already conducted in that context by other professionals (Raineri & Sala, 2019). Through this experience, students have to develop initiatives related not only to learning needs but also to *real* needs, with opportunities for the improvement of a community or a service (Corradini et al., 2020; Raineri & Sala, 2019; Scholar et al., 2014; Doel, 2010). In unconventional placements, students work with a network of people (professionals, volunteers, citizens, service users, and caregivers) to plan and implement an innovative project/intervention in a collaborative way.

All social work students must undertake practice placement and unconventional placement in the second and final years of the programme, and the placements are a crucial area of assessment for completing their degree. Both experiences are accompanied by group work among the students in the presence of an educator who is a social worker (Corradini et al., 2020). Each week, students group together with educators to share their experiences during the practice placement or unconventional placement. In these group meetings, equal exchanges and reciprocity between the participants are promoted and valued. In these groups, students elaborate their experience in light of other students' experiences. Educators and researchers at the Relational Social Work Research Centre (located in the department of Sociology at the Catholic University of Milan) have developed research projects aimed to study the social work education model, with particular interest in field education activities (Cabiati, 2016; Cabiati & Folgheraiter, 2016; Cabiati & Raineri, 2016; Cabiati & Tagliabue, 2017; Raineri & Sala, 2019).

Premises

The Value of Experiential Learning Activities to Prepare Students for Fieldwork Education

Assisting students to positively meet the reality of social work practice is a complex and dynamic process nurtured by the relationships between students, educators, practice teachers, and service users. It is a joint and dialogical process, like a whole orchestra (Hay, 2019). In the academic arena, the formal learning processes are highly structured and recognised as important, while the experiential learning processes within the university are less discussed, sometimes neglected, or considered as optional or less important activities.

In the transition from the classroom to the fieldwork environment, experiential learning activities could be an efficient means of introducing students to the reality of social work practice and testing and empowering their skills. Usually based on creative and less structured processes, the experiential learning activities can represent a space for active training of students' skills and a bridge between theoretical courses in the university and practice placement in the social work field. Experiential learning advances students' readiness for practice and promotes their proficiencies in preparation for their imminent future as social workers. Students learn from their reflection on their experiences, and their mistakes are a powerful opportunity to go beyond the surface of events and understand the essence of the profession (Sicora, 2019). The dialogic process, which requires teachers to be open and enter into dialogue with the students, helps to make links between theory and practice more concrete, which, in turn educators hope will prepare good social workers.

Creative and participative teaching and learning experiences can also benefit educators, for example, by allowing them to interact with the students as equals (Zapf, 2009).

As discussed in the conclusion section of this chapter, educators must provide students with guidance to reflect on the experiential learning activities so they can elaborate and create meaning from what they experienced.

Relational Social Work Method

Experiential learning (as theoretical learning) requires the methods to be effective toward specific goals and to be coherent with social work principles and challenges.

The five experiential learning activities described in this chapter have the relational social work method as a common root. Inspired by relational sociology (Donati, 2010), the relational social work method is consistent with social work principles such as, primarily, self-determination, subsidiarity, and respecting humanity (Folgheraiter, 2004). The relational social work method promotes the following key ideas: reciprocity, coping networks, freedom of action, and creativity (Folgheraiter & Raineri, 2017).

The principle of *reciprocity*, which is the core of the relational approach (Folgheraiter, 2004, 2017), refers to 'generating well-being in complex existential situations requires each person involved to leave the role of user or client to assume that of therapist or helper' (Folgheraiter, 2004). A *coping network* is a set of relationships between people concerned about a shared aim. In the relational social work perspective, the helping process is developed through the relationships between motivated people with good intention (service users, professionals, and citizens). Social work education programmes can be inspired by the same principles and key ideas, as shown by the experience already developed in the Italian framework at the Catholic University of Milan and Brescia (Cabiati, 2017).

To educate future social workers, in addition to practitioners already engaged in the field, it is beneficial 'to transfer' relational social work principles at the training level.

In relational social work education, teaching and learning become a simultaneous process focused on social work principles, such as empowerment, peer facilitation, reflexivity, auto-evaluation, valourisation and involvement of service users, and emotional elaboration (Cabiati, 2016).

According to the relational social work method, the undergraduate social work programme is planned as a path of education and not of 'technical training', with specific attention to the development of the students' human growth. If 'relational' means that both actors are in a truly mutual relationship, aiding each other (Folgheraiter, 2004), about field education and experiential learning activities, it is more appropriate to speak about a facilitator's role than a teacher's role and about group encounters rather than lessons. As part of social work education, Cabiati (2017, p. 74) underlined how the principles of relational social work have led to a 'relational teaching and learning approach' in which it is important to encourage the maximum possible degree of reciprocity between educators, practice teachers, and students, even in the university context.

The five experiential learning activities described below are consistent with these principles and have been constructed on these premises. Each activity has been inspired by the relational social work method.

Five Experiential Learning Activities to Prepare Students for Practice Placement Experience

The experiential activities presented here were developed with the aim to support students in gaining basic insights into the key principles of social work practice that will be useful for increasing their ability to cope with imminent future field education challenges.

To successfully cope with common practice placement challenges, students have to acquire many competences and skills that combine learning from theory and experiential activities (Trevithick, 2005; Thompson, 2002; Gambrill, 2013).

Without pretending to be exhaustive, to successfully cope with the challenges of the first practice placement, students must have developed at least these core social work skills:

- Being a reflective, critical thinker;
- Being resilient and constructive;
- Being collaborative and able to work in a group;
- Being able to listen and interact with service users and professionals;
- Being able to understand people's needs;
- Being able to welcome and manage their own emotions and those of and others;
- Being aware of the boundaries of professional practice and able to conduct themselves ethical, respecting the professional code of ethics;
- Being creative and being able to welcome the unknown and act in unpredictable circumstances.

Acquiring these skills is an ongoing process for professionals that occurs through continuing learning opportunities. Each social worker, even if experienced, must be engaged in a process of continuing education to address current knowledge and emerging developments related to social work practice and ethics. It is important that the development of these social work skills starts during the social work education pathway. The experiential activities described below can be the first steps to acquiring these specific social work skills.

A 75-hour Frontline Experience with People in Need

During the first year, before the beginning of the second semester of lessons, students are invited to participate in a 75-hour frontline experience (Cabiati, 2016).

The goal of this activity is to expose the students to real people in need.

For some students, this experience is the first real contact with people in need because they had never experienced it before in their personal lives.

Through guidance from academic tutors, students are invited to spend 75 hours at a non-profit organisation or charity in the community in which they live. These charities offer listening, essential services, and social support to people, families, and communities.

Students are required to spend 75 hours at a charity interacting with people in need and living the daily life (i.e., daily activities, community events, initiatives in the local community).

The frontline experience does not require students to use professional methods or techniques; it is not important, in this context, for students to experience the practitioners' work, and sometimes, students do not meet professionals, only volunteers. Through the frontline experience, students are encouraged to reflect on how encounters with men, women, and children in need stimulates them and to test their ability to stay in contact with those who are suffering, living in poverty, and are marginalised.

To facilitate students in engaging in conversations rather than only observation during their 75-hour frontline experience, they are required to hear the life story of at least one service user. The focus of the task is not on the details of the person's story or on the students' ability to make a professional interview – the aim of this close-encounter is to stimulate students' insights about what it means to talk face-to-face with a person in need.

At the beginning of the second semester of academic activities, students come back to the university to make an individual presentation about their 75 hour frontline experience to educators and colleagues. Educators encourage students to be creative, making it explicit that every style of presentation is welcome: the students are very creative and use songs, posters, videos, puppets, games, and poetry to elaborate their personal frontline experiences with other students.

A 21-hour Emotional Self-awareness Workshop

Thompson (2015) affirmed that working with people involves three dimensions: actions, thoughts, and feelings. Thompson (2015) went on to say that, in the professional practice, the emotional dimension is often neglected or reduced to only one aspect: the others' emotions. Gambrill stated that 'self-awareness is vital' (2013, p. x) because students can challenge their biases only if they are aware of them.

The path of self-exploration can contribute immensely to attentiveness (Sevenhuijsen, 2014). Emotional work and investment in the self are crucial to forming good social workers. With respect to this, it is problematic to think of social workers as people who are able to keep themselves above their own emotional experience. Educators noticed that, before beginning their fieldwork education experience, the fear of not being able to manage emotional content was a common anxiety among students.

The emotional self-awareness workshop was born from the wish to welcome students' emotional needs and to help them feel more prepared for meeting and managing strong emotional content (typical of social work encounters).

At the Catholic University of Milan and Brescia, social work students attend the emotional self-awareness workshop during the second semester of the first year. Students are divided in small groups (around 15 participants) led by psychologists with fieldwork experience in social welfare organisations. The goal of this 21-hour workshop is to work on the students' ability to manage emotional content, starting from the discovery of their own emotional world. Students are guided in making efforts to name their emotional states and to become more aware of the impact these have on their thinking and behaviour.

The emotional self-awareness workshop allows students to acquire a more accurate picture of themselves, even if it is not a therapeutic activity: the psychologists work with the students for educational purposes; in cases in which psychologists notice serious suffering in students, they meet individually with students to encourage them to start personal therapy with a professional. It is mandatory for all first-year students to attend the emotional self-awareness workshop, but the workshop does not include an assessment. At the end of the 21 hours, psychologists provide group feedback and individual feedback to each participant. The confidential feedback allows students to review, reflect, and improve their behaviour toward emotional content.

A Group Activity to Work on a Concrete Goal of Personal Change

According to global definitions, social work is focused, essentially, on social and existential change (I.A.S.S.W. & I.F.S.W., 2014). Social work is concerned with achieving change in the lives of people who suffer major difficulties.

Commonly, social work students may be driven by salvific, paternalistic, or benevolent attitudes, and their engagement in the education pathway could be motivated by the idea of learning to understand how to modify those who, in their opinion, would need them most: in other words, learning so that others can change.

Helping people to change for the better is right, but attempting to transform other people 'according to my ideas' can be a subtle form of violence (Rossiter, 2011).

To put in practice the idea that social workers are not literally 'agents of others' change' is a complex process. This process requires personal awareness combined with ethical and methodological knowledge about how to help others change while avoiding being paternalistic, manipulative, or oppressive. According to relational social work, social workers are effective when they realise that possible improvements in difficult situations emerge from the social relations involved (Folgheraiter, 2017). Learning how to help people, families, and communities improve cannot be fully achieved through only abstract content. It was on this premise that, in 2016, an experiential activity, in which participants try to change themselves, was launched (Cabiati & Folgheraiter, 2016). The focus of this activity is to help social work students try 'to change themselves first'.

Supported by a group activity, students are helped to directly experience with the challenge of making changes to themselves first, to prepare them to support life improvements in others in the future. The hypothesis of this experiential activity is that if students are able to make changes personally, they could be more able to understand the dynamics, resources, and limits connected to the topic of change, and they could become more attentive social workers in helping others to change.

It is made explicit to students that their personal goal of change must to be formulated in a positive way, realistic and reachable, referred to herself/himself, referred to a concrete and delimited aspect of their own and present lives, and not exclusively focused on the psychological sphere.

The activity has two main steps: the first is for the student to meet with an educator to identify a personal goal of change and the second is a group encounter in which students can reflect and receive reciprocal support.

In this activity, students proposed several goals of change (e.g., maintaining physical activity, following a diet, quitting smoking, dedicating more time to family, and avoiding watching TV during free time on weekends).

Students take part in the activity voluntarily so that they can understand that a personal path of change requires freedom and willpower. It is important to say whether there were any therapeutic goals through this experience of change. Our aim was an educational aim: helping young students in reflecting personally about the challenge of change, regardless of the single aim of change and the possibility of reaching it. Findings of the activity (Cabiati & Folgheraiter, 2016) show that, in trying to change themselves, the students gained basic insights into the key principles of social work practice. These results could inspire social work educators to promote creative opportunities for experiential learning for social work students to stimulate them to become effective and ethical guides for others' improvement.

Full-day Meetings with Experts by Experience

The involvement of service users and carers as experts by experience (E.B.E.) in social work education is an ethical and methodological choice that concerns bachelor's and master's programmes at the Catholic University of Milan (Cabiati & Raineri, 2016).

The E.B.E. involvement is grounded in social justice and the fundamental value placed on service users and carers' everyday experiences contributing to the knowledge and skills of social work students. The rationale for E.B.E. involvement is both epistemological and pedagogical. It emerges from the acceptance that knowledge is derived from a variety of different standpoints (Beresford & Boxall, 2012). Service users and carers are E.B.E., experts through living lives that have included additional social challenges leading to social work involvement. From receiving services, caring for a relative or a friend, to managing the relationship with practitioners, their knowledge and experiences can be utilised to enrich the learning of future social workers (Askheim et al., 2017; Heule et al., 2017; Irvine et al., 2015; Levy et al., 2020).

Full-day meetings represent a crucial learning activity to prepare students for education practice because it demonstrates, through example, the idea that educators must regard service users and carers as partners in social work students' educational journeys.

The concept of 'experiential competence' (Borkman, 1976; Folgheraiter, 2004) and the distinction between 'technical problems' and 'life problems' offered by the relational paradigm (Folgheraiter, 2004) support the social work educators in correctly channelling and enhancing the contributions from E.B.E. Taking up the words of Parton (2008), social workers should construct a process whereby the theory of how to help is generated mutually. For a social worker, understanding how to best help people in difficulties begins the moment they recognise that, as is true for himself/herself, all human beings give unique meaning to their world. It is important for social workers to keep in mind that service users are the first experts of the life problems they are dealing with. At the Catholic University of Milan and Brescia, all first-year students spend at least one full day meeting with E.B.E. The full-day meeting programme is divided into two parts. In the morning, each student is randomly matched with an E.B.E. The student and E.B.E. then share a two-hour face-to-face conversation. It is made clear to all the participants that this conversation is not a professional assessment or a research interview but a simple conversation aimed at getting to know one another and exchanging life experiences. Following the two-hour conversations, all participants eat lunch together in the university canteen. After lunch, two-hour group meetings occur with a mixture of students, E.B.E., and academics. In the initial years of the module, the group meetings were facilitated by academic tutors, but now E.B.E. take on this role. In the group meetings, all participants are asked to express their thoughts and feelings about the full day experience. Finally, all participants end the day together with greetings and thanksgiving. After the experience, the full day meetings are revisited in social work methodological courses and elaborated on with the support of academics in order to enable students to reach the value and the sense of E.B.E. involvement in their learning and future practice. The experience of the Catholic University of Milan shows that, beyond the common positive effects (McLaughlin, 2009; Preston-Shoot, 2007; Beresford & Boxall, 2012) the contact with E.B.E.

gives first-year social work students an opportunity to reduce discrimination and stigma against people with social life problems (Cabiati & Raineri, 2016; Cabiati & Panciroli, 2019).

Students' Self-managed Meetings on Social Work Themes

The idea of having students self-manage meetings on social work themes emerged in 2015 from a specific concern: the students were having difficultly working in group with their colleagues in an effective and respectful way.

Organising self-managed meetings on social work themes stimulates students to work collaboratively in groups, putting in practice creativity and negotiation skills (Cabiati & Tagliabue, 2017).

To plan a self-managed meeting, the students receive only three instructions from the educators: (1) organise a learning activity of three to five hours involving all of the class members in the planning through a democratic process; (2) choose an activity consistent with the first-year curriculum of the bachelor's degree programme; and (3) use creativity. Total freedom is given to the students regarding all of the remaining related aspects of the assignment. The students express both enthusiasm and concern about the assignment but usually show great initiative. Two or three days before, the students share with the educators some instructions about the planned activity (i.e., whether the meeting will occur in or outside of the university, whether equipment is needed, and the duration of the activity). In the past, the students' self-managed meetings have consisted of several activities including going to the Central Railway Station of Milan to meet homeless people, watching a movie and then discussing it as a group, interviewing citizens on the street, playing an interactive game constructed by the students, and visiting an exhibition. After the conclusion of the self-managed meeting, the educator asks the students to reflect on the experience in two ways: each student writes a self-reflection report and participates in a dedicated group discussion facilitated by the same educator.

The most interesting part of the activity is represented by the students' reflection on the decision-making process. Through the assignment to self-manage a meeting, students are involved in an active decision-making process. Regardless of the outcome of the self-managed meeting, through this assignment, students experience the challenges of thinking and acting with colleagues, they notice group and power dynamics, and they employ strategies to guide the decision-making process in a dialogical way. In some cases, the decision-making process is not dialogic, and the students experience the frustration of it, including the ability of overcoming misunderstandings and resolving conflicts.

Basic Insights into Key Issues of Social Work Practice

As mentioned above, the experiential learning activities presented here stimulate students in gaining basic insights into key issues of social work practice. These insights can help them to be more equipped for the practice placement experiences and for their imminent future as social workers.

The table below presents the educational goals of each activity with the link to what students can understand firsthand through these initiatives.

Conclusion

To find the way of 'being a social worker' is a multidimensional process that involves methodological, ethical, and relational aspects. It is not so easy for young students to fully reach these dimensions through abstract content. Educators must consider that social work methodology is

Table 24.1 Preparing Students for Practice Placement through Five Experiential Learning Activities: Educational Goals and Basic Insights into Key Issues of Social Work Practice

Five experiential learning activities to prepare students for practice placement experience	*Educational goals of the activities* *Educators aimed at developing and promoting the following.*	*Basic insights into key issues of social work practice* *Students discovered and learned the following concepts.*
A 75-hour frontline experience with people in need	Students' close, firsthand encounters with people who experience life problems.	Interaction with people in need is a delicate and complex process that requires self-awareness, prudence, and care. Welcoming others' vulnerabilities is crucial to taking care of themselves first and working on the personal motivation to become a social worker (overcoming salvific and paternalistic views).
A 21-hour emotional self-awareness workshop	Students' self-confidence about emotional needs and content (reducing personal feelings of fear and anxiety).	Personal positive and negative emotions can function as a 'brake' or an 'accelerator' in the helping relationships. Giving a response and a name to one's own emotions is a delicate and complex task.
A group activity to work on a concrete goal of personal change	Students' engagement in actions of self-care to support them in helping others make life improvements in an anti-oppressive way.	Changing other people according to one's own ideas is unethical and impossible. The change process is not a linear problem-solving process comprising a predictable sequence of steps. Working in groups with people who are undergoing a similar experience could represent a source of help (i.e., self- and mutual help groups). People require support, trust, self-confidence, and helping relationships when they try to change their lifestyle, opinions, or behaviours.
Full day meetings with Experts by Experience	Students' learning from the experiential knowledge of service users and carers; students' questioning how to overcome the dichotomy between 'helper' and 'helpee' to consider service users as partners in the helping process.	Knowledge is derived from a variety of standpoints. Service users not only have problems but also strengths and resources.
Students' self-managed meetings on social work themes	Students' ability to work collaboratively with groups, putting in practice creativity and negotiation skills.	Being dialogical with colleagues is demanding but crucial for the success of the collaborative and creative process. The helping process has a value regardless of the achievement of the specific goal. Creativity can be an answer to uncertainty, opening new ways of thinking and intervention.

not just a subject to be transmitted and that experiential learning is a way to assimilate theory and prepare students to welcome the practice. Guiding social work students into practice is an act of reciprocal responsibility, as suggested by the relational social work method. Reciprocal responsibility and influence among students, educators, and practice teachers go beyond formal collaborations. Imagining unexplored pathways to reach explicit social work education aims and working on students' preparedness for practice placement are important challenges for educators. Social work education programmes must prompt educators, students, and practice teachers to reflect on their preparedness for the forthcoming placement with a range of activities.

The five learning activities presented confirmed that if students' creativity and initiative are stimulated, they can work on their personal abilities as well as help educators to explore new ways to assist students prepare for their practice placement experience.

In several ways, international literature suggested that 'teaching social work is a science, an art form and a passion' (East & Chambers, 2007, p. 810) that requires courage and creativity in social work educators. Field education activities shape students' experience of the social work programme.

Students' success during the practice placement experience is unpredictable, even for the best performing students with the highest marks. Social work educators cannot regulate everything that happens on placement, so students need to be prepared and encouraged to exploit and recognise learning opportunities (McSweeney & Williams, 2018). The educators' responsibility is to work on the students' preparedness, from helping them to feel prepared to face practice placement to welcoming challenges while on placement. Because teaching and learning is a two-way relationship, educators cannot be solely responsible for the social work students' level of preparedness. Despite this, the problem of introducing undergraduate social work students to the field education practice, reducing poor experiences, and maximising their opportunities to learn is part of the educators' mission.

The experiential learning activities at the Catholic University of Milan and Brescia showed that the first undergraduate year of the programme represents an important time to invest in students' preparedness for their future fieldwork education experiences.

Working 'in advance' with first-year students to make the challenges of social work practice (not only through abstract content but also trough experiential activity) more explicit represents an antidote to 'practice shock' so that students welcome their first practice placement and are able to manage the impact of the experience.

Through the activities described in this chapter, students can be engaged early in some experiences. Learning from these preliminary experiences, students are stimulated to develop skills that will be useful for coping with the challenges they will encounter during their placements. For this to happen, introducing preparatory learning activities in the social work education curriculum is not enough. It is important to create dialogical environments in which these activities can find adequate room for students to reflect on the meaning of the experiences so that they can develop insights into key issues of social work practice. The model of the Catholic University of Milan and Brescia shows that students report enthusiasm for and overall satisfaction in the experiential learning activities but, for most of them, going beyond these feelings is not easy or automatic.

Supporting student reflection on what they live through during the experiential learning activities is crucial for the development of deep insights into key issues of practice; educators must provide students guidance to elaborate on content and meanings in order to enable them to fully reach the value and the sense of these opportunities.

In these processes, through peer-to-peer dynamics, students can learn from themselves and others because each experience is revisited in light of others' experiences.

References

Al-Ma'seb, H., Alkhurinej, A. & Alduwaihi, M. (2015). The gap between theory and practice in social work. *International Social Work*, 58(6), 819–830.

Askheim, O.P., Beresford, P. & Heule, C. (2017). Mend the gap – Strategies for user involvement in social work education. *Social Work Education: The International Journal*, 36(2), 128–140.

Barton, H., Bell, K. & Bowles, W. (2005). Help or hindrance? Outcomes of social work student placements. *Australian Social Work*, 58(3), 301–312.

Bellinger, A. (2016). *Practice Placement in Social Work. Innovative Approaches for Effective Teaching and Learning*. Bristol: Policy press.

Beresford, P. & Boxall, K. (2012). Service users. Social work education and knowledge for social work practice. *Social Work Education: The International Journal*, 31(2), 155–167.

Bogo, M. (2015). Evaluation of student learning. In: C. Hunter, Moen, J.K. & Raskin, M. S. (Eds.), *Social Work Field Directors: Foundations for Excellence* (pp. 154–178). Chicago: Lyceum Books.

Borkman, T. (1976). Experiential knowledge: A new concept for the analysis of self-help groups. *Social Service Review*, 50(3), 445–456.

Cabiati, E. (2016). Teaching and learning: An exchange of knowledge in the university among students, service users and professors. *European Journal of Social Work*, 19(2), 1–18.

Cabiati, E. (2017). Social work education. The relational way. *Relational Social Work*, 1(1), 61–79.

Cabiati, E. & Folgheraiter, F. (2016). Let's try to change ourselves first. An action-research on experiential learning with social work students. *Social Work Education*, 38(4), 439–452.

Cabiati, E. & Raineri, M.L. (2016). Learning from service users involvement: A research about changing stigmatizing attitudes in social work students. *Social Work Education*, 35(8), 982–996.

Cabiati, E. & Tagliabue, C. (2017). Learning from homeless people. Social work students at Milan's Central Railway Station. *Relational Social Work Journal*, 1(2), 92–101.

Cabiati, E. & Panciroli, C. (2019). Service users as collaborators in social work practice, research and education. *Socialinė Teorija, Empirija, Politika ir Praktika*, 19, 95–105.

Corradini, F., Landi, C. & Limongelli, P. (2020). Becoming a relational social worker. Group learning in social work education: Considerations from unconventional practice placements. *Relational Social Work*, 4(1), 15–29.

Doel, M. (2010). *Social Work Placements: A Traveller's Guide*. London: Routledge.

Doel, M. (2016). Foreword. In: A. Bellinger (Ed.), *Practice Placement in Social Work. Innovative Approaches for Effective Teaching and Learning* (pp.VII–IX). Bristol: Policy Press.

Donati, P. (2010). *Relational Sociology: A New Paradigm for the Social Sciences*. London: Routledge.

East, J. & Chambers, R. (2007). Courage to teach for social work educators. *Social Work Education*, 26(8), 810–826.

Folgheraiter, F. (2004). *Relational Social Work. Toward Networking and Societal Practices*. London: Jessica Kingsley.

Folgheraiter, F. (2017). The sociological and humanistic roots of relational social work. *Relational Social Work*, 1(1), 7–14.

Folgheraiter, F. & Raineri, M.L. (2017). The principles and key ideas of relational social work. *Relational Social Work*, 1(1), 15–22.

Flanagan, N. & Wilson, E. (2018). What makes a good placement? Findings of a social work student-to-student research study. *Social Work Education*, 37(5), 565–580.

Frost, E., Höjer, S. & Campanini, A. (2013). Readiness for practice: Social work students' perspectives in England, Italy, and Sweden. *European Journal of Social Work*, 16(3), 327–343.

Gambrill, E. (2013). *Social Work Practice: A Critical Thinker's Guide*. New York: Oxford University Press.

Geirdal, A., Nerdrum, P. & Bonsaksen, T. (2019). The transition from university to work; What happens to mental health? A longitudinal study. *BMC Psychology*, 7(1), 1–10.

Gelman, C.R. & Lloyd, C.M. (2008). Field notes: Pre-placement anxiety among foundation-year MSW students: A follow-up study. *Journal of Social Work Education*, 44(1), 173–183.

Grace, S. & O'Neil, R. (2014). Better prepared, better placement: An online resource for health students. *Asia-Pacific Journal of Cooperative Education*, 15(4), 291–304.

Grant, L., Kinman, G. & Alexander, K. (2014). What's all this talk about emotion? Developing emotional intelligence in social work students. *Social Work Education*, 33(7), 874–889.

Hay, K. (2019). 'It's a whole orchestra': what are the instrumental elements in quality field education? *Social Work Education, 39*(4), 1–13.

Heule, C., Knutagård, M. & Kristiansen, A. (2017). Mending the gaps in social work education and research: Two examples from a Swedish context. *European Journal of Social Work, 20*, 151–163.

Hughes, M. (2011). Do challenges to students' beliefs, values and behaviour within social work education have an impact on their sense of well-being? *Social Work Education*, 30(6), 686–699.

I.F.S.W. & I.A.S.S.W. (2014). Global definition of the social work profession. Retrieved from http://ifsw.org/get-involved/global-definition-of-social-work/.

Irvine, J., Molyneux, J. & Gillman, M. (2015). Providing a link with the real world: Learning from the student experience of service user and carer involvement in social work education. *Social Work Education*, 34, 138–150.

Kadushin, A. & Harkness, D. (2014). *Supervision in Social Work* (5th ed.). New York: Columbia University Press.

Kanno, H. & Koeske, G.F. (2010). MSW students' satisfaction with their field placements: The role of preparedness and supervision quality. *Journal of Social Work Education*, 46(1), 23–38.

Ketner, M., Van Cleave, D. & Coope-Bolinskey, D.C. (2017). The meaning and value of supervision in social work field education. *Field Educator*, 7(2), 1–18.

Laidlaw, K., Cabiati, E., Henriksen, O. & Shore, C. (2020). Preparing students for social work practice in contemporary societies: Insights from a transnational research network. *European Journal of Social Work*, *23*(6), 980–991.

Levy, S., Ferrier, C., Dowson, E. & Risbridger, J. (2020). Social pedagogy, collaborative learning and outcomes in service user and carer involvement in social work education. In: H. McLaughlin, Duffy, J., Beresford, P., Casey, H. and Cameron, C. (Eds.), *The Routledge Handbook of Service User Involvement in Human Services Research and Education*. London: Routledge.

Maidment, J. (2003). Problems experienced by students on field placement: Using research findings to inform curriculum design and content. *Australian Social Work*, 56(1), 50–60.

McLaughlin, H. (2009). What's in a name: 'Client', 'patient', 'customer', 'consumer', 'expert by experience', 'service user'—What's next? *British Journal of Social Work*, 39(6), 1101–1117.

McSweeney, F. (2018). Themes in the supervision of social care students in Ireland: Building resilience. *European Journal of Social Work*, 21(3), 374–388.

McSweeney, F. & Williams, D. (2018). Social care students' learning in the practice placement in Ireland. *Social Work Education*, 37(5), 581–596.

Parton, N. (2008). Rethinking professional practice: The contributions of social constructionismand the feminist ethics of care. *British Journal of Social Work*, 38(2), 253–269.

Preston-Shoot, M. (2007). Whose lives and whose learning? Whose narratives and whose writing? Taking the next research and literature steps with experts by experience. *Evidence and Policy: A Journal of Research, Debate and Practice*, 3(3), 343–359.

Raineri, M.L. & Sala, M. (2019). Unconventional practice placements. An Italian experience in social work field education. *Relational Social Work*, 3(2), 4–24.

Rossiter, A. (2011). Unsettled social work: The challenge of Levinas's ethics. *The British Journal of Social Work*, 41(5), 980–995.

Sarid, O., Anson, J. & Cohen, M. (2009). Reactions of students to different settings of field experience. *European Journal of Social Work*, 12(1), 101–111.

Scholar, H., McLaughlin, H., McCaughan, S. & Coleman, A. (2014). Learning to be a social worker in a non-traditional placement: Critical reflections on social work, professional identity and social work education in England. *Social Work Education*, 33(8), 998–1016.

Sevenhuijsen, S. (2014). *'Care and Attention' Paper for the Conference 'A Meaningful Life in a Just Society. Investigating Wellbeing and Democratic Caring'. Panel 'Rendering Care the Meaning of Politics'*. Utrecht: Universiteit voor Humanistiek.

Sicora, A. (2019). Reflective practice and learning from mistakes in social work student placement. *Social Work Education*, 38(1), 63–74.

Thompson, N. (2002). *Loss and Grief: A Guide for Human Services Practitioners*. Basingstoke: Palgrave Macmillan.

Thompson, N. (2015). *People Skills*. London: Palgrave MacMillan.

Trevithick, P. (2005). *Social Work Skills*. Berkshire: Open University Press.

Zapf, M.K. (2009). *Social Work and the Environment: Understanding People and Place*. Toronto: Canadian Scholar's Press.

25

Reflexivity Development Demonstrated in Examples of Field Placements of Social Work Students

Navrátil Pavel and Navrátilová Jitka

Czech Development: From Reflexivity to Competence?

Czech social workers are often a bit unsettled that 30 years after the reintroduction of the social work curriculum at the university level, it remains unclear what social work is (what it should be) and what its core social mission is (Chytil, 2007; Navrátil & Navrátilová, 2008; Punová et al., 2020; Matulayová & Musil, 2013; Musil, 2013; Punová & Navrátilová, 2014; Navrátilová & Navrátil, 2020).

The Czech and Slovak authors focusing on social work education and professional identity in this field seem to agree that social work is a socially constructed field (Navrátil, 1998, 2019; Matulayová & Musil, 2013), significantly determined by cultural and societal conditions. Such a premise allows for understanding social work as a profession that is continually updated with societal development and whose training encompasses various approaches to social work education and practice (Navrátilová & Navrátil 2020); however, it is also more difficult to discern its essential aim or meaning (Glumbíková, 2019). Social determination, moreover, makes social work sensitive to current societal trends, which may not reflect the aims, values, and needs of the profession. For example, today, much is said about the colonisation of public space (and of the social work world) by economic thinking, proceduralising strategies, and the logic of the natural sciences and some technical fields (Healy, 2014). Education and field placements remain among the most important areas in which we may preserve the distinctiveness of the field and its values while reacting to the changing context of social work. It is, therefore, necessary that the educational design, and especially that of field placements, result from prudent judgement.

Czech social work had to face multiple challenges following the fall of communism in late 1989. On one hand, newly recognised social problems emerged (e.g., drug abuse, unemployment, crime, prostitution, etc.); on the other hand, social work had to negotiate its new societal role in finding solutions. One of the first topics that needed to be debated and quickly resolved was the character of education as whole, including the question of field placements (Gojová et al., 2010).

It may be said that during the 30 years following the reintroduction of the social work curriculum at universities, many changes have taken place concerning not only the overall content

DOI: 10.4324/9781032164946-30

of university education but also the professional training of students in their field placements. While the early 1990s brought questions about whether field placements should be included as part of the academic training of social workers, the late 1990s and turn of the century witnessed questions related to the conceptualisation and organisation of field placements (Maroon, Matoušek, & Pazlarová, 2007; Navrátilová, 2010). The second decade of the twenty-first century has focused, in terms of the professional internship debates, on the role of field placements in the context of the understanding and development of the professional identity of social workers in post-modern conditions (Navrátil & Navrátilová, 2008; Matulayová & Balogová, 2013; Musil, 2013).

The internship debates brought about polarisation over the amount of emphasis to be placed on the theoretical grounding of professional internships. On one hand, the term *practical education* became typical for the Czech context, emphasising the necessity of linking field placements with systematic theoretical reflexion upon them (Navrátil & Šišláková, 2007)[1]. On the other hand, especially in the environment of vocational colleges, the prevalent model focused on competency-based field placements aimed at helping students learn specific skills and focusing on their practical training and testing (Havrdová, 1999).

In the Czech Republic, the basic document regulating the education of social workers is the so-called 'minimal standard'. Field placements are regulated according to two standards: the standard of professional training and the standard regulating the supervision of professional training. These standards have undergone significant changes during the last few years. At the beginning of the 1990s, their goals were formulated based on the idea of integrating professional training and theoretical knowledge. In this respect, the aim of field placements was mainly to 'provide students with experience of social relationships and ways of work, which exist or are used in existing organizations of social services and to stimulate students' efforts at reflecting on such experience' (A.S.V.S.P., 2009). From a contemporary perspective, we may understand this concept of the minimal standard as an effort to apply reflexive elements.

At the end of the second decade of the twenty-first century, a substantial shift took place in opinions about the aims of student internships and their supervision. While reflection is mentioned in the current standard, overall, the document clearly shows preference for a competency conceptualisation. The formulation of the aims of student field placements and supervision clearly shows this: 'To support professional qualification and develop students' competencies for their social work in given types of institutions and organizations' (A.S.V.S.P., 2009). This formulation of the minimal standard clearly emphasises the competency philosophy.

The development of social work in Czechia at the beginning of 1990s created conditions, we believe, for students not only to reflexively develop their knowledge and skills during their practical internships but also to creatively form their own professional identity. The gradual siding with the competency approach and the diminishing emphasis on reflexivity over time is now evident. Cooper (2008, p. 226) points out that 'a functional analysis of concrete, observable tasks and behaviours is simply inappropriate for complex 'professional activities';... it ignores the potential for professional judgment, takes no account of group processes and has no regard for the influence of social context or setting'.

Most importantly, the competency model of educating social workers will not allow future professionals to face new challenges and societal changes, which assail clients and social workers constantly in our post-modern conditions (Ferguson, 2003; Giddens, 1992). Furthermore, this model fails to respond to the crucial need for students to learn to reflect the structural and cultural life conditions of their clients (Fook, 2002; Thompson & Pascal, 2012).

The emphasis on competence, while taking into consideration reflexivity, mirrors another aspect of social worker education in the Czech Republic that we find troubling, namely the widespread insufficient understanding of what reflexive training actually means (Thompson & Thompson, 2008). Social workers consider any training in which students are encouraged to evaluate their internship without any reference to any methodical or theoretical model as being reflexive. Each subjective expression, opinion, or impression connected with the internship activity is, thus, considered an adequate indicator of reflexive practice, in our experience.

Reflexivity and Social Work

Reflexivity is attracting increasing interest and evokes great expectations in many areas of professional work. Interest in reflexive processes in the professional context started with authors who questioned the applicability of linear thinking in applied professions in which academic knowledge must be accompanied by experience and a sense of context (Argyris & Schön, 1974; Schön, 1983).

In the field of social work, the majority of authors showing interest in reflexive processes come from the English-speaking world (e.g., D'Cruz et al., 2007; Fook, 2002; Payne, 2005; Parton & O'Byrne, 2000; Thompson, 2002) where this approach germinated (Dewey, 1930, 1933; Argyris, 1957; Schön, 1983). Reflexive approaches quickly became a matter of interest in the area of scientific and educational social work publications because the idea that effective decision-making in social work must take into account not only knowledge but also experience (of both workers and clients) and the contextuality of the issues and problems seems naturally fitting for the area of social work (D'Cruz et al., 2007; Ferguson, 2003; Chow et al., & Chan, 2011; Morley, 2015; Nixon & Murr, 2006).

It was Donald Schön's (1983) ideas that initially shaped the discussion of reflexivity in the context of professions. Schön differentiated between 'reflection-on-action' and 'reflection-in-action'. Reflection on action is meant to lead to tested, objective knowledge, which can be regularly used in similar situations and cases. Such reflection is a one-time activity that takes place after meeting with the client, in other words, after the experience has been lived. It should help us to understand certain laws that appeared while working with the client. Schön (1983) characterises such reflection on action as an activity during which the worker examines why he/she acted the way he/she did and what happened during the process; on the basis of this information he/she considers his/her future strategy of action. These explicitly stated and conscious reflections upon the process form the basis for creating patterns, models, examples, and images that can help practitioners see better in future situations and offer possible courses of action in future work. This approach, rooted in technical rationality, is considered by Schön insufficient alone for helping professionals.

The second mode described by Schön is reflection in action. This type of reflection expects the social worker to keep track of internal and external influences during work with the client, as well as the theories and concepts that are currently influencing his/her actions. Reflection-in-action allows and supports creative processes, thanks to which the social worker adopts a situational view and can adjust his/her behaviour according to the developing situation. Reflection-in-action also makes 'legitimate' the insecurity and fears of social workers. Some authors go even further and consider these insecurities as sources of new knowledge (Lam et al., 2007).

During reflection-in-action, it is possible for the social worker to reflect on the changing situation in real time but also to pay attention to his/her own behaviour, feelings, and ways of thinking. According to Schön, this is in contrast to reflection-on-action, which distinguishes between thinking and acting as separate phenomena. According to reflection-on-action, the professional act is a result of rational construction. An example could be a social worker who acts on the basis of a previously thought-out strategy. Schön, however, believes that to be possible only when performing clear tasks of a technical nature and not in the world of complex problems, such as that encountered in social work.

Schön's contribution does not end with reflection by professionals; he also raised interest in factors influencing professional decision-making. Schön assumed that a professional does not perceive the 'problem situation' of his/her client completely 'objectively and clean', but that his/her perception is always coloured by previous experiences, knowledge, and values. These must be examined to understand their direct and indirect influences on practice.

In relation to reflexivity, many authors, therefore, also examine emotional introspection (Sewell, 2020), cognitive self-reflection (Nadan & Stark, 2017), theoretical and discursive contextualisation of professional phenomena (Navrátil & Janebová, 2010), and values (Thompson & Thompson, 2008). The key impulse in this area came from Fook (2002), noting that Schön's accent on modes of reflection should be complemented with interest in reflecting on structural and power influences. Fook, thus, defined what is now typically called critical reflexivity. The authors studying critical reflection encourage social workers to understand the power context of their work and in the lives of their clients and to make an effort to support more just conditions for their clients (Ferguson, 2008; Fook, 2002; Freire, 1996; Chytil, 2007; Keller, 2007; Laan, 1998; Lorenz, 2007; Payne, 2005).

A key feature of reflexive thinking is the ability to consider multiple perspectives from which a given situation or problem can be interpreted. Here also lies one of the objections to reflexivity – that it faces social workers with multiple options and interpretations but also with uncertainty over which of the possible interpretations and interventions is right for a client. Such a critique, however, is rooted in duality, an unnatural distinction between thinking and acting. If the duality of thinking and behaviour is overcome in the reflection-in-action mode, the duality ceases to exist (Bendelow et al., 2002).

Schön managed to distinguish between two types of gathering and processing data in professional practice. As for the further use of his assumptions about reflexivity, we agree with Fook (2002), who noticed that both concepts (reflection-in-action, reflection-on-action) can, in the practice of social work, be complementary and purposefully used. The continuous reflexive attitude of the social worker supports reflection on practice and vice versa. A reflexive attitude is, therefore, a kind of constant disposition to reflexivity, while reflection itself is a process of examining the practice (Redmond, 2006).

Reflexively Organised Field Placements as the Keystone of the Theoretical and the Practical

Even societies with a long social work tradition, such as Great Britain, have been engaging in lengthy debates over whether theoretical knowledge or practical training is more suitable for social workers' professional education. The applied nature of social work has often led to the field being perceived as 'insufficiently scientific' in academic circles. The current contradictory or dualistic ideas about social workers' professional training echo wide-reaching debates that took place in the Anglo-Saxon world in the 1980s. Thompson (1992), for example, sees the origins of this discussion in the early 1980s, pointing out two strong opposing ideas. On one hand, authors such as Martin Davis (1982) suggested that social work students should be trained primarily to gain practical competencies. Davis questioned the usefulness of academic study and the teaching of disciplines such as sociology and other rather theoretical subjects. In contrast, Sibeon (1982) pointed out that social work students should be educated in theory and intellectually fitted to be able to understand their professional practice in the context of social policy and other larger social themes.

One of the benefits of theoretical education is the development of critical judgement. Social workers undergoing such study learn about the problems and uncertainties inherent in the professional life of a social worker and may, thus, form a more holistic image of their practice and their profession. Proponents of this way of thinking expect social workers to have the capacity to understand their own role in its complexity and respond to challenges connected with the profession (Goddard & Carew, 1989).

Both contradictory currents find their expression in specific approaches to education and professional training, influencing not only students' education but even more so the formation of social work identity (Navrátilová & Navrátil, 2020). Training-based education crystallised into the competency-based approach to social work education, which has become dominant not only in the Czech context but is also supported by important EU directives based on the Bologna process. The theory-based current has found its expression, for example, in evidence-based social work education, according to which social workers are expected to have a theoretical scientific knowledge base when working with clients.

One possible way to answer which approach is more appropriate is to look at the question from the perspective of the aims of professional internships. Rotholz and Werk (1984) state that the main goals of professional training are professional socialisation, development of skills, and development of professional judgement. Such goals make it clear that the educational process cannot include only artisan-like training in certain competencies but also requires development of autonomous critical thinking abilities. Rotholz and Werke point out that students should, by all means, gain practical skills during their field placements and to be able to handle the demands of their daily work. To this end, the placements must include pragmatic tasks, often specific to the particular type of work or role. They suggest that alongside such practical competencies, field placement should also promote theoretical reflexivity. Theory-based education implies exposure to broader processes in which learning goes beyond immediate work tasks, and the demands are incorporated into a larger professional context. Theoretical education is characterised by two traits that distinguish it from technical practice: (1) a *research aspect*, in which the student and professional worker should be able to work with knowledge derived from research and to contribute to it, and (2) a *critical perspective* in which education helps the trainee to take things not only at face value but also to pose questions. Even though competencies are valuable as guides of professional behaviour, they are not sufficient in themselves. Alongside competencies, we also need knowledge that helps us fulfil our professional duties.

We argue that education and the field placement of social workers should integrate both approaches. Social workers need to master instrumental skills as well as learn how to use these skills when working with diverse clients in varied contexts. We believe that the integration of education emphasising the need for training and education based primarily in theoretical studies finds its realisation in education that is known as reflexive.

Reflexivity: A Competence or a Category of Capability?

We have explained that one of the defining aspects of the reflexive approach is taking into consideration various perspectives that may open unexpected and productive options. In the context of student field placement, the reflexive mode is applicable across all dimensions of professional performance. At this point, we would like to examine whether the reflexive approach to practice can be used in the context of competency-based models of education. We then attempt to identify an alternative, and finally we define the areas of professional development students are expected to master in which we advocate reflexive learning.

Speaking of professional development, there is a debate currently under way in the Czech Republic as to whether it is appropriate to use this term when considering development of professional competencies during social work education, or whether a different term should be used that would better express the complex nature of professionalism in social work (Navrátilová, 2014).

The concept of competency involves the acquisition of knowledge and skills. Competencies are stable structures characterising a normatively defined area of learning. Competencies may include, for example, professional elements such as 'effective communication' and 'intervention skills'. The main problem with the competency concept, in our view, is the static and narrow definition of the areas of learning, which quickly become irrelevant due to social developments and changes. Many authors also believe that the concept of competencies has become a tool of regulation and control rather than an expression of professional proficiency. Eraut (2002), for example, points out that the concept of competency can only be applied at the level of the newly qualified professional and cannot be used as a measure of his life-long progress.

One existing alternative is the concept of professional capabilities, which appears to broaden and enrich the professional competencies concept with other necessary attributes. Stephenson (2012, pp. 2–5) explains that the capabilities concept includes the idea of competence while complementing it with elements of creativity and potential: 'Capability is an integration of knowledge, skills, personal qualities and understanding used appropriately and effectively – not just in familiar and highly focused specialist contexts but in response to new and changing circumstances … to take action in uncertainty'. From our perspective, it is also important that the capabilities concept includes the reflexivity aspect. Capable people are those who know how to learn, are creative, have a high degree of self-efficacy, can apply competencies in novel as well as familiar situations, and work well with others. In comparison to competency, capability is a holistic attribute (Hase & Davis, 1999).

Despite some authors' doubts over the transferability of the capabilities theory into setting professional standards (Lester, 2014), England's Professional Capabilities Framework (P.C.F.) stands as an example of an attempt to apply the capabilities concept to the restructuring of social workers' education. In his two empirical studies of the P.C.F., Wiles (2017) describes how this application in England's social work education programmes contributed to the development of students' professional identities. In the Czech Republic, it is precisely the lack of professional identity among social work students that students themselves note and have asked the educational institutions to address (Kaňák, 2019).

Wiles (2017) considers as an innovative feature the fact that 'the PCF has been designed for use with both students and qualified practitioners. It progressively specifies the skills, knowledge and values expected at every stage of a social worker's career and professional development'.

P.C.F. consists of nine overarching and interdependent domains of capability that reflect the complexity of the social work profession and the interplay of knowledge, skills. and values: professionalism; values and ethics; diversity; rights, justice, and economic well-being; knowledge; critical reflection and analysis; intervention and skills; contexts and organisations; and professional leadership. P.C.F. includes not only these domains but also nine progression points representing professional development across a social worker's career. This starts with four 'student' levels (specifying entry criteria and the expectations for each year of qualifying education), followed by five 'qualified practitioner' stages ranging from newly qualified to senior (strategic level) (B.A.S.W., 2016).

Wiles (2017) stresses that P.C.F. was designed to be used holistically (in agreement with the capabilities philosophy). The domains are intentionally overlapping and interdependent rather than separate. Detailed descriptions of each capability are used diagnostically to help identify strengths and areas for potential development. There is no expectation that evidence must be produced for the domains/areas.

We believe it is important that this was a deliberate departure from the previous competence-based National Occupational Standards that were used across the U.K. starting in 2003.

Example of the Applied Reflexive Approach in the Practical Training of Social Workers

Let us consider how the P.C.F., as described by Willes (2017), is applicable during field placement. Due to space constraints, we focus on selected examples of applied reflexive questions in four areas (professionalism, values and ethics, intervention and skills, and contexts and organisations) as they are applied during the supervision of field placement.

Capability: Professionalism

The collective identity within a profession may be defined by various signs such as acceptance of the profession by the public, monopoly on certain types of work, professional autonomy, knowledge base, system of professional education, existence of professional organisations, and ethical standards, prestige, and rewards for work completed (Weiss-Gal & Welbourne, 2008). The key task of social work educators, according to many authors, is the socialisation of the student into the profession and helping the student create his individual professional identity (Šámalová, 2019). Professional identity is perceived by many authors as one form of social identity (Karpetis, 2014). Individual professional identity is constructed in reference to the group characteristics of the profession and requires personal creative effort not only of the educators but also active engagement by the student himself/herself. Professional identity is an abstract social construction, and its formation is a rather continuous, unfinished process that is sensitive to time (Webb, 2017).

REFLECTION OF PROFESSIONAL IDENTITY

The formation of professional identity and professionalisation have been complicated in the Czech Republic because of the insufficient public recognition of social work, negative evaluations of social workers' performance, unclear demarcation of social work, and the passiveness of professional organisations (Otava, 2016). The role of academic institutions is further complicated because of the lack of professional standards as a basis of the profession (Baláž, 2017; Elichová, 2017).

Under these circumstances, the formation of professional identity must be supported in two areas: defining the basic contours of the profession and self-reflection within the field.

Understanding social work as a profession may be furthered by the following reflexive questions: How do I understand the role of professional social work in society? Which social needs may be met by social work? What goals should social work aim at in society? Which personal and professional characteristics should a social worker have? What values and interests are represented by social work? Is there a difference between altruism and professional social work? What roles do personal dispositions and acquired qualifications play in social work practice?

Some authors consider personal self-reflection in the context of the profession an important part of the process of development of professional skills (Bowman, 1989). Some authors consider self-understanding a key prerequisite for work in helping professions (Dryden, 2008; Howe, 2008;Viner, Majzen, & Dakchém, 2006; Ševčíkova & Navrátil, 2010).

SELF-REFLECTION IN THE PROFESSIONAL CONTEXT

The development of self-reflection is part of the professional development process of a social worker and of an effective helping professional in general. Understanding oneself and one's personality and social resources can help a student discover the appropriate area(s) for his/her future engagement in social work. In the context of a reflexive field placement, the following questions and prompts may inspire growth in self-knowledge in regard to social work: What is motivating your interest in social work? Which areas of social work interest you and why? Reflect on your motivation for social work and formulate its advantages and risks. Are you conscious of an area of social work in which you would not want to work? Describe your personal perspective on social work. Do you have any qualities and personal resources that may make work in a particular area easier? Can you effectively use your abilities and talents in the workplace of your field placement? Does the workplace create opportunities for your personal growth? Which characteristics do you consider key for the profession of social work at the workplace?

Growth in self-understanding and uncovering the motives leading the student toward social work are necessary for future success. Neglecting to answer questions about why a student wants to direct his/her life to help others may result in attempts to solve his/her own problems through his/his clients. Research shows (Lambert & Ogler, 2004) that workers in helping professions may affect their clients both positively and negatively. Subconscious assertion of one's personality may be a source of negative influence on clients.

Capability: Reflection of Values and Ethical Contexts

We spoke about the necessity of *reflecting upon one's attitudes and values* as dimensions of the reflexive approach (Moss, 2007; Thompson & Thompson, 2008). Growing in understanding of one's own values goes hand-in-hand with improving the ability to reflect on and apply the values inherent in professional social work. Value reflection, thus, plays a significant role in the building of professional skills. Values can also influence the choice of workplace for field placement. Understanding one's own personality and social resources may help students find placements where they can optimally carry out their work in alignment with their abilities. When reflecting upon our own values and attitudes, we may find inspiration, for example, in the following questions: Which ethical dilemmas do you encounter in your field placement? Which ethical principles do you consider key in social work? Do some of the ethical principles of social work differ from your own values? Are your values, faith, and needs in agreement with values and requirements of your field placement? Which ethical requirement of social work practice is the least acceptable to you?

The formulation of these questions is a result of an effort to stimulate students' self-understanding and appreciation of the importance and role of values in personal life and in the life of a social worker. The crossover of values from personal life into professional social work should be an important topic of reflection.

Capability: Intervention and Skills

Social work education aims at preparing students for a future in the social work profession. Hence, during reflexively oriented field placement, great emphasis is placed on reflecting on individual aspects of work with clients. The student may, thereby, gain direct experience of work with clients and knowledge about the conditions under which such experience is lived and how it affects the work. It is, therefore, important to pay attention to such experiences and to reflect on what a particular instance of direct work with a client may mean for the client and for the student as well. The process of social work with a client takes place, as in other helping professions, in various phases (Gabura & Mydlíková, 2004), which should be reflected upon. Attention during work with clients may focus mainly on reflexion of each direct contact, assessing the client's life situation, continuous evaluation of the case, and the closing of the work with the client.

REFLECTING ON THE BEGINNING OF COOPERATION WITH A CLIENT

Work with a client begins with the first contact. Gabura and Pružinská (1995) state that the quality and effectiveness of the helping process is often directly related to the way the first contact with the client is handled. Therefore, students should be led to be aware of how the first contact went and what influenced its quality.

The following questions and prompts may help encourage such reflection: Is there any preparation for the first contact with the client in the organisation? What procedures must the client undergo before he/she becomes a client? Describe the first moments of contact with a client. In which ways does the professional express interest in the client and his/her problems? Describe the environment in which the first contact with the client takes place. Is it stimulating?

REFLECTION ON THE ASSESSMENT OF THE CLIENT'S LIFE SITUATION

Assessment constitutes a phase of the social work process that significantly influences the type and results of a social worker's actions. According to Parton and O'Byrn (2000), the practice of assessment distinguishes social work from counselling and therapy because the assessment outcomes from social work are often meant for use in court, by managers, or more generally in formal contexts. Barker (1995) defines assessment as a process in which the character, cause, development, and prognosis of a problem are determined, and further analysis is made of people and situations related to the problem.

During reflection, students should be led to become aware of how they judge client cases, and which information and knowledge they use to form an idea of the client's situation. In addition, the overall perception of the client should be reflected upon. From this perspective we may lead students to respond the following questions and prompts: State the main problems of the client and explain, using theoretical knowledge, how you understand the factors and circumstances which cause or influence them. Reason out an adequate approach (perspective, theory). Which information about the client, his/her family and life situation have you investigated? Do you consider the amount and quality of information adequate? Consider which sources of information about the client and his/her situation you are using. Who participates in the assessment as the assessor and the assessed? Which methods and techniques of assessment are used? Is assessment proceduralised? Does the social worker accord enough space for understanding the perspectives of the client and other actors in the client's life situation?

These questions orient the student's attention so as to see the client's problems not only as a separate part of his/her life that can, like a 'component part', be almost mechanically exchanged or fixed. The questions should inspire students to be open and willing to take into account the life situation of the client as a whole, and to search for the causes and consequences of problems in wider contexts. Client problems are becoming more and more complex, and solving them requires repeatedly renewed knowledge gathering, while the social worker is continuously exposed to changing conditions in his work and personal life.

REFLECTION ON ONGOING AND FINAL EVALUATIONS

Ongoing and closing evaluation of case development are significant processes that, together, play a key role in maintaining professional standards and improving social workers' practice. They are closely linked with assessment. While assessment identifies the needs of a client, evaluation examines to what extent the helping process fulfils them (Thompson, 2002). Students can use the following questions and prompts to reflect on the process of their work with a client so that they can continuously evaluate it from the standpoint of fulfilling goals: Describe the typical continuous evaluation of the development of the client's situation in the organisation. Which aspects of the situation or intervention are considered during continuous evaluation? What are the impacts of continuous evaluation on the future course of intervention? Who takes part in the continuous evaluation?

In addition to continuous evaluation, it is necessary to conduct a closing evaluation. Effective conclusion of an intervention is a qualified process that helps to reduce the probability of creating further problems (Caspi & Reid, 2002; Thompson, 2002). Ending the case or transferring it to another worker may be planned or unplanned, initiated by the client or the social worker, or mutually agreed upon or unilateral. Case closings and ending of relationships have not been extensively covered in the professional literature. The topic of case closing was examined in relationship to the topic of evaluation (Coulshed, 1991). Yet, the closing phase of work with a client has been underappreciated as a phase in the helping process, even though its importance is equal to that of the preceding phase. The key issue in the closing phase is preparing the client to solve his/her problems by himself/herself and to function without the support of helping workers. This places various demands on the client and underestimating the needed preparation to manage them may lead to new problems that can consequently cause imbalance in the social functioning of the client. Therefore, students should be encouraged during field placement to reflect upon the ways in which contact with a client is concluded and what such an ending to the cooperation means for both parties. This reflection should also aim at understanding the importance of the closing phase not only in the client's life but also in that of the social worker. The closing of a particular case may be a source of certain positive emotions or stresses. The following are some example questions appropriate for the closing phase: How is the closing evaluation carried out at the workplace? Which aspects of the client's case are evaluated at the end of the intervention? What is being monitored? Do you believe that the topic of ending the work with a client has been given sufficient attention at the workplace? How do helping professionals at the workplace prevent client dependence from forming? What situations associated with ending contact with the client can be difficult for social workers?

Capability: Reflection of the Institutional Context of Social Work Services

Thompson and Thompson (2008) consider accounting for questions about the context of social work services a key prerequisite of social work practice. This idea has been developed in the Czech context by Navrátil and Šišláková (2007) and is embodied also in the educational standards of the International Association of Social Work Schools (I.A.S.S.W.) and the International Federation for Social Workers (I.F.S.W.).

This dimension entails helping students develop the capacity to understand the legal norms, public and organisational policies, and accepted institutional practices in which social work takes place. Questions related to the context of social work services are aimed at discovering the conditions in which social work services are provided at field placement workplaces and the ways in which the local conditions of social work are taken into account there. This institutional approach, thus, creates a grounding framework defining the social work tasks in a given institutional environment (Healy, 2014).

Reflexivity in this domain is aimed at prompting students to consider social work in its larger context rather than as a set of mechanistic and narrowly focused acts.

REFLECTION OF ORGANISATIONAL POLICIES

Students reflecting in a reflexivity oriented field placement cannot bypass the organisational context of social work services. Examining the organisational background of the social work may help students to gain a basic orientation to the demands of the environment in which their professional field placement is carried out. Topics of reflexive examination will include: What are the goals of the organisation? What procedures does the organisation use in attempting to reach its goals? What is the organisation's philosophy of service (explicit, implicit)? How are clients' problems interpreted within the organisation? How do material resources and pressure limit the social workers? How is the social work limited by organisational or other pressures?

REFLECTION OF LEGAL NORMS AND PUBLIC POLICIES

The relationship between the practice of social work and legal norms or public policies has not been widely discussed in Czech social work. Those discussions that have emerged primarily describe dilemmas that social workers encounter in their practice (Janebová, 2019).

It seems advantageous that the relationship between social work practice and legal norms would be examined during the education of future professionals. Legal norms and public policies may be perceived as guiding points in unclear situations or as a complicating factor of the practice. Many authors comment that public policies and legal norms may be too removed from reality or simplistic, or have multiple meanings or may be irrelevant, colliding with social work values, complex, full of dilemmas, and stressful (Healy, 2014; Preston-Shoot et al., 1998). Such ambivalence, thus, underscores the necessity of the reflection.

Questions to reflect upon may include: Which legal norms are relevant in the specific social work environment? How do these legal norms mirror the knowledge and values of social work? Which procedures are established in this environment?

Understanding organisational policies leads to understanding of the meaning and influence that context may have on work with clients. Taking this information into account is necessary for the student to become capable of considering clients' problems from multiple perspectives. We can say that a contextual view inspired by the questions above may help prevent falling into a thoughtless routine that risks approaching every client with the same criteria and procedures. Reflexive thinking creates conditions for seeing the client not as an 'island' all by itself but as a being that exists within a larger milieu that affects him/her and that he/she himself/herself influences.

Encouraging students to apply the reflexive approach during professional field placement raises the question whether it is possible to conceptualise reflexivity as a competency. Based on our examples above, we lean toward the position that reflexivity cannot be understood as an independent competency. Rather, we consider it a principle that should guide both the education of social workers and professional field placement. The concept of capabilities enlarges the meaning of competency, bridging two banks of a river – theory and practice – and is anchored in the reflexive approach.

The Main Challenges Connected with the Integration of Reflexivity-Based Education into the Academic Environment in the Czech Republic

So far, we have presented examples of applying a reflexivity-based approach in social work student professional field placement. The examples demonstrate a limited selection of capabilities and their characteristics as they can be applied in the workplace. Below, we examine barriers limiting the implementation of a reflexivity-based approach to social worker education in the Czech Republic.

The following discussion describes the main barriers in the contemporary Czech academic setting that limit the development of reflexivity-based student professional field placement.

Low Value of Field Placement

One of the barriers to development of reflexivity-based student professional field placement in the Czech *university* setting appears to be the low value of the practicum experiences of social work students, despite the fact that such practical learning is required by the educational standards for schools training future social workers. We believe that professional field placement under supervision is the most important, productive, and most memorable component of social work education. The research also confirms that professional field experiences have the most pronounced effects on students (Tolson & Kopp, 1988). Schneck (1991) states that countries with the longest tradition of social work integrate professional training as an indispensable and valued part of education.

Rejecting Reflexivity

Even though student practicum in social work areas is considered an 'obvious' part of education, unresolved questions remain that necessitate professional discussion. One key question relates to the lack of clarity about how social work students should be educated during their field placement. The necessity of learning specific instrumental skills required for work with clients is a completely understandable demand that we encounter in the context of practicums. Field placement, however, is also the place where students quickly learn that their knowledge and learned procedures are insufficient when they are confronted with complex situations that are difficult to solve and, moreover, raise questions about the values, nature, and identity of social work. The social uncertainties and risks (Bauman, 1995; Giddens, 2003) of clients force social workers to step outside the security of well-trodden paths of set procedures and learn how to use new information. In student field placement, it is necessary for students to learn to react to the 'blurred' professional boundaries that formerly defined social work practice (Musil, 2004; Musil & Šrajer, 2008; Navrátil, 2005). Additionally, social work students should be led in their field placement to reflect upon their own person, practices, and social conventions. Reflection must become a means of feedback, which helps form a certain perspective on proper professional behaviour in 'blurred' (Musil & Šrajer, 2008) professional and societal circumstances. It is, thus, evident that social work students need to be taught reflexivity in their field placement, as without reflexivity the instrumental use of skills while working with clients may become an insufficient and even dangerous approach.

Unprepared System

Introducing reflexivity-based practical training into the academic environment has been a demanding task requiring a change in the entire educational system, including field placement.

In the Czech Republic, social service organisations offer field placement to social work students on a voluntary basis, which makes negotiating the form of field placement and the type of tasks for students to complete quite uneasy.

Absence of Models Integrating Theory into Practice

It is quite surprising that, despite the meaning of reflexivity, that is, integrating theory and practice (Thompson, 2000), there is a lack of sophisticated procedures for such reflection. Meanwhile, insufficient attention has been given to the theoretical basis of such integration (Thompson & Pascal, 2012). There is a richness of concepts of reflexive thinking left to us by John Dewey, Jürgen Habermas, Paolo Freire, Jack Mezirow, and Stephen Brookfield. For social work, however, it is necessary that this wealth of reflective approaches be transformed into concepts and models of reflexive practice. In this respect, the debate in the Czech environment about applying reflexivity models in student field placement has been influenced by the work of Donald Schön (1983), who introduced a new perspective to the ways of reflecting on the practice of professionals; Jane Fook (2002), who created a model of critical reflexivity; and the works of Neil Thompson (2002, 2012). Even though debates over reflexivity in the context of student field placement are topical in the Czech Republic, they have not resulted in the creation of applicable models of reflexivity.

Insufficient Theoretical Base

Thompson and Pascal (2012) called for development of a theoretical base for reflexivity-based field placement and its implementation. We believe that insufficient theorisation of reflexivity-based field placement is also a key challenge facing schools training social workers in the Czech Republic.

Thompson and Pascal (2012) pointed out that practices often described as reflexive practicum regularly lack a deeper theoretical dimension. They assert that simplified procedures came into being but not as a result of a reflexive way of thinking but, rather, through a superficial consideration of events that took place during the field placement. Authors identify 'Schön's heritage' as one of the reasons for a simplified understanding of reflexive practice. Despite the valuable contribution of Schön's findings about new types of thinking for professionals, some elements are lacking from his thought, such as planning social workers' activity, their language and meanings – but these have become prominent in reflexive practice. Furthermore, the Czech environment is typified by rejection of theorising social work (Elichová, 2017).

Neglecting Critical Reflection

Critical reflection focuses on critique and analysis of power and oppression in society with the goal of transforming society to overcome oppression, injustice, and exploitation. Social workers should help clients and be actively involved in the transformation of society so that their clients are not disadvantaged by structural pressures. Within this concept of practice, social workers should try not to reproduce by their acts oppressive practices rooted in the structural conditions of society (Healy, 2000; Fook, 2002). Such critical practice is gaining in intensity in the postmodern context, wherein social workers are expected to be all the more engaged reflexively in their practice. In other words, they should be capable of perceiving the life situations of clients in their complexity and from different perspectives. The need for critical stance during reflection is grounded in the value of questioning various aspects of social workers' service practices (Navrátil, 2010).

The demand for critical reflexivity in the context of student field placement in the Czech Republic is obstructed by the principles of managerialism and neoliberal logic that are becoming more pronounced in the organisations providing student field placement. Students are led to accept existing procedures as the only acceptable ones and taking a critical perspective is seen as undermining legitimate and good practices represented by set procedures and guidelines for work with clients.

Rejecting Ambiguity

Reflexively based social work leans on the principles of social constructivism (Berger & Luckmann, 1999), which is based on the assumption that social work in its perceptions and procedures is very closely tied to social reality and the ways in which this reality is formed through the processes of social construction. Constructivists refuse to believe that human affairs are unequivocal and easily accessible to be known. As the causes of problems in life situations are varied, according to constructivists, so the solutions may differ. Because a reflexive approach based on the constructivist assumes the existence of multiple equivalent truths and perspectives on life, Milner et al. (2015) require social workers to learn to accept this complexity and refrain from uncalled-for simplifications. In approaching reality, we should beware of so-called *false certainty* (Thompson, 1992). The reflexive approach favours understanding – that is, searching for the meaning(s) that clients assign to concrete events in their life.

In the Czech environment of social service providers where student field placements are carried out, the prevalent approach is that of using objective criteria and points of view, rather than acknowledging the idea of ambiguous reality. Procedures are normatively distinguished as effective or ineffective, desirable or undesirable, useful or useless. In this respect, practice is more oriented toward an objectivist viewpoint than the constructivist one.

Applying Managerialism and Neoliberalism in the Context of Field Placement

The education of professionals is closely linked with how we understand the profession itself. It concerns not only the perspective of the educators, but in the context of field placement, the educational experience is significantly influenced by the organisational structure of social work services. Especially those organisations active within the public sector are influenced by the model of the social welfare state in which they are operating. Since the 1980s, all welfare states have been influenced by neoliberal thinking. This process has been taking place across Europe, including the Czech Republic. The term 'new public management' describes the changes in conceptualising professional work and identities in associated professions. Many have already identified tendencies such as deprofessionalisation, proletarisation, and lowering of professional qualifications (Freidson, 1994).

Social work in the public sector has become more regulated and publicly accountable than ever before. New public management and new public governance place great emphasis on accountability to clients, employers, and the state. It may be considered highly problematic, however, that managerial jurisdiction and power have gained authority within social work, where emphasis has, subsequently, shifted to efficiency and economising (Hood, 1995), with saving money valued more than the client's interest. Public social services are becoming privatised. In the past, management and administration were understood to be subservient to the priorities of social work, but now the reverse is true.

In the context of student field placement, this development has limited the space for reflection as a genuine part of social work practice. Social work trainees are now often viewed as cheap labour that the organisation can, and sometimes even must, use to fulfil its stated mission. Field placement work is often directed toward proceduralised acts and not the development of reflexive professional judgement. In this respect, the field placement is becoming a prop for those arguing in favour of the competency-based approach in social work.

Conclusion

We see the barriers hindering the application of a reflexive approach in the Czech university setting as important areas of research interest. The development of a theoretical basis and the creation of models of reflexivity is a crucial task that we believe is a necessary prerequisite for further development of reflexive thinking and its further application in social work studies. Deeper theoretical understanding of reflexivity may build a bridge between the proponents of the competency and reflexivity-based approaches to education and field placement. This chapter was written in the belief that practical training and theoretical education differ only in emphasis and are not mutually exclusive relationships. Training and education may vary in their 'ideal' forms but, in reality, during the preparation of future professionals, both overlap. The relationship between theory and skills can be understood as a continuum. In one extreme, people may avoid knowledge and information, at the other, paralysis analysis makes people incapable of action until they have every piece of information. We believe that the middle way is most fruitful. And the specific form this golden middle way should take should be discussed by proponents of both positions.

We hope to contribute to this discussion with this chapter and to offer as a possible solution the concept of capabilities, which, from our perspective, expands the common understanding of competencies and opens up space for applying reflexivity. Introducing the reflexive approach as a basic principle of education of social workers, however, requires transformation of educational institutions and their policies – a long-term project, indeed!

Note

1 Many schools were successful in creating partnerships with organisations with good practices that were also open to critical reflection, where students were able to gain practical experiences during their professional education.

References

Argyris, C. (1957). *Personality and Organization: The Conflict between System and the Individual.* New York: Harper and Row.

Argyris, C., & Schön, D.A. (1974). *Theory in Practice: Increasing Professional Effectiveness.* San Francisco: Jossey-Bass Publishers.

ASVSP (2009). Základní cíle. [Main aims]. Retrieved September 20, 2015, from http://www.asvsp.org.

Baláž, R. (2017). Profesionalita sociálních pracovníků: Známka kvality, anebo procedurální berlička? [Professionalism of social workers: Quality mark or procedural crutch?]. *Czech & Slovak Social Work / Sociální Práce / Sociálna Práca, 17*(6), 131–151.

Barker, R. L. (1995). *The Social Work Dictionary.* Washington, DC: National Association of Social Workers.

Bauman, Z. (1995). *Úvahy o postmoderní době. [Reflections on Postmodern Times].* Prague: Slon.

Bendelow, G., Carpenter, M., Vautier, C., & Williams, S. (2002). *Gender, Health, and Healing: The Public/Private Divide.* New York: Routledge.

Berger, P. L., & Luckmann, T. (1999). *Sociální konstrukce reality. [The Social Construction of Reality].* Brno, Czech Republic: CDK.

Bowman, B.T. (1989). Self-reflection as an element of professionalism. *Teachers College Record, 90*(3), 444–451.

British Association of Social Work. (2016). Professional capabilities framework. Retrieved June 21, 2011, from https://www.basw.co.uk/pcf/.

Caspi, J., & Reid, W. J. (2002). *Educational Supervision in Social Work: A Task-Centered Model for Field Instruction and Staff Development*. New York: Columbia University Press.

Chow, A. Y. M., Lam, D. O. B., Leung, G. S. M., Wong, D. F. K., & Chan, B. F. P. (2011). Promoting reflexivity among social work students: The development and evaluation of a programme. *Social Work Education, 30*(2), 141–156. DOI:10.1080/02615479.2011.540377.

Chytil, O. (2007). Důsledky modernizace pro sociální práci. [Consequences of modernization for social work]. *Sociální Práce/Sociálna Práca, 8*(4), 64–71.

Cooper, B. (2008). Continuing professional development: A critical approach. In: A. W. Fraser & S. Matthews (Eds.), *The Critical Practitioner in Social Work and Health Care* (pp. 222–238). London: Sage.

Coulshed, V. (1991). *Social Work Practice: An Introduction*. London: Macmillan Press.

D'Cruz, H., Gillingham, P., & Melendez, S. (2007). Reflexivity, its meanings and relevance for social work: A critical review of the literature. *British Journal of Social Work, 37*(1), 73–90. DOI:10.1093/bjsw/bcl001.

Davies, M. (1982). A comment on heart or head. *Issues in Social Work Education, 2*(1), 57–60.

Dewey, J. (1930). *Human Nature and Conduct*. New York: Modern Library.

Dewey, J. (1933). *How We Think*. New York: Heath.

Dryden, W. (2008). *Poradenství: Stručný přehled. [Counseling in a Nutshell]*. Prague: Portál.

Elichová, M. (2017). *Sociální práce: Aktuální otázky. [Social Work: Topical Questions]*. Prague: Grada.

Eraut, M. (2002). *Developing Professional Knowledge and Competence*. London: Routledge.

Ferguson, H. (2003). Welfare, social exclusion and reflexivity: The case of child and woman protection. *Journal of Social Policy, 32*(2), 199–216.

Ferguson, H. (2008). The theory and practice of critical best practice in social work. In: K. Jones, B. Cooper & H. Ferguson (Eds.), *Best Practice in Social Work: Critical Perspectives* (pp. 15–37). New York: Palgrave Macmillan.

Fook, J. (2002). *Social Work: Critical Theory and Practice*. London: Sage.

Freidson, E. (1994). *Professionalism Reborn: Theory, Prophecy, and Policy*. University of Chicago Press.

Freire, P. (1996). *Pedagogy of the Oppressed*. London: Penguin Books.

Gabura, J., & Mydlíková, E. (2004). *Vedeni sociálního případu. [Social Case Management]*. Bratislava: Asociácia supervízorov a sociálnych poradcov.

Gabura, J., & Pružinská, J. (1995). *Poradenský proces. [Counselling Process]*. Prague: Slon.

Giddens, A. (1992). *The Transformation of Intimacy: Sexuality, Love and Eroticism in Modern Societies*. Cambridge: Polity.

Giddens, A. (2003). *Důsledky modernity. [The Consequences of Modernity]*. Prague: Slon.

Glumbíková, K. (2019). Postavení a cíle sociální práce v důsledku proměn společnosti. [Position and aims of social work as a result of societal changes]. *Sociální práce/Sociálna práca*. Retrieved from http://www.socialniprace.cz/zpravy.php?oblast=1&clanek=1175.

Goddard, C., & Carew, R. (1989). Social work: Mechanical or intellectual? *Social Work Today, 19*(1), 22–23.

Gojová, A., Holasová, V., Chytil, O., Keller, J., Sýkorová, D., & Krausová, A. (2010). Social work in Czech Republic. In: E. Brian & P. Littlechild (Eds.), *Social Work across Europe: Accounts from 16 Countries* (pp. 19–30). Ostrava, Czech Republic: University of Ostrava.

Hase, S., & Davis, L. (1999). From competence to capability: The implications for human resource development and management. Paper presented at Millennial challenges in management, education, cybertechnology, and leadership. 17th Annual Conference, San Diego. Retrieved from https://epubs.scu.edu.au/cgi/viewcontent.cgi?article=1126&context=gcm_pubs.

Havrdová, Z. (1999). *Kompetence v praxi sociální práce. [Competence in Social Work Practice]*. Prague: Osmium.

Healy, K. (2000). *Social Work Practices: Contemporary Perspectives on Change*. London: Sage Publications.

Healy, K. (2014). *Social Work Theories in Context: Creating Frameworks for Practice*. Houndmills, Basingstoke, Hampshire: Palgrave Macmillan.

Hood, C. (1995). Contemporary public management: A new global paradigm? *Public Policy and Administration, 10*(2), 104–117.

Howe, D. (2008). *The Emotionally Intelligent Social Worker*. Basingstoke: Palgrave Macmillan.

Janebová, R. (2019). Jak řešit kolize mezi praxí sociální práce a právem. [How to solve collisions between social work practice and the law]. *Czech & Slovak Social Work/Sociální Práce/Sociálna Práca, 19*(5), 87–103.

Kaňák, J. (2019). 'Ale hlavně, když se to trénuje': Výcviková profesionalita a primární profesní identita sociální práce. ['As long as it gets trained': Training professionalism and the primary professional identity of social work]. *Czech & Slovak Social Work/Sociální Práce/Sociálna Práca, 19*(3), 82–99.

Karpetis, G. (2014). Advocating the clinical social work professional identity: A biographical study. *Journal of Social Work Practice, 28*(1), 23–41. DOI:10.1080/02650533.2013.806888.

Keller, J. (2007). *Teorie modernizace. [Theory of Modernization]*. Prague: Slon.
van der Laan, Gert (1998). *Otázky legitimace sociální práce: Pomoc není zboží. [Questions of Legitimacy of Social Work: Help Is Not a Commodity]*. Boskovice, Czech Republic: Albert.
Lam, M. C., Wong, H., & Leung, T. T. F. (2007). An unfinished reflexive journey: Social work students' reflection on their placement experiences. *British Journal of Social Work, 37*(1), 91–105.
Lambert, M. J., & Ogler, B. M. (2004). The efficacy and effectiveness of psychoterapy. In: M. J. Lambert (Ed.), *Bergin and Garfiels Handbook of Psychotherapy and Behaviour Change* (5th ed.) (pp. 139–193). New York: Wiley.
Lester, S. (2014). Professional standards, competence and capability. *Higher Education, Skills and Work-Based Learning, 4*(1), 31–43.
Lorenz, W. (2007). Teorie a metody sociální práce v Evropě: Profesní profil sociálních pracovníků. [Theory and methods of social work in Europe: Professional profile of social workers]. *Sociální Práce/Sociálna Práca, 1*, 62–71.
Maroon, I., Matoušek, O., & Pazlarová, H. (2007). *Vzdělávání studentů sociální práce v terénu: Model pro praxi. [Field Education of Social Work Students: Model for Practice]*. Prague: Karolinum.
Matulayová, T., & Balogová, B. (2013). Education of social workers in Slovakia. In: T. Matulayoá & L. Musil (Eds.) *Social Work, Education and Postmodernity. Theory and Studies in Selected Czech, Slovak and Polish Issues* (pp. 88–110). Liberec: Technická univerzita v Liberci.
Matulayová, T., & Musil, L. (Eds.) (2013). *Social Work, Education and Postmodernity: Theory and Studies in Selected Czech, Slovak and Polish Issues*. Liberec, Czech Republic: Technical University of Liberec.
Milner, J., Myers, S., & O'Byrne, P. (2015). *Assessment in Social Work*. London: Palgrave.
Morley, C. (2015). Critical reflexivity and social work practice. In: J. D. Wright (Ed.), *International Encyclopedia of the Social and Behavioral Sciences* (2nd ed.) (pp. 281–286). United Kingdom: Elsevier Ltd.
Moss, B. (2007). *Values*. Lyme Regis: Russell House.
Musil, L. (2004). *'Ráda bych Vám pomohla, ale': Dilemata práce s klienty v organizacích. ['I would like to help you, but': Dilemmas of social work with clients in organizations]*. Brno, Czech Republic: Marek Zeman.
Musil, L. (2013). Challenges of postmodern institutionalisation for education in social work. In: T. Matulayová & L. Musil (Eds.), *Social Work, Education and Postmodernity: Theory and Studies in Selected Czech, Slovak and Polish Issues* (pp. 10–72). Liberec: Technical University of Liberec.
Musil, L., & Šrajer, J. (2008). Dimenze životní situace rodiny. [Dimensions of family life situation]. In: L. Musil & J. Šrajer (Eds.), *Etické kontexty sociální práce s rodinou. [Ethical Contexts of Family Social Work]* (pp. 9–17). Brno, Czech Republic: Albert.
Nadan, Y., & Stark, M. (2017). The pedagogy of discomfort: Enhancing reflectivity on stereotypes and bias. *British Journal of Social Work, 47*(3), 683–700. DOI:10.1093/bjsw/bcw023.
Navrátil, P. (1998). Sociální práce jako sociální konstrukce. [Social work as social construction]. *Sociologicky Casopis, 34*(1), 37–50.
Navrátil, P. (2005). Role sociální práce v pozdně moderní společnosti. [The role of social work in late modern society]. In: M. Smutek (Ed.) *Možnosti sociální práce na počátku. [Possibilities in Social Work at the Beginning of the 21st Century], 21. století* (pp. 37–52). Hradec Králové, Czech Republic: Univerzita Hradec Králové.
Navrátil, P. (2010). How helping workers construct the problems of Roma families: contribution of general and specific stereotypes about parenting. *Journal Of Social Policy Studies*. 8(3), 353–372.
Navrátil, P. (2019). Epistemic discourses of 'explanation' and 'understanding' in assessment models (p. 41–54) In: Malcolm Payne and Emma Reith-Hall, eds. *The Routledge Handbook of Social Work Theory*, Oxford: Routledge.
Navrátil, P., & Janebová, R. (2010). *Reflexivita v posuzování životní situace klientek a klientů sociální práce. [Reflexivity in Assessing Life Situation of Clients of Social Work]*. Hradec Králové, Czech Republic: Gaudeamus.
Navrátil, P., & Navrátilová, J. (2008). Postmodernita jako prostor pro existenciálně citlivou sociální práci. [Post-modernity as a space for existentially sensitive social work]. *Časopis Sociální Práce/Sociálna Práca, 8*(4), 124–135.
Navrátilová, J. (2010). *Pojetí praktického vzdělávání sociálních pracovníků. [Concept of Practical Education of Social Workers]*. Unpublished doctoral thesis. Brno, Czech Republic: Masaryk University.
Navrátilová, J. (2014). Kompetenční přístupy jako nástroj rozvoje dovedností studentů. [Competency approaches as a tool of skills development of students]. In: M. Punová & J. Navrátilová (Eds.), *Praktické vzdělávání v sociální práci optikou konceptu resilience. [Practical Education in Social Work under the Perspective of the Resilience Concept]* (pp. 79–100). Brno, Czech Republic: Masaryk University Press.

Navrátilová, J., & Navrátil, P. (2016). Educational discourses in social work. *Sociální Pedagogika/Social Education/Social Education, 4*(1), 38–56.

Navrátilová, J., & Navrátil, P. (2020). The concept of professional identity in selected approaches to the education of social workers. In: S. M. Sajid, R. Baikady, C. Sheng-Li & H. Sakaguchi (Eds.), *The Palgrave Handbook of Global Social Work Education* (pp. 456–471). New York: Palgrave Macmillan. DOI:10.1007/978-3-030-39966-5.

Nixon, S., & Murr, A. (2006). Practice learning and the development of professional practice. *Social Work Education, 25*(8), 798–811. DOI: 10.1080/02615470600915852.

Otava, L. (2016). Institucionalizace sociální práce a sebezkušenost sociálních pracovnic. [Institutionalization of social work and experience of self in female social workers]. *Sociální Práce/Sociálna Práca, 16*(3), 105–116.

Parton, N., & O'Byrne, P. (2000). *Constructive Social Work*. London: Macmillan.

Payne, M. (2005). *Modern Social Work Theory*. Basingstoke: Palgrave Macmillan.

Preston-Shoot, M., Roberts, G., & Vernon, S. (1998). Working together in social work law. *Journal of Social Welfare and Family Law, 20*(2), 137–150.

Punová, M., Navrátil, P. & Navrátilová, J. (2020). Capabilities and well-being of child and adolescent social services clients in the czech republic. *Children and Youth Services Review*, 117. DOI:10.1016/j.childyouth.2020.105280.

Punová, M., & Navrátilová, J. (Eds.) (2014). *Praktické vzdělávání v sociální práci optikou konceptu resilience. [Practical Education in Social Work under the Perspective of the Resilience Concept]*. Brno, Czech Republic: Centrum praktických a evaluačních studií.

Redmond, B. (2006). *Reflection in Action: Developing Reflective Practice in Health and Social Services*. Hampshire: Ashgate.

Rotholz, T., & Werk, A. (1984). Student supervision. *The Clinical Supervisor*, 2(1), 15–27.

Šámalová, K. (2019). Profesní identita budoucích sociálních pracovníků jako tekutý písek v rukách vzdělavatelů. [Professional identity of future social workers as liquid sand in the hands of educators]. *Sociální práce/Sociálna práca.* . Retrieved from https://1url.cz/uKgry

Schneck, D. (1991). Part I: Conceptual foundation for field education. In: D. Schneck, B. Grossman & U. Glassman (Eds.). *Field Education in Social Work: Contemporary Issues and Trends* (pp. 13–16). Dubuque, IA: Kendall/Hunt.

Ševčíkova, S., & Navrátil, P. (2010). Social work as the institutialisation of risk in the late modernity [Sociální práce jako institucionalizace rizika v pozdně moderní době]. *Socialni Studia*, 7(2), 115–133. DOI:10.5817/soc2010-2-115.

Schön, D. A. (1983). *The Reflective Practitioner: How Professionals Think in Action*. New York: Basic Books.

Sewell, K. M. (2020). Examining the place of emotions, affect, and regulation in social work education. *Journal of Social Work Education, 56*(1), 5–16. DOI:10.1080/10437797.2019.1627262.

Sibeon, R. (1982). Theory-practice symbolization: A critical review of the Hardiker-Davies debate. *Issues in Social Work Education, 2*, 119–147.

Stephenson, J. (2012). The context. In: J. Stephenson & M. Yorke (Eds.), *Capability and Quality in Higher Education* (pp. 1–14). Abingdon, Oxon: Routledge.

Thompson, N. (2000). *Theory and Practice in Human Services*. Maidenhead: Open University Press.

Thompson, N. (2002). *People Skills*. Basingstoke: Palgrave Macmillan.

Thompson, N. (1992). *Existentialism and Social Work*. Aldershot: Avebury.

Thompson, N., & Pascal, J. (2012). Developing critically reflective practice. *Reflective Practice: International and Multidisciplinary Perspectives, 13*(2), 311–325. DOI:10.1080/14623943.2012.657795.

Thompson, S., & Thompson, N. (2008). *The Critically Reflective Practitioner*. New York: Palgrave Macmillan.

Tolson, E. R., & Kopp, J. (1988). The practicum: Clients, problems, interventions and influences on student practice. *Journal of Social Work Education*, 24(2), 123–134.

Viner, D., Majzen, R., & Dakchém, D. (2006). *Supervizija supervizora: Praktika v poiske teorii. [Supervision of the Supervisor: Practice in Polish Theory]*. Moscow: Kogito-Centr.

Webb, S. (2017). *Professional Identity and Social Work*. New York: Routledge Academic.

Weiss-Gal, I., & Welbourne, P. (2008). The professionalisation of social work: A cross-national exploration. *International Journal of Social Welfare, 17*(4), 281–290. DOI:10.1111/j.1468-2397.2008.00574.x.

Wiles, F. (2017). Developing social work students' professional identity: the role of England's Professional Capabilities Framework. *European Journal of Social Work, 20*(3), 349–360.

26

Experiences of Social Work Fieldwork Education in Romania

Béla Szabó, Ágnes Dávid-Kacsó, and Éva László[1]

Introduction – The First Evidence of Social Work Professionalisation

Social work education in Romania looks back to nine decades of history. The modern era of social work education began in 1929, when the first higher education institution was established: the Principesa Ileana Superior School for Social Work. Three important actors brought this school to life: the Romanian Social Institute developed and supervised the curriculum and organised the seminars and field practices; the Ministry of Health bore the cost of organising and remunerating teaching staff; and the Association of Romanian Christian Women offered the classrooms and the student dormitory.

In the foreword of the first Romanian social work curriculum back in 1929, it is underlined that social work needs trained professionals in order to leave behind the primitive philanthropism which characterised the field at the time. The argument explains that this can be realised only by introducing modern social work methods. 'But we didn't even have to stop at this point. The ideal we are pursuing is a broader and more efficient social prophylaxis' (Buletinul 'Principesa Ileana', 1929, p. 9[2]).

This first school of social work had some interesting particularities. First of all, its form was equivalent to that of a college – the duration of training was three years and included theoretical courses and seminars, fieldwork, and internships. During the two month summer holiday, a month of internship had to be completed by the students. For this study programme, only women were accepted. The council of professors could accept external audiences of interested individuals who had different rights and obligations from regular students (e.g., they could not participate in exams). Among the members of this external audience, males were allowed.

Based on the available documents from this school (the curriculum of the study programme and the short analytical description of the disciplines), it can be concluded that the division between the theoretical formation (courses, seminars) and practice was equally distributed: including the weekly study hours during the whole six semesters, practical training (field practice) accounted for 51% of the programme. It also must be noted that the last semester (the sixth) was mainly fieldwork. The only classroom activity in this period was discussion of the specific problems of every type of field practice (family, infants, delinquents, industrial, psychiatric, health, and group assistance) in the frame of 2 hours.

DOI: 10.4324/9781032164946-31

After some fruitful years of professional and scientific development in the period after World War II, the caring professions in general and social work in particular were slowly erased. In 1952, the study period was reduced, and in 1969, the programme ceased completely, as the communist leadership thought that social problems could only be solved by certain administrative measures.

Actual Circumstances and Experiences Regarding Field Practice in Social Work

Social work education was (re)introduced in 1990. The curriculum of the first social work programmes included disciplines such as sociology, research methodology, psychology, legislation, and social medicine and very few basic social work disciplines, such as theories and practice of intervention in social work. The teaching staff included sociologists, psychologists, lawyers, and doctors but no social workers. The typical study period for full-time students was 4 years and 5 for distance learning (introduced after 2000). After the Bologna transformation, both programmes became 3 years long (Neamţu, 2007; Szabó, 2020).

Currently, the social work as a Bachelor of Arts (B.A.) specialisation is offered at 21 universities in Romania (Table 26.1), and some universities have more than one programme (e.g., type of programme: full time, distance learning; language: Romanian, Hungarian, German; combined with another domain: with different theological association), thus, there are 41 individual programmes available.

Table 26.1 Romanian Universities with Social Work Specialisations

University name/city	*Type of university*
Universitatea 'Ovidius' Constanţa	state-owned
Universitatea din Craiova	state-owned
Universitatea 'Dunărea de Jos' Galaţi	state-owned
Universitatea 'Al. I. Cuza' Iaşi	state-owned
Universitatea din Oradea	state-owned
Universitatea din Petroşani	state-owned
Universitatea din Piteşti	state-owned
Universitatea 'Eftimie Murgu' din Reşiţa	state-owned
Universitatea 'Lucian Blaga' Sibiu	state-owned
Universitatea 'Stefan cel Mare' Suceava	state-owned
Universitatea de Vest, Timişoara	state-owned
Universitatea din Bucureşti	state-owned
Universitatea '1 Decembrie 1918' Alba	state-owned
Universitatea 'Aurel Vlaicu' Arad	state-owned
Universitatea 'Transilvania' Braşov	state-owned
Universitatea 'Babeş-Bolyai' Cluj	state-owned
Universitatea 'Vasile Goldiş' Arad	private
Universitatea 'Petre Andrei' Iaşi	private
Universitatea 'Emanuel' Oradea	private
Universitatea Creştina 'Partium' Oradea	private
Universitatea 'Adventus' Cernica	private

The data in the table is based on the Governmental Decision no. 158/2018

Standards in Social Work Education

Since 1993, every university programme needs to be accredited by a national institution of evaluation. At the beginning, this institution was named the National Council for Academic Evaluation and Accreditation (C.N.E.A.A.), which carried out institutional and programme accreditation from 1993 to 2006. As Romania integrated the Bologna Process in line with the European higher education trends, there was a demand for new approaches and procedures in quality evaluation and assurance. Thus, the Romanian Agency for Quality Assurance in Higher Education (A.R.A.C.I.S.) was established in 2005. The new institution's mission is defined in compliance with the European trends established by higher education ministers in conferences held every 2 years since 2001.

According to the information presented on the A.R.A.C.I.S. website, the organisation's mission is:

> to carry out the quality external evaluation of education provided by higher education institutions and by other organizations providing higher education study programmes, which operates in Romania with the aim of:
>
> - certifying, according to quality standards, the capacity of education providing organizations to fulfil the beneficiaries' expectations;
> - contributing to the development of an institutional culture of higher education quality;
> - assuring the protection of direct beneficiaries of study programmes at higher education level by producing and disseminating systematic, coherent and credible information, publicly accessible, about education quality;
> - proposing to the Ministry of Education, Research and Innovation strategies and policies of permanently improving higher education quality, in close correlation with pre-university education.
>
> *(A.R.A.C.I.S., n.d.*[3]*)*

As can be deduced from the description above, A.R.A.C.I.S. is the only institution that is entitled to set standards for social work education. Regarding fieldwork in social work education, A.R.A.C.I.S. states that practical activities should be carried out throughout the whole training during internships. It can be organised either weekly (with a recommendation of—four to six hours/week) or combined for a period of three weeks for a total of 90 hours. The internships should represent at least 10% of the total number of specialised hours (they describe four types of disciplines: fundamental, domain, specialised, and complementary). The practice should be carried out under the coordination of a social worker who facilitates the learning of professional competences and a supervising teacher appointed by the faculty, based on practice conventions, and aligned to its own programmes, which must include objectives, types of activities, documents completed by students, and methods of evaluation at the place of practice and by the supervising teacher, which are based on the practice reports and tests. The analytical description of the disciplines should specify the following: the mission of the practice, the objectives, the theme, the types of activities and their scheduling, the student's tasks, the available resources (human, bibliographic, specialised sites, etc.), and the forms and criteria for evaluating the learning outcomes. Educational institutions are also required to have conventions or contracts with social services, providing a suitable framework for carrying out the practical internships. The evaluation of the practice should be made by a 'colloquium' with a rating ranging from 1 to 10 (A.R.A.C.I.S. Standards[4]).

The legal frame for the organisation and function of postsecondary education somewhat limits the ability of educational institutions to hire field instructors from the practice places. According to the Educational Law no. 1/2011, every academic teaching staff member should fulfil the requirement of having at least a Ph.D. and a few scientific publications in acknowledged journals/publishing houses. The field instructors fall under the same regulation. On the other hand, social workers in the field rarely fulfil these criteria. as their workload and life circumstances do not permit them to realise such prerequisites. In these conditions, the role of field instructor is fulfilled by a social worker from the agency who, in addition to their own professional obligations, agrees to volunteer as a field instructor, named 'tutor for practice'.

As Wayne, Bogo, and Ruskin (2010) stated, professional regulations usually offer few cues regarding the teaching/learning process in field education. The same was stated by Romanian specialists who argue that A.R.A.C.I.S. standards are mainly an enumeration of different types of disciplines, rules of hour-calculations, and requirements for teachers. Sorescu (2015), for example, underlines that there are no specifications regarding the competences to be formed, the fundamental disciplines differ from those considered internationally, and there are no guidelines regarding the content of the analytical programmes of the disciplines. She concludes that quality assurance is based on the entrance side, and emphasis should be moved to results, namely competences, abilities, and values that students learn.

The following sections present the results of a study conducted to assess the perception of students and tutors about their experiences regarding field education.

Methodology

This chapter is based on research which uses a mixed methodology to target the main actors in social work practice: students and tutors from the organisations. The research was conducted as part of a project financed by the European Commission through the Human Capital Operational Program, Romania, which provided funding that made it possible to hire field educators at the partner agencies but not their training for the work with students. The project's main objective was to improve students' professional competencies through practical training, professional orientation, and career counselling[5]. The Social Work Department of Babeş-Bolyai University of Cluj (as a member of the project) created a questionnaire-based survey and focus group techniques to collect data from all the third-year social work students (*N1* = 85 students) and their field tutors (*N2* = 17 tutors) from Babeş-Bolyai University. The survey and focus groups were conducted by the members of the department with the approval of the Ethical Commission for the project.

In this survey, 66 usable questionnaires were obtained from students and 12 from tutors. The tutors' questionnaire included data about the respondent, a section about the level of satisfaction with the internship (answer possibilities varied from 'not at all' to 'very much'), and open-ended questions regarding the strengths and weaknesses of the practice and possibilities for improvement.

The student questionnaires contained data about the respondent (age, gender, level of the study (B.S.W.) and the agency where the field training was fulfilled), a section with questions related to the level of satisfaction with the internship (the personal involvement of the parties), and a section about the extent to which the internship was perceived as contributing to the professional development of the student. The answer possibilities varied from 'not at all' to 'very much'. Two sections contained open-ended answers: the first referred to the strengths and weaknesses of the field experience, while the second referred to the possibilities for improvement. As only 33 students had filled in these sections, for a better understanding, the core data obtained in this project through the questionnaire was complemented with additional data gathered through focus groups (students) and semi-structured interviews (field tutors). Thus 14 randomly chosen social work students and all the tutors were contacted again.

In the focus groups for students, the topics explored were the link between the labour market and professional practice, the strengths and weaknesses of their field education, difficulties faced, support they received to cope with challenges, and recommendations to strengthen their field education. Questions in the interviews with tutors were grouped around the following topics: the strengths and weaknesses of social work students field education according to the identified needs of the labour market, the tutors' needs, and recommendations for improvement.

Results and Discussion

Student Feedback

More than 80% of the students considered the field placement to be important for deepening their knowledge, contacting employers, forming an image about the specific activities from one specific field, and observing the problem-solving modalities typical to the agency. Also, more than 80% of the students considered the field practice to be important for forming an image about their professional future.

Figure 26.1 presents students' perception of the importance of field practice for different aspects of their professional development.

As the percentages in Figure 26.1 show, more than 90% of the students questioned indicated that they considered internship important or very important in terms of becoming familiar with the culture of the organisation they attended, contact with the beneficiaries of the agency, and discovering and developing new skills.

To see the social workers' specific problems and the possibility of improving one's professional curriculum vitae (C.V.) were seen by more than 75% of respondents as important outcomes of the field practice, and more than three-quarters considered it important for future career-related decisions. About 70% of the students considered that field training was a good

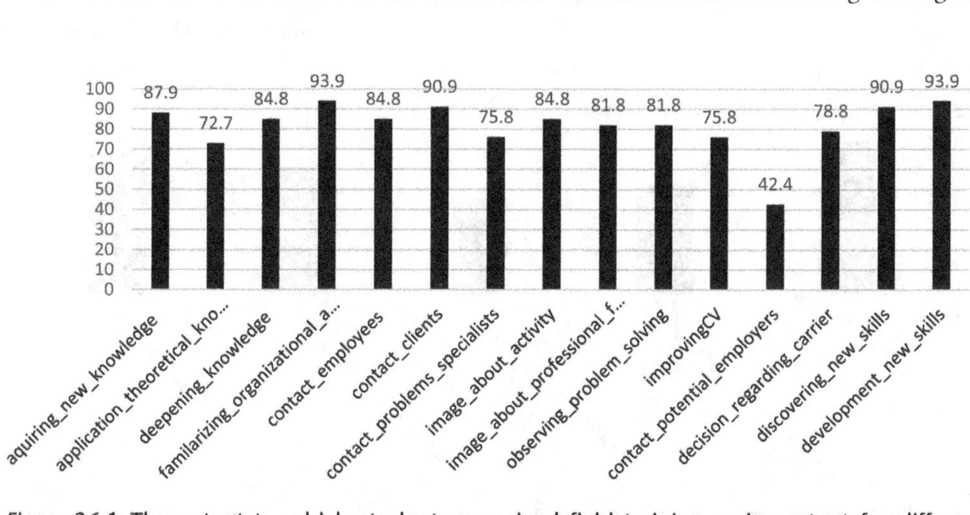

Figure 26.1 The extent to which students perceived field training as important for different aspects. The percentages represent the 'much' and 'very much' answers.

way to apply theoretical knowledge in practical settings. The field education was not perceived as a method of finding a potential workplace for the future, as fewer than half of the respondents considered the practical setting was important for contacting employers. Despite the fact that field practice was not seen by the students as their first step toward employment, all the respondents considered it important or very important for future career development (see Figure 26.2), and, according to more than 90% of respondents, field practice does create professional advantages.

Analysing these topics in focus groups, the results offer us some possible explanations: the majority of the students are not local to the city in which the university is located, they are intent on finding a job in/or close to their homes; the students do not think they have a real chance of employment in university cities, where they think competition for jobs is more intense, and some of them want to go abroad after graduation. For them, there is no direct link between field placement and any future workplace, but the experiences garnered are important professional resources. The following are typical answers on this topic:

> I would like to work in the future in a similar institution with disabled adults, but not here. Life is too expensive here and a social worker's salary is not enough even to cover the costs of living. (…) Maybe I'll start a new job in my hometown. The tutor from the N.G.O. [non-governmental organisation], where I had been an intern for the last year, promised to help me.
>
> *(Focus group student 1, third year)*

> A few days ago, we talked with two friends, also students of social work, but in another city. We would like to go to Germany or to the U.K., if it is possible, to work. Therefore, our fieldwork experience does not represent a direct opportunity for employment. It is, however, important and useful if we can receive a letter of recommendation.
>
> *(Focus group student 2, third year)*

> I'll move back home, for sure. I don't like it here, not only because it's expensive … I don't like living in such a big city … It is funny, as a student, there are parties, concerts, etc., but for me, it is more important to be closer to my family.
>
> *(Focus group student 7, second year)*

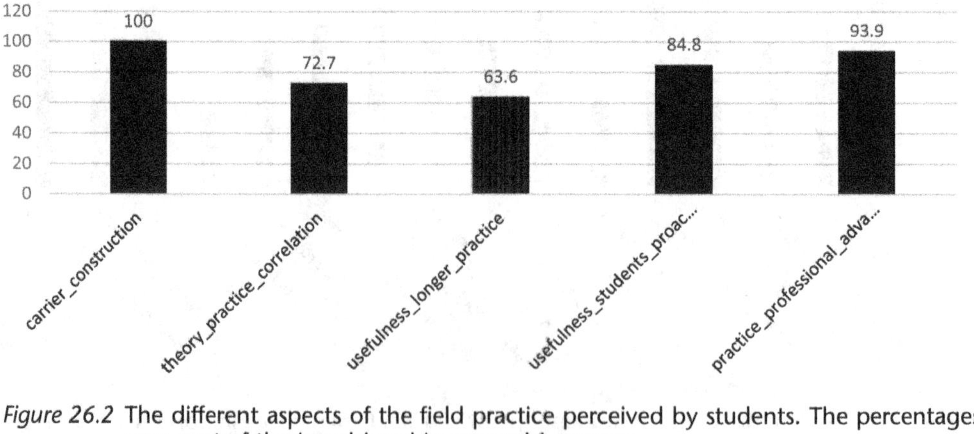

Figure 26.2 The different aspects of the field practice perceived by students. The percentages represent of the 'much' and 'very much' answers.

Students also presented positive experiences about the possibility of continuing cooperation with the internship provider:

> I would even like to continue working at the workplace where I had been practicing. I had been at the same institution from the beginning, and I have already talked to them, that I could stay here as a volunteer if I cannot be employed.
>
> *(Focus group student 8, third year)*

More than 70% of the students considered theoretical knowledge gained in the classroom and seminars is correlated with the demands of fieldwork, the same percentage as those who had seen the field practice as being important for the ability to apply their theoretical knowledge.

As the results presented in Figure 26.2 show, all students considered field practice important for career construction and more than 90% answered that the field practice contributes to the accumulation of experience and, thus, to professional advantage. For more than 70% of the respondents, the field practice was a good context in which to correlate theory and practice.

The proportion of students who believe that more hours of field practice would be useful for their professional development is relatively low, while more than 80% consider proactivity on the part of students contributes to a more positive outcome for the field practice. This importance accorded to proactivity, besides the recognition of one's own responsibility for the learning process, could reflect on the perceived lack of a structured programme for students in the practical setting. In these conditions, the students have the responsibility to optimise their own benefits.

When analysing the strengths of the internship mentioned by respondents, we could fit them into five themes: contact with beneficiaries, the development of new skills, accumulation of new knowledge and information, relationship with the staff, and the ability of applying theoretical knowledge. The contact with beneficiaries had three subthemes: better understanding of different categories of beneficiaries (disadvantaged, people with disabilities), professional attitudes toward beneficiaries, and empathy. The strengths related to the staff include the involvement of the tutor and the staff, respect toward the students, and flexibility in adapting the programme to the needs of the students. The ability to apply the theoretical knowledge was mentioned by two students.

The possibility of participating *in vivo* in social workers' daily professional lives was one major benefit of internship highlighted by the focus groups. Students' observation of qualified practitioners' work has been described in the literature as a special context of learning and acquiring professional skills. The observation, followed by debriefing and constructive feedback about their practice, helps to build professional confidence, contributes to developing students' practice competence, and enhances the quality of the learning process (Davys & Beddoe, 2015). Two reasons for this issue are presented below:

> It is quite interesting and captivating to actually be able to see their (social workers) work on site. I've learned a lot even by just observing and understanding what the social worker has explained to us or what we had been discussing and seen in our fieldwork.
>
> *(Focus group student 8, third year)*

> It is a unique experience to be able to just stand there, to assist, or just to observe the daily life. Truth be told, these experiences are more complex during practice time in the summer, when we are actually able to be there every day for a longer time.
>
> *(Focus group student 1, third year)*

The weaknesses mentioned can be grouped into three major themes: difficulties in fulfilment of the tasks received from the faculty, the time available for practice, and complaints of an administrative nature. While the strengths mentioned by the students were more general and are valid for the most field organisations, the weaknesses are more related to the specific aspects of the particular agencies. The difficulties related to the fulfilment of the tasks are typically associated with the reduced number of beneficiaries available for cooperation with the students—which strongly depends on the particularities of the organisation. One respondent stated:

> There were places where we couldn't talk to beneficiaries, nor take part in meetings. We were only doing office work, entering data, and that's it.
>
> *(Focus group student 2, third year)*

Some respondents mentioned their own feelings of unpreparedness or lack of support being provided by their tutors:

> It is a challenge being left alone. On the one hand, it is great to have the possibility to experience more, but on the other, there is this sense of huge responsibility and uncertainty. There were a lot of problems with children, and there were situations that even the employees couldn't handle. We should have guidance and training first and then practice.
>
> *(Focus group student 4, third year)*

Related to the time for practice, the weaknesses mentioned are varied: while some students considered the time for adaptation and fulfilment of tasks too short, others thought that there were too many hours assigned to the field practice. The complaints about administrative-related issues referred to the geographical place of the agency, which could be at the peripheral areas of the city that are difficult to access. Another observation concerned the room where the activities with the tutor took place, which were considered inappropriate. Some respondents also mentioned the students' lack of autonomy in choosing their field agency as a weakness.

The results of the focus groups revealed an important administrative problem in synchronising the educational programme and fieldwork. Most of the students were dissatisfied with the rigidity of the educational schedule. Their comments on this include the following:

> One day, we were out in the field with the social worker visiting families. To be able to follow the case better, I should have been visiting every day or at least many more times. However, the social worker could not schedule visiting hours after my programme.
>
> *(Focus group student 9, third year)*

> The activities that I am most interested in are usually on Fridays, once every month. We have classes, where participation is mandatory. I cannot just skip classes.
>
> *(Focus group student 5, third year)*

Students are best helped to overcome difficulties in the field through discussions and debates with the field teacher or university supervisor and support from peers. Although surveys show that there is no positive correlation between peer support and assessment of internship satisfaction and readiness (Flanagan & Wilson, 2018), the present results also show that social support is a very important resource for students. During the focus group, the students shared the following thoughts:

> When I was having difficulties at my practice, our colleagues' support and discussions with tutors from the institution or university offered me help.
>
> *(Focus group student 3, third year)*

> It was easier being able to prepare with our colleagues. For us, working in groups with children and in pairs, it would have been impossible to handle without helping each other and cooperating.
>
> *(Focus group student 6, third year)*

The measures proposed to the organisations to improve field education are grouped into two major themes: more access to the beneficiaries, meaning better involvement of the students in direct work with clients, and the relationship with the staff, stemming from typical statements such as more attention to the students', 'more social workers to work with students', and 'better availability of the staff'.

The recommendations targeting the faculty can be grouped into three themes: choice of field practice, flexibility in the timetable, and support on the part of the school. Related to the choice of the place of practice, the respondents said they need more autonomy in order to be able to follow their own professional interests. Also, the need for additional and more diverse options for field training were mentioned. The measures proposed for improvement suggest that time management was an important issue for students in field placement: the students had to match the timetable at school with the agency's programme, resulting sometimes in 'less time for practice'. The proposals also express an increased need for support and guidance on the part of the school, with about half of the respondents mentioning 'support for students', 'guidance in the choice of the place of field training', and 'supervision'. Two times students proposed the reduction of the theoretical knowledge in curricula.

Regarding the measures proposed for students, nearly all referred to more involvement and seriousness, once the importance of self-management and once the initiatives of the students to improve the agency's services were taken into account.

The feedback received from the students regarding their field experiences reflect three types of problems: one resulted from the consumer-like approach to students, the second from the shortcomings of the regulations, and the third from the lack of correlation between requirements on the part of the school and the concrete possibilities of the agencies.

The consumer-like approach to students is a result of the peculiarities of the funding of higher education, which depends on the number of students enrolled. This approach is reflected in the demands of the students related to the schedule and geographical placement of the field agency, as described also by Buck, Bradley, Robb West, and Shapiro (2012). Our subjects had very high expectations from the agencies regarding their access to the beneficiaries of the agency and the possibility of direct work with them, which is also an expectation mentioned by Buck et al. (2012).

A part of the shortcomings mentioned by students are due to the lack of appropriate regulations on field education in social work, which affect the availability of the staff and the diversity of available places for practice that are possible only if the agencies have not been adversely affected by underfunding for social services.

The third category of problems is related to the peculiarities of higher education: the busy schedule. The requirements of the courses and seminars are difficult to match with the schedule of the agency to which is added the travel time to and from the agency. This category of complaints can be integrated into the difficulties related to fulfilling field education tasks (e.g., too short a time, few available beneficiaries). These hardships were caused by the fact that the objectives, methods, and tasks described in the analytical programmes are in accordance with the curricula not with the possibilities of the particular social agencies. In this way, the tasks could be totally unsuitable for the organisations, e.g., an organisation that provides group activities will not meet a student's need to conduct individual interviews, or the ethical norms of the agencies do not permit students to access the files of the beneficiaries. What is clear from the feedback is that the students need support and supervision from the teachers responsible for field education.

Field Tutor Feedback

The tutors themselves had seen the strengths of the field education in the opportunity students have to become more familiar with the services particular organisations offer beneficiaries. The chance to learn when confronted with professional provocations and to apply theoretical knowledge were also mentioned among the strengths of field practice.

The main weaknesses perceived by tutors were related to insufficient time allocated to practice, the difficulty students faced in of fulfilling the tasks, and, as in the case of students, the problem of schedule synchronisation. Below are some examples of the tutors' feedback:

> Practice is too scarce. I would let students work in only one field. It would take hours of self-knowledge and personal development.
>
> *(Interview tutor 8, N. G. O.)*

> We would perhaps change the time allocated for practice hours; students and clients need more hours.
>
> *(Interview tutor 10, N. G. O.)*

> The number of mandatory courses should be increased for a better understanding and a deeper knowledge of our profession.
>
> *(Interview tutor 11, N. G. O.)*

> We would like for students to be able to spend more time at the institution, for example, a whole day (not two or four hours only) and for a longer period of time. If we include their training, preferably 30 hours, then there is not too much time left for practice and observation.
>
> *(Interview tutor 17, N. G. O.)*

> I believe that the practical side is well thought through, however, we face the same problem with our practitioners: we cannot fulfil our hours in a worthwhile fashion. Theory hours often overlap with our morning activities, which are our most important ones, where one can actually learn and experience.
>
> *(Interview tutor 7, N. G. O.)*

Representatives from two of the state-owned institutes were of the opinion that there were too many practice hours; one of them thought that field practice should be optional for students and, under these conditions, only motivated students would participate.

The interviews revealed a discrepancy between the students' expectations or tasks and their preparedness (abilities, skills, and knowledge). Respondents stated:

> Regarding the tasks of the students, we would bring out those topics that require a high level of knowledge and professional self-confidence that they do not have [e.g., in Year 2 to do intervention or case management].
>
> *(Interview tutor 14, N.G.O.)*

> Often, students' expectations are not in line with the specifics of the internship.
>
> *(Interview tutor 3, state institution)*

> Relatively ok, those [tasks] that help them in knowing the institution, the issues we deal with. But [the expectations of the educational institution and of the students are] unrealistic regarding the work with the beneficiaries of the institution.
>
> *(Interview tutor 8, N.G.O.)*

Our study reveals that supervising and guiding students during their fieldwork are perceived by some tutors as an additional workload that is unrecognised by their employers, the education institution, and, sometimes, the students as well. This perceived lack of valourisation of fieldwork was highlighted in other studies, also (Domakin, 2014). For some respondents, it is of great concern that these activities are not remunerated financially. Here are some examples of the feedback on this topic:

> Unfortunately, practice is often perceived as less important. Everyone passes; it's just three credits.
>
> *(Interview tutor 9, N.G.O.)*

> A remuneration of practical tutors/number of students/hours should be necessary.
>
> *(Interview tutor 8, N.G.O.)*

> The problem is that these protocols are signed at management level, and those who should put them into practice are us, working essentially onsite. We have got the impression that the management is not realising how much work it involves. Maybe not even those from the university. Moreover, sometimes they tell us that students are there to help, when actually they are there to learn, not be taken care of. It is a dissonance, if not a contradiction as a whole.
>
> *(Interview tutor 5, state institution)*

> In order for students to learn, they should be offered introduction, formation. They need more than just an introduction to the institution, field of work, and to assume they know what and how we are working. It is not like that, even though they have learned something at the university. There is too much work, which sometimes not even the management nor our university colleagues understand.
>
> *(Interview tutor 17, N.G.O.)*

Bellinger (2010) points out that, in order to prevent the polarisation of theoretical and practical education, educational institutions should pay more attention to practical aspects.

The measures proposed to the organisations to improve practice suggest the need of recognition of the status of field education. That would make better condition for work with the students possible: first, formal recognition of their work; second, providing a designated space for field education; and third, the ability to select the students' activities according to their needs.

More time for work with the students and to supervise them were also mentioned as factors that would improve practice.

The measures proposed to the educational institution focused on the need for communication and cooperation with the education provider institution and supervising teacher: 'monitoring students', 'support in evaluation of the students', 'debates' and 'supervision sessions with tutors', 'clarification of the expectations', and correlate the expectations with the profile of the field place. This need for cooperation between agencies is noted internationally by internship providers, as evidenced by other studies (Hay & Brown, 2015, Ross et al., 2019).

In order to avoid the awkward situation of students who are not interested in the particular topic of the placement field, the tutors, like the students themselves, proposed an increase of student autonomy in choosing the field of placement. A greater involvement of the education providers in guiding students in the choosing process is recommended to improve preparedness of students before internships (Ross et al., 2019).

The proposals for students were related to involvement, seriousness, and openness to learning.

Conclusion and Implications for Social Work Education

The agencies, which are under high pressure to rationalise their costs, often prefer not to accept students in practice because it is perceived as an additional burden. Even if students are accepted, the lack of regulation of the field instructor, with clear responsibilities for students' education in the job description, influences the involvement and performance of the tutor, whose only motivation for this task is his/her devotion to social work and to the development of future professionals. Social work departments at universities are not in a position to impose standards for practical settings, being grateful for all the possibilities because they have neither a legal right nor funds to pay the tutors. Using the available European Union funds to pay field instructors through different projects offers a temporary solution, but these possibilities are narrow; the projects are limited in time and can cover a maximum of a 3-year period, after which everything returns to the usual course of things.

After summarising the results, the need for a formal recognition of the field educator status is outlined in the feedback from both tutors and students. The integration of theory and practice, which is seen as one of the main objectives of the field education, presumes additional work on the part of the field educator because even the most competent practitioner could be overwhelmed by the task of linking the classroom content to the everyday experiences in the field (Domakin, 2014; Boysen & Koh, 2015). Better instrumental conditions and more time and energy investment in work with students—proposed both by tutors and students—is achievable only if there are paid professionals at the field organisations with the recognised task of organising and supervising student activities.

The other key aspect which could contribute to the improvement of the efficiency of practice is greater emphasis on communication between the educational institution and the field of placement. In this way, the tasks assigned by the latter could be adapted to the particularities of the organisations and the expectations of the students. Otherwise, due to the vagueness of the created situation, students perceive a gap between school and the 'reality of the field', which was expressed in their feedback about the weaknesses of field education – 'too much theory' – which is totally counterproductive to the foundation of theory-driven, reflexive social work practice.

Fieldwork education is an important part of social work education, and it has a major role in its efficiency. As one can conclude from the present chapter, the field tutor's motivation is greatly affected by the financing conditions from the universities. To ensure a highly efficient social work education, there is an indisputable need to have all involved partners comfortable and satisfied. We argue that this condition may be reached in several ways, one of which is creating a direct payment environment for field tutors (as it requires complex political negotiations to change national legislation). The National College of Social Workers has had the important role of consolidating the profession. Social workers, in order to practice, need to be a member of the College and, to achieve this status, they need to continuously participate in yearly trainings equivalent to at least 10 professional credits. A possibility to motivate the partners of the universities is to grant these credits (at least partially) to those social workers who work as field tutors.

Limitations

As a limitation of the research, we should note that the main aim of the programme 'SPiC – students in practice for the future career', which gave the framework for the research, was to increase the employability rate of the students with an emphasis on different actions and interventions but not on research.

Although the legislation and regulations presented in this chapter are valid nationally, the research was carried out at only one university centre and its partner institutes.

Notes

1 Acknowledgement: We would like to express our special gratitude to lecturer Anca Simionca, Ph.D., who is responsible of the SPiC project at the Faculty of Sociology and Social Work, Babes-Bolyai University Cluj Napoca; lecturer Corina Voicu; and associate professor Mihai Iovu, who is responsible for field education at the Department of Social Work, for permitting the use of the questionnaires for the purpose of this chapter.
2 The whole curriculum is available at the following link: http://www.swreview.ro/uploads_ro/1515/1004/Social_Work_no._1-1929.pdf.
3 https://www.aracis.ro/misiune/.
4 https://www.aracis.ro/wp-content/uploads/2020/05/30.04.2020-Standarde-specifice-Comisia-de-Stiinte-Sociale-Politice-si-ale-Comunicarii.pdf.
5 More can be found on the project's site: Project SPiC –Students in Practice for the Future Career - https://fspac.ubbcluj.ro/ro/cercetare/spic-studenti-practica-pentru-o-viitoare-cariera.

References

Bellinger, A. (2010). Talking about (Re)generation: Practice learning as a site of renewal for social work. *British Journal of Social Work*, 40(8), 2450–2466, https://doi.org/10.1093/bjsw/bcq072.

Boysen, L. A. & Koh, B. (2015). Integrating theory and practice methods in field education. In: Hensley, M. A. (Ed.), *The Social Work Field Instructor's Survival Guide* (pp. 63–82). New York: Springer Publishing Company.

Buck, P. W., Bradley, J., Robb West, L. & Shapiro, R. (2012). Complex and competing demands in field education: A qualitative study of field directors' experiences. *Field Educator*, 2(2), 1–17, https://doi.org/10.1080/08841233.2018.1436635.

Davys, A. M. & Beddoe, L. (2015). 'Going live': A negotiated collaborative model for live observation of practice. *Practice: Social Work in Action*, 27(3), 177–196, https://doi.org/10.1080/09503153.2015.1032234.

Domakin, A. (2014). Are we making the most of learning from the practice placement? *Social Work Education: The International Journal*, 33(6), 718–730, https://doi.org/10.1080/02615479.2013.869315.

Flanagan, N. & Wilson, E. (2018). What makes a good placement? Findings of a social work student-to-student research study. *Social Work Education*, 37(5), 565–580, https://doi.org/10.1080/02615479.2018.1450373.

Hay, K. & Brown, K. (2015). Social work practice placements in Aotearoa New Zealand: Agency managers' perspectives. *Social Work Education*, 34(6), 700–715, https://doi.org/10.1080/02615479.2015.1062856.

Neamţu, G. (2007). Formarea profesională a asistentului social din perspectiva Declaraţiei de la Bologna. In: Muntean, Ana, Sagebiel, Julian (Eds.), *Practici în asistenţa socială. România şi Germania* (pp. 138–150). Iaşi: Polirom.

Ross, B., Ta, B. & Oliaro, L. (2019). Institutional responsibilities: Providing placement for International students. *Social Work Education: The International Journal*, 39(5), 665–680, https://doi.org/10.1080/02615479.2019.1703931.

Sorescu, E.-M. (2015). Învăţământul românesc de asistenţă socială – Istoric, standarde şi perspective. *Revista de asistenţă socială*, XIV(1/2015), 23–34.

Szabó, B. (2020). Social work in Romania - Education, professional life, and challenges. In: Sajid, S. M., Baikady, R., Sheng-Li, C., Sakaguchi, H. (Eds.), *The Palgrave Handbook of Global Social Work Education*. Palgrave MacMillan, https://doi.org/10.1007/978-3-030-39966-5.

Wayne, J., Bogo, M. & Ruskin, M. (2010). Field education as the signature pedagogy of social work education. *Journal of Social Work Education*, 46/3(3), 327–339, https://doi.org/10.5175/JSWE.2010.200900043.

27

Reflexivity as a Pivotal Component of Fieldwork in Social Work Education

Jarosław Przeperski and Małgorzata Ciczkowska-Giedziun

Reflexivity in Social Work

It seems to be a truism to say that the modern world, including the social world, is constantly changing. This presents new problems and challenges that do not allow individuals and groups in societies to function independently and satisfactorily. Growing problems make it necessary to develop systems that offer support and assistance. An important element of the welfare system in most countries is social assistance (social work?) with a central role played by social workers. In their daily work, they tackle non-conventional, unique, and unpredictable problems. Preparing social workers to obtain one of the basic competences – being reflexive so that they are able to meet the needs of clients – becomes a major challenge. The ability to activate reflexivity is, therefore, an essential feature of current and future social workers who respond to the challenges that arise in an ever-changing society. Reflection is also a highly personal process that engages practitioners' insight into their own experiences and beliefs, assumptions, and values affecting their practice (Spray & Jowett, 2012; Howe, 2011; Kantowicz, 2005).

Reflexivity is an area/category that, over the years, has been systematically developed and subjected to scientific reflection. Today, the positive impact of reflection on thinking and human activity in various areas of life, including education (cf. Woronowicz, 2000) is highlighted. Reflective practice is highly linked with the practical action of social workers. This is not only a theoretical activity but, above all, allows the construction of recommendations (personal, professional, organisational, relational) that could be implemented in similar situations. A reflective social worker is aware of himself/herself, his/her role, and the assumptions, beliefs, and values that guide him/her (Howe, 2011). Moreover, professional reflexiveness requires social workers to listen more carefully and critically to themselves and to look at their actions (cf. White, 2012). Such an attitude favours being more sensitive and respectful toward others (Ruch, 2009).

Accepting the assumption that everyone understands the concept of the reflective practitioner raises the danger that this phrase will only be used at the level of a theoretical concept or will be used as a buzzword that sounds interesting but does not carry meaning. The gradual integration of the concept of 'the reflective practitioner' into the mainstream of social work practice was accompanied by the assumption that 'everyone knows what being a reflective practitioner involves and how becoming a reflective practitioner is facilitated and realized' (Ruch,

DOI: 10.4324/9781032164946-32

2009: 19). Therefore, it is necessary to adopt a specific concept of reflective practice. In social work and the inspiration for reflective social work, the concept of Schön's reflective practice (1983) became the main focus. This concept denies the limitation of practice as a radiance of theory or unconscious activity recognisable only through theory. The problem is that the action is not fully defined as its plan usually arises and is implemented. An important part of this concept is the use of hidden understanding, that is, *tacit knowledge*, derived from the construction and reconstruction of professional, personal, and intuition experience that is derived from the experience of practitioners. In other words, it's about learning from yourself. Practice is treated as a source of new knowledge. Thus, in a sense, the relationship between theory and practice is reversed. Reflection is not the application of scientific knowledge in practice, but it creates knowledge derived from personal experience, intuition, and unconscious processing of data emerging from problem solving.

Reflection is a central feature of good social work practice. Reflection on and in practice is not only important in the education process to become a social worker but should also be continued in professional development (Seden, 2005). Reflection can be understood as a tool for discovering the complexity of phenomena and constitutes a 'barrier against the force of what one sees immediately' (Kwiatkowska, 2008: 54), making it possible to 'uncover problematicness' and 'question obviousness' (ibid: 54). This approach allows the (future) social worker to act in ways in which the professional is neither a soulless programmed robot nor trusts improvisation, foreboding, and intuition. Its action is contained in the space between these extremes. Reflection helps the student, and then the practitioner, to bring to the surface and to intellectually process the principles guiding behaviour in practical situations, to become aware of the values that are guided, and to evaluate the effects to which these activities have led/lead/can lead (Mizerek, 1999: 54).

By analysing the relationship between social work and reflexiveness, several areas can be identified.

Reflexivity must become an immanent part of the implementation of social work practice because the theory and methodology of social work do not constitute a closed set of statements setting out practical actions. The social worker in his daily work has to face situations that are characterised by uncertainty, instability, and uniqueness. Solving such problems is not possible by simple application of well-known procedures. A reflective approach is necessary, which is based not only on basic theories of social work but also on concepts in other disciplines, e.g., psychology, sociology, psychiatry, and law (Sicora, 2010; Ruch, 2002; Chrostowska & Ciczowska-Giedziun, 2014; Krasiejko & Ciczkowska-Giedziun, 2016).

Social workers rarely face identical or similar problems or environmental conditions. Their activities are usually characterised by uncertainty, and the action plan is concreted in the course of the work carried out. During this time, therefore, the knowledge of a particular case is created, which explains the event. Such a situation should, at the same time, be accompanied by the conviction that updating past experience will be insufficient in resolving future problematic situations (cf. Ruch, 2002; Kantowicz 2005; Krasiejko & Ciczkowska-Giedziun, 2016).

In addition to the difficulties of variability and ambiguity of specific cases, the contexts of these cases are linked to the introduction of further assistance services. Without reflection, interinstitutional cooperation, which is often encapsulated in procedures, will not serve the client fully and meet his/her needs and, especially, the goals set by the institutions themselves (Przeperski & Taylor, 2020; Ciczkowska-Giedziun & Chrostowska, 2016).

The actions of a social worker are conditioned, more or less consciously, by a number of factors. They are related to the person of the social worker (e.g., his/her personal and professional experience, education, burnout, etc.), factors related to the relationship with the client, organisational and external factors (Graham et al., 2015), and the paradigms in which the social worker operates (Przeperski, 2021). Without a reflective attitude, the social worker is not aware of the influences that shape his/her practice and may be more vulnerable to cognitive disruption and the use of practices that do not fully respond to the customer's needs (Taylor, 2017).

Social work undoubtedly provides a space for reflective practice and the promotion of the social worker as a reflective practitioner. This is characterised by the fact that he/she:

1. Is an active thinker capable of initiating and responding to actions.
2. Is aware of the relationship with customers, with a clear understanding of their role and intentions.
3. Sees himself/herself as a participant in these activities and interactions.
4. Is capable of analysing the situation and evidence with an awareness of how his/her own participation affects the process; is aware of his/her own assumptions about customer relations (Connolly & Harms, 2012).
5. Reviews how he/she applies the theory in practice.
6. Looks at how he/she uses past experiences, skills, and knowledge in making decisions and doing his/her work.
7. He is capable of analysing the human conduct, motives, and effects of our actions (Howe, 2011).

Reflective social work refers to the above properties, the most important of which are self-knowledge, interpersonal skills, and alluding to one's own experiences. The ability to create partnerships with the customer is also important.

In conclusion, it can be said that the inclusion of reflexivity in the practice of the social worker will lead to the following effects:

1. The social worker is able, even in a situation of ambiguity, to assess the situation of the client more accurately and reliably (diagnosis), to develop a more effective assistance plan, and to carry out a reflective evaluation of his own actions.
2. Continuously develops his/her professional knowledge and skills through constant reflection on his/her actions (identification of effective and ineffective practices and attitude toward optimisation of activities).
3. Increases his/her motivation to help by understanding himself/herself and his/her needs (e.g., in the context of burnout) but also the client (he/she is able to see deeper and discover the dignity and value of each client).
4. Through self-insight, he/she achieves a higher level of personal development.

Social work, although carried out by individual social workers, takes place in an institutional context. The introduction of reflexivity into practice will have an impact not only on the social worker himself/herself but also on the aid system as a whole.

Better and more efficient social workers build better institutions that provide services more effectively. Reflexivity practised at the organisational level contributes to the continuous verification of the social worker's work and the implementation of activities that improve the quality of work done. In a situation in which reflexivity enters the level of the institution, it will also be important to acquire the skills of group reflection, which requires competences resulting from the need to include new actors. The reflection that is implemented by the groups will require, for example, the ability to accept the assessment of others, to regard important and reject irrelevant comments of other employees, or the ability to communicate their own thoughts and observations to colleagues in a way that will facilitate rather than block their development (Ryding & Wernersson, 2019).

In the theory and practice of social work, two approaches – reflective and statistical (technical) – are often considered to be opposites. Despite this view of the two approaches, it seems the optimal solution is their integration and use at work. The technical approach is associated with more objective, routinised, and measurable systems of accountability (Fook, Ryan, & Hawkins, 2000: 242). The use of a quantitative approach is also supported by arguments related to reducing variability in human judgement, increasing accuracy and reducing human bias, and benefitting from the practice experience of others (Søbjerg et al., 2020). On the other hand, reflective practice may, to some extent, respond to the need to make working with the client more structured and subjected to methodological rigour. The move toward reflective practice can be seen as part of the same imperative – making a professional practice more responsible (Fook et al., 2000).

It also seems important to distinguish between two notables: reflexivity and critical reflection. Both concepts combine the search for answers to questions on how we participate in the creation and generation of the knowledge we use and how that knowledge depends on the overall context in which it is produced. They differ in that critical reflection seeks to reveal the relationship of power and to show how the structures of domination are created and maintained (cf. Fook, 2002: 41). Understanding the dynamics of power is, therefore, an integral part of a critically reflective attitude and requires practitioners to study conscious and unconscious motivations, assumptions, and prejudices of themselves and others (Ruch, 2009: 25). To include critical reflection among students in the course of their apprenticeships means focusing on the interactive aspects of practice and situations in the context of power relations (Fook, 1999; Lam et al., 2007). Critical reflection has four dimensions: (1) reflective learning, which occurs during and after action – speaking the language of Schön (1983) is 'reflection in action' and 'reflection on action'; (2) emotionality perceived in different systems – toward oneself and toward others; (3) criticism relating to sources of power and ways of exercising this power and the resistance to it; and (4) reflexivity defined in a way, among many others, as focusing on one's own identity, beliefs, values, and attitudes affecting understanding and working in practice (cf. Hughes & Heycox, 2010). Reflexivity, on the other hand, will be understood more as a certain attitude associated with a critical approach to the professional practice (D'Cruz et al., 2007).

Reflexivity in Practical Education of Social Work Students

A reflective approach to learning reduces the distance between theory and practice. This approach also emphasises the importance of an active role for the practitioners (Cleak & Wilson, 2007: 56). On one hand, within education for social work, we strive to generalise the practice and create the theoretical basis of this teaching by accumulating experiences and trying to reflect on them. On the other hand, we emphasise the creative use of the theory of humanities and social disciplines by seeking references and explaining social phenomena with them. Different models of education emerge from these two approaches, among which the development model deserves special attention. It is based on a learning profile, in which it is possible to acquire skills and improve the ability to anticipate and shape future activities. Training in this model emphasises the improvement of reflexive, critical, creative, and alternative thinking skills (Kantowicz, 2001).

Student field education is an integral part of preparing students for work as social workers. During internships, students have the opportunity to get to know themselves, as well as the ways in which they generate and use knowledge. It is also a space to develop professional values, understand the specifics of the future role of practice, and deepen professional knowledge and skills (Cleak & Wilson, 2007: 2). Participation in apprenticeships fills the gap between theory and practice and enables the use of developed concepts and theories in real-world situations. The field placement not only provides students with the opportunity to integrate all the knowledge they have received while studying but also, equally importantly, helps them develop reflective thinking skills (Eltaiba & Ndoye, 2018: 171). It is, therefore, an important place of learning in which values and knowledge, skills and competences, ethics and a sense of professional identity are developed (Smith et al., 2014: 2).

The field placement is considered one of the main elements of education for social work and the main determinant of its quality. The implementation of these practices involves professionals who are often not university staff and usually do not participate in the development of practical curricula. Therefore, these trainers of student interns are often left to themselves when teaching and developing students' professional skills and creating links between theory and practice (Lam et al., 2007: 91–92). In order to improve this area of education for social work, it would be worth seeking closer cooperation between academia and representatives of practice on the ground (Eltaiba & Ndoye, 2018: 182). It is quite clear from the above position that field placement has always been part of training for social work and is an integral part of education for social work (Ajibo et al., 2017: 110).

Apprenticeships (field education) are spaces in which student learning occurs in a bidirectional way and knowledge and practice intersect and integrate. Students not only experience the real world of practice, where they gain competence to become social workers, but also have second thoughts about the knowledge gained during their studies. Thanks to this, they have the opportunity to deepen their knowledge of the theory of social work and to give meaning to their own practice. This type of knowledge is referred to as 'contextual knowing' and requires continuous reflection, examination, and expansion of their knowledge and practice in different situations and settings. Reflective learning during internships can also take place when students observe, critically evaluate, and question social work roles in the agency. Apprenticeships (field education) can also be a space for critical reflection on the values of social work and value conflict in practice situations. Being critically reflective also requires students to question privileged knowledge and deconstruct assumptions that knowledge is prioritised (Chan, 2017: 812–815). It is, therefore, crucial to place reflective practice in a critical analysis framework (Fook, 2002; Chan, 2017).

The importance of 'critical reflection' and 'reflective learning', in the context of students' apprenticeships, has always been underestimated (Lam et al., 2007: 93). To enable students to experience critical reflexivity during internships, the fieldwork agencies should be aware of the goal they want to achieve in the education process for social work. The action should, therefore, be carefully designed. This requires practitioners to think about their own philosophy of helping, their working methods, and to consider possible alternatives to help (Chan, 2017: 815). In addition, the curriculum should be designed to take into account the interaction between their experiences and the dynamic accounts of the ecstasy in which these experiences are embedded and to take into account uncertainty and dual ambiguity in the teaching process. One of the challenges teachers of social work face, therefore, is observing and analysing the dynamics that influence the design of the curriculum (Lam et al., 2007: 103).

The purpose of professional practice is to develop self-ownership, mastery, and understanding of the practice. At the same time, the practice supervisor must both facilitate students' reflection in the early stages of practice and trigger this reflection when performing the practical tasks that are assessed. Learning with the participation of 'real' recipients of social services requires good preparation; time to obtain feedback and provide practical experiences appropriate to the knowledge, skills, and comfort of students; and a number of structured educational activities (Beddoe et al., 2011: 514).

Learning during fieldwork requires students to put theory into practice and then reflect on practice through supervision (Beddoe et al., 2011: 514). The strengths of live supervision are that it is transparent, promotes critical reflection, and provides students with concrete guidance on their skills. The practice supervisor, thus, gains a complex insight into the student's skills, while students get to experience how to cope in a 'great' situation with the confidence that their supervisor will step in if needed. Skills of self-awareness and others in the professional environment are also developed. This promotes the preparation of students for future cooperation with social welfare users (Maidment, 2000: 209; Beddoe et al., 2011: 524–525; Davys and Beddoe, 2010).

Tools to Support Students' Reflexivity during Field Education

The characteristics of social work theory and practice described in the previous paragraph should be taken into account in the education of future social workers. They shall make particular reference to their traineeships. For this purpose, concepts of education for reflection seem to be helpful, such as models of reflective learning, learning from mistakes, or reflective writing.

The framework of the reflective approach has been defined by various authors including Graham Gibbs (1988), Christopher Johns (2009), Terry Borton (1970), and David Kolb (1984). For the purposes of this study, we will cite two of these concepts: Gibbs's reflective cycle (1988 and Johns's structural reflection model (2009). Gibbs' *reflective cycle* consists of six stages, during which a series of key questions are asked, thus setting the direction for the formation of reflection. These steps are presented in Figure 27.1.

The first stage consists of writing or narrating an event that took place during apprenticeship which is to be reflected on. It is important to indicate as many details as possible of this event. The following questions might be helpful to recall details of the event: What was the scene? Who else was there? Why were you there? What did you do there? What were other people doing there? What was the context of the event? What happened? What was your part in this? What was the outcome of this event?

In the second stage, it recalls and recognises what happened to the person during the analysed situation. These are usually questions about the feeling of satisfaction, or lack thereof, due to a given event. This is a stage in which we may find it difficult to share our thoughts with the other person. Useful questions in this phase are: How did you feel during this situation? What did you think at the time? How did it affect your well-being? How did other people's actions and statements affect you? What emotions did you have at the end of the event (resulting from the outcome of the meeting)? What do you think about it now?

The third stage is to identify the strengths and weaknesses of the situation under analysis. In other words, when evaluating an experience, we look at what has succeeded and what has not. Helpful questions include: How did the event proceed, and were there any problems? If there were any problems, could you solve them?

When analysing the experience – the fourth stage – it is important to make sense of this event. Therefore, in this phase, we look at our behaviour and the behaviour of others involved in the event. Helpful questions are: What factors influenced the outcome of the situation? What factors helped and made it difficult to overcome barriers? Can you explain why this happened? What did you want to achieve? Can you explain this experience by referring to your past experiences and future practice?

The fifth stage, the conclusions, proposes other ideas that can be used in a given situation. It is worth remembering that the purpose of reflection is to learn from one's own experience,

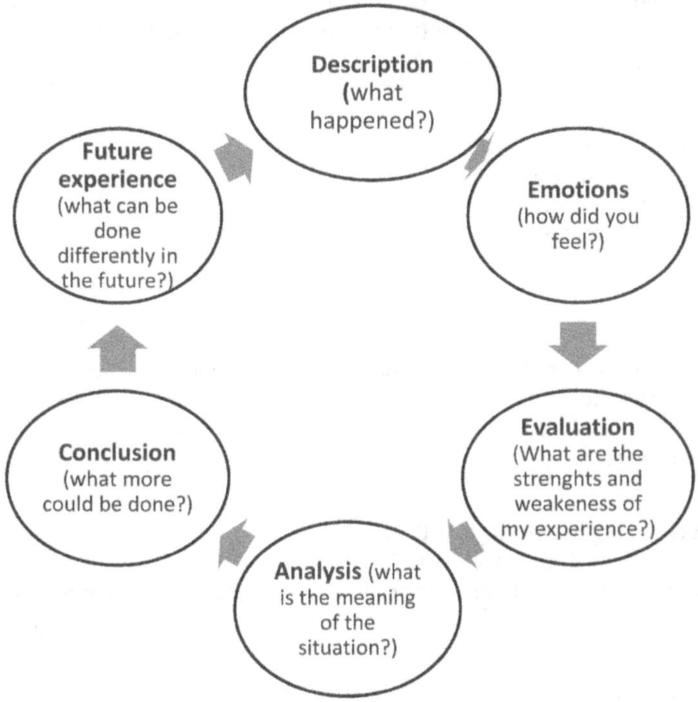

Figure 27.1 Gibbs's reflective cycle (Jasper, 2003: 77).

including mistakes of one's own. At this stage, particular importance is given to second thoughts about errors and mistakes. They are a special type of critical moment, during which reflection develops strategies that strengthen the professional skills of practitioners. Why? Because every mistake is like an open question about our way of looking at the world and acting (Sicora, 2010, 2017). This leads us to ask questions: Why? What can I do to change these negative effects? What can I do to avoid this in the future? Sicora (2010: 158) uses Columbus's discovery of America 'by mistake when looking for a new way to India as a metaphor to help better understand the potential of this kind of reflection and make it easier for future social workers to find ways to solve the complex problems of people receiving social assistance. Based on this example, the path is understood as 'right', which leads to the goal of a better understanding of reality and, consequently, to more effective assistance to those in need. It is, therefore, a mistake to move away from this 'road' (Sicora et al., 2020).

In the final stage, the whole situation is analysed in the perspective of a future occurrence. What could be done differently and what could be preserved as it is? Helpful questions are: What would you do in a similar situation in the future? How do you feel about this experience now? What have you learned? Gibbs's reflective cycle (1988) defines the stages of work on recognising a situation. This model ends with a theoretical reflection on action (cf. Schön, 1983).

The next model is Johns's *structured reflection* model (2009). In this model, the author goes a step further than Gibbs and puts reflection into action. This model offers a list of questions that are used to create reflections on an action as well as to develop reflective skills. These questions can also be used in the learning process based on apprenticeships. Detailed information on this concept is provided in Table 27.1.

Table 27.1 Johns's Structural Reflection Model (Brotherton, G., & Parker, S. (2008). Work-based learning/reflective practice. In G. Brotherton & S. Parker (Eds.), *Your foundation in health & social care: A guide for foundation degree students* (pp. 48–49). London: SAGE Publications)

Description:
1. Phenomenon/situation/event – write or talk about your experience.
2. Case – what are the main issues in this experience?
3. Context – what factors create the context of this experience?
4. Explanation – what are the key points for reflection in this experience?

Reflection:
1. What have I tried to achieve?
2. Why did I act like this?
3. What are the consequences of my actions for: client/clients, myself, the people I work with?
4. How did I feel during this experience?
5. How did customers feel?
6. How do I know what customers felt?

Significant factors:
7. What internal factors influenced my decisions and actions?
8. What external factors influenced my decisions and actions?
9. What are the sources of knowledge that have influenced or should affect my decisions and actions?

Alternative strategies:
10. Could I have done better in this situation?
11. What other choices did I have?
12. What would be the consequences of these other decisions?

Learning:
13. What kind of value would I give to my experience with regard to past and future ones?
14. How do I feel about this experience now?
15. Have I taken effective action to support myself and others as a result of this experience?
16. How has this experience changed my way of thinking about aesthetics, ethics, and myself (personal knowledge)?

In addition to methodical models, there are also approaches that raise awareness of reflection practices in the reflective education of social work students. As has already been pointed out, one such approach is to learn from mistakes. This concept was developed by Sicora (2019). Students participating in field education experience mistakes, and these mistakes offer a great opportunity to go beyond the surface of events and better understand the essence of the profession they are preparing for (Sicora, 2019). Realising that a mistake has been made is the starting point for triggering their reflexivity. It is worth noting that ignoring a situation that has gone wrong is much more dangerous than taking it into account and posing and taking the necessary steps to address it (Sicora, 2010: 159). Encouraging us to think about errors and disclose them when discussing practices is the first step in this process. The next step becomes a second look at the event being analysed. The frames of reflective approaches already described, as well as the reflective writing referred to later in the article, become useful tools (cf. Gibbs, 1988; Johns, 2009). Using these strategies, it can be said that the process of reflection begins when the subject articulates questions addressed to himself/herself. In the process of triggering reflexivity, it is more important to formulate 'the right questions' than 'the right answers'. Why is this happening? The 'right answer' will normally be appropriate for a particular situation, whereas the 'right question' can be applied in different contexts. This kind of question is of great value because it triggers a process of analysing and recalling memories, facts, and emotions that can help identify previously overlooked ways of interpreting an event (Sicora, 2010: 161–162). With regard to field education, it can be said that asking such questions promotes the widening of the 'field of vision' of the practice, as well as leading to a better understanding of it. This way of triggering reflexivity should be undertaken as a team, for instance, in practice recap classes or, if possible, during group discussions with other professionals or supervision at the place of professional practice. Without a detailed analysis and an in-depth assessment of the situation at the previous stages, it is impossible for all aspects of the event to be taken into account. This can cause valuable prerequisites for further learning to be omitted. Helpful questions are: What would you do differently? What other choices would you make? Would you adopt alternative strategies and approaches? What could you do to avoid the negative effects of the situation?

The models and approaches of reflective learning presented have many common points. In each of them, the reflection begins with a description of the situation. It is important to provide as much detail of the event as possible, as Gibbs's model does. The context in which the event took place is also important in the description. Both Gibbs (1988) and Borton (1970) draw attention to the importance of the emotions experienced during the event, which completes the description of the situation. Each model is also characterised by a situation analysis step. The questions that arise in the models presented are useful: What factors influenced the outcome of the situation? What could be learned during this event? The framework for reflective learning in each model ends with the answer to the questions: What's next? How can the situation be improved? What alternative behavioural strategies could be used in a given situation? Referring to these models, it can also be said that there are three different levels of reflection leading to a better understanding of the practice of social work. The first level of reflection is limited to the description of the facts. The second is done by exploring and explaining these facts, referring to theoretical concepts. The aim of the third level is to identify the extent to which the objectives have been achieved (cf. Sicora, 2010).

Triggering reflexivity during education for social work can also be done through reflective writing. Sicora (2010) proposes to use analytical and creative strategies for this purpose. The first category is characterised by a greater reference to objectivity: the social worker begins by describing the facts and, later, moves on to more personal and emotional elements. In turn, the separation of the narrative of analysis from the reflection itself and the use of imagination and metaphors characterise creative strategies. Among the analytical strategies, the researcher mentions: logs, analysis of critical moments, dialogue writing (creating conversations by asking questions and giving answers), 'working with chance' (recognising alternative perspectives of a given issue); strengths, weaknesses, opportunities, and threats (SWOT) analysis; identifying three things I learned that day; finding a title for each day of practice; or text messages from the day of practice. Creative strategies included writing letters or emails (without sending), writing to a friend, writing as if you were someone else (e.g., a journalist), writing poems and songs, writing articles in a certain style, and constructing mind maps (cf. Jasper, 2003).

Various exercises can also be used in education for social work to support students and practitioners in triggering reflection. Among these exercises are: creating a portfolio, writing a diary, and sharing reflection in a group. In creating a portfolio, components such as reflective writing, reading, listening, and sharing experience with peers and teachers are important. Mentors and 'critical friends' are also key, as they are needed for a reflective conversation that combines what is academic and practical. The introduction of a portfolio causes teachers to cooperate. This way of working engages lecturers to find new ways to respond and give feedback to students. These answers sometimes take the form of judgements but more often in the form of questions. Some students are more predisposed to using this technique. Those who find it more difficult need more support from teachers. This technique can also be an interesting experience in documenting your own learning process.

Writing a diary can be another useful way for (future) social workers to ask reflective questions. This tool can also be helpful in introducing reflective typing. Writing a diary is about describing one's own thoughts and reflections on the learning process. The journal also describes the doubts, thoughts, ideas, and feelings that accompanied the actions (Murphy, Dempsey, & Halton, 2010). Writing a diary is also an opportunity to record events and personal reactions during practice. Students should discuss and agree on how students use their practice logs at the beginning of the practice. Some caregivers encourage students to have a personal, reflective relationship with a practice that remains private. A diary can simply be a diary of daily events, meetings, and important dates to remember. Students should be encouraged to reflect and express a range of emotions, as this can be a good way for them to express their own feelings (Cleak & Wilson, 2007: 85).

Writing a diary can also be helpful in creating a portfolio. The third exercise is to read out loud the portfolio and diary records in the group. The purpose of this form of group work is to seek to construct reflective queries. Participants become more aware of what they are doing, answer questions about why they are doing this, and develop a specific style of work. They ask each other how they could have done differently. All this makes them more aware of how they worked that day (Murphy et al., 2010).

Another example of the use of reflective writing is the preparation by students of essays aimed at identifying and describing 'critical events' that occurred during professional practices (Boryczko, 2018, 2020). For this task, a model of critical deconstruction and reconstruction of Jan Fook's (2002, 2007) experience can be adapted. This model is based on four stages: (1) critical deconstruction, that is, the search for contradictions, different perspectives, and interpretations; (2) resistance, which consists of refusing to accept and participate in various aspects of dominant discourses which deprive power and sometimes results in a hopeless situation; (3) the challenge of identifying the existence and operation of hidden, mystified, or pre-established discourses; (4) reconstruction, based on the formulation of a new discourse, narrative, and structural change (Fook, 2002: 96). On the basis of this model, Boryczko (2020) proposed the following framework for the essay: introduction, description of the critical incident under analysis (a problematic situation that occurred during practice), critical deconstruction of thinking patterns (identification of different perspectives), resistance (finding ways to counter oppression, the relationship of power, and dominant discourses), the challenge (identification of discourses, power relationships, structure of oppression, and description of their role in relation to a critical incident), reconstruction (reflection on what we have learned, creation of new knowledge, new perspectives, new discourses, implications for practice), and conclusion. In critical reflection, the use of a critical incident as the basis for knowledge generation can be considered as 'reflection-on-action' rather than 'reflection-in-action' (Schön, 1983). The critical incident is firmly in the past and is represented as a learning opportunity for the future from this selected incident (D'Cruz et al., 2007: 83).

Although students are usually proficient in being reflective, a critical part of their reflection and analysis often needs to be strengthened. It is worth encouraging students, especially those who practice in recent years of study, to take a more informed approach to the critical part of reflection (Theobald et al., 2017: 303–304; Giles & Pockett, 2013). Integrating reflective approaches into social work curricula that combines critical thinking with experience becomes one of the most important challenges of modern education. This is facilitated by reflective writing, which is an effective tool combining different forms of knowledge and perspectives (cf. Theobald et al., 2017; Sicora, 2019; Boryczko, 2020).

Conclusions

In triggering reflection in education for social work, it is still important to pay attention to the relationship between academic knowledge and practical knowledge and to the quality of reflection proposed at the start of education for social work. On the first point, academic education provides general knowledge that enables one to be able to act in specific cases in social work. The role of practice in the education and development of a social worker is, therefore, important. According to Schön (1983), any practice, properly used, can have educational value, even a failed one, provided that the student is able to perceive the error and understand its logic. Otherwise, the wrong act may be regarded as a norm. On the second point, doubts can be raised as to the quality of the reflection proposed at the start of education. Because of a limited knowledge of theory and poor experience in social work, a student may find it difficult to receive the training qualities of the practice. Students may have difficulty reflecting in action when taking first practice. This ability is generally a feature of people with a certain level of intellectual creation (Ciczkowska-Giedziun & Chrostowska, 2016). Importantly, reflection 'feeds' on concepts – the richer the world of concepts and thoughts of the future social worker, the more he/she will be able to 'see' in a particular situation. Reflection also 'feeds' on cognitive contradictions, which is tantamount to having knowledge of different methodological origins. Such knowledge builds up slowly, and its understanding takes time (Kwiatkowska, 2008).

Therefore, it is easier to reflect at the outset on actions within selected subjects, e.g., social projects and practices (including failed versions of practice). Field trainers can become supportive of students in this area. It is also worth working on the deconstruction of colloquial concepts among students and to make reflection a tool for it.

References

Ajibo, H., Mbah, F. & Anazonwu, N. (2017). Field work practice in social work. In: U. Okoye, N. Chukwu & P. Agwu (ed.). *Social Work in Nigeria: Book of Readings* (pp. 104–113). Nsukka: University of Nigeria Press Ltd.

Beddoe, L., Ackroyd, J., Chinnery, S.A. & Appleton, C. (2011). Live supervision of students in field placement: More than just watching. *Social Work Education*, 30(5), 512–528.

Borton, T. (1970). *Reach, Teach and Touch*. London: Mc Graw Hill.

Boryczko, M. (2020). Critical thinking in social work education. A case study of knowledge practices in students' reflective writings using semantic gravity profiling. *Social Work Education*, DOI: 10.1080/02615479.2020.1836143.

Boryczko, M. (2018). Teoria przecięć – Myślenie krytyczne – Teoria Kodów Legitymizacji. O zastosowaniach teorii w kontekście analizy aktywności edukacyjnej studentów pracy socjalnej. *Praca Socjalna*, 2(33), 97–116.

Brotherton, G. & Parker, S. (2008). Work-based learning/reflective practice. In: G. Brotherton & S. Parker (ed.). *Your Foundation in Health et Social Care. A Guide for Foundation Degree Students*. London: SAGE Publications.

Chan, Y.-M. (2017). Enhancing critical reflective practice in fieldwork education: An exploratory study of the role of Social Work Agencies in the welfare context of Hong Kong. *International Journal of Humanities & Social Sciences*, 11(4), 811–821.

Chrostowska, B. & Ciczkowska-Giedziun, M. (2014). Refleksyjność w pracy socjalnej. In: A. Weissbrot-Koziarska & I. Dąbrowska-Jabłońska (eds.). *Słownik metod, Technik i form pracy socjalnej, opiekuńczej i terapeutycznej, Tom III*. Opole: Wydawnictwo Uniwersytetu Opolskiego.

Ciczkowska-Giedziun, M. & Chrostowska, B. (2016). Wyzwalanie refleksyjności w kształceniu do pracy socjalnej. *Praca Socjalna*, 31(7/8), 35–48.

Cleak, H. & Wilson, J. (2007). *Making the Most of Field Placement* (2nd ed.) Melbourne: Thomson Learning.

Connolly, M. & Harms, L. (2012). *Social Work. From Theory to Practice*. New York: Cambridge University Press.

D'Cruz, H., Gillingham, P. & Melendez, S. (2007). Reflexivity, its meanings and relevance for social work: A critical review of the literature. *British Journal of Social Work*, 37(1), 73–90, DOI: 10.1093/bjsw/bcl001.

Davys, A. & Beddoe, L. (2010). *Best Practice in Supervision: A Guide for the Helping Professions*. London: Jessica Kingsley.

Eltaiba, N. & Ndoye, A. (2018). The effectiveness of field education in social work education: A student perspective. *Advances in Social Work & Welfare Education*, 20(1), 170–184.

Fook, J. (1999). Critical reflectivity in education and practice. In: B. Pease & J. Fook (eds.), *Transforming Social Work Practice: Postmodern Critical Perspectives*. St Leonards: Allen and Unwin.

Fook, J. (2002). *Critical Deconstruction and Reconstruction*. London: Sage.

Fook, J. (2007). Reflective practice and critical reflection. In: J. Lishman (ed.), *Handbook for Practice Learning in Social Work and Social Care: Knowledge and Theory* (2nd ed.) (pp. 363–375). Jessica Kingsley.

Fook, J., Ryan, M. & Hawkins, L. (2000). *Professional Expertise: Practice, Theory and Education for Working in Uncertainty*. London: UK. Whiting & Birch.

Gibbs, G. (1988). *Learning by Doing: A Guide to Teaching and Learning Methods*. Further Educational Unit. London: Oxford Centre for Staff and Learning Development, Oxford Polytechnic.

Giles, R. & Pockett, R. (2013). Critical reflection in social work education. In: J. Fook & F. Gardner (eds.), *Critical Reflection in Context* (pp. 208–218). London: Routledge.

Graham, J. C., Dettlaff, A. J., Baumann, D. J. & Fluke, J. D. (2015). The decision-making ecology of placing a child into foster care: A structural equation model. *Child Abuse & Neglect*, 49, 12–23.

Howe, D. (2011). *Krótkie uprowadzenie do teorii pracy socjalnej*. Warszawa: Instytut Rozwoju Służb Społecznych.

Hughes, M. & Heycox, K. (2010). *Older People, Ageing and Social Work: Knowledge for Practice*. Sydney: Allen & Unwin.

Jasper, M. (2003). *Beginning Reflective Practice*. Cheltenham: Nelson Thomes Ltd.

Johns, Ch. (2009). *Becoming a Reflective Practitioner* (3rd ed.) Oxford: Wiley- Blackwell Publishing.

Kantowicz, E. (2001). Wybrane koncepcje i standardy kształcenia do profesji społecznych w Europie. In: W. E. Marynowicz-Hetka, A. Wagner, & J. Piekarski (red.), *Profesje społeczne w Europie. Europie problemów kształcenia i działania*. Katowice: Wyd„Śląsk.

Kantowicz, E. (2005). *Praca socjalna w Europie. Inspiracje teoretyczne i standardy kształcenia*. Olsztyn: Wydawnictwo Uniwersytetu Warmińsko-Mazurskiego.

Kolb, D. A. (1984). *Experiential Learning. Experience as the Source of Learning and Development*. Englewood Cliffs, NJ: Prentice-Hall, Inc.

Krasiejko, I. & Ciczkowska-Giedziun, M. (2016). Refleksyjność i refleksyjny praktyk w pracy socjalno-wychowawczej z rodziną. In: I. Krasiejko & M. Ciczkowska-Giedziun (eds.), *Praca socjalno-wychowawcza z rodziną w ujęciu wybranych koncepcji. Analiza metodycznego działania z osobami potrzebującymi pomocy* (pp. 195–221). Warszawa: Instytut Rozwoju Służb Społecznych.

Kwiatkowska, H. (2008). *Pedeutologia*. Warszawa: Wydawnictwa Akademickie i Profesjonalne.

Lam, C. M., Wong, H. & Fong Leung, T. T. F. (2007). An unfinished reflexive journey: Social work students' reflection on their placement experiences. *British Journal of Social Work*, 37(1), 91–105.

Maidment, J. (2000). Strategies to promote student learning and integration of theory with practice in the field. In: L. Cooper & L. Briggs (eds.), *Fieldwork in the Human Services: Theory and Practice for Field Educators, Practice Teachers and Supervisors*. St. Leonard: Allen & Unwin.

Mizerek, H. (1999). *Dyskursy współczesnej edukacji nauczycielskiej. Między tradycjonalizmem a ponowoczesnością*. Olsztyn: Wydawnictwo Uniwersytetu Warmińsko-Mazurskiego.

Murphy, M., Dempsey, M. & Halton, C. (2010). Reflective inquiry in social work education. In: N. Lyons (ed.). *Handbook of Reflection and Reflective Inquiry: Mapping a Way of Knowing for Professional Reflective Inquiry*. New York: Springer Science & Business Media, LLC.

Przeperski, J. (2021). Social work paradigms and their effect on decision making About out-of-home placement. *Research on Social Work Journal*, 31(4), 4, DOI: 10.1177/1049731520985607.

Przeperski, J. & Taylor, B. (2020). Cooperation in child welfare decision making: Qualitative vignette study. *Child Care in Practice*, DOI: 10.1080/13575279.2019.1701412.

Ruch, G. (2002). From triangle to spiral: Reflective practice in social work education, practice and research. *Social Work Education*, 21(2), 199–216, DOI: 10.1080/02615470220126435.

Ruch, G. (2009). Reflective practice and reflective spaces. In: G. Ruch (ed.). *Post-Qualifying Child Care Social Work: Developing Reflective Practice* (pp. 19–30). London: SAGE Publications.

Ryding, J. & Wernersson, I. (2019). The role of reflection in family support social work and its possible promotion by a research-supported model. *Journal of Evidence-Based Social Work*, 16(3), 3, DOI: 10.1080/26408066.2019.1606748.

Schön, D. (1983). *The Reflective Practitioner: How Professionals Think in Action.* New York: Basic Books.
Seden, J. (2005). *Counselling Skills in Social Work Practice* (2nd ed.) Berkshire: Open University Press.
Sicora, A. (2010). Self-evaluation of social work practice through reflection on professional mistakes. Practice makes 'perfect'? *Revista de Asistenţă socială*, IX(4), 153–164.
Sicora, A. (2017). *Reflective Practice and Learning from Mistakes in Social Work.* Bristol: Policy Press.
Sicora, A. (2019). Reflective practice and learning from mistakes in social work student placement. *Social Work Education*, 38(1), 63–74, DOI: 10.1080/02615479.2018.1508567.
Sicora, A., Lu, W. & Lei, J. (2020). Exploring mistakes and errors of professional judgement in social work in China and Italy: The impact of culture, organization and education. *Journal of Social Work*, DOI: 10.1177/1468017320919879.
Smith, D., Cleak, H. & Vreugdenhil, A. (2014). 'What Are They Really Doing?' an exploration of student learning activities in field placement. *Australian Social Work*, DOI: 10.1080/0312407X.2014.960433.
Søbjerg Mosegaard, L., Taylor, B., Przeperski, J., Horvat, S., Nouman, H. & Harvey, D. (2020). Using risk factor statistics in decision-making: Prospects and challenges. *European Journal of Social Work*, DOI: 10.1080/13691457.2020.1772728.
Spray, C. & Jowett, B. (2012). *Social Work Practice with Children and Families.* London: SAGE Publications.
Taylor, B. (2017). *Decision Making, Assessment and Risk in Social Work, Learning Matters.* Exeter: SAGE Publications.
Theobald, E. J., Eddy, S. L., Grunspan, D. Z,, Wiggins, B. L., & Crowe, A. J. (2017). Student perception of group dynamics predicts individual performance: Comfort and equity matter. *PLOS one*, 12(7), e0181336.
White, S. (2012). Analiza *dyskursu* i refleksyjność. In: M. Gray & S.A. Webb (ed.). *Praca socjalna. Teorie i metody.* Warszawa: Wydawnictwo Naukowe PWN.
Woronowicz, W. (2000). *Problemy edukacji refleksyjnej.* Koszalin: Bałtycka Wyższa Szkoła Humanistyczna.

28

Unconventional Practice Placements

Creativity, Partnership, and New Professional Opportunities in an Italian Experience of Social Work Field Education

M.L. Raineri, F. Corradini, C. Landi, and P. Limongelli

In social work education, the unanimous recognition of the importance of practical training (Goldstein, 2001; Dick et al., 2002; Clapton & Cree, 2004; Gui, 2009; Wayne et al., 2010) does not imply an actual uniformity in the educational and organisational models. Almost all decisions regarding the implementation of practice placements require mediation between different needs, which are difficult to reconcile with each other. There are, therefore, different configurations that present positive and negative or critical aspects concerning the learning process (Bogo & Vayda, 1998; Caspi & Reid, 2002; Shardlow & Doel, 2006; Wilson et al., 2009).

Practice placement activities can focus mainly on gathering information about the setting and observing supervisors and other professionals' work, or they can consistently imply that students carry out real professional tasks directly, first-hand. Whenever such autonomy is required, the choice of activities follows two main approaches. A 'training' approach, entailing the assignment of activities and tasks already performed in the practice placement location and that, therefore, would be carried out by the supervisor or by other social workers even if students were not present. A more innovative approach, broadly speaking, that requires students to develop a new activity or a new project, which, otherwise, would not have been carried out in that context. Consequently, it is not a question of reproducing the work of others, but of trying something new. It is unlikely (but not impossible) that it is new in an absolute sense. For example, it could be a project built along the lines of a plan that has already been successful elsewhere, or they could be activities that, although deemed useful, were ended because of a shortage of staff. In any case, students venture on a path that is not already fully traced.

Given the character of greater discretion in the planning and implementation of this second type of model, it can be defined as unconventional practice placement (U.P.P.) to distinguish it from traditional social work placements.

 DOI: 10.4324/9781032164946-33

Non-Traditional Placements and Service Learning in Social Work Education

Such experiences are well-documented in Britain (Skills for Care, 2009; Doel, 2010; Scholar et al., 2012, 2014; Hek, 2012; McLaughlin et al., 2014), where non-traditional placements were introduced to expand practice placement opportunities. These placements are carried out in settings with no social workers, as they do not provide social care services in the strict sense, such as police authorities, schools and colleges, unions and employment agencies (Scholar et al. 2012; Hek, 2012), and in local communities and groups with the involvement of services' users (Parker et al., 2003).

Despite the initial scepticism, over time, non-traditional placements have shown that they can offer good opportunities to aspiring social workers, providing field experiences that meet the requirements for traditional placements (McLaughlin et al., 2014). The activities that can be carried out in these settings (such as direct work with users and carers; assessment, planning, intervention, and final evaluation; teamwork; report writing; group work; project work) are remarkably similar to those carried out in traditional practice placements. The inter-professional work opportunities they provide are particularly interesting (Doel, 2010). With regard to professional social work, non-traditional placements offer the advantage of developing social work in unusual contexts. Sometimes students' activities result in the development of new services or the expansion of existing ones. It has also been found that students' presence can offer an additional benefit to host organisations in terms of public image improvement (Doel, 2010; Scholar et al., 2012, 2014).

A critical issue is the achievement of proper preparation for the experience, with the student, the host organisation, and the university knowing each other fairly well. Moreover, in a non-traditional placement, students need to be carefully assisted in linking the needs identified in the field, the activities carried out, and the training purposes envisaged in the practice placement's plan. To this end, in non-traditional placements, there is an in-place supervisor, although a non-professional, who accompanies the student day by day, and an offsite supervisor (at the university) who has experience both as a social worker and as a practice teacher (Doel, 2010). Group activities for students are also particularly useful, as they ensure peer support and the reworking of the lessons learned (Scholar et al., 2014).

In the U.S.A., U.P.P.s are implemented as service-learning experiences (Nadel, Majewski, & Sullivan-Cosetti, 2007; Petracchi et al., 2016). This pedagogical approach integrates class content with the experience of serving others, thus, developing collaborative and mutual relationships between students and members of the community (Hatcher & Bringle, 1997; Harkavy, 2004; Fiorin, 2016). While 'traditional' placements prioritise students' educational goals, service learning focuses on the needs of the community (Petracchi et al., 2016). Consequently, the realisation of service learning experiences requires intense collaboration and joint evaluation between universities and the local communities where these practices are performed (Campbell, 2012).

Service learning is certainly not exclusive to social work, as it is implemented at different educational levels, in different disciplines, and in many countries around the world. It is applied significantly in Spain and South America, where it is linked to the legacy of Paul Freire. North American experiences and reflexions are strongly influenced by John Dewey's theory and philosophy (Deans, 1999).

In 2008, the U.S. National Association of Social Workers recognised that the primary outcomes of service learning, and the civic and community commitment that it favours, are aligned with the fundamental principles of social work and the mission of social work education (Begun et al., 2010). Service learning's strengths include its ability to promote students' reflexivity, critical thinking, and problem-solving, which are considered essential elements of social work education (Lemieux & Allen, 2007). Social work students participating in service learning have shown a more significant civic commitment, perceived self-efficacy, and sense of responsibility, and they are more interested and confident in carrying out research activities (Byers & Gray, 2012; Ericson, 2011; Maccio, 2011). The reported critical aspects, for which improvements would be needed, include training methods that are not always adequate (Gerstenblatt & Gilbert, 2014) and the risk that the needs of universities and students prevail over those of local communities (Butin, 2010). Furthermore, Wayne and colleagues, drawing inspiration from the South American tradition that generally considers service learning as a group-class experience, suggest greater use of group learning, both among students and among them and the other subjects involved in service learning in the field (Wayne et al., 2010).

In Italy, U.P.P.s were the standard educational practice in the post-war years. At the time, the fact that professional social work was not widespread and institutionalised forced the field to tread new roads already in basic training. In more recent years, this kind of placement has been carried out at the University of Trent, the University of Turin (Dellavalle, 2011; Cola, 2015), the Bicocca University of Milan (Luppi, 2019), and the Catholic University of the Sacred Heart (U.C.S.C.) of Milan and Brescia. This chapter aims to describe those implemented at the latter, which are, as far as we know, the most significant experience in Italy for the number of U.P.P.s created and their formal integration in the social work academic curricula.

Data Collection and Analysis

The following description of U.P.P.s is based on the authors' first-hand knowledge, as they directly contributed to developing this model; the information informally collected by the teaching staff supervising the U.P.P.s; some quantitative and qualitative data collected in two extensive studies on the U.P.P.s performed at U.C.S.C. in bachelor's degree courses from 2008 to 2019.

The data supporting the description contained in the next paragraphs were collected through two surveys. The first, conducted by Sala (2016), studied the U.P.P.s that occurred between the academic years 2008–09 and 2014–15; the second (not yet published) studied the U.P.P.s between the academic years 2015–16 and 2018–19. The questionnaires consisted of closed-ended questions aimed at collecting information on the respondents' socio-personal data, their training, how their U.P.P.s were carried out (such as people involved, project goals, and interventions carried out), formal arrangements, and the U.P.P.s' outcomes. An open-ended question required respondents to briefly describe the U.P.P. project, its primary goals, and actions.

Data collection was carried out online, through the SurveyMonkey platform, between March and June 2016 for the first survey and between September 2019 and March 2020 for the second one. The collected data were analysed using the statistical software S.P.S.S.-version 25.

The questionnaires were submitted anonymously, however, the description of the U.P.P. projects could make the respondents identifiable. Consequently, the questionnaires were administered after the formal U.P.P. assessments and the European Credits Transfer System[1] (E.C.T.S.) awarding, when the relationship between students and teachers/researchers had ended. The two surveys were carried out in compliance with the standards set by the Code of Ethics of the Catholic University (Rectoral Decree no. 9350/2011).

U.P.P.s Performed at the Catholic University of Milan and Brescia: A Brief Overview

Non-traditional placements and service learning, combined, summarise the two peculiar characteristics of the U.P.P.s carried out at U.C.S.C. for the following reasons. First, students do not merely reproduce the social work activities already present in their practice placement context, as they are expected to carry out something 'new'. Second, students develop a project that is related not only to their training needs, but also, above all, to some *real* needs of a local community or some *real* opportunities for improvement. Consequently, U.P.P.s are based on a collaborative approach. Students' learning depends on the cooperation with the other subjects involved in the project (citizens, operators, volunteers, or service users and their family members) while these subjects must be able to gain something useful from the students' work.

A third peculiar characteristic of U.P.P.s is the high autonomy required of the students, even in relation to educational supervision. Therefore, students are expected to conceive and develop the project by themselves from the beginning, and eventually negotiate its contents with the various stakeholders: the university, on the one hand. and the citizens, community, users, and/or social services on the other.

U.P.P.s were introduced in U.C.S.C. bachelor's degree courses in social work starting from the 2008–09 academic year, becoming mandatory from the 2009–10 academic year. They are worth 9 E.C.T.S., with 175 hours in the field and 40 hours of classroom training; further, an optional 2 or 4 E.C.T.S. (50 or 100 hours) can be added. U.P.P.s are assessed and graded by a commission of practice teachers.

Unconventional placements are carried out in the third year of the course, after students have attended an introductory placement in the first year and a traditional placement in the second year. Although one U.P.P. may differ from the other, in October, November, and December, students generally prepare for unconventional placements with classroom work and individual study and identify the first ideas for their projects. In January and February, the actual planning is performed, and, from February onward, they proceed to the implementation of the project, which usually ends between June and September.

A range of educational supports is provided: a 40-hour classroom workshop with a social worker tutor, in groups of 15–25 students, from October to May; three to four individual (or in a small group) interviews with the tutor; an administrative assistant helps students with the necessary bureaucratic requirements. Furthermore, a social work professor coordinates all the practice education related to the U.P.P.s.

Some Data on the U.P.P.s Performed from 2008 to 2019

Based on the administrative records of the university, between the academic year 2008–9 and the 2018–19 one, 1,058 students were engaged in U.P.P.s. The course is held at two locations, both in Lombardy (a region in northern Italy): one in Milan and one in Brescia. The two surveys concern all the students of these two locations. Although two or more students could collaborate on projects connected and with similar goals, each one of them needed to develop a specific part of the work entrusted to his/her responsibility. On this basis, we can assume that each respondent created a distinct U.P.P. from that of his/her colleagues.

A total of 311 students participated in the first survey (203 in Milan and 108 in Brescia) and 191 in the second, for a total of 502 respondents. The response rate was 48% in the first survey and 55.5% in the second.

Of the respondents, 40.5% did not indicate the number of their work hours, 64% of the rest achieved a 175-hour U.P.P., while 22.8% of the U.P.P.s had a duration of 225 hours, and 13.4% were for 275 hours.

All U.P.P.s took place in parallel with lessons or exams. Therefore, no student was involved full-time in his/her U.P.P. Two days a week were reserved for U.P.P.s in the academic calendar. Students could organise their schedule according to the project needs (and possibly according to their preferences) compatibly with their other academic tasks. Such a flexible schedule led to different completion times: more than half of the respondents ($N = 401$) carried out their U.P.P. over 4 to 6 months (59%); 32.4% of U.P.P.s lasted 7–11 months, while the U.P.P.s that took only 3 months (3.8%) or 12 or more months (4.7%) were less frequent.

The First Step in the U.P.P. Process: Finding a Suitable Setting

First, each student has to identify a setting for his/her U.P.P., that is the agency or informal organisation which could host it. They also must get an idea of the people who could be interested in such a project, the social characteristics of that geographical area, the type of problems to be addressed, and the resources available.

At this stage, the following essential guideline is given to students: their starting point should be people's problems or aspirations, not what they, the students, would like to learn. This indication is important because students sometimes get confused about the great 'autonomy' they experience in U.P.P.s (Raineri, 2015). It might, perhaps, sound paradoxical to say that, although students must define the project independently, the project must be shared, that is, built collaboratively. Precisely, students are independent in creating the collaborative connections necessary to conceive and develop their U.P.P. project. Therefore, autonomy does not mean being able to do whatever they want, doing it literally 'on their own': otherwise, what kind of *social* work would it be? Their task is to find somebody (an organisation, families, a local community, a group) who is interested in their project, considers it useful, and is available to participate. Consequently, students' project planning autonomy consists of identifying their own U.P.P. project by combining their training needs and interests with the needs and aspirations of others (Raineri, 2015).

Once they identify the problems or issues around which they deem it realistic and interesting to develop their U.P.P.s, students make first contacts with people who are potentially interested in helping them or who can provide useful information. The goal is to probe the 'social basis' of the possible project (Folgheraiter & Raineri, 2017). In other words, it is essential to understand whether the issue is of interest and the stakeholders (as individuals and/or representatives of their organisations) are willing to collaborate and whether the neighbourhood, informal group, association, or agency could be a suitable setting for developing a project, and what type of project could be more appropriate. In general, students should take some time to 'explore the field', without immediately settling for the first available opportunity, in order to have some choices.

Once students have identified in principle the type of work to perform, they examine the possible settings and decide where to start the project. The possible options are essentially a public, non-profit, or market organisation, with a formal agreement between this agency and the university, or, alternatively, an internship formally based at the university, without a formal agreement with an external organisation.

Some Data about Targets and Formal Settings

The data on formal settings of our U.P.P.s seem to confirm that social work can take place anywhere as long as there is an 'issue' identified by a 'social' entity and a relational guide capable of connecting motivated people and catalysing a coping network to address that social problem (Folgheraiter & Raineri, 2017). This Italian experience, like the ones in the U.K. (McLaughlin et al., 2014), also seems to disprove the widespread conception that professional training is possible only in conventional social services. As shown in Figure 28.1, 25.2% of the students carried out their U.P.P.s without a formal agreement with an external organisation from 2008 to 2015, while from 2016 to 2019 such U.P.P.s made up 60.3%. If we consider the total number of students from 2008 to 2019, the 'free U.P.P.s were 38.5%. These U.P.P.s were carried out in collaboration with informal groups of citizens, users, and carers. In the other U.P.P.s, there was a formal agreement, which was entered, in the majority of cases, with private or third-sector organisations, which seldom host traditional placements.

Figure 28.2 also relates to the settings where the U.P.P.s were performed, but in terms of the project targets (the type of recipients and problems). Although some of the U.P.P.s were not implemented in traditional settings, most of the problems that students worked on are typical of social work. This fact seems to confirm the hypothesis that there are many different settings in which social work can be performed.

Some of the targets were unusual for social work, which are seldom considered in traditional practice placement. These targets are the 'general population of a local area' (10%), 'young people

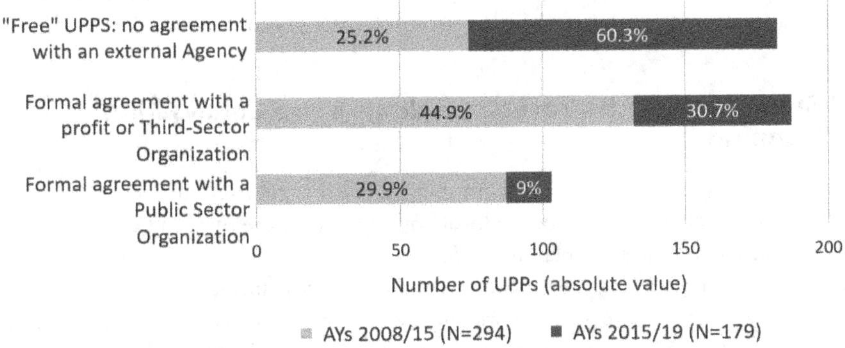

Figure 28.1 Formal arrangements of U.P.P.s realised in U.C.S.C. from 2008 to 2019; absolute and percentage values from the two surveys.

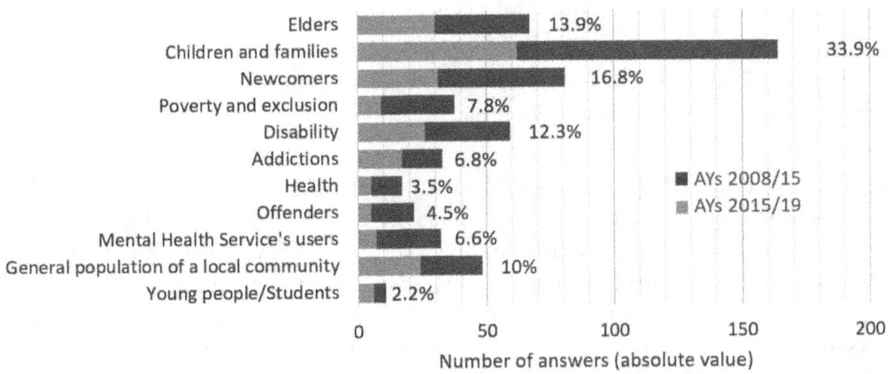

Figure 28.2 Targets of U.P.P.s realised in U.C.S.C. from 2008 to 2019; number of answers and their percentage values on total respondents (*N* = 483; multiple answers were allowed).

and/or students' (2.2%; this category was detected from the answers to the open-ended question given under the item: other). These data show that U.P.P.s can offer an opportunity to experience new forms of social work, sometimes borderline between social work and socio-cultural animation (Lorenz, 1994).

A Brief Example: Maria Looks for Her U.P.P.

Maria, a social work student, was interested in community work with people in poverty and offered her collaboration to some local social services that worked in a run-down estate on the outskirts of her city. Unfortunately, none of these services was available to collaborate with her on any community work, but social workers suggested that Maria turn to the parish volunteer group. The volunteers asked Maria if she wanted to help them in their counselling service and distribution of used clothes, and the parish priest asked her to accompany him to visit the families of the neighbourhood. So, Maria got to know many inhabitants of the area, but she was worried about wasting time on all these visits, without having a specific purpose. She talked about this concern in the classroom workshop, where the other students and the tutor helped her to reflect on the importance of building a community profile starting from meeting people, in order to create the basis for building a shared project. Therefore, Maria decided to implement her U.P.P. without a formal agreement, in collaboration with the volunteers and the parish.

The Second Step in the U.P.P. Process: Guiding-group Catalysation and Project Planning

Students are asked to study and learn about the problems and the socio-cultural characteristics of the identified target, the characteristics of the local community where they will work, and the type of activities or initiatives that they plan to perform.

After this preliminary preparation, they move on to the project planning.

Consistent with what is taught in social work theory courses, students are invited to adopt an 'open' and participatory programming approach. That is, an approach able to deal with what, at the beginning, is not entirely predictable and that could change, such as the decisions and the choices made by citizens, users, caregivers, and sometimes even by other professionals or other services. To carry out this kind of project planning, students must find people who are:

- interested in the field they have chosen;
- somewhat expert in that field, as experts by experience or as professionals; and
- available to collaborate with them in the project planning.

First contacts can be quite difficult and stressful for students, as they are uncertain of how to introduce themselves and what to ask. After all, people are used to being offered already well-defined programmes, while it is quite unusual to be asked to collaborate on a project still to be planned. The main suggestions that are offered to students to help them manage these first contacts are to present themselves to potential collaborators as someone *asking for their help* to build a project together and to start from what interests people. In U.P.P.s, students should perform work that is useful, significant, and appropriate not only for them but also for their collaborators (Raineri, 2015).

In the end, if all goes well, students invite a small group of people interested in collaborating, the so-called 'guiding group', to a meeting. In this meeting, they discuss the possible *goals* of the U.P.P. project, which now is not just the single student's project anymore, but a shared one. After agreeing on the goals, the group discusses the strategies to achieve them, and then it defines the project implementation. Finally, students will have the task of drafting the project plan (also indicating whether there are non-essential issues to be decided later) to be submitted to the approval of the guiding group, the university, and any host organisation. This process can have several variations. For instance, one or more meetings may be necessary to reach a concrete decision; the initial guiding group may change because some members were not interested or available and left, or other people joined, often at the suggestion of the first members. It is also possible to agree on a brief initial project, which can be expanded later if things go well.

Such shared planning involves a negotiation to find a balance between the training needs of the social work student, the peculiar characteristics of the U.P.P., and the needs or desires expressed by the guiding group. This negotiation is, in itself, a valuable opportunity to learn how to promote collaboration between people, which is a fundamental skill in social work.

A Brief Example: The Guiding-Group in Maria's U.P.P.

After a few weeks, a local charity asked the volunteer group if they were available to collect the unsold groceries left every evening from two supermarkets and redistribute them to the people in poverty who lived in the neighborhood. The group consisted of some elderly ladies, and not all of them drove a car. They couldn't accept this offer because it was too demanding. So, Maria proposed to involve some families in poverty who seemed eager to do something for their community. She also talked about this idea with the parish priest, and, with his help, Maria put together a guiding-group made up of the volunteers, five people in poverty, the parish priest, and her.

With Maria's facilitation, the group assessed the pros and cons of accepting the supermarkets' offer and, once they decided to accept, people began to reflect on the criteria to follow in food distribution. This led to a heated discussion, which seemed to never end. Maria talked about it in her class and asked for help. By reasoning with the other students, she focused on valuing people's resources and skills. Thus, in the following meeting, Maria proposed that people who received the food for free should, in return, collaborate to manage the distribution and/or to improve their local community. The group was enthusiastic about this idea. They worked on it together, and a detailed project was defined.

The Third Step in the U.P.P. Process: Working Together

Whatever the actions planned, the project is carried out with the constant 'guidance' of the guiding group through periodic meetings. Students are responsible for facilitating the guiding group in this task. In essence, they should act as a contact point with the various people involved and take care of the project organisation to facilitate their participation. In this phase, additional collaborators are often involved who sometimes join the guiding group; other times, they do not have a planning role, except for some parts of the overall project.

In the academic years between 2008–09 and 2014–15, the U.P.P.s offered many examples of projects characterised by a participatory approach (Warren, 2007; Fawcett et al., 2017), according to relational social work (Folgheraiter, 2004, 2017).

Such participatory perspective is consistent with the ethical principles of international and Italian social work. However, although it has its roots in the history of social work (Bortoli,

2013), there is still a long way to go for it to translate into effective social work practices. In Italy, participatory policies are often just declarations of principles or fail to define a coherent framework. At the field level, many social workers tend to work in a 'professional-centred' way, that is, following the general principle by which experts should be the ones to decide what is best to do when addressing users' difficulties. Therefore, projects with the general purpose of promoting participation have often a significant innovative relevance, especially when they promote the participation of the most vulnerable people, those who apparently seem to have truly little to offer, and much to receive.

The following are the most representative types of projects described in the open-ended questions of the two surveys.

- Projects aimed at participatory planning (of services, guidelines, specific social care initiatives) and/or participatory evaluation. The people involved can be those living in specific areas (a neighbourhood, a village) or people facing the same issues. About 9.5% of the U.P.P.s dealt with this type of project.
- Projects aimed at addressing some needs in a new way – an entirely new way or new for that context – and projects aimed at introducing typical social work tasks (such as counselling interviews, referring to other services, social work assessments, and so on) in entirely new contexts (such as a parish, a local association) or in contexts in which they are not yet provided, although, elsewhere, experiences have already been made in this regard. About 30.8% of the U.P.P.s dealt with this type of project.
- Projects aimed at informing, promoting, or sensitising a local community about a social problem, with the participation of experts by experience; 19% of the U.P.P.s dealt with this type of project.
- Projects aimed at creating opportunities for relationships, exchanges, and dialogue between people, such as spaces for gathering and socialising, community mediation, community development initiatives, community advocacy, and promotion of active citizenship initiatives. About 28.6% of the U.P.P.s dealt with this type of project.

Figure 28.3 shows a classification of U.P.P.s in four levels of intervention. Categories were inductively identified from the projects' descriptions written by students in questionnaires, and frequencies were obtained by classifying each description in the category that most represented it. There are very few U.P.P.s (3% of respondents) primarily based on casework. Most of the students promoted groupwork experiences (45%), community work experiences (32%), or both (18%). These data are interesting because Italian social work is mainly focused on casework (Allegri, 2015). Until recently, groupwork and community work were considered marginal work areas for social workers, and, consequently, it is difficult for students to experience community work in traditional practice placements.

Some Data about Professional and Informal Collaborators

The two surveys detected how many collaborators were engaged by the students in creating their U.P.P.s (Figure 28.4). In the first survey (Sala, 2016), 44.9% of the respondent students ($N = 216$) had from one to three collaborators and 35.6% from four to six, the remaining U.P.P.s had a higher number. In the second survey, the number of collaborators in the 191 U.P.P.s was, on average, eight people. Overall, the two surveys reported 2,597 collaborators.

This large number is a significant difference compared to traditional practice placements, in which the protagonists are mainly two: the student and his/her supervisor, while in U.P.P.s a

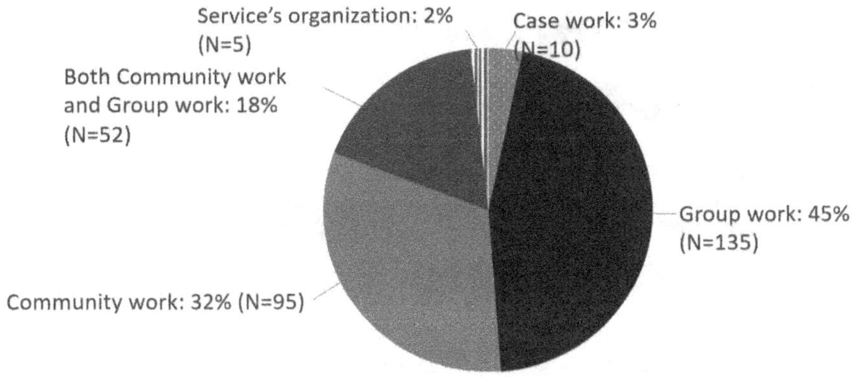

Figure 28.3 Social work levels experimented in U.P.P.s realised in U.C.S.C. from 2008 to 2019 ($N = 297$).

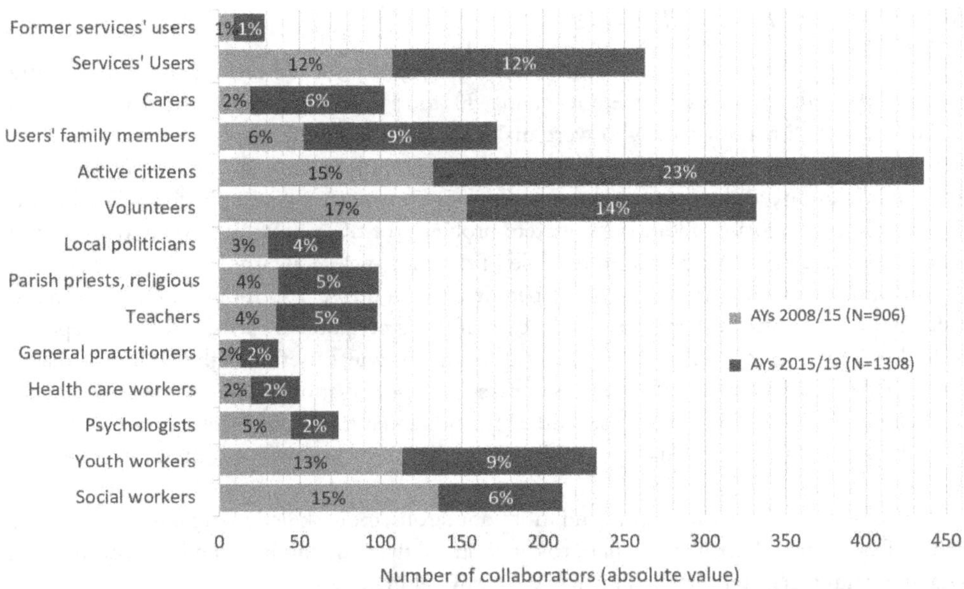

Figure 28.4 People who collaborated with students for realisation of U.P.P.s realised in U.C.S.C. from 2008 to 2019 (absolute and percentage values from the two surveys).

'learning community' approach seems prevalent. Such an approach makes it possible for the student to learn from different people, professionals, and non-professionals, and for the latter to get some useful insight from the student on how to improve their local communities, services, or life situations.

Figure 28.5 summarises what the collaborators involved by the students did in the U.P.P.s. Such activities concern the shared reflection on project design, its planning, and implementation. It is interesting to note that activities aimed at increasing the number of participants are well represented. In essence, it seems that the students were able to get help from their collaborators to 'widen the network' (Folgheraiter, 2004) and to involve additional people.

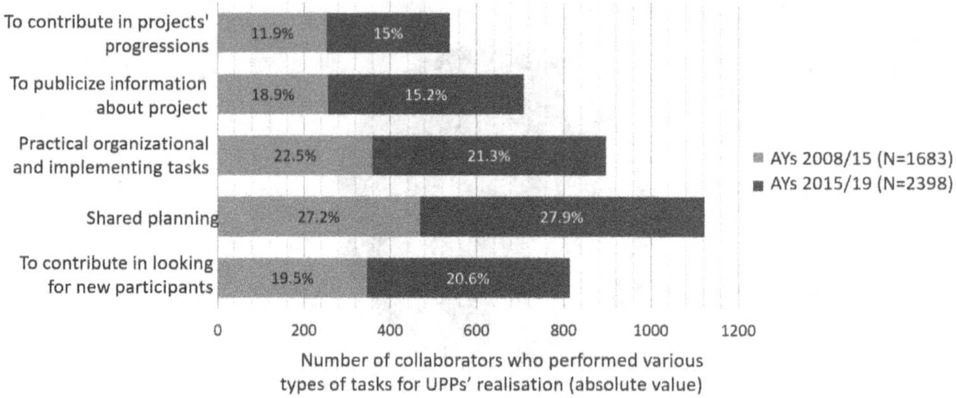

Figure 28.5 Tasks performed by people who collaborated with students for U.P.P.s' realisation, from 2008 to 2019 (absolute and percentage values from the two surveys).

A Brief Example: Maria's U.P.P. Goes On

After a public presentation of the project, the guiding group started to organise a fortnightly meeting with all the people who were receiving the food and, in return, were collaborating to its collection and distribution or who were making something useful for the local community. These aims and activities for the local community development were decided by all members of the guiding group, so the meetings became not only a time to organise the food distribution but also a discussion forum about the concrete problems of the neighbourhood and about the ways to cope with them. Maria played the role of the meetings' facilitator.

Many initiatives were carried out. Some people cleaned up a parish room for children to use for after-school activities, other people took care of the green, others played a role as keeper of the children's playground, others were involved in small services useful for the course of Italian language for foreigners, which was proposed by a local organisation. Moreover, people created small helping networks to support each other in individual situations of temporary difficulty, e.g., for health problems or to manage children. The parish made available some rooms and two vehicles.

The people involved became more and more numerous, more skilled in organising, and more trusting of each other. This allowed them to carry out all the activities independently, even when Maria, the volunteers, and the parish priest ware busy elsewhere.

The Fourth Step in the U.P.P. Process: Learning Evaluation

At the end of the U.P.P., each student individually prepares a written report of about 20 pages, documenting the project and what he/she has learnt from it. Students are required to connect the experience in the field with the curricula content of the courses.

Students' self-assessments and the assessments made by the university tutor are made on a specific form. This form is divided into four broad areas of expertise, with a list of some professional skills. For each skill, some indicators are listed that describe more directly observable learning goals (Figure 28.6). This form is like a 'guide' that helps students and tutors to link the activities experienced in the U.P.P. with the relevant professional skills expected of a social worker. The effectiveness (or not) with which these activities have been addressed in the U.P.P. suggests that the student has acquired (or not) the related professional skills.

SKILLS	ITEMS	WAS THE ITEM OBSERVED?				NOTES
		YES: NOT GOOD ENOUGHT	YES: PARTLY GOOD	YES: COMPLETLY GOOD	NO, IT ISN'T	*On what occasions was it possible to observe what this item describes?*
B.6 *Skills in working with informal helpers*	1. The student is able to identify informal helpers, such as carers, family members, neighbourhood, peers etc. who could collaborate in carrying out UPP's project.					
	2. The student knows about voluntary or self-help/mutual-aid initiatives relevant to the internship.					
	3. The student takes care of involving carers, family members, neighbours, peers, or volunteers in planning and carrying out the project.					
	4. The student is able to facilitate a small network of people (informal helpers and professionals) interested in developing a project, helping them to come together and keep in touch with each other.					

Figure 28.6 Example of some items in a section of the assessment form (Raineri, 2015: 369 (author's translation))

Connecting the performed activities with professional skills is a crucial operation in field education, particularly for U.P.P.s, for which there is no senior social worker already carrying out such activities and, therefore, testifying with his/her presence that these are examples of social work activities. Highlighting the connection between activities and skills helps the student to reflect on how these skills can also be transferred to contexts other than that of the U.P.P.: both to more traditional work fields and different innovative fields.

At the same time, focusing on professional skills helps to connect theory with practice, as it is a sort of 'intermediate conceptual bridge' between them. Performing a complex professional task requires a specific range of skills, and focusing on what these skills are solicits a reflection about social work theories for practice.

The evaluation is also an assessment of the opportunities offered to the student in that specific setting. In other words, it is not only an evaluation of the student but also of the practice placement. From this point of view, it is also an opportunity for the tutor to receive feedback about the individual student as well as useful information for planning future U.P.P.s.

A Brief Example: What Maria Learnt Thanks to Her U.P.P.

Maria's assessment form highlighted that her U.P.P. allowed her to improve her professional skills in many typical areas of social work. During the home visits with the parish priest, she experienced a range of interview skills. Thanks to the meetings, she learnt a range of groupwork skills. The whole project taught her a lot about community social work, about the facilitator's role, and about what it means, in practice, to work for the empowerment of people in poverty.

U.P.P.s' Overall Outcomes

A different level of assessment regards the overall impact of U.P.P.s 'outside the university environment': on the local communities, the organisations in which they are carried out, and the professional community. The two surveys collected some data about the social relevance of U.P.P.s, which can contribute to the university's third mission (Pinheiro et al., 2015; Inman & Schütze, 2010).

There are no available data related to the effective level of achievement of the project goals. However, the students' perception of this topic was recorded. According to 81% of the respondents ($N = 368$), the project goals had been completely (32%) or somewhat (49%) achieved, and about as many ($N = 366$) thought their project raised good (34%) or quite good (47%) participation. Around 9.5% made a negative evaluation. Further investigation on the students' points of view is needed to better understand these assessments.

The wide range of collaborators identified by the survey (see Figure 28.4) seems to indicate that U.P.P.s encouraged people (professionals and non-professionals) to get involved and take up responsibilities for improving their communities.

The fact that, in 45 cases (16% of respondents), funding was obtained from an organisation or foundation or through a public contract shows the interest generated by at least part of the U.P.P. projects. Furthermore, 214 projects could continue even at the end of the U.P.P. thanks to the availability of material resources (structures/premises, work material, promotional material, small professional services) provided by public or third-sector organisations or even private citizens. These data are to be considered relevant also because the search for funding and resources was never among the priority objectives of the projects, and the students had no specific training or guidance in this regard.

The U.P.P.s' potential enabling effect also seems to be confirmed by the continuation of the majority of the projects after the end of the students' mandatory hours in a practice placement, as shown in Figure 28.7.

In absolute terms, over the seven years examined by the first survey (Sala, 2016), the U.P.P.s that continued were 160, which is an encouraging result, considering that these projects were started by bachelor's degree students with minimal experience, driven, mainly, by training reasons. Furthermore, the data of the first survey (Sala, 2016) show that the 160 continued projects lasted over three years in 13.3% of cases, from one to three years in 13.9% of cases, from six months to one year in 26.5% of cases, and for less than six months in 22.9% of cases, while 23.5% of the respondents did not know whether their project had continued or not. It should be noted that these data could underestimate the effective duration of the U.P.P.s because they also include projects that had started less than six months before the survey.

In the second survey, 92 projects continued after the end of the students' mandatory hours in a practice placement, equal to 48% of the sample. However, this figure is less significant than the previous one because the data were collected close to the end of the curricular hours of part

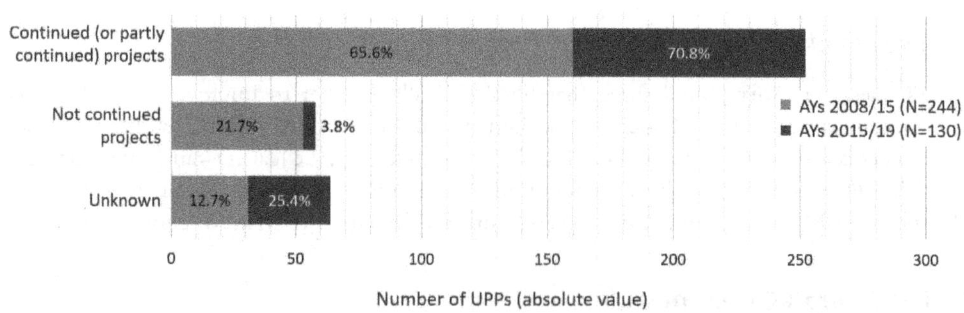

Figure 28.7 Projects that did or did not continue after the student's work was completed (absolute and percentage values from the two surveys).

of the U.P.P.s. Consequently, the students involved were not sure whether their projects would continue or not.

As shown in Figure 28.5, approximately 13% (A.V. = 538) of the total activities carried out by the collaborators involved by the students in their U.P.P.s were aimed at allowing the continuation of the projects even beyond the end of the curricular hours. In 58% of cases, the projects continued over time thanks to the people engaged in the U.P.P.s. In 27% of U.P.P.s, the continuation took place thanks to the former student, who remained as a volunteer (in 22% of the total of the continued projects) or as a paid social worker (in a small but very interesting 5.7% of the total of the continued projects; see below).

The third sector seems to be the most favourable setting for the continuation of the projects launched in the U.P.P.s, as it hosted 43.9% of the continued projects. It is also relevant to note the continuation of many projects that started as U.P.P.s without a formal agreement with the university (32.8%). It might have been expected that these projects, initiated by a student with little experience and lacking even the formal support of an organisation, had no chance of continuing. On the contrary, the data collected revealed the continuation of 83 initiatives of this kind. More data would be needed to explain these results. However, our hypothesis (according to the reflections of the practice teachers) is that students have been able to capture the interest of motivated collaborators and have given value to their experiential knowledge.

Finally, almost a fifth of U.P.P.s (19.2%, corresponding to 73 cases) had also an impact on the job opportunities that opened up for students once they graduated – or, in some cases, even earlier. Of the 73 students who declared that they had found employment thanks to the U.P.P., 8.2% were hired as social workers and 11.1% as youth or care workers or with other tasks connected to their U.P.P. projects.

Figure 28.8 shows that the percentage of U.P.P.s which turned into job opportunities in the 2008–2015 period is a little higher (21.6%) than the one in the 2016–2019 period (14.6%). This fact could be explained by the higher number of U.P.P.s just concluded at the time of the second survey, which, therefore, could turn into job placements for the students at a later time.

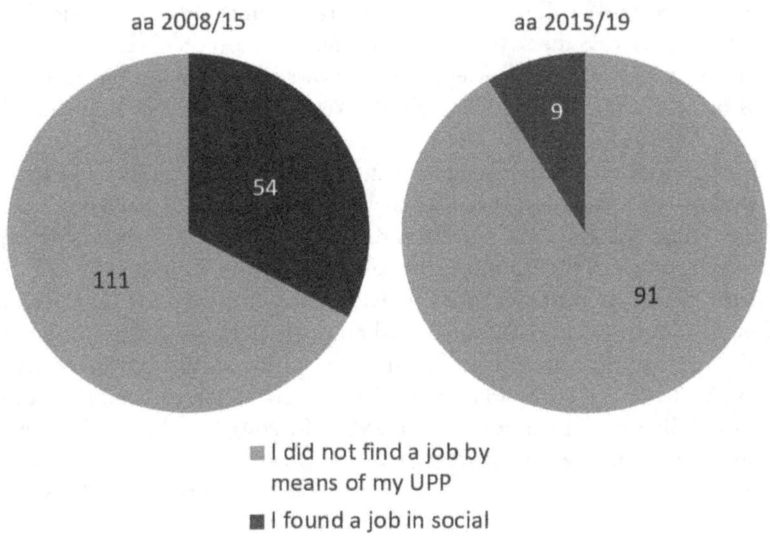

Figure 28.8 Job opportunities found by students thanks to their U.P.P.s: Absolute values (*N*) from the two surveys.

Of the 73 students who found work thanks to the U.P.P., 22% were hired to continue the work already started. The projects entrusted to them, therefore, correspond to that 5.7% of the total projects continued beyond the end of the formal placement. This figure is relevant and allows us to hypothesise that, without the creative work required by the U.P.P., these jobs would not have opened.

A Brief Example: A Paid Job for Maria

The local charity organisation – the one that had initially received the food offer from supermarkets – learned from the parish priest of the excellent work carried out thanks to Maria. So, it decided to hire her as a social worker to continue the project and to develop others similar to it. More than five years have passed, and the project is still in place.

U.P.P.s' Strengths and Critical Issues

With regard to student learning, the creative autonomy of U.P.P.s allows practising professional skills of critical importance (Nino et al., 2011; Poulin et al., 2006; Schelbe et al., 2014), such as knowing how to analyse individual or collective situations to devise new caring or promotional actions, different from usual standard processes or provisions. Without this skill, a social worker could become a bureaucrat, at risk for burnout. U.P.P.s train students to consider social work with a view to continuous improvement and innovation. U.P.P.s teach to avoid settling into routines, to exercise creativity, and to seek alliances for developing new ideas (Billingham & Roberts, 2002).

In addition, the creative discretion required by U.P.P.s is a way for students' empowerment (Williams et al., 2002; Anderson, 2006): the student is not someone who 'does not know anything', and who is there just to 'observe and reproduce' the work of others. He/she is someone who is asked to examine reality, be critical, and engage in planning and acting, with the confidence that his/her planning and acting can have a positive outcome. A parallelism often arises between the attitude adopted toward us during our social work training and the attitude that later we will adopt toward our service users. If students are treated too protectively, they will tend to hyper-protect in turn. If students experience an empowerment relationship in their practice placement, it is more likely that they will apply the same kind of relationship toward the people they will help.

The data presented in the previous section suggest that one of the advantages of U.P.P.s is that students learn to explore and create new social work settings (Jones, 2011). Knowing how to explore new avenues is a vital skill given the current turbulence in the public welfare system, which is causing significant changes in the labour market of social care professions.

The new job opportunities opened thanks to the U.P.P.s shows that they can be a useful way to promote professional social work. U.P.P.s are based on the hypothesis that professional social work can both find new contexts, in addition to those currently consolidated (Beverley & Worsley, 2007; Bellinger, 2010a, 2010b; Scholar et al., 2014; McLaughlin et al., 2014), and find new ways to use its skills even in traditional contexts. Moreover, for better development of professional social work in the future, new graduates must start work equipped to search for new ideas and not to settle for what they find in the field, as if they could not do it differently.

Alongside these strengths, U.P.P.s also show some critical issues that need to be addressed. According to the experience of the practice teachers who guide the U.P.P.s at our university, the difficulty felt by most students is the initial anxiety caused by having to 'create' a real project without having a precise example to reproduce and without having instructions to follow that 'guarantee' a successful outcome. The above is an experience that social workers have to face very often in their practice, but the majority of students face it for the first time when they are asked to start a U.P.P. It may happen that some students – who find the 'looking and repeating' approach, typical of the traditional placement, much more reassuring – complain of not feeling guided enough. They may also feel uncomfortable in having to develop a project that will not only depend on them but also on the people from the local community that they have to identify and involve. These feelings of anxiety and discomfort are usually overcome as the project takes shape and students realise that they can do it.

Another critical issue is time. Even in traditional practice placements, students' work schedules need to be adapted to the actual work progress. However, in a conventional field practicum, the students' tasks are more predictable. In U.P.P.s, it is not so, precisely because U.P.P.s take students off the beaten path. Thus, it may be difficult to reconcile the training schedule (lessons, exams, academic year deadlines) with the schedules of informal collaborators, volunteers, services' users and carers, and the local communities involved in the projects. In some cases, this problem can be addressed by differentiating the moment of the formal end of the U.P.P. (with the university exam) from the moment in which the student disengages from the project. However, this strategy is not always feasible.

A final critical point of our experience is the puzzled look that the professional social work community has sometimes given to U.P.P.s. It is perhaps inevitable for untrodden paths to be considered with caution and suspicion, as if they were outside the boundaries of 'real' social work. But, on the other hand, professional social work needs to explore new territories to develop, and such a task is mainly undertaken by younger generations in all societies and cultures. So, it is important to support new social workers and understand that they can provide good practices even in unusual contexts, as U.P.P.s propose (Scholar et al., 2014).

Limits

The description proposed in this chapter was based only in part on a systematic collection of data. Some of the information was collected from the authors' direct experience and the informal narratives by their colleagues engaged in guiding the U.P.P.s at U.C.S.C. Qualitative data collected and analysed more rigorously would be necessary for a description less influenced by the authors' point of view.

The quantitative data offer only a first picture of the U.P.P.s, which should be expanded by gathering the opinion of the different subjects involved: for example, the people of the local communities, users, carers, and professionals.

Conclusions

Although further studies are needed to evaluate the educational and social impact of U.P.P.s, the experiences that have been carried out at U.C.S.C. for more than a decade suggest that it is an effective training method to develop students' creativity and professional discretion in a shared project. In U.P.P.s, students *ask for help* from service users and carers, active citizens, and local communities, inviting them to collaborate in projects useful both for the students' training and for a greater well-being of the same users and citizens. In this way, U.P.P.s open new opportunities for social work practices. New opportunities in terms of new jobs in contexts for which social work was not performed before and new ways of developing social help.

Note

1 The European Credit Transfer and Accumulation System (E.C.T.S.) is a tool of the European Higher Education Area for helping students to move between countries and to have their academic qualifications and study periods abroad recognised. For more information visit https://ec.europa.eu/education/resources-and-tools/european-credit-transfer-and-accumulation-system-ects_en.

References

Allegri, E. (2015). *Il servizio sociale di comunità*. Roma: Carocci.

Anderson, D. K. (2006). Mucking through the swamp: Changing the pedagogy of a social welfare policy course. *Journal of Teaching in Social Work, 26*(1–2), 1–17. https://doi.org/10.1300/J067v26n01_01

Begun, A. L., Berger, L. K., Otto-Salaj, L. L., & Rose, S. J. (2010). Developing effective social work university—Community research collaborations. *Social Work, 55*(1), 54–62. https://doi.org/10.1093/sw/55.1.54

Bellinger, A. (2010a). Studying the landscape: Practice learning for social work reconsidered. *Social Work Education, 29*(6), 599–615. https://doi.org/10.1093/sw/55.1.54

Bellinger, A. (2010b). Talking about (re)generation: Practice learning as a site of renewal for social work. *British Journal of Social Work, 40*(8), 2450–2466. https://doi.org/10.1093/bjsw/bcq072

Beverley, A., & Worsley, A. (2007). *Learning and Teaching in Social Work Practice*. New York: Macmillan International Higher Education.

Billingham, J., & Roberts, S. (2002). Creative practice learning: Exploring opportunities to fulfil students' requirements. *Practice, 14*(4), 29–41. https://doi.org/10.1080/09503150208411540

Bogo, M., & Vayda, E. (1998). *The Practice of Field Education in Social Work*. Toronto: University of Toronto Press.

Bortoli, B. (2013). *I giganti del lavoro sociale. Grandi donne (e grandi uomini) nella storia del welfare 1526–1939* (2nd ed.) Trento: Erickson.

Butin, D. W. (2010). *Service Learning in Theory and Practice: The Future of Community Engagement in Higher Education*. New York: Palgrave MacMillan.

Byers, L. G., & Gray, K. (2012). The meaning of service learning in an MSW course. *Journal of Teaching in Social Work, 32*(3), 257–267. https://doi.org/10.1080/08841233.2012.688095

Campbell, E. M. (2012). Implementing service learning into a graduate social work course: A step-by-step guide. *Journal of Teaching in Social Work, 32*(3), 300–313. https://doi.org/10.1080/08841233.2012.688935

Caspi, J., & Reid, W. J. (2002). *Educational Supervision in Social Work: A Task-Centered Model for Field Instruction and Staff Development*. New York: Columbia University Press.

Clapton, G., & Cree, V. E. (2004). *Integration of Learning for Practice: A Literature Review*. Dundee: Scottish Institute for Excellence in Social Work Education.

Cola, P. (2015). Tirocinio sperimentale e supervisione delegata. In: M. Tognetti Bordogna (Ed.), *Il tirocinio come pratica situata. Le esperienze dei Corsi di laurea in Servizio Sociale* (pp. 176–184). Milano: FrancoAngeli.

Deans, T. (1999). Service-learning in two keys: Paulo Freire's critical pedagogy in relation to John Dewey's pragmatism. *Michigan Journal of Community Service Learning, 6*, 15–29.

Dellavalle, M. (2011). *Il tirocinio nella formazione al servizio sociale*. Roma: Carocci.

Dick, E., Headrick, D., & Scott, M. (2002). Practice learning for professional skills: A literature review: A report commissioned by the Scottish Executive. *Scottish Executive*. Retrieved from: https://www.scotland.gov.uk/Resource/Doc/1135/0010021.doc. Accessed November 2014.

Doel, M. (2010). *Social Work Placements: A Traveller's Guide*. London: Routledge.

Ericson, C. B. (2011). Pura Vida with a purpose: Energizing engagement with human rights through service-learning. *Advances in Social Work, 12*(1), 63–78. https://doi.org/10.18060/671

Fawcett, B., Fillingham, J., & Ward, N. (2017). *Service User and Carer Involvement in Health and Social Care: A Retrospective and Prospective Analysis*. London: Palgrave Macmillan.

Fiorin, I. (2016). *Oltre l'aula. La proposta pedagogica del Service Learning*. Milano: Mondadori Education.

Folgheraiter, F. (2004). *Relational Social Work: Toward Networking and Societal Practices*. London: Jessica Kingsley.

Folgheraiter, F. (2017). The sociological and humanistic roots of relational social work. *Relational Social Work, 1*(1), 4–11. https://doi.org/10.14605/rsw111601

Folgheraiter, F., & Raineri, M. L. (2017). The principles and key ideas of relational social work. *Relational Social Work, 1*(1), 12–18. https://doi.org/10.14605/rsw111602

Gerstenblatt, P., & Gilbert, D.J. (2014). Framing service learning in social work: An interdisciplinary elective course embedded within a university–community partnership. *Social Work Education, 33*(8), 1037–1053. https://doi.org/10.1080/02615479.2014.935731
Goldstein, H. (2001). *Experiential Learning: A Foundation for Social Work Education and Practice.* Alexandria: C.S.W.E.
Gui, L. (2009). Tirocinio tra mandato, competenze sul campo e nuova formazione dell'assistente sociale. In: A. Campanini (Ed.), *Scenari di welfare e formazione al servizio sociale in un'europa che cambia* (pp. 235–269). Milano: Unicopli.
Harkavy, I. (2004). Service-learning and the development of democratic universities, democratic schools and democratic good societies in the 21st century. In: M. Welch, S. H. Billig (Eds), *New Perspectives in Service Learning: Research to Advance the Field* (pp. 3–22). Greenwich: Information Age.
Hatcher, J. A., & Bringle, R. G. (1997). Reflection: Bridging the gap between service and learning. *College Teaching, 45*(4), 153–158.
Hek, R. (2012). Is it possible to develop and sustain non-traditional placements? An evaluation of the development of practice learning opportunities in partnership with the police and probation services in the West Midlands. *Social Work Education, 31*(4), 512–529. https://doi.org/10.1080/02615479.2011.570328
Inman, P., & Schütze, H. G. (Eds) (2010). *The Community Engagement and Service Mission of Universities.* Leicester: NIACE.
Jones, S. H. (2011). Life is experienced until we die: Effects of service-learning on gerontology competencies and attitudes toward aging. *Advances in Social Work, 12*(1), 94–112. https://doi.org/10.18060/672
Lemieux, C. M., & Allen, P. D. (2007). Service learning in social work education: The state of knowledge, pedagogical practicalities, and practice conundrums. *Journal of Social Work Education, 43*(2), 309–326. https://doi.org/10.5175/JSWE.2007.200500548
Lorenz, W. (1994). *Social Work in a Changing Europe.* London: Routledge.
Luppi, M. (Eds) (2019). *Innovare il tirocinio. La formazione di base degli assistenti sociali di fronte a nuovi bisogni e a nuove politiche.* Retrieved from: https://www.secondowelfare.it/edt/file/2WEL_WP_3_2019_Luppi.pdf. Accessed April 2020.
Maccio, E. M. (2011). Graduate social work students' attitudes toward service-learning. *Journal of Teaching in Social Work, 31*(2), 163–177. https://doi.org/10.1080/08841233.2011.560539
McLaughlin, H., Scholar, H., McCaughan, S., & Coleman, A. (2014). Are non-traditional social work placements second-best learning opportunities for social work qualifying students? *British Journal of Social Work, 45*(5), 1469–1488. https://doi.org/10.1093/bjsw/bcu021
Nadel, M., Majewski, V., & Sullivan-Cosetti, M. (Eds) (2007). *Social Work and Service Learning: Partnerships for Social Justice.* Lanham: Rowman & Littlefield.
Nino, M., Cuevas, M., & Loya, M. (2011). Transformational effects of service-learning in a university developed community-based agency. *Advances in Social Work, 12*(1), 33–48. https://doi.org/10.18060/590
Parker, J., Hillison, K., & Wilson, L. (2003). SWiSP: The social work students in schools project. *Practice, 15*(4), 69–87. https://doi.org/10.1080/09503150308416935
Petracchi, H. E., Weaver, A., Schelbe, L., & Song, H. A. (2016). Service learning in baccalaureate social work education: Results of a national survey of accredited programs. *Journal of Social Work Education, 52*(3), 325–336. https://doi.org/10.1080/10437797.2016.1174628
Pinheiro, R., Langa, P. V., & Pausits, A. (2015). The institutionalization of universities' third mission: Introduction to the special issue. *European Journal of Higher Education, 5*(3), 227–232. https://doi.org/10.1080/21568235.2015.1044551
Poulin, J., Silver, P., & Kauffman, S. (2006). Field notes: Serving the community and training social workers: Service outputs and student outcomes. *Journal of Social Work Education, 42*(1), 171–184. https://doi.org/10.5175/JSWE.2006.200400486
Raineri, M. L. (2015). *Tirocini e stage di servizio sociale. Manuale per studenti e supervisori.* Trento: Erickson.
Sala, M. (2016). *Lo Stage Sperimentale Nella Social Work Education. Una Ricerca Esplorativa Sul Modello dell'Università Cattolica del Sacro Cuore* (Unpublished doctoral dissertation). Milan: U.C.S.C.
Schelbe, L., Petracchi, H. E., & Weaver, A. (2014). Benefits and challenges of service-learning in baccalaureate social work programs. *Journal of Teaching in Social Work, 34*(5), 480–495. https://doi.org/10.1080/08841233.2014.954689
Scholar, H., McCaughan, S., McLaughlin, H., & Coleman, A. (2012). 'Why is this not social work?' The contribution of 'non-traditional' placements in preparing social work students for practice. *Social Work Education, 31*(7), 932–950. https://doi.org/10.1080/02615479.2011.608123

Scholar, H., McLaughlin, H., McCaughan, S., & Coleman, A. (2014). Learning to be a social worker in a non-traditional placement: Critical reflections on social work, professional identity and social work education in England. *Social Work Education, 33*(8), 998–1016. https://doi.org/10.1080/02615479.2014.926320

Shardlow, S., & Doel, M. (2006). *Practice Learning and Teaching* (2nd ed.) Basingstoke: Palgrave.

Skills for Care. (2009). *How New Projects and Initiatives in Social Work Practice Learning Successfully Mature, Leeds*. Retrieved from: https://www.skillsforcare.org.uk. Accessed November 2014.

Warren, J. (2007). *Service User and Carer Participation in Social Work*. London: Sage.

Wayne, J., Bogo, M., & Raskin, M. (2010). Field education as the signature pedagogy of social work education. *Journal of Social Work Education, 46*(3), 327–339. https://doi.org/10.5175/JSWE.2010.200900043

Williams, N. R., King, M., & Koob, J. J. (2002). Social work students go to camp: The effects of service learning on perceived self-efficacy. *Journal of Teaching in Social Work, 22*(3–4), 55–70. https://doi.org/10.1300/J067v22n03_05

Wilson, G., O'Connor, E., Walsh, T., & Kirby, M. (2009). Reflections on practice learning in Northern Ireland and the Republic of Ireland: Lessons from student experiences. *Social Work Education, 28*(6), 631–645. https://doi.org/10.1080/02615470903027348

29

Construction and Evaluation of Knowledge in Social Work from the Evidence of Professional Internships in Spain

Enrique Pastor Seller

The creation of the European Higher Education Area (henceforth E.H.E.A.) has meant the restructuring of official university undergraduate, graduate, and doctoral degrees based on the learning of skills that society calls for in order to pursue a profession (Tuning Project 2009; Taylor, Catherine, & Fleming 2010; O.C.D.E. 2012; Escudero, Aparicio, Grosso de la Vega, & Rodríguez 2019; Álvarez 2019) as well as a focus on job placement (Comisión Europa 2011). This is a new type of higher education in which students are at the fore of their progress toward assimilating content and concepts as well as the acquisition of skills, abilities, and aptitudes that prepare them for future professional practice. These skills facilitate the development of a comprehensive education in all its dimensions—knowledge, know-how, and knowing how to be—and, at the same time, they promote a sustainable and responsible university system (Álvarez & Arreguit 2019).

The evolution toward this skills-based approach (also called the learning experience approach) underscores significant, collaborative-cooperative learning processes (Pegalajar 2018) which are continuous and transformative, based on a multiplicity of resources and activities open to interaction with the environment and the co-responsibility of all participants (Council for Social Work Education 2015; Marion 2018; International Association of Schools of Social Work 2019; Zayas et al. 2019). Teachers no longer act as mere transferrers of knowledge but, rather, as guides who encourage and promote learning and the acquisition and development of skills. For their part, students play a central role as active participants in discovering, understanding, creating, and developing skills and abilities. This approach necessarily requires changes to higher education. Specifically, pedagogical and organisation strategies must be revised, active methodologies must be advanced, innovation in learning processes must be promoted, and a greater nexus between institutions and professional service providers must be created. This means lifelong learning (in line with the European Parliament and European Council's Recommendations from December 18th, 2006) related to professional skills (Manninen & Hobrough 2000, Instituto Nacional de Administración Pública 2014; Tynjälä et al. 2006; O.C.D.E. 2017; Kinni 2020). In this context, internships enable students to train in a context similar to what they will encounter in the future, integrating real reference frameworks to develop and acquire professional skills (Egido

DOI: 10.4324/9781032164946-34

2017; Sierra et al. 2017; Ferrández et al. 2019; Latorre & Blanco 2011). This learning model fosters the creation of broad networks and involved communities through active and collaborative methodologies highlighting the relevance of internships.

The Spanish higher education system in general, and university degrees in social work in particular, have been no exception to this new dynamic process of change. Starting in 2007, the undergraduate degree in social work—as was the case with all undergraduate degrees—was adapted to the E.H.E.A., and in the 2008–9 academic year, the process for implementing new social work curricula at Spanish universities began. The undergraduate degree in social work was lengthened from three years to four, and expanded from a total of 180 to 240 credits from the European Credit Transfer and Accumulation System (E.C.T.S.). The entity responsible for accreditation, monitoring, assessment, and certification of university degrees is the National Agency for Quality Assessment and Accreditation of Spain (henceforth A.N.E.C.A.), attached to the Ministry of Universities. To fulfil this responsibility, three main programmes are used:

- Verification—assesses degree curricula in accordance with the E.H.E.A.;
- Accreditation—assesses official university degrees for the renewal of their accreditation. This assessment is carried out cyclically and has a twofold objective—verify whether the degree is being implemented according to the objectives established in its initial project memo and verify whether the results are adequate and contribute to students' attainment and the achievement of the stated objectives. A favourable or unfavourable report is issued to support or deny the renewal of accreditation.
- Monitoring—provides universities with external evaluation on how they are implementing their official degrees with the goal of offering an additional resource for improving their academic offering.

This new framework has helped to provide access to graduate and doctoral programmes, to standardise studies across degree offerings, and to equalise salaries and professional recognition.

One of the most substantial changes is that of learning professional skills through an increase in internship training programmes carried out at social institutions. The intention of these internships is to offer real-life situations to promote skills and abilities related to professional practice as a social worker. Specifically, the goal is to promote the correct usage and application of social work methods, procedures and techniques while training to design, diagnose, programme, implement, coordinate, supervise, and evaluate social centres, services, and policies. Ultimately, it is an education that provides students with new methods to acquire professional skills and teachers with new teaching challenges in the classroom and immediate social environment.

Skills learning is addressed from a holistic and integrative (Booth, McLean & Walker 2009) approach (Fook 2002; Barber 2012; Niehaus et al. 2017), guiding what future professionals will have to know, know how to do, and know how to be to maximise effectiveness and efficiency in their actions as professionals. Päivi Tynjälä, who developed the integrative pedagogy model, states that theory and practice are not separate (Tynjälä et al. 2011, p. 305) and that the theories should be considered in the light of practical experiences and vice versa (Tynjälä et al. 2016, p. 370). Instead of separating theory from practice, knowledge can be split up into different categories (Tynjälä et al. 2011, p. 305). Professional experience requires the 'integration of different types of knowledge and interaction between theory and practice' (Tynjälä 2008, p. 131). As such, the integrative pedagogy model illustrates and emphasises the importance of learning that takes place in different educational and work settings throughout the overall experience (Hood & Littlejohn 2017, p. 1586).

The lessons learned and synergies from internships for degrees in social work were analysed in this frame of reference. The skills for undergraduate degrees in social work, as indicated in the *White Paper on Undergraduate Degrees in Social Work* (A.N.E.C.A. 2004, pp. 189–192) are related to the following skills: working and jointly assessing the needs and circumstances of individuals, families, groups, organisations, and communities; planning, implementing, reviewing, and evaluating the practice of social work with individuals, families, groups, organisations, communities, and other professionals; encouraging individuals to express their needs, points of view, and circumstances; acting to resolve situations of risk for individuals, as well as for their themselves and their colleagues; and managing and being responsible for the practice of social work itself within the organisation, with supervision and support.

Internships result in students having more significant contact with professional work experience during their academic training. Internships are clearly important, as they are considered one of the degree's quality process criteria and indicators; a specific programme for internships is required and must include teaching content as well as the necessary conditions for professionals from collaborating entities to take part in internships (A.N.E.C.A. 2004; Conferencia de Decanos/as y Directores/as de Trabajo Social de las Universidades Españolas, henceforth C.D.T.S., 2007). They provide for the development of professional skills and abilities as well as methodological quality in analysis, intervention, and assessment with the necessary ethical framework that professional activity requires. However, to do so requires adequate professional supervision and tutelage on the part of academic and collaborating entities. The various International Social Work Conventions held in Spain (I Murcia, 2014[1]; II La Rioja, 2016[2]; and III Deusto, 2018[3]) and their related publications (Pastor-Seller 2014; Carbonero et al. 2016; Sobremonte & Rodríguez 2019) and studies (Ovejas et al. 2012; C.D.T.S. 2013; Torralba & Pastor-Seller 2019; Aguilar et al. 2020; Hidalgo 2020; Pérez & Martínez 2020) demonstrate that internships are a transversal element in the training process for social work degrees at every Spanish university and a nexus for professional activity and skills transfer.

Social work's consideration as a core subject has implied complex internal and external processes of design, organisation, planning, coordination, supervision, and tutelage at universities because of its dual nature—academic and institutional. In these strategic planning processes, the direct or indirect participation of different actors, such as students, professors, administrative staff, alumni, professionals, the university, the public administration, businesses, social entities, and professional associations stands out. It involves building learning environments that integrate different types of knowledge, all of which are necessary for professional practice. Four basic skills stand out from the professional experience of internships: theoretical, practical, self-regulatory, and sociocultural (Tynjälä et al. 2016, p. 370). In this particular case, theoretical knowledge about social work casework elaborated in the classroom is combined with practical knowledge when students see their supervisors and other professionals solving social work problems in their own professional practice and developing their own practical skills. In addition to problem-solving skills, a mediation process between theoretical and practical knowledge takes place in the opposite direction: practical problems encountered in day-to-day professional practice are conceptualised. In these processes, self-regulation skills and the ability for reflection are also necessary (Tynjälä et al. 2016, p. 370). These skills help to integrate theoretical and practical knowledge at the same time that students reflect on their own actions, make sense of what they have achieved, apply knowledge (Hood & Littlejohn 2017, pp. 1586–1587), and recognise their strengths and weaknesses.

The objective of this study is to understand the structure and offering of internships for undergraduate degrees in social work at Spanish universities as well as the skills students acquire during their studies, which is essential to guarantee a quality education for future professionals.

Methods

Study Objectives and Scope

This study analyses the educational offering of internships for undergraduate degrees in social work at Spanish universities, the skills and knowledge acquired in connection with social entities, and the evidence that enables monitoring and assessment of those skills. From this analysis, the following objectives were established:

- Identify the universities and educational institutions that offer undergraduate degrees in social work in Spain;
- Typify the courses related to internships;
- Analyse, relate, and classify internship skills and produce typologies related to professional skills;
- Describe the objectives, skills, and evidence that enable monitoring and assessment of the applied learning.

The parameters of the study were: course offerings; implementation, monitoring, modification, and accreditation processes; organisation and structure; course length and integration in the curriculum; academic organisation; monitoring and professional areas; skills analysis and description of skills; and monitoring and assessment evidence.

Scope and Data Sources

This chapter analyses internship offerings at Spanish universities that have undergraduate programmes in social work, regardless of whether they are public or private, affiliated to A.N.E.C.A. or not. The data was gathered from the following public, accredited, trustworthy sources: The Ministry of Universities (2020), A.N.E.C.A. (2020), the Committee of Social Work Faculty Deans and School Directors of Spanish Universities, the Committee of Spanish University Chancellors (C.R.U.E.), and the official websites of each of the universities that were analysed. According to the latest *Spanish Universities in Figures Report* (Universidad Española en Cifras) from 2019, the Spanish university system is comprised of a total of 82 universities, 50 of which are public (47 on-site, one online, and two special universities: Universidad Internacional Menéndez Pelayo (U.I.M.P.) and Universidad Internacional de Andalucia (U.I.A.) and 32 are private (27 on-site and five online) (Hernández & Pérez 2019, p. 16).

Investigation Procedure and Instruments and Techniques for Data Collection and Analysis

After the range of universities offering undergraduate degrees in social work was identified (37), the teaching guides from the 2019–20 school year were used to identify and analyse the courses defined as or associated with the category 'internship' or 'practicum' (units of analysis). In other words, those courses related to internships in social institutions and entities were selected (85 courses). The methodological decision to use the teaching guide for the skills and knowledge analysis is based on the following criteria:

1 Uniformity and transparency—they are public academic records issued by the governing bodies of the set of universities;

2 Descriptive—they present the content, skills, and knowledge of each course; and
3 Coherent—they identify the courses character and integration in curricula.

In this way, the teaching guide represents a logical opportunity for the present study. Two regulatory, academic, and professional reference documents on higher education in social work in Spain were used to systematise and analyse the skills identified. The first was *The White Paper on Undergraduate Degrees in Social Work* (A.N.E.C.A. 2004), and the second was the set of criteria for designing curricula for undergraduate programmes in Social Work (C.D.T.S. 2007).

Data logging was based on an ad hoc systematic data collection protocol. It was validated in a trial run and applied after verifying coherence and validity with the study's objectives.

The data analysis technique was based on content systematisation and analysis carried out on the 572 skills identified in the teaching guides of 85 courses, which, after analysing for similarities, enabled the construction of a typology of 42 integrating skills from the overall set.

Finally, the learning objectives were presented together with the skills and evidence that enable adequate monitoring, supervision, and assessment of the professional skills used uniformly by both the supervisor from the social entity and the advisor; their design and development are known to the student to promote transparency and coherence in the educational process and the students own self-assessment.

Results

Offering of Undergraduate Degrees in Social Work in Spain

Of the 82 Spanish universities that currently exist, 37 (45.13%) offered an undergraduate degree in social work (2019–20 academic year), 29 (78.4%) of which are public, and eight (21.6%) of which are private and/or affiliated. Analysis of the data from the Registry of Universities, Centers and Degrees (R.U.C.T.) of the Ministry of Universities (2020), A.N.E.C.A. (2020), and official websites of Spanish universities shows that there are 38 universities (public and private) and their respective management centres where an undergraduate degree in social work is taught, one of which did not offer the degree in the 2019–20 academic year.

Implementation, Monitoring, Modification, and Accreditation Processes for Undergraduate Degrees in Social Work

From the data analysed in this study, we identified the implementation of an undergraduate degree in social work at the University of Saragossa and the University Pontificia Comillas in Madrid in 2008. From 2009–2011, 35 universities (92%) put a programme in place—the University Rey Juan Carlos was the last to do so in 2015–16. These universities implemented their undergraduate programmes after they were assessed and verified. As shown in Table 29.1, 30 universities (80.1%) were verified between 2009 and 2010 (15 each year), five were verified in 2008, one in 2011, and one in 2015.

There are four universities whose degree programmes have been approved/verified by A.N.E.C.A. but were not offered in the 2019–20 academic year.

We found that 36 universities have renewed their accreditation, and one is pending approval because of its recent implementation. As shown in Table 29.2, of the 36 universities mandated to renew their accreditation, 30 have done so: five in 2015, 19 in 2016, 11 in 2017, and one in 2018. Modifications and assessments preceded these renewals. Specifically, 22 (61%) of the universities carried out one or more substantial modifications to their degrees in this process, as follows: nine

Table 29.1 Social Work Undergraduate Degrees Verified with a Favourable Assessment

2008	5 (13.5%)
2009	15 (40.5%)
2010	15 (40.5%)
2011	1 (2.7%)
2015	1 (2.7%)
Total	37 (100 %)

Source: Prepared by the authors based on the Ministry of Universities (2020), A.N.E.C.A. (2020) and official university websites (Anexo1)

Table 29.2 Modifications to Social Work Undergraduate Degrees

2015	5 (13.5%)
2016	19 (51.4%)
2017	11 (29.7%)
2018	1 (2.7%)
Pending	1 (2.7%)
Total	37 (100 %)

Source: Prepared by the authors based on the Ministry of Universities (2020), A.N.E.C.A. (2020) and official university websites

universities (one modification), eight universities (two modifications), three universities (three modifications), and two universities (four modifications). In summary, there were substantial variations in the implementation process prior to the renewal of accreditations, which indicates the dynamic nature of these studies and the desire to adapt them to social realities.

Structure and Organisation of Internship Courses in Social Entities

After analysing the course offerings from the teaching guides for the undergraduate degree in social work at the different universities, we found that all 37 universities (100%) offer a course tied to an internship, although under different names. Some use generic names ('practicum', 'internship', 'placement', 'work experience'), some allude to advancement in levels of knowledge (professional internships/practicum I, II, III), while others employ specific terminology related to their methodological process (research work placement, internship in social work intervention, internship in social diagnosis, internship in social work interventions, internship in analysing reality, internship in observation and knowledge of reality, experimental internship, internship in institutional training, etc.), and still others combine several categories (general internship I, specialty internship II, practicum III: contexts in social intervention, practicum IV: social analysis of a territory, practicumV: institutional and supervisory framework, and practicum VI: internship in social action and monitoring, etc.)

Course Integration in the Curriculum

As shown in Table 29.3, the majority of the internship courses are taught in the fourth year of studies; overall, 18 universities (48.7%) chose the fourth year, followed by 15 universities (40.5%)

Table 29.3 Course Integration in the Curriculum

Year of study when the courses take place	*Universities*
Integrated in all years of study	1 (2.7%)
2, 3, and 4	2 (5.4%)
2 and 4	1 (2.7%)
4	18 (48.7%)
3 and 4	15 (40.5%)
Total	37 (100.0%)

Source: Prepared by the authors from the results of the study.

Table 29.4 Length of the Internship Courses

Total E.C.T.S. credits for internship courses	*Universities*
12–17	2 (5.4%)
18–23	12 (32.4%)
24–29	2 (5.4%)
30–35	9 (24.3%)
36–40	5 (13.5%)
More than 40	7 (18.9%)
Total	37 (100.0%)

Source: Prepared by the authors from the results of the study.

that spread them over the third and fourth years, while two universities did so over three years, and finally two universities did so in the second and fourth years of studies. Thus, 33 universities (89.2%) placed these courses in the second half of the degree, and all of them offer courses in the fourth year of studies.

Length of the Courses (E.C.T.S.)

The length of courses varied between 12 and 44 E.C.T.S. As shown in Table 29.4 below, the majority of the courses were worth between 18–23 credits: (12 courses, 32.4%), followed by those with between 30–35 credits (nine courses, 24.3%), then those with more than 40 credits (7 courses, 18.9%), followed by those with between 36–40 credits (five courses, 13.5%), and finally those with between 12–17 and 15–29 credits, with two courses each.

Organisation, Monitoring, and Professional Areas

Internships are planned and carried out in a curricular programme through teaching guides that define the competencies, learning outcomes, content, abilities, skills and aptitudes, methodology, evaluation system, and educational supervisory processes. In this last respect, progressive monitoring, tutelage, and assessment of the internship through shared supervision between the professional from the social entity and the student's advisor was found to be important. The functions of both are complementary and direct coordination ensures adequate, continuous, and comprehensive monitoring and assessment. This requires an organisational structure based on the participation of all the parties and institutions involved. Institutional collaboration was noted on the part of the universities (practical teaching guides, specific training, management of agreements with entities, support for professors and social entities that have to commute, recognition for professionals in internship supervisory roles and collaborating entities) as well as the collaborating social entities (agreements, job openings, making professionals available to supervise students). This structure necessitates the presence of a vice-chancellor of internships, or a similar position, and a participating body, such as an internship committee, for the actors involved – professionals, teachers, and students. Internships are organised using a process that starts by recruiting interested centres and professionals and later assigning the students' placements according to their preferences. Subsequently, the students start their internships at the centre they were assigned and create an individual internship project as a signed commitment between the student, the professional, and the academic advisor. During the internship, active supervision ensures assistance for all the parties involved through seminars, individual and group monitoring sessions, and meetings with supervisors. Finally, internships are evaluated, taking into account the processes, results, lessons learned, and the overall impact by way of an assessment document that the professionals and the advisor share and the student knows about.

The present study has found that students are undertaking internships in different increasingly complex areas of professional activity in social work. Thus, in addition to the traditional options (social and health services), other alternatives of recent relevance have come to the fore, such as mediation, social appraisal, prisons, businesses, social exclusion, dependence, and housing, among others, which is in line with social changes (Pastor-Seller, Verde & Lima 2019).

Skills Analysis

A total of 572 specific skills, objectives, or differentiated learning outcomes were identified from the teaching guides of the 85 courses at the 37 universities that offer specific internship courses. After a content analysis, they were grouped according to semantic coincidence, content and professional ties using *The White Paper on Undergraduate Degrees in Social Work* (A.N.E.C.A. 2004) and the *Set of Criteria for Designing Curricula for Undergraduate Programs in Social Work* (C.D.T.S. 2007). A total of 42 convergent skills were identified from the content analysis and later grouped into skills, capacities, abilities, and attitudes.

General skills were classified into the following 18 groups according to their characteristics:

- create and support professional relationships, identifying problems, difficulties, and conflicts with a view to identifying the most appropriate means to intervene at an individual, family, group, and community level;
- correctly use social work methods, models, and techniques in the different areas of intervention;
- encourage and support the development of community organising networks, groups, and dynamics;
- create, organise, and manage social welfare services and entities, monitoring their effectiveness and ensuring their quality;
- evaluate needs and possible options to guide an intervention strategy;
- individual, family, group, organisational, and community interventions to help actors make well-informed decisions about their needs, circumstances, risks, preferable options, and resources;

- encourage individuals' growth, development, and independence by identifying opportunities to create groups, using group programme planning and dynamics for individual growth and strengthening interpersonal skills;
- design, implement, and assess policies, plans, research projects, and social interventions with the participation of the individuals concerned and the parties involved;
- prepare and participate in decision-making meetings with a view to defending the individuals, groups, organisations, and communities' best interests;
- respond to crisis and emergency situations by assessing their urgency while planning and performing actions to deal with these situations and reviewing the results of said actions;
- manage and take responsibility for one's own work by prioritising, meeting professional obligations, and assessing the effectiveness of the work programme itself;
- contribute to the management of resources and services by collaborating in the procedures involved in obtaining them while supervising their efficiency and ensuring their quality;
- systematise information obtained from professional practice and promote best practices for innovative professional strategies that advance the disciplined development of social work while strengthening the exchange and transmission of acquired knowledge;
- manage, present, and share social assessment reports and social histories while ensuring that they are complete, accurate, accessible, and updated in order to ensure decision-making and professional reviews;
- identify and manage conflicts, dilemmas, and complex ethical problems and design coping strategies while reflecting on the results;
- work effectively in 'multiorganisational' and interdisciplinary systems, networks, and teams aiming to collaborate in the establishment of goals, objectives, and their target dates while contributing to a constructive approach to possible disagreements that arise;
- reflect on professional activities and duties, identifying personal and professional limits while constantly pushing these limits;
- work in accordance with agreed standards for social work and ensure one's professional development by using professional assertiveness to justify one's decisions and supervision as a means of responding to professional development needs.

Specific capacities were grouped into the following ten categories:

analysis, synthesis, and supervision;
organisation, planning, and assessment;
manage and interpret data and knowledge;
problem, conflict, and ethical dilemma management and resolution;
responsible and ethical decision making;
teamwork;
interpersonal skills;
ethical commitment;
adapting to new situations; and
creativity and innovation.

Abilities and attitudes were grouped into the following 14 categories:

- empathy in the face of situations of need;
- ethical behaviour and an active attitude for learning;

- verbal and non-verbal communication, listening, and observation skills;
- anticipation, decision-making, and problem-solving in unforeseen situations;
- knowing one's limits;
- participative and cooperative attitude during the internship and working on teams;
- adequate use of supervision and internship systematisation;
- challenge and argue the validity of data;
- appreciate, respect, and evaluate cultural, religious, and sexual diversity, among others;
- promote respect for personal dignity and the value and uniqueness of every human being;
- reflect on the relationships between social work, social policy, and the contexts in which their activity takes place;
- ability to learn and continuously renew and stay up-to-date;
- ability to work independently; and
- collect and interpret relevant data to make sound judgements.

Learning outcomes and evidence-based assessment

From the data obtained in the present study, the following learning skills connected to internships were identified by synthesis:

Professional institutional and regional context analysis. Students should be capable of performing applied analysis of the structure and dynamics of social institutions and organisations where they work as social workers.

Professional profile analysis. Students should analyse professional profiles (functions and roles), networking and working on interdisciplinary teams.

Emergency attention internship analysis and systematisation. Introduce students to the process of professional intervention in social work through active observation in direct and indirect care activities.

Individual and family interventions. Practical implementation of social work methodological processes, techniques, and instruments for individuals and families, including investigation, analysis, planning, intervention, and assessment of professional performance.

Group and community social work. Students should acquire specific knowledge, strategies, and abilities about the analysis and intervention process for groups and communities (creating social research and/or intervention projects).

Ethical principles and professional skills analysis. Acquire and practice social and communication skills, apply ethical principles, and solve ethical problems.

Discussion and Conclusions

As the results of this study have shown, internships constitute substantive required training included in all curricula at Spanish universities. They represent the most important framework for introducing students to professional practice during their academic development, which is evident from the significant teaching load of this subject matter as well as the organisation and responsibility they demand.

In a manner similar to other university degrees, students' learning outcomes in relation to the nature of social work and the skills necessary to effectively pursue a future career are addressed in curricula through internships. The context in which internships take place (institutions, services, professionals/supervisors) should also be considered during their implementation. In line with Tynjälä et al. (2016, p. 371), this set of factors represent socio-cultural knowledge that is developed though interactions with individuals, groups, and institutions; discussions and deliberations, cooperation, and problem-solving are relevant in this process (Hood & Littlejohn 2017). Other studies on the topic (Cleak & Smith 2012; Smith et al. 2015; Wayne et al. 2010) have shown the importance of institutional contexts, professional references, and the supervisor's profile for learning processes. The present study has shown how important it is for the professionals in charge of supervision at the social entities to have up-to-date training with the goal of offering students an appropriate context for the acquisition of professional skills and abilities. Internships in Spain are structured and organised according to a collaborative, open, and cooperative model that enables significant attainment based on close coordination between social work schools and social entities. This model provides clear experiences, knowledge, and shared social skills (teachers and professionals but also students) that are essential to pursue a future career in the field. In this way, teaching tied to internships is rooted in social interaction, and the professors involved must have the necessary skills in this respect.

Internships allow students to develop a range of professional skills and abilities at different types of social institutions: public, private, and all of the social protection systems, including social services, health care, training-employment, education, justice, and housing, among others. Formal agreements with centres that collaborate on internship training programmes are established with the respective universities, which favours real-life work contexts that are duly supervised. In turn, the universities' ties to professional practice allow them to develop innovative learning-service programmes.

As has been shown in this study, internships are places of collaborative learning that generate clear potential for all the parties involved (professors, professionals, schools, and social entities). The acquisition of skills, abilities, and capacities through internships enables understanding how to apply methodologies to the different levels of intervention (individual, family, group, and community) as well as the previously mentioned professional areas. On the other hand, the use of ethical problem-solving principles and strategies encourages students to acquire different skills that will benefit them in their future careers, regardless of the area chosen. At any rate, internships are highly valued by participants, and satisfaction is closely related to the quality of the supervision provided (Miller et al. 2005; Kanno & Koeske 2010; Cleak & Smith 2012; Cleak et al. 2016; Spector & Infante 2020). However, to do so requires knowledge and a specific skill set to provide adequate guidance. The data analysis from this study shows a continual adaptation of curricula to the different areas of professional practice: judicial, gender violence, health, education, dependence, and disability. On the other hand, a shared monitoring and assessment protocol via a rubric, known to students, professors, and supervisors, has proven to be effective at teaching (Expósito et al. 2017; Fraile et al. 2017) and, based on the participants' remarks, has shown evidence of satisfaction in monitoring and continuous assessment processes due to its participative, transparent, and reflective nature.

In the context of adapting studies to society, teaching in the area of social work has assimilated the consequences from the implementation or modification of social policies and the recognition of social rights. The enactment of or changes to laws that affect social protection systems in general or specific sectors thereof, (groups with social problems) has meant the emergence and development of centres, services, and programmes in which social workers have clear opportunities for job placement. Without a doubt, the continual renewal and assessment of theory and practice allows for the improvement of teaching-learning processes and the consolidation of internships as a privileged 'space' for competent professional training.

Notes

1 Available at https://eventos.um.es/event_detail/687/detail/i-congreso-internacional-de-facultades-y-escuelas-de-trabajo-social_-andquot%3Bel-trabajo-social-ante.html.
2 Available at http://cifets.unirioja.es/1/CIFETS-2016.
3 Available at https://cifets2018.deusto.es/18900/detail/cifets-2018.html.

References

Agencia Nacional de Evaluación de la Calidad y Acreditación [A.N.E.C.A]. (2004). *Libro blanco título de Grado de Trabajo Social. [White Paper on Undergraduate Degrees in Social Work].* Madrid: A.N.E.C.A. http://www.aneca.es/var/media/150376/libroblanco_trbjsocial_def.pdf. Accessed May 5, 2020.

Agencia Nacional de Evaluación de la Calidad [A.N.E.C.A]. (2020). *Registro de Títulos de las universidades españolas. [Title Registry of Spanish Universities].* http://srv.aneca.es/ListadoTitulos/. Accessed April 15, 2020.

Aguilar, M.V., Erro, A. & Pérez, R.M. (2020). Social work educational programmes aimed at the young: Redefining programmes to succeed? *Social Work Education*, 39(1), 41–59.

Álvarez, E. (2019). Evolución de la Universidad en la Sociedad del Aprendizaje y la Enseñanza. El valor de las competencias en el desarrollo profesional y personal. [The evolution of universities in the learning society and knowledge economy. The value of skills in personal and professional development]. *Aula Abierta*, 48(4), 349–372.

Álvarez, E. & Arreguit, X. (2019). El Futuro de la Universidad y la Universidad del Futuro. Ecosistemas de formación continúa para una sociedad de aprendizaje y enseñanza sostenible y responsable. [The future of universities and universities of the future. Continuous education ecosystems for a sustainable learning society and knowledge economy]. *Aula Abierta*, 48(4), 447–480.

Barber, J.P. (2012). Integration of learning: A grounded theory analysis of college students' learning. *American Educational Research Journal*, 49(3), 590–617.

Booth, A., McLean, M. & Walker, M. (2009). Self, others and society: A case study of university integrative learning. *Studies in Higher Education*, 34(8), 929–939.

Carbonero, D., Raya, E., Caparros, N. & Gimeno, C. (2016). *Respuestas transdisciplinares en una sociedad global. Aportaciones desde el Trabajo Social. [Transdisciplinary answers for a global society].* La Rioja: Universidad de La Rioja. https://publicaciones.unirioja.es/catalogo/online/CIFETS_2016/publicaciones.shtml. Acessed May 5, 2020.

Cleak, H., Roulston, A. & Vreugdenhil, A. (2016). The inside story: A survey of social work students' supervision and learning opportunities on placement. *British Journal of Social Work*, 46(7), 2033–2050. https://doi.org/10.1093/bjsw/bcv117.

Cleak, H. & Smith, D. (2012). Student satisfaction with models of field placement supervision. *Australian Social Work*, 65(2), 243–258.

Council for Social Work Education. (2015). Educational policy and accreditation standards (EPAS). https://www.cswe.org/Accreditation/Standards-and-Policies/2015-EPAS. Accessed May 15, 2020.

Conferencia de Decanos/as y Directores/as de Trabajo Social de las Universidades en España [CDTS] (2013). La formación universitaria en Trabajo Social. Estándares de calidad en las prácticas curriculares externas del título de grado en trabajo social. [University studies in social work. Quality standards for internships in undergraduate degrees in social work.] *AZARBE, Revista Internacional de Trabajo Social y Bienestar*, 2, 99–108.

Conferencia de Decanos/as y Directores/as de Trabajo Social de las Universidades en España [C.D.T.S.]. (2007). *La formación universitaria en Trabajo Social. Criterios para el diseño de planes de estudios de títulos de Grado en Trabajo Social. [University Studies in Social Work. Criteria for the Design of Curricula in Undergraduate Degrees in Social Work].* Barcelona: C.D.T.S.

Egido, I. (2017). El prácticum como elemento clave en la iniciación al desarrollo profesional docente: Debate y líneas de futuro. [Internships as a key element in the introduction to professional development training: Debate and a vision for the future]. In: Hector Monarca & Blanca Thoillez, *La profesionalización dicente: Debates y propuestas [Spoken Profesionalization: Debates and Proposals]* (pp. 133–147). Madrid: Síntesis.

Escudero, A., Aparicio, P., Grosso-de-la-Vega, R. & Rodríguez, M. (2019). La colaboración Universidad-Empresa Como Elemento motivador. Un estudio De Caso. [A case study: University-Business collaboration as a motivating element]. *Aula Abierta*, 48(4), 435–446.

European Commission. (2011). Supporting growth and jobs – An agenda for the modernisation of Europe's higher education systems. https://eur-lex.europa.eu/LexUriServ/LexUriServ.do?uri=COM:2011:0567:FIN:EN:PDF. Accessed May 15, 2020.

Expósito, M., Nicolau, D. & Tomás, J.V. (2017). La evaluación por competencias en los grados. Desarrollo de una experiencia mediante el uso de rúbrica. [Skills assessment in undergraduate degrees. Experiences with rubrics]. *Revista Complutense de Educación*, 28(4), 1155–1171.

Ferrández, R. & Sánchez, L. (2019). Las prácticas externas desde la perspectiva de las entidades colaboradoras. [Internships from the perspective of collaborating entities]. *RELIEVE: Revista Electrónica de Investigación y Evaluación Educativa*, 25(1), 5. http://doi.org/10.7203/relieve.25.1.13189.

Fook, J. (2002). Theorizing from practice: Towards an inclusive approach for social work research. *Qualitative Social Work*, 1(1), 79–95.

Fraile, J., Pardo, R. & Panadero, E. (2017). ¿Cómo emplear las rúbricas para implementar una verdadera evaluación formativa? [How to use rubrics to implement true formative assessment]. *Revista Complutense de Educación*, 28(4), 1321–1334.

Hernández, J. & Pérez, J.A. (Dirs.) (2019). *La universidad española en cifras. [Spanish Universities in Figures]*. Madrid: C.R.U.E. Universidades Españolas. http://www.crue.org/Documentos%20compartidos/Publicaciones/Universidad%20Espa%C3%B1ola%20en%20cifras/UEC%201718_FINAL_DIGITAL.pdf. Accessed February 15, 2020.

Hidalgo, A. (2020). Presence and competences of social workers in Spanish educational centres. Laws vs. reality. A research approach. *Social Work Education*, 39(3), 378–391.

Hood, N. & Littlejohn, A. (2017). Knowledge typologies for professional learning: Educators (re)generation of knowledge when learning open educational practice. *Educational Technology Research & Development*, 65(6), 1583–1604.

Instituto Nacional de Administración Pública [I.N.A.P.]. (2014). *Catálogos de competencias genéricas para el conjunto de la Administración General del Estado. [Directories of General Skills for the Central State Administration]*. Madrid: I.N.A.P. file:///D:/Usuarios/epastor/Downloads/Informe_Perfiles_de_Competencias_INAP%20(1).pdf. Accessed March 1, 2020.

International Association of Schools of Social Work [I.A.S.S.W.]. (2019). Global standards of for the education and training of the social work profession. https://www.iassw-aiets.org/global-standards-for-social-work-education-and-training/. Accessed June 5, 2020.

Kanno, H. & Koeske, G. F. (2010). MSW students' satisfaction with their field placements: The role of preparedness and quality of supervision. *Journal of Social Work Education*, 46(1), 23–38.

Kinni, R.-L. (2020). Integration of theory and practice in social work education. Analysis of Finnish social work students' field reports. *Social Work Education*. https://doi.org/10.1080/02615479.2020.1754385.

Latorre, M.J. & Blanco, F.J. (2011). El prácticum como espacio de aprendizaje profesional para docentes en formación. [Internships as a professional learning space for teachers in training]. *Revista de Docencia Universitaria*, 9(2), 35–54.

Manninen, J. & Hobrough, J. (2000). Skills gaps and overflows? A European perspective of graduate skills and employment in SMEs. *Industry & Higher Education*, 14(1), 51–57.

Marion, B. (2018). *Social Work Practice: Integrating Concepts, Processes and Skills*. New York: Colombia University Press.

Miller, J., Corcoran, J., Kovacs, P.J., Rosenblum, A. & Wright, L. (2005). Field education: Student and field instructor perceptions of the learning process. *Journal of Social Work Education*, 41(1), 131–135.

Ministerio de Universidades. (2020). *Registro de Universidades, Centros y Títulos* [Registry of universities, centres and degrees]. https://www.educacion.gob.es/ruct/consultaestudios?actual=estudios. Accessed February 10, 2020.

Niehaus, E., Holder, C., Rivera, M., Garcia, C. E., Woodman, T., Dierberger, J. & Dierberger, J. (2017). Exploring integrative learning in service-based alternative breaks. *The Journal of Higher Education*, 88(6), 922–946.

Organization for Economic Cooperation and Development [O.E.C.D.]. (2012). *Fostering Quality Teaching in Higher Education: Policies & Practices*. O.E.C.D. Publishing. http://www.oecd.org/education/imhe/QT%20policies%20and%20practices.pdf.

Organization for Economic Cooperation and Development [O.E.C.D.]. (2017). *Skills for a High Performing Civil Service*. OECD Public Governance Reviews. Paris: O.E.C.D. Publishing. https://doi.org/10.1787/9789264280724-en. Accessed March 10, 2020.

Ovejas, C., Fernández, J., De La Rosa, P. P., Facal, T., Raya, E. & Sobremonte, E. (2012). Encuesta sobre prácticas externas y trabajo fin de Grado en trabajo social. [Survey on internships and a final project for undergraduate degree in social work.]. *Alternativas*, 19, 95–113.

Pastor-Seller, E. (Ed.) (2014). *El Trabajo Social ante el Reto de la Crisis y la Educación Superior. [Social work in the face of crisis and higher education].* Madrid: Universitas.

Pastor-Seller, E., Verde, C. & Lima, A. I. (2019). Impact of neo-liberalism in Spain: Research from social work in relation to the public system of social services. *European Journal of Social Work*, 22(2), 277–288.

Pegalajar, M.C. (2018). Formación en competencias en alumnado universitario mediante prácticas basadas en aprendizaje cooperativo. [University students skills training through internships based on cooperative learning]. *Revista Complutense de Educación*, 29(3), 829–845.

Pérez, B. & Martínez, L. (2020). Social work education in Spain: Evaluation and challenges for a new generation of social workers. *Social Work Education*. https://doi.org/10.1080/02615479.2020.1724931.

Recommendation of the European Parliament and of the Council of 18 December. (2006). *On Key Competences for Lifelong Learning*. Official Journal of the European Union L 394 of 30 December 2006. https://eur-lex.europa.eu/LexUriServ/LexUriServ.do?uri=OJ:L:2006:394:0010:0018:ES:PDF. Accessed May 15, 2020.

Sierra, J.E., Caparrós, E., Molina, D. & Blanco, N. (2017). Aprender a través de la escritura. los diarios de prácticas y el desarrollo de saberes experienciales. [Learning through writing, internship journals and the development of experiential wisdom]. *Revista Complutense De Educación*, 28(3), 673–688.

Smith, D., Cleak, H. & Vreugdenhill, A. (2015). 'What are they really doing?' An exploration of student learning activities in field placement. *Australian Social Work*, 68(4), 515–531.

Sobremonte, E. & Rodriguez, A. (Eds.) (2019). *El Trabajo Social en un mundo en transformación. ¿Distintas realidades o nuevos relatos para la intervención? [Social Work in a Transforming World. Different Realities or New Narratives for Internvention?]*Valencia: Tirant lo Blanch.

Spector, A.V. & Infante, K. (2020). Community college field placement internships: Supervisors' perspectives and recommendations. *Social Work Education*, 39(4), 462–480.

Torralba, J.M. & Pastor-Seller, E. (2019). Estrategias y oportunidades para el acercamiento entre universidad y práctica profesional en la disciplina de Trabajo Social. [Strategies and opportunities for bringing universities and professional practice closer in the field of social work.]. In E. Sobremonte y A. Rodriguez (Eds). *El Trabajo Social en un mundo en transformación. ¿Distintas realidades o nuevos relatos para la intervención? [Social Work in a Transforming World. Different Realities or New Narratives for Intervention?]* (pp. 647–674). Valencia: Tirant lo Blanch.

Taylor, B.J., Catherine, J. & Fleming, G. (2010). Partnership, service needs and assessing competence in post qualifying education and training. *Social Work Education*, 29(5), 475–489.

Tuning Project. (2009). *Una introducción a Tuning Educational Structures in Europe. [La contribución de las universidades al proceso de Bolonia]. [An Introduction to Tuning Educational Structures in Europe. Universities' Contribution to the Bologna Process].* Bilbao: Publicaciones de la Universidad de Deusto.

Tynjälä, P. (2008). Perspectives into learning at the workplace. *Educational Research Review*, 3(2), 130–154. https://doi.org/10.1111/bjet.12164.

Tynjälä, P., Slotte, V., Nieminen, J., Lonka, K. & Olkinuora, E. (2006). From university to working life: Graduates' workplace skills in practice. In P. Tynjälä, J. Välimaa & G. Boulton-Lewis (Eds.), *Higher Education and Working Life: Collaborations, Confrontations and Challenges* (pp. 73–88). Amsterdam: Elsevier.

Tynjälä, P., Heikkinen, H.L. & Kiviniemi, U. (2011). Integratiivinen pedagogiikka opetusharjoittelussa opettajan autonomisuuden tukena. *Kasvatus*, 42(4), 302–315.

Tynjälä, P., Virtanen, A., Klemola, U., Kostiainen, E. & Rasku-Puttonen, H. (2016). Developing social competence and other generic skills in teacher education: Applying the model of integrative pedagogy. *European Journal of Teacher Education*, 39(3), 368–387.

Wayne, J., Marion, B. & Raskin, M. (2010). Field education as the signature pedagogy of social work education. *Journal of Social Work Education*, 46(3), 327–339.

Zayas, B., Gozálvez, V. & Gracia, J. (2019). La Dimensión Ética y Ciudadana del Aprendizaje Servicio: Una apuesta por su institucionalización en la Educación Superior. [The ethical and citizen dimensions of service learning: A bid for their institutionalization in higher learning]. *Revista Complutense de Educación*, 30(1), 1–15.

30

Character Strengths and Virtues for Competent Fieldwork Education

Perspectives of Undergraduate Students from Two University Departments of Social Work in Greece

Eleni Papouli, Sevaste Chatzifotiou, and Charalampos Tsairidis

Character strengths and virtues are qualities of character that guide and affect a person's behaviour in positive ways in order to achieve desired goals in different aspects of life, including education and work (Peterson & Seligman, 2004; Peterson & Park, 2012). Regarding the education of social workers, character strengths are considered to be critical virtuous skills for achievements in all curriculum areas of social work, with a particular focus on fieldwork education. As is well known, fieldwork education is an essential component of social work graduate programmes across the world and is, thereby, recognised as the signature pedagogy of social work (Bogo, 2010; Council on Social Work Education, 2015). Fieldwork as part of the educational preparation of students for professional practice provides them with unique opportunities to identify, develop, and apply the character strengths needed to be competent social workers in the future. This is particularly important for students, as character strengths such as virtuous professional skills are best learned and developed through active engagement in real-world tasks and problems, though they can be taught in the classroom.

Overall, it can be argued that focusing on their character strengths, students are most engaged in fieldwork learning and, therefore, perform their tasks not because someone else is asking them to but because, in addition to the academic knowledge they have acquired throughout their studies, they feel confident about themselves and their abilities to deal with various situations that could arise during the field placement. Also, they feel less anxious about the field placement experience and, thereby, more ready to act in ways to make sure that they obtain the tools and learning experiences necessary for working life. Given their importance in relation to the achievement of learning and performance, in recent years, a number of academic disciplines (e.g., education, psychology, business management, and neuropsychology) have started to turn their attention to the study of strengths-based approaches in education and fieldwork practice, seeking to build on character strengths of students, rather than their

DOI: 10.4324/9781032164946-35

weaknesses, to actively engage them in the learning process, inside and outside the university classroom, and inspire in them positive action for change. Yet, despite the growing interest of researchers from various disciplines in the subject at present, character strengths and virtues remain a neglected area of social work research, including education and fieldwork, both in Greece and internationally. Therefore, taking into account both the research gaps and the need for exploring such issues with social work students, too, we sought to identify and highlight the character strengths and virtues considered as important for achievement in fieldwork education. Once they are identified by the students themselves and properly analysed, they will constitute the solid ground on which the rest of the professional and academic strengths and virtues will be developed. For its purposes, the study was based on Peterson and Seligman's (2004) list of 24 character strengths, grouped within six core virtues, and literature relevant to the topic under study.

Before we present and discuss the results of the study, we briefly review the literature on the concepts of character strengths and virtues and look at their relations to empower individuals to take ownership of learning and practice responsible roles, having a positive attitude. We also discuss Peterson and Seligman's (2004) list of 24 character strengths and how it is associated with core human virtues.

Literature Review

Character strengths and virtues are placed in the foreground and are both fundamental parts of good social work practice, though they differ in meaning. Character strengths, also called soft skills or social-emotional skills (Thiers, 2018), are positive personality traits that are reflected in thoughts, feelings, and behaviours and are valued in their own right (Peterson & Seligman, 2004; Snyder & Lopez, 2002). Character strengths are components of a positive, good character and, therefore, are considered as important ingredients of virtues, which, in their turn, are necessary to flourishing (or eudaimonia), according to Aristotle's virtue ethics theory (Peterson & Seligman, 2004; Papouli, 2019). In the professional field, particularly in the social work profession, virtues are often described as:

> qualities, character, good habits or attributes of practitioners that help them to achieve excellence in their practice [...] the concept of virtues is constructed by linking values/principles and qualities and attributes and roles and functions.
>
> *(Pawar, Hugman, Alexandra, & Anscombe, 2020, p. 9)*

Character strengths and virtues are essential to both personal and professional well-being, though they have been neglected topics in the social sciences and research, including social work practice and education throughout much of the twentieth century, as mentioned earlier. This might partly be explained by the fact that both concepts were explicitly connected with religious beliefs and morals, as well as with the ideologies of social conservatism that, for so long, have dominated human systems. So, until recently, most research focused primarily on 'rectifying' weaknesses or what is wrong – the deficit model according to Langley (2016) – rather than identifying strengths of character or what people do well and can do better. But thanks to recent trends in the fields of moral philosophy and positive psychology in particular, character strengths and virtues have been revived over the last decades (Carr, Arthur, & Kristjánsson, 2017; Papouli, 2019; Pawar et al., 2017; Peterson & Seligman, 2004).

Peterson and Seligman (2004), pioneers of positive psychology, were the first to examine character traits and their relations to human flourishing. Drawing on their studies, as well as the global literature review, Peterson and Seligman developed the values in action (V.I.A.) classification of character strengths, a classification of positive traits of character. The V.I.A. classification includes 24 ubiquitously recognised character strengths that all people have to a greater or lesser degree that lay the foundation of positive psychology and well-being (Table 30.1). In order to be regarded as ubiquitously recognised and valued, each character strength must meet most of the following criteria:

Table 30.1 The Six Core Virtues and Their Associated Character Strengths

Wisdom: Cognitive strengths involving acquisition and use of knowledge.	**Courage:** Emotional strengths that involve the exercise of will to accomplish goals in the face of opposition, external or internal.	**Humanity:** Interpersonal strengths that involve 'tending and befriending' others.
• **Creativity:** thinking of novel and productive ways to do things • **Curiosity:** taking an interest in all of ongoing experience • **Judgement:** weighing all aspects objectively in making decisions, including arguments that are in conflict with my convictions • **Love of learning:** mastering new skills, topics, and bodies of knowledge • **Perspective:** being able to provide wise counsel to others	• **Honesty:** speaking the truth and presenting oneself in a genuine and sincere way • **Bravery:** not shrinking from threat, challenge, difficulty, or pain • **Perseverance:** finishing what one starts • **Zest:** approaching life with excitement and energy	• **Kindness:** doing favours and good deeds for others • **Love:** valuing close relations with others • **Social intelligence:** being aware of the motives and feelings of self and others
Justice: Civic strengths that underlie healthy community life.	**Temperance:** Strengths that protect against excess.	**Transcendence:** Strengths that forge connections to the larger universe and provide meaning.
• **Fairness:** treating all people the same according to notions of fairness and justice • **Leadership:** organising group activities and seeing that they happen • **Teamwork:** working well as member of a group or team	• **Forgiveness:** forgiving those who have done wrong • **Humility:** letting one's accomplishments speak for themselves • **Prudence:** being careful about one's choices; not saying or doing things that might later be regretted • **Self-regulation:** regulating what one feels and does	• **Appreciation of beauty and excellence:** noticing and appreciating beauty, • excellence, and/or skilled performance in all domains of life • **Gratitude:** being aware of and thankful for the good things that happen • **Hope:** expecting the best and working to achieve it • **Humour:** liking to laugh and joke; bringing smiles to other people • **Spirituality:** having coherent beliefs about the higher purpose and meaning of life

(Adapted from V.I.A. Institute on Character and Peterson & Seligman, 2004)

> fulfilling, morally valued, does not diminish others, has no felicitous opposites, trait-like, distinctive from other strengths, have paragons who exemplify it, has prodigies, selective absence of it in some situations, and has institutions/rituals to celebrate or express it.
>
> *(Niemiec, 2013, p. 12)*

Moreover, the 24 character strengths are clustered into six broad virtue categories as follows: wisdom, courage, humanity, justice, temperance, and transcendence. These six core virtues are universal across cultures and nations and exist irrespectively of socio-economic status of people (Dahlsgaard, Peterson, & Seligman, 2005; Park, Peterson, & Seligman, 2006; Peterson & Seligman, 2004). Peterson and Park (2012) argue that the six core virtues are 'grounded in biology through an evolutionary process that selected for these predispositions toward moral excellence as means of solving the important tasks necessary for survival of the species' (p. 279). Finally, of the 24 character strengths, the five strengths that people use most frequently based on self-report are often referred to as 'signature strengths' (Thun & Kelloway, 2011, p. 271). Table 30.1 includes the six core virtues and their associated character strengths.

Today, there is strong evidence that character strengths and virtues are positively related to both general and specific outcomes and can be used as protective factors to foster resilience and to help reduce risk factors. For instance, character strengths such as kindness, hope, and perspective have been shown to be associated with protective factors against the impacts of stress and trauma (Park & Peterson, 2008). In addition, several strengths – hope, curiosity, love, zest, and gratitude – are associated with overall job satisfaction (Heintz & Ruch, 2019; Park et al., 2004; Peterson & Park, 2012; Thun & Kelloway, 2011). Of them, particularly, the strengths of zest for life, curiosity, and hope are most related with greater life satisfaction and eudaimonic well-being (Shogren et al., 2017). Moreover, many character strengths have been linked with students' academic achievement and performance (e.g., perseverance, temperance, love, gratitude, hope) (Peterson & Park, 2009; Shogren et al., 2017; Tang et al., 2019; Yotsidi et al., 2018). Overall, research on the subject in the educational sector has confirmed that helping students find and use their personal strengths and virtues to do what they do best has a direct positive impact on their engagement, learning, and performance, regardless of their academic discipline or educational stage (Park, 2004).

Methodology

Aims and Objectives of the Study

Character strengths and virtues is an important, but largely neglected area of research in social work fieldwork education across the world, as mentioned earlier. Thus, the study aimed at filling this research gap by gathering information and views on character strengths and virtues that are important to students for competent fieldwork practice. The study used the following objectives to ascertain this:

- Identify the character strengths and their associated virtues according to Peterson and Seligman's (2004) list of 24 character strengths;
- Evaluate and identify the top five character strengths (known as signature strengths), considered as the most important for accomplishing tasks and goals in the field placements;
- Check for similarities/differences between the two university departments regarding the signature strengths of students;
- Search for a shared division for strength-based fieldwork education.

Research Approach and Methods

The study was descriptive in nature and, thereby, its objective was focused on gathering information and views of students regarding the research topic. To this end, the survey method was used as the most suitable quantitative research method to collect the required data and achieve the objectives of the study (Babbie, 2014).

Data Collection Methods and Instruments

Data were collected using a questionnaire which was created and configured based on Peterson and Seligman's (2004) list of 24 character strengths, grouped within six core virtues. This list is available online in different languages, including the Greek language, from the V.I.A. Institute (www.viacharacter.org). The design of the questionnaire was also based on the review of the current literature on the role of fieldwork education in social work. At the social work department at the University of West Attica (U.N.I.W.A.), teaching staff, having the role of academic supervisors for students placed in field agencies, were informed about the study aims by the researcher, who was a faculty member, and helped to answer questions and deliver/collect the questionnaires to all students present in their classes. At the social work department of Democritus University of Thrace (D.U.T.H.), the researchers, who were also faculty members, distributed and collected the questionnaires themselves. The questionnaires were completed anonymously and voluntarily by more than 98% of students from both universities during November 2019 (U.N.I.W.A.) and December 2019 (D.U.T.H.) during the 2019–2020 academic year. Finally, the questionnaires were completed by hand, and the median completion time was 25 minutes.

Instrument

The questionnaire was divided into three sections. Section A dealt with demographic data of the students (i.e., gender, age, and nationality), academic information (i.e., semester of studies), types of field placement (e.g., education/school, disability, health and mental health, etc.), and sector provider (i.e., public sector, private sector, non-governmental organisation (N.G.O.)). Section B included the list of 24 character strengths (see Table 30.1), each of which had its own definition, asking students to report on the degree to which they embody each of the 24 character strengths, using a Likert scale from 1 to 5 (strongly disagree = 1, disagree = 2, undecided = 3, agree = 4, strongly agree = 5). This was an important step in the research process, as it gave the opportunity to students to familiarise themselves with the concept of each character strength included in the V.I.A. classification and choose the answer which really represents them. Finally, Section C enabled students to rank, in hierarchical order, their top five character strengths related to the skills needed in fieldwork placement and then to provide analytically written statements to rationalise their choices as mentioned earlier, using an open-ended question. The use of the open-ended question was very helpful, as it allowed (a) students to express themselves freely on the given subject and (b) researchers to collect and yield more reliable and valid information.

Sampling and Participants

Participants were drawn from two university departments: the departments of social work at U.N.I.W.A. and D.U.T.H., located, respectively, in Athens (the capital city of Greece) and

Komotini (an established university city in the north of Greece) – two cities with different historical-geographical dynamics. Researchers used convenience sampling because it was easy to gain access to the population because of their positions as university faculty members. All students (210 students) who were doing their first placement (of two field placements over the course of the two academic semesters) were invited to participate in the study through an email sent from the offices of field placement of the universities.

Data Analysis Techniques

Data analysis was conducted using quantitative and qualitative processes as follows.

Quantitative

The researchers used the statistical package for social sciences (S.P.S.S.) to analyse the data collected for Sections A and B of the questionnaire, as well as to analyse the question in Section C of the questionnaire related to the five most important character strengths of students (i.e., 'signature' character strengths). Quantitative data were analysed using descriptive statistics and multiple response data analysis techniques. Because the gender ratio of male students to female students was very high (1 to 9), it was not statistically feasible to test for gender differences and character strengths.

Qualitative

All data derived from the open-ended question were analysed using the content analysis method (Krippendorff, 2019). Following the literature guidelines on conducting content analysis to analysing data derived from the open-ended question on our questionnaire, we familiarised ourselves with the data by reading the qualitative material several times. Then, for the organising phase, we proceeded to use open coding and the creation of codes, subcategories, and categories. Further, we found similarities through the subcategories, and we grouped them together creating categories resulting from coding together in relation to the entire data set. Finally, we selected typical examples from participants' answers which we presented in the main body of the paper, highlighting the participant's own voices and interconnecting them with the research questions and the existing relevant literature.

Research Ethics

Ethics protocol was approved by the assemblies of the two university departments with written informed consent obtained from each student prior to participating in the study. Students' voluntary participation in the study could be withdrawn at any time.

Results and Analysis

Student Demographics

The results of the study showed that, of the sample (*N*), comprised of 196 undergraduate social work students, 48% (95) were from the U.N.I.W.A., and 52% (101) were from D.U.T.H. With regard to gender, 10% were men, and 89% were women (overall, women comprise the majority of enrolled social work students for both departments), and their mean age was 23.54 years with a standard deviation of 6.48 years. In addition, the overwhelming majority of students were Greeks (97%), with a very small percentage of students having different nationalities such as Albanian (2%), Cypriot (1%), Armenian (1%), and Israeli (1%). Regarding the semester of studies, 41% were in the fifth semester, 46% were in the seventh semester, and 13% were in the final (eighth) semester. Students from both universities were basically placed in the same type of field placements such as education/school (18%), disability (14%), health (12%), child protection (11%), mental health (10%), social protection services (9%), community organisation and development (8%), refugees and migration services (4%), and elder services (4%). In addition, a very small percentage of students were placed in probation/juvenile services (2%) and other field agencies (e.g., addiction services, municipality social services, etc.). Finally, 4% of students were placed in the 'laboratory of social and community work and counselling'. This lab exists only in D.U.T.H. and functions as a field placement as well. Lastly, the majority of social services providing field placements belong to the public sector (65%), while 20% of them belong to the private sector, and 15% were NGOs active in different social fields.

Quantitative Results

The results derived from the statistical analyses are displayed in frequency tables (Tables 30.2, 30.3, 30.4 and 30.5) as follows: Table 30.2 shows the frequencies (as a percentage) of Likert-type scale responses based on the whole sample for each item (strength), while Table 30.3 provides

Table 30.2 Frequency of Students' Views of Their Character Strengths (N = 196)

Character strengths	*Strongly disagree = 1* N *(%)*	*Disagree = 2* N *(%)*	*Undecided = 3* N *(%)*	*Agree = 4* N *(%)*	*Strongly agree = 5* N *(%)*
Creativity	0 (0)	7 (4)	49 (25)	89 (45)	51 (26)
Judgment	0 (0)	5 (3)	18 (9)	93 (48)	78 (40)
Love of learning	0 (0)	12 (6)	45 (23)	76 (39)	61 (31)
Perspective	3 (2)	11 (6)	55 (29)	83 (43)	41 (21)
Curiosity	4 (2)	15 (8)	62 (32)	73 (37)	42 (21)
Bravery	2 (1)	9 (5)	43 (22)	88 (45)	54 (28)
Perseverance	2 (1)	11 (6)	38 (20)	78 (40)	66 (34)
Honesty	0 (0)	1 (1)	22 (11)	89 (46)	83 (43)
Zest	2 (1)	30 (15)	59 (30)	67 (34)	37 (19)
Love	0 (0)	3 (2)	13 (7)	50 (26)	130 (66)
Kindness	0 (0)	2 (1)	30 (15)	85 (43)	79 (40)
Social intelligence	1 (1)	6 (3)	41 (21)	99 (51)	49 (25)
Teamwork	0 (0)	4 (2)	28 (14)	93 (47)	71 (36)
Fairness	1 (1)	1 (1)	35 (18)	79 (40)	80 (41)
Leadership	6 (3)	22 (11)	55 (28)	76 (39)	37 (19)
Forgiveness	2 (1)	22 (11)	74 (38)	62 (32)	35 (18)
Humility	4 (2)	21 (11)	50 (26)	81 (42)	38 (20)
Prudence	9 (5)	29 (15)	70 (36)	57 (28)	31 (16)
Self-regulation	7 (4)	24 (12)	72 (37)	56 (29)	37 (19)
Appreciation of beauty and excellence	4 (2)	21 (11)	65 (33)	67 (34)	38 (19)
Gratitude	1 (1)	10 (5)	37 (19)	76 (39)	71 (36)
Hope	7 (4)	15 (8)	71 (36)	62 (32)	41 (21)
Humour	1 (1)	10 (5)	29 (15)	60 (31)	96 (49)
Spirituality	2 (1)	4 (2)	53 (27)	96 (49)	40 (21)

Table 30.3 Frequency of Character Strengths Scores

Character strengths	*Strongly disagree/disagree* N *(%)*	*Strongly agree/agree* N *(%)*
Creativity	7 (4)	140 (71)
Judgment	5 (2)	171 (88)
Love of learning	12 (6)	137 (71)
Perspective	14 (7)	124 (64)
Curiosity	19 (10)	115 (59)
Bravery	11 (6)	142 (72)
Perseverance	13 (7)	144 (74)
Honesty	1 (1)	172 (88)
Zest	32 (16)	104 (53)
Love	3 (2)	180 (92)
Kindness	2 (1)	164 (84)
Social intelligence	7 (4)	148 (76)
Teamwork	4 (2)	164 (84)
Fairness	2 (1)	159 (81)
Leadership	28 (14)	113 (58)
Forgiveness	24 (12)	97 (50)
Humility	25 (13)	119 (61)
Prudence	38 (19)	88 (44)
Self-regulation	31 (16)	93 (47)
Appreciation of Beauty and Excellence	25 (13)	105 (54)
Gratitude	11 (6)	147 (75)
Hope	22 (11)	103 (53)
Humour	11 (6)	156 (80)
Spirituality	6 (3)	136 (70)

score levels (low/high) for each item (strength). As evident in Tables 30.2 and Table 30.3, 'love' (92%), 'honesty' (88%), 'judgement' (88%), 'kindness' (84%), and 'teamwork' (84%) are the five most common strengths that students reported they hold strongly. On the contrary, 'prudence' (44%), 'self-regulation' (47%), 'forgiveness' (50%), 'zest' (53%), and 'appreciation of beauty and excellence' (54%) are the five most common strengths that students reported they hold less.

Table 30.4 (resulting from multiple response analysis) shows, in descending order, the frequencies of the hierarchy of responses based on the whole sample of students (N = 196). In Table 30.4, the percentages are given by responses and by respondents (cases). Finally, Tables 30.5 and 30.6 present the character strengths of students for each university department separately.

As shown in Tables 30.4–30.6, character strengths are listed from the most common to the least common. In examining the whole sample, 'honesty' (10%), 'fairness' (10%), 'love' (9%), 'humour' (8%), and 'kindness' (7%) are seen as the five most frequent character strengths (i.e., signature strengths) that students deem necessary for their success in the field placements (Table 30.4). Interestingly, the same character strengths are also reported by the U.N.I.W.A. students but with a different rank order (Table 30.5). For example, 'love' (10%) is ranked the first character strength, followed by 'honesty' (10%), 'fairness' (9%), 'humour' (7%), and 'kindness' (7%). Regarding the sample of D.U.T.H. students, we observed that except for the strength of 'perseverance', the remaining four character strengths are the same as those reported by the sampled student of U.N.I.W.A., while the two samples differ only in order of the strengths' preference. For example, the strength of 'fairness' (11%) is ranked first among D.U.T.H. students' preferences, followed by 'honesty' (11%), 'humour' (9%), and 'perseverance' (8%), while the

Table 30.4 Character Strengths of the Whole Sample of Students (N = 196)

		Responses		
Core virtues	*Character strengths*	N	*Percent (%)*	*Percent of cases (%)*
Courage	Honesty	101	10	52
Justice	Fairness	97	10	50
Humanity	Love	84	9	43
Transcendence	Humour	78	8	40
Humanity	Kindness	67	7	34
Courage	Perseverance	64	7	33
Wisdom	Judgment	49	5	25
Wisdom	Creativity	43	4	22
Humanity	Social intelligence	40	4	20
Transcendence	Hope	39	4	20
Temperance	Self-regulation	37	4	19
Justice	Teamwork	35	4	18
Temperance	Humility	34	4	17
Wisdom	Love of learning	31	3	16
Temperance	Forgiveness	31	3	16
Transcendence	Gratitude	29	3	15
Transcendence	Spirituality	21	2	11
Courage	Zest	19	2	10
Courage	Bravery	19	2	10
Wisdom	Curiosity	17	2	9
Wisdom	Perspective	14	1	7
Justice	Leadership	13	1	7
Temperance	Prudence	13	1	7
Transcendence	Appreciation of beauty and excellence	5	1	3
	Total	980	100.00	500.00

strength of 'love' (7%) is ranked last among top five character strengths of D.U.T.H. students (Table 30.6). Commenting on the above findings, there were no significant differences in preference of strengths between the two samples, as the students' responses differed slightly across the two samples. The results showed that there is a relative balance between the two university departments in terms of students' views on the preferences of signature character strengths for success in fieldwork education.

Qualitative Results

This section is concerned with presenting and discussing the results of the content analysis of the open-ended question of the questionnaire. The results are presented based on the signature strengths preferences of the two samples and include the conceptual categories that were derived from the data and the selected quotes that were picked up during the coding process. Characters strengths are presented according to the ranking order ofTable 30.4.

Honesty

Honesty is an emotional character strength, which falls under the virtue category of courage. It is about speaking the truth and presenting oneself in a genuine and sincere way (Peterson &

Table 30.5 Character Strengths by the U.N.I.W.A. Students ($N = 95$)

	Responses		
Character strengths	N	*Percent (%)*	*Percent of Cases (%)*
Love (Humanity)	48	10	51
Honesty (Courage)	47	10	50
Fairness (Justice)	42	9	44
Humour (Transcendence)	35	7	37
Kindness (Humanity)	34	7	36
Perseverance (Courage)	26	6	27
Judgment (Wisdom)	25	5	26
Hope (Transcendence)	24	5	25
Humility (Temperance)	21	4	22
Social intelligence (Humanity)	20	4	21
Love of learning (Wisdom)	18	4	19
Gratitude (Transcendence)	18	4	19
Creativity (Wisdom)	18	4	19
Self-regulation (Temperance)	16	3	17
Teamwork (Justice)	15	3	16
Forgiveness (Temperance)	14	3	15
Zest (Courage)	11	2	11
Spirituality (Transcendence)	9	2	10
Perspective (Wisdom)	8	2	8
Prudence (Temperance)	8	2	8
Curiosity (Wisdom)	7	2	7
Bravery (Courage)	4	1	4
Leadership (Justice)	4	1	4
Appreciation of beauty and excellence (Transcendence)	3	1	3
Total	475	100	500

Seligman, 2004). The results presented below are consistent with previous studies showing honesty to be of critical importance for effective working relationships and communication, especially to the professions that serve society (Arthur & Earl, 2020; Molina & McKeown, 2012; Wells & Molina, 2017). According to the results obtained, honesty is the highest character strength in terms of the overall ranking of U.N.I.W.A. and D.U.T.H. (Table 30.4). Also, it has been ranked second in the list of top five character strengths in both rankings (Tables 30.5 and 30.6).

Students' responses indicated that honesty is at the very heart of good collaboration and professional relationships based on trust and credibility. It also contributes to communication with others (clients, colleagues) and empathy.

> With honesty you can create a professional relationship based on trust and cooperation.
>
> *(D.U.T.H., Int. 14)*

Additionally, honesty as the top character strength, is connected to justice and safety, as well as to the emancipation of clients and life change.

> Honesty is the highest principle of social work profession for achieving social justice and safety.
>
> *(U.N.I.W.A., Int. 25)*

Table 30.6 Character Strengths by the D.U.T.H. Students ($N = 101$)

Character strengths	*Responses* N	*Responses* *Percent (%)*	*Percent of Cases (%)*
Fairness (Justice)	55	11	55
Honesty (Courage)	54	11	54
Humour (Transcendence)	43	9	43
Perseverance (Courage)	38	8	38
Love (Humanity)	36	7	36
Kindness (Humanity)	33	7	33
Creativity (Wisdom)	25	5	25
Judgment (Wisdom)	24	5	24
Self-regulation (Temperance)	21	4	21
Teamwork (Justice)	20	4	20
Social intelligence (Humanity)	20	4	20
Forgiveness (Temperance)	17	3	17
Hope (Transcendence)	15	3	15
Bravery (Courage)	15	3	15
Humility (Temperance)	13	3	13
Love of learning (Wisdom)	13	3	13
Spirituality (Transcendence)	12	2	12
Gratitude (Transcendence)	11	2	11
Curiosity (Wisdom)	10	2	10
Leadership (Justice)	9	2	9
Zest (Courage)	8	2	8
Perspective (Wisdom)	6	1	6
Prudence (Temperance)	5	1	5
Appreciation of beauty and excellence (Transcendence)	2	1	2
Total	505	100	500

> Everybody deserves a second chance, we all deserve equal opportunities and we, social workers, through honesty, need to bring people's strengths as well as our owns into light.
>
> *(U.N.I. W.A., Int. 10)*

Moreover, the strength of honesty is associated with the self-image of students and professionals. Furthermore, the strength of honesty provides a positive attitude toward life and respect for others and gives a helping hand to those who need it.

> Honesty makes a better person and I feel good about myself and my colleagues.
>
> *(D.U.T.H., Int. 99)*

Finally, honesty is connected to the effectiveness of services provided in the fieldwork.

> My work effectiveness as a social worker is much greater when I am honest and fair…
>
> *(D.U.T.H., Int. 27)*

Fairness/Justice

It is necessary to mention here that, as fairness and justice express almost identical concepts, in the Greek language, the word *fairness* has been replaced by justice in the questionnaire used in our study. Fairness is civic character strength within the justice virtue and involves what is right and equal (Peterson & Seligman, 2004). Fairness (in terms of justice), which lies at the heart of social work practice, is the first major strength chosen by D.U.T.H. students (Table 30.6). It also ranks second in the preferences of U.N.I.W.A. students (Table 30.5) and in the whole sampled students, respectively (Table 30.4).

According to content analysis, several categories of data derived from the students' descriptions about fairness and justice such as: guaranteeing equal opportunities for all without prejudice, bias, and discrimination; respect for others; and learning from mistakes. The following quotes illustrate the types of responses provided by students at both university departments.

> The Justice spirit is very strong with me and helps me see all people as equal and helps me fight for their rights.
>
> *(U.N.I. W.A., Int. 75)*

> We treat all people as equal ... all people have the same rights. So, there is no room for discrimination, prejudices or personal feelings that might lead someone to social exclusion.
>
> *(D.U.T.H., Int. 1)*

Moreover, fairness/justice as a civic strength is associated with empowering clients to assert their rights and advocating for social change and equality.

> The social injustice is synonymous to the immigrants' life, and I believe that the sense of justice that I have in me will help for the advocacy of these people...
>
> *(U.N.I. W.A., Int. 48)*

Finally, the strength of fairness/justice is connected with the importance of making right decisions and solving problems, which are usually related to good cooperation by putting boundaries in professional relationships.

> Justice helps me to take right decisions and solve problems after careful and multifaceted thought and research.
>
> *(D.U.T.H., Int. 31)*

Love

Love is an interpersonal character strength that involves tending and befriending others and is included in virtue of humanity (Peterson & Seligman, 2004). Love is also one of the most important strengths for success in the field experience. Love holds the third position in the overall preferences of students, the first position in the list of top five among the U.N.I.W.A. students, while it occupies the last position in the list of top five preferences of D.U.T.H. students (Table 30.6). Students' responses showed that love is an important character strength and is in the following categories: It helps them develop positive energy to do things they like to do and achieve greater self-optimisation and self-awareness. Furthermore, it allows them to familiarise with others and care for them, as well as to build safe relationships with clients.

> I love this profession and I want to do whatever I can to help people in need of our services.
>
> *(D.U.T.H., Int. 15)*

Also, the value of love helps create good professional relationships and promote good cooperation and progress, whether as a team or an individual. Moreover, love is associated with spirituality, which is an important contemporary topic in health care according to van der Weegen et al. (2019) as well as a basic element of caring as a spiritual concept (O'Brien, 2018). Finally, the kind of love students have for their clients is often referred to in literature as compassionate love that 'centers on the good of the other' (Fehr, Sprecher, & Underwood, 2008; Underwood, 2008, p. 3; Rindt-Hoffman, Kernes, & Bui, 2019) and is a core value for social and health care interactions.

> Love is the only perspective for developing a good cooperation with your service users as well as for my personal and professional development.
>
> *(D.U.T.H., Int. 53)*

> Love for your fellow human being is the most important virtue at the social work profession.
>
> *(U.N.I.W.A., Int. 55)*

Humour

Humour was also seen as a very important character strength by students. The character strength of humour is amongst the strengths under the virtue of transcendence that provides meaning through connection to the larger universe. Humour has been shown to have many mental, physical, and social benefits for professionals and students, though its use in social work practice has not been extensively explored (Gilgun & Sharma, 2012). In our study, humour ranked third in the D.U.T.H. students' choices and fourth in the U.N.I.W.A. students' choices and the whole sample, respectively (Tables 30.4 and 30.5). The content analysis showed that humour is associated with the following categories: ice-breaking and breaking monotony at work. According to students, these functions can help to create a sense of intimacy and trust when working with clients (children and adults) and others, as well as contributing to the establishment of a good therapeutic relationship.

> Humour makes me approachable and so people around me feel comfortable and trustful.
>
> *(U.N.I.W.A., Int. 1)*

> Humour is always very useful … especially in a job environment with many problems it can work therapeutically.
>
> *(U.N.I.W.A., Int. 6)*

Humour is also related to coping with difficult situations at work. For many students, for example, humour is seen as a defence mechanism that helps in rejuvenating and engaging team members and acts as a discharge and resting tool.

> Humour can help you take the stress away and create a pleasant environment at work.
>
> *(U.N.I.W.A., Int. 63)*

Lastly, humour is considered as an element of personal and professional development.

> I believe humour helps you to move on and develop.
>
> *(D.U.T.H., Int. 51)*

Kindness (U.N.I.W.A. Students Only)

Kindness is an interpersonal character strength under the virtue of humanity. Kindness is doing favours and good deeds for others (Peterson & Seligman, 2004). Literature recognises kindness as a powerful tool for building and maintaining healthy relationships and supporting the well-being of individuals and communities (Ferguson, 2017). In this study, kindness ranked last among the top five strengths of U.N.I.W.A. students and the whole sample of students, but it didn't appear in the top five strengths of D.U.T.H. students; it appears, though, in the sixth position (Table 30.6). U.N.I.W.A. students indicated kindness as important character strength for success in the field placements for a variety of reasons related to issues such as communication with others and intimacy, trust, respect, empathy, and positive attitudes toward life. The following quotes reflect the variety of students' views on the importance of kindness in fieldwork.

> Kindness helps me with my communication with others and my positive influence on them.
>
> *(U.N.I. W.A., Int. 1)*

> Kindness helps me develop a great sense of empathy so that I can be of help to clients.
>
> *(U.N.I. W.A., Int. 76)*

> Kindness has a great effect on holding a positive stance to life so you can transfer that stance to the rest of the people.
>
> *(U.N.I. W.A., Int. 14)*

Perseverance (D.U.T.H. Students Only)

Perseverance is among the emotional strengths that accompany the virtue of courage. It is not giving up, even when things get hard (Peterson & Seligman, 2004). As already seen, perseverance is one of the strengths most associated with students' academic achievement and performance. In this study, it is noticeable that perseverance only appeared in the list of top five character strengths of D.U.T.H. students, where it was ranked fourth following fairness, honesty, and humour. As the content analysis showed, D.U.T.H. students considered persistence to be a necessary element for a variety of things that were categorised in the following: Their success in achieving personal and professional goals and achieving desired change(s) during fieldwork education and professional development. The quotes below are indicative of how D.U.T.H. students perceived the role of perseverance in the fieldwork setting and professional practice.

> The skill of persistence adds to the everlasting effort for professional development.
>
> *(D.U.T.H., Int. 5)*

> means to persist in achieving what you really want, that is the change you want for society.
>
> *(D.U.T.H., Int. 22)*

> hard work and persistence are the means for achieving wonderful things in your work.
>
> *(D.U.T.H., Int. 61)*

Discussion

This study sought to identify and highlight the character strengths and associated virtues of undergraduate students for achievement in fieldwork education. To do this, the study, first, asked students from two university departments of social work in Greece to identify their greatest character strengths based on Peterson and Seligman's list of 24 character strengths. Second, the study asked students to write down the top five character strengths most important for their success in fieldwork education, prompting them to defend and explain their answers. The results of the study were interesting for many reasons.

First, the results showed that, overall, three out of five character strengths that students stated they possess strongly, such as honesty, love, and kindness, were also viewed as key strengths needed for fieldwork education (see Tables 30.2 and 30.3). Evidently, students acknowledged some of their character strengths as qualities that are essential skills required for effective fieldwork practice as well. From the perspective of students, honesty, love, and kindness are seen as character strengths that reflect personal virtuous qualities, which are important parts of building strong and valuable relationships with both clients and colleagues in social work practice. Surprisingly, however, character strengths such as judgment and teamwork, which are also important skill-based strengths in any health and social care profession, didn't appear in any of the lists of top five character strengths required for fieldwork education. Perhaps we can speculate that this was because such character strengths are under the virtue of justice, which appears, later, in the top five character strengths needed for fieldwork education and which, in broader terms, covers many of these concepts. For example, justice is seen as a prelude to teamwork in medical centres (Delbecq & Gill, 1985) and other organisations, including social services, and is essential for good judgement. Also, justice (social), in terms of treating people as equals in civic society (Mason, 2012), is a core value of the social work profession that all practitioners should use in advocating on behalf of people who are unable to advocate for themselves (I.F.S.W., 2014).

Second, the results indicated that character strengths such as honesty, fairness/justice, love, and humour are seen as common essential strengths for the majority of students of both university departments. In our judgement, this finding clearly shows that, despite their historical-geographical differences, the two departments seem to have common ground on the question of fieldwork education concerning the strengths-based approach to being a social worker. However, kindness and perseverance were found to be the highest strengths for each sample of students separately. But this difference in findings between the two samples of students had positive outcomes for the study; it helped us to perceive that there are not more or less important character strengths for students. Therefore, we can infer that all the strengths included in each of the top five lists of character strengths of the two university departments should be seen as equally important virtuous skills for fieldwork education, i.e., honesty, fairness/justice, love, humour, kindness, and perseverance. Clark (2006) notes that 'the requirements of the social work role include demonstrating a virtuous character' (p. 75) and, thereby, our results agree excellently with current approaches to virtue ethics for today's social workers and students (Hugman et al., 2020; Papouli, 2019; Pawar et al., 2017). Related to the above, future research might usefully explore how those character strengths are transmitted through the educational process (both directly and indirectly) and what the student is learning about them during fieldwork in different areas of social work practice (e.g., social protection services, mental health services, child protection services, etc.).

Third, the results identified four factors of character strengths contained under different virtues and associated with effective fieldwork education: emotional strengths (honesty and perseverance) under the virtue of courage, interpersonal strengths (love and kindness) under the virtue of humanity, civic strengths (fairness/justice) under the virtue of justice, and connection strengths (humour) under the virtue of transcendence. Our study further highlighted that these factors and the associated virtues are all interrelated and strong predictors of fieldwork performance for our undergraduate students. Emotional strengths and interpersonal strengths, along with connection strengths, include positive personal, active behaviours (e.g., being honest, being kind, being persistent, or to love the people you care for, having humour) that give students the skills they need to enable them to communicate and interact with others effectively in fieldwork practice from a base of loving relationships. By the same token, civic (or social) strengths, such as justice/fairness include social behaviours that positively impact others' lives and, therefore, help bolster a healthy community well-being. During fieldwork, students engage with social problems (e.g., social inequality, poverty, discrimination, racism) and their impacts on the lives of individuals, families, groups, and communities. Consequently, they have to reflect their competence on their commitment to justice as both an individual virtue and social virtue.

In light of the above evidence, the study makes a unique contribution to understanding the interrelated and interconnected nature of character strengths that are needed to fulfil the fieldwork goals. But at the same time, it recognises that each character strength is conceptualised as a basic skill, which is unique in how it helps students to meet their fieldwork requirements. Given that character strengths are also related to specific fieldwork skills and achievements, future research should focus on what types of different character strengths are used by students and how they are combined with each other when working with diverse clients and communities. Despite the limitations and the context-specific nature of the study, our findings appear to be well supported by previous studies on the benefits of using characters strengths and virtues across education and fieldwork for developing a positive and responsible attitude toward learning and achievement.

Conclusion

As mentioned previously, fieldwork education helps students to achieve competence in applying their character strengths as virtuous professional skills (most of them) they developed through their classroom learning. Also, fieldwork education facilitates the transition from the role of student to that of social work practitioner. Under this spectrum, we educators, along with field instructors and supervisors, need to organise and support learning initiatives that will encourage our students to identify their character strengths as good qualities in themselves and teach them to use them so that they can be ready for the transition into professional life. Taking into account the results presented here, we believe that it is necessary to develop new innovative programmes and projects that correspond to modern trends in social work fieldwork education. Such fieldwork education will be based on the strengths perspective that focuses on student's abilities and skills and allows them to identify their personal strengths and virtues and, at the same time, apply them in practice. In conclusion, we hope this study provides a useful starting point for future research on developing a shared language of strengths and virtues between universities to deliver effective strength-based fieldwork programmes and ensure consistency with the mission and vision statements of the social work profession.

References

Arthur, J., & Earl, S. (2020). *Character in the Professions: How Virtue Informs Practice*. Research Report. Birmingham: Jubilee Centre for Character and Virtues, University of Birmingham.

Babbie, E. (2014). *The Basics of Social Research* (6th ed.) Wadsworth: Belmont-Cengage.

Bogo, M. (2010). *Achieving Competence in Social Work through Field Education*. Toronto: University of Toronto Press.

Carr, D., Arthur, J., & Kristjánsson, K. (2017). Varieties of virtue ethics: Introduction. In: Eggleston, B., & Miller, D. E. (Eds.). *Varieties of Virtue Ethics* (pp. 1–13). Basingstoke: Palgrave Macmillan.

Clark, C. (2006). Moral character in social work. *British Journal of Social Work*, 36(1), 75–89.

Council on Social Work Education (C.S.W.E.). (2015). Educational policy and accreditation standards for baccalaureate and master's social work programs. Retrieved from https://www.cswe.org/getattachment/Accreditation/Standards-and-Policies/2015-EPAS/2015EPASandGlossary.pdf.aspx.

Dahlsgaard, K., Peterson, C., & Seligman, M. (2005). Shared virtue: The convergence of valued human strengths across culture and history. *Review of General Psychology*, 9(3), 203–213. DOI: 10.1037/1089-2680.9.3.203.

Delbecq, A. L., & Gill, S. L. (1985). Justice as a prelude to teamwork in medical centers. *Health Care Management Review*, 10(1), 45–51.

Fehr, B., Sprecher, S., & Underwood, L. G. (Eds.) (2008). *The Science of Compassionate Love: Theory, Research, and Applications*. Malden: Wiley-Blackwell.

Ferguson, Z. (2017). *The Place of Kindness: Combating Loneliness and Building Stronger Communities*. Carnegie Trust.

Gilgun, F. J., & Sharma, A. (2012). The uses of humour in case management with high-risk children and their families. *British Journal of Social Work*, 42(3), 560–577. DOI: 10.1093/bjsw/bcr070.

Heintz, S., & Ruch, W. (2019). Character strengths and job satisfaction: Differential relationships across occupational groups and adulthood. *Applied Research in Quality of Life*, 15(2), 503–527. DOI: 10.1007/s11482-018-9691-3.

Hugman, R., Pawar, M., Anscombe, A. W., & Wheeler, A. (2020). *Virtue Ethics in Social Work Practice*. London: Routledge.

International Federation of Social Workers (I.F.S.W.). (2014). Global definition of the social work profession. Retrieved from https://www.ifsw.org/what-is-social-work/global-definition-of-social-work/.

Krippendorff, K. (2019). *Content Analysis: An Introduction to Its Methodology* (4th ed.). London: Sage publications.

Langley, S. (2016, July 1). Four strengths tools based on positive psychology. Retrieved from https://langleygroup.com.au/four-strengths-tools-based-on-positive-psychology/.

Mason, C. (2012). Social work and the 'art of relationship': Parents' perspectives on an intensive family support project. *Child and Family Social Work*, 17(3), 368–377. DOI: 10.1111/j.1365-2206.2011.00791.x.

Molina, A. D., & McKeown, C. L. (2012). The heart of the profession: Understanding publicservice values. *Journal of Public Affairs Education*, 18(2), 375–396.

Niemiec, R. M. (2013). VIA character strengths: Research and practice (The first 10 years). In: H. H. Knoop & A. Delle Fave (Eds.), *Well-Being and Cultures: Perspectives on Positive Psychology* (pp. 11–30). New York: Springer.

O'Brien, M. E. (2018). *Spirituality in Nursing: Standing on Holy Ground* (6th ed.) Burlington: Jones & Bartlett Learning.

Papouli, E. (2019). Aristotle's virtue ethics as a conceptual framework for the study and practice of social work in modern times. *European Journal of Social Work*, 22(6), 921–934. DOI: 10.1080/13691457.2018.1461072.

Park, N. (2004). Character strengths and positive youth development. *Annals of the American Academy of Political and Social Science*, 591(1), 40–54. DOI: 10.1177/0002716203260079.

Park, N., & Peterson, C. (2008). Positive psychology and character strengths: Application to strengths-based school counseling. *Professional School Counseling*, 12(2), 85–92.

Park, N., Peterson, C., & Seligman, M. E. P. (2006). Character strengths in fifty-four nations and the fifty US states. *The Journal of Positive Psychology*, 1(3), 118–129. DOI: 10.1080/17439760600619567.

Pawar, M., Hugman, R., Alexandra, A., & Anscombe, A. (2017). Virtue-led social work practice. In: M. Pawar, R. Hugman, A. Alexandra, & A. W. B. Anscombe (Eds.), *Empowering Social Workers: Virtuous Practitioners* (1st ed.) (pp. 193–204). Singapore: Springer. DOI: 10.1007/978-981-10-3809-9.

Pawar, M., Hugman, R., Alexandra, A., & Anscombe, A. W. (2020). *A Search for Virtue Ethics: Social Work Ethics Curriculum and Educators' Survey*. Monograph, I.L.W.S. Report 128. Albury: Charles Sturt University.

Peterson, C., & Park, N. (2009). Classifying and measuring strengths of character. In: S. J. Lopez & C. R. Snyder (Eds.) *Oxford Handbook of Positive Psychology* (2nd ed.) (pp. 25–33) New York: Oxford University Press.

Peterson, C., & Park, N. (2012). Character strengths and the life of meaning. In: P. T. P. Wong (Ed.), *The Human Quest for Meaning: Theories, Research, and Applications* (2nd ed.) (pp. 277–295). New York: Routledge.

Peterson, C., & Seligman, M. E. P. (2004). *Character Strengths and Virtues: A Handbook and Classification*. American Psychological Association. Oxford University Press.

Rindt-Hoffman, S., Kernes, J. L., & Bui, N. H. (2019). Attachment style, spirituality, and compassionate love among mental health professionals. *Journal of Mental Health Counseling*, 4(2), 112–126. DOI: 10.17744/mehc.41.2.02.

Shogren, A. K., Singh, N., Niemiec, R., & Wehmeyer, L. M. (2017). Character strengths and mindfulness. *Clinical Psychology*. DOI: 10.1093/oxfordhb/9780199935291.013.77.

Snyder, C. R., & Lopez, S. J. (2002). *Handbook of Positive Psychology*. New York: Oxford University Press.

Tang, X., Li, Y., Duan, W., Mu, W., & Cheng, X. (2019). Character strengths lead to satisfactory educational outcomes Through strength use: A longitudinal analysis. *Frontiers in Psychology*, 10, 1829. DOI: 10.3389/fpsyg.2019.01829.

Thiers, N. (2018). Reader's guide/the social-emotional learning moment. *Educational Leadership*, 76(2), 7–7. Retrieved from http://www.ascd.org/publications/educational_leadership/oct18/vol76/num02/The_Social-Emotional_Learning_Moment.aspx.

Thun, B., & Kelloway, E. K. (2011). Virtuous leaders: Assessing character strengths in the workplace. *Canadian Journal of Administrative Sciences/Revue Canadienne des Sciences de l'Administration*, 28(3), 270–283.

Underwood, L. G. (2008). Compassionate love: A framework for research. In: B. Fehr, S. Sprecher, & L. G. Underwood (Eds.) *The Science of Compassionate Love: Theory, Research, and Applications* (pp. 3–25). Wiley-Blackwell. DOI: 10.1002/9781444303070.ch1.

van der Weegen, K., Hoondert, M., Timmermann, M., & van der Heide, A. (2019). Ritualization as alternative approach to the spiritual dimension of palliative care: A concept analysis. *Journal of Religion and Health*, 58(6), 2036–2046. DOI: 10.1007/s10943-019-00792-z.

V.I.A. Institute on Character. (n.d.). The 24 character strengths. Retrieved from https://www.viacharacter.org/character-strengths.

Wells, D. D., & Molina, A. D. (2017). The truth about honesty. *Journal of Public and Nonprofit Affairs*, 3(3), 292–308. DOI: 10.20899/jpna.3.3.292-308.

Yotsidi, V., Pagoulatou, A., Kyriazos, T., & Stalikas, A. (2018). The role of hope in academic and work environments: An integrative literature review. *Psychology*, 9(3), 385–402.

31

Supervision About Culture and Culture in Supervision

International Field Placement

Gurid Aga Askeland and Elsa Døhlie

In the Global North, it has been increasingly common for social work educational programmes to offer students field placement abroad. To a large degree, students travel from the Global North to the Global South. This illustrates a lack of reciprocity in opportunities for learning possibilities for students, and the same accounts for supervisors from the Global South. It seems like publications on international field placement are more focused on the students' learning from various perspectives than on the supervisors and their roles (Magnus, 2009; Das & Anand, 2014; Zuchowski, 2016; Cleak et al., 2016; Mathews & Lough, 2017). The significance of partnership between the sending and receiving institutions and consequences for training and quality of supervision seem to be lacking.

In this chapter, we will refer to Norway, and particularly use VID Specialized University as a case study. Internationalisation of education is a political aim in Norway, in accordance with the Bologna Process (White Paper no. 14, 2008–2009). The Norwegian framework for social work education addresses the increased immigration of people with various ethnic, cultural, and religious backgrounds, which will influence society's development. A multicultural competence is, therefore, required in social work (*Forskrift for nasjonal retningslinje for sosionomutdanning*, 2019). International field placement is expected to contribute to this competence.

Since the 1980s, VID Specialized University[1] has had students in field placements in various countries in the Global South. Between 15% and 20% of students choose placement abroad, which last 4.5 months.

To prepare for these field placements, representatives from universities in the Global North visit and approve institutions for collaborations in the Global South. However, we are not aware of studies regarding supervisors from the Global South being invited to the Global North to develop a common understanding of field placement supervision.

In this chapter, by referring to students travelling from the Global North to the Global South, we will focus on the preparation and education of supervisors in the receiving countries. Based on a pilot study exploring students' learning experiences from field placement in the Global South (Askeland et al., 2018), we decided to invite field supervisors from the same countries to a week's intensive seminar on supervision in Norway. The intention of the seminar was to offer supervisors from the Global South some insights into the cultural background of the students

DOI: 10.4324/9781032164946-36

they receive, and for the participants to learn more about the Norwegian contextual nature of social work in general and supervision more specifically.

The purpose of this chapter is to highlight the importance of how culture influences supervision. In international field placement, we expect discrepancies between the supervisors and students' cultural backgrounds. This might be implicit, and in supervision, it is important to address it explicitly. We will discuss how a partnership between the sending and receiving institutions may contribute to the development of supervision. We are aware that power relations play a role in partnerships between educational institutions in the Global North and receiving organisations in the Global South and between students and supervisors. However, power relations will not be focused on in this chapter, as it has not been dealt with in the empirical material to which we are referring.

Culture is a set of norms, traditions, and values transferred in a somewhat changed form from one generation to the next within a community (Klausen, 1992). Culture has a stabilising and a dynamic function in a society. This implies that transfer of behaviour makes it possible for people to communicate without necessarily accepting each other's points of view (Eriksen, 2001). Culture may be regarded as socially constructed and, thus, under constant change, as it is created by human beings in their contexts (Askeland & Døhlie, 2006).

We consider social work as contextually and socially constructed. When social work is performed in a context different from what the supervisors and students are respectively familiar with, the supervision must open up a space for exchange about cultural differences. This is demanding for the supervisors. However, it might lead to a clearer picture of how social work is socially constructed differently in various countries (Payne & Askeland, 2008). This is challenging for students, as they have access to knowledge primarily from their own context when they arrive in a new environment and vice versa for the supervisors.

Our main question is what structures and content may contribute to support the supervisors in students' learning in a foreign cultural context. To respond to this question, we will discuss experiences from the educational supervision project in relation to students' experiences and relevant educational theories and models.

The authors are both experienced in international social work and have been involved in preparing students for international field placement. We conducted the students' pilot study and, together with colleagues, organised and implemented the project for supervisors.

We will first introduce some educational and supervision theories and models and include culture and partnership as significant elements in supervision.

Theories and Models

The main content of the seminar, and the theories and models on which we based the programme, will constitute the background for the analysis and discussion of how to recognise culture and improve supervision.

Learning is an individual and a social process. It is interactional, which implies that supervisors and students mutually influence how and what students learn. Together, they create the learning situation. In international field placement, transformation of learning is a two-way process, from the theoretical studies in the home country to the practical experiences in a foreign setting and vice versa.

Learning in Different Contexts

Two well-known concepts frequently used in learning theory are the transmission metaphor and the participation metaphor (Lahn & Jensen, 2008). The transmission metaphor presupposes passive conveyance of established knowledge from experts to students, while the participation metaphor expects students to actively partake in their own learning processes and in knowledge creation. The latter has its parallel in Dewey's (2014) and Freire's (1978) thinking (in Askeland et al., 2018).

The participation metaphor is dominant in higher education in Norway, with the permeating concept that students are responsible for their own learning. Students are expected to acquire learning through reading, collaborating, discussing, reflecting, and even opposing and criticising the teachers' lecturing. Nevertheless, the transmission metaphor is also the basis for conveying professional theories and competence in Norway. However, in many countries and cultures, the transmission metaphor will be the dominant one.

Supervision could be based on either or both metaphors. The transmission metaphor is recognised by transference of knowledge, instructions, and advice from supervisors to students. The participative metaphor is recognised by process orientation, reflection, and dialogue between supervisors and students.

Experiential Learning

Experiential learning is in line with the participation metaphor. It is a useful approach for students' learning in field placement. Learning is a confluent process in which an intellectual activity and emotional and bodily reactions mutually influence each other and create a holistic understanding (Grendstad & Sandven, 1986). When experiential learning is the basis for supervision, the intention is to link theoretical knowledge, experiences in practice, and personal development. It also stresses the role of formal education and professional development (Kolb, 1984). Kolb's definition of experiential learning theory is 'the process whereby knowledge is created through the transformation of experience. Sustainable knowledge results from the combination of grasping and transforming experiences' (Kolb, 1984: 41 in Askeland et al., 2018: 694).

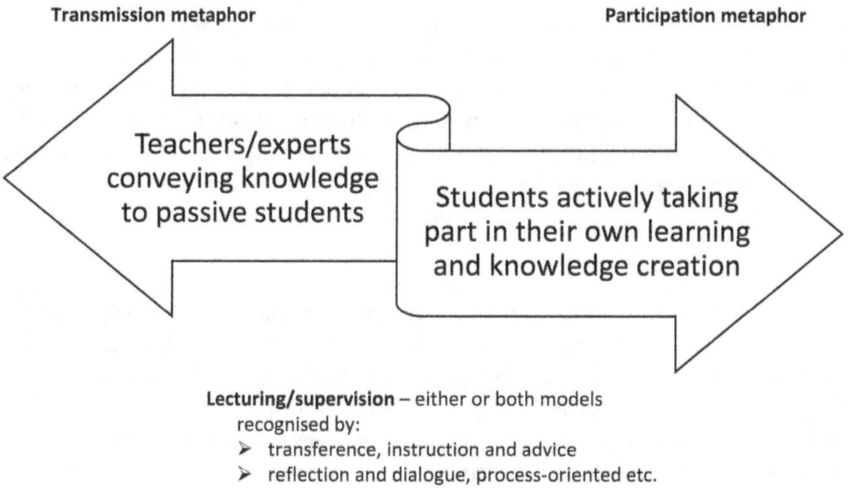

Figure 31.1 Two educational metaphors. Source: Askeland, G. A. A. (2017) *Transforming International Experiences into Professional Competence: Quality and Sustainability.* Oslo: SIU conference: Borderless education 15–16 March.

Personal experiences take place in a cultural context. The experiential learning process starts with identifying a personal experience of concern for the students. This has to be reflected upon from divergent perspectives in order to transform the experience from a happening to sustainable knowledge.

Figuratively, reflection means throwing-back, consideration, or second thoughts. Reflection, in this meaning, is used to change taken-for-granted ways of thinking, feeling, and acting that people bring with them from their own culture into a new context. Schøn (1995, 1987) distinguishes between reflection on action and reflection in action (Fook & Gardener, 2007; Fook & Gardener, 2012). The former is what takes place in supervision when reflecting on action after the experiences have taken place within a cultural framework. A step further in professional competence is reflection in action, which happens when a person is able to reflect continuously in the situation, simultaneously changing one's thinking and, thereby, action. In reflection in action, it is taken for granted that a cultural understanding will be integrated.

Additionally, according to Schøn, there is a difference between knowing *what* and knowing *how* and between knowledge in action and knowing in action. The former refers to having general knowledge as knowing what, while the latter is the ability to apply knowledge in a specific situation, meaning knowing how. Knowledge about different cultures will be considered knowing *what* and is what the students learn about the culture in preparation for the field placement. In doing so, they might have knowledge in action when they arrive. Reflection on learning and living in a new culture may contribute to transforming *what* to *how* and, thereby, enable them to practice knowing in action.

Situated Learning

Situated learning is a participative learning model in which teaching takes place in real life surroundings outside the classroom, such as in international field placement, where students live and work in a foreign society. Various factors influencing the field placement will become visible for students, such as the cultural, economic, and political context (Payne & Askeland, 2008). The advantages of such an approach are that the 'distinction between learning and doing, between social identity and knowledge, between education and professional practice' (Lave, 1997: 143) are broken down, which makes learning in the community important (Wenger-Trayner et al., 2015). Supervision, in relation to situated learning, gives the opportunity to learn about and in culture. In situated learning, the supervisors become role models for the students in the new culture. However, it is not enough for the students to copy the supervisors. To learn *how* and be able to practise knowing in action requires that students reflect on what they observe and how they may transform it into their own competence.

Supervision

A main purpose of supervision, according to the participative metaphor, is to help students bridge the gap between practice and theory. It contributes to the integration of basic knowledge, working methods, and ethical principles. Another purpose of supervision is to promote a learning process for a personal and professional development and identity. This presupposes respectful interaction between supervisors and students. The basis for supervision will be the students' experiences and related reactions in order to learn from it.

Supervision is influenced by the culture in which it takes place. Culture in supervision is a mode of supervision process in which students and their supervisors represent different cultures. The students are supported by actively initiated exchanges and sharing of cultural differences with their supervisors. Thus, culture becomes the overarching atmosphere of the supervision (Davys & Beddoe, 2010). Mutual sharing and reflection with the local supervisors in an atmosphere of openness and curiosity are what constitute culture in supervision. Accomplishing this is demanding for supervisors, and requires:

- Awareness of the differences between the supervisors and students in terms of values, styles of communication, learning theories and emotional reactions;
- Knowledge about one's own and the students' social and cultural contexts;
- Relationship building and performance in supervision;
- Skills and ability to support the students' professional training in a new cultural setting while respecting the students' own cultural identity.

(Arkin, 1999: 12 in Davys & Beddoe, 2010: 44)

This is unlike supervision about culture, which would be more like the introduction students receive before they go abroad.

Culture in supervision might allow for the integration of emotional and bodily reactions to experiences as well as an intellectual reflection. This could contribute to a more holistic approach to sustainable learning as it lays the ground for broader understanding and acceptance of differences in and between cultures.

Supervision, and particularly in culture, might cause changes in understanding, opinions, values, and prejudices. It might, therefore, cause ambivalence, both for the students and the supervisors. Understanding people and contexts that are different from one's own is paramount in social work. Supervision in culture enables this to take place.

Supervisors' Roles

For various reasons, supervisors may practise different approaches to supervision, which may take the form of one of three approaches. First, giving planned information and advice. Second, quick responses to the students' questions 'on the go'. This might be superficial, as it focuses on the immediate challenges students experience. Both of these approaches could be related to the transmission metaphor. Third, structured and systematic approaches, which imply time set aside for prioritised and prepared sharing and reflection. The latter is the most demanding approach for both supervisors and students.

The approaches may be connected to the supervisors' performance of different roles. Frequently used roles in supervision are administrator, teacher, and supporter (Kadushin & Harkness, 2014; Davys & Beddoe, 2010).

The administrator role organises and structures the field placement, provides tasks, and makes sure that the users get the service for which they are eligible. Supervisors are responsible for the quality of the students' performance (Killén, 2017). In this role, the supervisors make sure that students get necessary instruction and advice. This is particularly important in the beginning and decreases as the students become familiar with the tasks. It belongs to the administrator role to instruct the students about rules and regulations. The cultural context is subordinated.

The teacher role is important in conveying knowledge and practice wisdom as part of supervision. The role includes both transfer of concrete knowledge as well as getting the students to reflect in order to discover their own knowledge and competence and to integrate theory and practice, including cultural knowledge. Presupposing that there is a cohesion between teaching and learning for the supervisors and students, the supervisors could be perceived as a role model for the students. Apprenticeship is a basic phenomenon in social work education.

The supervisors, as supporters or helpers, challenge and encourage the students to get insight into their personal and professional role. This implies becoming aware of attitudes, prejudices, feelings that influence the situation, and the analysis of and reactions to it. Emotions and bodily reactions are important sources of knowledge that are very easily overlooked. The supervisors might need to assist students to be able to value and convert their personal involvement and commitment into professional practice. Personal support might be necessary for students to perform tasks that are new and frightening to them, emotionally provoking, or personally demanding. In international social work, students might also need support in distinguishing between their backgrounds and themselves, what is generally valid, and what is culturally specific. The supporter role is a prerogative for students for learning in culture.

These three roles overlap and, in combination, ensure that various sides of supervision are taken care of. The supervisors' competence is to find out which role fits best in which situation. However, the choice of role is also a cultural issue. In more hierarchical societies in which teaching is primarily lecturing, the supervisors might feel most familiar with the administrative and teacher roles. The supporter role is more demanding and time consuming in any culture. It implies sound preparation and profound reflection for both parties and may provoke ambivalence and resistance. However, learning, for supervisors and students, might be more exciting and give new insight.

Partnership Model

The idea of partnership is to build cooperation between partners with joint interests. In international field placement, the partners might not be equivalent, such as educational institutions on one side and practice organisations on the other. Building a fruitful cooperation between partners in different cultures, and under different structures, with stakeholders at different levels in their organisations, is demanding. A model, called 'The five 'i's', was developed for analysing the progression of investment in international exchange in higher educational institutions (Payne & Askeland, 2008: 129). To get an indication of the comprehensiveness and the amount of investment in building a functioning partnership in international field placement, we have simplified the model.

- *In time*: Allocated time for achieving partnership goals.
- *In commitment*: Personal and organisational commitment of both stakeholders and resources.
- *In mutuality*: Balance between imposed and mutual consent.
- *In complexity*: Demands on the participants and organisations of the cross-national activity.
- *In equality*: Distribution of power between the parties.

(Payne & Askeland, 2008: 129).

In partnerships, goals may be formulated demanding different degrees of involvement. For the purpose of this chapter that analyses cooperation with the supervisors in the Global South, we have simplified a model of 'objectives in cross-national work' (Payne & Askeland, 2008: 130). In the hierarchy of goals, the formulations will develop from less demanding to more comprehensive. Goal obtainment will be influenced by the investment of the 'the five i's'.

- *Interest*: Providing a well-rounded understanding of the cross-national work.
- *Information*: Gaining information may be used to pursue one's own objectives.
- *Instruction*: Providing information that helps the other.

- *Interaction*: Providing an opportunity for cross-national relationships for social development.
- *Integration*: Achieving joint development and enabling progress for both parties.

(Payne & Askeland, 2008: 130).

Challenges in building partnerships are influenced by different cultures in the cooperating countries as well as in the partners' organisations. The cultural influences may be related to social conventions, power distributions, gender equality, and conceptualisation of social work in the organisations.

An Educational Project

In 2015, VID Specialized University arranged an educational project for 13 supervisors from five countries in Africa, Asia, and the Middle East, with a minimum of two participants from each country. Approximately half of the participants did not hold a passport and had never been abroad before. The main element of the project was a seminar on supervision and contextual social work. The participants had already been supervisors for our students and other Norwegian social work students or committed themselves to work in this context in the future. In addition, seven Norwegian participants from two other Norwegian universities were invited. This was a unique event, in that, for the first time, supervisors from the Global South attended such an event in Norway. The seminar facilitated an unprecedented meeting point between supervisors from three continents and, thus, creating a multi-cultural arena for sharing.

From our own background, we know that international teaching and learning approaches differ. This is in congruence with the students' reported experiences over time. The aim of the project was to develop a common understanding of field placement supervision and to strengthen the partnership. The subjects we decided to emphasise in the seminar were selected from what we revealed as significant points in the students' study and from our own experiences. The educational theories and models presented above were the basis for the content and the learning and teaching approaches in the project.

The seminar programme covered subjects such as professional supervision roles, structure, and content, including challenges in supervising students from a different culture. Another subject was partnership and mutual expectations between institutions sending and receiving students. The participants were informed about the preparatory course the students go through before leaving for international field placement. The teaching methods at the seminar were a mix of theoretical input, group discussions, reflections, and feedback sessions.

Most of the international participants stayed in the homes of Norwegian colleagues, and common dinners were hosted by Norwegian families. These arrangements aimed to enhance the participants' insight into Norwegian culture.

Originally, this was meant to be an internal experiential learning project. Therefore, we wanted to collect as much information as possible for our own development process. We decided to get the participants' written feedback throughout the process of the project. When we analysed the material, we found that publishing it might inspire others to develop it further.

At the starting point of the seminar, the participants filled in a questionnaire about their expectations. Semi-structured questionnaires were systematically prepared beforehand. During the seminar, we systematically collected written individual and group responses and written reports from plenary discussions. At the end of the seminar, the participants filled in a semi-structured evaluation form covering different subjects of the seminar and their reflections on the organisation, process, and content of the project. All responses were anonymous. All the material has been summarised and analysed. One project researcher collected and systemised all the written material from the seminar. We have both gone through and discussed how to interpret the material. For the purpose of this chapter, we have only used the evaluation forms filled in by the international participants and not those filled out by Norwegian participants.

The findings from the seminar will be discussed in relation to the former pilot study of students' learning in international field placement (Askeland et al., 2018). In this study, we conducted focus group discussions with 12 students who had spent their field placement in the same countries as the supervisors represented, with one exception. This pilot study concluded that supervision is paramount for transforming learning experiences into sustainable competence.

Even if the material from these two sources is limited due to selected sampling, we find the experiences and results they highlight important for further discussion and follow up.

Supervisors and Students – What Did They Tell Us?

We first present the supervisors' experiences from the seminar, and then see them in light of the study of students' experiences in field placement, which had been published earlier (Askeland et al., 2018).

Supervision – Various Expectations

At the beginning of the seminar, the participants expressed some expectations. First, they expected to strengthen their supervision skills. Further, they wanted to understand how to address students' supervision needs, including understanding their responsibility for the students, both in the organisation and outside. These responses were connected to the cultural challenges they experienced with the students.

Quotes from the evaluation forms about the benefits of the seminar were: 'Useful for my career and supervision'. 'Learnt what to tackle with the students'. 'Great eye opener'. 'Learning from different experiences, which helped me to strengthen my supervision skills'.

Further, in the written evaluation, the participants were asked about competences and strengths they had discovered in themselves. Some reported that they had become aware of their function as a role model, while others said that they had strengthened their personal flexibility and ability to adjust and handle difficult issues with the students. Others stated that they had learned about the various roles in supervision and how to 'adjust and facilitate [a] learning ground'.

When challenged about what they would like to try out in the future, they referred to 'Systematic and structured supervision'. 'Trying out the supervisors' various roles'. 'Have more group discussions and reflection with students'. 'Support the students' in their understanding of context and culture'. 'Give them systematic feedback and perform mid-term evaluation'.

Some also emphasised during the seminar that they would have liked to learn about social work in Norway.

VID expects students to receive 1.5 hours of individual supervision each week, or alternatively converted into some group supervision. In our study of students' experiences in international field placement, most of the students missed being encouraged by the supervisors to reflect on their experiences and performances in the given cultural context. Most of the students experienced supervision as lecturing, practical information, and receiving advice on how to perform their tasks. They were hardly asked about their own reflection on their experiences and performances and what learning they could draw from it. Nevertheless, some students reported having been encouraged to share their feelings and reflections on their cultural experiences.

Culture in Supervision

Supervisors' Experiences

To learn about culture and cultural differences was the main expectation expressed at the beginning of the seminar. During the seminar, culture appeared to be the main challenge in supervision and, for them, the most surprising and provoking in the students' behaviour.

The supervisors realised that culture is an underlying issue for students struggling with acknowledging what is social work in the new context: 'Assuming that our system will work like their systems. The thought of thinking you know what you don't know'. Another issue that came up was their surprise that the students 'do not want to talk about religion'. Likewise, the supervisors were concerned about the students' straightforwardness, which might indicate a lack of respect 'for authorities and food', and 'how they choose to dress', and 'assuming that it is OK to take pictures everywhere. They got so excited about coming to Africa and feel they have a lot of freedom to do anything they want'.

In the evaluation of the seminar, the supervisors stated that the introduction and focus on culture had given them an understanding of the significance of cultural influence in supervision. 'Understanding the students' culture will help me understand them more and how to handle our culture with them and relate [to] the context'. While the participants stated that they became better able to see culture integrated in supervision, they would have liked to have learned more about it.

The international supervisors were exposed to elements of the Norwegian culture by staying at colleagues' homes. The supervisors shared their experiences related to time, differences in food, social codes, weather, and seasons. Examples given included the bus arriving and the seminar starting on time. 'Cold food in a cold climate'. 'Grey trees without leaves'. 'Nobody talked to each other in public transportation'.

Students' Experiences

Culture was also a main concern for the students in the international field placement study (Askeland et al., 2018). The motivation for going abroad in this student group was curiosity about other cultures and living in a foreign country over time. One main learning experience was being a newcomer in a foreign country.

> They felt insecure and powerless when not understanding what was going on in the society. They connected this to not being part of the culture and not understanding the behaviour and the languages.
>
> *(Ibid. p. 697)*

Working through and reflecting on their experiences after they returned home, they related this experience to how it is to be a newcomer in their home country. In hindsight, the students became aware that they interpreted what was going on from their own cultural perspectives and became conscious of their own prejudices. The students became aware of how the contextual setting is forming social work and the role of the local social worker. They had to think through whether what they were assigned to do could be considered social work from their Norwegian perspectives. Reflecting upon the meaning of context, students got a clear picture that clients, local social workers, and they themselves all belong to different cultures. They realised that, as social workers, they cannot assume that the clients' contexts are similar to their own not only in an international setting but also when doing social work at home. This could be considered a groundbreaking discovery.

All students in this study discovered that religion – whether it be Christianity, Hinduism, or Islam – was a more integrated part of peoples' identity and culture than they were used to at home. It permeated clients' lives, organisational systems, and collegial relationships. The students were unprepared for how to relate to religions. What they had learned in their training in Norway was that religion should be an issue only if the clients brought it up.

Partnership

Some of the expectations for the seminar were to establish further cooperation and better links for networking with the Norwegian partners. This should be initiated by the sending institutions.

It was expressed during the seminar that it is important to improve and escalate the dialogue between supervisors in the Global South and the responsible person in the educational institution. Before the students arrive, the VID's supervisors abroad receive a manual containing rules and regulations for the field placement, including students' assignments and evaluation form. This is a direct translation of what the Norwegian supervisors receive. The participants revealed that they had not fully understood the content, as they did not have an intimate knowledge of the Norwegian framework in which it was developed. In the evaluation, it was expressed that the interaction between the sending and the receiving partners had been long awaited and 'most of the expectations were met' by holding the seminar.

The supervisors expressed that they realised that they were hardly involved in the communication that took place between the students and the educational institution during the field placement.

Discussion

Supervision

Several studies have revealed a lack of qualified supervision in international students' exchanges in social work (Panos et al., 2004; Yeom & Bae, 2010 in Mathew & Lough, 2017; Cleak et al., 2016). It is, therefore, relevant to question whether the training of supervisors abroad has the same priority for the sending institutions as training of supervisors at home. Yet, supervision in international field placement is more demanding, as they have to manage in a multicultural atmosphere. In sending students abroad in international field placement, we must respect that the local models of supervision will be shaped by their cultural system, learning theories, and social conventions. Nevertheless, the sending institutions are responsible for the students' learning according to the Norwegian standard and for supporting the supervisors in fulfilling the job.

The main question in this chapter is what structures and content may contribute to the support of supervisors in the students' learning in a foreign cultural context.

If the supervision abroad had a clearer inclusion of cultural reflections, a breakthrough of what the supervisors reported as missing in the students' approaches, understanding and adjusting to the new context might have happened. This could have enhanced the satisfaction of both the supervisors and the students. However, it is important not to overlook that distance in time and space between experiences and reflection contributes to transforming experiences into sustainable knowledge. When the students worked through their experiences on their return home, they showed that they had reached a mature reflection that might not necessarily take place while in the situation abroad. This includes their own adjustment to the local culture that the supervisors reacted to as described above. The supervisors do not learn about this unless the partnership includes feedback from the sending institution after the termination of the field placement.

In addition, the analysis shows how important it is to have a close partnership with regular exchanges in which the supervisors abroad report unresolved issues to the educational institutions. Equally important is, at the end of the field placement, providing the supervisors, in return, with feedback about what the students have learned and what contributed to it. This might strengthen the supervisors in the supporter role. Likewise, it creates mutual responsibility for the students' learning by moving from information, via instruction, to integration, according to the 'five i's' model. When the sending institutions prioritise contacting the students and not involving the supervisors during the field placement, a bonding seems to take place that may create a barrier to supervision. In the worst case, this might influence the supervisors' self-confidence. The contact person at the sending institution has to be sensitive to when this occurs and then take a mediating role between the students and the supervisors.

Culture is an underlying factor, which influences the relationships in the supervision setting, within the organisation where the students are to work, and in the society in which they are to live. Nevertheless, both supervisors and students report this as a topic missing in their communication. How culture permeates the experiences and the learning outcome is easily overlooked.

The students were concerned that most of the supervision they received was different from what they expected. Magnus (2009) maintains that students must be prepared to accept cultural differences in approaches to supervision. We cannot demand that supervisors apply a participative learning approach without any introduction from the sending institutions if that is not a familiar approach. It explains that a cultural misunderstanding might occur in supervision. To prevent this, students are now given a somewhat more specific preparation in our educational institution. The students are now better prepared to understand and relate to different approaches to supervision. On one hand, in a culture where the transmission model is dominant, the students must take an active responsibility for preparing issues and questions on which they need to reflect. On the other hand, the sending institutions must prepare the supervisors for the students' learning approaches without taking it to be at the expense of their authority as supervisors. Learning by living in a culture presupposes that the supervisors have the authority to guide the students to acceptable behaviour in the local culture.

In the evaluation of the seminar, the participants reported that the whole arrangement had contributed to their cultural understanding, professional growth, and competence in supervision. We, therefore, might hope that, for these supervisors, what they learned may be reflected in their future supervision. However, we are aware that long-lasting effects would rely on a continuous follow-up.

The students learn about cultural aspects in their pre-departure training. However, to identify and acknowledge how a culture pervades a society has to be encountered and reflected on. Situated learning about a culture means learning by living in the culture. To live in a culture is a holistic experience, which engages intellectual, emotional, and bodily reactions. We observed this in both the supervisors' reactions during their one-week stay in Norway and their reflections on the students' behaviours, as well as in the students' study. In relation to a holistic approach, a reminder from supervisors, as well as from students, was that students were unprepared to deal with religion as an integrated aspect of the societies and people's lives. Religion is a contextual factor that international social work has to take into account, as, for many people, it is an integrated part of their lives (Askeland & Døhlie, 2015).

Living in a new culture may easily provoke a comparison with what is known from home. We then may end up with an ethnocentric or relativistic attitude to the local culture (Døhlie & Askeland, 2006). In the seminar, supervisors referred to students who recommended their home systems to be superior. To prevent this, Western assumptions need to be challenged, and supervision becomes paramount for acknowledging the holistic experience in order to develop a multicultural competence.

By arranging for the participants to stay with Norwegian colleagues during the seminar, the intention was to give them a sense of living in another culture, particularly those who had not been abroad before, and a parallel experience to what the students go through. This may have contributed to making supervision a two-way learning experience for both students and supervisors (Matthew & Lough, 2017).

When culture has a prominent place in supervision, it may contribute to a multicultural competency for students and for supervisors. Following the requirements above by Arkin (1999 in Davys & Beddoe, 2010: 43) have their parallels in social work in relationship building. When practised by supervisors, they are acting as role models for students by giving them a real-life experience of good social work practice.

Partnership

The educational policy of higher education in Norway requires international exchanges for both students and academic staff. This implies the necessity for developing and analysing partnerships. Generally, social work partnerships between educational institutions and local agencies seem to be weak (Mathew & Lough, 2017).

A seminar was a significant step in trying to establish an equal platform for sharing and integrating different cultural experiences in order to build a reciprocal partnership. Visits, so far, had been from the Global North to the Global South. We wanted to turn this around. Investing in mutual commitment could result in equality between the partners, which, again, may nourish interaction and, hopefully, lay the ground for integration. One of the participants' views on partnership was that it 'was long awaited for'. By this, we obtained an interaction hoping to lay the groundwork for a goal of integration.

Evaluation from the participants at the seminar shows that the partnerships between the sending and the receiving institutions do not function sufficiently. We would, therefore, look more closely at the connection between the comprehensiveness of our investment in the partnership in relation to the level of goal attainment.

The allocated time for achieving partnership has been spent visiting institutions in the Global South, negotiating contracts and financial compensations and have, thus, obtained the goals of interest and information for both parties. This requires limited time and degree of commitment from both sides.

Written material about the study programme, including requirements for field placement, students' assignments, and information about the students were provided to the supervisors, expecting it to be self-explanatory. It was meant to fulfil the goal of instruction. The feedback at the seminar showed that the sending institution had not understood and not taken seriously into account mutuality in developing a study material for a context different from a Norwegian one. The complexity in doing this became obvious when the participants expressed that, because they did not know the Norwegian culture and teaching and learning approaches, they had not been able to use the written material sent to them. At the seminar, the participants expressed that they missed information about Norwegian social work. We realise that this would have helped them to understand the frame of reference for the understanding of social work the students brought with them. Such an introduction would acknowledge the complexity of the partnership. The complexity is also related to the fact that several partners represent their own organisations, political systems, and cultures, which would be unfamiliar to the other partners.

To achieve the goal of integration, enabling joint development and progress for both partners require interaction over time.

During the field placement period, the educational institution has regular follow-up communications on Skype, primarily with the students, but sometimes the supervisors are included. The supervisors reported that they felt that the educational institution bonded more with the students than with them. Their experiences were rarely requested, unless related to the students' personal and professional development. This reveals a one-way interest and communication lacks exploration of each other's understanding. If the students are unsatisfied, it may result in closing the partnership without discussing it with the supervisors. It does not contribute to fulfilling the goal of interaction in order to develop the quality of supervision. A mutual exchange, including students, supervisors in the host country, and the educational institutions would contribute to moving from the goal of instruction to the goal of interaction.

Conclusion

Supervisors and students are concerned about culture missing in the supervision, respectively from different perspectives. The supervisors' and students' lack of knowledge about each other's culture effects their relationship and learning. When culture is an implicit and not an explicit basis in supervision, it becomes a barrier for the supervisors' feedback and for the students' learning.

Supervision in an international field placement requires that various aspects of learning about as well as living in a culture play a significant role. To live in a culture is a holistic experience which engages intellectual, emotional, and bodily reactions. To transform holistic experiences into sustainable knowledge and competence requires reflection both during the field placement and on the return home. Supporting supervisors in integrating culture in supervision means that supervision training and partnership building are required.

Inviting the supervisors from the Global South to a seminar with the teaching staff responsible for international exchanges at the educational institution was a first step in offering supervision training. A benefit for them and the sending institution was to realise, through the exchanges, how cultural understanding could become a barrier or a facilitator for students' sustainable learning.

By offering supervisors a one-time event for training and cultural experiences, without following it up systematically, complicates the dynamic process of building competence and a reciprocal partnership. To obtain a satisfying benefit for the students' learning, partnerships must become valuable for both partners.

The sending institutions are responsible for the quality of the students' learning, and therefore also for the supervisors' ability to understand and handle the students' challenges in a new culture. To follow up this responsibility is a prerequisite for a partnership over time that allows for a respectful atmosphere for sharing and development. Mutual partnership is an underdeveloped condition for student exchanges. A satisfying supervision for both supervisors and students depends on a well-developed and respectful partnership between the receiving and sending institutions.

The conclusions in this chapter are based on selected material. We, therefore, see the need for developing partnerships and ways of highlighting supervision in culture and culture in supervision followed by systematic research.

Note

1 Formerly Diakonhjemmet University College.

References

Arkin, N. (1999). Culturally sensitive students' supervision: Difficulties and challenges. *The Clinical Supervisors* 18(2), 1–16.

Askeland, G. A. A. & Døhlie, E. (2006). *Internasjonalt sosialt arbeid–når sosialarbeidaren kryssar grenser. Internasjonalt sosialt arbeid. Innsats på andres Arena.* Universitetsforlaget.

Askeland, G. A. A. & Døhlie, E. (2015). Contextualising international social work: Religion as a relevant factor. *International Social Work* 58(2), 261–269.

Askeland, G. A. A., Døhlie, E.& Grosvold, K. (2018). International field placement in social work: Relevant for working in the home country. *International Social Work* 61(5), 692–705.

Cleak, H., Anand, J. & Das, C. (2016). Asking the critical questions: An evaluation of social work evaluation in an international placement. *British Journal of Social Work* 46(2), 389–408.

Das, C. & Anand, J. C. (2014). Strategies for critical reflection in international contexts for social work students. *International Social Work* 57(2), 109–120.

Dewey, J. (2014). *How We Think.* Revised edition. D.C. Heath.

Davys, A. & Beddoe, L. (2010). *Best Practice in Professional Supervision: A Guide for the Helping Professions.* Jessica Kingsley Publishers.

Døhlie, E. & Askeland, G. A. (2006). *Internasjonalt sosialtarbeid. Innsats på andres Arena.* Universitetsforlaget.

Eriksen, T. H. (2001). *Flerkulturell forståelse.* Universitetsforlaget.

Fook, J. & Gardener, F. (2007). *Practising Critical Reflection: A Resource Handbook.* Open University Press, McGraw-Hill House.

Fook, J. & Gardener, F. (eds.) (2012). *Critical Reflection in Context: Applications in Health and Social Care.* Routledge.

Forskrift for Nasjonal Retningslinje for Sosionomutdanning. (15.03.2019). https://lovdata.no/dokument/SF/forskrift/2019-03-15-409; https://www.regjeringen.no/contentassets/32eda0b38b8349e39e8ca18667b19890/forskrift-om-felles--sosialfagutdanninger.pdf (accessed 20.03.2019).

Freire, P. (1978). *De undertrygtes pædagogik.* Christian Eilers' Forlag.

Grendstad, N. M. & Sandven, G. J. (1986). *Å lære er å oppdage: Prinsipper og praktiske arbeidsmåter i konfluent pedagogikk.* Didakta.

Kadushin, A. & Harkness, D. (2014). *Supervision in Social Work.* Columbia University Press.

Killén, K. (2017). *Profesjonell utvikling og faglig veiledning. Et fellesfaglig perspektiv for helse-, sosiale og pedagogiske profesjoner.* Gyldendal.

Klausen, A. (1992). *Kultur, mønster og kaos.* Ad Notam Gyldendal.

Kolb, D. (1984). *Experiential Learning – Experience as the Source of Learning and Development.* Prentice Hall.

Lahn, L.Ch. & Jensen, K. (2008). Profesjon og Læring. In: A. Molander & L.I. Terum (Eds.), *Profesjonsstudier.* Universitetsforlaget.

Lave, J. (1997). Learning, apprenticeship, social practice. *Nordisk Pedagogik* 17(3), 140–151.

Magnus, P. (2009). Preparation for social work students to do cross-cultural social work education. *International Social Work* 52(3), 375–385.

Matthew, L. E. & Lough, B. J. (2017). Challenges social work students' encounter in international field placement and recommendations for responsible management. *Journal of Social Work Education* 53(1), 18–36.

Panos, P.T., Petty, G. L., Cox, S. E. & Jones-Hart, E. (2004). Survey of international field education placement accredited social work programs. *Journal of Social Work Education* 40(3), 467–478.

Payne, M. & Askeland, G. A. A. (2008). *Globalization and International Social Work: Postmodern Change and Challenge*: Aldershot.

Schøn, D. (1995). *The Reflective Practitioner.* Arena, 2. Reprint.

Schøn, D. (1987). *Educating the Reflective Practitioner.* Jossey-Bass Publishers.

Wenger-Trayner, E., Fenton-O'Creevy, M. & Hutchinson, S. (eds) (2015). *Learning in Landscapes of Practice: Boundaries, Identity, Knowledgeability in Practice-Based Learning.* Routledge.

White Paper No 14. (2008–2009). *Internationalisation of Education in Norway.* Summary in English: Report No. 14 (2008–2009) to the Storting. Norwegian Ministry of Educaatiom and Research.

Yeom, H. S. & Bae, H. (2010). Potential issues in field practicum students exchange between Korean and the USA. *International Social Work* 53(3), 311–326.

Zuchowski, I. (2016). Getting to know the context: The complexities of providing off-site supervision in social work practice. *British Journal of Social Work* 46(2), 409–426.

32

Resilience Enhancement in Social Work Field Education

Monika Punová[1]

In the early days of building social work, the focus was on the client and the client's needs, with the social worker helping them deal with difficult situations in life. As the discipline has gradually established itself, more attention is also paid to the worker. This change of perspective is accompanied by questions such as: 'Who is mindful of the needs and well-being of the social worker?' and 'How can the social worker deal with the demands of their profession?' This shift in perception reflects the fact that the social worker is now seen as a human being and a key instrument of assistance; like their clients, the worker also pursues goals (whether personal, professional, or social), has needs, perceives and experiences situations uniquely, and lives in a social context that affects them and influences their actions.

As observed by Beddoe and Davys (2016), the perception of social workers' well-being has developed over the past decade or two from an initial focus on the effects of traumatic professional experiences toward career-long well-being. This key shift from clients to workers ('caring for caretakers') became the underlying factor driving interest in the social worker's resilience and later also in the subject of resilience in social work education. This primary interest in strengthening the client's resilience with the help of a professional, thus, directed attention toward strengthening the worker's resilience as well. Consideration of how to cultivate resilience has then led to the conclusion that the subject of resilience needs to be implemented in social work education.

The fact that the work of social workers is demanding has been proven in a number of studies. They are exposed to many stressful situations in the conduct of their work that make them vulnerable to exhaustion (Adamson 2012; Collins 2008; Duffy et al. 2009; Morrison 2007; Punová 2020; Rose & Palattiyil 2020). It has also been shown that their work is more demanding, and they are more vulnerable to burnout, as compared with other helping professions (Bennett et al. 1993; Coffey et al. 2004; Kinman & Grant 2017; Grant & Kinman 2012, 2014). Curtis et al. (2010) examined the retention rate of British helping professionals after graduation. The number of years of professional experience in the field of study was lowest among social workers – only 8–13 years, followed by nurses (15 years), physicians (25 years), and pharmacists, who lasted longest (28 years). It is hardly surprising that the demands of social work extend to education, particularly field education. In this context, Punová (2019) speaks of a conflict between the students' expectations, often idealised, and the harsh reality of practice.

DOI: 10.4324/9781032164946-37

Dziegielewski et al. (2004) and Collins et al. (2010) believe that practice is harsher for students of social work, as compared with students of other disciplines.

On the other hand, the difficulties associated with the conduct of social work and field education cannot be viewed as an a priori source of distress and risk for the individual but can also be understood as a source of eustress and a challenge to be conquered. Overcoming life's adversities is the very basis of resilience. As we will show in the following section, resilience refers to dynamic developmental processes through which a person (e.g., a social work student) adapts and positively responds to explicit internal and external pressures (risks, adverse experiences). Not only does resilience help one overcome difficult life events, but it may also bring about psychosocial well-being, prosperity, and benefits generated through these difficult experiences. Indeed, research on social workers has also confirmed that adverse professional experiences can be a source of not only surviving but also thriving (McAllister & McKinnon 2009; Rose & Palattiyil 2020; Wendt et al. 2011).

Resilience is the focal point of this chapter. Its aim is to find the answer to the question: 'How to strengthen the resilience of students of social work in field education?' First, the concept of resilience will be introduced, both in general and in the context of practical training for students of social work. The justification for including resilience in the field education of students will also be covered. The next section of this chapter will present selected empirical knowledge on the subject. It will demonstrate that scholars from different parts of the world focus on different aspects of resilience-building in students undertaking practical training. The concluding section provides a recommendation for the development of a field-education curriculum for social work students that builds on the cultivation, support, and strengthening of their capacity for resilience not only in relation to the current practical training but also to their future professional careers. The term 'curriculum', which comes from Latin and originally referred to running, can be understood as meaning a combination of 'educational strategies, course content, learning outcomes, educational experiences, assessment, the educational environment and the individual students' style, personal timetable and program of work' (Harden 2001, p. 123). Building on Harden (2001) and Prideaux (2003), Ballantyne et al. (2019) further distinguish between *declared* (what educators want students to learn), *taught* (what tutors present to students), and *learned* (what students actually learn) components of the curriculum. In this context, the *curriculum* will be conceived as a planned pathway toward education, both in terms of its content and the outcome that the student is to achieve through field education. In this chapter, the term *field education* refers to the conduct of practical training and supervision of social work students. The term *conduct of practical training* refers to practical education of students in the field – in organisations providing social services to clients under the guidance of experienced professionals. *Supervision* is understood as meaning professional guidance by an experienced supervisor provided within the framework of tertiary education at a college or university.

The Subject of Resilience in Field Education

The demands of the social work profession are reflected in practical training. Students often find themselves in the position of novices discovering a whole new world, quite different to how they imagined it before starting the training. Their enthusiasm and desire to help and to change the world around them encounter reality, presenting them with a difficult challenge in making a career choice. For example, how should they behave when they encounter situations in practice that are so emotional that they linger for a long time? How are they to deal with the fact that social workers have insufficient access to resources and, therefore, cannot intervene as effectively as they would like? They are witness to many instances in practice when social workers are so overloaded with unnecessary bureaucracy that they have insufficient time left for clients. For some students, the situation may be all the more difficult because reflecting on practice confronts them with their own personal history, with which they may have not come to terms. Experiences from practice may exacerbate old wounds and leave the students feeling at a loss. We could also talk about organisational culture and how it may, to say the least, cause students to become surprised and even resentful. In other words, some students come to a relatively clear realisation that real social work does not compare with their expectations and that organisations providing practical training operate rather differently than they expected. In some cases, they also realise that their practical training experience may touch them on a very personal and private level. We could carry on listing further demands imposed on the student (cf. Collins 2015; Dziegielewski et al. 2004; Grant et al. 2015; Navrátil & Šišláková 2007; Navrátilová 2010; Maidment 2003; Punová 2014). However, the challenges of field education, in relation to students building their professional identities, are not the subject matter of this chapter. Rather, the focus is on setting up those segments of the curriculum that deal with practical training and supervision to help equip students to cope with these challenges and not succumb to them; the chapter is dedicated to avoiding the pitfalls of professional field education and exercising resilience in building professional identity.

The key concept of this chapter is *resilience* (from the Latin *re-salire*, meaning 'the act of rebounding or springing back'); the opposite of resilience is *vulnerability*. Resilience was initially studied in high-risk children and adolescents (Werner & Smith 1982; Garmezy & Rutter 1983) in which researchers first examined why the subjects behaved well despite adverse circumstances. Later on, research was extended to also include other areas (e.g., family or community resilience). As already mentioned, we have come across research studies examining the resilience of students and practitioners in social work in recent decades. Their aim is to find out why some workers are able to effectively cope with work-related problems, while others are faced with risky outcomes that may manifest themselves as illness, burnout, compassion fatigue, vicarious trauma, or retention (Adamson 2012; Beddoe & Adamson 2016; Collins 2008; Grant et al. 2015; Punová 2019). The initial cornerstone of research into workers' resilience is aptly characterised by the question: 'What might enable some workers to persist, endure, and thrive in their careers, compared to others who may become ill and sometimes eventually leave the profession?' (Collins 2007, p. 257).

Defining resilience is not easy because there is no single concept. It is generally defined in terms of the process, ability, and outcome of successful adaptation in the face of adverse conditions (Masten 1990; Norman 2000; Werner & Smith 1992). However, resilience is not only about favourable outcomes despite adversity but also encompasses recovery from the experience and the capacity and capability to manage similar future adverse conditions. In the context of this chapter, we shall define it as *a concept that includes dynamic relational developmental processes through which the student is able to adapt and achieve their desired level of personal well-being, despite having experienced a difficult life situation in connection with the conduct of field education.* As stated by Beddoe and Adamson (in Taylor et al. 2006), the student's resilience can be characterised as a process in which the student develops the skills needed to cope with stressors in the workplace of the training and, at the same time, develops the ability to be reflexive, which is a necessary part of identity-building in social work within the framework of competing interactions between different system levels (organisational, community, and government policies).

When we refer to *the dynamic aspect of resilience*, we mean the fact that resilience cannot be considered a static personality trait or human attribute. No one can be said to be inherently resilient because every new adverse event is a test of how we will respond, whether we will succumb to it or be resilient. It is a manifested ability to adapt in a situational framework, the character of which is always different; at the same time, the dispositions, abilities, and possibilities available to a person at that given moment to handle a certain situation are also different. As Luthar (2003) adds, it is a hypothetical construct manifested in the fact that an individual maintains positive functioning despite significant adversity. Resilience can be imagined as a process that has three basic stages.

The first stage is exposure to a stressor, adversity, or a difficult life situation. In the face of these adverse conditions, the risk and protective factors, both personal and environmental, interact (Stage 2). The number, intensity, and chronicity of individual factors are key at this stage. Risk factors can be understood as various situations of stress, such as the student's difficult personal circumstances, marginalisation of the importance of practical training and supervision by the school or the workplace, disharmony in relationships at the workplace, unclear organisational culture of the organisation, or clients' aggressive behaviour toward the student, etc. We can see that these adversities (whether originating in the student's micro-system level or in more distal environments) are not universal but situational and can generate different types of response. In addition to risk factors, protective factors are also key. They consist of a set of resources, capabilities, possibilities, capacities, and potential. Again, they are to be found in both the individual and their environment and can be thought of as airbags that cushion the impact of adversity. If the protective factors are strong enough and sufficiently numerous, they can help the individual to manage the situation, in which case we speak of the manifestation of resilience, and we say that the person has demonstrated resilience (Stage 3). The individual protective factors will be discussed below in the sections devoted to research aimed at strengthening students' resilience.

Speaking of the factors underlying resilience, it is important to note that their nature and effects are viewed from the perspective of the *socio-ecological concept*, which is a key element of the concept of resilience (Bronfebrenner 1979; Corcoran & Nichols-Casebolt 2004; Fraser et al. 2004; Punová 2014). A distinction is, thus, made between micro-level factors (in the context of our topic, these are inborn or acquired factors on the student's side, such as the level of cognitive skills, health, and emotional intelligence), mezzo-level factors (these are factors found in the student's family, among friends, classmates, in the training workplace, at school, community, etc.) and macro-level factors (for example, factors related to the legislative framework for the state's educational policy regulating the qualifications of future social workers, to national and international standards, and the media image of social work in society). It is precisely this socio-ecological thinking that underlies both the concept of resilience and social work. Beddoe and Adamson (in Taylor et al. 2006) speak of philosophical synergy in this context. They list a number of other aspects that apply equally to both areas, including a complexity of theories, emphasis on social justice and human rights, and strength-based approach.

Having said that, the *strength-based perspective* is another source of the resilience approach. Strength-based social work is particularly connected with the name of Saleebey (1996, 2000, 2006). It does not build on earlier deficient models but focuses on a paradigmatic shift 'from weak to strong'. While this approach does not overlook the weaknesses of individuals, it concentrates mainly on the strengths that they can draw on for vigour and that help them achieve the desired change because each person has the capabilities and internal resources to help them face challenges (Brun & Rapp 2001). Under this approach, great emphasis is placed on empowering the client, which is seen as an instrument helping the client use assets, define barriers, and harmonise internal and external resources (Saleebey 2000). Capabilities can also be resources (Navrátilová et al. 2021; Navrátilová 2018; Punová et al. 2020). The role of the professional lies in developing how the client sees their resources and providing guidance on how to use them. The professional also encourages the client to be aware of the barriers to the use of resources. The basic starting point is that no matter how difficult a person's situation may be, there always is some potential, and it is always possible to find a positive outlook. These may also be desires, visions, and hopes. After all, as stated by Seligman and Csikszentmihalyi (2000), human potential can best be used not when a person is doing well but, on the contrary, in difficult moments of life when the person really needs it. Here, we can see a direct link with the resilience theory because it is in those difficult moments in life when we see the need to draw on resilience. The theories also have in common the assumption that a human being is predisposed to prosper and to overcome the pitfalls of life. Norman (2000, p. 3) has also observed mutual synergy in that resilience is the 'attribute, the concept, the process that epitomises and operationalises the strengths perspective. In fact, resiliency enhancement is probably the most reasonable way that social work can put the strengths into practice'.

In discussing resilience-building in students during field education, one point to consider is that educational curricula should include the aspects where resilience intersects with the above-mentioned socio-ecological perspective and strength-based social work. We will present these in the final recommendation for a field-education curriculum, but first we will present selected research examining various factors that enhance or undermine students' ability to exercise resilience.

Field Education in the Light of Research

Risks of Field Education as Seen by Students: A Study by Maidment

Maidment (2003) conducted a survey of 39 social work students from Victoria, Australia, focusing on three contexts of workplace training. The first was the demographic characteristics of the respondents, the second was the organisations providing field placements (the focus was on how students perceive their role in the organisation and how they interact with clients and with those who guide them through the placement) and the last area of research focused on the university environment (theoretical education, field placement arrangements). The students reported that the greatest problems were exposure to verbal assaults by the organisation's clients and the considerable demands, leading to stress, made by the field placement. The greatest upsides were the experience of personal growth, the acknowledgement of field placement as an integral part of their degree course, and the fact that the placement was well aligned with their educational needs. Based on this empirical evidence, the author recommends that attention must be paid to enhancing students' resilience to help them cope with the hardships associated with workplace training, clients' behaviour, and organisational cultures.

The advantage of the concept is the fact that the recommendations are organised along specific areas of the social work curriculum. They focus on: (1) work safety (e.g., insurance coverage, discussion of examples of risks during supervision), (2) stress management (e.g., raising awareness of stress and its impact on behaviour, practising self-care techniques, consultations with workers who went through the burnout syndrome process), and (3) working context and agency culture (emphasising the presentation of various types of organisations before field placement; as part of their training, the students critically reflect on the workplace).

Stress, Personal Well-being and Student Support: A Study by Collins et al.

Collins et al. (2010) surveyed first and second year students at the University of Wales. They specifically focused on the following areas: (1) experienced demands, (2) support from colleagues, university teachers, family, and friends, (3) students' feelings about their fieldwork, (4) students' self-reflection, (5) level of student's well-being, and (6) factors that could contribute to reducing the stress associated with practical education. Their empirical study showed that many students experienced higher levels of stress and mental discomfort associated with emotional exhaustion and impaired self-image. On the other hand, however, field placement also benefited students. They saw it as an important component of their study, were active participants in the training, and showed interest in the agency's clients. Fellow students, persons guiding them through the training, and teachers were regarded as the most important sources of social support. The possibility to take courses aimed at coping with stress was also seen as beneficial.

Based on the research findings, the authors recommended that attention should be paid to the issue of excessive demands and addressing them by, e.g., developing coping strategies, improving job satisfaction, and strengthening resilience. Collins (2008, 2010, 2015) then developed these concepts further not only in relation to students but also to social work practitioners. As regards resilience-building at the level of internal factors, Collins (2015) recommends turning to concepts related to the sense of coherence, challenge appraisals, self-efficacy, and sense of control. In general, she recommends dealing with excessive demands by accentuating positive topics: 'Education and training in resilience, in the management of positive emotions and optimism, could help both students and qualified workers cope more readily with the demands made by their work' (Collins 2007, p. 266).

The Impact of Education on Resilience in Students and Staff: A Study by Palma-García and Hombrados-Mendieta

Palma-García and Hombrados-Mendieta (2014) examined the correlation between the nature of education and resilience-building in 613 university students of social work, as well as in social work practitioners from Spanish Malaga. The authors conducted a longitudinal cross-sectional study in which they explored a basic attributive feature of resilience, which is the presence of protective factors. Their objective was to find out how education affects the presence and cultivation of these factors. In identifying relevant factors, they built on Grotberg's (2003) concept that highlights the dynamic aspect of resilience – it varies depending on how the protective factors interact with each other. First, they focused on examining the respondents' level of resilience, which they then compared through repeated measurements in the course of the following years. In the group of respondent social workers, the study showed the amplifying effect of field experience: the social workers' resilience grew ever stronger with years of experience. As regards the students, the same effect manifested itself in relation to the year of study: as they progressed through their degree course, their resilience to hardships increased. The most marked increase in the degree of resilience was observed in recent graduates who had gone through all the pitfalls of their studies. The authors conclude their research study by validating the fact that 'adversity can be perceived not only as a source of distress, but it can also be used to become stronger and resilient' (Palma-García and Hombrados-Mendieta 2014, p. 394).

Enhancing Students' Resilience: Research Studies by Grant and Kinman

Grant and Kinman are among important proponents of the role of resilience in professionalisation of social work. As they observed: 'building resilience in the future workforce should be a key element of social work education' (2012, p. 605). In their research studies, they, therefore, focused on the characteristics of resilience, the ways and extent to which it can enhance the well-being of the student and the worker, and gave a number of recommendations for the social work curriculum. One of the authors' research studies was conducted among 240 British students in the first and second year of social work (Grant & Kinman 2012). The authors examined the influence of emotional intelligence, reflective ability, empathy, and social confidence on the manifestation of resilience. They showed that students who had higher levels of emotional intelligence, had developed more advanced reflective thinking skills, and had confidence in their abilities were more likely to demonstrate resilience in adverse circumstances. The students were also shown to be mentally healthier.

Another of their studies explored the views of 48 social work educators working in English universities and examined the role of an emotional curriculum in promoting students' resilience (Grant et al. 2015). As the authors emphasise, cultivation of the emotional curriculum and of the overall affective domain is important not only because of its effects on the development of resilience, but especially now when 'social work education tends to prioritise the cognitive (knowing and thinking) domain' (Grant et al. 2015, p. 2352). The study showed that the majority of educators considered it helpful for them to further their education in the topic of resilience. Knowledge of the topic is seen as a prerequisite for them to be able to facilitate resilience-building in their students. The authors also discussed techniques to enhance resilience. According to them, the techniques seen as particularly useful are reflective supervision, time management, sources of support and work life balance, reflective writing, and emotional literacy. In their educational course, they usually cover reflective writing and supervision, sources of support, and time management. Teachers also gave their opinion on who was most accountable for enhancing students' resilience: they believed students themselves should bear the most responsibility, with field-training educators the second most important actors.

Based on the empirical evidence, the authors made specific recommendations for authors of social work curricula. Although they did not focus exclusively on field education, their proposals are inspiring. In particular, they recommend 'development of a toolbox or repertoire of strategies which social workers can draw upon when needed' (Grant et al. 2015, p. 2363). According to them, it is important to emphasise the key role of resilience in relation to well-being (not only on a personal level, but also in the context of a professional curriculum), and emphasis should also be placed on the development of emotional and social skills and especially reflectivity. They used their empirical findings to formulate a project proposal, 'well-being days', targeted at students of social work. The objectives should be: (1) emphasising the importance of self-care and resilience for current and future well-being and the conduct of the social work profession, (2) acquainting students with techniques that can help them develop their resilience and well-being, and (3) teaching students to determine how to apply resilience in relation to the situations they experience. According to the authors, these days should take the form of an interactive experience and focus on the development of the following skills: meditation and mindfulness, thinking skills (cognitive behavioural techniques), utilising supervision for reflective practice, peer coaching, goal-setting and personal organisation, action-planning, and self-knowledge.

From analysing the authors' approach, we can conclude that they primarily studied those resilience factors that are related to personality attributes of the individual. This micro-system perspective is all the more apparent when we compare it, for example, with the abovementioned concepts of Collins et al. (2010) and Maidment (2003), which also placed great emphasis on other system levels – the context of the training workplace and university environment. Indeed, Grant and Kinman (2012, p. 617) themselves admitted some drawbacks of this micro view: 'It should be acknowledged, however, that interventions that aim to enhance individual coping abilities without recognising and addressing the structural causes of stress are likely to fail'. On the other hand, the value of Grant and Kinman's concept resides in having provided educators with specific, evidence-based input for designing social work curriculum content, even if only for the sections concerning micro-system resilience factors.

Field Education Aiming at Enhancing Resilience in New Zealand Research

The most comprehensive treatment of the concept of resilience in relation to field education can be found in the work of New Zealand authors Beddoe, Adamson, and Davys. Their research builds on the basic idea that the study of social work should equip graduates to be able to show resilience. As part of their research (Adamson et al. 2014), they interviewed student field supervisors and social workers with at least three years of professional experience. A total of 21 respondents was interviewed. The research aimed to show respondents' resilience levels and explore the methods through which resilience can be strengthened as part of study. The questions examining the parameters of resilience in the respondents generated a 'map of resilience'. The authors used this to summarise their findings in the form of three basic systems that interact with one another. The first area concerns the personality profile of the worker, including their personal and work history and moral characteristics. This is where resilience can possibly manifest itself. In addition to these 'internal' factors, the second system, consisting of external factors of the practice context are also important. These structural characteristics of the environment, organisational culture, and formation of the social worker's professional identity create a framework in which social workers may exercise their resilience. The last area consists of mediating factors between the person of the worker and the surrounding context. The research participants characterised this third systemic level as one of the most important because it fosters the sustainability of resilient practice (Adamson et al. 2014). The authors then turned their attention to the tools that enhance students' resilience. Based on their empirical findings, they recommend developing a knowledge base of resilience, strengthening the skills needed for self-care and reflective thinking, and, last but not least, creating space for reflective processes (such as supervision and professional development). These tools can help students cultivate resilience even after they graduate and begin to fully experience the demands of the profession first hand.

In a similar study (Hay et al. 2019), the authors examined 27 educators and 35 students from eight New Zealand schools. They focused mainly on the evaluation of taught and learned field education curricula. Unsurprisingly, they found that field placement and supervision were key for students' future careers. The authors' main interest was supervision. Here, the students pointed out that there was a big difference between the taught curriculum (presented as part of supervision before starting the placement) and the learned curriculum (the real on-placement situation). Teachers and students, for the most part, expressed dissatisfaction with the difference between the taught curriculum and the reality in the placement organisations. In addition, many students stated that they were happy when supervision was regular and of good quality because they considered it a very important component of their practical training. A chance for an inspiring placement that provides opportunities to learn new things and an opportunity for peer-comparison were among other aspects of field education that the students considered important. The basic application of the research by Hay et al. (2019, p. 23) was the recommendation 'that students should be able to consistently access effective placement supervision rather than consider this a matter of luck'.

As already mentioned, the approach of these authors is the most elaborate contribution to the discussion of including the resilience concept in social work field education. The added value lies mainly in the fact that the authors have provided a broader range of suggestions for fieldwork curriculum. Here are some of them (Beddoe & Adamson 2016):

- Field education should not be based on the mere transmission of information but should be practical – transformational in nature. Related to this is an emphasis on reflective thinking. Through this way of thinking, in the context of professional identity formation, students develop realistic expectations of the exercise of their future profession. The approach of educators, from both the school and field placement, should build on the promotion of altruism, setting a good example, mentoring, leadership, coaching, and motivation. At the same time, the workplace should be safe for students, and they should not be overloaded with responsibility.

- A fieldwork curriculum should address concepts related to personal development – e.g., development of emotional intelligence, adaptability, positive identity, use of social support, development of coping strategies, development of personal spirituality, and reflection on the meaning of suffering, self-denial, and one's own personal path and motivation to study, as well as reflection on personal history; discussion of topics related to e.g., inappropriate emotional response or triggers of prejudicial behaviour should not be avoided. Supervision plays a key role in this context.
- The importance of the 'preparatory phase' before the student begins their placement should be emphasised – it is advisable to focus on students' previous experience with challenges and their response to them. At this stage, it is also helpful to turn to the identification of protective factors (such as dispositional optimism) that can help students cope with difficulties.
- Knowledge of resilience-related topics should be fostered, including general topics (coping, well-being, work-life balance), stress (and its effects on coping and burnout), self-care, personal professional boundaries, ethical aspects of the profession, mindfulness, and other techniques. It is appropriate to encourage students' desire for further theoretical and practical education (which should be a lifelong learning process).

A reflection on this subchapter leads us to the conclusion that the concept of empirical validation of the subject matter differs from author to author, with each of them accentuating different risk or protective factors of field education. The resilience-enhancing factors, as highlighted in the above-outlined studies, are, nevertheless, based on shared principles. First and foremost, resilience has been shown to stem from interactions between the risk and protective factors found at different socio-ecological levels. The authors of the above studies focused on micro-system factors of the student, as well as mezzo-systemic factors at the level of the school and placement organisations. Reflection on the macro-systems, though currently lacking empirical knowledge, will also be covered in the following section. It has also been shown that the primary prerequisite for the development of resilience is awareness of the topics related to it. There is a consensus across the different studies that the topic of resilience and its strengthening should play an important or even a key role in the field education of students. It is important that the topic of resilience be covered not only in field education but also in theoretical classroom instruction. In the following section, we will focus precisely on the issue of the defining features of resilience and propose principles for the field education curriculum.

Field Education Curriculum for Social Work Students

When considering the answer to the central question of this chapter, which is 'How to strengthen the resilience of students of social work in field education?', we need to keep in mind several aspects. *The primary prerequisite for the development of resilience is awareness of the topics related to it.* As shown in the above-described research, there is a consensus that the topic of resilience and its strengthening should play an important or even a key role in the field education of students. In this context, it is important that the topic of resilience be covered not only in field education but also in theoretical classroom instruction. Another important aspect of the curriculum should be that *the development of resilience should be integrated into all stages of field education*, i.e., take place throughout the study of social work (cf. McAllister & McKinnon 2009). It is important to cultivate resilience from the first year of study onward because, as a number of studies have shown, the early stages of the studies are associated with considerable demands on students. Tobin and Carson (1994), for example, focused on first-year social work students and found that a third of them experienced high levels of stress after completing the first year. Barefoot (2004), Cooke et al. (2006), and Mlcek and Pulla (2014) also describe the situation of first-year students as the most difficult. Senior students are expected to become more resilient as their experience coping with the demands of field education grows; it is, nevertheless, important to acknowledge the need to support students' coping strategies in all years of study.

Another aspect of the curriculum is related to a systematic view of the effects of risk and protective factors. The socio-ecological (also referred to as ecosystem) concept, which feeds into the concept of resilience, provides a complex perspective on the curriculum because it reflects a host of factors from within different environments. Therefore, the first starting point is that *the educational curriculum should reflect all socio-ecological frameworks in which the risk and protective factors of field education are located*. Based on this starting point, Figure 32.1 shows the basic areas of the curriculum, which are based on a reflection of literature and the abovementioned research.

The above figure provides a summarised and not entirely exhaustive view of the subject matter. It essentially indicates that an interplay of multiple factors is needed to strengthen the student's resilience. As we know from the resilience theory, these include both risk and protective factors. Let us take an example of a selected factor – the student's self-care. Some situations on placement are very exhausting, generating risk potential (e.g., the placement organisation is a hospice and there is a sudden death of a close relative in the student's family). In this situation, it is important that the student also has protective factors available. In this particular case, it is advisable that the curriculum provides for the possibility of extra individual supervision sessions in addition to the standard supervision time allocation or that the student is allowed to change the placement. Supervision is one of the key factors in field education (a number of

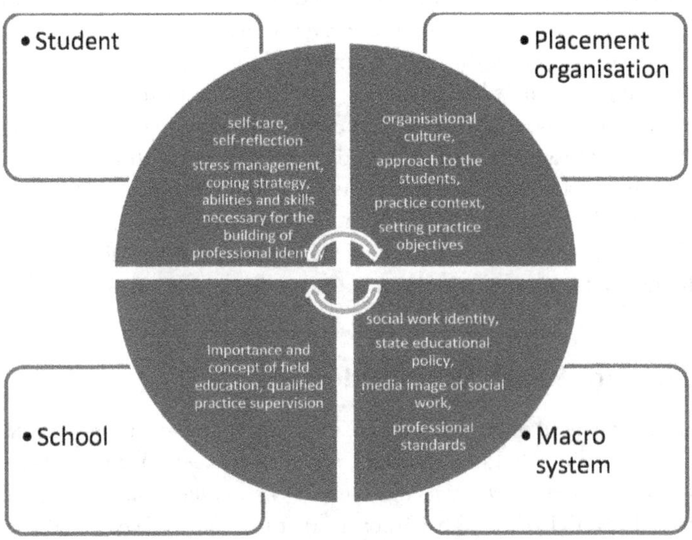

Figure 32.1 Ecosystems of the field education curriculum for social work students.

studies were conducted on the role of supervision in strengthening students' resilience, see e.g., Adamson 2012; Collins 2007; Maidment & Beddoe 2012). It is during supervision that self-care, in terms of attention to personal well-being, stress management, and resilience development, can be fostered. Indeed, these topics should not be limited to the domain of supervision but should also be included in theoretical teaching.

Bogo (2015) focused on the basic protective factors on the part of the placement organisation. According to him, it is important that placement organisations perceive field education as mutually beneficial and that field educators are experienced practitioners and have a good relationship with students. At the same time, students should be able to actually practice with clients during the placement and use a variety of methods (direct observation, writing, and review of records and verbal reports). Reflection on the practice, feedback, and future planning should take place through mutual reflective dialogues. On the contrary, Punová (2014) points out the risk factors on the part of the organisation. She speaks about risks arising from organisations' ambivalent attitude toward student placements, inadequate definition of the intern's role, insufficiently meaningful and thought-provoking positions (e.g., administrative overload), inadequate guidance on placement, inappropriate communication with the student, and inadequate safety measures to protect the student (e.g., practice insurance or protection of the student from clients' aggression). This author also mentions risks on the part of the educator, which include marginalisation of the importance of field education and prioritisation of the theoretical component of teaching, imperfect integration of the theoretical and practical component of teaching, deficient organisation, too low or too high demands placed by the fieldwork curricula and the related low or too high number of hours of practice, and, last but not least, lack of competence concerning supervision arrangements (unqualified supervisor, inadequate number of hours, or inadequate form of supervision, etc.).

We can see that the curriculum alone cannot influence all aspects of practical education. It cannot change the sometimes distant attitude of organisations' representatives to students, regarding students as extra work that brings no benefits and value to the organisation. Even more so, it cannot influence the macro-framework, e.g., opinion leaders who could report on social workers' failures in the media, thus, forming a negative image of the profession in the eyes of the general public. It also has no direct influence on legislators in the area of social work education. However, the curriculum and, particularly, the teachers' and supervisors' compliance with it have a fundamental impact on how these factors form the resilience of the student.

Another principle of resilience is the strength-based perspective that highlights the power of unwavering human potential. We believe that a *field education curriculum should not be based on the deficit model but should centre around students' strengths and apply the strength-based perspective.* Saleebey (1996) summarised the differences between the deficit- and strength-based approaches of social workers to clients. In Table 32.1, we use these two models to describe the supervisors' approach to students on placement.

We can see that the approach is very different when the focus is on students' strengths and potential than when the educator focuses on addressing their 'weaker areas' (this is certainly not limited to the supervisor at school but also applies, e.g., to a tutor at school or in the placement organisation). With some simplification, we can illustrate the principles presented in the above table using an example of a supervision session with a student. Under the deficit approach, the supervisor will act as an expert seeking to identify the problem, its causes, and solutions. They will ask the student questions exploring the student's perception of the problem, will listen to the student, assess the situation, and present the student with their own view on the matter. It is likely that the supervisor, as a 'situation expert', will have more room to voice their opinion. Under the strength-based approach, the supervisor will listen more carefully and will

Table 32.1 The Principles of Field Education Curriculum from the Deficit- and Strength-Based Perspectives

Deficit-based	*Strength-based*
The supervisor perceives the student as 'a member of the supervision group'.	The student is seen as a singular individual with unique features and talents who has strong points on which they can build.
The supervisor addresses problem situations with the student (problem-focused).	During supervision, the supervisor focuses on the student's positive potential (possibility-focused).
The student's observations are interpreted by the supervisor, and they help search for a solution to the given situation.	The student's self-reflection is the key method to understanding and assessing the given situation.
The supervisor is only interested in the problematic situation reported by the student.	The supervisor is interested in the student's life story.
Childhood trauma affects the student's later behaviour.	Childhood trauma does not predict a negative future; it can activate and strengthen the student
The supervisor has a more direct style of leadership and applies their own versions of desirable solutions in the forefront.	The student's assessment of the situation is in the forefront.
It is the supervisor who is an expert on the student's situation.	It is the student who is an expert on the situation.
The process of change is based on the knowledge and skills of the supervisor.	The process of change is based on the capacity, strengths, and adaptability of the student and the characteristics of the student's surroundings (e.g., placement organisations, families).
The supervisor guides the student to minimise the impact of risk factors related to the execution of the placement.	The supervisor directs the student's attention to their own potential as well as the potential within environments related to the placement.

tend to guide the student to a more in-depth reflection and encourage the verbal expression of thoughts. The supervisor's questions will seek to identify the student's potential and to find a positive side to even the most negative experience from the placement. The supervisor will be guided by the assumption that the variability, intensity, and amount of healing potential in students and their environments can be considerable.

The resilience approach puts at the forefront the importance of identifying, activating, cultivating, and increasing the presence of the student's empowering (protective) factors, which may help them be able to cope with even the toughest challenges of their professional identity formation. It can certainly be argued that there do exist factors that threaten the student (many have been mentioned in this chapter) and ignoring them would mean denying reality. However, application of the strength-based approach does not mean marginalising or ignoring risks. It simply builds on the assumption that, just as there are real problems and risks experienced in field education, so, too, are there also real potential and resources to tackle the problems.

The current era of fluid modernity presents social workers with a number of challenges, which must necessarily be reflected in their education. As pointed out by Chytil (2007), Navrátil (2019), Navrátil et al. (2021), and Navrátilová and Navrátil (2020), it is not enough to pass a set of expertise and abstract knowledge on to students and develop some predefined set of competencies. It is necessary to lead them to become sensitive to the changes in society and to be able to critically reflect on the social challenges faced by both their clients and themselves. The above principles of the fieldwork curriculum should lead students to develop reflective life-management skills in order to be able to 'read the signs of the times' and respond adequately.

Conclusion

Antoine de Saint Exupéry is believed to be the author of a quote that involves deeply resilient elements. According to him, a man will only discover his full potential when he measures himself against an obstacle. The same can be said about a social work student. Their professional identity cannot fully form only through reflection on literature and attendance of lectures and seminars but needs confrontation with the pitfalls of practice, where the student steps out of the safe space of theoretical teaching and experiences the everyday reality of social workers. For some students, navigating this difficult reality is a touchstone of their professional identity, which needs to go through this strenuous test in order to be able to rest on realistic ground. If this shaking of the foundation of professional identity through field education and supervision is not sufficiently reflected in educational curricula, it can affect the student's personal life and, in extreme cases, lead to the student even choosing a different career. The resilience enhancement should be part of social work education. At the end of the day, being resilient is about the social worker's continuing relevance to the service user as well as to the whole profession. The capacity to help is always contingent upon the ability of the social worker to respond to situations and how he/she deals with the service user.

This chapter focused on how students' resilience can be strengthened through field education. It explored how students can be supported in coping with the demands presented by this specific form of study in practice. Grant et al. (2015) compare some aspects of field education to an 'oxygen mask' and point to the fact that, in order for social work professionals to be able to provide clients with services, to help others 'put on an oxygen mask', they sometimes need the mask for themselves during their studies. In this chapter, we first introduced the topic of resilience and its principles. We focused on why it is necessary to discuss the need to strengthen it in the field education of social work students. We also examined approaches underlying resilience – the socio-ecological model and strength-based social work. Building on the evidence-based approach, we then presented studies that deal with the validation of various concepts related to the education of social work students.

The end result of our discussion of the topic was the last part of the chapter, where we summarised the basic principles that should inform the field education curriculum. We pointed out that the concept of resilience and resilience-building should play an important or even key role not only in the practical but also in the theoretical education of students at all stages. We highlighted the significance of selected risk and protective factors for resilience and described their effect spanning all socio-ecological levels. Last but not least, we addressed the principle of focusing on students' potential, abilities, and capacity for change. The aim of this chapter was also to point to the fact that strengthening students' resilience, as yet a rather marginal issue, is more key than ever for the formation of their professional identities. A fully qualified graduate cannot get by with only having knowledge and understanding the strategies for avoiding the difficulties of the profession. The graduate also needs to experience difficulties as a natural part of professional life, along with the need to brave them. Social work is a very challenging profession with high demands on the resilience of the worker. The role of education is precisely to prepare the student for that reality: to remain vulnerable (as is their human nature) but, at the same time, unhurt in the face of the difficulties of the profession.

Note

1 Acknowledgment: The text was financially supported from institutional support for long-term conceptual development of the research organisation for the period 2018–2022; it is part of the project 'Research of the attractiveness of social work disciplines for students of secondary schools, colleges and universities, professional competences, and personality prerequisites' which was realised by the Research Institute of Labor and Social Affairs, vvi, Brno, Czech Republic.

References

Adamson, C. (2012). Supervision Is Not Politically Innocent. *Australian Social Work*, 65(2), 185–196.

Adamson, C., Beddoe, L., & Davys, A. (2014). Building Resilient Practitioners: Definitions and Practitioner Understandings. *British Journal of Social Work*, 44(3), 522–541.

Ballantyne, N., Hay, K., Beddoe, L., Maidment, J., & Walker, S. (2019). Mapping and Visualising the Social Work Curriculum. *Journal of Technology in Human Services*, 37(2/3), 184–202.

Barefoot, B. O. (2004). Higher Education's Revolving Door: Confronting the Problem of Student Dropout in U.S. Colleges and Universities. *Open Learning*, 19(1), 9–18.

Beddoe, L., & Adamson, C. (2016). Educating Resilient Practitioners. In: I. Taylor, M. Bogo & B. Lefevre (Eds.), *The Routledge International Handbook of Social Work Education* (pp. 343–354). London: Routledge.

Beddoe, L., & Davys, A. (2016). *Challenges in Professional Supervision: Current Themes and Models for Practice*. London and Philadelphia: Jessica Kingsley Publishers.

Bennett, P., Evans, R., & Tattersall, A. (1993). Stress and Coping in Social Workers: A Preliminary Investigation. *British Journal of Social Work*, 23(1), 31–44.

Bogo, M. (2015). Field Education for Clinical Social Work Practice: Best Practices and Contemporary Challenges. *Clinical Social Work Journal*, 43(3), 317–324.

Bronfebrenner, U. (1979). *The Ecology of Human Development*. Cambridge: Harvard University Press.

Brun, C., & Rapp, C. (2001). Strengths-Based Case Management: Individuals' Perspectives on Strengths and the Case Manager Relationship. *Social Work*, 46(3), 278–288.

Coffey, M., Dugdill, L., & Tattersall, A. (2004). Stress in Social Services: Mental Well-Being, Constraints and Job Satisfaction. *British Journal of Social Work*, 34(5), 735–746.

Collins, S. (2007). Social Workers, Resilience, Positive Emotions and Optimism. *Practice*, 19(4), 255–269.

Collins, S. (2008). Statutory Social Workers: Stress, Job, Satisfaction, Coping, Social Support and Individual Differences. *British Journal of Social Work*, 38(6), 1173–1193.

Collins, S. (2015). Alternative Psychological Approaches for Social Workers and Social Work Students Dealing with Stress in the UK: Sense of Coherence, Challenge Appraisals, Self-Efficacy and Sense of Control. *British Journal of Social Work*, 45(1), 69–85.

Collins, S., Coffey, M., & Morris, L. (2010). Social Work Students: Stress, Support and Well-Being. *British Journal of Social Work*, 40(3), 963–982.

Cooke, R., Bewick, B. M., Barkham, M., Bradley, M., & Audin, K. (2006). Measuring and Managing the Psychological Well-Being of First Year University Students. *British Journal of Guidance and Counselling*, 34, 505–517.

Corcoran, J., & Nichols-Casebolt, A. (2004). Risk and Resilience Ecological Framework for Assessment and Goal Formulation. *Child and Adolescent Social Work Journal*, 21(3), 211–234.

Curtis, L., Moriarty, J., & Netten, A. (2010). The Expected Working Life of a Social Worker. *British Journal of Social Work*, 40(5), 1628–1643.

Duffy, B., Oyebode, J. R., & Allen, J. (2009). Burnout among Care Staff for Older Adults with Dementia. *Dementia*, 8(4), 515–541.

Dziegielewski, S., Tornage, B., & Roest-Mari, S. (2004). Addressing Stress with Social Work Students: A Controlled Evaluation. *Journal of Social Work Education*, 40(1), 105–119.

Fraser, M.W. (Ed.) (2004). *Risk and Resilience in Childhood: An Ecological Perspective*. Washington DC: N.A.S.W.

Garmezy, N., & Rutter, M. (Eds.) (1983). *Stress, Coping and Development in Children*. New York: McGraw Hill.

Grant, L., & Kinman, G. (2012). Enhancing Wellbeing in Social Work Students: Building Resilience in the Next Generation. *Social Work Education*, 31(5), 605–621.

Grant, L., & Kinman, G. (2014). *Developing Resilience for Social Work Practice*. London: Palgrave Macmillan.

Grant, L., Kinman, G., & Baker, S. (2015). 'Put on Your Own Oxygen Mask before Assisting Others': Social Work Educators' Perspectives on an 'Emotional Curriculum'. *British Journal of Social Work*, 45(8), 2351–2367.

Grotberg, E. H. (2003). *Resilience for Today: Gaining Strength from Adversity*. Westport, CT: Praeg.

Harden, R. M. (2001). AMEE Guide No. 21: Curriculum Mapping: A Tool for Transparent and Authentic Teaching and Learning. *Medical Teacher*, 23(2), 123–137.

Hay, K., Maidment, J., Ballantyne, N., Beddoe, L., & Walker, S. (2019). Feeling Lucky: The Serendipitous Nature of Field Education. *Clinical Social Work Journal*, 47(1), 23–31.

Chytil, O. (2007). Důsledky modernizace pro sociální práci. [The Consequences of Modernisation for Social Work.]. *Czech and Slovak Social Work*, 8(4), 64–71.

Kinman, G., & Grant, L. (2017). Building Resilience in Early-Career Social Workers: Evaluating a Multi-Modal Intervention. *British Journal of Social Work*, 47(7), 1979–1998.

Luthar, S. (Ed.) (2003). *Resilience and Vulnerability. Adaptation in the Context of Childhood Adversities*. Cambridge: Cambridge University Press.

Maidment, J. (2003). Problems Experienced by Students on Field Placement: Using Research Findings to Inform Curriculum Design and Content. *Australian Social Work*, 55(1), 5–59.

Maidment, J., & Beddoe, I. (2012). Is Social Work Supervision in 'Good Heart'? A Critical Commentary. *Australian Social Work*, 65(2), 163–170.

Masten, A. S. (1990). Ordinary Magic: Resilience Processes in Development. *American Psychologist*, 56(3), 227–238.

McAllister, M., & McKinnon, T. (2009). The Importance of Teaching and Learning Resilience in the Health Disciplines. A Critical Review of the Literature. *Nurse Education Today*, 9, 371–379.

Mlcek, S., & Pulla, V. (2014). Knowledge Building for Practice: Resilience in Social Work Engagement. *International Journal of Innovation, Creativity and Change*, 4(1), 57–74.

Morrison, T. (2007). Emotional Intelligence, Emotion and Social Work: Context, Characteristics, Complications and Contribution. *British Journal of Social Work*, 37(2), 245–263.

Navrátil, P., & Šišláková, M. (Eds.) (2007). *Praktické Vzdělávání v Sociální Práci. [Field Education in Social Work.]*. Brno: Tribun.

Navrátil, P. (2019). Epistemic Discourses of 'Explanation' and 'Understanding' in Assessment Models. In: M. Payne & E. Reith-Hall (Eds.). *The Routledge Handbook of Social Work Theory* (1st ed.) (pp. 69–83). Oxon, New York: Routledge, Routledge International Handbooks.

Navrátilová, J. (2010). *Pojetí praktického vzdělávání sociálních pracovníků. [Disertační Práce. [The Concept of Field Education of Social Workers. Dissertation.]*. Brno: Masarykova Univerzita.

Navrátilová, J. (2018). Využití capability přístupu při posouzení dětského well-beingu. [Using capability approach in child well-being assessment]. *Sociální práce*, 18(6), 65–77.

Navrátilová, J., & Navrátil, P. (2020). The Concept of Professional Identity in Selected Approaches to the Education of Social Workers. In: S. M. Sajid, R. Baikady, C. Sheng-Li & H. Sakaguchi (Eds.). *The Palgrave Handbook of Global Social Work Education*. (pp. 456–471). New York: Palgrave Macmillan.

Navrátilová, J., Navrátil, P., & Punová, M. (2021). The well-being of children and young people: The context of social services from the perspective of the capability approach. *Clinical Social Work and Health Intervention*, 12(4), 49–61.

Navrátil, P., Pazlarová, H., Matulayová, T., & Matoušek, O. (2021). Reflektivní praxe v ČR a její důsledky pro vzdělávání v sociální práci. [Reflective Practice in the Czech Republic and it's consequences for education in social work.] *Sociální práce*, 21(6), 42–61.

Norman, E. (Ed.) (2000). *Resiliency Enhancement. Putting the Strengths Perspective Into Social Work Practice*. New York: Columbia University Press.

Palma-García, M. O., & Hombrados-Mendieta, I. (2014). The Development of Resilience in Social Work Students and Professionals. *Journal of Social Work*, 14(4), 380–397.

Prideaux, D. (2003). ABC of Learning and Teaching in Medicine: Curriculum Design. *British Medical Journal*, 326(7383), 268–270.

Punová, M. (2014). Rizika ve vzdělávání studentů na praxi. [Risks in Students' Field Education]. In: M. Punová & J. Navrátilová (Eds.), *Praktické Vzdělávání v Sociální Práci Optikou Konceptu Resilience [Social Work Field Education in the Context of Resilience Concept]*. (pp. 130–144). Brno: MUNI Press.

Punová, M. (2019). Resiliency Enhancement in Field Education of Social Work Students. *Czech and Slovak Social Work*, 19(2), 5–20.

Punová, M. (2020). The Personality Dispositions and Resilience of Social Workers. *Czech and Slovak Social Work*, 20(5), 88–107.

Punová, M., Navrátil, P., & Navrátilová, J. (2020). Capabilities and Well-Being of Child and Adolescent Social Services Clients in the Czech Republic. *Children and Youth Services Review*. London: Elsevier, 117.
Rose, S., & Palattiyil, G. (2020). Surviving or Thriving? Enhancing the Emotional Resilience of Social Workers in Their Organisational Settings. *Journal of Social Work*, 20(1), 23–42.
Saleebey, D. (1996). The Strengths Perspective in Social Work Practice: Extensions and Causations. *Social Work*, 41(3), 296–305.
Saleebey, D. (2000). Power in the People: Strengths and Hope. *Advances in Social Work*, 1(2), 127–136.
Saleebey, D. (Ed.) (2006). *The Strengths Perspective in Social Work Practice* (4th ed.) Boston: Allyn and Bacon.
Seligman, M. E. P., & Csikszentmihalyi, M. (2000). Positive Psychology: An Introduction. *American Psychologist*, 55(1), 5–14.
Tobin, J., & Carson, J. (1994). Stress and the Student Social Worker. *Social Work and Social Sciences Review*, 3(3), 246–256.
Wendt, S., Tuckey, M. R., & Prosser, B. (2011). Thriving, Not Just Surviving, in Emotionally Demanding Fields of Practice. *Health and Social Care in the Community*, 19(3), 317–325.
Werner, E. E., & Smith, R. S. (1982). *Vulnerable but Invincible: A Study of Resilient Children*. New York: McGraw-Hill.
Werner, E. E., & Smith, R. S. (1992). *Overcoming the Odds: High Risk Children from Birth to Adulthood*. Ithaca and London: Cornell University Press.

33

Social Work Field Instruction in Turkey

Challenges, Problems, and Implications

Cemre Bolgün and Buğra Yıldırım

Social work is a distinctive profession, with its efforts to improve the well-being of individuals, groups, and communities under pressure, and the quality of social work education is based on two principles: theory and practice. The aim of such education is to provide theoretical knowledge to the social worker and to improve performance skills. In this process, field instruction plays a critical role. With field instruction, students can apply the theoretical knowledge they learned in the classroom environment into practice; they are prepared for real life, and independently take their first steps toward understanding social work practice at different levels. However, many problems can be encountered today through the social work field instruction process.

Understanding the current problems of a profession and its role in the new social order is possible by knowing the past stages of that profession's education. Social work has emerged as a profession and discipline as a beneficial result of the social and political climate created by the philanthropy movement brought by the Industrial and French Revolutions in the nineteenth century. It developed and matured in the twentieth century as a result of the need for professional provision of social services. On the other hand, the infrastructure of social work education in Turkey was created by the United Nations in the late 1950s, and the education process began in 1961. Since then, the concept of 'social work practice' in Turkish social work education has been the subject of many discussions. In this chapter, first, the past stages of social work education in Turkey and the current situation of social work field instruction will be summarised, and then challenges, problems, and implications will be discussed.

Social Work Education in Turkey: The Beginning and Development

Social work education began in 1961 in Turkey, and in this period, there were important political and social changes. It is possible to say that the 'social' state principle, brought by the 1961 Constitution, with the political and social atmosphere experienced in 1960s, was effective (Hacettepe University Social Work Department, 2020). The 1960s were the years when the 'planned development periods' were accepted as a state policy, and the community development practices were mainly applied to problems of migration and slums (S.H.U.D.E.R., 2020). In fact,

DOI: 10.4324/9781032164946-38

social work education in Turkey began nearly 50 years later than the West and 15 years later than Egypt and India in the East. In 1950, social work education was provided at approximately 373 schools in 46 countries around the world, but none were in Turkey.

The beginning of social work education in Turkey was carried out by the Law on the Establishment of the Social Services Institute, No. 7355, dated 1959, which was a result of the efforts of consultants coming to Turkey from the United Nations. The law's provision of 'establishing a Social Services Academy of high and secondary level education for training social work specialists and social assistants' constituted the legal basis of social work education (Karataş & Erkan, 2005; Resmi Gazete, 2020). Based on this law, the Social Services Academy was established in 1961 under the Ministry of Health and Social Assistance, and a 4-year undergraduate education programme was created.

At the beginning, four education consultants were assigned by the United Nations technical assistance programme. In addition, with the Fulbright Commission, Dutch technical assistance programme, and bilateral agreements, six faculty members from the U.S.A. and one each from the Netherlands, Pakistan, and India have been on the academic staff of the Academy. The United Nations was effective in the creation of the first syllabus during the establishment of the Social Services Academy. The Academy was accepted as a member of the International Association of Social Work Schools in 1965, after the programme was shown to comply with the organisation's standards (Koşar & Tufan, 1999; Hacettepe University Department of Social Work, 2020; S.H.U.D.E.R., 2020).

The Social Work College was founded at nearly the same time as the Social Services Academy. The Social Work College initially started as a college within Hacettepe University and later organised as a department within the Faculty of Economics and Administrative Sciences. Founded in 1967 by Professor Emre Kongar, the Social Work College had the distinction of being the second social work school in Turkey and the first social work school[1] to provide social work education under the umbrella of a university.

As a result of the changing socio-political environment after the 1980 coup d'état, reconstruction has begun in the field of social work in Turkey. In this process, the Social Services and Child Protection Law No. 2828, which was adopted in 1983 and is still in force today, and the Social Services and Child Protection Agency was established under the Ministry of Health and Social Assistance. In this environment, the Social Services Academy and Social Work College were merged under Hacettepe University in 1982, and named the Social Work College, and social work education in Turkey was given under the umbrella of a single school until 2002 (Çengelci, 1996; Özbek, 2006).

Consequently, although the first social work school in Turkey started education in 1961, it was not possible to expand social work education in Turkey until the 2000s, as a result of the social and political atmosphere in those years. Therefore, the number of social workers and social work academicians trained in this process has been limited. On the other hand, in the 2000s, there has been a rapid increase in the number of universities providing social work education and the number of personnel working in this field within the framework of the European Union membership perspective. As of 2020, the number of social work departments in Turkey is more than 60.

Knowledge, Skill, and Value: The Basis of Social Work Field Instruction

Knowledge is necessary for professional practice. It is not possible to talk about a profession that is not based on knowledge (Duyan, 2010; Thompson, 2009). The common definition of social work by the International Federation of Social Workers (I.F.S.W.) and the International Association of Schools of Social Work (I.A.S.S.W.), dated July 2014, marks the knowledge base of social work (I.F.S.W. & I.A.S.S.W., 2014). The relevant part of the definition states: 'Underpinned by theories of social work, social sciences, humanities and indigenous knowledge, social work engages people and structures to address life challenges and enhance wellbeing'. In this context, in its most general sense, the knowledge base of social work refers to information produced by practitioners, theorists, and researchers. In this scope, the social work profession uses social work theories and methods, the information created by the social work practice, as well as the knowledge of many disciplines such as sociology, psychology, social anthropology, medicine, biology, social policy, law, public administration, economics etc. Moreover, the knowledge base of social work is not context independent. Therefore, it continues to evolve and change over time.

Thompson (2009) emphasised the need to support the knowledge base of social work with the skill base. If it does not become skill, knowledge will not have much value on its own. Skill can be defined as the ability to do a certain activity effectively and continuously in a certain period of time (Yolcuoğlu, 2012) and the ability to use information immediately and effectively in practice. In other words, it is the competence to do something. Skills can be developed and nurtured over time (Thompson, 2009). Social work skills require both the selection of appropriate techniques for a particular situation and the effective use of techniques (Duyan, 2010). Because the field of social work is a complex, versatile, and continuously changing area, the skill base of the field may present some difficulties.

The role of skills in social work education is very important in terms of the lack of disconnection between theory and practice. Thompson (2009) states that skill development in social work education includes two basic components: (1) basing, reinforcing, strengthening, and sharpening existing skills on a particular basis; and (2) recognising, understanding, and developing new skills. Therefore, it is very important for students to learn and develop some skills, and social work education plays a critical role in this process.

In the context of social work, the concept of value is used to express a number of basic moral/ethical principles to which social workers are bound (Banks, 2001). Values that complement the elements of knowledge and skill are the basic criteria for controlling the profession and for professional staff to work in a certain discipline (Duyan, 2010). Having a value base is one of the important components that makes the social work discipline a profession (Thompson, 2009).

With the addition of value, the knowledge-skill-value combination is completed – magnificent trio of social work practice. Social work education changes the approaches, techniques, and information that it uses according to the conditions of the day and even the client population it serves. Social work practices take a position according to which social problem hurts people that day and determines the approaches, techniques, and information from which they will benefit. Social work education can be a complex behavioural organisation, but when the skill base of generalist social work practice integrates with the knowledge and value base, this leads us to the concept of an intervention repertoire with direct or indirect practice competencies.

Intervention Repertoire and Direct and Indirect Practice in Field Instruction

Assessment of factors related to the individual's situation is within the direct practice of social work. Direct generalist social work practice involves working with individuals, families, and groups. With direct practice, behavioural changes that we expect and want in the clients and the solutions for social, emotional, or psychological problems can be performed easily because the experience of face-to-face practice is provided on behalf of both the client and the social worker. Being able to work face-to-face with the client allows people to maintain their freedom and improve their social functionality. The opposite of direct practice is indirect practice. While direct practice develops clinically focused work strategies and skills, indirect practice addresses working with the environment, organisations, and society and displays a socio-political context.

In other words, people have immediate and distant environments, and it is more difficult to change in the distant environment compared to the immediate environment. First of all, ensuring change in the distant environment is a laborious process that requires patience. Therefore, the immediate environment is a direct practice field, and the distant environment is the indirect practice field. Sometimes, it is important to remember that in generalist social work practice, we have two main areas of action that deal with direct practice (direct treatment: work with the client) and indirect treatment with the client's environment (indirect treatment: work with the client's environment). Direct practice includes micro- and mezzo-level field instruction elements, while indirect practice involves macro-level competencies (Butrym, 1968; Duyan, 2010; Yıldırım, 2018).

On the other hand, in social work practice, the intervention repertoire concept is used to characterise the presentation of knowledge, skills, and values together to respond to client's social dysfunction problems (Dewees, 2006; Duyan, 2010). In fact, the intervention repertoire is a monolithic perception consisting of technique, method, and practice skills. This concept incorporates already existing social work practice knowledge into skills that effectively put them into action. Thus, the transformation of information into practice is illustrated by an intervention repertoire.

Social Work Field Instruction and the Situation in Turkey

Field instruction is considered the central and essential component of social work education (Cleak & Smith, 2012; Fortune et al., 2001; Wayne et al., 2010). Social work field instruction allows the application of the knowledge, skills, and values learned in the social work departments in the process of social work education (Bogo, 2015). It is one of the most critical stages of social work education. It provides the opportunity to put the theory taught in the classroom into practice for the student who gets the support of both the agency supervisor he/she practices with and the educational supervisor at the school (Hemy et al., 2016; Homonoff, 2008). In the final analysis, the student learns to think and act like a social worker during the field instruction process (Bogo, 2015).

In the field instruction process, students can take the role of practitioner or assistant practitioner, thus, having the opportunity to truly experience social work practice, learn the profession through active participation, and observe successful social work practices. Wayne et al. (2010) refer to two interconnected processes at this point. The first is the subjective reflection about students' understanding and reactions to the practice situation. The second is the process of understanding social work practice by connecting the theory and getting support from the field supervisor. In the field instruction process, students learn to transform the theoretical framework they have acquired into practice to examine, criticise, and test the social work knowledge, skills, values, and principles discussed in academic courses (Bogo, 2006).

Savaya et al. (2003) describe three basic approaches to field instruction. The first is the apprenticeship model, in which students observe an experienced social worker prior to theoretical training. It is an inductive approach to learning in which the students deduce theory from practice. The second is the academic model, in which students first receive theoretical training in the classroom and then start field instruction. This model emphasises the cognitive development of the student. The third is the articulated approach in which field instruction is carried out simultaneously with theoretical training. This model proceeds from a simpler theory and progresses to more complex ones. Within the scope of the model, education is applied in the classroom and in the field at the same time. The model used widely in social work education in Turkey is the academic model. After three years of receiving theoretical training, students are placed at a variety of social service agencies for the field instruction process in the last year of their four-year degree programme.

The field instruction supervision process around the world is handled in different ways. In this context, besides individual supervision practice, there are also group supervision or task supervision practices in social work education (Abram et al., 2000; Bogo et al., 2004; Fortune & Kaye, 2002). The method that is widely used in social work education in Turkey is known to be individual supervision that corresponds to one-on-one supervision with students.

In the context of individual supervision, in general, four parties are involved in the social work field instruction experience (Garthwait, 2008): social work student, agency supervisor, educational supervisor, and field instruction coordinator. Each of these individuals who take part in the field instruction process is critical to the successful and quality execution of the field practice. In this context, in all the social work departments in Turkey, these four parties, working to provide quality education, are the main actors of the field instruction process. Thus, responsibilities of these parties in the field instruction process in Turkey can be explained as follows.

First, the main goal of field instruction is the social work student. The student conducts weekly interviews with both the agency supervisor and the educational supervisor in the field instruction process. In this process, he/she prepares reports and presents them to his/her supervisors and has the opportunity to discuss the practice process with both the educational supervisor and the agency supervisor. In the process, he/she has the opportunity to implement the theoretical knowledge that they learned in the classroom in a safe environment. At the end of the process, is for the student to be able to perform social work practice at micro, mezzo, and macro levels.

The second is the agency supervisor. The agency supervisor is selected from people who have actively participated in social work practice in a governmental or nongovernmental organisation that provides services in at least one of the social work areas. They are preferably selected from graduates of social work departments. In determining the agency supervisors, the field instruction coordinator of the social work department and the representatives of the relevant agency to which the student is appointed act together. The agency supervisor provides supervision and guidance for students in the field instruction process. He/she allows the student to participate directly in the intervention process as a practitioner or co-practitioner. In this process, he/she creates learning opportunities for the student.

The third is the educational supervisor. He/she advises the student during the field instruction process. In the field instruction process, he/she examines the weekly reports prepared by the student, regularly conducts interviews with the student, and gives feedback to the student. Moreover, the educational supervisor also supports the student's agency supervisor.

The last participant is the fieldwork coordinator in the social work departments of universities. The coordinator coordinates the field instruction process and enables students to be placed in agencies. Moreover, he/she deals with problems that may arise during placement and in the field instruction process.

Challenges, Problems, and Implications

One of the main responsibilities of social work is to strengthen society by meeting the needs of vulnerable and at-risk individuals and poor and oppressed people. In this process, social work practice targets both the individual and the society. Thus, as individuals' needs are met, society will be strengthened, and as structural problems are eliminated, the well-being of individuals will be increased. As a result, both individual and social welfare will increase. Accordingly, social work draws attention to the individual, social, and environmental structures, formations, and factors that raise and contribute to social problems. In Turkey, social work education, especially in the context of the practice environment, emerged with the aim of solving social problems and meeting the needs of individuals. However, some challenges are encountered in reaching this aim. These challenges will be addressed under the topics of structural issues; consultancy and supervision; performance evaluation and education/training indicators; record keeping, reporting, and remittance.

Structural Issues

An important issue that must be addressed is that a number of structural problems in social work education and practice in Turkey (Bolgün & Şahin, 2019) affect social work field instruction directly. One of these problems is the rapid increase of social work schools in recent years. In fact, the expansion of social work education in Turkey can be considered a very positive development. However, until 2002, there was only one social work school in Turkey, but today, this number has exceeded 60. Moreover, the number of adequate social work academicians did not increase at the same rate. In today's Turkey, while there are more social work schools, some were formed by academics who did not receive social work education. This situation, which directly affects social work education and the curriculum of the departments, may eventually lead to the emergence of social work departments and graduates that do not comply with international standards.

The ability of social work education to graduate ethical, competent, innovative, and effective social workers is highly dependent on the quality of the field experience (Bogo, 2015). However, some of the social work departments' curriculum in Turkey is entirely composed of theoretical courses, which means there are no practical courses in the curriculum. This means that an intervention repertoire – direct and indirect practice skills of students – cannot be developed sufficiently. Considering that the main goal in field instruction is the development of the student, it should be essential for the students to have basic competencies in social work practice.

On the other hand, departments that have practical courses in their curriculum may face other problems. As discussed before, while the number of social work schools has increased rapidly in Turkey, there are not enough adequate academicians. On the other hand, the number of students admitted to the social work graduate programmes in Turkey has increased rapidly in parallel with the number of schools. As a result, there may be difficulties in the process of providing theoretical education in the social work departments where the number of academicians is limited. In addition, the high number of students per academician poses problems in placing students in agencies by social work departments' fieldwork coordinators in the field instruction process. This situation adversely affects the quality of field instruction in two aspects. First, the counselling time allocated by educational supervisors to each student and agency supervisor becomes shorter, and the student follow-up process becomes more difficult. Secondly, in agencies that accept a large number of students for field practice, the number of students per agency supervisor is increasing. As a result, the agency supervision process may also be damaged.

Another important problem is that the changes made in social work legislation in the 2000s has paved the way for some professional groups who are not graduates of social work education programmes to implement social work (Karakuş, 2015). In this context, graduates of various departments, such as family and consumer sciences, psychological counselling and guidance, psychology and sociology, operate in social work practice environments under the name of 'social work attendant'. These professional groups have started to work to fulfil the tasks, just because their profession is regarded as close to the social work field in order to meet the need of personnel. The reflection of this process, which limits the employment of social workers to field instruction, is that students sometimes have to perform their field practices under agency supervisors who are not social workers. However, a recent study (Tanga, 2012) draws attention to the fact that the agency supervision by a social worker increases the quality of education within the scope of social work education.

Consultancy and Supervision

In Turkey, within the scope of field instruction, there are a number of challenges in terms of responsibilities in the consulting and supervision process. The knowledge and competence of educational and agency supervisors are at the top of these challenges. Social work educators who provide counselling and supervision to the student face-to-face, remotely, directly, or indirectly should have high-level knowledge and competence primarily in their practice fields. In Turkey, in the last two or three semesters of social work education at schools that provide four-year undergraduate programmes, social work students develop skills in the practice environment and work with agency and educational supervisors. However, given the high number of students studying in the social work departments in Turkey and the insufficient number of academicians, it would be a dream to think that all educational supervisors master their own application field in terms of knowledge and competence.

A second issue related to the consulting and supervision process is that it is quite difficult to find a qualified agency supervisor for undergraduate students. In Turkey, due to the large number of social work departments and the large number of students, it is a priority for students to fulfil their practice hours that will enable them graduate rather than to practice next to a social worker.

Third, in Turkey, some issues related to social workers providing consultancy and supervision do not yet have a controllable status. These issues are (1) protecting open, appropriate, and culturally sensitive boundaries in practice; (2) avoiding bilateral or multiple relationships in risky situations, especially in social media and other electronic environments; and (3) being fair and respectful when evaluating students' performance (N.A.S.W., 2017).

Fourth, supervision has guidance (educational), consultancy (support), and controlling (administrative) functions. However, in Turkey, the controlling function by educators sometimes overtakes other functions. The responsibilities of the supervisors regarding the field instruction should not be described only with reports and through a limited supervision process which is to control attendance and routine work of students (Tuncay, 2017). In the supervision process, the supervisors should be aware of the student's interest in the field, their personal abilities, orientations, and desires in addition to their skills. However, in Turkey, this expectation is not seen by supervisors among the issues that should be followed closely during the supervision process.

Finally, it is beneficial to talk about the training of agency supervisors regarding the consulting and supervision process. Agency supervisors must be competent to ensure the success of the educational process. Thus, the training of new agency supervisors is critical to this success (Abramson & Fortune, 1990). However, in Turkey, it is seen that the agency supervisors are not included in any additional training programme within the scope of field instruction in any social work department. Unfortunately, this affects the quality of the field instruction process negatively.

Performance Evaluation and Education-Training Indicators

Social work educators aim to help students cope with the problems they face in the professional environment while providing counselling to students. An integral part of social work education is field instruction, or sometimes called field practice. Therefore, social work is a discipline with a holistic curriculum consisting of both theory and field practice components (Dhemba, 2012).

In field instruction, which is a dimension of social work education, the criteria for evaluating students' performance are directly proportional to their learning competencies, that is, on the analysis of the practice technique. For example, in field instruction, supervisors focus on how the student uses social work theories and what he/she learns. With such a vague understanding of performance evaluation, students' practice scores are either too high or too low. As a matter of fact, when many social work programmes in the world are examined, it is seen that the students get very high grades from the field practice courses (Regehr et al., 2007; Tuncay, 2017). The situation is similar in Turkey, and the grades of the students in social work programmes are generally high. This is a serious ethical challenge because, for field instruction, social work knowledge, skills, management, and organisational competencies; multicultural awareness and sensitivity; and effective communication level must play an effective role in assessing student performance (Brenner, 2020).

Perhaps the biggest challenge in field instruction in Turkey, in terms of education and training indicators, is that social work students have problems in finding an agency for field practice. The reason for this problem, which violates the right of education of social work students and creates ethical dilemmas, is a change in the legislation. With the amendment made in the Vocational Education Law No. 3308, the practical courses in social work departments are considered as 'internships', which makes agencies compulsory to pay fees to students. On the other side, social work agencies in Turkey are not willing to pay the social work students the internship fee. At this point, students have difficulties in finding an agency for field instruction. Thus, the quality of the small number of agencies and agency supervisors cannot be ignored in the context of social work field instruction.

Record Keeping, Reporting, and Remittance Issues

Social workers in the practice environment should carefully address the issue of record keeping and reporting. Thus, they can place their client's concerns on a planned basis. However, this issue is not sufficiently discussed. In our country, there are colleagues who graduated from some social work schools without seeing the Social Analysis Report sample. Although the students present some reports (such as process reports, annual reports, and field and agency promotion reports) to the supervisors during the field instruction periods, the reality of the professional life and the problem area to be assigned is completely different. Sharing examples of recording and reporting more frequently in Turkish social work education would be the right step. Also, another important point in this step is that record keeping and reporting provide the client's privacy in the most appropriate way. Records and reports include sensitive information, such as the client's private topics, the content of the interview, and the determinants of the service delivery. In Turkey, the students face very strict suggestions about the confidentiality of records and reports throughout their education life, and this is an indispensable part of social work education. However, it is also important that students have information about what should be recorded and documented.

According to Barsky (2017), the social worker may have many clients working at the same time. Organising records and reports helps the professional by preventing clients from getting mixed up in such a situation. In addition, the easiest way for other social workers to continue working with clients is, again, to reference the records and reports. In some cases, clients may return to social work after months or years and may need social work again. Records and reports make it easier for the social worker to remember returning clients and reassess the services provided (Barsky, 2017).

Another current problem in social work practice in Turkey is the remittance issue, and Turkish social work education has serious responsibilities for the clarification of this issue. In the implementation of social work, it may be possible to transfer clients from one agency or social worker to another. This action can cause serious risks and a number of adversities. Golden (1976) lists these risks from simple to complex, and that client transfer can cause risks from disrupting the therapeutic process to harming to the client. In order to prevent these risks, the old and new social worker need to constructively approach in the client transfer process, which occurs in two stages.

First, is the termination of the client's relationship with the former social worker and agency, and second is to shape the practice process with the new social worker and agency. If possible, it is useful for the former social worker to participate in the interview process of the new social worker for at least one time. It is important to encourage the client to express their feelings clearly in the transfer process. Therefore, sufficient time should be given to the client for the transfer to be carried out. After the transfer is made, the new social worker should inform the client of his/her freedom of choice regarding the practice to prevent any insecurity that may occur in the client during the transfer process (Golden, 1976).

Conclusion and Implications for the Future

In this chapter, the challenges and problems experienced in social work field instruction in Turkey are emphasised. In this context, some structural problems stand out and affect the Turkish field instruction process negatively. One of these problems is the number of social work schools increased rapidly in 2000s. Unfortunately, this increase was not accompanied by the increase in the number of qualified and suitable academicians. As a result, today, there are social work departments in Turkey established from academicians who have not received social work education. This situation is reflected in social work education and educational curriculum. On the other hand, the number of students enrolled in social work programmes has also increased rapidly. The high number of students affects the success and effectiveness of the supervision process provided by educational supervisors and agency supervisors within the scope of field instruction. Therefore, both prioritising postgraduate education in social work and increasing the number of qualified social work academics and limiting the number of students of social work undergraduate programmes are considered important for the future of social work education.

Another issue is that some professional groups who are not graduates of social work have had the way paved for them to practice social work. As a result, within the scope of field instruction, it is seen that the students sometimes practice with supervisors who are not social workers. This situation affects the quality of education negatively. Therefore, taking steps to overcome the problems arising from the legislation is also vital for the future of both social work practice and social work education.

Consultancy and supervision are also important within the scope of field instruction. Considering the high number of students studying and the insufficient number of academicians, a number of shortcomings may occur regarding the knowledge and competence of educational supervisors. Moreover, the selection of qualified supervisors is also an important problem for students to be put into practice. In this context, it is also important to organise consultancy training programmes for agency supervisors. On the other hand, Turkish social work education needs mechanisms to control the supervision environment. Qualified field instruction is provided for students who have received consulting and supervision support and have adopted critical concepts such as intervention repertoire and direct and indirect practice.

There are some political and legislative challenges for social work field instruction that prevent finding a desired social work agency for students. If the process continues in this way, both social work education and social work practice will suffer from this wound. Solving the problem in the coming periods can be possible by the efforts of Turkish social work schools collectively rather than individual initiatives.

Other critical issues for field instruction are record keeping, reporting, and remittance issues. Well-prepared records and reports will continue to help students, social workers, and clients and ensure that services are provided effectively. As a matter of fact, it is necessary to focus more on the issues of record keeping, reporting, and remittance in Turkish social work education. Thus, within the scope of field instruction, students can better grasp the issues of record keeping, reporting, and transfer and actively use them in their future practices.

In conclusion, it is vital to provide qualified social work practice and social work education. In this context, it is seen that many social work schools and academics in Turkey try to overcome all these problems and to carry out the social work field instruction process in the best possible way. Fortunately, there are academics who work through the problems, challenges, and follow-up processes of social work field instruction in Turkey.

Note

1 In 2006, Hacettepe University Social Work College became the Department of Social Work after being a part of Hacettepe University Faculty of Economics and Administrative Sciences.

References

Abram, F.Y., Hartung, M. R., & Wernet, S. P. (2000). The non-MSW task supervisor, MSW field instructor, and the practicum student: A triad for high quality field education. *Journal of Teaching in Social Work*, 20(1–2), 171–185.

Abramson, J. S., & Fortune, A. E. (1990). Improving field instruction: An evaluation of a seminar for new field instructors. *Journal of Social Work Education*, 26(3), 273–286.

Banks, S. (2001). *Ethics and Values in Social Work*. Palgrave: Carfax Publishing.

Barsky, A. (2017). Ethics alive! To record or not to record: The ethics of documentation. Retrieved 11.04.2018, from https://www.socialworker.com/feature-articles/ethics-articles/to-record-or-not-to-record-the-ethics-of-documentation/.

Bogo, M. (2006). Field instruction in social work. *The Clinical Supervisor*, 24(1–2), 163–193.

Bogo, M. (2015). Field education for clinical social work practice: Best practices and contemporary challenges. *Clinical Social Work Journal*, 43(3), 317–324.

Bogo, M., Globerman, J., & Sussman, T. (2004). Field instructor competence in group supervision: Students' views. *Journal of Teaching in Social Work*, 24(1–2), 199–216.

Bolgün, C., & Şahin, F. (2019). Public perception and attitudes about social work in Turkey. *International Social Work*, 62(5), 1329–1342.

Brenner, L. (2020). Performance review questions for social workers. Retrieved 8.04.2020, from https://work.chron.com/performance-review-questions-social-workers-14685.html.

Butrym, Z. (1968). *Medical Social Work in Action*. London: Bell & Sons.

Çengelci, E. (1996). *Cumhuriyet Türkiyesinde sosyal hizmetlerin örgütlenmesi*. Ankara: Şafak Matbaacılık.
Cleak, H., & Smith, D. (2012). Student satisfaction with models of field placement supervision. *Australian Social Work*, 65(2), 243–258.
Dewees, M. (2006). *Contemporary Social Work Practice*. New York: McGraw-Hill.
Dhemba, J. (2012). Fieldwork in social work education and training: Issues and challenges in the case of Eastern and Southern Africa. *Social Work and Society International Online Journal*, 10(1), 1–16.
Duyan, V. (2010). *Sosyal hizmet: Temelleri-yaklaşımları-müdahale yöntemleri*. Ankara: Sosyal Hizmet Uzmanları Derneği Yayını.
Fortune, A. E., & Kaye, L. (2002). Learning opportunities in field practica: Identifying skills and activities associated with MSW students' self-evaluation of performance and satisfaction. *The Clinical Supervisor*, 21(1), 5–28.
Fortune, A. E., McCarthy, M., & Abramson, J. S. (2001). Student learning processes in field education: Relationship of learning activities to quality of field instruction, satisfaction, and performance among MSW students. *Journal of Social Work Education*, 37(1), 111–124.
Garthwait, C. L. (2008). *The Social Work Practicum. A Guide and Work Book for Students*. Boston: Allyn and Bacon.
Gazete, Resmi (2020). Resmi gazete kanunlar. Retrieved 18.02.2020 from https://www.resmigazete.gov.tr/arsiv/10233.pdf.
Golden, K. M. (1976). Client transfer and student social work. *Social Work*, 21(1), 65–66.
Hacettepe University Social Work Department. (2020). Sosyal hizmet bölümü tarihçe. Retrieved 18.02.2020, from http://www.shy.hacettepe.edu.tr/tr/menu/tarihce-108.
Hemy, M., Boddy, J., Chee, P., & Sauvage, D. (2016). Social work students 'juggling' field placement. *Social Work Education*, 35(2), 215–228.
Homonoff, E. (2008). The heart of social work: Best practitioners rise to challenges in field instruction. *The Clinical Supervisor*, 27(2), 135–169.
I.F.S.W. (International Federation of Social Workers), & I.A.S.S.W. (International Association of Schools of Social Work) (2014). Global definition of social work. Retrieved 26.04.2020, from http://www.iassw-aiets.org/global-definition-of-social-work-review-of-the-global-definition and http://ifsw.org/policies/definition-of-social-work/.
Karakuş, B. (2015). Sosyal hizmet mezunlarının kadro ve ünvanı 'sosyal hizmet uzmanı/sosyal çalışmacı'. *Toplum ve Sosyal Hizmet*, 26(2), 169–190.
Karataş, K., & Erkan, G. (2005). Türkiye'de sosyal hizmet eğitiminin tarihçesi. In: Ü. Onat (Ed.), *Sosyal hizmet eğitiminde yeni yaklaşımlar* (pp. 112–133). Ankara: Aydınlar Matbaacılık Ltd. Şti.
Koşar, N., & Tufan, B. (1999). Sosyal Hizmetler Yüksek Okulu tarihçesine genel bir bakış. In: Yaşam Boyu Sosyal Hizmet (Ed.). Ankara: HÜSHYO Yayını.
N.A.S.W. (National Association of Social Workers). (2017). Code of ethics of the national association of social workers. Retrieved 4.04.2020, from https://socialwork.utexas.edu/dl/files/academic-programs/other/naswcode-of-ethics.pdf.
Özbek, N. (2006). *Cumhuriyet Türkiye'sinde sosyal güvenlik ve sosyal politikalar*. İstanbul: Emeklilik Gözetim Merkezi.
Regehr, G., Bogo, M., Regehr, C., & Power, R. (2007). Can we build a better mousetrap? Improving the measures of practice performance in the field practicum. *Journal of Social Work Education*, 43(2), 327–344.
Savaya, R., Peleg-Oren, N., Stange, D., & Geron, Y. (2003). Congruence of classroom and field instruction in social work: An empirical study. *Social Work Education*, 22(3), 297–308.
S.H.U.D.E.R. (Ulusal Sosyal Hizmet Uzmanları Derneği). (2020). Sosyal hizmet uzmanları derneğinin tarihçesi. Retrieved 18.02.2020, from https://shuder.org/shuder/tarihce.html.
Tanga, P. T. (2012). The challenges of social work field training in Lesotho. *Social Work Education: The International Journal*, 10(1), 1–22.
Thompson, N. (2009). *Kuram ve uygulamada sosyal hizmeti anlamak*. Ankara: Dipnot Yayınları.
Tuncay, T. (2017). Sosyal hizmet eğitiminin etik yönleri [Ethical aspects of social work education]. *Sosyal Çalışma Dergisi*, 1(2), 1–9.
Wayne, J., Bogo, M. S., & Raskin, M. (2010). Field education as the signature pedagogy of social work education. *Journal of Social Work Education*, 46(3), 327–339.
Yolcuoğlu, İ. G. (2012). *Sosyal Hizmete giriş*. Ankara: SABEV Yayınevi.
Yıldırım, B. (2018). Hastane sosyal hizmetinin işlevi ve bakım veren ebeveynlerde pediatrik astım yönetimi [Function of hospital social work and paediatric asthma management in caregiver parents]. *Toplum ve Sosyal Hizmet*, 29(2), 364–385.

Part V

Social Work Field Education under COVID-19

34

The Self-Directed Practicum

An Innovative Response to COVID-19 and a Crisis in Field Education

Beth Archer-Kuhn, Angela Judge-Stasiak, Lorraine Letkemann, Jennifer Hewson, and Jessica Ayala

We are approaching the end of 2020 and what a year it has been – a year of the unexpected, of worry and grief, but also a time of coming together, transformation, and resilience. It seems we ride the spectrum of emotions routinely now, perhaps even unnoticed, as we continue to adjust to our new context in the time of COVID-19. We practice social distancing, wear masks in public, and mostly stay home. Having navigated the initial shock and force of the pandemic as well as the traumatic first wave, we are now in the midst of the second wave of the pandemic in our communities. In social work education, our courses are taught primarily online, and we utilise technology such as Zoom to engage in multiple meetings each day as we continue to educate, carry out research, and provide service.

Field education, a critical part of our integrated social work education model in Canada (C.A.S.W.E., 2014), has been challenged to respond to student learning needs and agency capacity both prior to (Ayala et al., 2017) and during the pandemic. This chapter will provide an overview of some of our experiences and innovative responses in Canadian social work education, as we present a new model for cutting-edge field education that does not rely solely on agency capacity. Recommendations existed for field educators to respond to the challenges facing this essential component of social work education and alternatives were being explored prior to the pandemic (Ayala et al., 2018), yet the challenges of providing quality field education during a world health crisis have highlighted the urgency of implementation.

In Canada, there has been consensus across regions on messaging about the severity of the COVID-19 outbreak and social distancing practices (Merkley et al., 2020). Slowing the spread of the outbreak through social distancing, as noted by the World Health Organization (W.H.O., 2020), has informed our response. Prior to the pandemic, we were already facing a field education crisis. There was an already overloaded system with increasing numbers of students needing field practicum placements along with diminished community capacity to host those students in practicum due to losses of funding resulting from government budget cuts (Government of Alberta, 2020). The pandemic restrictions added opportunities for both urgency and innovation. Our colleagues in medicine illustrated how telemedicine technologies have contributed to improved core competencies in medical students (Waseh & Dicker, 2019). Indeed, we learned how technology can guide and support students to continue their education journey, even

DOI: 10.4324/9781032164946-40

during COVID-19 (Mian & Khan, 2020). Our supervised, self-directed practicum model allows students and faculty to embrace the opportunity to continue their learning in meaningful ways despite a lack of capacity in the community – be it as a result of the pandemic or budget cuts.

Field Practicum in Social Work

Higher education trends continue to include a focus on employability, experiential learning, and accountability of teaching and learning outcomes with some emphasis on the use of technology (Regehr, 2013). In social work, field education or practicum placements are utilised for the application of knowledge, values, and skills in supervised practice settings (Wayne et al., 2010). Typically, this occurs in a dyad between the student and the supervisor hosted in an agency where students complete a predetermined number of hours of unpaid professional experience. Ayala et al. (2017) reported challenges in securing agency hosted practicum opportunities for students including, but not limited to, competition for placements, funding and budget restraints in agencies, lack of space for or managerial support for accepting students, and the need to grow the culture and expectations of supervision across the profession. This has created pressure for field educators to think creatively about how to respond to these constraints in the community while continuing to offer quality education placements that fulfil accreditation standards and appropriate skill development of emerging social work practitioners (Ayala et al., 2018).

In Canada, researchers are sounding the alarm that field education is in a state of crisis with increased numbers of students entering social work programmes, while field education has been unable to keep pace and meet the demand for practicum placements (Ayala et al., 2017). The COVID-19 pandemic has not only amplified the field education crisis but also the impetus of much-needed innovation (Archer-Kuhn et al., 2020). Such innovation can be found in recent studies within social work education. Ayala et al., (2018) explored the challenges within field education and strategies to address the crisis through a mixed methods study with field educators across nine Canadian provinces. They reported the following themes: (1) collaborating to create change within the neoliberal context; (2) developing innovative alternative practicum models and partnerships, particularly models with students as partners; and (3) enhancing field education resources and supports. Together these strategies form the sustainability model of field education, which will be discussed further below.

Other social work studies have identified various models of field education, such as a hub model (George et al., 2013), online cyber counselling (Mishna et al., 2013), workplace practicum (Pelech et al., 2009), and rotational models of field education (Birkenmaier et al., 2012). Further, a number of studies have identified pedagogical practices for field education and include positive learning environments, collaborative relationships with field instructors, shadowing, and debriefing (Bogo, 2015); simulations and role play to prepare students for practicum (Bogo et al., 2016; Fulton et al., 2019); education in caring, training in reflective practice, video interaction (Hermsen & Embregts, 2015); and feedback during simulation-based activities (Kourgiantakis et al., 2018). Researchers in Sweden (Rehn & Kalman, 2018), in Canada (Archer-Kuhn et al., 2020), and in the U.K. (Wilson, 2013) contend that reflective practice, which includes critical thinking, remains an essential component in supporting students in their transformation to professional social workers.

Indeed, much attention has been drawn to re-imagining field education. During this time of COVID-19, the need for alternative practicum models is amplified to address the limited access to community agency practicums and the increased reliance on technology and online practicum placements. In this chapter, we focus on one such alternative model for field education that considers many components reflected in a humanising response, including: empathic and collaborative supervisory relationships; education in caring; students as partners; reflective practices and the development of critical thinking; and increased student responsibility, choice, and agency in the development of their practicum and learning plan. These characteristics are also found in inquiry-based learning principles.

Inquiry-Based Learning

Inquiry-based learning (I.B.L.) approaches encourage students to design and lead their own inquiry process with the support of the instructor (Ellis, 2016; Saunders-Stewart et al., 2012). Falling within a constructivist paradigm, I.B.L. is student-centred, and knowledge is constructed from experience (Apedoe & Reeves, 2006; McKinney, 2014; Spronken-Smith & Walker, 2010). As a pedagogy, students learn to critically examine and deconstruct knowledge as power is shifted between the student and teacher (Little, 2010), leaving students as co-constructors of knowledge, not passive recipients (Apedoe & Reeves, 2006; Buckner & Kim, 2014). This is particularly important in applied disciplines, including social work in which students develop critical thinking skills that are necessary for professional competence and ethical practice.

In a recent explanatory mixed methods study of seven cohorts of undergraduate, graduate, and doctoral students in social work education, students embraced the structured and guided approach to I.B.L. This turned out to be an important aspect when shifting from traditional teacher-centred to student-centred methods of teaching (Archer-Kuhn, Lee, Finnessey & Liu, 2020). Not only did student engagement increase with the level of choice and agency inherent in I.B.L., but the researchers also found an increase in higher order learning among students after participating in the I.B.L. courses, regardless of their levels of education and gender. Also, there was a significant increase in students' reflective and integrative learning after participating in the inquiry-based learning courses. Additionally, the experiential and intentional nature of their learning increased students' confidence as they became more comfortable as independent learners and took ownership of their learning. All of this, students said, led to much deep learning as they (1) made linkages into the everyday, (2) utilised multiple sources, (3) broadened the learning environment, (4) had their curiosity sparked, and (5) learned together with peers and the instructor.

We propose that many of these same outcomes can be found in the model of field education that will be presented next in this chapter. Although students developing their own learning plan do not necessarily have an inquiry question that they are seeking to answer throughout their field education, the process of the new model contains many principles of I.B.L., including being student-centred, the instructor offering structure and guidance, student choice and agency, student engagement, collaborative learning, peer and instructor feedback, and the development of critical thinking skills.

Theoretical Grounding

The model is grounded in the principles of a guided and structured I.B.L. approach (Archer-Kuhn et al., 2020; Spronken-Smith & Walker, 2010) while maintaining the existing framework based in experiential learning and reflective practice (Wayne et al., 2010). These principles include being student-centred, providing student choice, and emphasising student curiosity and empowerment. Students have choice over the areas of learning they want to explore; need to be curious about the topic of interest; and are provided with the encouragement, support, and trust from the faculty field instructor that, indeed, students know what it is that they need to learn. This approach fits well with our social work values of social justice, integrity, competence, and service to humanity (C.A.S.W., 2005) and prioritising student well-being (Archer-Kuhn et al., 2020).

Field Practicum in Canada: Current Situation

The Faculty of Social Work, University of Calgary offers social work programming including Bachelor of Social Work (B.S.W.) and Master of Social Work (M.S.W.) programmes that are delivered face-to-face, online, and via blended learning. Students who apply to the online programme options are often working full-time and have career experience and family responsibilities. These responsibilities can create challenges for leaving paid employment or the ability to be available for unpaid full-time practicums. Despite evidence to support excellent learning opportunities for students in paid work field placements (Pelech et al., 2009) in Canada, most field practicums remain unpaid in social work education. The constraints in supervision capacity also limit the availability of agency-hosted practicums.

The journey toward a supervised, self-directed practicum model began in 2017. Two field education coordinators from the Faculty of Social Work (F.S.W.), University of Calgary began imagining new ways of aligning the long-standing history of field education with new opportunities to meet the needs of both students and community stakeholders, particularly to meet the needs in rural and remote communities. What emerged was the concept of a supervised, self-directed practicum in which the F.S.W. managed the responsibility for the supervision of students. Students would create an individual learning plan under the guidance of a social work faculty field instructor which included both indirect practice opportunities (e.g., readings, training opportunities, webinars, workshops, podcasts) and direct practice opportunities (e.g., volunteer service, research practice) in the social work profession.

A pilot of the supervised, self-directed practicum began for five students in the spring semester of 2019, and another was offered to three students in the winter semester of 2020. These eight students were able to explore areas of practice they were deeply passionate about or had never thought to explore prior to the practicum, and each student had been unable to secure a practicum in a traditional agency setting either because of agency capacity or personal circumstances. The areas explored by students ranged greatly and included trauma and mental health, post-traumatic stress disorder (P.T.S.D.) in first responders, palliative care and grief, adverse childhood experiences, youth resilience, and trauma-informed practice.

In March 2020, the COVID-19 global pandemic had an abrupt impact on students who were currently in field education and those scheduled to begin practicum in spring (May) and summer (July) 2020. Following the national directives of our accrediting body, the Canadian Association of Social Work Education (C.A.S.W.E.), the policies of the University of Calgary, and local public health directives, all in-person practicum placements were suspended over the spring and summer semesters. Some agencies were able to offer student field practicums using remote technology to offer services, but the majority of agency-hosted placements were lost. The pressures impacting the availability of social work field placements (Ayala et al., 2017) were amplified, and hundreds of students faced the possibility of not being able to complete their social work programme. The F.S.W. field education team offered the option of the supervised, self-directed practicum as a pathway for students to complete their field education placements. This model allowed the field education team to navigate through the abrupt suspension of in-person or onsite practicum options for students and mitigate the loss of community capacity for placements in the upcoming semesters. This response allowed students to obtain direct practice experience, learn alongside peers in the same learning configuration, and receive reflective supervision from a registered social work practitioner at a time when the community was navigating the pandemic crisis. As such, the COVID-19 crisis created an opportunity to offer students a choice in how their practice hours were completed, including (1) remote, agency-hosted practicum; (2) remote, workplace-hosted practicum; or (3) supervised, self-directed practicum.

Supervised, Self-Directed Model in Fieldwork

Description

In the initial pilot, the eight self-directed students were supported by volunteer field instructors or practicum supervisors (members of the F.S.W. field education team). The supervised, self-directed practicum was grounded in the learning plan created by each student under the supervision of their social work faculty field instructor. Students were empowered to choose their own learning activities and engage in peer support and supervision consultation to ensure activities were dedicated to the practice objectives (set out by the F.S.W. for the practicum) that would guide their practicum learning journey. Students were responsible for keeping track of their weekly hours, reporting on their weekly activities and learnings from those activities, and actively contributing to a learning environment through peer support. Each week, students would offer a written log of their activities and engage in group supervision sessions with their field instructor (via Zoom or telephone). Students were also supported through individual telephone supervision consultations, as needed.

When COVID-19 impacted field education and the solution to continuing to offer quality field education placements was decided upon via the supervised, self-directed practicum, the F.S.W. created a new role to support self-directed practicum students: the *faculty field instructor* (F.F.I.). The decision to create this role was based on the volume of students requiring this type of learning, feedback from the students and instructors involved in the previous pilot offerings of self-directed options, and the core importance of supervision to help students reflect on their weekly accomplishments and how this impacts practice. This role served to offer the support and supervision previously offered in an agency hosted practicum. To ensure continuity and appropriate support for the new team of F.F.I.s hired for the spring and summer terms, the original field instructors who supported the pilot students offered training sessions, ongoing consultation support, and developed and shared resources to offer support for all F.F.I.s and students.

The learning plans created by each student were as diverse as the individual learner. Some students chose to focus on a primary theme and dedicated volunteer service and professional development to a specific topic area. Other students chose to seek out breadth in their experiences, volunteering and learning in a wide range of areas. At times, students would volunteer in one place for a significant component of the hours and have less in the way of professional development (training, etc.). In other instances, students volunteered with several places while enhancing their knowledge by completing professional development modules and certifications relevant to social work practice.

Opportunities that would not usually be available for field placements – for example, due to a lack of social work supervision or lack of sufficient opportunities to sustain the full hours of placement – became available as part of self-directed placements, including contributions to research projects on social work and social justice concepts, anti-oppressive community development movements, workshops and initiatives, telephone and in-person outreach, seniors' centres, children's aid, gender-based violence, shelters and advocacy groups, crisis lines, illness-focused agencies, and committee work.

Implementation

Feedback from the supervised, self-directed practicum pilot showed that the first few weeks were the most challenging for students, as they began to take charge of their learning and started to create their own learning plan. Building on this experience and feedback, the field education team ensured that additional resources and sessions were created to help support the student and the F.F.I. This support included tutorials and resource lists for developing a learning plan incorporating direct practice options (i.e., volunteer opportunities based in the student's community or remote options) and self-directed learning opportunities based on the student's interest and indirect practice (e.g., webinars, online courses, readings, articles, websites, etc.). Once the learning plan was created, additional learning opportunities could be added that may become available throughout the semester, but the roadmap was clear and offered structure to inform the student's weekly reporting responsibilities on their time, learning activities, and reflection on learnings.

Based on student and field instructor feedback from the initial pilot, two components emerged as critical to the implementation of the self-directed practicum model: peer support and supervision. Supervision was provided by the F.F.I. and included weekly supervision sessions for students (group and/or individual) and feedback on student weekly reflection logs and evaluation on learning progress at mid-term and upon completion of practicum. Supervision was recognised as a mutual responsibility, and students were encouraged to prepare for meetings with their supervisor and learn with the peers in the small group sessions. These sessions were focused on discussing social work competencies and professional identity, debriefing learning activities from the previous week, and providing support to reflect and integrate social work theory, practice, and research into the student's practice identity. The main components of the supervised, self-directed model are outlined below (Figure 34.1).

New Innovative Fieldwork Model During Covid-19 Pandemic

The experiences of students and field instructors participating in the supervised, self-directed practicum were collected each term. The field education team invited feedback through a student survey, individual debrief consultations, group debrief sessions, and written testimonials about the self-directed practicum experiences. Feedback indicated both benefits and challenges of this format for field education. This knowledge helped to inform orientation and onboarding information, including resources and handouts to support students and instructors with lists of possible direct or indirect practice opportunities, learning plan samples, self-directed practicum tips, and a rubric for successfully completing the practicum.

Students emphasised the importance of reflection and supervision for (1) integrating key learning in their programme with their emerging professional social work identity and processing indirect and direct practice opportunities; (2) uncovering areas of practice that either the field could not support (agency capacity) or the student had not been aware of or even considered as an area of practice, such as approaching mental health practice from a research lens or the ability to attend virtual international conferences to understand social justice issues in international social work; and (3) the ability to have more space to explore work with diverse populations and social justice than their peers experienced in an agency hosted setting, which increased confidence in their skills in these practice areas.

Students described their learning journey as empowering (the student sets the pace and is free from agency constraints of practice), flexible (allowing for a fit with their life and balance), and motivating (the inquiry and learning activities are chosen by the student). Many who thrived in this type of learning were given opportunities to learn in areas of practice new to them. One

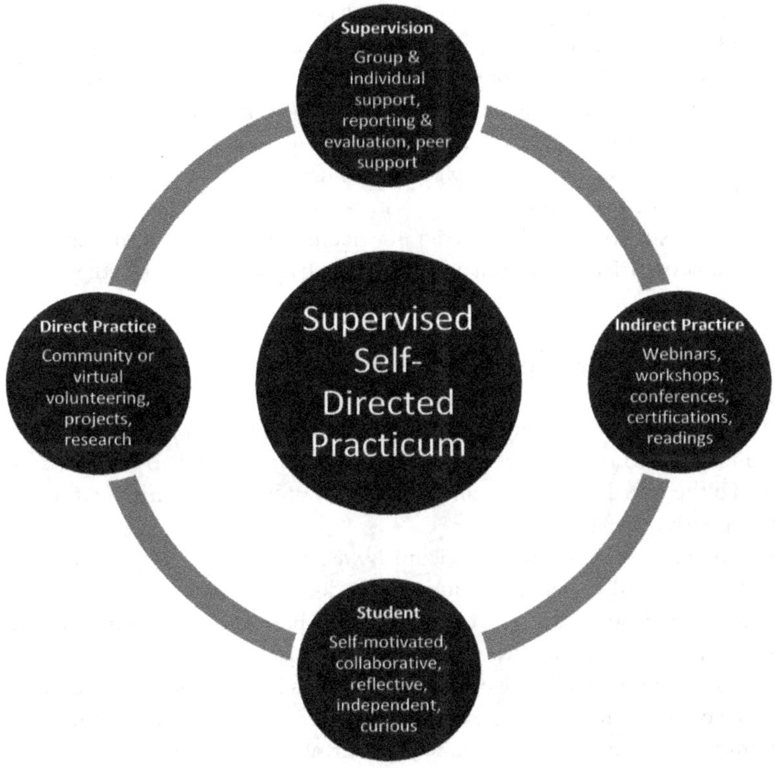

Figure 34.1 Faculty of social work, supervised, self-directed model in fieldwork.

unintended consequence from the supervised, self-directed practicum was the unexpected shift in higher education plans or career trajectory (e.g., deciding to pursue graduate studies or dedicate practice to a previously unexplored area of social work practice). Students explained that the characteristics which supported their success in this learning configuration were self-motivation, the ability to work independently and engage in supervision, as well as innate curiosity.

Field education coordinators and F.F.I.s observed some resistance from both community partners and social work educators to support supervised, self-directed practicums in favour of agency hosted practicums. The beliefs about the new method for offering practicum experiences was met with criticism and uncertainty about the quality of the learning experience for students. Field educators from the F.S.W. working with the supervised, self-directed practicum model received spirited reactions from colleagues elevating agency-hosted or specific agency-hosted practicum options claiming that this model did not offer the same rigour as agency-hosted practical experiences. Efforts were made to increase information available about what the supervised, self-directed practicum involved in order to recognise this concept as a parallel pathway to practicum, offering an alternative to meet students learning needs and the needs of the community in a new way to align with the learning outcomes of the programme and the national accreditation standards.

F.F.I.s supervising self-directed students witnessed student transformation evidenced in group supervision; individual mastery for their own learning; and the integration of this learning into their emerging practice framework of competence, ethics, and social justice. Weekly written reports and dialogue in group supervision allowed students to process the activities for the week by asking questions, considering the implications of their activities, and creating intentions to include the knowledge in their ongoing practice. These field instructors observed the unexpected outcome that students were able to delve more deeply into concepts of oppression, diversity, and social justice as they had the ability to direct and select their learning activities.

From a field coordination standpoint, the direct practice (experiential learning) components of the practicum were based on what opportunities existed in the community (volunteer opportunities). The practicum became a bridge between community needs and a student-centred approach to learning in field education.

The challenges faced in the supervised, self-directed practicum were identified in responses from field education coordinators, F.F.I.s, and students, and these challenges related to the initial journey to arrive at the learning plan that guided the practice hours. Students and their supervisors struggled in the first few weeks to create the learning plan and have a sense of how the practicum and the learning would transpire. Both patience and a willingness to embrace uncertainty was required. Once the student had a clear learning plan to guide the direction of their learning activities, there was engagement, clarity, and ability to take on new opportunities. This momentum was then sustained through the weekly supervision meetings. Similarly, supervisors who were able to embrace the initial discomfort and uncertainty and trust the momentum in the process had the most positive experiences.

This concept of the supervised, self-directed practicum is well aligned with the field education literature with respect to a need to reimagine how field education is delivered and brings opportunities to further refine, evaluate, and improve this model. We have an opportunity to lead a change in the way social work practice is understood, how agencies relate to and connect with the university, increase the participation in practical learning opportunities for all students regardless of the community capacity or personal circumstances, and fill volunteer positions in the community.

There is an opportunity to expand this as an option and create more choice in how field education is delivered. The support of students to align with the knowledge development and mobilisation of faculty members and the increased intersection with research and practical experience is promising. During the spring and summer semesters of 2020, the self-directed practicum was the primary model via which students were able to gain direct practice experience. Perhaps the greatest promise is to partner with agencies in the community and meet our stakeholders directly with what they need through their volunteer service, public outreach, consciousness-raising and social justice initiatives, rather than competing with other schools requiring a student placement.

In terms of meeting the challenges we face within the context of the pandemic, this innovation offered the flexibility demanded of us as a faculty. Building on this experience, we can look to increased partnership with community agencies through volunteer opportunities, the use of role playing and technology for simulation and instructional debrief, and the continued work to recognise this learning format as equally valuable to that of agency-hosted practicum opportunities, regardless of pandemic necessity.

Conclusion

Despite the challenges presented by COVID-19, to offer practicum placements, the supervised, self-directed practicum was the primary pathway for students to complete their programme while actively contributing to their own professional development and the needs of the community. It required passionate and dedicated individuals to think creatively despite the adversity and trauma faced by both students and the community and to continue to focus on the importance of supervision and reflection to integrate skills into an emerging practice framework for emergingsocial workers.

The supervised, self-directed model for field education allowed for an enactment of our social work values of self-determination and social justice, whereby students were provided with a choice about their learning and encouragement to drive their own learning process. This student-centred approach to learning using structured and guided I.B.L. principles has been shown to be effective in other components of social work education (Archer-Kuhn et al., 2020). The application of the model may fill a niche in social work education for students with a natural curiosity and who thrive on self-discovery. We propose this learning-centred approach to field education as an option for meaningful social work education during this pandemic time and moving forward in response to the ongoing crisis in social work field education.

References

Apedoe, X. S., & Reeves, T. C. (2006). Inquiry-based learning and digital libraries in undergraduate science education. *Journal of Science Education and Technology*, *15*(5/6), 321–330. https://doi.org/10.1007/s10956-006-9020-8

Archer-Kuhn, B., Ayala, J., Hewson, J., & Letkemann, L. (2020). Canadian reflections on the Covid-19 pandemic in social work education: From tsunami to innovation. *Social Work Education*, *39*(8), 1010–1018. https://doi.org/10.1080/02615479.2020.1826922

Archer-Kuhn, B., Lee, Y., Finnessey, S., & Liu, J. (2020). Inquiry-based learning as a facilitator to student engagement in higher education. *Teaching and Learning Inquiry*, *8*(1). https://doi.org/10.20343/teachlearninqu.8.1.x

Archer-Kuhn, B., Lee, Y., Hewson, J., & Burns, V. (2020). Growing together: Cultivating inquiry-based learning in social work education. *Social Work Education*. https://doi.org/10.1080/02615479.2020.1839407

Archer-Kuhn, B., Samson, P., Damianakis, T., Barrett, B., Matin, S., & Ahern, C. (2020). Transformative learning in field education: Students bridging the theory/practice gap. *The British Journal of Social Work*, 1–20. https://doi.org/10.1093/bjsw/bcaa082

Ayala, J., Drolet, J., Fulton, A., Hewson, J., Letkemann, L., Baynton, M., Elliott, G., Judge-Stasiak, A., Blaug, C., Gérard Tétreault, A., & Schweizer, E. (2017). Field education in crisis: Experiences of field education coordinators in Canada. *Social Work Education*, *37*(3), 281–293. https://doi.org/10.1080/02615479.2017.1397109

Ayala, J., Drolet, J., Fulton, A., Hewson, J., Letkemann, L., Baynton, M., Elliott, G., Judge-Stasiak, A., Blaug, C., Gérard Tétreault, A., & Schweizer, E. (2018). Restructuring social work field education in 21st century Canada: From Crisis Management to Sustainability. *Canadian Social Work Review*, *35*(2), 45–65. https://doi.org/10.7202/1058479ar

Birkenmaier, J., Curley, J., & Rowan, N. L. (2012). Knowledge outcomes within rotation models of social work field education. *Journal of Gerontological Social Work*, *55*(4), 321–336. https://doi.org/10.1080/01634372.2011.625596

Bogo, M. (2015). Field education for clinical social work practice: Best practices and contemporary challenges. *Clinical Social Work Journal*, *43*(3), 317–324. https://doi.org/10.1007/s10615-015-0526-5

Bogo, M., Lee, B., McKee, E., Baird, S. L., & Ramjattan, R. (2016). Field instructors' perceptions of Foundation Year students' readiness to engage in field education. *Social Work Education*, *35*(2), 204–214. https://doi.org/10.1080/02615479.2015.1123689

Buckner, E., & Kim, P. (2014). Integrating technology and pedagogy for inquiry-based learning: The Stanford mobile inquiry-based learning environment (SMILE). *Prospects*, *44*(1), 99–118. https://doi.org/10.1007/s11125-013-9269-7

Canadian Association for Social Work Education. (2014). Standards for accreditation. https://caswe-acfts.ca/wp-content/uploads/2013/03/CASWE-ACFTS.Standards-11-2014-1.pdf

CASW. (2005). *Social Work Code of Ethics*. Ottawa: Canadian Association of Social Workers (CASW). Available at https://www.casw-acts.ca/sites/default/files/attachements/casw_code_of_ethics.pdf

Ellis, R. A. (2016). Qualitatively different university student experiences of inquiry: Associations among approaches to inquiry, technologies and perceptions of the learning environment. *Active Learning in Higher Education*, *17*(1), 13–23. https://doi.org/10.1177/1469787415616721

Fulton, A. E., Dimitropoulos, G., Ayala, J., McLaughlin, A. M., Baynton, M., Blaug, C., Collins, T., Elliott, G., Judge-Stasiak, A., Letkemann, L., & Ragan, E. (2019). Role-playing: A strategy for practicum preparation

for Foundation Year MSW students. *Journal of Teaching in Social Work, 39*(2), 163–180. https://doi.org/10.1080/08841233.2019.1576573
George, P., Siver, S., & Preston, S. (2013). Reimagining field education in social work: The promise unveiled. *Advances in Social Work, 14*(2), 642–657
Government of Alberta. (2020). Budget 2020. https://www.alberta.ca/budget.aspx
Hermsen, M., & Embregts, P. (2015). An explorative study of the place of the ethics of care and reflective practice in social work education and practice. *Social Work Education, 34*(7), 815–828. https://doi.org/10.1080/02615479.2015.1059804
Kourgiantakis, T., Sewell, K. M., & Bogo, M. (2018). The importance of feedback in preparing social work students for field education. *Clinical Social Work Journal, 47*(1), 124–133. https://doi.org/10.1007/s10615-018-0671-8
Little, S. (2010). *Inquiry-Based Learning in the Social Sciences: A Meta-Analytical Study*. CILASS: Centre for Inquiry-Based Learning in the Arts and Social Sciences, University of Sheffield. Retrieved from www.shef.ac.uk/polopoly_fs/1.122795!/file/IBL_in_SocSci-FINAL.pdf
McKinney, P. (2014). Information literacy and inquiry-based learning: Evaluation of a five-year programme of curriculum development. *Journal of Librarianship and Information Science, 46*(2), 148–166. https://doi.org/10.1177/0961000613477677
Merkley, E., Bridgman, A., Loewen, P. J., Owen, T., Ruths, D., & Zhilin, O. (2020). A rare moment of cross-partisan consensus: Elite and public response to the COVID-19 pandemic in Canada. *Canadian Journal of Political Science, 53*(2), 1–8. https://doi.org/10.1017/S0008423920000311
Mian, A., & Khan, S. (2020). Medical education during pandemics: A UK perspective. *BMC Medicine, 18*(100). https://doi.org/10.1186/s12916-020-01577-y
Mishna, F., Levine, D., Bogo, M., & Van Wert, M. (2013). Cyber counselling: An innovative field education pilot project. *Social Work Education, 32*(4), 484–492
Pelech, W. J., Barlow, C., Badry, D. E., & Elliot, G. (2009). Challenging traditions: The field education experiences of students in workplace practica. *Social Work Education: The International Journal, 28*(7), 737–749. https://doi.org/10.1080/02615470802492031
Regehr, C. (2013). Trends in higher education in Canada and implications for social work education. *Social Work Education: The International Journal, 32*(6), 700–714
Rehn, M., & Kalman, H. (2018). Social work students' reflections on challenges during field education. *Journal of Social Work: JSW, 18*(4), 451–467
Saunders-Stewart, K. S., Gyles, P. D. T., & Shore, B. M. (2012). Student outcomes in inquiry instruction: A literature-derived inventory. *Journal of Advanced Academics, 23*(1), 5–31. https://doi.org/10.1177/1932202x11429860
Spronken-Smith, R., & Walker, R. (2010). Can inquiry-based learning strengthen the links between teaching and disciplinary research? *Studies in Higher Education, 35*(6), 723–740. https://doi.org/10.1080/03075070903315502
Waseh, S., & Dicker, A. P. (2019). Telemedicine training in undergraduate medical education: Mixed methods review. *JMIR Medical , 5*(1), e12515. https://doi.org/10.2196/12515
Wayne, J., Bogo, M., & Raskin (2010). Field education as the signature pedagogy of social work education. *Journal of Social Work Education, 46*(3), 327–339. https://doi.org/10.5175/JSWE.2010.200900043
Wilson, G. (2013). Evidencing reflective practice in social work education: Theoretical uncertainties and practical challenges. *British Journal of Social Work, 43*(1), 154–172. https://doi.org/10.1093/bjsw/bcr170
World Health Organization. (2020). Critical preparedness, readiness and response actions for COVID-19. Interim guidance. https://apps.who.int/iris/bitstream/handle/10665/331511/Critical%20preparedness%20readiness%20and%20response%20actions%20COVID-10%202020-03-22_FINAL-eng.pdf

35

COVID-19 Pandemic

A Threat or an Opportunity to Fieldwork Education in England?

Paula Beesley

The year 2020 saw an unprecedented global pandemic sweep the world and impact life in a previously unimagined way. Social isolation and distancing became a requirement, unemployment and poverty rose significantly, and the worldwide death count continued to rise. The impact on every country's emotional and physical welfare cannot be underplayed. At such a time, the profession of social work was more important than ever to support and safeguard the vulnerable members of our society. In parallel to this, social work education continued.

Fieldwork education in England occurs when the student applies the learning and knowledge from their academic input to their skill development in a practical social work placement. It enables learning through observation, modelling, and practise of skills, which is developed further through reflective discussion within social work student supervision (Davys & Beddoe, 2009). Fieldwork education in England is supported by the new English social work regulatory body, Social Work England (S.W.E.) and a brief context of fieldwork education in England is first provided.

The main body of the chapter will reflect chronologically on solutions to the impact of the COVID-19 pandemic on English fieldwork education. It will first provide discussion on the crisis-based decision-making in relation to the initial governmental response of a national lockdown in England. Furthermore, the directive that placements could be continued, shortened, suspended, or replaced, which empowered individual social work education providers to make decisions about placement provision on a cohort by cohort basis, will be considered (S.W.E., 2020a). The chapter will then discuss an alternative learning package that some English social work education providers opted to use in place of a social work placement in the spring/summer of 2020. The chapter will also consider the longer term planning in relation to fieldwork education and implementation of social work placement provision within a socially distanced environment. A style of blended experiential placement learning has emerged, which will be discussed.

The chapter will conclude with a reflection that English social work educators and fieldwork educators have embraced the changes in social work placement provision to identify solutions. Whilst the chapter will focus on the impact of COVID-19 on the English social work fieldwork education and placement provision, many of the lessons can be applied across the world.

DOI: 10.4324/9781032164946-41

The Context of Fieldwork Education in England in 2020

In order to understand the significant impact that COVID-19 has had on learning within fieldwork education in England in 2020, the context of learning within social work placement is explored briefly. Social work students in England are required to successfully complete a recognised and ratified social work course in which they will undertake a significant amount of their social work education undertaking a practice learning *placement* (S.W.E., 2020b). This is located in a social care or social work office and is often a 70-day first placement, further academic teaching, and 100-day final placement. However, this is by no means the sole pattern of teaching, as the new regulations provide greater flexibility and creativity for social work education (S.W.E., 2020b).

Whilst on placement, the student is expected to undertake the social work role to develop skills in an experiential manner. This requires firstly learning through observation and modelling before holding a small caseload that enables the student to practice and develop their social work skills. This is enhanced through reflective discussion within social work student supervision (Davys & Beddoe, 2009). Social work placement is a critical aspect of learning within social work education, as, indeed, reviews of social work education recommended that the quality of social work student placement is to be promoted (Narey, 2014; Croisdale-Appleby, 2014).

> It is the quality of the placement and the supervision received that is most frequently cited both by students and recently qualified social workers as key in the initial formation of their own professional practice – it is that important!
>
> *(Croisdale-Appleby, 2014, p. 49)*

When students begin their social work placement, they will be unfamiliar with team norms, practices, and procedures. The induction period is designed to familiarise the student with these practices, which is primarily undertaken through observation of practice. In the first weeks of placement, the student will accompany the practice educator and other colleagues to a variety of meetings and service-user appointments. This enables the student to observe and reflect upon different styles of intervention in different settings. It is recognised that it is beneficial if the student is aware of their own areas for development and discuss them early in placement with the practice educator (Beesley, 2020b). Furthermore, taking account of a student's cultural, social, and educational history enables student-centred practice education (Tedam, 2011). The development of an understanding of the student enables the practice educator to adapt the learning within the placement to ensure that it is relevant and appropriate for the student's learning needs.

Once the induction is completed, there is often a period of co-working. This enables the student to model the observed intervention styles in a supportive environment. During this time, the practice educator is undertaking a formative assessment (Sadler, 1989) of the student's strengths and areas for development through observation and reflective discussion. Furthermore, the practice educator is able to provide feedback, which enables the student to reflect on and adapt their social work skills (Sadler, 1989; Turner-Daly & Jack, 2017). Finally, they will take lead on a small, but increasingly complex, caseload with oversight from their practice educator.

An important factor, here, is that the quality of the teaching on placement impacts the students' development (Usher, 2018). Moreover, the importance of the supervisory (practice educator–student) relationship is highlighted in fieldwork education research (Litvack et al., 2010; Beddoe et al., 2016; Heron et al., 2015). This was seen to be most effective when it was professional but approachable and where there was an open and honest relationship (Ketner et al.,

2017). As an interactive induction is less viable in 2020, the facilitation of observation of practice and development of an informal working relationship outside social work student supervision can be seen to be more challenging.

Reflection on practice is a core task for social work students and is, indeed, entrenched in the English developmental and assessment criteria, the Professional Capability Framework (P.C.F.) (B.A.S.W., 2018), as *critical reflection and analysis* is the sixth developmental domain. Frequently, social work students are asked to write reflective pieces on their learning from interventions, which is experiential learning (Kolb, 1984). There are a wide variety of reflective models that are recommended to students to facilitate their reflection (Beesley, 2020b). Within social work placement, the student is required to link theory to practice as it is by the understanding of the application of theory to practice that the student can best learn on placement (Lee & Fortune, 2013).

However, it can be argued that independent experiential learning alone is insufficient when developing social work skills and knowledge. Reflective supervision can enhance the student's development within experiential learning (Boud et al., 1985; Davys & Beddoe, 2009). The practice educator develops the student's learning by asking questions to stimulate the student's reflection and offers observations and thoughts that the student may not have considered. Furthermore, they will ask the student to think from different perspectives, for example, having an empathic approach to why service users react the way they do. A strong reflective supervision discussion will incorporate social work theories, values, social policy, legislation, and ethical dilemmas (Beesley, 2020b). This enables the social work student to learn from both positive and negative experiential outcomes, which results in deep learning (Biggs, 1987; Race, 2020).

The impact of remote learning due to the COVID-19 pandemic on reflective learning was centred on an anxiety about reduced intervention opportunities for social work students to undertake. As fieldwork education moved forward, consideration had to be given by placement providers on ensuring that students still had learning opportunities and a working caseload.

It can, therefore, be seen that social work student learning in fieldwork education in England is centred on supported practical interventions with service users and reflection on the interventions. The learning is dependent on observation of practice to model interventions and the opportunity to undertake interventions with service users. Furthermore, this is supported by the development of the supervisory relationship and reflective discussion within social work student supervision. The aim for the student is to develop both practical skills and an understanding of the knowledge that underpins the skills development. However, the COVID-19 pandemic was a significant threat to the viability of English fieldwork education.

Threats to Fieldwork Education

As the world started to adapt to a *new normal*, we faced a diminished world economy and increased unemployment and poverty which would inevitably impact the most vulnerable sectors of society. Social work students faced the same challenges that the world population did, including loss of loved ones or fear for the well-being of themselves or their families and friends. There was an emotional impact of social isolation, including loss of social interaction and loss of routine (Williams et al., 2020) However, students faced additional COVID-19-related stressors. A moral panic occurred in England about students as super-spreaders of the virus, and consequentially, some social work students have become isolated in unfamiliar towns away from family support. In contrast, social work attracts many mature students, who had to contend with a variety of other stressors, including fluctuating school attendance by their children and financial worries.

Whilst social work students experienced stressful new teaching strategies in academic teaching, they faced a different set of challenges in fieldwork education due to the impact of COVID-19 on service provision. Interestingly, there were a range of responses from students during the initial crisis, veering from a desire to stop placement completely through to a desire to carry on as normal (Beesley, 2020a). The duty of care to social work students was complex, as it required deliberation of both the students' welfare and their progression. Similarly, there were differing responses from placement providers and practice educators amid reduced service provision. Many social care service providers were impacted by decreased finances and social distancing (C.A.F., 2020), resulting in fewer fieldwork education opportunities in social care settings. Social work service providers reduced the required number of direct interventions, and much work was undertaken remotely. For those offices that were open, they operated at reduced capacity.

Furthermore, practice educators were anxious about their ability to support a social work student in uncertain times and without established remote educating strategies within frequently changing national COVID-19 policy directives. The opportunities to observe the practice educator undertaking a direct intervention were significantly limited due to social distancing and changed service provision delivery. The ability to have weekly reflective supervision within the office was eradicated, as offices were shut or at reduced capacity. Consideration had to be given to whether there were sufficient learning opportunities available to a social work student to ensure that the fieldwork education was viable.

In summary, the COVID-19 pandemic has created worldwide health, employment, and social isolation issues that have impacted every stratum of society and have created new challenges to fieldwork education. Learning within social work placement in England is based on observing, modelling, and undertaking practical tasks and intervention with service users. This is supported through reflective social work student supervision that enhances knowledge and understanding of how the task was undertaken, to promote further development of social work skills. It can be seen that fieldwork education was under threat from reduced placement capacity and diminished learning opportunities.

Fieldwork Education Responses to COVID-19 Problems

This section will now reflect on solutions to the problems that impacted fieldwork education during the COVID-19 pandemic. Decisions had to be made by social work education providers that took account of the students' competing needs, service provision, and placement availability in an environment of often rapidly changing social policy (Beesley, 2020a) in partnership between social work education providers and placement providers (Beesley & Devonald, 2020). However, the impact of the COVID-19 pandemic on fieldwork education was a 'wicked problem' (Rittel & Webber, 1973), as it was not one that had been faced previously within modern history, and there were not immediately available solutions.

Leeds Beckett University fieldwork education provision is used as a case study, but knowledge of other social work educators' provision is utilised. It will outline the crisis decision-making that occurred in the initial crisis, before considering alternatives developed to replace fieldwork education in the short term. It will then reflect on decision-making in relation to fieldwork education in England as a *new normal* pattern of placement provision and practice developed.

Initial Crisis Management

In March 2020, English social work education providers began making decisions about the short-term future of fieldwork education based on the individual needs of each cohort. Of merit to English social work educators and the placement providers was that decision-making was undertaken quickly and disseminated immediately (Beesley & Devonald, 2020; Durham M.S.W. Collective, 2020). Evidence suggests that collaborative decision-making within a multi-stakeholder partnership enhances outcomes and the ability to provide services across the partnership (MacDonald et al., 2019), particularly in a crisis (Grint, 2010). Nevertheless, research undertaken at the time showed that social work students were anxious about an uncertain future and a lack of knowledge about placement (Blackwell, 2020). It was important to remember that people's stress in relation to how COVID-19 would affect them increases with lack of information (Wu et al., 2020) and that social work education providers had a duty of care to keep their students informed of decisions.

S.W.E., the new English social work regulatory body, had only three months earlier come into effect and was perceived by some as understandably slow to react to the crisis. Nevertheless, they provided guidance that placements could be continued, shortened, suspended, or replaced, which empowered individual social work education providers to make decisions about placement provision on a cohort-by-cohort basis (S.W.E., 2020a). This meant that, across England, there was a variety of responses. At Leeds Beckett University, for example, Master of Arts (M.A.) final year students had just completed placement; Bachelor of Arts (B.A.) final year students were just over halfway through their final placement, and negotiation resulted in a shorter placement with increased support in the first year of qualified practice, and the M.A. and B.A. first placement students, who were only three weeks into induction, had their placement terminated and replaced with an alternative learning package (Beesley & Devonald, 2020). However, other universities had different solutions that included completing the full placement days as originally planned or suspending the placement until the crisis passed.

However, even for placements that continued, learning was immediately transformed to taking place within a remote placement. The English government had, on the advice of world health professionals, introduced a *lockdown*, meaning that only essential travel and personal interaction was permitted (P.H.E., 2020a). The impact on fieldwork education was immediate. Social work offices stood empty. Social workers and social work students alike were creating makeshift office space on kitchen tables, whilst often juggling unexpected childcare commitments as schools were also closed. Home visits to service users and interprofessional meetings were replaced with Zoom calls.

Practice educators were anxious that they could not assess students robustly, as they were themselves orientating to remote working (Beesley & Devonald, 2020), and short-term solutions were created to counter these fears. For example, at Leeds Beckett University, a daily sheet was completed by the student to monitor tasks and interventions undertaken within the day and regular check-ins advocated to keep the practice educator and social work student communicating. Furthermore, increased support in the first year of qualified practice was negotiated for the affected cohort (Beesley & Devonald, 2020). Whilst a policy was written to advise practice educators on assessing remotely in a shorter time frame, individual support was also offered, where required, to ensure confident support and assessment was provided.

However, remote placements also raised concerns for the students, who were anxious that they would miss out on learning opportunities and leave them less prepared for qualified practice. Indeed, they were no longer able to observe and model practice with their practice educator, as practice was undertaken remotely. Practice educators were unable to observe the student's practice and provide feedback to the student to enhance development of skills and knowledge. Nevertheless, reflective supervision (Davys & Beddoe, 2009) was critical to support students to learn from their practice and was prioritised. This immediately became telephone supervision, with lengthy discussion supporting students on how to continue to engage with their caseload and learning within it. It was acknowledged that, whilst their practical learning of social work skills may have been impacted, students developed skills in other areas: resilience, flexibility, telephone communication, and creativity. Furthermore, they developed an understanding of how vulnerable service users were impacted by the COVID-19 pandemic. These skills, whilst not the learning goals that may have been set for students at the start of the placement were, nevertheless, invaluable learning for social work students and would prepare them for qualified practice in a new social work environment (Banks et al., 2020).

In summary, English social work educators, in partnership with placement providers, were empowered to make flexible decisions about each of their cohorts in relation to fieldwork education. Within a very short period, fieldwork education was transformed from a long-established pattern to a responsive one that was primarily based on remote learning. The organisational and individual adaptive commitment to the changes was remarkable.

Short-Term Solutions to Terminated Placement Provision

Whilst it is acknowledged that many English social work education providers completed existing placements and some suspended placements with a view to resuming after the initial crisis, the focus here will be on the placements that were replaced with an alternative teaching strategy than fieldwork education. This also applied to those courses in which the placement was due to start in the period of March to September 2020 but felt unable to do so for COVID-19 related reasons and/or limited placement provision.

It is recognised that it is impossible to replace fieldwork education, as the benefits of learning within social work placement are multiple (Narey, 2014). Nevertheless, in some circumstances, social work educators had to do just that due to the impact of the COVID-19 pandemic. As such, alternative learning packages were developed by some English social work educators. These often took the form of academic blended learning (Race, 2020) in which live webinars were delivered and/or narrated lectures were recorded and supplemented by a range of reading, videos, and activities. Within Leeds Beckett University, this followed a structure in which each learning package addressed a different domain from the national developmental and assessment criteria P.C.F. (B.A.S.W., 2018).

The learning packages had to be undertaken remotely, as university teaching spaces were not available. The advantage to a remote teaching package was that students, who often had complex lives due to COVID-19, could engage with the learning at a time of their choice, so it was a flexible option within a complex world. Nevertheless, students also raised concerns about the self-directed nature of the study. As such, revised iterations provided by other social work educators also embedded weekly tutorials with academic staff and/or practice educators. This enabled the reflective discussion and application of theory of social work student supervision to be applied to the learning packages. Whilst learning strategy for these alternative learning packages was firmly rooted in academic teaching models (Race, 2020), the application of reflective discussion (Davys & Beddoe, 2009) enhanced student learning.

In summary, alternative learning packages were quickly developed by English social work educators to replace fieldwork education where required. These were mapped against the placement assessment criteria and based on self-directed study and enhanced by practice educator input.

The New Normal for Fieldwork Education

As 2020 continued, with no apparent cure or vaccination for COVID-19, English social work educators recognised the need to develop a fieldwork education model that enabled social work placements to occur within remote working conditions. This final section will consider the issues that had to be considered when developing remote and blended placement models.

The first deliberation was that consideration had to be given to students who were shielding (P.H.E., 2020b). Whilst national advice suggested that, since August 2020, shielding was no longer necessary, there were still a few students who self-assessed as clinically extremely vulnerable. Clinically extremely vulnerable people were advised to minimise their interactions where possible (P.H.E., 2020b). One option for these students was the identification of a telephone service to enable them to work remotely. However, when that could not be facilitated, and they were unable to work within the agreed blended home and office arrangements, it was agreed that their placement would have to be delayed until such time that it was assessed as safe for them to undertake the placement. Naturally, COVID-19 personal protective equipment (P.P.E.) and training was required by all placement providers to facilitate safe home visits to service users.

The Placement Learning Agreement (P.L.A.) meeting is scheduled before the student begins placement and facilitates the discussion of organisational issues. As such, the P.L.A. form and meeting had a designated section to ensure P.P.E. and training were addressed, and patterns of working were considered to ensure clarity of understanding. The student's learning needs had always been an important part of the P.L.A. meeting but were now afforded even greater priority. The P.L.A. meetings, which had always taken place in the placement location, were now undertaken remotely by video call to reduce risks. The lack of need to allocate tutor travel time meant that additional tutor support could be afforded to students whilst they were on placement.

Social work offices in England had reduced capacity because of distancing rules, and practice educators were often only in the office one day per week or one week per month. Indeed, there were ethical challenges to working remotely and limited direct work in P.P.E. (Banks et al., 2020). This meant learning opportunities to observe and model practice would be limited but, with careful planning, would be viable. Social workers have adapted to a pattern of case management that requires mainly telephone calls, with home visits in P.P.E. only to be undertaken when required. It was agreed that social work students could practice in the same way. It was recognised that they may not be developing the traditional social work skills, for example, assessing a service user in their home environment. However, they would be learning the contemporary and relevant social work skills of the COVID-19 working environment, for example, assessing by telephone. It was agreed that a remote placement would prepare social work students for qualified practice, as was the new normal of service delivery.

Previously to the COVID-19 pandemic, social work students were rarely allowed to work at home. Negotiation with placement providers had to occur to develop new practices. Whilst concerns were raised that social work students' commitment to the working day and the quality and quantity of work would not be monitored to the same level, it was recognised that there had to be an element of trust from practice educators in the students' professionalism. Mechanisms were put in place, including the previously initiated daily worksheets and daily check-ins. Once the practice educator had undertaken a positive formative assessment of the student's ability, it was often felt that this overt monitoring could reduce. Indeed, informally, practice educators reflected that they observed no difference in the range of student commitment. Perhaps an explanation for this comes from an andrological understanding that adult learners are seen to be motivated and autonomous learners (Knowles, 1973). Students are committed to developing social work skills and knowledge to prepare them for qualified practice, and the remote nature of learning did not impact this. Furthermore, as students are valued by the practice educator for their achievements, building *social capital* (Lesser & Storck, 2001), they are rewarded and continue to be motivated to enhance their practice to retain and enhance their position as successful social work students.

Each student received a placement laptop, which had been the norm across the statutory placements before the COVID-19 pandemic. However, previously they had not been allowed to take it home. This raised issues of security. Students were, therefore, asked to have a secure location to store their placement laptop when not using it. Furthermore, issues of confidentiality rose from students working remotely. Negotiations agreed that students must have a private space to work within, where confidential telephone calls could not be overheard by family or shared house members. Finally, students with childcare commitments were informed that they could not be a carer within placement hours and had to have childcare arrangements in place, as they would if they were in the office. Naturally, this caused difficulties for some students, but all adhered to the philosophy.

It was inevitable that a number of the students on placement would be asked to remain in isolation due to symptoms, a positive result, or having been in proximity to some who subsequently tested positive (P.H.E., 2020a). This meant that, during that time, students were unable to attend the office or undertake service user home visits. It was agreed that if the student was asymptomatic that they could continue to work remotely. However, if the student had symptoms s/he would need to take the time off sick and add the missed days to the end of the placement. This caused further pressures on placement provision mapping, which has a tight annual schedule.

The availability of learning opportunities for students had been a concern for practice educators. However, social workers had established a new normal of remote working that involved a mixture of weekly office-based work, home visits to service users, and working from home on a work laptop to undertake emails and telephone calls. This was, then, replicated by social work students. It was recognised that the opportunities for observing and modelling of practice educator's practice were reduced, but, with careful planning, this was viable. In addition to accompanying the practice educator on a home visit, the student would listen to a telephone call or remote meeting and observe and model the practice educator's practice.

Reflective supervision, which had always involved the observation of the student's non-verbal communication and responses, initially raised concerns for practice educators. They felt that supervision would not be effective if it was not *in person*. However, it was agreed that limited office time should be afforded to co-working to facilitate student learning and assessment tasks. Instead, reflective social work supervision (Davys & Beddoe, 2009) was transferred to video telephone calls within a remote working day. By this time, practice educators were often skilled in telephone service user appointments, so they were able to transfer learning to social work student supervision.

Finally, the assessment of students in fieldwork education in England had raised concerns for practice educators, as they were not situated close to the student in an office environment. However, the schedule of weekly office days facilitated focused time together when informal assessment could occur. Similarly, concerns were raised about the ability to undertake direct observations. Where opportunities to co-work were limited, the expectations for direct observations had to be reviewed. In England, practice educators are required to undertake a minimum of three direct observations of the student (S.W.E., 2020b). It was agreed that a minimum of one direct observation had to be undertaken within a service user home visit with the practice educator present. However, a second direct observation could be a shared telephone call to a service user and a third could be a remote interprofessional meeting. With the agreed pattern of daily check-ins, weekly supervision, office days, and direct observations, it became apparent that the practice educator had ample opportunity to assess the student's social work knowledge and skills.

In summary, fieldwork education had to adapt to a new normal. This included remote placements in which social work students undertook a blended approach to placements of office-based and home-based working. Whilst home visits to service users were undertaken when required, telephone interventions became the norm. Social work students were supported remotely by their practice educator, using frequent video calls for check-ins and supervision. Whilst the impact of these remote placements on students' readiness for qualified practice should be assessed in the near future, it is recognised that remote placements are superior to an alternative, self-directed learning package.

Conclusion: A Threat or an Opportunity to Fieldwork Education in England?

It can be seen that the initial practice educator responses to the impact of the COVID-19 pandemic created a significant level of concern across a range of social work placements. The initial threats were centred around a lack of direct contact between practice educator and student and a lack of learning opportunities. Short-term solutions were developed that included a variety of responses in English fieldwork education including continuing, terminating, suspending, and shortening social work placement. However, longer term solutions have now been established that facilitate social work student learning in fieldwork education. Indeed, a second lockdown in November 2020 demonstrated the resilience of the newly developed English fieldwork education. During that time, social work placements continued with established, robust remote learning for students.

The impact of the COVID-19 pandemic on fieldwork education was seen as an opportunity to develop new and flexible ways of working. Social work service delivery became remote, and non-essential visits and assessments were undertaken by telephone and video call. This new way of working was applied to student working. Skill and knowledge development remained accessible for social work students, who could observe and model practice educator practice through carefully managed office time and telephone calls to enable an independent caseload once the student was deemed ready. Reflective supervision and scheduled check-ins were undertaken by video call, and carefully planned direct observations were viable.

Whilst the longer term impact of COVID-19 on service provision and, thus, placement provision will be dependent on the identification of a cure and/or vaccination, it is anticipated that remote placements will be around beyond 2020. It is expected that social work students will, for example, be afforded greater flexibility to mirror the placement team's working from home patterns. Additionally, remote meetings have become acceptable means of communication, and tutor support patterns, which have changed and increased, could be adapted for the benefit of the student. Established norms can prevent the development of creative, flexible new patterns of learning. It is recommended that research is undertaken into the impact of remote learning on student development of knowledge and skills in fieldwork education. However, it should be seen that there are clear indicators that different ways of learning and assessing students can and should be available to enable social work educators to be responsive to meet the needs of contemporary fieldwork education.

References

Banks, S., Cai, T., de Jonge, E., Shears, J., Shum, M., Sobočan, A.M., Strom, K., Truell, R., Úriz, M.J. & Weinberg, M. (2020) Practising ethically during COVID-19: Social work challenges and responses. *International Social Work*, 63(5), 569–583.

B.A.S.W. (2018, July 20) Student PCF level descriptors for pre-qualifying levels and ASYE. B.A.S.W. Retrieved from https://www.basw.co.uk/system/files/resources/pcf-student-asye.pdf.

Beddoe, L., Karvinen-Niinjkoski, S., Ruch, G. & Tsui, M. (2016) Towards an international consensus on a research agenda for social work supervision: Report on the first survey of a Delphi study. *British Journal of Social Work*, 46(6), 1568–1586.

Beesley, P. (2020a) Covid-19: The impact on social work placements. *Social Work 2020 under Covid-19 Magazine*. Retrieved from https://sw2020covid19.group.shef.ac.uk/2020/04/24/covid-19-the-impact-on-social-work-placements/.

Beesley, P. (2020b) *Making the Most of Your Social Work Placement*. London: Sage.

Beesley, P. & Devonald, J. (2020) Partnership working in the face of a pandemic crisis impacting on social work placement provision in England. *Social Work Education*, 1–8. DOI: 10.1080/02615479.2020.1825662.

Biggs, J. (1987) *Student Approaches to Learning and Studying*. Research Monograph. Hawthorne: Australian Council for Educational Research.

Blackwell, A. (2020, April 1) Placements closing, online lectures and uncertain futures: Covid-19's impact on social work students. *Community Care*. Retrieved from https://www.communitycare.co.uk/2020/04/01/failed-placements-online-lectures-uncertain-futures-covid-19s-impact-social-work-students/.

Boud, D., Keogh, R. & Walker, D. (1985) Promoting reflection in learning: A model. In: Boud, D., Keogh, R. & Walker, D. (eds.) *Turning Experience into Learning*. Oxon: Routledge, 18–40.

Charities Aid Foundation (CAF). (2020) CAF Charity coronavirus briefing 3 months into lockdown, how are charities in the UK faring? Retrieved from https://www.cafonline.org/docs/default-source/about-us-publications/caf-charity-coronavirus-briefing-june-2020.pdf.

Croisdale-Appleby, D. (2014) *Re-Visioning Social Work Education: An Independent Review*. London: Department of Health.

Davys, A. & Beddoe, L. (2009) The reflective learning model: Supervision of social work students. *Social Work Education*, 28(8), 919–933.

Durham MSW Collective. (2020, April 24). Lessons in resilience: Supporting social work students during the Covid-19 crisis. *Social Work 2020 under Covid-19 Magazine*. Retrieved from https://sw2020covid19.group.shef.ac.uk/category/second-edition-article/durham-msw-collective/.

Grint, K. (2010) Wicked problems and clumsy solutions: The role of leadership. In: Brookes, S. & Grint, K. (eds.) *The New Public Leadership Challenge*. London: Palgrave.

Heron, G., McGoldrick, R. & Wilson, R. (2015) Exploring the influence of feedback on student social workers' understanding of childcare and protection. *British Journal of Social Work*, 45(8), 2317–2334.

Ketner, M., Cooper-Bolinskey, D. & VanCleave, D. (2017) The meaning and value of supervision in social work field education. *Field Educator*, 7(2), 1–18.

Knowles, M. (1973) *The Adult Learner: A Neglected Species*. Texas: Gulf Publishing.

Kolb, D.A. (1984) *Experiential Learning: Experience as the Source of Learning and Development* (Vol. 1). New Jersey: Prentice-Hall.

Lee, M. & Fortune, A. (2013) Do we need more 'doing' activities or 'thinking' activities in the field practicum? *Journal of Social Work Education*, 49(4), 646–660.

Lesser, E. & Storck, J. (2001) 'Communities of practice and organizational performance'. *IBM Systems Journal*, 40(4), 831–841.

Litvack, A., Bogo, M. & Mishna, F. (2010) Emotional reactions of students in field education: An exploratory study. *Journal of Social Work Education*, 46(2), 227–243.

MacDonald, A., Clarke, A. & Huang, L. (2019) Multi-stakeholder partnerships for sustainability: Designing decision-making processes for partnership capacity. *Journal of Business Ethics*, 160(2), 409–426.

Narey, M. (2014) Making the education of social workers consistently effective. Retrieved from https://assets.publishing.service.gov.uk/government/uploads/system/uploads/attachment_data/file/287756/Making_the_education_of_social_workers_consistently_effective.pdf.

Public Health England (P.H.E.). (2020a) *Guidance on Social Distancing for Everyone in the UK*. P.H.E. Retrieved from https://www.gov.uk/government/publications/covid-19-guidance-on-social-distancing-and-for-vulnerable-people/guidance-on-social-distancing-for-everyone-in-the-uk-and-protecting-older-people-and-vulnerable-adults.

P.H.E. (2020b) *Guidance on Shielding and Protecting People Who Are Clinically Extremely Vulnerable from Covid-19*. Retrieved from https://www.gov.uk/government/publications/guidance-on-shielding-and-protecting-extremely-vulnerable-persons-from-covid-19/guidance-on-shielding-and-protecting-extremely-vulnerable-persons-from-covid-19.

Race, P. (2020) *The Lecturer's Toolkit. A Practical Guide to Assessment, Learning ad Teaching*. London: Sage.

Rittel, H. & Webber, M. (1973) Dilemmas in general theory of planning. *Policy Sciences*, 4(2), 155–169.

Sadler, D. (1989) Formative assessment and the design of instructional systems. *Instructional Science*, 18(2), 119–144.

Social work England (S.W.E.). (2020a) *Information for Education Providers and Social Work Students*. S.W.E. Retrieved from https://www.socialworkengland.org.uk/coronavirus/information-for-education-providers-and-social-work-students/.

Social work England (S.W.E.). (2020b) *Practice Placements Guidance*. S.W.E. Retrieved from https://www.socialworkengland.org.uk/media/2973/practice_placements_guidance_final.pdf.

Tedam, P. (2011) The MANDELA model of practice learning: An old present in new wrapping? *Journal of Practice Teaching and Learning*, 11(2), 60–76.

Turner-Daly, B. & Jack, G. (2017) Rhetoric vs. reality in social work supervision: The experiences of a group of childcare social workers in England. *Child and Family Social Work*, 22(1), 36–46.

Usher, R. (2018) Chapter Fourteen Experience, pedagogy and social practices. In: Illeris, K. (ed.) *Contemporary Theories of Learning: Learning Theorists in their own words*. Abingdon: Routledge.

Williams, S., Armitage, C., Tampe, T. & Dienes, K. (2020) Public perceptions and experiences of social distancing and social isolation during the COVID-19 pandemic: A UK-based focus group study. *British Medical Journal Open*, 10(7), 1–8.

Wu, A., Connors, C. & Everly Jr, G. (2020) COVID-19: Peer support and crisis communication strategies to promote institutional resilience. *Annals of International Medicine*. DOI: 10.7326/M20-1236.

36

Performance of Volunteering and Work Duties During the Pandemic of COVID-19 in the Czech Republic

Lived Experience of Social Work Students

Marie Špiláčková, Kateřina Glumbíková, Veronika Zegzulková, Iva Tichá, and Pavlína Rabasová

The profession of social work is legitimised and maintained through what we call 'professional knowledge', which can be defined as specialised knowledge generated and disseminated by a particular profession (Fook, 2002). This knowledge has a dual nature in social work: it is 'knowing that', which includes general theories and facts, and 'knowing how', which includes specific applications of 'knowing that' in a certain context of social work practice (Healy, 2005). Students are being prepared for performance in their profession by gaining both types of knowledge, and it is the practical education that allows students to acquire know-how. It is this confrontation of 'knowing that' and 'knowing how' that can bring students unique experience, whether in a positive or negative sense.

Social work as a practical activity and its education has had a tradition of more than a century in the Czech Republic. We live in a new century, but one thing, in terms of the content of studies, has remained the same for more than 100 years: professional practice as an integral and indispensable part of training for the profession. In accordance with the Act on Social Services No. 108/2006 Sb., social work in the Czech Republic is a regulated profession, which has a defined education based on European values of freedom and solidarity and an emphasis on human and civil rights. The professional level of universities and higher vocational schools has been guaranteed since 1993 by the Association of Educators in Social Work in the Czech Republic, which is based on the Minimum Standard of Education in Social Work. The purpose of the standard is to define the expected minimum quality of study programmes in the field of social work education. According to the standard, the professional practice must make up at least a quarter of the total teaching time.

In 2020, social work students experienced a completely unprecedented situation. Their theoretical and practical studies were disrupted by the first wave of the COVID-19 pandemic in the spring months (March–May 2020) and by the state of emergency declared by the Czech

 DOI: 10.4324/9781032164946-42

government (see Section 36.1). As part of the declared state of emergency, full-time students had to perform work duty, without any prior knowledge of the content, assigned to them by the governor of the relevant region. The second way to help was to participate in volunteer activities, such as sewing masks, delivering shopping to people in need, distributing disinfection, telephoning lonely seniors, etc.

No one had prepared the students or the educators for this new situation. The students met new challenges in practice, not only in the form of specific activities but also in the form of contact with target groups with which they may not have had any experience. The concurrence of studies and the performance of work duty or volunteer activities as specific performances of professional practice have affected the lives of students both in terms of their studies and their mental state. This created situations that were burdensome for the students. Because– (a) there is currently no systematic evaluation of the impact of work duty on students in the Czech Republic, (b) there is no information on this topic in foreign expert articles because of the new nature of the coronavirus pandemic, and (c) it can be assumed that the situation may recur, it is necessary to evaluate the effects of work duty on students in order to provide recommendations for the (possible) next period of the coronavirus pandemic.

Comprehensive data on work duty and volunteering in the Czech Republic are absent. With regard to the absence of these data and the fact that the work duty was always imposed by regional governors, we focused on an analysis of the Moravian-Silesian Region (M.S.R.), where the Faculty of Social Studies of the University of Ostrava (hereinafter F.S.S. O.U. or 'faculty') is located.

The aim of the presented chapter is to analyse the experience of social work students of the F.S.S. O.U. gained during their performance of work duty or volunteering in the 'first wave' of the COVID-19 pandemic and to draw recommendations for social work educators.

A Description of the Situation of the Students in the Spring of 2020

The Czech Republic has 14 territorial self-governing units, called regions. The M.S.R., with the regional city of Ostrava, is in the northeast of the Czech Republic and has more than 1.2 million inhabitants. The study programme of social work in M.S.R. is provided by the Higher Vocational School in Ostrava, the F.S.S. O.U.

Pursuant to the Constitutional Act No. 110/1998 Sb., on the Security of the Czech Republic, the Government of the Czech Republic declared a state of emergency on 12 March 2020 for the territory of the Czech Republic regarding the coronavirus (S.A.R.S. C.o.V.-2) health threat – the first wave of which lasted for a total of 66 days until 17 May 2020. In practice, it was accompanied by a number of measures. An example is the Resolution of the Government of the Czech Republic No. 207, which imposed work duty on students at higher vocational schools and university students in the full-time form of study in the fields of education according to the Act No. 108/2006 Sb., on Social Services. The resolution also concerned study programmes that are provided at the F.S.S. O.U., namely full-time forms of social work and health and social care programmes at the bachelor's, master's, and doctoral levels. The implementation of the resolution was entrusted to the M.S.R. Regional Authority. According to the available data, the M.S.R. Regional Authority addressed a total of 600 students in the region, and 98 began to perform work duty, 33 of them being F.S.S. students. It was possible to refuse work duty for certain reasons, which primarily included the health condition of the students or their families. Failure to participate in work duty was punished by a fine of C.Z.K. 50,000, which is approximately 1.5 times the average gross salary of an employee in the Czech Republic. The students worked in facilities of social services in the M.S.R., most often in homes for the elderly with regard to vulnerable groups declared by the World Health Organization (W.H.O.). Another large group of students (not registered, therefore, not quantified) carried out various volunteer activities in Ostrava or at their places of residence. All the students involved contributed to mitigating the consequences of the spread of the infection and the security measures imposed, thus, being of great help and support for both the clients and the social services staff. By showing solidarity, they contributed to the fulfilment of the mission of their future profession.

To cope with this difficult situation, the faculty offered its students an opportunity to use online psychological and supervisory support in the form of telephone or Skype interviews, which were offered voluntarily in the evenings by qualified experts of the faculty. The faculty also expressed support for these students by rewarding their work (the Rector's Award of the O.U. for the activities of students for the civic society) and by taking into account their activities in fulfilling their study obligations.

The Heuristic Context of the Data Analysis: System of Professional Practice at F.S.S. O.U.

To understand the experience of students during the COVID-19 pandemic, it is necessary to present the heuristic context of the system of professional practice at F.S.S. O.U. In 2020, the faculty had a total of six study programmes, of which two were bachelor's (social work and health and social care), three master's (social work with two specialisations – the family and development and management in social work and health and social care and rehabilitation), and one doctoral (social work).

For the performance of the regulated profession of social workers and health and social workers, it is sufficient to complete a bachelor's degree programme in the Czech Republic, therefore, we will continue to deal with the system of professional practice at the bachelor's level.

Compulsory practice is a part of the abovementioned study programmes. The system of professional practical education at F.S.S. O.U. is based on three pillars: professional internships, case seminars, and supervision of internships. Specifically, professional practical education is carried out in the form of excursions – continuous and permanent internships.

The aim of professional practice is to gain experience in the performance of social work – to acquire, use, and further develop the competencies necessary for the performance of the profession of social workers and health and social workers; to build a professional identity; and to be able to combine theoretical knowledge with practice. The internships are carried out in state or non-state organisations in which social and health work is performed. They take place mainly in inpatient acute and follow-up care facilities, palliative care facilities, social services, the state administration in the field of social care, social and legal protection of children, etc. (Qualification Standard, p. 1; Decree No. 39/2005 Sb). The internship can be performed both in the Czech Republic and abroad.

The practical training of students takes place in a minimum range of 1,008 hours for a health and social worker and 537 hours for a social worker, while 100% participation is mandatory. The complex structure of practical education is further completed by supervision and case seminars.

Professional practice takes two forms: continuous and permanent. Continuous practice is realised in the range of eight teaching hours for each teaching week of the semester. Permanent practice is performed in the total range of 80–120 teaching hours. The internship can be completed only once at one workplace. In connection with the epidemiological situation and the occurrence of COVID-19, this rule was waived in the emergency state. Even after completing one block of internship, students may return to the workplace repeatedly in connection with participation in volunteering or work duty imposed on students by the regulation of the Government of the Czech Republic.

The internship is usually performed by the student under the guidance of a mentor, who is an experienced social worker or health and social worker of the given organisation, who accompanies the student throughout his/her internship. Mentors provide support to students in creating study plans, formulating individual educational goals, and fulfilling the conditions of the internship. The student is expected to take initiative and a positive approach to the internship.

In the emergency state, due to the epidemiological situation, the faculty did not expect such a degree of participation from the mentors in the practical education of students.

Internships are reflected through case seminars and through supervision of internships. Case seminars are usually run by experts from practice with many years of professional experience in the field of social work and health and social work.

Supervision support is provided to students by a supervisor with 500 hours of supervisory training in the third year of study after gaining experience in practical training.

Administrative support for internships is provided by the coordinator of professional internships. Students complete practical education with the support of the textbook *Guide to Vocational Practical Education* (Kaniová, Recmanová, & Vaňharová, 2019). Further support is provided by e-learning courses and websites. According to evidence-based practice (E.B.P.), the goal of professional practical education is to develop students' skills in dealing with difficult social situations of clients/patients arising primarily in connection with illness, disability, risky lifestyles, and others.

Methodology of the Research with Students

The data were obtained in the research which was focused on the evaluation of work duty and volunteering. To gain insight into the experience of students in a situation in which it was not realistic to conduct interviews with students, we used a questionnaire with open-ended questions. Because of the use of this technique, our approach to the analysed data should be seen in the context of a qualitative research strategy.

The informants were selected on the basis of intentional criteria sampling which served to select research participants according to certain characteristics and guaranteed the selection relevance in relation to the research subject (see e.g., Rubin & Babbie, 2011). The sampling criteria for the informants were set out as follows: (a) performance of work duty or volunteering during the pandemic of COVID-19 in the summer semester, (b) being a student in one of the study programmes of social work at the O.U., and (c) voluntary involvement in the research. As part of the research, we addressed all 58 students who performed volunteering or work duty.

The research group consisted of a total of 58 students of the faculty (three men and 55 women) – 33 of whom carried out work duty and 35 carried out some volunteer activities, and the faculty registered them (it included e.g., distribution of protective equipment to seniors, delivering shopping, issuing disinfection to citizens, etc.). The questionnaires were filled in by a total of 33 students, which represents a return of 56.89%. Of these, 84.8% were bachelor's degree students and 15.2% master's degree students. Students who performed work duty in the spring were second-year students (62.5%) and third-year students (34.4%). One respondent stated that he was a first-year student. Out of the total number, there were 18 students aged 18–22, 10 students aged 23–26, two students aged 31–40, and three students over 40.

As for the facilities where students performed their work duty, homes for the elderly significantly dominated (69.7%). The vast majority of students (29 students, i.e., 87.9%) stated that they worked with the target group of seniors as part of their work duty. Three students worked with the target group of families with children and people with disabilities, and one student worked with homeless people.

In addition, students performed activities related to the protection of high-risk groups of the population, such as making masks (12.1%), delivering shopping to persons in need (15.2%), distributing disinfectants (15.2%), and providing telephone assistance (9.1%).

For the data collection, we used a tailor-made questionnaire, which consisted of 26 questions aimed at evaluating various aspects and experiences of work duty and volunteering during the COVID-19 pandemic. These were questions aimed at the place of help, the target group of help, the content of work, new experience, reasons for refusal of an activity or of the whole work duty, experience in vocational training, preparedness by the previous studies to perform work duty or volunteering, impact on studies, and recommendations for organisers of work duty or volunteering.

Qualitative data were analysed using a thematic analysis according to Braun and Clarke (2006), in which data were subject to open coding and then grouped to specific topics (i.e., content-meaning units in the data) based on their similarity or difference. We used the content analysis of Braun and Clarke (2006) because it is based on constructivist principles of working with data that are considered to be interpretively co-created in the interaction between the researcher and the content items communicated by the informants. To deepen the data analysis and make an analytical conclusion, we also used position maps from Clarke and colleagues' situation analysis, which is also based on the constructivist tradition. The position maps make it possible to look at the diversity of semantic positions held or not held by actors in given situations on the semantic axes identified in the researched situation (Clarke, Friese, & Washburn, 2018).

The research was conducted in accordance with the Ethical Principles of Human Research, adopted by the American Psychological Association (A.P.A.) in 2016 and in accordance with the applicable Czech laws. Participation in the research was voluntary. Special attention was paid to maintaining anonymity and confidentiality in relation to the communication partners.

To ensure the research validity, we reflected on the possible social desirability response set (the level of readiness of the informants to behave as they think the researcher expects or wishes) and on the demands posed by the research topic on the self-reflection of the informants. The data were also validated by triangulation of people analysing the data, in which the data were independently analysed by two researchers, and the resulting analysis was subject to their consensus. The validity was confirmed in the sense of gaining a good understanding from different perspectives of the investigated phenomenon. As for the description of the research methodology, it can also be stated that despite the fact that the generated data cannot be generalised, they bring a unique insight into the researched topic.

Analysis and Interpretation of Results

The following interpretation of the results is divided into three basic topics, namely (1) work duty, (2) volunteering, and (3) job description, and final reflection, which are then analytically divided according to the categories.

Work Duty

Motives for the Performance of Work Duty

Students stated that the main reason for the performance of work duty was the threat of financial sanctions for refusal of performance, up to C.Z.K. 50,000. This reason was repeatedly given in the entire questionnaire and the possibility of a fine was seen very negatively as unfair: 'Under the financial penalty of 50,000 … ? I really don't have so much money' (S33); or as another student stated: 'The refusal was under the threat of a fine, which would be really unpleasant' (S11).

Students also mentioned other reasons, but they were rather individual, such as the *possibility of having the performance of work duty recognised as practice* or their own *need of solidarity*, 'Because I think helping is good and I have known since I was a child that I want to *help* others' (S26); 'I felt I could help someone, so why not' (S15); and the need for 'helping where it was needed' (S20). Despite the fact that work duty was imposed, some of the students contacted the regional authorities on their own initiative and started performing the work duty voluntarily: 'I volunteered even before the work duty was imposed' (S30). The students also talked about the *opportunity to test their professional readiness*: 'I wanted to test my potentials and limits, to confirm my minimum experience with this target group' (S15).

Positive Evaluation of Work Duty Performance

According to the students, the greatest benefit of performing the work duty was *gaining new experience or knowledge or skills*: 'The knowledge I have learned while performing the work duty will certainly come in handy' (S11); 'I evaluate it quite positively, it brought me a lot of new experience' (S30). Another student in his statement appreciated the fact that he gained an overview of the operation of the organisation: 'Thanks to the pandemic, I found out how things actually work in homes for the elderly' (S31). At the same time, students largely agree on the usability of the newly acquired knowledge in their professional life: 'Because it was very beneficial for my future work' (S26).

Students also spoke, in line with the initial motives for the performance of work duty, about fulfilling a certain need for *solidarity with clients* and a need for *helping them in the difficult situation* caused by the pandemic: 'I was in a direct contact with clients and communicated with them. Visits were forbidden, so I could make their day at least a little more pleasant' (S18).

Another significant positive factor was the *possibility of financial rewards*, which also played a motivating role before starting the performance of work duty: 'And money also played a role' (S28).

Students also appreciated the *opportunity to participate in any activity*, which they missed due to the government regulations, for example, 'It was killing me only to sit at home sewing masks, I wanted to go somewhere' (S29); or 'At least I do something and am not sitting idly at home' (S16).

Some students see the work duty ambiguously, speaking of achieving a gradual balance of negative experiences and positive consequences, such as: 'It's an ill wind that blows nobody any good' (S7); or 'It was terrible, but it was good for something' (S33).

The students' statements show that the atmosphere in the workplace and the attitude of employees, especially social workers, was also important, as evidenced by this statement: 'In the spring I worked in the department where I was feeling well, the team was great, and I can say nothing wrong about the department. Then I moved to another department, and I must say that it was terrible there and I felt bullied there' (S26).

Negative Evaluation of the Performance of Work Duty

The most mentioned factor of the negative evaluation of the performance of work duty was the unfriendly atmosphere in the workplace and the unfriendly attitude of social workers to students:

> In one incident, when the client did not want to get up for the morning hygiene, I agreed with him saying that I would come later. Another nurse noticed that and warned me, and especially the client, very roughly that it was not possible and treated him very improperly, and she was very upset at how cheeky the client was. She said that he would be in bed all day anyway and she had to get her job done.
>
> *(S28)*

Another student's comment noted this negative aspect: 'Yes, the improper treatment from the part of the social workers' (S26).

Speaking of the inappropriate attitude of social workers, students also mentioned the fact that they had to perform activities that did not fall within the job of social workers:

> The female social workers in the department were aggressive, arrogant and uncompromising … no agreement was possible, when I did something wrong without having been told how to do it beforehand, I was told off, despite not having completed a social worker course.
>
> *(S32)*

'The management didn't say anything about us to the staff, and they were upset that we weren't as good at work as they were' (S9); or as another student states:

> it has little to do with my future profession, you just need to know what kind of work nurses do, but in my case, I know this job very well and I think a lot of students did not help in these activities because they were recruited as activation workers. For me, the internship is more important.
>
> *(S29)*

Some students also stated that they had been forced to perform some activities despite their disapproval or refusal to do certain tasks:

> We were not allowed to say that we could not. I refused to change a diaper, which made me sick, so another employee did it for me as part of camaraderie. Otherwise, we had to do basically everything, even if we didn't like it or we were not skilled at that. They did not care.
>
> *(S28)*

Another student said that, after being pressured, she carried out the activity: 'Even if I refused to do that (e.g., hygiene, cleaning – the job of a cleaner), I still had to do it' (S9). These were most often activities related to direct service care for clients, which will be discussed in more detail below. 'Changing diapers, washing private parts, bathing … I was forced to do that due to the aggressiveness of the workers, because as they said I was doing nothing there and still got paid' (S32). This is also linked to the students' feeling that they were working instead of social workers: 'I felt as if I was doing someone else's job and they are were just loitering about … I was coping with the feeling that some of them did not do anything and I did their job' (S29). Another student said: 'I worked instead of three workers who were just sitting on their butts drinking coffee and smoking' (S33).

Recommendations to Work Duty Organisers

As part of the questionnaire survey, the students also had an opportunity to make recommendations for a more efficient or better organisation of work duty in the future. One of the main recommendations arising from the students' answers is to provide a job that would really correspond to the nature of the profession of social work: 'To explain to organisations that a university student has no experience with clients' hygiene (therefore we were called useless)' (S9); or: 'Not to call students just for cleaning' (S22). The students also suggested calling for work duty students of other disciplines that would correspond to the nature of work in various organisations. 'Although I am a health and social care student, I think that after the first semester we were absolutely unsuitable for the work we did, maybe I could have used my knowledge of ergotherapy' (S11). They also suggested calling for work duty people who could not find a job in the labour market:

> To place in the necessary positions people who are, for example, registered at the Labor Office (these people need money, they can go and help in social facilities and earn something, thus improving their economic situation); I do not criticize the ordering of work duty as such, however, there are so many people who are unable to find work, they can help in various social facilities, even if it is work duty intended for students. Students should be the last option.
>
> *(S16)*

The students also call for taking into consideration the complexity of their studies so there should be a clearly defined period for the performance of work duty: 'to determine the number of hours per week really needed in individual organizations' (S29); 'A better work schedule, a work schedule for students' (S30). Another suggestion was to end the work duty immediately when there is no shortage of employees in the organisation: 'At a later stage when employees previously on sick leave were returning to work, there were a lot of us there and I felt redundant, instead of that I could have been studying' (S23).

The students also mentioned in their statements the need for better communication and information about the organisation of work duty: 'To improve communication, a better systematicity' (S21); or 'To be better informed' (S13).

Volunteering

Motives for Volunteering

Unlike work duty, the main motive for volunteering was, according to the students, the possibility of help/solidarity. The students described providing help as a matter of course: 'I offered my help because I take it as my moral duty, also when considering what I study' (S20); 'The urge to get involved, to help' (S3). Another factor was the possibility of volunteering to be recognised as the internship: 'It was one of the ways to do the internship' (S12); this motive also appeared in students performing work duty.

Likewise, the same motive in both categories is the opportunity for being active: 'I wanted to be useful and not just sit at home' (S7).

Positive Evaluation of Volunteering

The positive evaluation of volunteering included the possibility of gaining new experience, knowledge, or skills: 'It is an enriching experience for me' (S4); 'Experience is non-transferable, so any experience in social services is beneficial for me. Seeing the functioning of social services in a crisis is an interesting experience. I felt accepted and welcomed in the working team' (S20).

Students also positively assessed the opportunity to gain a holistic view of the social work profession in the given organisations: 'It helped me to understand work in social services. I also worked with a social worker from whom I learned many things in practice' (S8). They were also positive about the opportunity see how work is managed in crisis situations, or: 'to work under great pressure' (S21).

Negative Evaluation of Volunteering

In opposition to the performance of work duty, the statements of students about volunteering were rarely negative. They only concerned the situation when they did not carry out direct activities of social workers: 'Almost no contact with the job of the social worker' (S6); 'I was not in such a position where I could work in the future, what I gained was more personal experience' (S18).

Job Description and Final Reflection

When being asked questions related to the job description, students (performing work duty) often criticised the fact that they performed activities that did not relate to the profession of the social worker. According to them, the job most often included direct service care for the clients: 'Direct service care, serving food, preparing food, morning and afternoon hygiene (changing diapers, washing intimate areas, bathing, shaving men, etc.)' (S32). Some students refused to perform these activities, and they often criticised the fact that, despite their refusal, they were either forced to perform the activity or they were then trained for these activities due to the length of work duty (see Section 36.4.1.3).

Other activities performed by students as part of their volunteer work included ensuring the day-to-day running of the organisation: 'Laundry work and day-to-day operations' (S6); 'cleaning the wards (dusting, washing dishes, etc.)' (S9); 'assistance in technical activities - kitchen' (S26); or cleaning work. Other activities included work intended to prevent the spread of the coronavirus: 'I measured temperature, helped the visitors to put on protective suits, disinfected protective equipment and certain rooms' (S20). Direct service care and activities ensuring the day-to-day running of the organisation are among the activities that students do not normally encounter in internships: 'from disinfecting and changing beds to assisting in feeding clients' (S2).

According to the students, various forms of communication were also frequent, e.g., with foster parents (S25), but most often with seniors, with whom telephone assistance was carried out (S31, S12), or field assistance such shopping delivery, providing masks, and disinfection, etc.

As part of volunteering, students were most often included in the sewing of masks and their subsequent distribution together with disinfectants: 'Sewing masks, their distribution according to the itinerary supplied by the municipal authority, occasional assistance in the distribution of lunches, disinfectants' (S10).

The biggest benefit, as shown by the students' statements, is the prioritisation of the target group of clients, either in a positive or negative sense. On the one hand, the students were able to try working with different target groups: 'To try working with a target group that I would never choose for my internship' (S22); 'Due to the pandemic, I found out how things actually work in homes for the elderly' (S31). First of all, they also realised what target group of clients they would like to work with in the future: 'Based on this experience I want to work with children after graduating from school' (S7); or groups they would rather not work with: 'Because it strengthened my opinion that I really never want to work with this target group again, I found out that I really don't have a relationship with seniors and I would burn out very soon, as I actually burned out last time' (S32).

In the analysis, we also used the position maps of Clarke's situation analysis (Clarke, Friese, & Washburn, 2018) and discovered four positions of motivation for the performance of work duty and volunteering in social work (see Figure 36.1). The positions are created on the basis of the intersection of two axes. One of the axes represents the content of the work performed, which could range from work completely unsuitable for a social worker (the students compared it to the performance of service work and cleaning, or the job of a worker in social services) to work corresponding to the qualifications of a social worker. The second axis is the possibility of choice, for which one of the poles of the axis was stated by the students as the absolute impossibility of choice, both in the target group, facility, or independent activity. It was also typical of the pole characterised in this way that the workplace had a 'harsh and coercive atmosphere'. The opposite of this axis was the possibility of full choice, in which the students could choose both the target group and the facility or activity in the workplace.

Using the position map created in this way, we revealed four positions of motivation for the performance of social work, namely those that are instrumental, professional, solidarity-based, and holistic. The instrumental motivation was characterised by an effort to achieve a certain result or, on the contrary, an effort to avoid a sanction in the conditions set for the performance of work duty or professional activities. The professional motivation was characterised by the desire to further develop professionally in an environment that the students themselves would not choose (which was perceived by them as a certain challenge). The solidarity motivation was based on the inner motivation of students to help those in need. Finally, the holistic motivation consisted in the desire to gain a holistic view of the practice of social work and a wide range of new experience in an environment that fully enabled development by giving students the opportunity to fully choose a specific setting for the performance of professional work.

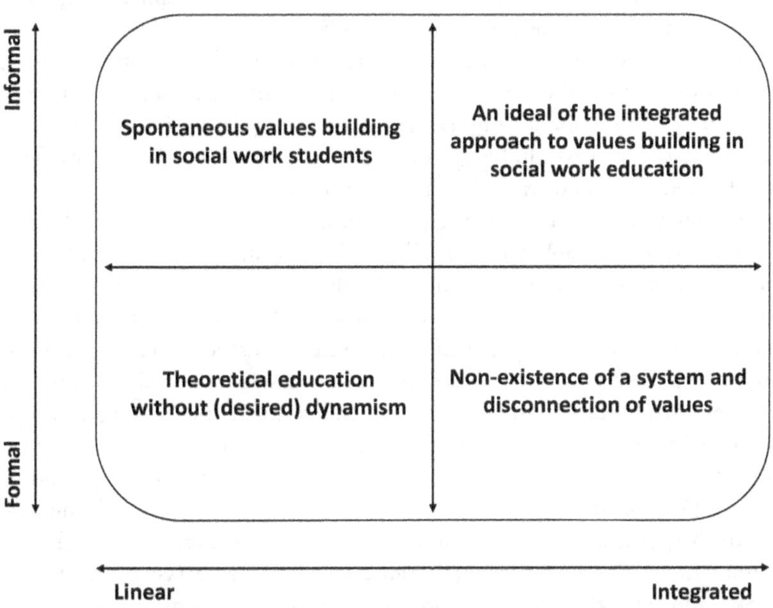

Figure 36.1 Position map of students' motivational factors. Source: Authors

Implications, Discussion, and Conclusion

The results of the research revealed four positions of motivation for the performance of social work, namely those that are instrumental, professional, solidarity-based, and holistic.

It is obvious that work duty and volunteering had both positive and negative aspects for students, such as gaining new experience, knowledge, and skills that they may apply in their professional life; an opportunity to gain a holistic view of the profession of social work within the given organisations, and a unique opportunity to learn to manage work in crisis situations. Financial remuneration is also a significant element. The atmosphere in the workplace and the attitude of employees toward students can also influence the ratio of negative experiences and positive consequences (similarly, see Musil, 2004). An unfriendly atmosphere in the workplace and an unfriendly attitude of social workers toward students are certainly negative factors that may affect the students' enthusiasm for their profession. It is, therefore, necessary to pay attention to quality communication. The promoters and managers of health and social services should continuously ensure the readiness of the staff to cooperate with students, strengthen the possibility of education in the workplace in the field of mentoring and development of communication skills, and prepare the staff for a possible increased influx of students in the workplace. A necessary condition for that is an explicitly defined type and scope of work performed which the staff can expect from students.

During the performance of work duty and volunteer activities, students may encounter activities that do not fall within the competencies of the profession of the social worker. These are mainly activities connected with direct service care for clients, which students do not normally encounter in their internships. The students are given mentally and physically demanding tasks and get into a situation in which they are expected to cope with various challenges and, at the same time, provide professional assistance to the clients (similarly, see Punková, 2019). The overall complexity of the work makes it difficult for them to study. The result can be a higher level of stress from lagging behind in their studies, especially in fulfilling their study obligations. When preparing study programmes, it would be appropriate to include specific subjects in which students would be trained for activities that appeared to be important during their work duty (dealing with the clients' hygiene, preparing and serving meals, communicating with clients, and others). It is possible to use interdisciplinary interconnections, simulation centres, training flats and, last but not least, virtual reality, which offers opportunities for a more effective achievement of educational goals, as evidenced by Dalgarno and Lee (2009), among others. To be prepared for the emergency state, it would be appropriate to give students a short but effective course in the basic theoretical and practical skills in direct service care of clients.

Educational institutions should prepare their study programmes so that they are as flexible as possible for students who would be able to fulfil their study obligations even in crisis situations. The starting point can be the optimisation of study obligations using interdisciplinary coherence. Then it could be recognising the performance of work duty or volunteer activities as internships, even though the students will perform, in some situations, activities that will not fall within the expected competencies in their future profession or will not reach professional qualities. At the same time, it would be useful to enable students to prioritise the target groups of clients to realise their preferences for further professional development. Last, but not least, in case of failure in their studies, it would be useful to enable students to extend the period of their studies free of charge. Despite the abovementioned, it is essential to comply with the legislative rules governing the acquisition and recognition of competence to perform the selected regulated profession (Act No. 96/2004 Sb.; Act No. 108/2006 Sb.; Decree No. 39/2005 Sb.; Decree No. 55/2011 Sb.) and with the standards and the accreditation file of the study programme approved by the National Accreditation Office. It follows that the readiness and ability of educators to provide studies in times of epidemiological crisis situations depend on systemic changes on the national and international levels.

An integral part of this preparedness must be an optimisation of crisis plans within the framework of crisis management not only at the level of educational institutions but also at the level of regional and national authorities. For example, as to the imposition of work duty, the best methodological practices for effective communication should be developed for the state administration and educational institutions and their mutual cooperation. The system should be uniform at least at the regional levels. If a student performs an internship in a certain type of facility and an emergency situation arises with the need to call students to perform work duty, it seems more effective to keep the student in that facility if students are expected to participate there in the performance of work duty. Other students can then be kept in reserve filling the missing positions. It would also be appropriate to call students from various disciplines to certain types of facilities and, thus, strengthen interdisciplinary cooperation. For example, students from various disciplines (medical doctor, general nurse, social worker, occupational therapist, and others) would gather in a home for the elderly at a given moment, and the division of labour would be more efficient within their competencies. Mutual consensus on the readiness of the state administration, the integrated rescue system, the promoters of health and social services, educators, and others is a necessity for steady management of emergencies.

We consider the goal of the chapter to be fulfilled. The results of the presented work provide a basis of recommendations for educators in social and health social work. This topic is a challenge both for the practice of social work and for educators in social work and deserves more attention from researchers.

References

Act No. 108/2006 Sb. on Social Services. Retrieved from: https://www.mpsv.cz/documents/20142/225517/Zakon_o_socialnich_sluzbach-stav_k_1._10._2017.pdf/a538a1ee-153e-a989-b2b5-c62ae97d5262

Act No. 96/2004 Sb. on the Conditions for Acquiring and Recognizing Competence to Perform Non-Medical Health Professions and to Perform Activities Related to the Provision of Health Care and on Amendments of Certain Related Acts (Act on Non-Medical Health Professions). Retrieved from: https://ppropo.mpsv.cz/zakon_96_2004

American Psychological Association (APA). (2016). *Ethical Principles of Psychologists and Code of Conduct.* Available at: http://www.apa.org/ethics/code/.

Braun, V., & Clarke, V. (2006). Using Thematic Analysis in Psychology. *Qualitative Research in Psychology, 3*(2), 77–101.

Clarke, A., Friese, C., & Washburn, R. (2018). *Situational Analysis in Practice: Grounded Theory after the Interpretative Turn.* London: SAGE.

Constitutional Act No. 110/1998 Sb. Constitutional Act on the Security of the Czech Republic. Retrieved from: https://www.psp.cz/en/docs/laws/1998/110.html

Dalgarno, B., & Lee, M. J. W. (2009). What Are the Learning Affordances of 3-D Virtual Environments? *British Journal of Educational Technology, 41*(1), 10–32. https://doi.org/10.1111/j.1467-8535.2009.01038.x.

Decree 55/2011 Sb. On the Activities of Healthcare Workers and Other Professionals. Retrieved from: https://www.psp.cz/sqw/sbirka.sqw?cz=55&r=2011

Decree No. 39/2005 Sb. Decree Laying down the Minimum Requirements for Study Programs to Acquire Professional Competence to Perform the Non-Medical Medical Profession. Retrieved from: https://www.psp.cz/sqw/sbirka.sqw?cz=39&r=2005

Fook, J. (2002). *Social Work Critical Theory and Practice.* London: Sage.

Healy, K. (2005). *Social Work Theories in Context: Creating Frameworks for Practice.* Houndmills: Palgrave Macmillan.

Musil, L. (2004). *Ráda bych Vám pomohla, ale: Dilemata práce s klienty v organizacích.* Brno: Marek Zeman.

Punková, M. (2019). Posilování odolnosti v praktickém vzdělávání studentů sociální práce. *Sociální Práce / Sociálná Práca, 19*(2), 5–20.

Rubin, A., & Babbie, E. R. (2011). *Research Methods for Social Work.* Belmont: Brooks/Cole Cengage.

Conclusion

Technological Advancement and Changing Landscape of Social Work Practice – Challenges Ahead of Next-generation Practitioners

Rajendra Baikady, Varoshini Nadesan, Sajid S.M., and M. Rezaul Islam

As we draw this handbook to a close, we see concerted effort across the globe in making fieldwork practicum a true learning experience for students and graduates. It also gives us a feeling that 'our future is in safer hands' as we witness innovative and new initiatives taking place all over the world. This undoubtedly promises quality, capable, and competitive social work professionals for the next generation. Social work, as a service profession, has a huge responsibility of preparing its students for working in a globalised, neoliberal society with diverse populations. Further, the global agenda for social work and social development (IFSW, IASSW, & ICSW, 2012, 2020; Jones & Truell, 2012) and the Global Standards for Social Work Education and Training (IASSW & IFSW, 2004, 2020; Sewpaul & Jones, 2004) recognises social work as a profession that responds to new social issues as a part of global development. It is evident from contributions in this volume that schools of social work across the globe are aligning their curriculum and teaching strategies to address the issues related to global inequality and social justice.

Schools of social work around the globe are obliged to produce skilled, competent, and value-oriented graduates. In a constantly changing education system, social work educators as supervisors play a crucial role in the development of skills, competencies, and capability of social work students. This responsibility is also evident in their assessments of students, who, in turn, will respond to societal dysfunctions within the boundaries of values and ethics of professional practice. Notwithstanding these responsibilities, educators and supervisors internationally face the reality of the scarcity of placement opportunities which hinders quality learning opportunities for social work students in their fieldwork practicum. Understandably, literature characterises this issue as a 'crisis' in fieldwork education (Ayala et al., 2018a; Bellinger, 2010). Opportunities are fewer for social work graduates in agencies as schools of social work in close proximity compete for suitable placement opportunities. Similarly, many disciplines other than social work are encouraging experiential learning as a component in their teaching programmes, some of which may be at the same placement organisation (Ayala et al., 2018a; Zuchowski et al., 2019).

DOI: 10.4324/9781032164946-43

It is, therefore, imperative that social work as a practice-based profession with 'fieldwork' at its heart needs to ensure a higher degree of competence for its graduates.

The key concerns raised in international literature is about the quality of fieldwork training, the availability of trained faculty supervisors and agency supervisors, and difficulties in finding placement agencies. All of these issues are covered in the present volume. A number of authors address various challenges faced by social work field practicum educators in different countries (Chapter 8 Canada; Chapter 13 Aotearoa, New Zealand; Chapter 15 Australia), whereas other authors focus on educators (Chapter 17), students (Chapter 22, Chapter 32), and ethical responsibilities (Chapter 33) in field instruction. In an effort to introduce specific focus on health care social work curriculum and arranging fieldwork education in China, Wong (Chapter 2) elaborates on a number of possibilities and challenges. Jordan and colleagues in their chapter (Chapter 1) evaluate the possibility and need for training social workers to intervene in multilevel practice in addressing the multidimensional complexity of Hong Kong's social issues.

Understandably, social work is a practice profession committed to adherence to principles of social justice and equality. However, there are many occurrences in which social work students and educators experience deferential treatment during their practice learning and teaching. Tedam and her colleague evaluate black African students' perspectives on fieldwork (Chapter 16) based on an empirical study. Literature had documented the need for developing alternative ways to teach social workers in engaging with anti-oppressive social work learning (Schwartz, Kreitzer, Barlow, & Macdonald, 2014; Smith & Ferguson, 2016). Further, while discussing the challenges faced by social work education it is also important to note that, in some countries, social work education is a new academic discipline and neither the government nor the general public understand the importance of social work education and practice in a development context. In an effort to better understand the development of social work education, this handbook attempts to deliver a clear understanding of fieldwork education in different countries across the globe with a blend of country-specific case studies, cross-cultural comparison, and international perspective.

Information and Communication Technology in Social Work Field Education

Technology in the twenty-first century has altered almost every aspect of human life. The integration of information technology in teaching and learning is highly encouraged and promoted at all levels of education, but mostly in parts of the world with more privileges and facilities. In many developing countries, social work is still attached to charity, and social workers are considered as helping people in the society, and they do not need special skill sets and capabilities. While there are many context-specific reasons for low recognition, respect, and acceptance of the profession, issues related to capability, competency, and efficacy play a major role. Social work in many countries is not considered equal to any other educational discipline because of the differences in competences and capability of the graduates that social work produces parallel to graduates in other educational disciplines. The reason for this probably lies in the face-to-face interventions as opposed to technological interventions in social work. Technical skill training in social work education is a less emphasised area in many countries. These may be attributed to a lack of resources, lack of skilled educators and competences of the students. However, it is expected that the social work curriculum builds competency levels. One way of building competency and skillsets for social work graduates is to empower them with up-to-date technical tools in assessment, evaluation, and intervention while working with clients and community.

Information and communication technology (ICT), when used effectively by trained social workers, may lead to improved access to care and better outcome on treatments (Taylor, 2015). Further technology is also proven to be effective and useful in reaching out to different marginalised communities, such as persons with disabilities and marginalised gender identity (Berzin et al., 2015). Given the changes taking place in contemporary society and advancement of teaching learning methods, the use of information technology may result in consistent and high quality service by the social work professionals across the globe. Used with due care and respect for privacy, ICT proves to be effective in delivering ethical and value-oriented services by next generation social workers in international social work.

Further studies have debated the use of digital technology in social work education and its importance for practice efficiency. Transfer of information using a computer and performing different functions such as access, store, produce, present, and exchange are considered as important skills required for the graduates in any profession (Gallardo-Echenique et al., 2015, p. 9). Unfortunately, there are no contributions directly addressing technological aspects in fieldwork training in this volume; however, many of the cross-cutting issues discussed in these 36 chapters align with the need for incorporating more advanced training and education in technology-focused education for social work graduates. We feel this is an opportunity for the authors in this volume to collaborate and explore the areas in the fourth industrial revolution that will take social work into the twenty-first century.

Why We Need to Strengthen Field Education in Social Work

Fieldwork education is an opportunity to integrate theory with practice (Lager & Robbins, 2004; Edmond et al., 2006). However, in terms of capability, efficiency, and efficacy, there is a gap between these two aspects. Social work educators as supervisors are expected to bridge these gaps through teaching and practice supervision (Lager & Robbins, 2004). Social work's commitment is for social justice and equality in the global society. For ensuring equality of opportunities, availability of justice, and basic human rights for all social work students, educational programmes teach basic principles of social, economic, and political justice across the regimes and regions. Further studies (D'Aprix et al., 2004; Wilson & McCrystal, 2007) reveal that students enrolled in social work were driven by their desire to help other people and contribute to the social development agenda as per the core value of the social work profession. However, due to limited exposure, low skill training, and limited international perspectives in teaching and learning programmes, some social work graduates leave the social work profession for other means of living. This is an area that needs more research which we hope to cover in other publications. A range of contributions in this volume provide insight into social work as the most promising human service profession committed to the principles of social justice and equality. Strengthening the fieldwork practicum and providing the best possible agency and supervisory support to students during their studies play a vital role in their future professional career. Competency of students and graduates from a school of social work largely depends on the quality of the field education agency, availability of faculty support, competent supervisors, and expertise in introducing an innovative fieldwork practicum. This is an important aspect in students' professional development because field practicum literally performs the gatekeeping function while evaluating students' competence and readiness to graduate (Sowbel, 2012). Further, Jennifer Boddy (Chapter 14 in this volume) raises the importance of simulated learning and its relationship to social work field education. The author provides examples of simulations that have helped prepare students for social work field education and professional practice while suggesting a framework for defining the various forms of simulation that contribute to practice learning.

Contributions in this handbook also alert social work academia to new approaches to fieldwork education, factors that contribute to maintaining a professional commitment to delivering the best possible service. Schools of social work largely depend on the voluntary service of the fieldwork agency and supervisors at agency; this may impact the commitment and involvement of fieldwork supervisors. Helen Cleak (Chapter 11 in this volume) explores issues related to field education in Australia and addresses some common difficulties experienced between the schools of social work and field practice agencies. A further analysis of the content of this chapter reveals that there should be a workable, healthy, and mutual relationship between the schools of social work and the field practice agency. Without the support of the fieldwork agency, it is challenging to provide experiential learning opportunities to social work graduates and, in many countries, practicing in open communities may need the support of fieldwork agencies, particularly in instances in which the community may not welcome students without an agency introduction. It is also expected that cordial and mutual learning relationships between the agency supervisor and faculty supervisor may lead to a tightened connection between the theory and practice curriculum, which is the ultimate aim of the social work field practicum in any context.

Field learning occupies a central role in the social work curriculum across the globe. However, the emphasis of scholars is on indigenous or context-specific focus in both theory and practice teaching and learning. The hegemony of a Western influence and the lack of context-specific focus has certainly influenced practice and theory. It was also true that, until recently, few academics took up the cudgels of seeking indigenous knowledges. Nevertheless, as social work education started spreading in many countries across the globe, innovations and new approaches to educating social work graduates and the internationalisation of the social work academia occurred; international social work organisations committed to transforming practice and education in social work. Kylie Agllias and colleagues (Chapter 12 of this volume) discuss indigenous students' experiences in field education. The authors address the little-attended-to subject of the 'experience of First Nations students' in fieldwork education with an effort to bring their experiences, struggles, and challenges to the mainstream literature on fieldwork education. These efforts are rather important in documenting and developing indigenous and context-specific social work education.

On the whole, we see this *Handbook of Field Work Education in Social Work* as a collective effort in debating, discussing, and devising alternative and innovative models of social work field education while documenting the challenges and opportunities faced by social work across the regions and regimes. Last, we recall our opening remark in this chapter, viz, 'we believe our future is in safer hands' and are assured that the contributions in this handbook are the actual evidence behind our confidence in the growing importance and standards of social work education across the globe. We are unconditionally convinced that the efforts put forward by educators and supervisors in ensuring quality, compatibility, and capacity-building of future generations of social work practitioners will result in the discipline of social work as a strongly committed profession for social justice and equality across the globe. We believe that this handbook itself is a rich source of information on fieldwork education across the globe, and we urge educators, fieldwork supervisors, practitioners, students, graduates, and policymakers to engage in international debates on strengthening field education in social work.

References

Ayala, J., Drolet, J., Fulton, A., Hewson, J., Letkemann, L., Baynton, M., Elliott, G., Judge-Stasiak, A., Blaug, C., Gérard Tétreault, A., & Schweizer, E. (2018a). Field education in crisis: Experiences of field education coordinators in Canada. *Social Work Education*, 37(3), 281–293. https://doi.org/10.1080/02615479.2017.1397109

Bellinger, A. (2010). Studying the landscape: Practice learning for social work reconsidered. *Social Work Education*, 29(6), 599–615. https://doi.org/10.1080/02615470903508743

Berzin, S. C., Singer, J., & Chan, C. (2015). *Practice Innovation through Technology in the Digital Age: A Grand Challenge for Social Work*. Grand Challenges for Social Work Initiative Working Paper No. 12. Columbia: American Academy of Social Work and Social Welfare.

D'Aprix, A., Dunlap, K.M., Abel, E., & Edwards, R.L. (2004). Goodness of fit: Career goals of MSW students and the aims of the social work profession in the United States. *Social Work Education*, 23(3), 265–80.

Edmond, T., Megivern, D., Williams, C., Rochman, E., & Howard, M. (2006). Integrating evidence-based practice and social work field education. *Journal of Social Work Education*, 42(2), 377–396. https://doi.org/10.5175/jswe.2006.200404115

Gallardo-Echenique, E. E., de Oliveira, J. M., Marqués-Molias, L., Esteve-Mon, F., Wang, Y., & Baker, R. (2015). Digital competence in the knowledge society. *MERLOT Journal of Online Learning and Teaching*, 11(1), 1–16.

International Association of Schools of Social Work (I.A.S.S.W.) & International Federation of Social Workers (I.F.S.W.). (2004). Global standards for social work education and training. Retrieved from http://cdn.ifsw.org/assets/ifsw_65044-3.pdf

International Association of Schools of Social Work (I.A.S.S.W.) & International Federation of Social Workers (I.F.S.W.). (2020). The Updated Global Standards For Social Work Education And Training: The New Chapter In Social Work Profession. Retrieved from https://www.iassw-aiets.org/wp-content/uploads/2020/11/IASSW-Global_Standards_Final.pdf

International Federation of Social Workers (I.F.S.W.), International Association of Schools of Social Work (I.A.S.S.W.), & International Council on Social Welfare (I.C.S.W.) (2012). The global agenda for social work and social development: Commitment to action. Retrieved May 2017, from, http://www.globalsocialagenda.org

International Federation of Social Workers (I.F.S.W.), International Association of Schools of Social Work (I.A.S.S.W.), & International Council on Social Welfare (I.C.S.W.) (2020). 2020 TO 2030 Global Agenda for Social Work and Social Development Framework: 'Co-Building Inclusive Social Transformation'. retrieved from https://www.iassw-aiets.org/consultation-on-next-global-agenda-2020-2030/5734-2020-to-2030-global-agenda-for-social-work-and-social-development-framework-co-building-inclusive-social-transformation/

Jones, D. N. , & Truell, R. (2012). The global agenda for social work and social development: A place to link together and be effective in a globalized world. *International Social Work*, 55(4), 454–472. https://doi.org/10.1177/0020872812440587

Lager, Patricia B. & Virginia Cooke, Robbins (2004). Field education: Exploring the future, expanding the vision. *Journal of Social Work Education*, 40(1), 3–12.

Schwartz, K. , Kreitzer, L. , Barlow, C. A., & Macdonald, L. (2014). *Sherpa in My Backpack: A Guide to International Social Work Practicum Exchanges and Study Abroad Programs* . Whitby: Sitter Publications.

Sewpaul, V., & Jones, D. (2004). Global standards for social work education and training. *Social Work Education* , 23(5), 493–513. https://doi.org/10.1080/0261547042000252244

Smith, L., & Ferguson, I. (2016). Practice learning: Challenging neoliberalism in a turbulent world. In: I. Taylor, M. Bogo, M. Lefevre, & B. Teater (Eds.), *Routledge International Handbook of Social Work Education* (pp. 197–208). New York: Routledge.

Sowbel, L. R. (2012). Gatekeeping: Why shouldn't we be ambivalent? *Journal of Social Work Education*, 48(1), 27–44. https://doi.org/10.5175/jswe.2012.201000027

Taylor, K. (2015). *Connected Health: How Digital Technology Is Transforming Health and Social Care*. London: Deloitte Centre for Health Solutions

Wilson, G. & McCrystal, P. (2007). Motivation and career aspirations of MSW students in Northern Ireland. *Social Work Education*, 26(1), 35–52.

Zuchowski, I., Cleak, H., Nickson, A., & Spencer, A. (2019). A national survey of Australian social work field education programs: Innovation with limited capacity. *Australian Social Work*, 72(1), 75–90. https://doi.org/10.1080/0312407X.2018.1511740

Index

Note: **Bold** page numbers refer to tables; *Italic* page numbers refer to figures and page numbers followed by "n" denote endnotes.